Dissension in the House of Commons

1974-1979

DISSENSION IN THE HOUSE OF COMMONS 1974–1979

PHILIP NORTON

CLARENDON PRESS · OXFORD

1980

Oxford University Press, Walton Street, Oxford OX2 6DP

OXFORD LONDON GLASGOW
NEW YORK TORONTO MELBOURNE WELLINGTON
KUALA LUMPAR SINGAPORE JAKARTA HONG KONG TOKYO
DELHI BOMBAY CALCUTTA MADRAS KARACHI
NAIROBI DAR ES SALAAM CAPE TOWN

*Published in the United States
by Oxford University Press, New York*

British Library Cataloguing in publication Data

Norton, Philip
   Dissension in the House of Commons,
   1974–1979
   1. Great Britain. Parliament. House of Commons – Voting
   2. Great Britain – Politics and government – 1964
   I. Title
   328.41'07'75   JN675   79-41754

   ISBN 0-19-827430-0

*Typeset by Enset Ltd., Midsomer Norton, Bath
Printed in Great Britain by Lowe & Brydone Printers Ltd., Thetford, Norfolk*

To my parents

PREFACE

I first began my research of intra-party dissent in the House of Commons in 1972, and my research has since continued. My first reference work, covering intra-party dissent in the Commons' division lobbies in the period from 1945 to 1974, was published in 1975. The kind reviews which the work received, the use to which it was put by researchers, and the findings of my own initial research of dissent in the last Parliament, encouraged me to produce another volume covering the Parliaments of 1974 and 1974–9. This work constitutes that further volume.

It is usual for authors to make formal declarations of responsibility for any errors, omissions or misinterpretations in their work. In this case, such a declaration is more than a formality. Given the nature of the work, based on research of more than 1,600 division lists and probably in excess of half-a-million names (the numbers voting in a division ranging sometimes from fewer than forty to more than six-hundred), I am very conscious of the possibility that, however thorough the research and the checking of it, errors may occur. Further, I have been responsible for the compilation of this work at all stages, from the initiation and research through to the typing and indexing, prior to its submission to the publisher. While one may take a certain pride in claiming something to be one's own work, the corollary is that any accompanying errors or omissions are one's own work as well. Hence, the blame for any faults found in this work can and must be given to me. Harry S Truman, of course, put a similar declaration of responsibility somewhat more succinctly.

While any weaknesses in this work are my responsibility, I think I can safely say that it would have had many more, and would not have seen the light of day, but for the kind help of others, to whom my grateful thanks are due. For accepting this volume for publication, I wish to express my gratitude to the Delegates of the Oxford University Press and to their advisors; and to Mr Ivon Asquith of the Press for his help in seeing it through to publication. I am very grateful also to the Director of Publishing of Her Majesty's Stationery Office for permission to make use of and quote from *Hansard*, without which this work would not have been possible. My thanks go also to those Members of Parliament who gave of their time to assist in confirming or commenting upon their voting behaviour on certain occasions during the period of this study. More generally, my thanks for their continued help and encouragement go to various friends and colleagues, in particular S. A. Walkland, Reader in Politics at the University of Sheffield, and F. W. S. Craig, of Parliamentary Research Services, and, for various helpful and insightful comments in the course of conversations, my fellow members of the Study of Parliament Group who are officers of the House of Commons.

For me, this work (as with my other works) has been something of a labour of love. I have greatly enjoyed it, and my research will continue. So long as Members of Parliament continue to demonstrate that they are not the 'lobby fodder' that some believe them to be, I think there will be a need for it.

PHILIP NORTON

Department of Politics
University of Hull.

August 1979.

CONTENTS

LIST OF TABLES

INTRODUCTION

The role of political parties, and especially of behaviour *within* as well as *between* parties, is central to an understanding of the modern House of Commons. However, despite the development of organized political parties in the nineteenth century and their consolidation in the twentieth, the importance of party, and particularly internal party behaviour and organization, in the House of Commons has been much neglected in the study and literature of Parliament.

In the nineteenth century, the growth of a mass electorate helped transfer elsewhere some of the functions of the Commons identified by Walter Bagehot in his classic work *The English Constitution* in 1867. Although the increase in the size of the electorate in 1832 helped encourage the development of embryonic party organizations, it was the increase in consequence of the Second Reform Act of 1867 that made necessary highly organized, and centralized, political parties. If voters were to be contacted, organization was necessary. If their votes were to be forthcoming, the parties had to promise them something (and the new electors were of a different sort to those of earlier days); if these promises were to be fulfilled, party members had to be returned in sufficient number to, *and display voting cohesion in*, the House of Commons. During the latter half of the century, party came to dominate politics, serving as the conduit for the transfer of the legislative and the elective functions of the Commons, the former going to the Cabinet and the latter to the electorate. Party became the determinant of voting, both in the country and in the division lobbies of the House of Commons. Whereas Members had displayed a large degree of freedom in their voting behaviour in the period between the two Reform Acts (except for the period between 1841 and 1846), their independent voting habits disappeared rapidly in the last quarter of the century.[1]

The growth in party cohesion in the division lobbies of the House of Commons was demonstrated by Lawrence Lowell at the beginning of this century, and more recently by another distinguished American academic, Samuel Beer.[2] During the last quarter of the nineteenth century, 'party votes' as defined by Lowell (ninety per cent or more of the members of one party voting in a division doing so in the same lobby) became increasingly common. Whereas the percentage of party votes cast by both parties on opposite sides had actually declined in one period between the two Reform Acts (from a little over twenty-two per cent of divisions in 1836 to less than seven per cent in 1860), the percentage after the Second Reform Act increased notably, from over thirty-five per cent in 1871 to over forty-six per cent in 1881, and to more than seventy-six per cent in 1894.[3] By the turn of the century, as Beer noted, 'party whips, although used more sparingly when the party was in Opposition than at present, could produce results comparable to the monolithic unity of recent times'.[4] The 'recent times' referred to by Beer were the immediate post-war years, or rather the immediate post-war year, with the figures in his tables not extending beyond the parliamentary session of 1945–6. Attention to the more recent incidence of party cohesion has been sparse. Given the knowledge that party unity had become, as Ergun Ozbudun noted, 'a well-established norm in British politics'[5]—a norm which ensured that the Commons no longer constituted a regular part of the decision-making process, decisions made by the Cabinet being agreed to almost as a matter of course by a party majority in the House—political scientists have tended to turn their attention elsewhere. Those who have written on the House of Commons have tended to underemphasize or ignore the importance of party, concentrating instead upon the constitutional formality in preference to the political reality and emphasizing the role of the House as a collective entity rather than the role of the elements within it. The nineteenth edition of *Erskine May*, published in 1976, devoted less than five of its 1,156 pages to a consideration of party machinery in Parliament.[6] The academic literature, as Anthony King has observed in a highly pertinent article on the subject, has tended to concentrate upon the Commons in its 'non-party' mode, to the neglect of its more important 'Opposition' and 'intra-party' modes.[7] For the purposes of our study, it is the neglect of this latter mode that is of especial importance.

When reference has been made to party in the context of the House of Commons, it has, in recent years, been often in a negative or critical sense. Some observers, aware of the cohesiveness of the parties, have viewed the Commons as an arena in which the relationship between the two largest parties, between the Government and Opposition, is of the greatest significance, with the two main parties engaging in what is now termed an 'adversary' style of politics, with the Government winning automatically the division at the end of the day. References to 'lobby fodder' appear not uncommon (similarly, references to 'the tyranny of the whips'), and a new school of thought has developed recently opposed to the adversary style of parliamentary politics, seeking to replace it with what may be termed a 'consensus' style of politics.[8]

The literature of those who concentrate upon the formal role of the Commons and of those who have pressed and do press for a reform of the House (be it through internal institutional reform or through electoral reform as favoured by those opposed to 'adversary' parliamentary behaviour) has demonstrated a tendency either to ignore or to take for granted party cohesion in the Commons' division lobbies. Since the researches of Lowell, and prior to the recent research of the compiler of this work, little original comprehensive research was undertaken; even Samuel Beer's data was derivative rather than original. Works or articles which incorporated empirical research of cohesion and, following from that, which sought to identify and explain any significant incidence of non-cohesion, of *dissent*, within parties— the 'occasional deviations' from the norm, as Ozbudun expressed it— were few and far between. Ronald Butt in his highly readable if perhaps inaptly titled *The Power of Parliament* appreciated the importance of dissent within parties, but his work was not designed to provide a comprehensive analysis, concentrating instead upon the more important occasions of intra-party dissent pertinent to his study.[9] R. J. Jackson's work, *Rebels and Whips*, was an attempt at a systematic study of cohesion and intra-party dissent in the period from 1945 to 1964, but regrettably was an attempt that was not altogether successful: there were too many errors and omissions for it to be treated as in any sense definitive.[10] A small number of articles appeared covering different aspects of dissent, the more substantial ones generally (though not exclusively) being written by American academics,[11] but none that sought to provide data upon which one could seek to generalize about the incidence of cohesion and, concomitantly of course, intra-party dissent in the division lobbies in the whole of the post-war period since 1945.

In order to try to fill this gap in the study of parliamentary behaviour, providing data on which generalizations could be based, this author researched all occasions of intra-party dissent (expressed by vote) in the division lobbies in the period covering the parliamentary sessions from 1945–6 to 1973–4 inclusively, a period of eight Parliaments. This data was published in 1975.[12] It revealed that in the post-war period up to 1970, party cohesion was indeed a well-established norm in the House of Commons, though with the 'occasional deviations' not as rare as was perhaps popularly supposed. In only one Parliament did the percentage of divisions in which one or more Members of either main party cast dissenting votes exceed ten per cent of all divisions; when Members did dissent, they rarely did so in a manner that would embarrass seriously the Government's majority, dissenting in large numbers usually only when the opponent party abstained from voting or when the Government's overall majority was such that it could sustain a sizeable dissenting vote. The cohesion of the parties in the division lobbies was especially noticeable in the 1950s (see table 1 in the conclusions); indeed, in two sessions in the 1950s there was not one dissenting vote cast by any Conservative Member. However, the work revealed a significant change in the Parliament of 1970–4. Although party cohesion was still the norm, there was a marked increase in the incidence of dissent by Government backbenchers, an increase that may be described as both qualitative as well as quantitative—not only was there an increase in the number of divisions involving dissenting votes (over thirty-six per cent of all divisions in the 1971–2 session), and the dissenters more persistent than had previously been the case with Conservative Members, but Conservative backbenchers proved willing to dissent in sufficient numbers to join with the Opposition and actually defeat the Government in the division lobbies in whipped votes, doing so on six occasions. These defeats were not the first defeats in post-war history: there had been ten in the period from 1945 to 1970, but these had resulted from poor organization by the whips or deliberate Opposition ploys (as in 1953 and 1965)[13] and were concentrated in the two Parliaments of small Government majorities (1950–1 and 1964–6). The six defeats experienced in the 1970–4 Parliament were the first to be inflicted as a result of dissent by Government backbenchers. Three of the defeats took place on three-line whips, the most important being on the immigration rules in 1972.[14] A more detailed analysis of the intra-party dissent by Conservative Members in the 1970–4 Parliament was undertaken, and the findings published in 1978.[15] This research identified the variable responsible for the increase in, and the seriousness of, dissent as the leadership of the Prime Minister, Edward Heath: the measures he introduced, the manner in which they were introduced and the way in which they were pushed through the House, his failure to communicate with his backbenchers (either at the personal level of friendship or at the intellectual level of explaining and justifying his actions), and his failure to use judiciously his powers of appointment and patronage, all coalesced to produce serious dissent by Conservative Members. (This dissent was facilitated by the articulation of an alternative intra-party view to challenge Mr Heath by Enoch Powell.)[16] Although Mr Heath ceased to be leader of the Conservative Party in February 1975, the foregoing factors contributing to his loss of leadership,[17] the work suggested that the incidence of Government defeats and the manner of their infliction during his premiership may have helped set a precedent which Government backbenchers in subsequent Parliaments might be prepared to follow. As the author concluded, 'Conservative intra-party dissent within the 1970 Parliament may not have had much effect upon the particular measures involved, but its effect in terms of parliamentary behaviour may yet prove to be lasting.'[18]

Given the change in the incidence of dissent in the first Parliament of the 1970s (and an awareness that such change was taking place within the context of wider political and constitutional changes),[19] and the speculation that Government defeats in that Parliament may have set a precedent for later years, there was clearly a need to monitor dissent in subsequent Parliaments. This need was commented upon by *The Parliamentarian* in 1976, expressing the hope that a further volume, covering intra-party dissent in the division lobbies in the post-1974 period, would be forthcoming.[20] This work constitutes that further volume, covering the short Parliament of March to October 1974 and the five-session Parliament of 1974–9. The short 1974 Parliament was the first Parliament of minority government since that of 1929 to 1931. The 1974–9 Parliament was the only Parliament of the century in which a Government slipped from having a majority to being in a minority and continued to govern for a full five-session Parliament. It was the first Parliament since 1924 in which a Government was defeated on a vote of confidence. Both Parliaments were thus very different to that of 1970–4 in which a Conservative Government governed with a clear overall majority. How does cohesion and intra-party dissent in the subsequent Parliaments compare with that of 1970–4? Given Labour administrations, and the failure of Mr Heath to be re-elected as leader of the Conservative Party, was there an absence of serious intra-party dissent, at least not comparable to that of 1970–4? And were there any further defeats in consequence of dissent by Government backbenchers as opposed to defeats that might be expected as a result of opposition parties combining against a minority government? This work contains the data on the basis of which we can attempt to answer such questions, as well as testing other generalizations that were applicable in previous Parliaments. The author's own tentative analysis of the data, undertaken in the summer recess following the dissolution of the 1974–9 Parliament, is provided in the Conclusions, including an assessment of the political and constitutional implications of the dissent and its wider implications for the movement for parliamentary reform.

Format of the volume

This volume follows largely the format of the author's 1975 compilation, *Dissension in the House of Commons 1945–74*, with only minor changes having been made. Each division in which one or more Members of either the Parliamentary Labour or Conservative Parties cast a dissenting vote is recorded, with the names of the dissenter or dissenters being preceded by a precis or explanation of the debate, emphasis being given to the views expressed (if any) by dissenting Members; for reasons of space, the summaries of debates have, where possible, been condensed by comparison with those of the earlier volume. Given the increased importance of intra-party dissent, the author's own analysis has been extended to form a concluding chapter.

As with our earlier volume, our definition of intra-party dissent in the division lobbies encompasses those occasions when one or more Labour or Conservative Members entered a lobby to vote against their party whip or the apparently clear wishes (sometimes implicit)[21] of their own Front Bench. This definition is employed to ensure that while genuine free votes are excluded, those divisions in which the whips are applied *de facto* (even though not employed *de jure* for tactical or cosmetic purposes) are not. Most instances of dissent which fall within this definition are clearly recognizable. It is perhaps pertinent to note, though, that there is a small grey area between what are clearly free votes and those which are not. For example, it is not unknown for whips to act as tellers (the normal indication of a whipped vote) in divisions on certain House of Commons' matters on which Members, in practice, are allowed a free vote. Where the debate suggests that a vote is a free one in practice, then it has been excluded from our compilation. On other occasions, whips may or may not act as tellers in divisions on issues which are normally considered suitable for free votes, but in the debates on which specific Front Bench advice has been proferred and Members have given some indication that they regard disagreement with such advice as constituting dissent from the wishes of their party leaders, and in which there may be some evidence of *de facto* whipping;[22] such instances have been included in this compilation. The author's own judgement, based upon his research of post-war parliamentary debates and divisions, has been the determining factor in those few cases in which the dividing line between a free vote and what may be termed a non-free vote has not been clear on the basis of the foregoing criteria.[23]

As provided for by our definition, this work seeks to identify dissenting votes cast by Members in receipt of either the Labour or the Conservative whip in the House of Commons. However, in view of the importance of the minority parties in the two Parliaments of 1974 and 1974–9, more attention has been given to identifying the party composition of each lobby in the divisions covered by this work. The party composition of the House in both Parliaments is detailed below.

The data in this work are based upon research of every division to have taken place in the division lobbies of the House of Commons in the 1974 Parliament (109 divisions) and that of 1974–9 (1,505 divisions), a total of 1,614 divisions. Background material on parliamentary procedure and related matters pertinent to the divisions covered in this volume is provided in the introductory notes.

Party composition of the House of Commons

The general election of February 1974 (the new Parliament meeting in March) resulted in the return of 301 Labour Members, 296 Conservatives, 14 Liberals, 11 United Ulster Unionist Coalition Members, 7 Scottish National Members, 2 Plaid Cymru Members, 1 Social Democratic and Labour Party (SDLP) Member (G. Fitt at Belfast, West), 1 Independent Labour Member (E. Milne at Blyth), 1 Social Democratic Labour Member (D. Taverne at Lincoln), and the Speaker, Mr Selwyn Lloyd. A minority Labour Government was consequently formed, and after six months in office went to the country in October 1974. It was returned with a small overall majority, the election results being as follows: Labour 319, Conservative 276, Liberal 13, Scottish National 11, United Ulster Unionist Coalition 10, Plaid Cymru 3, Social Democratic and Labour Party 1, Irish Independent 1 (F. Maguire at Fermanagh and South Tyrone), and the Speaker, Mr Lloyd.

During the course of the 1974–9 Parliament, the ranks of the governing Labour Party were depleted by occasional by-election losses (a total of seven, six being lost to the Conservatives, and one to the Liberals), and by what Burton and Drewry have described as 'less conventional processes'.[24] On 7 April 1976, Mr John Stonehouse, the Member for Walsall North, resigned the Labour whip (the event which deprived the Government formally of an overall majority),[25] sitting subsequently as an English National Party Member until he was convicted and gaoled for seven years on theft and false pretences charges on 6 August 1976; he resigned his seat on 27 August. In September 1975, the Labour Member for Ayrshire South, Mr James Sillars, became a founder member of the breakaway Scottish Labour Party, being joined in January 1976 by the Member for Paisley, Mr John Robertson. They retained the Labour whip until both resigning it on 26 July 1976. In October 1977, the Labour Member for Newham North-East, Mr Reg Prentice (a member of the Cabinet until 21 December 1976), crossed the Floor of the House to take the Conservative whip. In addition to the changes within the ranks of the Labour Party, the Unionist Members from Northern Ireland experienced certain changes in their nomeclatures; on 4 May 1977 the United

Ulster Unionist Coalition broke up following an abortive Loyalist strike in the province.[26]

When the House was dissolved in April 1979, its party composition was as follows: Labour 306, Conservative 282, Liberal 14, Scottish National 11, Ulster Unionists (using this nomeclature as an umbrella category) 9, Plaid Cymru 3, Scottish Labour Party 2, Democratic Unionist 1 (I. Paisley), Social Democratic and Labour Party 1, Irish Independent 1, and the Speaker, Mr George Thomas (formerly a Labour Member); there were four vacancies, two in formerly Labour-held seats and two in formerly Conservative-held seats. The results of the general election of 3 May 1979—though not directly pertinent to this volume (albeit very relevant to a future one)—resulted in the formation of a Conservative Government with an overall majority of 43.[27] The implications of intra-party dissent in the 1974–9 Parliament for its successor Parliament will be considered in our concluding analysis.

[1] This paragraph is based upon chapter two of Philip Norton, *The Commons in Perspective* (Martin Robertson, forthcoming 1981).

[2] A. Lawrence Lowell, *The Government of England*, Vol. II (Macmillan, 1924), pp. 74–81. Sanuel H. Beer, *Modern British Politics* (Faber, 1969 ed.), pp. 256–63.

[3] Lowell, *op. cit.*, pp. 76–8.

[4] Beer, *op. cit.*, p. 261.

[5] Ergun Ozbudun, *Party Cohesion in Western Democracies: A Causal Analysis* (Sage Publications, 1970), p. 316.

[6] Sir David Lidderdale (ed), *Erskine May's Treatise on the Law, Privileges, Proceedings and Usage of Parliament*, 19th edition (Butterworths, 1976), pp. 242–6.

[7] Anthony King, 'Modes of Executive-Legislative Relations: Great Britain, France, and West Germany', *Legislative Studies Quarterly*, Vol. 1(1), February 1976, pp. 20–21.

[8] The main literature of this school of thought is represented by S. E. Finer (ed.) *Adversary Politics and Electoral Reform* (Anthony Wigram, 1975), and various articles by S. A. Walkland, e.g. 'The Politics of Parliamentary Reform', *Parliamentary Affairs*, Vol. 29(2), Spring 1976, pp. 190–200, and 'Whither the Commons?' in S. A. Walkland and Michael Ryle (eds), *The Commons in the Seventies* (Fontana, 1977), pp. 238–56.

[9] *The Power of Parliament* (Constable, 1967). 'The Influence of Parliament' might have been more appropriate as a title. The work covers instances where Governments have made concessions in response to backbench pressure, but in which the decision-making capacity has remained with the Government and with the underlying assumption that if the concessions had not been made the Government would still have been able to have its way. Only when the House exercises its decision-making capacity through the division lobbies can it be said to be exercising power, albeit largely a negative power. See the Conclusions to this volume.

[10] *Rebels and Whips* (Macmillan, 1968). See the comments in Philip Norton, *Dissension in the House of Commons 1945–74* (Macmillan, 1975), p. 614, and, for an example, p. 163n.

[11] E.g. Robert T. Holt and John E. Turner, 'Change in British Politics: Labour in Parliament and Government', in W. G. Andrews (ed.), *European Politics II: The Dynamics of Change* (Van Nostrand Reinhold, 1969), pp. 23–116; John E. Schwarz and Geoffrey Lambert, 'The Voting Behavior of British Conservative Backbenchers', in Samuel C. Patterson and John C. Wahlke (eds), *Comparative Legislative Behaviour: Frontiers of Research* (Wiley, 1972), pp. 65–85; Jorgen S. Rasmussen, 'The Relations of the Profumo Rebels with their Local Parties', *University of Arizona: Comparative Government Studies No. 1* (University of Arizona, 1966); and J. Richard Piper, 'Backbench rebellion, Party Government and consensus politics: the case of the Parliamentary Labour Party, 1966–70', *Parliamentary Affairs*, Vol. 27 (4), Autumn

1974, pp. 384–96. Other important articles have been contributed by writers such as Leon D. Epstein, Harry Lazer, James J. Lynskey, and, on the British side, R. K. Alderman and (on the nineteenth century) Hugh Berrington. See the Select Bibliography.

[12] Philip Norton, *Dissension in the House of Commons 1945–74* (Macmillan, 1975).

[13] See Lord Wigg, *George Wigg* (Michael Joseph, 1972), pp. 165–7, and *The Times*, 8 July 1965. It appears also to have been the case in the 1950–1 Parliament as well. See Colin Thornton-Kemsley, *Through Winds and Tide* (Standard Press, 1974), p. 234.

[14] See Philip Norton, "Intra-Party Dissent in the House of Commons: A Case Study. The Immigration Rules 1972", *Parliamentary Affairs*, Vol. 29 (4), Autumn 1976, pp. 404–20.

[15] Philip Norton, *Conservative Dissidents: Dissent within the Parliamentary Conservative Party 1970–74* (Temple Smith, 1978).

[16] *Ibid.*, Ch. 9.

[17] See Philip Norton, 'Reflections on Mr Heath's loss of the Conservative Party Leadership, 1975', *British Politics Group Newsletter* (U.S.A.), No. 6, Fall 1976, pp. 3–4, and *Conservative Dissidents, op. cit.*, p. 242.

[18] *Conservative Dissidents, op. cit.*, p. 274.

[19] See, e.g., Dennis Kavanagh, 'New Bottles for New Wines: Changing assumptions about British Politics', *Parliamentary Affairs*, Vol. 31 (1), Winter 1978, pp. 6–21; and Gillian Peele, 'Change, Decay and the British Constitution', *Hull Papers in Politics No. 1* (Hull University Politics Department, 1978), and 'The Developing Constitution', in Chris Cook and John Ramsden (eds), *Trends in British Politics Since 1945* (Macmillan, 1978), pp. 1–27.

[20] *The Parliamentarian*, Vol. 57 (1), January 1976, p. 72.

[21] On occasion the Opposition abstains from voting without the Front Bench offering advice during the course of debate. It is normally clear from the division lists when the Opposition has abstained (as opposed to allowing an unwhipped vote) due not only to the numbers absent but also to who is absent. The absence of members of the Shadow Cabinet and Opposition whips is an indication usually of official abstention, and such abstention the whips usually seek to enforce.

[22] Such evidence may be forthcoming from Members' comments, newspaper reports, and the composition of the lobbies in the divisions themselves.

[23] This judgement has been based upon an assessment of the debates, the issues involved, and the voting behaviour of Members in the lobbies. The dividing line between what to include and what to exclude has, in one or two instances, been a very thin one indeed. For example, on a number of amendments to the motion establishing an inquiry into Rhodesian oil sanctions' breaking, although Government whips acted as tellers, the Government issued no whip, a fact confirmed during the debate, and the Opposition allowed explicitly a free vote. See especially *HC Deb.* 961, c. 1731. The divisions have been excluded from this compilation, though given the issues involved (albeit concerned more with how to proceed than with the principle of the matter) and the presence of whips as tellers, it could be argued that they fall very much on the line between a free and a non-free vote, and might justify inclusion.

[24] Ivor Burton and Gavin Drewry, 'Public Legislation: A Survey of the Sessions 1975/6 and 1976/7', *Parliamentary Affairs*, Vol. 31 (2), Spring 1978, p. 142.

[25] Philip Norton, 'Standing Committees and "The Composition of the House" ', *The Parliamentarian*, Vol. 57 (4), October 1976, p. 293.

[26] Philip Norton, 'Party Organization in the House of Commons', *Parliamentary Affairs*, Vol. 31 (4), Autumn 1978, p. 413. Following the ending of the Coalition, the Unionist Members were divided into six official Ulster Unionists, 1 Independent Ulster Unionist, 1 Vanguard Progressive Party Member (subsequently becoming an official Ulster Unionist), 1 United Ulster Unionist Movement Member, and 1 Democratic Unionist. For convenience, the foregoing Members, with the exception of the Democratic Unionist (Ian Paisley), are subsumed under the heading of Ulster Unionists after 4 May 1977 in the text.

[27] The results were as follows: Conservative 339, Labour 268, Liberal 11, Ulster Unionist 5, Democratic Unionist 3, Scottish National 2, Plaid Cymru 2, United Ulster Unionist 1, Independent Ulster Unionist 1, Social Democratic and Labour Party 1, Irish Independent 1, and the Speaker, Mr Thomas. Election figures in this section have been based upon the relevant editions of *The Times Guide to the House of Commons* and 'The General Election 1979', *Politics Today*, No. 8, 4 June 1979 (Conservative Research Department, 1979).

INTRODUCTORY NOTES

These notes are included as a means of providing background material relevant to understanding procedural and other points touched upon in the text. For the authoritative works on parliamentary procedure, readers are referred to *Erskine May*, the *Manual of Procedure*, and the *Standing Orders* of the House.[1]

Abstentions

If, in addition to a number of Members casting dissenting votes, a number of others abstain from voting, then this, where known, is indicated in the text. Abstentions, unlike dissenting votes, are frequently difficult to detect or estimate. Absence from a division does not, in itself, denote a deliberate abstention—Members may be 'paired', ill or inadvertently delayed on the way to vote—and the only accurate or near-accurate information on abstentions, which is not publicly available, is maintained by the whips, and even they, on occasion, may not be certain whether a Member's absence is a deliberate abstention or not.

The means by which abstentions may be detected are usually those of reading Members' speeches in debate (declarations of intended abstention sometimes being made), by comparing the names of those speaking in debate with the names in the division lists (speaking and then not voting usually but not always suggests deliberate abstention),[2] by comparing division lists with those of immediately preceding and succeeding divisions, and by monitoring press accounts of proceedings — Members and whips may sometimes reveal the number of abstentions to correspondents in the aftermath of a division, and on occasion some Members abstain ostentatiously by remaining in their seats, attracting publicity in so doing.

Business motions

At 10.00 p.m. on Mondays to Thursdays, and 4.00 p.m. on Fridays, the proceedings on any business then under consideration are interrupted, unless the business constitutes 'exempted business'.[3] Proceedings on non-exempted business may continue, though, if a Minister tables what is known as a business motion (referred to in the text as the procedural exemption motion) to the effect that any specified business 'may be entered upon and proceeded with at this day's sitting though opposed' either until any hour, until a specified hour, or until either a specified hour or the end of a specified period after it has been entered upon, whichever is the later. The motion is decided without amendment or debate. All such motions appear under the heading of 'Business of the House'.

Closure motions

A Member wishing to bring a debate to a close and have a vote taken may move 'That the Question be now put'. The motion for closure, if accepted by the Chair, is put forthwith and, if carried, the Question before the House is divided upon without further debate. For a closure motion to be carried it must be supported by at least one hundred Members.

Collective responsibility

The principle of collective responsibility applies to members of the Cabinet, each being bound to support a decision of the Cabinet once taken. In practice, the principle is applied to other members of the Government in that they may not (on pain of dismissal) speak or vote against Cabinet decisions. Thus, Ministers will not be found in dissenting lobbies. The only exceptions to this (unprecedented in post-war history) have been in 1975 and 1977 when the principle was suspended in order to allow Ministers to dissent from the Government on the issue of European Community Membership and the Second Reading of the first European Assembly Elections Bill respectively. Both occasions are covered in this volume.

The principle of collective responsibility is now also applied as a rule to members of the Shadow Cabinet. On occasion, though, members of the Shadow Cabinet do dissent from the decisions of their colleagues, and on such rare occasions it is up to the Leader of the Opposition to decide to what extent the principle should be enforced.[4] On very rare occasions, the Leader of the Opposition may extend the principle to junior Opposition spokesmen (as Mrs Thatcher did in the division on Rhodesian oil sanctions in December 1978), but usually does not do so. It is thus not uncommon to find junior Opposition spokesmen voting in a number of dissenting lobbies.

Committee stage

The Committee stage of most Bills is usually taken in Standing Committee. For the more important Government Bills, especially measures of constitutional importance, Committee stage is taken on the Floor of the House (in Committee of the whole House). All divisions taking place in Committee of the whole House are encompassed by this work.

In Committee, each clause of a Bill is considered separately, and the Question 'That the clause (or the clause as amended) stand part of the Bill' has to be put for each one. These motions are referred to generally as the 'stand part' motions.

Cross-votes

The term "cross-votes" refers to votes cast by Members in the lobby of their opponents in a division in which both main parties voted in opposing lobbies.

Emergency debates

Under Standing Order No. 9, a Member may rise in his place at the commencement of Public Business and ask leave to propose a motion for adjournment for the purpose of 'discussing a specific and important matter that should have urgent consideration'. If Mr Speaker is satisfied that the matter is a proper one to be so discussed, and the leave of the House given (or, failing that, forty Members or more rising in their places to support it, or upon a division if less than forty but more than ten Members rise), the motion stands over for discussion at the commencement of Public Business on the following day (or the following Monday if raised on a Thursday) or, if the Speaker deems it sufficiently urgent, at 7.00 p.m. the same day. Debate on such motions for adjournment, commonly referred to as emergency debates, is restricted to three hours.

Free votes

Free votes are those on which the whips are not applied and on which usually but by no means always Members are under no pressure from their Front Bench to vote in a particular manner. Free votes are normally, but not always, allowed on Private legislation, on Private Members' motions and legislation, House of Commons' matters (such as procedure and privilege), Ten Minute Rule Bills, Church of England measures, and various 'conscience' issues. In votes which are genuinely free votes, there is no party line and hence they do not fall within the scope of this study.

Guillotine motions

In order to ensure that discussion of a measure is completed within a certain period, the Government may introduce an allocation of time motion, commonly known as a guillotine motion, stipulating the time within which the remaining stage or stages should be completed and the time at which the parts of it should be completed. (Under Standing Order No. 44, discussion on allocation of time motions is limited to three hours.) The effect of a guillotine is that, once it falls, the remaining relevant Questions must be put forthwith without debate.

Lords Amendments

If the House of Lords amends a Bill originating in the Commons, the Lords return the Bill to the Commons requesting the concurrence of the House in the amendments. Amendments to amendments proposed by the Lords may be tabled. If none are forthcoming (or are disposed of), each Lords amendment is dealt with on the motion 'That this House doth agree (or disagree) with the Lords in the said amendment'.

Members' names

The names of Members who cast dissenting votes in a division are listed alphabetically in this volume. For consistency, the surname and first initial of each Member is given. Exceptions have been made (and other initials added) in cases where two Members of the same party share the same surname and initial and/or where Members are specially well known by a middle name or initial.[5] In the name index, Members' constituencies are also given.

Prayers

The term 'prayer' is applied normally to a motion to approve or annul a Statutory Instrument promulgated by a Government Department or body,[6] but is also applied commonly to any other motion to approve or annul a rule, order, or regulation, and it is given this wider application in this work.

Quorum of the House

The quorum of the House (including in Committee of the whole) is forty Members. Since 1971, it has not been possible for Members to call a count of the House, but if it appears on a division that forty Members are not present the Question is declared not decided. In determining the number of Members present, the Tellers and the occupant of the Chair are included.[7]

Reasoned amendment for rejection

On Second (or Third) Reading of a Bill, an amendment for rejection may be moved. This may take the form of a straightforward amendment for rejection (to read the Bill 'upon this day six (or three) months') or one in which a reason for rejection is outlined, commonly referred to as a 'reasoned amendment'. Examples of such amendments are to be found in the text.

Strangers

A Member may rise to call attention to Strangers (those who are not Members), and the Question 'That Strangers do withdraw' must be put forthwith.

'Take note' motions on EEC Documents

The texts of draft European Community legislation and other documents published by the EEC Commission for submission to the Council of Ministers are transmitted to Parliament by the Government, and considered in the Commons by the Select Committee on European Secondary Legislation. The Committee has the duty of recommending whether documents to which they have drawn attention as raising questions of legal or political importance should be further considered by the House. The Government tries, save in exceptional circumstances, to provide time for such debate, and it is held on 'take note' motions. Ministers are expected to take into account views expressed in debate. The effectiveness of this method of scrutinizing EEC documents has sometimes been questioned, especially though not exclusively by Members opposed to British membership of the European Communities.

Tellers

The official voting figures in a division do not include the Tellers (those who do the counting, two for the 'Ayes' and two for the 'Noes'), but they have been incorporated in this work. The names of dissenting Members who act as Tellers are identified by asterisks.

Voting in both lobbies

On occasion, the division lists record a Member as having voted in both lobbies. In some instances, this may be a mistake in the printing of the lists (see 'Note on Sources'), but in the remaining instances such dual voting has occurred. A Member may inadvertently enter the wrong Lobby, and once he has passed the Tellers his or her vote cannot be expunged. The only recourse a Member has who has voted in the wrong Lobby is to enter immediately the other Lobby, and in effect cancel out the other vote.[8] Where a Member has entered a dissenting Lobby apparently by mistake, and voted in the other Lobby as well, his or her name has not been included in the list of dissenters.

---

[1] Sir David Lidderdale (ed.), *Erskine May*, 19th edition, *op. cit.*, *House of Commons Manual of Procedure in the Public Business 1974*, 11th edition (Her Majesty's Stationery Office, 1974), and *Standing Orders of the House of Commons: Public Business* (Her Majesty's Stationery Office, 1976); there are separate Standing Orders for Private Business.

[2] A Member may speak without announcing his subsequent voting intentions, and in exceptional circumstances may be unavailable to take part in the division. It is not unknown, for instance, for a Member who is 'paired' to have taken part in a debate, though being unable to vote by virtue of being paired.

[3] Exempted business comprises proceedings on a Bill brought in on a Ways and Means resolution or a Consolidated Fund or Appropriation Bill; proceedings in pursuance of any Standing Order which provides for proceedings though opposed to be decided after the expiration of the time for opposed business; proceedings in pursuance of an Act of Parliament and proceedings on a motion authorizing expenditure in connection with a Bill, though with certain time limits operating.

[4] For example, Iain Macleod was allowed to retain his membership of the Shadow Cabinet in 1968 after voting against the Second Reading of the Commonwealth Immigrants Bill, whereas in 1976 Alick Buchanan-Smith was required to resign as Shadow Scottish Secretary because of his support for the Scotland and Wales Bill.

[5] The names to be distinguished because of the same surname and first initial (or commonly used middle initial in preference to the first) are, on the Labour benches: R. C. Brown (Newcastle-Upon-Tyne, West) and R. Brown (Hackney, South and Shoreditch); L. J. Callaghan (the Prime Minister, Cardiff, South-East) and J. Callaghan (Middleton and Prestwich) (this is the best known example, both Members being known as James Callaghan, but perhaps the least pertinent as the Prime Minister's name can be found only in the summaries of debate and not in a dissenting lobby); R. J. Hughes (Newport) and R. Hughes (Aberdeen, North); Mrs M. Miller (Ilford, North) and M. Miller (East Kilbride); A. L. Williams (Hornchurch) and A. Williams (Swansea, West); and on the Conservative side, R. G. Page (Crosby) and by-election returnee R. Page (Workington).

[6] The term derives from the fact that the House formally presents an address to the monarch 'praying' that an instrument be annulled.

[7] For a quorum to be present, a total of 35 Members must actually vote; the four Tellers and the occupant of the Chair bring the number up to forty.

[8] According to *Erskine May*, a Member who votes in both lobbies may be allowed on the following day to state as a matter of personal explanation in which lobby he or she intended to vote, 'and the numbers of the division have been directed to be corrected accordingly'

(19th ed., p. 401). In practice, this method of proceeding has not been employed in recent years, and it appears generally accepted that the only thing a Member voting in the wrong lobby can do is enter the other one and then leave it at that. See the comments of Mr Speaker on 15 May 1978, *HC Deb*. 950, c. 178–9.

NOTE ON SOURCES

The primary source of information contained in this work is *Parliamentary Debates: House of Commons*, fifth series, otherwise known as *Hansard*. This is cited in the text as *HC Deb.*, followed by the volume number and the column numbers of the division, in addition to the session and the division number.

'Roll call votes', as David Truman noted, 'have the great advantage of being 'hard' data. Like statistics on elections, they represent discrete acts the fact of whose occurrence is not subject to dispute. . . . Taken in quantity, therefore, they can be examined statistically with more confidence than can be granted to data whose reliability depends upon the objectivity of visual observations or verbal reporting.'[1]

It is, however, necessary to enter a small caveat. The division lists as published in *Hansard* are necessary and usually sufficient to determine which Members have cast dissenting votes in divisions. On occasion, though, mistakes occur during the holding of a division and in the publication of the division lists. The Tellers in one lobby may make a mistake in counting Members through (as the text will illustrate, the number of names listed in one lobby on occasion does not correspond with the voting figures given); a Clerk may tick off the name of a similarly-named Member to the one going through in the division; an error may occur at the printers. The result is that a Member may sometimes be listed as having voted in a dissenting lobby, his name being added by mistake or in place of a similarly-named Member on the other side of the House. (For example, the name of Conservative Member Paul Dean appeared on one occasion in error for Labour Member Joe Dean, similarly the name of Conservative Member Robert Cooke for Labour Member Robin Cook.) Sometimes, the mistake is obvious from the division list itself; e.g. the listing of a Deputy Speaker as having voted, or of a person no longer a Member of the House.[2] On other occasions, it is not. Where it appears (on the basis of the issue involved, the debate, the division lists, and the Member concerned—his or her interests and past voting behaviour) that there may have been a mistake in a Member's name appearing in the lobby of the opponent party, an attempt has been made to confirm the accuracy of the list in question. The division list as published in the weekly edition and the bound volume of *Hansard* (the responsibility for which lies with *Hansard*) has been compared with that as published in the *Votes and Proceedings* (the responsibility for which lies with the Clerks and, of the two, is the 'official' list); if a name appearing in the former does not appear in the latter, it has been omitted. If a name is published in both lists, the Member (or Members) in question has been contacted. In most cases, the communication from the Member(s) concerned has provided the definitive answer. In those few cases where Members have been unable to recall or comment upon their voting behaviour,[3] their names have been included on the basis of what appears in the printed division lists.

This approach serves also as a means of identifying those exceptional cases where a Member *has* entered the lobby of the opponent party but not in order to cast a dissenting vote, doing so either by mistake or for procedural or other reasons; e.g. voting in the opponent lobby in order to cancel out the vote of a colleague who has voted inadvertently while paired. Such cases are very rare.[4]

Other supporting sources, for material on events surrounding debates, names of abstainers and the like, are cited in the text as appropriate.

---

[1] *The Congressional Party: A Case Study* (Wiley, 1959), quoted in Ergun Ozbudun, *op. cit.*, p. 305.

[2] On occasion during the 1974–9 Parliament the names of the Chairman of Ways and Means, Oscar Murton, and the Deputy Chairman, Sir Myer Galpern, appeared in whipped divisions (both, by virtue of their positions, being non-voting Members), and on one occasion the name of Mr Christopher Tugendhat appeared in a division list after he had ceased to be a Member of the House.

[3] One or two Members failed to respond to the author's enquiries. It is presumed that if a Member was informed of his name being recorded as having cross-voted and knew it to be a mistake he or she would wish that fact to be known. Hence the presumption of accuracy unless informed otherwise by the Member(s) concerned.

[4] Most cases of voting by mistake (in the wrong lobby or voting while paired) would result in the same Member entering the other lobby as well, hence being identified and excluded at an early stage in our study (see 'Voting in both Lobbies' in the introductory notes). The process of contacting a Member is involved only when such dual voting does not take place.

ABBREVIATIONS

c.	column number
C.	Conservative
CAP	Common Agricultural Policy
Cmnd.	Command Paper
Dem. U.	Democratic Unionist
EC	European Communities
EEC	European Economic Community
HC Deb.	*Parliamentary Debates: House of Commons* (*Hansard*)
Hon.	Honourable
IMF	International Monetary Fund
Ind.	Independent
IRA	Irish Republican Army
Lab.	Labour
Lib.	Liberal
MP	Member of Parliament
NATO	North Atlantic Treaty Organization
PLP	Parliamentary Labour Party
PR	Proportional Representation
SDLP	Social Democratic and Labour Party
SI	Statutory Instrument
SLP	Scottish Labour Party
SNP	Scottish National Party
SO	Standing Order
STV	Single Transferable Vote
TUC	Trades Union Congress
UK	United Kingdom
UU	Ulster Unionist
UUUC	United Ulster Unionist Coalition
Vol.	Volume

The Parliament of March–October 1974

RATE SUPPORT GRANT   [1]

Prayer: 25 March 1974

The Secretary of State for the Environment, A. Crosland, moved 'That the Rate Support Grant Order 1974, a copy of which was laid before this House on 14th March, be approved.'

The motion was approved by 292 votes to 217. 1 Conservative cross-voted to support the motion, and at least one Labour Member (L. Huckfield) abstained from voting.

Conservative to vote for the motion:

Townsend, C.

HC Deb. 871. 195–200
1974, No. 3.

Mr Townsend was not called to speak during the debate, but is known to have voted for the motion for constituency reasons (the order benefitting his constituency).

NORTHERN IRELAND   [2]

4 April 1974

The Government initiated a debate on Northern Ireland on an adjournment motion. At the end of the debate, critics of the Government's Northern Ireland policy forced the adjournment motion to a division.

The adjournment motion was negatived by 190 votes to 9, with the Opposition abstaining from voting. The 11 Members (including tellers) to support adjournment comprised 10 United Ulster Unionist Coalition Members and 1 Conservative. At least 1 Conservative (C. Mather) abstained from voting.

Conservative to vote for adjournment:

Bell, R.

HC Deb. 871, 1581–2
1974, No. 7.

ADJOURNMENT (EASTER)   [3]

9 April 1974

The Lord President of the Council and Leader of the House, E. Short, moved 'That this House at its rising on Thursday do adjourn till Monday 29th April.'

The motion permitted Members the opportunity to raise disparate issues, with a number of Conservative Members pressing for a statement from the Minister of Agriculture on a guaranteed or intervention price for beef and related matters before the House rose for the Easter recess.

After the Lord President had replied to the various points raised, after four hours of debate, the Government Chief Whip moved 'That the Question be now put'.

(1) The closure motion was carried by 247 votes to 60, with the Opposition abstaining from voting. The 62 Members (including tellers) to oppose closure comprised 53 Conservative, 7 Liberal and 2 UUUC.

Conservatives to vote against closure:

Ancram, M.	Goodhart, P.	Oppenheim, Mrs S.
Baker, K.	Gorst, J.	Page, R. G.
Berry, A.	Gow, I.	Pattie, G.
Biffen, J.*	Hampson, K.	Redmond, R.
Boardman, T.	Hawkins, P.	Rees, P.
Boscawen, R.	Kellett-Bowman, Mrs E.	Rhys-Williams, Sir B.
Brittan, L.	King, T.	Ridley, N.
Channon, P.	Knight, Mrs J.	Sainsbury, T.
Cooke, R.	Lawrence, I.	Shersby, M.
Cormack, P.*	Lewis, K.	Silvester, F.
Crouch, D.	MacGregor, J.	Stanley, J.
Durant, T.	Miller, H.	Stewart, I.
Eden, Sir J.	Moate, R.	Tebbit, N.
Emery, P.	Money, E.	Temple-Morris, P.
Farr, J.	Moore, J.	Viggers, P.
Fenner, Mrs P.	Morgan-Giles, M.	Waddington, D.
Fowler, N.	Morrison, C.	Winterton, N.
Gardiner, G.	Morrison, P.	

(2) The motion was then put and carried by 238 votes to 28, with the Opposition abstaining from voting. The 30 Members (including tellers) to oppose the motion comprised 23 Conservative, 6 Liberal and 1 UUUC Member.

Conservatives to vote against the motion:

Berry, A.	Hampson, K.	Rhys-Williams, Sir B.
Biffen, J.*	Hawkins, P.	Ridley, N.
Cormack, P.*	King, T.	Rifkind, M.
Eden, Sir J.	Lawrence, I.	Silvester, F.
Emery, P.	Miller, H.	Stanley, J.
Farr, J.	Moore, J.	Temple-Morris, P.
Gorst, J.	Morgan-Giles, M.	Winterton, N.
Gow, I.	Pattie, G.	

HC Deb. 872, 249–54
1974, Nos. 8 and 9.

BUSINESS OF THE HOUSE [4]

9 April 1974

At 10.00 p.m., during the Second Reading debate of the Prices Bill, a Government whip moved formally the procedural exemption motion 'That the Prices Bill and Motion relating to Ways and Means may be proceeded with at this day's Sitting, though opposed, until any hour'.

The motion was carried by 220 votes to 31, with the Opposition abstaining from voting. The 33 Members (including tellers) to oppose the motion comprised 24 Conservative, 8 Liberal and 1 UUUC.

Conservatives to vote against the motion:

Bell, R.	Gow, I.	Redmond, R.
Biffen, J.	Hawkins, P.	Ridley, N.
Bruce-Gardyne, J.*	King, T.	Shaw, G.
Budgen, N.	Lawrence, I.	Shersby, M.*
Cormack, P.	Miller, H.	Sims, R.
Crouch, D.	Morrison, P.	Waddington, D.
Fenner, Mrs P.	Page, J.	Wakeham, J.
Gorst, J.	Page, R. G.	Winterton, N.

HC Deb. 872, 295–8
1974, No. 10.

The Prices Bill was subsequently given a Second Reading without a division, but with the Money Resolution for the Bill being divided upon (see below).

PRICES (MONEY)   [5]

Ways and Means: 9 April 1974

After the Prices Bill had been given a Second Reading, a junior Minister moved the Money Resolution for the Bill.

The Resolution was carried by 217 votes to 12, with the Opposition abstaining from voting. The 14 Members (including tellers) to oppose the Resolution comprised 10 Liberal and 4 Conservative.

Conservatives to vote against the Resolution:

Biffen, J.   Gow, I.   Ridley, N.
Bruce-Gardyne, J.

HC Deb. 872, 371–4
1974, No. 11.

NATIONAL INSURANCE BILL   [6]

Committee: 10 April 1974

New Clause 4 (Increase of death grant)

R. Boscawen (C., Wells) moved the new clause, designed to increase to £30 the death grant for those who were within ten years of retirement in 1948.

The clause was opposed by the Government. The Minister of Health and Social Security, B. O'Malley, said it dealt with only a fraction of the problem. The Government was prepared to consider the matter of death grants as a matter of priority before the next uprating.

The new clause was negatived by 253 votes to 36, with the Opposition abstaining from voting. The 38 Members (including tellers) to support the clause comprised 35 Conservative and 3 Liberal.

Conservatives to vote for the clause:

Aitken, J.	Hurd, D.	Page, R. G.
Ancram, M.	Kellett-Bowman, Mrs E.	Pattie, G.
Baker, K.	Knight, Mrs J.	Renton, T.
Boscawen, R.*	Knox, D.	Rhys-Williams, Sir B.
Chalker, Mrs L.	Lawrence, I.	Sainsbury, T.
Clarke, K.*	Lester, J.	Shaw, G.
Cockroft, J.	McCrindle, R.	Sims, R.
d'Avigdor-Goldsmid, J.	Marshall, M.	Steen, A.
Durant, T.	Mayhew, P.	Warren, K.
Dykes, H.	Moate, R.	Winterton, N.
Fletcher, A.	Morrison, C.	Worsley, Sir M.
Hampson, K.	Nicholls, Sir H.	

HC Deb. 872, 583–8
1974, No. 13.

COMPLAINT OF PRIVILEGE (MR SPEAKER'S RULING) [7]

30 April 1974

On 29 April 1974, Sir H. Nicholls (C., Peterborough) raised as a matter of privilege comments made publicly by J. Ashton (Lab., Bassetlaw) about fees received by Members of Parliament.

On 30 April, Mr Speaker ruled that he would permit a motion on the matter to take precedence over the Orders of the Day, and the Lord President of the Council and Leader of the House of Commons, E. Short, moved 'That the matter of the complaint made by the hon. Baronet the Member for Peterborough relating to statements made by the hon. Member for Bassetlaw in a broadcast interview be referred to the Committee of Privileges'.

The motion was supported by both the Government and the Opposition, but a number of Labour backbenchers forced it to a division.

The motion was carried, with the Government whips on, by 283 votes to 94, with the Opposition supporting the Government. The 96 Members (including tellers) to oppose the motion comprised 76 Labour, 10 Liberal, 5 Scottish National, 3 UUUC and 2 Plaid Cymru.

Labour Members to vote against the motion:

Allaun, F.
Atkins, R.
Atkinson, N.
Barnett, G.
Bates, A.
Bennett, A.
Bidwell, S.
Blenkinsop, A.
Boothroyd, Miss B.
Callaghan, J.*
Carter-Jones, L.
Clemitson, I.
Cohen, S.
Cryer, R.
Cunningham, G.
Davies, B.
Dean, J.
Duffy, P.
Edge, G.
Edwards, R.
Ellis, T.
Evans, F.
Evans, J.
Flannery, M.
Fletcher, T.
Garrett, J.

Garrett, W.
George, B.
Ginsburg, D.
Hamilton, W.
Hatton, F.
Hooley, F.
Huckfield, L.
Hughes, R. J.
Hunter, A.
Jones, A.
Kelley, R.
Kerr, R.*
Kinnock, N.
Lamond, J.
Lee, J.*
Lestor, Miss J.
McMillan, T.
Madden, M.
Marks, K.
Mendelson, J.
Mikardo, I.
Ovenden, J.
Park, G.
Prescott, J.
Radice, G.

Richardson, Miss J.
Roberts, G.
Roderick, C.
Rodgers, G.
Rooker, J.
Rose, P.
Sedgemore, B.
Shaw, A.
Sillars, J.
Silverman, J.
Skinner, D.
Snape, P.
Spriggs, L.
Stott, R.
Swain, T.
Thorne, S.
Tinn, J.
Torney, T.
Walker, T.
Whitehead, P.
Williams, W.
Wilson, A.
Wilson, W.
Woodall, A.
Young, D.

HC Deb. 872, 949–54
1974, No 14.

CHANNEL TUNNEL BILL [8]

Second Reading: 30 April 1974

The Minister for Transport, F. Mulley, moved the Second Reading of the Bill. He explained that it was identical to the one introduced in the last Parliament (Second Reading, 5 December 1973), and was essentially a technical Bill to enable the Government to fulfil its obligations if it agreed that construction of the Tunnel should be authorized. However, the Government believed there was a need for a full reassessment of the project before considering whether to go beyond phase two.

For the Opposition, Mrs M. Thatcher supported the measure.

A number of backbenchers rose to oppose the measure. L. Huckfield (Lab., Nuneaton) felt they should be considering more important matters. He thought the Tunnel could be a monumental fire hazard, that its profitability was open to doubt, that its escalation in cost could be great, and that its environmental benefits were doubtful. A. Clark (C., Plymouth, Sutton) thought the proposed Tunnel could affect the country's natural defence barrier.

The Bill was given a Second Reading by 287 votes to 62,[1] with the Opposition supporting the Government. The 64 Members (including tellers) to oppose the Bill comprised 33 Labour, 13 Conservative, 9 Liberal, 6 Scottish National, 2 Plaid Cymru and Democratic Labour Member D. Taverne.

Labour Members to vote against Second Reading:

Colquhoun, Mrs M.
Craigen, J.
Cryer, R.
Edge, G.
Evans, J.
Flannery, M.
George, B.
Hamilton, W.
Hatton, F.
Huckfield, L.
Kerr, R.

Kilroy-Silk, R.
Kinnock, N.
Lee, J.
Lewis, A.
Loyden, E.
Madden, M.
Newens, S.
O'Halloran, M.
Parry, R.
Prescott, J.
Rodgers, G.

Rooker, J.
Sandelson, N.
Sedgemore, B.
Selby, H.
Silverman, J.
Skinner, D.
Stallard, A.
Thorne, S.
Walker, T.
Wilson, A.
Wise, Mrs A.

Conservatives to vote against Second Reading:

Ancram, M.
Bell, R.
Body, R.
Clark, A.
King, E.

Latham, M.
Macfarlane, N.
Marten, N.
Mawby, R.

Moate, R.
Morgan, G.
Redmond, R.
Stanley, J.

HC Deb. 872, 1037–40
1974, No. 15.

[1] *Hansard* gives the number as 63, but lists only 62 names.

FINANCE BILL [9]

Second Reading: 9 May 1974

The Chancellor of the Exchequer, D. Healey, moved the Second Reading of the Bill.

For the Liberals, J. Pardoe (Lib., Cornwall, North) moved a reasoned amendment for rejection, 'That this House declines to give a Second Reading to a Finance Bill which does nothing to stop the rate of inflation rising to a level which is a danger to democracy, fails to protect those on lower incomes who suffer most from inflation, and yet increases the danger of an unacceptable level of unemployment'.

The amendment for rejection was negatived by 120 votes to 12, with the Opposition abstaining from voting. The 14 Members (including tellers) to support the amendment comprised 13 Liberal and 1 Conservative.

Conservative to vote for the amendment:

Redmond, R.

HC Deb. 873, 739–42
1974, No. 21.

FINANCE BILL [10]

Committee: 21 May 1974

Clause 7 (Charge of Corporation Tax for financial year 1973)

J. Pardoe (Lib., Cornwall, North) moved an amendment to provide that the tax should be levied on the basis of profits calculated in real terms on the basis of assets valued by reference to the movement of the Retail Price Index since the date of purchase.

The amendment was negatived by 239 votes to 24, with the Opposition abstaining from voting. The 26 Members (including tellers) to support the amendment comprised 13 Liberal, 11 Conservative and 2 Plaid Cymru.

Conservatives to vote for the amendment:

Biggs-Davison, J.
Langford-Holt, Sir J.
Lawson, N.
Maxwell-Hyslop, R.

Meyer, Sir A.
Morgan, G.
Nicholls, Sir H.
Redmond, R.

Stanbrook, I.
Taylor, E.
Winterton, N.

HC Deb. 874, 267–70
1974, No. 27.

PRICES BILL [11]

Third Reading: 12 June 1974

The Secretary of State for Prices and Consumer Protection, Mrs S. Williams, moved formally the Third Reading of the Bill.

During the debate, J. Bruce-Gardyne (C., South Angus) declared that it was a Bill with 'virtually no redeeming features'. 'I have no doubt that in time it will be destroyed in the way that we have seen happen to all these attempts to deal with inflation by passing laws against it. It will only be destroyed, ultimately, by public ridicule. The sooner that happens, the better.'

For the Opposition, Mrs S. Openheim said that despite their misgivings they did not wish to see the Bill fail.

After the Government's reply, the Bill was given a Third Reading by 209 votes to 20, with the Opposition abstaining from voting. The 22 Members (including tellers) to oppose the Bill comprised 13 Liberal and 9 Conservative.

Conservatives to vote against Third Reading:

Biffen, J.
Bruce-Gardyne, J.
Cormack, P.

Eden, Sir J.
Gow, I.
Latham, M.

Lawrence, I.
Shaw, G.
Winterton, N.

HC Deb. 874, 1787–90
1974, No. 40.

HEALTH AND SAFETY AT WORK ETC. BILL [12]

Report: 18 June 1974

Clause 1 (Preliminary)

R. Cryer (Lab., Keighley) moved formally an amendment to the clause to provide 'Nothing in this Act shall permit the Secretary of State to remove, or limit the application of any of the provisions imposing absolute liability contained in any of the relevant statutory provisions or any regulations, orders or other instruments made thereunder.'

The amendment was opposed by the Government, and negatived by 222 votes to 37, with the Opposition abstaining from voting. The 39 Members (including tellers) to support the amendment were all Labour Members. 9 Conservatives entered the Government lobby to oppose the amendment.

Labour Members to vote for the amendment:

Allaun, F.	Fletcher, T.	Roberts, G.
Ashton, J.	Huckfield, L.	Roderick, C.
Atkinson, N.	Kelley, R.	Rodgers, G.
Bennett, A.	Kerr, R.	Rose, P.
Bidwell, S.	Lambie, D.	Sedgemore, B.
Carter-Jones, L.	Latham, A.	Sillars, J.
Clemitson, I.	McNamara, K.	Skinner, D.
Cook, R.	Madden, M.*	Swain, T.
Cryer, R.*	Marks, K.	Tomlinson, J.
Davies, B.	Mikardo, I.	Torney, T.
Douglas-Mann, B.	Newens, S.	Wainwright, E.
Edge, G.	Price, C.	Wilson, A.
Fernyhough, E.	Richardson, Miss J.	Wise, Mrs A.

Conservatives to vote against the amendment:

Clark, A.	Godber, J.	Ridley, N.
Costain, A.	Macfarlane, N.	Rifkind, M.
Glyn, A.	Mayhew, P.	Winterton, N.

HC Deb. 875, 345–8
1974, No. 43.

HOUSING (SCOTLAND) BILL　　　　　　　　　　[13]

Report: 26 June 1974

Clause 5 (Amount of improvement grant)

R. Cook (Lab., Edinburgh, Central) moved an amendment to increase the level of maximum allowable expenditure on which improvement grants were calculated from £2,400 (as proposed in the clause)to £3,000.

The Minister of State at the Scottish Office, B. Millan, said the figure was under review, and could be amended if the Bill went through.

Mr Cook subsequently asked leave to withdraw his amendment, but a number of Members objected.

The amendment was negatived by 130 votes to 16, with the Opposition abstaining from voting. The 18 Members (including tellers) to support the amendment comprised 7 Liberal, 7 Scottish National, 3 Conservative and 1 UUUC.

Conservatives to vote for the amendment:

Crowder, F. P.　　　　Stanbrook, I.　　　　Winterton, N.

HC Deb. 875, 1663–4
1974, No. 56.

EEC (ECONOMIC POLICY)　　　　　　　　　　　[14]

3 July 1974

The Paymaster-General, E. Dell, moved 'That this House takes note of Commission Documents Nos R/1253/74, R/1474/74 and COM (74) 696.'

The documents dealt with guidelines for co-ordination of short-term economic policies, the draft Council decision on Practical Rules for Prior Notification of Exchange Rate Changes, and the Commission Communication on Urgent Economic and Monetary Measures.

A number of backbench opponents of British membership of the EEC forced the motion to a division, in which it was carried by 107 votes to 70, with the Opposition supporting the Government. The 109 Members (including tellers) in the Government lobby comprised 54 Labour, 50 Conservative and 5 Liberal. The 72 Members (including tellers) to oppose the motion comprised 49 Labour, 8 UUUC, 7 Scottish National, 5 Conservative, 2 Plaid Cymru, and 1 Independent Labour.[1]

Labour Members to vote against the motion:

Allaun, F.	Hughes, M.	Richardson, Miss J.
Atkins, R.	Hughes, R. J.	Roberts, G.
Atkinson, N.	Jay, D.	Roderick, C.
Barnett, G.	Lambie, D.	Rodgers, G.
Butler, Mrs J.	Lamond, J.	Rooker, J.
Colquhoun, Mrs M.*	Latham, A.	Sedgemore, B.
Cook, R.	Leadbitter, T.	Sillars, J.
Cryer, R.	Lee, J.	Silverman, J.
Davies, B.	Loughlin, C.	Skinner, D.
Davies, D.	Loyden, E.	Spearing, N.
Dunwoody, Mrs G.	McElhone, F.	Spriggs, L.
Evans, J.	McNamara, K.	Thorne, S.
Ewing, H.	Madden, M.*	Tierney, S.
Flannery, M.	Mikardo, I.	Tuck, R.
Fletcher, T.	Newens, S.	Wise, Mrs A.
George, B.	Ovenden, J.	Woof, R.
Hooley, F.		

Conservatives to vote against the motion:

Bell, R.	Marten, N.	Mudd, D.
Body, R.	Moate, R.	

HC Deb. 876, 527–30
1974, No. 65.

[1] E. Milne, returned as the Independent Labour Member for Blyth.

RENT BILL   [15]

Second Reading: 8 July 1974

The Minister for Housing and Construction, R. Freeson, moved the Second Reading of the Bill.

At 10.00 p.m., the Government moved 'That the Question be now put.'

The closure was carried by 155 votes to 6, with the Opposition abstaining from voting. The 8 Members (including tellers) to oppose closure were all Conservatives.

Conservatives to vote against closure:

Bell, R.	James, D.	Rees-Davies, W.*
Cordle, J.*	Maxwell-Hyslop, R.	Winterton, N.
Emery, P.	Morgan-Giles, M.	

HC Deb. 876, 1087–8
1974, No. 68.

The Bill was then given a Second Reading without a division.

STATUTORY INSTRUMENTS [16]

9 July 1974

A Government whip moved formally 'That the draft European Communities (Definition of Treaties) Order 1974 be referred to a Standing Committee on Statutory Instruments.'

The motion was carried by 153 votes to 52, with the Opposition supporting the Government. The 54 Members (including tellers) to oppose the motion comprised 41 Labour, 6 Scottish National, 5 UUUC, 1 Conservative[1] and 1 Plaid Cymru.

Labour Members to vote against the motion:

Allaun, F.	Fletcher, T.	Roberts, G.
Ashton, J.	Garrett, W.	Roderick, C.
Bennett, A.	Hatton, F.	Rooker, J.
Colquhoun, Mrs M.	Hughes, R. J.	Sedgemore, B.
Cook, R.	Jay, D.	Sillars, J.
Cryer, R.	Kerr, R.	Skinner, D.
Davidson, A.	Kinnock, N.	Snape, P.
Davies, B.	Lambie, D.	Spearing, N.
Dean, J.	Latham, A.	Stoddart, D.
Edge, G.	Lee, J.*	Thomas, J.
Ellis, J.	Madden, M.	Tuck, R.*
Evans, J.	Ovenden, J.	Wise, Mrs A.
Fernyhough, E.	Prescott, J.	Young, D.
Flannery, M.	Richardson, Miss J.	

Conservative to vote against the motion:

Biffen, J.

HC Deb. 876, 1155–8
1974, No. 69.

---

¹ The *Hansard* division lists record R. Cooke (C., Bristol, West) as voting against the motion,
but his name is listed in error for R. Cook (Lab., Edinburgh, Central).

NORTHERN IRELAND   [17]

Prayer: 9 July 1974

The Secretary of State for Northern Ireland, M. Rees, moved 'That
the Northern Ireland (Emergency Provisions) Act 1973 (Continuance)
Order 1974, a copy of which was laid before this House on 4th July, be
approved.'

Mr Rees said that the Act should be renewed until the Gardiner
Committee which he had set up had reported. It was the Government's hope to introduce new legislation in the not-too-distant future.

A number of Labour backbenchers opposed the order, and forced it
to a division. The order was approved by 98 votes to 17, with the
Opposition supporting the Government. The 19 Members (including
tellers) to oppose the order comprised 18 Labour and 1 SDLP.

Labour Members to vote against the order:

Atkinson, N.	Loyden, E.	Prescott, J.
Bennett, A.	McGuire, M.	Richardson, Miss J.
Colquhoun, Mrs M.*	McNamara, K.*	Skinner, D.
Cook, R.	Madden, M.	Stallard, A.
Cryer, R.	Newens, S.	Thorne, S.
Latham, A.	O'Halloran, M.	Wise, Mrs A.

HC Deb. 876, 1315–8
1974, No. 70.

The division took place at 12.23 a.m.

NORTHERN IRELAND BILL [18]

Committee: 15 July 1974

Schedule 2 (Convention on future Government of Northern Ireland)

H. West (UUUC, Fermanagh and South Tyrone) moved an amendment to increase the size of the Northern Ireland Assembly from 78 to 81.

The Secretary of State for Northern Ireland, M. Rees, opposed the amendment. He contended that such matters were best left to the Boundary Commission.

The amendment was negatived by 131 votes to 11, with the Opposition abstaining from voting. The 13 Members (including tellers) to support the amendment comprised 10 UUUC and 3 Conservative.

Conservatives to vote for the amendment:

Fairgrieve, R.	Taylor, E.	Winterton, N.

HC Deb. 877, 153–6
1974, No. 82.

FINANCE BILL [19]

Report: 16 July 1974

Clause 2 (Increase of certain duties on betting)

R. Eyre (C., Birmingham, Hall Green) moved an amendment to restrict the rate of pool betting duty from 40% to $33\frac{1}{3}$% for holders of licences under the 1971 Pool Competitions Act and any person approved by the Secretary of State on the recommendation of the Gaming Board.

W. Wilson (Lab., Coventry, South-West) rose to support the amendment. He said the pools concerned were worthy of support, and if the amendment was accepted the Chancellor might receive more revenue.

The Financial Secretary to the Treasury, Dr J. Gilbert, expressed sympathy with the aims of the amendment, but said he would need to see the financial implications in more detail. The best way to proceed would be by a general review of the law on the matter.

The amendment was *carried* by 291 votes to 274, *a majority against the*

Government of 17. 1 Labour Member cross-voted to support the amendment.

Labour Member to support the amendment:

Wilson, W.

HC Deb. 877, 355–60.
1974, No. 84.

FINANCE BILL [20]

Report: 17 July 1974

Clause 15 (Restrictions on relief for interest)

J. Pardoe (Lib., Cornwall, North) moved an amendment designed to provide that interest on a loan up to £25,000 for house purchase or improvement would be allowed against the basic rate of tax only, and not all rates of tax.

The Financial Secretary to the Treasury, Dr J. Gilbert, said there were various administrative reasons why the amendment was not acceptable, including the complications that would be introduced in the PAYE system.

The amendment was negatived by 274 votes to 24, with the Opposition abstaining from voting. The 26 Members (including tellers) to support the amendment comprised 15 Liberal,[1] 6 Scottish National, 3 Conservative, 1 UUUC and Democratic Labour Member D. Taverne. 11 Conservatives entered the Government lobby to oppose the amendment.

Conservatives to vote for the amendment:

Mudd, D.	Normanton, T.	Redmond, R.

Conservatives to vote against the amendment:

Boardman, T.	Marten, N.	Rifkind, M.
Hutchison, M. C.	Mills, P.	Shaw, M.
Lamont, N.	Miscampbell, N.	Stewart, I.
Macmillan, M.	Nott, J.	

HC Deb. 877, 583–6
1974, No. 88.

---

[1] Including C. Mayhew, returned as Labour Member for Woolwich, East, who took the Liberal whip on 9 July 1974.

FINANCE BILL [21]

Report: 17 July 1974

Schedule 1 (Relief for Interest)

The Financial Secretary to the Treasury, Dr J. Gilbert, moved an amendment to delete subsection (2) (inserted in Committee by Opposition Members) which linked the ceiling provided under the schedule to changes in the official retail price index.

Dr Gilbert said that for reasons covered in Committee, he was unable to recommend the House to accept the subsection.

The amendment was carried by 102 votes to 29, with the Opposition abstaining from voting. The 31 Members (including tellers) to oppose the amendment comprised 24 Conservative, 6 Liberal and 1 UUUC.

Conservatives to vote against the amendment:

Body, R.	Lamont, N.*	Nicholls, Sir H.
Churchill, W.	Lawrence, I.	Normanton, T.
Cooke, R.	Lawson, N.*	Page, J.
Cope, J.	Lester, J.	Page, R. G.
du Cann, E.	Lloyd, I.	Ridley, N.
Durant, T.	MacGregor, J.	Scott-Hopkins, J.
Hannam, J.	Mitchell, D.	Wiggin, J.
King, T.	Newton, T.	Winterton, N.

HC Deb. 877, 615–8
1974, No. 91.

EUROPEAN COMMUNITIES (TREATIES) [22]

Prayer: 18 July 1974

A Government whip moved formally 'That the European Communities (Definition of Treaties) Order 1974, a draft of which was laid before this House on 8th July, be approved.'

The motion was carried by 90 votes to 24, with the Opposition supporting the Government. The 92 Members (including tellers) in the Government lobby comprised 70 Labour, 14 Conservative and 8 Liberal. The 26 Members (including tellers) to oppose the motion comprised 25 Labour and 1 UUUC.

Labour Members to vote against the motion:

Ashton, J.	Huckfield, L.	Richardson, Miss J.
Atkinson, N.	Kelley, R.	Rodgers, G.
Carter-Jones, L.	Kerr, R.*	Sedgemore, B.
Colquhoun, Mrs M.	Latham, A.	Skinner, D.
Cryer, R.	Lee, J.*	Snape, P.
Dunwoody, Mrs G.	McNamara, K.	Spearing, N.
Ellis, J.	Madden, M.	Stoddart, D.
Flannery, M.	Parry, R.	Wise, Mrs A.
Fletcher, R.		

HC Deb. 877, 841–2
1974, No. 95.

ECONOMIC SITUATION   [23]

Supply: 24 July 1974

The Leader of the Opposition, E. Heath, moved 'That this House regrets that the measures announced by Mr Chancellor of the Exchequer on Monday are irrelevant to the underlying problems of the economy, make no attempt to restore business confidence, and do nothing to encourage the industrial investment which alone can safeguard the jobs and future prosperity of the nation.'

The Prime Minister, H. Wilson, moved an amendment to make the motion read 'That this House welcomes the statement of the Chancellor of the Exchequer of 22nd July in relation to the extension of rate relief, the reduction in value added tax, the extension of food subsidies, the doubling of regional employment premium, and the easing of dividend restraint.'

At the end of the debate, the Government amendment was put and carried by 269 votes to 28, with the Opposition abstaining officially from voting. The 30 Members (including tellers) to oppose the amendment comprised 27 Conservative, 2 Liberal and Democratic Labour Member D. Taverne.

Conservatives to vote against the amendment:

Aitken, J.	Gow, I.	Ridley, N.
Bennett, Sir F.	Hordern, P.	Rost, P.
Biffen, J.*	Iremonger, T.	Royle, Sir A.

Body, R.	Lawson, N.	Sims, R.
Budgen, N.	Miller, H.	Skeet, T.
Churchill, W.	Morgan, G.	Tapsell, P.*
Cormack, P.	Page, J.	Tebbit, N.
Dodsworth, G.	Redmond, R.	Viggers, P.
Fraser, H.	Renton, T.	Wells, J.

HC Deb. 877, 1731–4
1974, No. 100.

The amended motion was then accepted without a division. *See* also *The Times*, 25 July 1974.

ROAD TRAFFIC BILL   [24]

Committee: 26 July 1974

New Clause 4 (Compulsory wearing of seat belts)

J. Wiggin (C., Weston-super-Mare) moved the new clause to make compulsory (with certain exceptions) the wearing of seat belts.

The clause was opposed by the Government, and negatived by 65 votes to 3, with the Opposition abstaining from voting. The 5 Members (including tellers) to support the clause were all Conservatives. 2 Conservatives entered the Government lobby to vote against it.

Conservatives to vote for the clause:

Moate, R.*	Waddington, D.
Page, R. G.	Wiggin, J.*
Sinclair, Sir G.	

Conservatives to vote against the clause:

Bell, R.	Body, R.

HC Deb. 877, 2119–20
1974, No. 102.

The Parliament of 1974–1979

The Session of 1974–5

DEBATE ON THE ADDRESS   [25]

5 November 1974

From the Opposition Front Bench, Mrs M. Thatcher moved an amendment to the Address, regretting that the Speech 'in no way measures up to the perils facing the country, and that its doctrinaire proposals will divide rather than unite the country.' On a straight party vote, the amendment was negatived by 310 votes to 268.

The substantive motion (the traditional Humble Address) was then put: 'That an humble Address be presented to Her Majesty, as follows: Most Gracious Sovereign, We, Your Majesty's most dutiful and loyal subjects, the Commons of the United Kingdom of Great Britain and Northern Ireland, in Parliament assembled, beg leave to offer our humble thanks to Your Majesty for the Gracious Speech which Your Majesty has addressed to both Houses of Parliament.'

The Liberals divided the House on the motion, which was carried by 308 votes to 14, with the Opposition abstaining from voting. The 16 Members (including tellers) to oppose the motion comprised 12 Liberals, 3 Conservatives and 1 UUUC Member.

Conservatives to vote against the motion:

Rost, P.   Scott-Hopkins, J.   Winterton, N.

HC Deb. 880, 1025–8
1974–5, No. 3.

RHODESIA   [26]

Prayer: 8 November 1974

The Secretary of State for Foreign and Commonwealth Affairs, L. J. Callaghan, moved 'That the Southern Rhodesia Act 1965

(Continuation) Order 1974, a draft of which was laid before this House on 29th October, be approved.'

The order provided the authority under which sanctions against Rhodesia could be maintained. The Foreign Secretary noted that it was the tenth occasion on which the House had been asked by successive Governments to approve the order.

A number of Conservative backbenchers rose to oppose the Order. In a maiden speech, M. Brotherton (C., Louth) declared that he thought sanctions had failed, and that it was time to tell the United Nations so. S. Hastings (C., Mid-Bedfordshire) said that at the outset he had argued that sanctions would achieve nothing except to toughen the resolve of white people in Rhodesia, and so it had proved. 'Therefore, as usual, I shall vote against the order.' P. Wall (C., Haltemprice) felt that sanctions would make it impossible to achieve the objectives of avoiding a race war in Southern Africa and maintaining British interests in that strategically important part of the world.

Two Conservative backbenchers also rose to support the Order. I. Stanbrook (C., Orpington) declared that the vast majority of the people of Rhodesia were Africans, and sooner or later the Government of that country would be African. 'If we believe in democracy, we must believe in majority rule and what it amounts to in Africa and elsewhere. If continuation of sanctions helps to bring about this change of attitude on the part of white Rhodesians, I believe that the order is justified.' C. Townsend (C., Bexleyheath) argued that if a settlement that would last was to be reached the best way was through a maintenance of the status quo.

The Order was approved by 124 votes to 23, with the Opposition abstaining from voting. The 25 Members (including tellers) to vote against the Order comprised 23 Conservative and 2 UUUC Members. 3 Conservatives also entered the Government lobby to support it.

Conservatives to vote against the Order:

Bell, R.	Fell, A.	Skeet, T.
Bennett, Sir F.	Goodhew, V.	Stokes, J.
Biggs-Davison, J.*	Hastings, S.*	Taylor, R.
Boyson, R.	James, D.	Tebbit, N.
Brotherton, M.	Lloyd, I.	Wall, P.
Clark, A.	Montgomery, F.	Warren, K.
Clark, W.	Ridley, N.	Wiggin, J.
Emery, P.	Sims, R.	

Conservatives to vote for the Order:

Dykes, H.   Stanbrook, I.   Townsend, C.

HC Deb. 880, 1505–6
1974–5, No. 5.

OFFSHORE PETROLEUM DEVELOPMENT   [27]
(SCOTLAND) BILL

Second Reading: 19 November 1974

The Minister of State at the Scottish Office, B. Millan, moved the
Second Reading of the Bill, which was designed to provide certain
controls over the development of oil exploration and exploitation in
and around Scotland.

For the Opposition, A. Buchanan-Smith welcomed the principles
behind the Bill, though expressing the fear that the Government had
allowed itself to be carried away in the provisions of Clause 1, which
concerned the public acquisition of land.[1] He expressed a qualified
welcome for the measure.

Scottish National Members rose to oppose the Bill, as did Liberal
Members. A number of Conservative backbenchers also criticized the
measure. Miss B. Harvie Anderson (C., Renfrewshire, East) said she
would not vote against it, but felt that the powers provided were
excessive. A. Fletcher (C., Edinburgh, North) felt individuals should
be considered more in such legislation, and M. Rifkind (C., Edinburgh,
Pentlands) contended that, in its existing form, it was a dangerous Bill,
asking for Draconian powers of a kind which no previous Government
had sought to exercise.

The Bill was given a Second Reading by 201 votes to 30, with the
Opposition abstaining from voting. The 32 Members (including tellers)
to oppose the Bill comprised 12 Liberal, 11 Scottish National, 6
Conservative and 3 Plaid Cymru. According to the division lists, one
of the Conservative dissenters (N. Ridley) voted in both lobbies.

Conservatives to vote against Second Reading:

Adley, R.   Corrie, J.   Rost, P.
Bowden, A.   Ridley, N.   Winterton, N.

HC Deb. 881, 1239–42
1974–5, No. 11.

¹ Under Clause 1(2), the Secretary of State was empowered to acquire by agreement or compulsorily any land in Scotland needed for the exploration or exploitation of offshore oil, and, where required because of urgency, to proceed by means of an expedited compulsory acquisition procedure, under which there would be no requirement to hold a public inquiry related to the order, but subject to parliamentary approval under the negative resolution procedure.

TEA SUBSIDY   [28]

Prayer: 19 November 1974

The Under-Secretary of State for Prices and Consumer Protection, R. Maclennan, moved 'That the Food Subsidies (Tea) (No. 2) Order 1974 (S.I., 1974, No. 1913), a copy of which was laid before this House on 18th November, be approved.'

The Order permitted the Secretary of State to continue to pay a consumer subsidy on tea. For the Opposition, T. Raison announced that, as they had not opposed the introduction of tea subsidies before the General Election, they did not propose to vote against the Order.

R. Wainwright (Lib., Colne Valley) opposed the Order, arguing that the cost of the subsidy—£29 million—could be much more effectively spent 'on relieving specific ascertained needs'. Dr K. Hampson (C., Ripon) made a similar point, and argued that everything that could be saved should be saved; if there was a division, he would vote against the Order. A number of Conservative Members also rose to question what the position was in the four day period between the expiration of the previous Order and the one currently before them.

The Order was approved by 141 votes to 15, with the Opposition abstaining from voting. The 17 Members (including tellers) to oppose the Order comprised 12 Liberals and 5 Conservatives.

Conservatives to vote against the Order:

Hampson, K.   Skeet, T.   Winterton, N.
Rodgers, Sir J.   Stanbrook, I.

HC Deb. 881, 1273–4
1974–5, No. 12.

PREVENTION OF TERRORISM (TEMPORARY PROVISIONS) BILL [29]

Committee: 28 November 1974

Clause 4 (Right to make representations to Secretary of State)

F. Hooley (Lab., Sheffield, Heeley) moved an amendment to provide for the establishment of an Appeal Tribunal to hear appeals against exclusion orders made by the Home Secretary, and for the Tribunal to have power to revoke or confirm such orders.

Mr Hooley said he could not accept that the Home Secretary could adequately discharge the task of appeal as well as the original onerous task of taking the decision to exclude a person from the country. He did not think the House should pass such legislation without a safeguard of that kind.

A. Bennett (Lab., Stockport, North) said it was important that someone should not be making the orders and then judging whether they had been made fairly. Miss J. Richardson (Lab., Barking) observed that the Home Secretary had said many times that he did not want to infringe more than was absolutely essential the rights of ordinary law-abiding citizens. 'The best way of ensuring that is to remove any idea that he may be prosecutor, judge and jury.'

The Home Secretary, R. Jenkins, said that persons who had been served exclusion orders could make representations to the Home Secretary, who had to refer them to advisers whom he nominated. In making orders, matters of grave national security were involved, and advice had to be sought from people to whom secrets affecting national security could be entrusted. There could be no question of open proceedings or the public presentation of evidence. 'I would not think it reasonable to tell the House that I was presenting an emergency Bill in order to deal with the gravest terrorist situation we have ever confronted and then to propose executive powers less powerful, less effective, than those which apply in cases in which I and every other Home Secretary have been able, wherever someone's entry is non-conducive to the public good, to make a decision. . . . What is concerned here goes much more to the heart of our national life and danger to the structure of society than the issues dealt with in that way. If these powers are to be effective at all, basically, I must retain as much executive power here over the matters I have mentioned.'

The amendment was negatived by 218 votes to 51, the Conservatives voting with the Government. The 220 Members (including tellers) in the Government lobby comprised 196 Labour, 15 Conservative, 8

UUUC and 1 Liberal. The 53 Members (including tellers) to support the amendment comprised 52 Labour and 1 SDLP.

Labour Members to vote for the amendment:

Atkinson, N.	Hoyle, D.	Ovenden, J.
Bennett, A.	Huckfield, L.	Parry, R.
Bidwell, S.*	Jackson, Miss M.	Prescott, J.
Buchan, N.	Jeger, Mrs L.	Richardson, Miss J.
Canavan, D.	Kerr, R.	Roderick, C.
Clemitson, I.	Kilroy-Silk, R.	Rodgers, G.
Colquhoun, Mrs M.	Kinnock, N.	Rooker, J.
Cook, R.	Lee, J.	Sedgemore, B.
Corbett, R.	Litterick, T.	Short, Mrs R.
Cryer, R.	Loyden, E.	Sillars, J.
Davies, B.	McNamara, K.	Skinner, D.
Delargy, H.	Madden, M.	Stallard, A.
Edge, G.	Marshall, J.	Thomas, R.
Flannery, M.	Maynard, Miss J.	Thorne, S.
Fletcher, T.	Mendelson, J.	Watkinson, J.
Garrett, J.	Mikardo, I.	Wise, Mrs A.
Gould, B.	Miller, Mrs M.	
Hooley, F.*	Newens, S.	

HC Deb. 882, 895–8
1974–5, No. 17.

The division took place at 5.58 a.m., during an all-night sitting.

PREVENTION OF TERRORISM (TEMPORARY PROVISIONS) BILL [30]

Committee: 28 November 1974

New Clause 5 (Independent Tribunals)

J. Prescott (Lab., Hull, East) formally moved the new clause, which read: 'The Secretary of State shall establish a tribunal independent of the police to review allegations of abuse by persons who have been detained under section 7 of this Act.'

The new clause had been discussed earlier in conjunction with other amendments, and opposed by the Government.[1]

The new clause was negatived by 193 votes to 61, Conservative Members voting with the Government. The 195 Members (including tellers) in the Government lobby comprised 174 Labour, 13 Conservative and 8 UUUC. The 63 Members (including tellers) to support the clause comprised 61 Labour, 1 Liberal and 1 SDLP.

Labour Members to vote for the new clause:

Bates, A.	Huckfield, L.	Parry, R.
Bean, R.	Jackson, Miss M.	Prescott, J.*
Bennett, A.	Janner, G.	Richardson, Miss J.
Bidwell, S.	Jeger, Mrs L.	Roderick, C.
Buchan, N.	Kerr, R.	Rodgers, G.
Callaghan, J.	Kilroy-Silk, R.	Rooker, J.
Canavan, D.	Kinnock, N.	Sedgemore, B.
Clemitson, I.	Lee, J.	Short, Mrs R.
Colquhoun, Mrs M.	Litterick, T.	Sillars, J.
Cook, R.	Loyden, E.	Skinner, D.
Cryer, R.	McElhone, F.	Spearing, N.
Davies, B.	McNamara, K.	Stallard, A.
Delargy, H.	Madden, M.	Taylor, Mrs A.
Edge, G.	Marshall, J.	Thomas, R.
Edwards, R.	Maynard, Miss J.	Thorne, S.
Evans, F.	Mendelson, J.	Walker, T.
Flannery, M.	Mikardo, I.	Watkinson, J.
Fletcher, T.	Miller, Mrs M.	Whitehead, P.*
Garrett, J.	Newens, S.	Wise, Mrs A.
Hooley, F.	Noble, M.	
Hoyle, D.	Ovenden, J.	

HC Deb. 882, 929–34
1974–5, No. 18.

1 Prescott had argued that it was crucial that the law be seen as being fair to all. "To go forward with these extraordinary powers without bringing in extraordinary means of protection is wrong." The Home Secretary had replied that the matter was very complicated and required full-scale legislation. He was in favour of such a proceeding as was proposed, but the clause would not be a practical or appropriate way of achieving it.

POST OFFICE (COMPENSATION) [31]

Prayer: 2 December 1974

The Under-Secretary of State for Industry, G. Mackenzie, moved 'That the Compensation for Limitation of Prices (Post Office) Order

1974, a draft of which was laid before this House on 29th October, be approved.'

The order, made under section 2 of the Statutory Corporations (Financial Provisions) Act of 1974, provided for payment of £123m. in compensation to the Post Office for the year 1973–4.

From the Opposition Front Bench, M. Heseltine raised certain queries about the order, though the Opposition did not divide the House on it; a number of backbenchers nevertheless took it to a division.

The order was approved by 43 votes to 11, with the Opposition abstaining from voting. The 45 Members (including tellers) in the Government lobby comprised 43 Labour and 2 Liberal. The 13 Members (including tellers) to oppose the order were all Conservatives.

Conservatives to vote against the order:

Clarke, K.	Marshall, M.	Shaw, G.
Eyre, R.	Mayhew, P.	Stanley, J.*
Gow, I.	Montgomery, F.	Tebbit, N.
James, D.	Renton, T.	Young, Sir G.
King, T.*		

HC Deb. 882, 1289–90
1974–5, No. 20.

NORTHERN IRELAND (EMERGENCY POWERS)   [32]

Prayer: 5 December 1974

The Secretary of State for Northern Ireland, M. Rees, moved 'That the Northern Ireland (Various Emergency Provisions) (Continuance) Order 1974, a draft of which was laid before this House on 28th November, be approved.'

The order sought to continue the provisions of the Northern Ireland (Emergency Provisions) Act 1973 and the Northern Ireland (Young Persons) Act 1974 for a period of six months. The Secretary of State announced that he hoped to do everything possible within that time to introduce legislation based on the anticipated report of the Gardiner Committee.[1]

L. Huckfield (Lab., Nuneaton) rose to express his concern about the renewal of the emergency provisions. He was not happy with the Government's policy of 'watching, waiting and hoping'. K. McNamara

(Lab., Hull, Central) expressed the view that the powers which the order sought to renew had never worked. Under the powers, the Secretary of State had condemned nine men 'without trial, without a shred of evidence, accusing them of mass murder and sectarian crimes of the worst possible sort'; they had not been able to say a word in their own defence or see the evidence against them. He also expressed concern about the emphasis placed upon the Gardiner report, and what might be in it. He announced that he would vote against the order.

The order was approved by 91 votes to 22, the Opposition voting with the Government. The 93 Members (including tellers) in the Government lobby comprised 71 Labour, 11 Conservative, 9 UUUC and 2 Liberal. The 24 Members (including tellers) to oppose the order comprised 23 Labour and 1 SDLP.

Labour Members to vote against the order:

Atkinson, N.	Kerr, R.	Richardson, Miss J.
Bidwell, S.	Litterick, T.	Sedgemore, B.
Clemitson, I.	Loyden, E.	Skinner, D.
Colquhoun, Mrs M.	McNamara, K.	Stallard, A.*
Cryer, R.*	Madden, M.	Thomas, R.
Flannery, M.	Maynard, Miss J.	Thorne, S.
Gould, B.	Newens, S.	Wise, Mrs A.
Huckfield, L.	O'Halloran, M.	

HC Deb. 882, 2101–4
1974–5, No. 23.

¹ The Committee had been asked to make recommendations on powers to deal with terrorism and subversion, while maintaing the civil liberties and human rights of the people of Northern Ireland "to the maximum practicable extent". *HC Deb.* 882, c. 2071.

OFFSHORE PETROLEUM DEVELOPMENT (SCOTLAND) BILL   [33]

Committee: 10 December 1974

Clause 1 (Acquisition of land for purposes connected with offshore petroleum)

G. Wilson (SNP, Dundee, East) moved an amendment designed to limit the powers available to the Secretary of State under the clause.

The effect of the amendment would be to limit the power of compulsory purchase to certain specified cases, and the Government contended that this would impose an excessive restriction.

The amendment was negatived by 193 votes to 18, with the Opposition abstaining from voting. The 195 Members (including tellers) in the Government lobby were all Labour Members. The 20 Members (including tellers) to support the amendment comprised 9 Liberal, 9 Scottish National and 2 Conservative.

Conservatives to vote for the amendment:

Goodhart, P.   Winterton, N.

HC Deb. 883, 259–70
1974–5, No. 24.

OFFSHORE PETROLEUM DEVELOPMENT (SCOTLAND) BILL   [34]

Committee: 10 December 1974

Clause 1 (Acquisition of land for purposes connected with offshore petroleum)

G. Wilson (SNP, Dundee, East) moved an amendment designed to remove the power under the clause to make expedited acquisition orders.

The Government claimed that the amendment struck at the heart of the Bill, and resisted it.

The amendment was negatived by 179 votes to 15, with the Opposition abstaining from voting. The 181 Members (including tellers) in the Government lobby comprised 180 Labour and 1 Conservative. The 17 Members (including tellers) to support the amendment comprised 9 Scottish National, 6 Liberal and 2 Conservative.

Conservative to vote against the amendment:

Maxwell-Hyslop, R.

Conservatives to vote for the amendment:

Eyre, R.   Mudd, D.

HC Deb. 883, 313–6
1974–5, Nʳ. 25.

OFFSHORE PETROLEUM DEVELOPMENT [35]
(SCOTLAND) BILL

Committee: 10 December 1974

Clause 11 (Supplementary provisions as to acquisition and appropriation of land)

Miss B. Harvie Anderson (C., Renfrewshire, East) moved an amendment to delete subsection (3) of the clause, which extended the power to make expedited acquisition orders on inalienable land.

Miss Harvie Anderson contended that much of the land involved, held by the National Trust, had been given in the belief that inalienability would stand the test of time. The provision had given rise to great concern.

She was supported from the Labour benches by A. Blenkinsop (Lab., South Shields). The provision, he said, breached undertakings given in the past, and he could see no reason why the existing procedure should not be left to operate as it did. He would find it difficult to support the Minister on this issue. N. Buchan (Lab., Renfrewshire, West) also rose to declare that 'some kind of apparatus of investigation and ministerial intervention should be provided before we proceed further'.

The Minister of State at the Scottish Office, B. Millan, argued that full parliamentary protection was provided under the Bill. There was already a special parliamentary procedure available to set inalienability aside. The Government was seeking to apply another parliamentary procedure and in principle it was right that it should apply to inalienable land. He asked the Committee not to accept the amendment.

The amendment was negatived, on a whipped party vote, by 151 votes to 105. 1 Labour Member entered the Opposition lobby to support the amendment, and at least one other (N. Buchan) abstained from voting.

Labour Member to vote for the amendment:

Blenkinsop, A.

HC Deb. 883, 425–8
1974–5, No. 29.

The division took place at 12.50 a.m. during an all-night sitting on Committee stage of the Bill.

DEFENCE   **[36]**

16 December 1974

The Secretary of State for Defence, R. Mason, moved 'That this
House takes note of the Secretary of State for Defence's Statement on
Tuesday 3rd December 1974.'[1]

From the Opposition Front Bench, P. Walker moved an addendum,
to add at the end 'and regrets that the proposals contained in the
Statement will imperil the nation's security'.

During the debate, a number of Labour backbenchers rose to
criticize the Government's defence policy. F. Allaun (Lab., Salford,
East) argued that the cuts in defence expenditure announced by the
Defence Secretary were 'phoney', and that spending on defence in
real terms would increase. An increase in arms spending would increase
tension and reduce hopes of detente. S. Newens (Lab., Harlow) said
he believed that they must seek to achieve the withdrawal of all forces
from western and eastern Europe to their own countries; he thought
the Government should be prepared to embark on real initiatives to
bring about mutual force reductions. Proper social services could be
provided if more far-reaching defence cuts were made. R. Cook (Lab.,
Edinburgh, Central) said he had not been persuaded by the Secretary
of State that his increase in defence expenditure came within the scope
of the word 'savings'. Miss J. Richardson (Lab., Barking) suggested
that Britain would gain much more respect if it rejected its role of
trailing behind the United States and NATO and instead stood on its
own. More could then be spent on social services. J. Lee (Lab.,
Birmingham, Handsworth) contended that the retention of a unilateral
nuclear deterrent was madness. Because the Government had not
decided that it was time to bring an end to the nuclear deterrent 'some
of us are going to find ourselves in revolt tonight'.

The Opposition amendment was negatived, on a straight party vote,
by 316 votes to 256, with no cross-votes or apparent abstentions.

The main motion was then put, and forced to a division by a number
of Labour backbenchers. The Opposition abstained from voting. The
motion was carried by 241 votes to 58. The 243 Members (including
tellers) in the Government lobby comprised 232 Labour, 7 Liberal
and 4 Scottish National.[2] The 60 Members (including tellers) to
oppose the motion comprised 54 Labour, 3 Scottish National and 3
Plaid Cymru. 14 Labour Members who voted in the first division were
also absent from the division.[3]

Labour Members to vote against the motion:

Allaun, F.	Garrett, J.	Newens, S.
Ashton, J.	Grocott, B.	Noble, M.
Atkins, R.	Hoyle, D.	Parry, R.
Atkinson, N.	Huckfield, L.	Prescott, J.
Bennett, A.	Hughes, M.	Richardson, Miss J.
Bidwell, S.	Hughes, R. J.	Roberts, G.
Callaghan, J.	Kerr, R.*	Roderick, C.
Canavan, D.	Kinnock, N.	Rodgers, G.
Carter-Jones, L.	Lamond, J.	Rooker, J.
Clemitson, I.	Latham, A.	Sedgemore, B.
Colquhoun, Mrs M.	Lee, J.	Selby, H.
Cook, R.	Litterick, T.	Sillars, J.
Corbett, R.	Loyden, E.	Snape, P.
Cryer, R.	McNamara, K.	Thomas, R.
Davies, B.	Madden, M.	Thorne, S.
Edge, G.	Marshall, J.	Watkinson, J.
Flannery, M.	Maynard, Miss J.	Wilson, W.
Fletcher, T.	Mikardo, I.*	Wise, Mrs A.

HC Deb. 883, 1295–8
1974–5, No. 36.

  1 The statement constituted a report on a defence review instigated in March 1974, and included an announcement that the Government had decided that they should reduce defence expenditure as a proportion of gross national product from its existing level of $5\frac{1}{2}$ per cent to $4\frac{1}{2}$ per cent over the next ten years. See *HC Deb.* 882, c. 1351–69.
  2 According to the *Hansard* division lists, W. Roberts (C., Conway) voted in the Government lobby. This is an apparent error.
  3 The fourteen were: L. Abse, Sir A. Broughton, R. Brown, N. Buchan, H. Delargy, M. Edelman, R. Edwards, I. Evans, B. Gould, A. Lewis, J. Mackintosh, Mrs R. Short, J. Silverman and T. Torney.

FINANCE BILL [37]

Second Reading: 17 December 1974

The Chief Secretary to the Treasury, J. Barnett, moved the Second Reading of the Bill.

From the Opposition Front Bench, Mrs M. Thatcher moved a reasoned amendment for rejection, 'That this House declines to give a Second Reading to a Bill whose provisions, in the present critical state of the economy, are inadequate and in some respects damaging and which also provides, without good reason, for the retrospective repayment of tax to one section of taxpayers.'

The Opposition reasoned amendment was negatived, on a straight party vote, by 312 votes to 269.

Second Reading was then carried by 303 votes to 14,[1] with the Opposition abstaining from voting. The 16 Members (including tellers) to vote against the Bill comprised 12 Liberal, 3 Conservative and 1 UUUC.

Conservatives to vote against Second Reading:

Maxwell-Hyslop, R.   Stanbrook, I.   Stewart, I.

HC Deb. 883, 1495–8
1974–5, No. 39.

None of the three Conservatives to vote against had taken part in the debate.

[1] *Hansard* gives the number voting against as 13, but 14 names are listed.

BRITISH LEYLAND MOTOR CORPORATION LIMITED   [38]

18 December 1974

The Industry Secretary, A. Benn, moved 'That this House authorizes the Secretary of State to pay or undertake to pay by way of financial assistance under section 8 of the Industry Act 1972 in respect of a guarantee or guarantees to be given to the bankers of British Leyland Motor Corporation Limited and any of its subsidiaries covering borrowing facilities made available by the bankers to those companies, insofar as the amount paid or undertaken to be paid under the guarantee or guarantees is in excess of £5 million but does not exceed £50 million.'

From the Opposition Front Bench, M. Heseltine said that, in the circumstances, the Government's suggestion of a guarantee was the right course to take, as long as it was seen as a holding operation while the inquiry appointed by the Secretary of State did its work. The Opposition was not saying it would commit itself to a particular form of Government intervention on a particular scale until it had seen the report of the inquiry.

N. Budgen (C., Wolverhampton, South-West) said he found himself in the position of not agreeing with Mr Heseltine that it was a holding operation. It was wrong to pretend that it was just a mere holding operation; it would be seen as leading to public control of the whole industry. 'I believe it to be a preliminary to massive Government expenditure and nationalization which are wholly wrong in the circumstances in which the debate takes place.' The proposals were wrong in every way.

The motion was approved by 149 votes to 13, with the Opposition abstaining from voting. The 151 Members (including tellers) in the Government lobby comprised 143 Labour, 3 UUUC, 2 Conservative, 2 Scottish National and 1 SDLP. The 15 Members (including tellers) to oppose the motion comprised 10 Conservative, 4 Liberal and 1 UUUC.

Conservatives to vote for the motion:

Eyre, R.   Miller, H.

Conservatives to vote against the motion:

Biffen, J.*	Howell, R.	Nelson, A.
Brotherton, M.	Lawrence, I.	Tebbit, N.
Budgen, N.	Morgan-Giles, M.	Winterton, N.
Gow, I.*		

HC Deb. 883, 1771–2
1974–5, No. 41.

BUTTER PRICES   [39]

Prayer: 13 January 1975

From the Opposition benches, Mrs S. Oppenheim moved 'That an humble Address be presented to Her Majesty praying that the Butter Prices Order 1974 (S.I., 1974, No. 1984), dated 29th November 1974, a copy of which was laid before this House on 6th December, be annulled.'

Mrs Oppenheim declared that there existed in the order a conflicting and tangled web of enforcement anomalies. It represented for the most part an exercise which appeared to be a combination of bureaucratic lunacy and a party political public relations exercise.

Although the Opposition did not intend to divide the House on the prayer—confirmed from the Opposition Front Bench by T. Raison at the end of the debate—a number of Conservative backbenchers rose to support it, and N. Ridley (C., Cirencester and Tewkesbury) declared his intention to enter the lobby in support of it. The order, he contended, was a mistake. Price control was not necessary. He disagreed with the point made by Mrs Oppenheim [and later by Mr Raison] that where there was a subsidy there must be price control. 'I shall be happy to divide the House if my hon. Friends will support me in registering a protest against legislation of this kind, which is totally out of keeping and unnecessary.'

The prayer was negatived by 136 votes to 22, with the Opposition abstaining officially from voting. The 138 Members (including tellers) in the Government lobby comprised 137 Labour and 1 UUUC. The 24 Members (including tellers) to vote for the prayer comprised 22 Conservative, 1 Liberal and 1 UUUC.

Conservatives to vote for the prayer:

Budgen, N.	Lawrence, I.	Miller, H.
Cormack, P.	Marten, N.	Mills, P.*
Crowder, F. P.	Mates, M.	Neave, A.
Douglas-Hamilton, Lord J.	Mawby, R.	Page, J.
Hurd, D.	Maxwell-Hyslop, R.*	Page, R. G.
Jessel, T.	Mayhew, P.	Shepherd, C.
Kaberry, Sir D.	Meyer, Sir A.	Skeet, T.
Knight, Mrs J.		

HC Deb. 884, 141-4
1974-5, No. 42.

OFFSHORE PETROLEUM DEVELOPMENT (SCOTLAND) BILL　　　　　　　　　　　　[40]

Report: 14 January 1975

Clause 5 (Terms and effect, etc. of licences under s. 4)

G. Wilson (SNP, Dundee, East) moved an amendment designed to extend the right to compensation to fishermen exercising public fishing rights in addition to those exercising private rights, should those rights be interfered with.

From the Opposition Front Bench, A. Buchanan-Smith said he hoped the Minister would accept the spirit of the amendment, though he appreciated the difficulties involved.

The Minister of State at the Scottish Office, B. Millan, said it was not normal to compensate public rights, and he was not persuaded that the point of principle should be set aside. He was not persuaded either that it was easy or possible to produce a formula that would produce the result intended by the amendment. He could not advise the House to accept it.

The amendment was negatived by 180 votes to 23, with the Opposition abstaining from voting. The Government lobby comprised solely Labour Members. The 25 Members (including tellers) to support the amendment comprised 9 Scottish National, 7 Conservative, 7 Liberal and 2 Plaid Cymru.

Conservatives to vote for the amendment:

Brotherton, M.	Corrie, J.	Hall, Sir J.
Budgen, N.	Gray, H.	Sproat, I.
Clark, A.		

HC Deb. 884, 295–8
1974–5, No. 47.

EEC (AGRICULTURAL PRICES) [41]

16 January 1975

The Minister of Agriculture, Fisheries and Food, F. Peart, moved 'That this House takes note of Commission Documents Nos. R/3358/74, R/3470/74, and R/3408/74.' [The Documents dealt with the European Commission's proposals for the common agricultural prices for 1975–6, including an overall proposal to raise prices in the EEC by an average of between 9 and 10 per cent.]

From the Labour backbenches, N. Buchan (Lab., Renfrewshire, West) moved an addendum, to add 'but declines to approve proposals for Regulations still subject to possible and unforseeable alteration by the Council of Ministers before enactment, which would raise even further the price of a number of major foodstuffs, including milk, butter, pigmeat and beef, and which accepts the principle of permanent intervention buying of beef by member states including the United Kingdom'.

The debate had commenced at 10.15 p.m. and was restricted to one-and-a-half hours' duration. Shortly before 11.45 p.m., in an attempt to obtain a vote on his amendment, Mr Buchan moved 'That the Question be now put.' The motion was accepted by the Speaker.

Voting on the closure motion was 54 in favour and 1 against, Government whips acting as tellers against. The 56 Members (including tellers) to vote for closure comprised 39 Labour, 5 Conservative, 5 UUUC, 4 Scottish National and 3 Plaid Cymru. The one Member to enter the lobby against closure was a Conservative.

Labour Members to vote for closure:

Atkinson, N.	Jeger, Mrs L.	Richardson, Miss J.
Bennett, A.	Kerr, R.*	Roderick, C.
Bidwell, S.	Kinnock, N.	Sedgemore, B.
Buchan, N.	Lamond, J.	Skinner, D.
Cryer, R.	Latham, A.	Snape, P.
Davies, B.	Lee, J.	Spearing, N.
English, M.	Madden, M.	Stallard, A.
Flannery, M.*	Mendelson, J.	Stoddart, D.
Fletcher, R.	Mikardo, I.	Taylor, Mrs A.
Gould, B.	Miller, Mrs M.	Thomas, R.
Hooley, F.	Molloy, W.	Weetch, K.
Jackson, Miss M.	Prescott, J.	White, F.
Jay, D.	Price, C.	Wise, Mrs A.

Conservatives to vote for closure:

Biffen, J.	Hutchison, M. C.	Moate, R.
Body, R.	Marten, N.	

Conservative to vote against closure:

Maxwell-Hyslop, R.

HC Deb. 884, 851-2
1974-5, No. 60.

One hundred Members not having supported closure, the Speaker declared that the Question had not been decided in the affirmative. The motion, in consequence, became what was described as a 'dropped order'.

CHANNEL TUNNEL [42]

20 January 1975

After Questions, the Environment Secretary, A. Crosland, made a statement about the Channel Tunnel. He announced that he had informed the French Government that he saw no alternative to accepting the claim of the companies involved that the existing arrangements had been abandoned; that there was not the slightest prospect of the tunnel being taken over as a directly Government-financed project, and that the project would be run down as soon as possible.

E. Ogden (Lab., Liverpool, West Derby) sought leave to move the adjournment under S.O. 9 to discuss 'the announcement made by the Secretary of State for the Environment today that the British Government have unilaterally abandoned the Channel Tunnel project'. Mr Speaker announced he was satisfied it was a proper matter to be discussed under S.O. 9, and more than forty Members having risen to support the motion, directed that it be held over for discussion at 7.00 p.m. that evening.

In moving the adjournment, Mr Ogden declared his faith in the Channel Tunnel project. For the ordinary British people, he said, a fixed-link Tunnel would be a growing asset for their work, employment and leisure.

S. Cohen (Lab., Leeds, South-East) said the decision was a tragic blow for the railway industry. J. Prescott (Lab., Hull, East) welcomed the Minister's statement. He had, he said, constantly questioned the economic viability of the project. P. Snape (Lab., West Bromwich, East) said it was a sad day for the British people, for the future prospects of British industry, and for British Rail in particular. D. Crouch (C., Canterbury) said it was a tragic day in the history of the country; the Minister had made a wrong decision. R. Moate (C., Faversham) rose to welcome the Government's decision. He did so, he declared, for financial and environmental reasons. He believed, on balance, it would be beneficial to Kent.

For the Opposition, J. Peyton said that the Government had stumbled into their decision with a mixture of relief and irresponsibility. He invited his right hon. and hon. Friends to condemn the Government 'for their irresponsible handling of this matter'.

The motion for adjournment, moved by Mr Ogden, was negatived by 294 votes to 218, the Government voting against and the Opposition voting in support of it. The 296 Members (including tellers) to vote against adjournment comprised 264 Labour, 13 Conservative, 10 Scottish National, 7 Liberal and 2 UUUC. The 220 Members (including tellers) to vote for adjournment comprised 211 Conservative and 9 Labour. A number of Members (including, on the Labour benches, S. Cohen) abstained from voting.

Conservatives to vote against adjournment:

Biffen, J.	Fell, A.	Moate, R.
Body, R.	Hutchison, M. C.	Morgan, G.
Brotherton, M.	Marten, N.	Mudd, D.
Clark, A.	Mawby, R.	Ridley, N.
Cormack, P.		

Labour Members to vote for adjournment:

Atkins, R.	Crawshaw, R.	Ogden, E.*
Bradley, T.	Lewis, R.	Snape, P.*
Buchanan, R.	Mackintosh, J.	Spriggs, L.

HC Deb. 884, 1157–62
1974–5, No. 61.

FINANCE BILL   [43]

Committee: 21 January 1975

Clause 17 (Capital Transfer Tax)

J. Pardoe (Lib., Cornwall, North) moved an amendment to provide that capital transfer tax should be paid by the donee rather than the donor.

The Chancellor of the Exchequer, D. Healey, opposed the amendment. It would produce a lower yield and would be more costly to administer. There would also be a delay in collecting it, which would not occur with a donor-based tax. He asked the House to resist the amendment.

The amendment was negatived by 259 votes to 76, with the Opposition Front Bench abstaining from voting.[1] The Government lobby comprised solely Labour Members. The 78 Members (including tellers) to support the amendment comprised 54 Conservative, 11 Scottish National, 10 Liberal and 3 Plaid Cymru.

Conservatives to vote for the amendment:

Bell, R.	Grist, I.	Mudd, D.
Biffen, J.	Grylls, M.	Price, D.
Body, R.	Hall, Sir J.	Renton, T.
Brittan, L.	Hawkins, P.	Rhys Williams, Sir B.
Cormack, P.	Howell, R.	Ridley, N.
Corrie, J.	Irving, C.	Ridsdale, J.
Costain, A.	King, E.	Rost, P.
Eden, Sir J.	Lamont, N.	Shaw, M.
Fairgrieve, R.	Langford-Holt, Sir J.	Skeet, T.
Fell, A.	Lawson, N.	Spence, J.
Fraser, H.	Lloyd, I.	Spicer, J.
Fry, P.	McCrindle, R.	Stanbrook, I.
Galbraith, T.	MacGregor, J.	Stanley, J.
Gardner, E.	Macmillan, M.	Stewart, I.
Glyn, Dr A.	McNair-Wilson, P.	Viggers, P.
Goodhew, V.	Mitchell, D.	Walker-Smith, Sir D.
Gow, I.	Morgan, G.	Winterton, N.
Gower, Sir R.	Morris, M.	Young, Sir G.

HC Deb. 884 1365-8
1974-5, No. 67.

[1] No Opposition Front Bench spokesman rose to speak on the amendment.

SOCIAL SECURITY BENEFITS BILL [44]

Report: 29 January 1975

Clause 1 (Rates of basic scheme benefits)

The Minister of State for Health and Social Security, B. O'Malley, moved an amendment to restore the earnings rule limit for retired persons to £13, and thus reverse an amendment carried against the Government in committee.[1]

Mr O'Malley said the Government was not defending the earnings rule in principle, but he opposed the amendment carried in committee on grounds of cost. Complete abolition of the rule, in April 1975 terms, would cost £225 million. The Department had to decide its order of priorities, and consider completing claims.

Opposition Members—including the Opposition Front Bench spokesman, K. Clarke—rose to oppose the amendment, as did a number of Labour backbenchers. G. Cunningham (Lab., Islington, South and Finsbury) said the House should help the Ministers involved to achieve an objective which in their hearts they wanted to achieve. He would vote against the earnings rule. Dr C. Phipps (Lab., Dudley, West) pleaded with the Minister to think again. 'If he wants my vote and the votes of some of my hon. Friends, he will have to do something.' B. Douglas-Mann (Lab., Mitcham and Morden) asked the Secretary of State to reconsider, and at least take steps to accept an increase in the earnings rule to £20 for 1975–6. D. Lambie (Lab., Central Ayrshire) said he had not made up his mind how to vote; he hoped the Government would make a concession to enable him to support the Secretary of State.

The Minister of State at the Treasury, R. Sheldon, said that he and the Chancellor accepted the case for phasing out the rule, but in existing economic circumstances could not commit the Government to a precise amount or to precise timing.

The amendment was *negatived* by 280 votes to 265, *a majority of 15 against the Government.* The 267 Members (including tellers) in the Government lobby comprised 265 Labour, 1 SDLP and 1 Irish Independent. The 282 Members (including tellers) in the Opposition lobby comprised 239 Conservative, 12 Liberal, 10 Scottish National, 9 UUUC, 9 Labour and 3 Plaid Cymru. At least 5 Labour Members also abstained from voting.[2]

Labour Members to vote against the amendment:

Cunningham, G.[3]	Hooley, F.	Spriggs, L.
Douglas-Mann, B.	Huckfield, L.	Tinn, J.
Hamilton, W.	Phipps, C.	Walden, B.

HC Deb. 885, 525–30
1974–5, No. 77.

[1] In committee, an amendment had been carried to increase the earnings rule from £13 to £20 in 1975–6, to £35 in the following year, £50 in the year after that, and for the earnings rule to be abolished in April 1980.

[2] The five known abstainers (who voted in an immediately succeeding division) were R. Crawshaw, J. Lee, E. Luard, B. Magee and P. Whitehead.

[3] Following the division, Mr Cunningham resigned his position as Parliamentary Private Secretary to the Secretary of State for Education. *The Times,* 30 January 1975.

PRICES BILL [45]

Second Reading: 30 January 1975

The Secretary of State for Prices and Consumer Protection, Mrs S. Williams, moved the Second Reading of the Bill, designed to enable food subsidies to be continued into 1975-6.

From the Opposition Front Bench, T. Raison moved a reasoned amendment for rejection, 'That this House, believing that indiscriminate food subsidies have proved an extravagant way of helping those in need, are liable to create distortions and shortages, and conceal rather than deal with inflation, declines to give a Second Reading to a Bill which fails sufficiently to secure their progressive reduction.'

Mr Raison announced that the Opposition would press the reasoned amendment to a division. A number of Conservative backbenchers rose to oppose the Bill, and one or two indicated their willingness to vote for the amendment *and* against Second Reading. I. Gow (C., Eastbourne) contended that, once embarked upon, it would be impossible to escape from the policy of ever-escalating food subsidies. The Bill would distribute money primarily to those households with an income of more than £50 per week, and could be put, he said, to other uses. 'For those reasons, my hon. Friends and I will most certainly oppose the Bill in the Division tonight.' G. Dodsworth (C., Hertfordshire, South-West) declared that the Bill was yet another licence to spend, and one which they could not afford. He saw no alternative but to vote for the amendment and against Second Reading.

The Opposition amendment for rejection was negatived by 281 votes to 214, with no cross-votes.

The motion for Second Reading was then put, and carried by 270 votes to 50, the Opposition abstaining from voting. The 272 Members (including tellers) in the Government lobby comprised 268 Labour, 3 Scottish National and 1 Plaid Cymru. The 52 Members (including tellers) to vote against Second Reading comprised 41 Conservative, 8 Liberal and 3 UUC.

Conservatives to vote against Second Reading:

Alison, M.	Knox, D.	Renton, Sir D.
Biffen, J.	Lawrence, I.	Ridley, N.
Biggs-Davison, J.	Lester, J.	Sainsbury, T.
Brittan, L.	Macfarlane, N.	Shersby, M.
Budgen, N.	McNair-Wilson, M.	Sims, R.
Carlisle, M.	Meyer, Sir A.	Spicer, J.

Chalker, Mrs L.	Miller, H.	Sproat, I.
Crowder, F. P.	Moate, R.	Stanbrook, I.
Dodsworth, G.	Moore, J.	Stewart, I.
Drayson, B.	More, J.	Wakeham, J.
Farr, J.	Morgan, G.	Warren, K.
Glyn, A.	Morrison, P.	Winterton, N.
Goodhew, V.	Price, D.	Young, Sir G.
Hampson, K.	Rathbone, T.	

HC Deb. 885, 755–8
1974–5, No. 81.

IMPORT DUTIES [46]

Prayer: 3 February 1975

D. Jay (Lab., Battersea, North) moved 'That an humble Address be presented to Her Majesty, praying that the Import Duties (General) (No. 5) Order 1974 (S.I., 1974, No. 2020), dated 4th December 1974, a copy of which was laid before this House on 6th December, be annulled.'

Mr Jay explained that the order increased the import duty on a number of foodstuffs including beef and veal from outside the EEC. The Government, he said, may be bound to introduce higher food prices, but Parliament was not so bound. He suggested the Minister withdraw the order, and re-introduce it without the provisions for an increase in the taxation of food.

The Secretary of State for Trade, P. Shore, said that the Government had intended to postpone the upward movement of tariffs until after British membership of the European Communities was re-negotiated, but the European Commission had been insistent that that could not be done. The Government was also locked in by the treaty as a matter of Community law. To reject the order would not be justified, and to reject it would have large and damaging consequences. He asked those who intended to vote for the prayer not to do so.

Supporters of the prayer forced it to a division, in which voting was 34 for the prayer, and none against, Government whips acting as tellers against.[1] The 36 Members (including tellers) to vote for the prayer comprised 19 Labour, 8 Scottish National, 5 UUUC and 4 Conservative.

Labour Members to vote for the prayer:

Allaun, F.
Atkinson, N.
Flannery, M.*
Gould, B.
Hoyle, D.
Jay, D.
Kinnock, N.

Lee, J.
Madden, M.
Mendelson, J.
Mikardo, I.
Miller, Mrs M.
Richardson, Miss J.

Rodgers, G.
Sedgemore, B.
Spearing, N.
Thomas, R.
Walker, T.
Wise, Mrs A.

Conservatives to vote for the prayer:

Biffen, J.
Body, R.

Marten, N.

Moate, R.

HC Deb. 885, 1107–8
1974–5, No. 82.

Forty Members (a quorum) not having taken part in the division, the Deputy Speaker declared that the Question was not decided.

¹ This appears a tactical move by the whips, forcing the prayer to a division while ensuring that Government supporters do not vote, apparently in the expectation that an insufficient number of Members would vote for the prayer for the House to be quorate.

INDUSTRY (FINANCIAL ASSISTANCE) [47]

Prayer: 18 February 1975

The Minister of State for Industry, E. Heffer, moved 'That the Financial Assistance for Industry (Increase of Limit) Order 1975, a draft of which was laid before this House on 31st January, be approved.'

The Minister explained that since the passing of the 1972 Industry Act, the aggregate of assistance on the basis defined under section 8(6) of the Act stood at just over £125 million. 'The Government consider it prudent to invite the House to approve the order increasing the limit from £150 million to £250 million.'

Conservative Members rose to criticize the order, and P. Rost (C., Derbyshire, South-East) declared that the House should reject it. The Department of Industry, he contended, had already abused the 1972 Act and it was obviously intending to abuse it further. 'There can be no doubt that the Government intend indiscriminately to grant themselves public funds through Parliament, to avoid accounting for the expenditure and to spend the money in a way which will allow them to pursue their political objectives.'

The order was approved by 245 votes to 13, with the Opposition abstaining from voting. The 247 Members (including tellers) in the Government lobby comprised 242 Labour, 3 Plaid Cymru and 2 Scottish National. The 15 Members (including tellers) to oppose the order were all Conservatives.

Conservatives to vote against the order:

Budgen, N.	Hordern, P.	Mitchell, D.
Fairgrieve, R.	Lawrence, I.	Ridley, N.
Farr, J.*	Lawson, N.	Rost, P.
Gow, I.	Lester, J.	Townsend, C.
Hampson, K.	Marshall, M.	Winterton, N.*

HC Deb. 886, 1295–8
1974–5, No. 97.

LOCAL GOVERNMENT (SCOTLAND) BILL [48]

Report: 19 February 1975

Schedule 6 (Adaptation and amendment of enactments)

D. Steel (Lib., Roxburgh, Selkirk and Peebles) moved an amendment to provide for the Lothians Region and the Borders Region each to have a police force of its own, instead of a joint police board proposed by the Government.

Mr Steel argued that the Government's proposed joint police board would be costly and unnecessary. He was supported from the Labour benches by J. Mackintosh (Lab., Berwick and East Lothian). He regarded all joint boards as fundamentally unsatisfactory, he said, and also pointed out that the two police forces did not wish to be joined. It was contrary to the desires of the people in the area, and he hoped the Minister would give way on the issue. R. Cook (Lab., Edinburgh, Central) also rose to support what had been said. He pointed out that the two regional councils involved had come to the clear opinion that they did not wish their police forces to be amalgamated.

The Minister of State at the Scottish Office, B. Millan, said the decision to confirm the previous Government's decision in favour of amalgamation had been taken for reasons which had already been well explained. His information was that the authorities concerned had accepted that amalgamation should go ahead, and that the police in the area concerned were not against it. He saw no reason to make any change in the Bill.

The amendment was negatived by 96 votes to 12, with the Opposition abstaining from voting. The 98 Members (including tellers) in the Government lobby comprised solely Labour Members. The 14 Members (including tellers) to support the amendment comprised 7 Liberal, 5 Scottish National, 1 Labour and 1 UUUC. At least 1 Labour Member (R. Cook) abstained from voting.

Labour Member to vote for the amendment:

Mackintosh, J.

HC Deb. 886, 1511–4
1974–5, No. 100.

The division took place at 11.47 p.m.

HOUSING RENTS AND SUBSIDIES BILL   [49]

Lords Amendment: 24 February 1975

Clause 9 (Certain amenties to be disregarded in determining fair rent)

The Under-Secretary of State for the Environment, G. Kaufman, moved for the House to agree with a Lords amendment (and related ones) designed to require rent officers and rent assessment committees in fixing fair rents to disregard not only provisions of and improvements in neighbourhood amenities since the material date to which the landlord had contributed nothing, but also deterioration in or disappearance of such amenities for which he was not to blame.

B. Douglas-Mann (Lab., Mitcham and Morden) rose to oppose the Lords amendment. When an amenity had disappeared, it was reasonable for a tenant to say he was entitled to have a rent reduction. He urged the Government to reject the amendment. He was supported by G. Cunningham (Lab., Islington, South and Finsbury) who said he would prefer to have neither provisions [i.e. to disregard both improvements and deterioration in a locality] but would prefer to give up the logic of that position rather than see tenants suffer a disadvantage in an area such as his. He intended, he said, to vote against the amendment.

The motion to agree with the Lords amendment was carried by 407 votes to 42, the Opposition voting with the Government. The 409 Members (including tellers) in the Government lobby comprised 231 Labour, 172 Conservative and 6 Liberal. The 44 Members (including tellers) to oppose the Lords amendment were all Labour Members. At least a further 6 Labour Members also abstained from voting.[1]

Labour Members to vote against the Lords amendment:

Allaun, F.	Jeger, Mrs L.	Robertson, J.
Buchan, N.	Kinnock, N.	Rodgers, G.
Canavan, D.	Lambie, D.	Rooker, J.
Clemitson, I.	Latham, A.	Sedgemore, B.
Colquhoun, Mrs M.	Lee, J.	Selby, H.
Cook, R.	Madden, M.	Silverman, J.
Cunningham, G.*	Mendelson, J.	Skinner, D.
Davies, B.	Mikardo, I.	Snape, P.
Douglas-Mann, B.*	Miller, Mrs M.	Thomas, R.
Evans, J.	Molloy, W.	Thorne, S.
Faulds, A.	Newens, S.	Wainwright, E.
Fernyhough, E.	Noble, M.	Watkinson, J.
Flannery, M.	Ovenden, J.	Weetch, K.
Fletcher, R.	Price, C.	Wise, Mrs A.
Hoyle, D.	Roberts, G.	

HC Deb. 887, 209–14
1974–5, No. 104.

[1] G. Barnett, R. Brown, Mrs R. Short, N. Spearing, L. Spriggs and J. Wellbeloved. (All six particpated in preceding and subsequent divisions.)

HOUSING RENTS AND SUBSIDIES BILL [50]

Lords Amendment: 24 February 1975

Schedule 6 (Repeals)

The Under-Secretary of State for the Environment, G. Kaufman, formally moved for the House to disagree with a Lords amendment designed to affect the provisions of the Bill for the termination of general decontrol by reference to rateable value.[1]

The motion to disagree with the Lords amendment was carried by 114 votes to 8, with the Opposition abstaining from voting. The

Government lobby comprised solely Labour Members. The 10 Members (including tellers) to vote against the motion were all Conservative.

Conservatives to vote against the motion:

Body, R.
Bowden, A.
Budgen, N.
Bulmer, E.

Cope, J.
Durant, T.*
Hurd, D.

Latham, M.*
Mawby, R.
Mayhew, P.

HC Deb. 887, 247–8
1974–5, No. 106.

¹ The Lords amendment had been included for discussion with an earlier related one, though in the short discussion no direct mention was made of it. *HC Deb.* 887, c. 213–22.

LOTTERIES BILL   [51]

Second Reading: 26 February 1975

The Under-Secretary at the Home Office, Dr S. Summerskill, moved the Second Reading of the Bill. She said that the Bill introduced three major changes: it increased substantially the financial limits on small public lotteries, it permitted local authorities to promote lotteries within the same financial limits as those applying to other bodies, and it introduced a new system of registration involving the Gaming Board. Lotteries held not more frequently than weekly were permitted a limit of £10,000 on the total value of tickets sold, with a maximum single prize of £1,000 and a ticket price of 25p. For lotteries held at less frequent intervals, the turnover and prize limits would be higher. The main objective of the Bill, she explained, was to restore the potential of the provisions on small lotteries for the many voluntary bodies which benefited from lottery revenue.

For the Opposition, M. Alison criticized the limits imposed by the Bill and the complicated provisions for registration, but gave the measure a guarded welcome. The Opposition, he said, would seek to improve it in committee.

Despite Government and Opposition support for the measure, a number of Members rose to oppose it. E. Ogden (Lab., Liverpool, West Derby) objected to the Bill in principle. It was designed to increase the facilities for gambling, and it had to do without his support. He also queried the effect of the measure on employment in Liverpool, which housed the headquarters of one football pools organization and the major part of another. A Shaw (Lab., Ilford,

South) felt the Bill was a 'non-event', and thought councils would have enough to do without organizing lotteries. 'All in all, it would be a mercy if the Bill were quietly forgotten.' J. Farr (C., Harborough) argued that lotteries held by social, sporting and other bodies would be swamped by lotteries which local authorities could now organize. He said 8,600 local authorities would be entitled to promote lotteries. He had grave reservations about the whole of the Bill. K. Marks (Lab., Manchester, Gorton) said the provisions would constitute an incitement to local authorities to spend more, and a local authority lottery would be wasteful in terms of manpower and costly in administration.

The Bill was given a Second Reading by 305 votes to 64, the Opposition voting with the Government. The 307 Members (including tellers) in the Government lobby comprised 199 Labour, 103 Conservative and 5 Liberal. The 66 Members (including tellers) to oppose Second Reading comprised 39 Labour, 19 Conservative, 6 UUUC and 2 Liberal.

Labour Members to vote against Second Reading:

Bennett, A.	Gould, B.	Ogden, E.
Bidwell, S.	Hamilton, W.	Parry, R.
Campbell, I.	Hatton, F.	Rodgers, G.*
Cartwright, J.	Janner, G.	Roper, J.
Clemitson, I.*	Kilroy-Silk, R.	Sandelson, N.
Colquhoun, Mrs M.	Kinnock, N.	Shaw, A.
Cook, R.	Lamond, J.	Sillars, J.
Dalyell, T.	Lewis, R.	Thorne, S.
Dempsey, J.	Litterick, T.	Walker, T.
Dunwoody, Mrs G.	Loyden, E.	White, F.
Fernyhough, E.	McGuire, M.	White, J.
Garrett, J.	Marks, K.	Wilson, A.
Golding. J.	Miller, Mrs M.	Woodall, A.

Conservatives to vote against Second Reading:

Body, R.	Gardner, E.	Monro, H.
Brotherton, M.	Gower, Sir R.	Morris, M.
Clark, A.	King, E.	Mudd, D.
Cordle, J.	Kitson, Sir T.	Nelson, A.
Costain, A.	McAdden, Sir S.	Rhys Williams, Sir B.
Fairgrieve, R.	Mills, P.	Stainton, K.
Farr, J.		

HC Deb. 887, 571–4
1974–5, No. 111.

CIVIL LIST **[52]**

Prayer: 26 February 1975

J. Wellbeloved (Lab., Erith and Crayford) moved 'That an humble Address be presented to Her Majesty, praying that the Civil List (Increase of Financial Provisions) Order 1975 (S.I., 1975, No. 133), dated 5th February 1975, a copy of which was laid before this House on 12th February, be annulled.'

Mr Wellbeloved contended that the order should be annulled on four basic grounds: the manner of its presentation to Parliament, its effect on the social contract, the absence of any detailed evidence of the effect on wage and salary rates of employees of the Royal Household, and the availability of other sources of revenue to finance certain requirements of the Royal Household. He argued that there should be a change in the provision of tax exemptions for the Sovereign and members of the Royal Family, and also contended that the matter had been handled very badly by the Prime Minister.

The prayer received support from a number of Labour backbenchers. J. Lee (Lab., Birmingham, Handsworth) felt it unfortunate that the order should be sprung upon the House at a time when the Government was seeking to sustain the social contract. Its maladroit introduction would do the Government, the economy, the Monarchy and the country no good. W. Hamilton (Lab., Fife, Central) declared that members of the Royal Family were no more 'than glorified civil servants', and suggested having a referendum on the issue of taxation of the Royal Household. N. Kinnock (Lab., Bedwellty) said they were considering paying an extra award to one of the richest women in the world.

For the Opposition, Sir G. Howe opposed the prayer. He pointed out that the provisions of the order did not constitute a 'pay rise'; the sum proposed would meet the huge rise, because of inflation, in the Queen's expenses, incurred as a result of her official functions and duties. He offered whole-hearted support for the order.

The Chancellor of the Exchequer, D. Healey, agreed with Sir G. Howe that the order did not provide for an increase in the Queen's pay. Three-quarters of the sum involved was for the wages and salaries of members of the Household. The order was designed only to cope with the demands made by an unprecedented rate of inflation on the purely official element of the financial arrangements made with the Crown. He also pointed out that the total expenditure by the Exchequer or the taxpayer from all sources on the Monarchy was about the cost of one General Election.

The prayer was negatived by 427 votes to 90, with both the Government and Opposition voting against it. The 429 Members (including tellers) in the Government lobby comprised 250 Conservative, 153 Labour, 10 Scottish National, 9 UUUC and 7 Liberal. The 92 Members (including tellers) to support the prayer comprised 91 Labour and 1 Liberal. At least a further 16 Labour Members would also appear to have abstained from voting.[1]

Labour Members to vote for the prayer:

Allaun, F.	Hoyle, D.	Price, C.
Ashton, J.	Huckfield, L.	Richardson, Miss J.
Atkins, R.	Hunter, A.	Roberts, G.
Bagier, G.	Jackson, C.	Rodgers, G.
Bean, R.	Jeger, Mrs L.	Rooker, J.
Bennett, A.	Johnson, W.	Rose, P.
Bidwell, S.	Kelley, R.	Sedgemore, B.
Buchan, N.	Kerr, R.	Selby, H.
Callaghan, J.	Kilroy-Silk, R.	Shaw, A.
Canavan, D.	Kinnock, N.	Sillars, J.
Cartwright, J.	Lambie, D.	Silverman, J.
Clemitson, I.	Lamond, J.	Skinner, D.
Cohen, S.	Latham, A.	Snape, P.
Colquhoun, Mrs M.	Lee, J.	Spriggs, L.
Conlan, B.	Loyden, E.	Thomas, J.
Cook, R.	McCartney, H.	Thomas, R.
Corbett, R.	Madden, M.	Thorne, S.
Cryer, R.*	Marquand, D.	Tierney, S.
Dunwoody, Mrs G.	Marshall, J.	Wainwright, E.
Edwards, R.	Mikardo, I.	Walker, T.
Evans, I.	Mitchell, R.	Watkins, D.
Evans, J.	Molloy, W.*	Watkinson, J.
Fernyhough, E.	Moonman, E.	Weetch, K.
Flannery, M.	Newens, S.	Wellbeloved, J.
Fletcher, T.	Noble, M.	White, F.
Forrester, J.	Orbach, M.	White, J.
Garrett, W.	Ovenden, J.	Whitehead, P.
George, B.	Palmer, A.	Wilson, A.
Grocott, B.	Park, G.	Wilson, W.
Hamilton, W.	Parry, R.	Wise, Mrs A.
Hatton, F.		

HC Deb. 887, 631–6
1974–5, No. 112.

[1] The following were absent from the division but took part in another division twenty minutes later: G. Barnett, A. Blenkinsop, H. Boardman, J. Craigen, B. Ford, J. Golding, B. Gould, Mrs H. Hayman, D. Jay, R. MacFarquhar, M. McGuire, Mrs M. Miller, C. Phipps, J. Robertson, C. Roderick and D. Young.

FINANCE BILL   [53]

Report: 3 March 1975

Clause 2 (VAT: special rate for light hydrocarbon oil, etc.)

N. Ridley (C., Cirencester and Tewkesbury) moved an amendment to reduce from 25 per cent to 15 per cent the VAT on petrol.

Mr Ridley asked the House to accept the amendment, and to cease persecuting the private motorist. Socialists, he said, disliked private motorists, and were trying to price them out of the market.

The Paymaster-General, E. Dell, replied that the objective of the measure was to encourage economy in the use of oil and so to help the balance of payments. A second objective was to raise money and assist with the public sector borrowing requirement. Passing the amendment would create a serious practical problem, since it would require the refunding of the difference between the two rates since 18th December. He asked Mr Ridley to withdraw the amendment.

For the Opposition, J. Nott had already informed the House that it was not the intention of the official Opposition to reduce the Government's revenue, though they believed the principles behind the clause in question deserved scrutiny.

After the Minister's speech, Mr Ridley asked leave to withdraw the amendment, but a number of backbenchers refused leave. The amendment was negatived by 275 votes to 54, with the Opposition abstaining from voting. The Government lobby comprised solely Labour Members. The 56 Members (including tellers) to support the amendment comprised 27 Conservative, 10 Liberal, 10 Scottish National, 6 UUUC and 3 Plaid Cymru.

Conservatives to vote for the amendment:

Brotherton, M.	Gower, Sir R.	Maxwell-Hyslop, R.
Clark, A.	Grylls, M.	Morgan, G.
Corrie, J.	Hawkins, P.	Morris, M.
Costain, A.	Kellett-Bowman, Mrs E.	Mudd, D.
Durant, T.	Latham, M.	Rodgers, Sir J.
Emery, P.	Lawrence, I.	Spence, J.

Fairbairn, N.   Lester, J.   Spicer, J.
Fry, P.   Lewis, K.   Walker-Smith, Sir D.
Gardner, E.   Macfarlane, N.   Winterton, N.

HC Deb. 887, 1197–1202
1974–5, No. 116.

EEC MEMBERSHIP (REFERENDUM)   [54]

11 March 1975

On a motion for adjournment, the House discussed the Government's White Paper on the proposed referendum on continuing Britain's membership of the EEC.

For the Government, the Lord President of the Council and Leader of the House, E. Short, said that the consent of the British people for entry into the EEC had not previously been obtained, and that was the essence of the case for having a referendum. Only by means of a referendum could they discover whether the British people did or did not consent to continued membership; a General Election could not give them the answer. The referendum was wholly consistent with parliamentary sovereignty; the Government would be bound by its result, but Parliament could not be bound by it. The issue involved was a unique one.

The Leader of the Opposition, Mrs M. Thatcher, said that the Government's White Paper on the matter made no attempt to deal with the constitutional decision of the referendum. She queried the effects of a referendum upon parliamentary sovereignty, the principle of collective responsibility, representative Government and treaty obligations. The referendum, she said, was a tactical device to overcome a split in the Labour Party. 'The White Paper has come about because of the Government's concern for internal party interests. It is a licence for Ministers to disagree on central issues but still stay in power. I believe that the right course would be to reject it and to consider the wider constitutional issues properly and at length.'

During the debate, a number of Members rose to depart from the line taken by their respective Front Benches. P. Rose (Lab., Manchester, Blackley) believed that the Labour Party should take a decision, and that it should be a Cabinet decision. The first indictment of the referendum, he said, was that the principle of collective Cabinet responsibility had been destroyed in this country. N. Marten (C.,

Banbury) supported the referendum. Sovereignty belonged to the people, who gave it to MPs at election time. By agreeing to a referendum it was handing back sovereignty to the people; after the referendum, the people handed sovereignty back to Parliament. W. Hamilton (Lab., Fife, Central) said he was against the referendum in principle. 'I think it is a constitutional outrage.' He greatly regretted the White Paper. R. Brown (Lab., Hackney, South and Shoreditch) declared that he found it impossible to accept the arguments for attaching a referendum to our parliamentary system. If they wanted to discover what people were thinking, they should have a General Election. J. Mackintosh (Lab., Berwick and East Lothian) argued that the referendum as such was a bad thing. 'It is a defeat for the parliamentary system of government and that is why I cannot vote for it.'

The motion for adjournment was negatived, on a whipped party vote, by 312 votes to 262. The 314 Members (including tellers) in the Government lobby comprised 290 Labour, 11 Scottish National, 6 Conservative, 4 UUUC and 3 Liberal. The 264 Members (including tellers) in the Opposition lobby comprised 252 Conservatives, 7 Liberal, 3 Plaid Cymru, 1 Labour and 1 UUUC. A small number of Members on both sides of the House would also appear to have abstained from voting.[1]

Conservatives to vote against adjournment:

Bell, R.	Farr, J.	Marten, N.
Body, R.	Goodhart, P.	Moate, R.

Labour Member to vote for adjournment:

Mackintosh, J.

HC Deb. 888, 451–6
1974–5, No. 141.

---

[1] The Labour abstainers included R. Brown and W. Hamilton. (P. Rose voted in the Government lobby.) Known Conservative opponents of British membership of the EEC absent from the division included P. Fry, M. C. Hutchison, D. Mudd, E. Taylor and Sir D. Walker-Smith. According to *The Times*, the Government's majority of 50 'was markedly lower than the two main parties had expected'. 'There were some Labour abstentions that still have to be explained after allowing for pairs and members absent through illness.' *The Times*, 12 March 1975.

CALF SUBSIDIES [55]

Prayer: 25 March 1975

The Minister of State for Agriculture, Fisheries and Food, E. Bishop, moved 'That the Calf Subsidies (United Kingdom) (Variation) Scheme 1975, a draft of which was laid before this House on 19th February, be approved.'

The scheme was designed to remove the £10 increase in the calf subsidy, following agreement in the EEC of new support arrangements for beef.

G. Howells (Lib., Cardigan) said that on the one hand the Government were trying to encourage beef production and on the other doing away with some of the most important subsidies in the agricultural industry. He and his colleagues on the Liberal benches intended to vote against the motion.

The motion was carried by 171 votes to 11, with the Opposition abstaining from voting. The 173 Members (including tellers) in the Government lobby comprised 172 Labour and 1 Conservative. The 13 Members (including tellers) to vote against the prayer comprised 8 Liberal, 2 Scottish National, 1 Conservative, 1 Plaid Cymru and 1 UUUC.

Conservative to vote for the prayer:

Mawby, R.

Conservative to vote against the prayer:

Maxwell-Hyslop, R.

HC Deb. 889, 405–8
1974–5, No. 160.

CENSUS [56]

Prayer: 25 March 1975

The Minister of State for Health and Social Security, Dr D. Owen, moved 'That items 7, 8, 9(d)(e)(f)(g)(h)(i)(j), 10, 11(a)(b)(c)(d), 14, 15, 17(a)(b), 18(vi), 19, 20, 21(a)(b)(c) in Schedule 2 and items 6, 8, 10(c)(d)(e)(f)(g)(h)(i), 11(vi), 12, 13, 14(a)(b)(c)(d)(e), 16 and 17 in Schedule 4 to the Order in Council entitled the Census Order 1975, a draft of which was laid before this House on 20th February, be approved.'

Dr Owen explained that the order providing for a census had been laid before the House under the 1920 Census Act, and was subject to negative resolution. Some of the items of information which it was proposed to include in the census returns were not specifically authorized in the Act and required approval by affirmative resolution of both Houses, and the motion before them covered those items.

A. Beith (Lib., Berwick-upon-Tweed) moved an amendment designed to deny the Government authority to put on the census all but one of the questions that could not be included by negative resolution. Mr Beith explained that the reasoning behind the amendment was that certain basic questions should be answered compulsorily, but that others should be answered voluntarily.

(1) The amendment moved by Mr Beith was negatived by 66 votes to 13, with the Opposition abstaining from voting. The Government lobby comprised solely Labour Members. The 15 Members (including tellers) to support the amendment comprised 8 Liberal and 7 Conservative.

Conservatives to vote for the amendment:

Brittan, L.	Mayhew, P.	Taylor, R.
Chalker, Mrs L.	Morrison, P.	Winterton, N.
Durant, T.		

HC Deb. 889, 441–4
1974–5, Nos. 161 & 162.

(2) The motion was then put and carried by 66 votes to 13, with the Opposition abstaining from voting. The Government lobby comprised solely Labour Members, and the 15 Members (including tellers) to vote against comprised the same 8 Liberals and 7 Conservatives.

Conservatives to vote against the motion:

Brittan, L.	Mayhew, P.	Taylor, R.
Chalker, Mrs L.	Morrison, P.	Winterton, N.
Durant, T.		

The division took place at 12.32 a.m.

SEX DISCRIMINATION BILL   [57]

Second Reading: 26 March 1975

The Home Secretary, R. Jenkins, moved the Second Reading of the Bill, designed to give effect to the principles outlined in the Government's White Paper *Equality for Women*. The Bill, the Minister explained, made sex discrimination unlawful in employment, training and related areas, and extended to the fields of education, licensing bodies and the provision of services and facilities to the public. He believed it was probably the most comprehensive Bill of its kind in the world.

For the Opposition, I. Gilmour rose to query certain provisions of the Bill, while welcoming the principle which it embodied. 'Our anxiety is to ensure that this is a workable piece of legislation because we think the principles behind it are right.'

Members on both sides of the House rose to welcome the Bill, the only outright opposition to the measure being expressed by E. Powell (UUUC, Down, South) and R. Bell (C., Beaconsfield). The Bill, declared Mr Bell, 'has as its purpose the regulating of the minds and judgments of the citizens of a free society and telling them that they may not exercise their judgments freely.' Equality could not be created by legislation. They were embarking upon a path, he said, which would not stop there.

The Bill was given a Second Reading by 104 votes to 5, with the Opposition voting with the Government. The 106 Members (including tellers) to vote for the Bill comprised 78 Labour, 19 Conservative, 5 Liberal, 2 Scottish National, 1 UUUC and 1 SDLP. The 7 Members (including tellers) to vote against the Bill comprised 4 Conservatives and 3 UUUC Members.

Conservatives to vote against Second Reading:

Bell, R.*   Morgan-Giles, M.   Stanbrook, I.*
Gow, I.

HC Deb. 889, 615–8
1974–5, No. 163.

EUROPEAN COMMUNITY (MEMBERSHIP)   [58]

7–9 April 1975

The Prime Minister, H. Wilson moved 'That this House approves the recommendation of Her Majesty's Government to continue Britain's

Membership of the Community as set out in the White Paper on the Membership of the European Community (Command No. 5999).'

The Prime Minister explained that the Government had re-negotiated the terms of Britain's membership of the Community, and he declared that, in the Government's view, they had substantially achieved the objectives set out in 1972. The objectives had covered changes in the common agricultural policy, the Community budget, the movement for economic and monetary union, regional and industrial policies. Since joining the Community, the Community itself had changed as had the Commonwealth. His judgment, he said, on an assessment of all that had been achieved and all that had changed, 'is that to remain in the Community is best for Britain, for Europe, for the Commonwealth, for the Third World and the wider world'.

For the Opposition, W. Whitelaw said that the improvements obtained through re-negotiation could have been gained in the normal development of the Community; he also felt the referendum on the subject could provide a dangerous precedent. However, he supported the motion, arguing that the case for remaining in the Community was a compelling one, even more so than before. 'I hope that my right hon. and hon. Friends will take the only course open to us and unite with right hon. and hon. Members on both sides of the House, vote massively in favour of the White Paper, and so give a really powerful lead to the nation in support of Britain's staying in Europe.'

Although official Government and Opposition advice was in favour of the motion, a number of backbenchers on both sides of the House, especially the Government side, rose to oppose it. D. Jay (Lab., Battersea, North) declared that re-negotiation had changed almost nothing; the Treaty of Rome and the European Communities Act remained unamended. R. J. Hughes (Lab., Newport) said Britain needed to be free to make whatever agreements it could with any country in the world. 'We must withdraw,' he declared. E. Taylor (C., Glasgow, Cathcart) viewed the White Paper as simply a propoganda document. He did not look forward, he said, to a future in which Britain was absorbed by the EEC in a united Europe. F. Hooley (Lab., Sheffield, Heeley) said that it was primarily because he was an internationalist that he was an anti-Marketeer; he wanted to see the country play a role in 'genuine international organizations'. The EEC had developed an inward-looking approach to the great international problems facing them. N. Marten (C., Banbury) argued that the anti-Marketeers had been right in 1971, and were right again on this occasion. J. Ovenden (Lab., Gravesend) argued that to say that there was no future for Britain outside the EEC ignored the economic facts of life. W. Molloy (Lab., Ealing, North) declared himself of the opinion that if the British people voted to remain within the Common Market 'they will have been the victims of delusionists'. The Minister of State for Industry, E. Heffer, also rose to speak against the motion. He did not believe there had been any fundamental re-negotiation. He was convinced that the British people would vote 'No' in the referendum, 'and they will be right to do so'.

At the conclusion of the three-day debate, the Foreign & Commonwealth Secretary, L. J. Callaghan, re-stated the case for the motion. The Government, he said, was faithfully carrying out the Labour manifesto. 'We have attempted to discharge our responsibilities both in our re-negotiations and now, as the Government are giving the British people the opportunity to declare themselves. That is why the Government ask for support from every hon. Member in the Lobby tonight.'

Labour Members were permitted a free vote, although official Government advice was to support the motion. The principle of collective Cabinet responsibility was suspended in order that members of the Cabinet could vote as they wished.

The motion was carried by 396 votes to 170, Opposition Members voting in the Government lobby. The 398 Members (including tellers) in the Government lobby comprised 248 Conservative, 138 Labour and 12 Liberal. The 172 Members (including tellers) to vote against the motion comprised 145 Labour, 11 Scottish National, 8 Conservative, 6 UUUC and 2 Plaid Cymru. 18 Conservatives abstained from voting.[1] A similar number of Labour Members would also appear to have abstained from voting. Thus, an absolute majority of Labour Members either voted against or abstained from voting on the motion.[2]

Conservatives to vote against the motion:

Bell, R.	Clark, A.	Moate, R.*
Biffen, J.	Hutchison, M. C.	Taylor, E.
Body, R.	Marten, N.	

Labour Members to vote against the motion:

Ashton, J.	Gould, B.	Newens, S.
Atkins, R.	Gourlay, H.	Noble, M.
Atkinson, N.	Hamilton, J.[4]	O'Halloran, M.
Barnett, G.	Hardy, P.	O'Malley, B.[4]
Bates, A.	Harrison, W.[4]	Orbach, M.
Benn, A.[4]	Hart, Mrs J.[4]	Orme, S.[4]
Bennett, A.	Hatton, F.	Ovenden, J.
Bidwell, S.	Heffer, E.[4]	Pavitt, L.[4]

Booth, A.[3]
Buchan, N.
Butler, Mrs J.
Callaghan, J.
Campbell, I.
Carmichael, N.[4]
Carter-Jones, L.
Castle, Mrs B.[3]
Clemitson, I.
Cocks, M.[4]
Colquhoun, Mrs M.
Cook, R.
Corbett, R.
Cox, T.[4]
Cryer, R.
Cunningham, G.
Davies, B.
Davies, D.
Davis, C.[4]
Dean, J.
Dempsey, J.
Douglas-Mann, B.
Dunwoody, Mrs G.
Eadie, A.[4]
Edge, G.
Ellis, J.[4]
English, M.
Evans, F.
Evans, I.
Evans, J.
Ewing, H.[4]
Fernyhough, E.
Flannery, M.
Fletcher, T.
Foot, M.[3]
Forrester, J.
Fraser, J.[4]
Freeson, R.[4]
Garrett, W.
George, B.
Gilbert, J.[4]

Hooley, F.
Hoyle, D.
Huckfield, L.
Hughes, M.
Hughes, R.[4]
Hughes, R. J.
Hunter, A.
Irvine, Sir A.
Jackson, Miss M.[4]
Jay, D.
Jenkins, H.[4]
John, B.[4]
Jones, A.[4]
Judd, F.[4]
Kaufman, G.[4]
Kelley, R.
Kerr, R.
Kilroy-Silk, R.
Lambie, D.
Lamond, J.
Latham, A.
Leadbitter, T.
Lestor, Miss J.[4]
Lewis, A.
Lewis, R.
Lipton, M.
Litterick, T.
Loyden, E.
McElhone, F.
McMillan, T.
McNamara, K.
Madden, M.
Marshall, E.
Maynard, Miss J.
Meacher, M.[4]
Mikardo, I.
Miller, M.
Miller, Mrs M.
Molloy, W.
Morris, C.[4]

Pendry, T.[4]
Prescott, J.
Price, C.
Richardson, Miss J.
Roberts, G.
Robertson, J.
Roderick, C.
Rodgers, G.
Rooker, J.
Ross, W.[3]
Ryman, J.
Sedgemore, B.
Selby, H.
Shaw, A.
Shore, P.[3]
Short, Mrs R.
Silkin, J.[3]
Silverman, J.
Skinner, D.
Snape, P.
Spearing, N.*
Spriggs, L.
Stallard, A.
Stoddart, D.
Stott, R.
Swain, T.
Thomas, R.
Thorne, S.
Tierney, S.
Torney, T.
Urwin, T.
Varley, E.[3]
Walker, H.[4]
Watkinson, J.
Weetch, K.
Weitzman, D.
Wilson, A.
Wilson, W.
Wise, Mrs A.
Woof, R.

HC Deb. 889, 1365–70
1974–5, No. 164.

Following the division, for having spoken against the motion in debate, Mr Heffer was dismissed from his post of Minister of State for Industry. *The Times*, 10 April 1975.

1 *Financial Times*, 11 April 1975. The abstainers included E. du Cann (C., Taunton), Chairman of the 1922 Committee.
2 Note the comments of *The Spectator*, 19 April 1975, p. 463. *The Times*, 10 April 1975, put the number of Labour abstainers at 'about 30'.
3 Member of the Cabinet.
4 Member of the Government.

REFERENDUM BILL   [59]

Second Reading: 10 April 1975

The Lord President of the Council and Leader of the House, E. Short, moved the Second Reading of the Bill, which provided for a national referendum on the question of whether or not Britain should remain a member of the European Community.

For the Opposition, J. Peyton rose to oppose the Bill. 'We regard the Bill as a wretched little measure.' The Opposition, he said, regarded the whole idea of a referendum as damaging to Parliament and damaging to the country.

The debate on the measure followed party lines, with the exception of two speeches, one from either side of the House. P. Goodhart (C., Beckenham) said that over the years he had advocated a referendum on this particular issue. He did not believe the referendum to be a major threat to the sovereignty of Parliament. 'In 1911 the Conservative Party firmly believed that any measure which seriously altered the constitutional balance at that time should be submitted to a referendum. I believe that we were right then and we would be right to adopt that practice now.' W. Hamilton (Lab., Fife, Central) rose to attack the Bill. 'This is a miserable, bastard, little Bill and the parent has not even attended a minute of the debate. I say no more than that, except that it shows all evidence of another shambles. Whoever devised the wording or the machinery should be locked up in a mental institution.' After criticizing details of the Bill, he declared that 'I am so disgusted that I shall shortly go home.'

The Bill was given a Second Reading, on a whipped party vote, by 312 votes to 248, a Government majority of 64. 4 Conservatives cross-voted to vote for Second Reading, and a small number of Members on both sides of the House (including W. Hamilton) abstained from voting.1

Conservatives to vote for Second Reading:

Bell, R.   Marten, N.   Moate, R.
Goodhart, P.

HC Deb. 889, 1543–8
1974–5, No. 165.

[1] On the Labour side, in addition to W. Hamilton, the abstainers would appear to have included R. Brown and J. Mackintosh. On the Conservative side, R. Body and J. Farr abstained; other anti-Marketeers absent from the division, who had also been absent from the division on 11 March (No. 141), were P. Fry, M. C. Hutchison, D. Mudd and E. Taylor.

BUDGET RESOLUTIONS   [60]

Ways & Means: 21 April 1975

After debate on the Budget Resolutions and Economic Situation, the Budget Resolutions were put.

Scottish National Members divided the House on Resolution number three, *Spirits (Customs and Excise)*, designed to increase the rate of duty of excise chargeable on British spirits and the rate of customs duty chargeable on imported spirits.

The resolution was carried by 287 votes to 15, the Opposition abstaining from voting. The 17 Members (including tellers) to oppose the resolution comprised 10 Scottish National and 7 Conservative.

Conservatives to vote against the resolution:

Brotherton, M.   Gray, H.   Kimball, M.
Fairbairn, N.   Hutchison, M. C.   Morgan-Giles, M.
Gilmour, Sir J.

HC Deb. 890, 1123–6,
1974–5, No. 172.

REFERENDUM BILL   [61]

Committee: 22 April 1975

Clause 1 (Holding of referendum)

R. MacFarquhar (Lab., Belper) moved an amendment to provide for British passport holders living abroad, but with an address in the U.K., to be eligible to vote in the referendum.

Mr MacFarquhar argued that in the unique circumstances of the referendum there should be a unique extension of the franchise to British citizens living and working abroad.

For the Opposition, Sir M. Havers said they would like to hear about the difficulties the proposals might entail, but, on principle, subject to certain safeguards, they would be prepared to support the amendment. 'The official Opposition's view is that British people overseas working for Britain should be entitled to vote in this most important referendum.'

M. Edelman (Lab., Coventry, North-West) rose to indicate his support for the amendment. 'What is happening now is that we are agreeing that if we allow them to be excluded, there will be some arbitrary constitutional distinction between Britons in London and Britons abroad.' He believed the amendment should be supported. Dr C. Phipps (Lab., Dudley, West) also rose to support the amendment. British citizens working abroad would resent being unable to vote in a referendum which would uniquely determine the future of the country in which they and their children would spend the majority of their lives.

The Lord President of the Council and Leader of the House, E. Short, rose to oppose the amendment. To introduce such a provision, the Government believed a minimum of five conditions had to be met, four of which could not be checked in the time remaining before the referendum. There was also the problem created by the small number of posts throughout the world at which voters could attend to vote, which would create further anomalies. 'The Committee should be in no doubt that if the amendment is carried and the referendum result is close, the vulnerability of the scheme to abuse and its anomalies will undermine confidence in the result and acceptance of the result. For those reasons I ask the Committee to reject the amendment.'

The amendment was negatived, after further debate, by 251 votes to 211. The 253 Members (including tellers) in the Government lobby comprised 235 Labour, 11 Scottish National, 3 Conservative, 3 Plaid Cymru and 1 UUUC. The 213 Members (including tellers) to support the amendment comprised 191 Conservative, 12 Liberal and 10 Labour. A small number of Members on both sides of the House (including M. Edelman) also appear to have abstained from voting.

Conservatives to vote against the amendment:

Bell, R.   Marten, N.   Moate, R.

Labour Members to vote for the amendment:

Ellis, T.   Marquand, D.   Stewart, M.
Hamilton, W.   Phipps, C.*   Strauss, G.*
MacFarquhar, R.   Rose, P.   Walden, B.
Mackintosh, J.

HC Deb. 890, 1375–80
1974–5, No. 176.

REFERENDUM BILL [62]

Committee: 22 April 1975

Clause 1 (Holding of referendum)

At 1.00 a.m., following a day's discussion on amendments to clause 1 of the Bill, the 'stand part' motion for the clause was moved.

P. Emery (C., Honiton) rose to speak on the motion, querying certain provisions of the clause, objecting to the Committee having to deal with it at that hour, and arguing that people had no desire for the provisions of the clause.

After he had spoken for almost half-an-hour, a Government whip rose to move 'That the Question be now put.'

The closure motion was carried by 209 votes to 3, with the Opposition abstaining from voting. The 5 Members (including tellers) to oppose closure were all Conservatives.

Conservatives to vote against closure:

Brotherton, M.   Gow, I.   Lawrence, I.*
Emery, P.*   Gower, Sir R.

HC Deb. 890, 1437–40
1974–5, No. 180.

The 'stand part' motion was then put, and carried without a division.

REFERENDUM BILL [63]

Committee: 23 April 1975

Clause 3 (Grants towards cost of campaign)

N. Buchan (Lab., Renfrewshire, West) moved an amendment to increase the grant of public money to the two umbrella organizations campaigning for and against remaining in the EEC respectively in the referendum from £125,000 to £500,000 each.

Mr Buchan argued that the purpose of the amendment was to show that they were not dealing with a fair situation. They had a situation in which one side had access to unlimited wealth and power, and that was being used in order to carry a 'Yes' vote in the referendum. The amendment, he declared, must be carried.

The Parliamentary Secretary, Privy Council Office, W. Price, replied that the Government believed it would be possible to have a reasonable display of leaflets, hire halls, employ secretaries and pay for limited press advertising with £125,000. The money was meant to supplement the resources which the organizations would seek to raise from other sources; the grant would also be more than quadrupled by the decision to circulate to every household a booklet setting out both sides of the case. 'Under the circumstances, we believe this to be the maximum amount of public money we can justify spending in this way, bearing in mind the need for curbs on public expenditure.' He asked the Committee to reject the amendment.

The amendment was negatived by 195 votes to 60, the Opposition abstaining from voting. The 62 Members (including tellers) to support the amendment comprised 53 Labour, 7 Scottish National, 1 Liberal and 1 Plaid Cymru. 21 Conservatives entered the Government lobby to oppose the amendment.

Labour Members to vote for the amendment:

Atkins, R.	Hoyle, D.*	Roderick, C.
Barnett, G.	Hughes, R. J.*	Rodgers, G.
Bennett, A.	Irving, S.	Rooker, J.
Buchan, N.	Kerr, R.	Ryman, J.
Callaghan, J.	Lambie, D.	Sedgemore, B.
Canavan, D.	Leadbitter, T.	Selby, H.
Clemitson, I.	Lee, J.	Short, Mrs R.
Cook, R.	Litterick, T.	Skinner, D.
Cryer, R.	Loyden, E.	Spearing, N.
Davies, B.	Madden, M.	Stallard, A.
English, M.	Marquand, D.	Swain, T.
Evans, I.	Miller, Mrs M.	Taylor, Mrs A.
Evans, J.	Newens, S.	Thomas, R.
Fernyhough, E.	Noble, M.	Torney, T.
Flannery, M.	Ovenden, J.	Walker, T.
Fletcher, T.	Parry, R.	Weetch, K.
George, B.	Richardson, Miss J.	Wise, Mrs A.
Hatton, F.	Roberts, G.	

Conservatives to vote against the amendment:

Blaker, P.	Dykes, H.	Rees, P.
Braine, Sir B.	Emery, P.	Rhys Williams, Sir B.
Brotherton, M.	Gow, I.	Ridley, N.
Buck, A.	Mates, M.	Shaw, G.
Budgen, N.	Mayhew, P.	Stanbrook, I.
Butler, A.	Mudd, D.	Winterton, N.
Clarke, K.	Osborn, J.	Wood, R.

HC Deb. 890, 1627–30
1974–5, No. 184.

The House then divided upon a related amendment, to increase the amount from £125,000 to £250,000 (see below).

REFERENDUM BILL [64]

Committee: 23 April 1975

Clause 3 (Grants towards cost of campaign)

A. L. Williams (Lab., Hornchurch) moved formally an amendment to increase the grant of public money to the two umbrella organizations campaigning for and against remaining in the EEC respectively in the referendum from £125,000 to £250,000 each.

The amendment had been discussed with a preceding one, and had been resisted by the Government (see above).[1]

The amendment was negatived by 161 votes to 81, the Opposition abstaining from voting. The 83 Members (including tellers) to support the amendment comprised 67 Labour, 7 Liberal, 7 Scottish National, 1 Plaid Cymru, and 1 Minister entering the wrong lobby. 12 Conservatives voted in the Government lobby.

Labour Members to vote for the amendment:

Ashton, J.	Hatton, F.	Roderick, C.
Atkins, R.	Hooley, F.	Rodgers, G.
Atkinson, N.	Hoyle, D.	Rooker, J.
Barnett, G.	Hughes, R. J.	Ryman, J.
Bennett, A.	Jay, D.	Sedgemore, B.
Buchan, N.	Jeger, Mrs L.	Selby, H.

Callaghan, J.

Canavan, D.

Clemitson, I.

Cook, R.

Cronin, J.

Cryer, R.*

Davies, B.

Ellis, T.

English, M.

Evans, I.

Evans, J.

Fernyhough, E.

Fitch, A.

Flannery, M.

Fletcher, T.

Forrester, J.

George, B.

Kerr, R.

Lambie, D.

Lee, J.

Litterick, T.

Loyden, E.

McNamara, K.

Madden, M.

Marquand, D.

Miller, Mrs M.

Newens, S.

Noble, M.

Ovenden, J.

Parry, R.

Radice, G.

Richardson, Miss J.

Roberts, G.

Short, Mrs R.

Silverman, J.

Skinner, D.

Spearing, N.

Stallard, A.

Swain, T.

Taylor, Mrs A.

Thomas, R.

Thorne, S.

Tinn, J.

Torney, T.

Walker, T.

Watkins, D.

Weetch, K.

Williams, A. L.*

Wise, Mrs A.

Conservatives to vote against the amendment:[2]

Brotherton, M.

Budgen, N.

Butler, A.

Clarke, K.

Emery, P.

Mates, M.

Mawby, R.

Mayhew, P.

Osborn, J.

Ridley, N.

Winterton, N.

Wood, R.

HC Deb. 890, 1631–4
1974–5, No. 185.

[1] In a brief speech in support of his amendment, Mr Williams had said that, contrary to press reports, the Labour Committee for Europe was not flush with money. The Committee hoped to get some money from the Government, but did not want the debate to be just about money. They wanted both sides to have adequate funds, and to have a debate about the issues.

[2] During the debate on the preceding amendment, P. Emery and N. Budgen had made it clear that they opposed the use of public money in the way proposed, and hence opposed any suggestion that the amount should be raised; they felt no public money should be expended. D. Hurd (C., Mid-Oxon) had risen in the same debate to incicate that Opposition Members believed that if there was to be a referendum it should be conducted in conditions of fairness. *See* the subsequent division on the 'stand part' motion for the clause (below).

REFERENDUM BILL   [65]

Committee: 23 April 1975

Clause 3 (Grants towards cost of campaign)

D. Hoyle (Lab., Nelson and Colne) moved an amendment designed to cut off public money for maintaining the special information unit set up to answer questions concerning the re-negotiated terms of EEC membership and the like.

Mr Hoyle contended that the unit had become a propaganda unit, and had started to volunteer information without being asked. The Government, he contended, were putting the civil servants involved in an impossible position. 'The Government should now drop the idea.'

The Parliamentary Secretary to the Privy Council Office, W. Price, replied that somebody had to answer the questions that were coming in. They had received more than a thousand questions in the first two weeks from the press and public. The unit had been set up because it was felt that the task would best be carried out centrally. Its terms of reference were to provide the facts, whether they supported the Government's case or not. 'What we are saying is that this is not a propaganda unit, as has been alleged, and we ask the Committee to reject the amendment.'

The amendment was negatived by 164 votes to 63, with the Opposition abstaining from voting. The 65 Members (including tellers) to support the amendment comprised 52 Labour, 6 Scottish National, 4 Conservative and 3 UUUC. 6 Conservatives entered the Government lobby to oppose the amendment.

Labour Members to vote for the amendment:

Atkinson, N.	Jay, D.	Rooker, J.
Barnett, G.	Kerr, R.	Ryman, J.
Bennett, A.	Lee, J.	Selby, H.
Buchan, N.	Litterick, T.	Shaw, A.
Callaghan, J.	Loyden, E.	Short, Mrs R.
Canavan, D.	McNamara, K.	Silverman, J.
Clemitson, I.	Madden, M.*	Skinner, D.
Cook, R.	Miller, Mrs M.	Spearing, N.
Cryer, R.	Newens, S.	Spriggs, L.
Davies, B.	Noble, M.	Swain, T.
English, M.	Ovenden, J.	Taylor, Mrs A.
Evans, I.	Parry, R.	Thomas, R.*
Evans, J.	Richardson, Miss J.	Thorne, S.
Flannery, M.	Roberts, G.	Walker, T.
Fletcher, T.	Robertson, J.	Weetch, K.
George, B.	Roderick, C.	Wise, Mrs A.
Hatton, F.	Rodgers, G.	Young, D.
Hoyle, D.		

Convervatives to vote for the amendment:

Brotherton, M.   Marten, N.   Townsend, C.
Gow, I.

Conservatives to vote against the amendment:

Hurd, D.   Osborn, J.   Winterton, N.
Meyer, Sir A.   Renton, T.   Wood, R.

HC Deb. 890, 1641-4
1974-5, No. 186.

REFERENDUM BILL [66]

Committee: 23 April 1975

Clause 3 (Grants towards cost of campaign)

On the motion that the clause stand part of the Bill, E. Powell (UUUC, Down, South) and M. English (Lab., Nottingham, West) rose to query the operation of subsection (2) of the clause concerning the accountability and publication of sums spent in the referendum campaign by the umbrella organizations. The Lord President of the Council and Leader of the House, E. Short, responded that the grants could only be used for purposes connected with the referendum, and the organizations concerned had to keep accounts of all sums received or spent since 26th March. The organizations concerned had accepted the various conditions laid down; the conditions, he said, were tight but fair.
    P. Emery (C., Honiton) said there were no sanctions if the money was not spent as intended. He also voiced objection to the principle of the clause. 'We are allowing taxpayers' money to be spent by political parties and to be provided to them for a political campaign. I believe that that is not the wish of the majority of people in this country.' He felt it would be incorrect for the clause to stand part of the Bill, and expressed sorrow that his party was not officially objecting to the clause. N. Budgen (C., Wolverhampton, South-West) rose to associate himself with Mr Emery's speech.
    The 'stand part' motion was carried by 195 votes to 9, with the Opposition abstaining from voting. The 197 Members (including tellers) in the Government lobby comprised 189 Labour, 6 Liberal and 2 Scottish National. The 11 Members (including tellers) to oppose the clause were all Conservatives.

Conservatives to vote against the clause:

Brotherton, M.	Goodhart, P.	Mates, M.
Budgen, N.*	Gow, I.	Stanbrook, I.
Clarke, K.	Lawrence, I.	Winterton, N.
Emery, P.*	Marshall, M.	

HC Deb. 890, 1657–8
1974–5, No. 187.

The division took place at 12.25 a.m.

REFERENDUM BILL [67]

Report: 24 April 1975

Clause 1 (Holding of referendum)

From the Opposition Front Bench, Sir M. Havers moved an amendment to extend the right to vote in the referendum to British passport holders, aged 18 and over, employed by the U.K. Government or international organizations, who were resident outside the U.K.

Sir M. Havers said the amendment was framed in order to overcome the objections raised by the Lord President of the Council in resisting an earlier amendment in committee.[1]

The Minister of State, Privy Council Office, G. Fowler, replied that Crown servants resident overseas were entitled to make a service declaration and register in that way. The basic objection to the amendment, he said, was one of principle. 'We decided in Committee to reject any extension of the franchise to persons who would not be entitled to register to vote under existing electoral law.' If endless anomalies were to be avoided, one had to confine the franchise to persons entitled to be registered to vote under the Representation of the People Acts.

The amendment was negatived, on a straight party vote, by 231 votes to 142. 1 Conservative cross-voted to oppose the amendment.

Conservative to vote against the amendment:

Body, R.

HC Deb. 890, 1803–6
1974–5, No. 189.

[1] See above, division no. 176, 22 April, *HC Deb.* 890, 1375–80.

DEFENCE [68]

6–7 May 1975

The Defence Secretary, R. Mason, moved 'That this House, recognizing the need both to provide adequately for the nation's security and to ensure that the level of public expenditure is contained within available resources, welcomes the statement on the Defence Estimates 1975 (Command Paper No. 5976); notes the circumstances in which further financial savings have since become necessary; and endorses the Government's determination to maintain efficient and well-equipped armed forces for the security of the United Kingdom.'

On the second day of the two-day debate, S. Newens (Lab., Harlow) moved an amendment, to leave out everything from 'House', and to insert 'declines to approve the statement on the Defence Estimates 1975 (Command Paper No. 5976) on the grounds that in the present critical economic circumstances it proposes an increase in arms expenditure in real terms over future years; that it commits Great Britain for the next 10 years to spend a higher proportion of the gross national product on defence than any of our major European allies; that it fails to propose significant reductions in major weapons projects; that it still leaves Great Britain to maintain unjustifiable commitments east of Suez; and that it fails to make adequate provision for a smooth transfer of the real resources and skilled manpower which would be released by more far-reaching cuts to alternative forms of employment, above all those which will directly assist economic growth and exports.'

The amendment was negatived by 489 votes to 57, the Opposition voting with the Government. The 491 Members (including tellers) in the Government lobby comprised 250 Conservatives, 224 Labour, 9 Liberal and 8 UUUC. The 59 Members (including tellers) to support the amendment comprised 56 Labour and 3 Plaid Cymru.

Labour Members to vote for the amendment:

Atkinson, N.	Hoyle, D.	Roberts, G.
Bennett, A.	Hughes, R. J.	Robertson, J.
Bidwell, S.	Jeger, Mrs L.	Rodgers, G.
Buchan, N.	Kelley, R.	Rooker, J.
Callaghan, J.	Kerr, R.*	Sedgemore, B.
Canavan, D.	Kilroy-Silk, R.	Selby, H.
Clemitson, I.	Kinnock, N.	Short, Mrs R.
Colquhoun, Mrs M.	Lambie, D.	Sillars, J.
Cook, R.	Lamond, J.	Silverman, J.
Corbett, R.	Lee, J.	Skinner, D.

Cryer, R.	Litterick, T.	Snape, P.
Davies, B.	Loyden, E.	Swain, T.
Edge, G.	Madden, M.	Thomas, R.
Evans, I.	Maynard, Miss J.	Thorne, S.
Fernyhough, E.	Mikardo, I.*	Tierney, S.
Flannery, M.	Newens, S.	Walker, T.
Fletcher, T.	Parry, R.	Wise, Mrs A.
Garrett, J.	Price, C.	Woof, R.
Hatton, F.	Richardson, Miss J.	

HC Deb. 891, 1567-72
1974-5, No. 199.

The main question was then put, and carried on a straight party vote by 291 votes to 251. Of the 56 Labour Members to vote for the amendment, 54 (in company with Liberal Members) voted in the Government lobby; the two exceptions were Mrs L. Jeger and I. Mikardo, who were absent from the division. There were no cross-votes.

FINANCE (No. 2) BILL [69]

Second Reading: 8 May 1975

The Chancellor of the Exchequer, D. Healey, moved the Second Reading of the Bill, and explained its main provisions. Clause 1 provided for an increase in the duties on tobacco and alcoholic drink, clauses 5 and 6 gave effect to substantial increases in revenue being sought from road users, clauses 17 to 20 covered changes in value added tax, clause 31 removed the tax benefit enjoyed by shareholders who had been able to take their dividends in the form of additional shares, and other clauses dealt with changes in income tax rates and the amounts of personal allowances; the Chancellor said he had sought to protect the most vulnerable members of the community by simultaneously raising the tax thresholds.

For the Opposition, Sir G. Howe said that possibly no Budget had been more rapidly overtaken by the progress of events than that one had been. He criticised the Chancellor for his lack of urgency in the attack on inflation, and argued the case for a decisive onslaught on the size of the public sector borrowing requirement. There was a gap between expenditure and revenue which could only be bridged by raising taxes or reducing public expenditure. The Chancellor had taken the first course. 'That is why in our responsible judgment of the present situation—because we recognize the equation with which the Chancellor is confronted—we did not vote against the Budget as a whole, and we shall not vote against the Bill, although we shall challenge the way in which the additional taxes have been levied.' He felt they were at about the limit of the nation's taxable capacity.

The Bill was given a Second Reading by 182 votes to 22, the Opposition abstaining officially from voting. The 184 Members (including tellers) in the Government lobby comprised 175 Labour and 9 UUUC. The 24 Members (including tellers) to oppose Second Reading comprised 12 Liberal, 9 Scottish National and 3 Conservative.

Conservatives to vote against Second Reading:

Biggs-Davison, J.   Stewart, I.   Winterton, N.

HC Deb. 891, 1755–6
1974–5, No. 201.

None of the three Conservative dissenters participated in the debate.

PREVENTION OF TERRORISM   [70]

Prayer: 19 May 1975

The Home Secretary, R. Jenkins moved 'That the Prevention of Terrorism (Temporary Provisions) Act 1974 (Continuance) Order 1975, a draft of which was laid before this House on 1st May, be approved.'

Mr Jenkins said he did not wish the exceptional powers provided under the Act to remain in force a moment longer than was necessary, but he was satisfied that it would not be right to allow the provisions of the Act to lapse as early as 28th May. The security situation continued to give cause for concern. The ceasefire in Northern Ireland was fragile, and following the discovery of an IRA bomb factory in Britain they had to assume plans existed for the resumption of terrorist operations should the cease-fire come to an end. He reminded the House of the provisions of the Act, and said that the essence of it was prevention. 'I do not like special powers legislation of this sort. But I am convinced that the Act has helped to protect us in a difficult position, and that in a fragile situation it continues to be necessary for the immediate future. Therefore, I ask the House to accept the order.'

From the Opposition Front Bench, I. Gilmour announced that the

Opposition supported the continuance of the powers for a further six months. 'They are,' he said, 'a disagreeable necessity.'

A number of Labour Members rose to criticise or oppose the order. A. Bennett (Lab., Stockport, North) questioned whether the Act had worked well, and noted that there were rumours in the Irish community that unfairness had occurred. He felt it was time to get rid of the Act. The only way to defeat terrorists was to isolate them. R. Thomas (Lab., Bristol, North-West) objected to persons served with exclusion orders not being given any indication of the evidence against them. He said it was completely unacceptable and he would not be voting for the extension. 'Given the opportunity, I will vote against it.' F. Hooley (Lab., Sheffield, Heeley) said he regarded the Act as a serious potential danger to civil liberties in Britain, and believed it was passed in panic in a manner unworthy of the House. S. Thorne (Lab., Preston, South) declared that the Act was a further erosion of civil liberties, and should never have been put on the statute book. He took the view that the Act should not be renewed, 'and I urge hon. Members not to give it a renewal when a Division takes place later this evening.'

The order was approved by 161 votes to 10, the Opposition voting with the Government. The 163 Members (including tellers) in the Government lobby comprised 137 Labour, 20 Conservative and 6 UUUC. The 12 Members (including tellers) to oppose the order comprised 10 Labour, 1 SDLP and 1 Plaid Cymru.

Labour Members to vote against the order:

Bennett, A.	Loyden, E.	Selby, H.
Bidwell, S.	Maynard, Miss J.*	Thomas, R.
Callaghan, J.	Richardson, Miss J.	Thorne, S.*
Flannery, M.		

HC Deb. 892, 1159–61
1974–5, No. 210.

FINANCE (No. 2) BILL [71]

Committee: 20 May 1975

Clause 28 (Alteration of personal reliefs)

N. Lawson (C., Blaby) moved an amendment designed to provide for various personal allowances to be increased in subsequent financial years according to the rise in the retail price index.

Mr Lawson said the Committee had already heard the arguments for indexation at some length, and it was clear that the argument had been won by those who supported it. He hoped the Government would accept the amendment.

The Minister of State at the Treasury, R. Sheldon, replied that there was no need for indexation. There could be a case for it, he said, if they were so foolish as to accept a continual, high and regular level of inflation of a kind which they did not have and which the Government were determined not to have. He also contended that an attempt to force the Government to forgo some of its independent power of action must be self-defeating, and that the amendment would severely limit the function of trade unions.

The amendment was negatived by 148 votes to 37, with the Opposition apparently abstaining from voting.[1] The Government lobby comprised solely Labour Members. The 39 Members (including tellers) to support the amendment comprised 33 Conservative, 3 Liberal, 2 Plaid Cymru and 1 UUUC.

Conservatives to vote for the amendment:

Arnold, T.	Fisher, Sir N.	Page, R. G.
Awdry, D.	Gow, I.	Rees, P.
Carlisle, M.	Gray, H.	Renton, Sir D.
Chalker, Mrs L.	Hampson, K.	Shaw, G.
Clegg, W.	James, D.	Sims, R.
Cooke, R.	Lawrence, I.	Skeet, T.
Cope, J.*	Lawson, N.*	Stainton, K.
Cormack, P.	Lester, J.	Stanbrook, I.
Corrie, J.	Mitchell, D.	Townsend, C.
Dean, P.	Morgan, G.	Wiggin, J.
Farr, J.	Morrison, P.	Winterton, N.

HC Deb. 892, 1345–8
1974–5, No. 213.

[1] Voting in a division 23 minutes earlier had been 151 to 133.

BRITISH LEYLAND (FINANCIAL ASSISTANCE) [72]

Prayer: 21 May 1975

The Under-Secretary of State for Industry, M. Meacher, moved 'That this House authorizes the Secretary of State to pay or undertake to pay sums by way of financial assistance under section 8 of the Industry Act

1972 in respect of a guarantee or guarantees to be given to the bankers of British Leyland Motor Corporation Limited and any of its subsidiaries covering borrowing facilities made available by the bankers to those companies, insofar as the amount paid or undertaken to be paid under the guarantee or guarantees is in excess of £50 million being the maximum amount authorized by resolution of this House on 18th December 1974, but does not exceed £100 million.'

Mr Meacher said they had had a full debate on the Bill which enabled the Government to acquire a substantial share in the enlarged equity of the company, and he did not intend to rehearse the arguments. The motion provided essentially an interim arrangement to meet British Leyland's requirements while the longer-term scheme and the steps necessary for its implementation were considered by the various parties concerned.

For the Opposition, T. King rose to express substantial reservations about the Government's proposals in the British Leyland Bill. The Opposition had opposed the proposals in the Bill; however, he said, 'we think it right to let this motion proceed, as it is essential'. The Opposition wanted a much more realistic approach to the British Leyland problem than was contained in the Ryder report, but felt that appointing a receiver, as some backbenchers wanted, was not the best policy in the existing situation.

A number of Conservative Members rose to oppose the motion. Dr R. Boyson (C., Brent, North) said he and other Members felt strongly about the order because they did not like the inverted funnel syndrome: that once money was put into something it was in there permanently because, as it went down, the funnel got wider to take more in. There were two reasons for British Leyland's existing state, he said: one was the result of Government intervention, and the other was the worship of size. He argued that the money should not be paid. N. Fairbairn (C., Kinross and West Perthshire) said they were being asked to approve an order which fined every man, woman and child in the United Kingdom £1 a head to sustain an organization which had been brought into being by an absurd civil service fantasy. I. Gow (C., Eastbourne) opposed the order on the grounds that it had not been sufficiently justified by the Minister, that it demonstrated that the Industry Secretary was running the Government, and that it would add still further to the public sector borrowing requirement. K. Warren (C., Hastings) declared that it was ridiculous that they should be asked to authorize paying the money when the Industry Secretary had already failed. If there was so much money available, some of it should be used to back firms in which hard work and success did not find the reward from the Government that was needed.

The motion was approved by 226 votes to 58, the Opposition abstaining from voting. The 228 Members (including tellers) in the Government lobby comprised 219 Labour, 6 Scottish National, 2 UUUC and 1 Conservative. The 60 Members (including tellers) to oppose the motion comprised 50 Conservative, 8 Liberal and 2 UUUC.

Conservative to vote for the motion:

Miller, H.

Conservatives to vote against the motion:

Aitken, J.	Hannam, J.	Osborn, J.
Biffen, J.	Hordern, P.	Ridley, N.
Biggs-Davison, J.	Howell, R.	Rost, P.
Body, R.	Knight, Mrs J.	Shepherd, C
Bowden, A.	Lawrence, I.	Sims, R.
Boyson, R.	Lawson, N.	Skeet, T.
Brotherton, M.	Lloyd, I.	Spence, J.
Budgen, N.	Macfarlane, N.	Spicer, J.
Clark, A.	McNair-Wilson, P.	Stanbrook, I.
Cope, J.	Marshall, M.	Stokes, J.
Cormack, P.	Mather, C.	Taylor, R.
Fairbairn, N.	Mayhew, P.	Tebbit, N.
Fletcher, A.	Mills, P.	Townsend, C.
Fletcher-Cooke, C.	Moate, R.	Warren, K.
Glyn, A.	Morris, M.	Wiggin, J.
Gow, I.	Morrison, P.	Winterton, N.
Grieve, P.	Nelson, A.	

HC Deb. 892, 1575-8
1974-5, No. 217.

STANDING COMMITTEE ON REGIONAL AFFAIRS [73]

9 June 1975

The Lord President of the Council and Leader of the House, E. Short, moved a motion to establish a Standing Committee on Regional Affairs, comprising all Members representing English constituencies plus five others.

Mr Short said that recent pressure on parliamentary time had meant that the prospect for debates on English regional issues was poor. The proposal was designed to try to improve the situation by making provision for a Standing Committee to consider any matters relating to English regional affairs which might be referred to it. It would be a sessional committee, and the proposal was being put forward on an experimental basis.

From the Opposition Front Bench, J. Peyton declared that the proposal was just another device to facilitate life for the executive and to chip away at the powers of Parliament and its rights. It would mean more pressure on the time, resources and energies of Members, and would mean less pressure on the Government to find time which would afford adequate opportunity for Members to discuss matters of urgent public interest.

During the debate, one Conservative rose to support the motion. A. Fletcher (C., Edinburgh, North) said he supported the motion because he was anxious that English regional business should be given the same amount of time, discussion and emphasis as was given to Scottish and Welsh business in the House, and also because he thought it was the beginning of the re-shaping of attitudes. He thought the debate could have far-reaching consequences for devolution.

(1) After one-and-a-half hour's debate, the Government deputy chief whip moved the closure which was carried, on a whipped party vote, by 143 votes to 112. 1 Labour Member cross-voted to oppose closure, and at least one other (E. Ogden) abstained from voting.

Labour Member to vote against closure:

Leadbitter, T.

(2) The motion was then put, and although ostensibly a House of Commons' matter, carried on a whipped party vote by 154 votes to 104; Liberal Members, having opposed closure, voted with the Government. 2 Conservatives cross-voted to support the motion, and 1 Labour Member cross-voted to oppose it.

Conservatives to vote for the motion:

Fletcher, A.   Sproat, I.

Labour Member to vote against the motion:

Leadbitter, T.

HC Deb. 893, 199–204
1974–5, Nos. 220 & 221.

FINANCE (No. 2) BILL [74]

Committee: 10 June 1975

Clause 60 (Introductory)

On the motion for the clause to stand part of the Bill, N. Ridley (C., Cirencester and Tewkesbury) rose to oppose it. That and following clauses were designed to stop tax abuses, but the clause had implications for the 'lump sum contract' system, he said, and he made it clear that he supported the principle underlying the 'lump' system. He noted two defects in the clause: it was totally wrong to require one citizen to be the tax collector on behalf of another with whom he had no relationship other than contractual, and it would be extremely difficult to collect the money from private individuals who had done work and were not large and registered businesses in the sense that builders were. He would vote against the clause because he felt it was time the Committee demonstrated in favour of the 'lump'. J. Biffen (C., Oswestry) said that the message from the debate was that the Government should look again at the overwhelming necessity for an early reduction in the totality of public spending, and they should move very warily with regard to taxing self-employment, which was a growth area in the economy.

The Financial Secretary to the Treasury, Dr J. Gilbert, said they were not establishing any great new principle. They were tightening up the arrangements under the existing scheme because they had manifestly proved inadequate to prevent tax evasion on a massive scale.

The clause was approved by 189 votes to 28, the Opposition abstaining from voting. The 30 Members (including tellers) to oppose the clause were all Conservatives.

Conservatives to vote against the clause:

Benyon, W.	Gower, Sir R.	Mudd, D.
Biffen, J.	Howell, R.	Newton, T.
Boscawen, R.	Knight, Mrs J.	Normanton, T.
Brotherton, M.	Latham, M.	Rees-Davies, W.
Budgen, N.	Lawrence, I.	Ridley, N.*
Clegg, W.	Lawson, N.*	Roberts, W.
Corrie, J.	Macfarlane, N.	Rossi, H.
Costain, A.	Miller, H.	Townsend, C.
Durant, T.	.Mitchell, D.	Wiggin, J.
Goodhew, V.	Monro, H.	Winterton, N.

HC Deb. 893, 361–2
1974–5, No. 224.

BUSINESS OF THE HOUSE [75]

11 June 1975

At 10.00 p.m., a Government whip moved the business motion to permit the Social Security Pensions Bill to be proceeded with, though opposed, until any hour, and the Motion relating to Economic Policy Guidelines to be proceeded with, though opposed, until 11.30 p.m. or one-and-a-half hours after it had been entered upon, whichever was the later.

Scottish National Members divided the House, and the motion was carried by 145 votes to 9, with the Opposition abstaining from voting. The 11 Members (including tellers) to oppose the motion comprised 8 Scottish National, 2 Plaid Cymru and 1 Conservative.

Conservative to vote against the motion:

Brotherton, M.

HC Deb. 893, 545–8
1974–5, No. 228.

INDUSTRY BILL (ALLOCATION OF TIME) [76]

18 June 1975

The Under-Secretary of State for Industry, G. Kaufman, moved a motion to increase the time allocated for report stage and Third Reading of the Industry Bill from two to three days.

Mr Kaufman said the Government had concluded that it would be appropriate to extend the time to three days in order to assure an adequate opportunity for the discussion of amendments.[1]

From the Opposition Front Bench, M. Heseltine moved an amendment to increase the time allocated for report and Third Reading to four days.

Mr Heseltine said that the Industry Secretary had given an assurance that if substantial amendments were to be introduced he would recommend that adequate time be given on report. So the Minister, without spelling it out, was saying the Government had decided upon extensive amendments, which took them back to the position which had provoked the suspension of the Standing Committee on three occasions the previous week.[2] The House and the Standing Committee had been treated in a regrettable way, and he contended that the House should show its unwillingness to be treated in that way by voting for four days instead of three.

E. Heffer (Lab., Liverpool, Walton) rose to say that, as long as amendments on report arose from discussions and commitments given in Committee, he and his hon. Friends would not press for any additional time; however, he warned the Government not to come forward with any fundamental changes 'which reflect the opinions of the CBI.' I. Mikardo (Lab., Bethnal Green and Bow) agreed with Mr Heseltine that the Government's handling of the Bill at that stage was an insult to the Members who served on the Standing Committee. It seemed the Government's intention to introduce *de facto* a different Bill. The changes made would not, he contended, be in the direction that he wanted, and he declared his intention to vote against the motion.

The Opposition amendment was negatived, on a straight party vote, by 192 votes to 162. The Government lobby comprised solely Labour Members. The 164 Members (including tellers) in the Opposition lobby comprised 144 Conservative, 11 Liberal and 9 Scottish National.

The main question was then put, and carried by 185 votes to 6, with the Opposition abstaining from voting. The 187 Members (including tellers) in the Government lobby comprised 178 Labour and 9 Scottish National. The 8 Members (including tellers) to oppose the motion were all Labour Members. A further 8 Labour backbenchers were absent from the division, having voted in the preceding one.[3]

Labour Members to vote against the motion:

Bidwell, S.	Richardson, Miss J.	Thomas, R.
Colquhoun, Mrs M.	Selby, H.	Thorne, S.*
Mikardo, I.*	Skinner, D.	

HC Deb. 893, 1425–8
1974–5, No. 238.

[1] Although spending more time in winding-up the debate, the Minister spoke for only one minute in moving the motion.

[2] On 9 June, the Industry Secretary had said, in answer to a parliamentary Question, that the Government would consider the publication of a further White Paper on the working of the proposed Bill; *HC Deb.* 893, c. 14–15. In consequence, the Standing Committee on the Bill had demanded to have further information as to what was likely to be in the White Paper. The Secretary of State could not be found, and the Under-Secretary of State was unable to answer questions on it, so Members of the Committee walked out, causing the Committee to be suspended. (One Member went to the Chamber to ask for guidance from the Chair; *HC Deb.* 893, c. 271–2.)

[3] The eight were: N. Atkinson, S. Irving, R. Kerr, J. Lee, E. Loyden, C. Phipps, R. Tuck and J. Wellbeloved. At least four of these (Messrs Atkinson, Kerr, Lee and Loyden) would appear to be deliberate abstainers.

SEX DISCRIMINATION BILL [77]

Report: 18 June 1975

New Clause 5 (Codes of practice, guidelines and rules of practice)

Miss J. Richardson (Lab., Barking) moved the new clause, which gave the Equal Opportunities Commission the power to issue codes of practice 'containing such practical guidance as the Commission thinks fit for the purpose of eliminating discrimination and promoting equality of opportunity,' and also prescribed a number of matters on which the Commission should issue codes of practice, guidelines or rules of practice.

Miss Richardson said the Bill went some way towards setting certain legal guidelines, but she would like the Government to accept that it ought to go somewhat further. She wanted the EOC to be able to issue guidance on how discrimination could be prevented by employers, bodies responsible for educational establishments, and avoided in advertisements and audio and visual material. She believed the new clause was an important one which would considerably strengthen the role of the Commission.

The Under-Secretary of State at the Home Office, Dr S. Summerskill, replied that the Commission could, if it wished, issue voluntary codes. The Government was doubtful about the practicality of the clause, and whether there was a role for statutory codes in the Bill. A code of practice for equal opportunity employers would not help a court or tribunal in deciding whether a woman had been treated less favourably than a man on grounds of sex, and complying with the provisions of a code would not necessarily mean that an act of unlawful discrimination had not taken place. She could not recommend that the House accept the clause.

The new clause was negatived by 150 votes to 31, with the Opposition abstaining from voting. The 33 Members (including tellers) to support the clause were all Labour Members. 5 Conservatives entered the Government lobby to vote against the clause.

Labour Members to vote for the clause:

Allaun, F.	Flannery, M.	Noble, M.
Bidwell, S.	George, B.	Prescott, J.
Butler, Mrs J.	Hayman, Mrs H.	Price, C.
Canavan, D.	Heffer, E.	Richardson, Miss J.*
Colquhoun, Mrs M.*	Hoyle, D.	Roderick, C.

Cook, R.	Janner, G.	Rooker, J.
Cryer, R.	McCartney, H.	Skinner, D.
Davies, B.	McMillan, T.	Taylor, Mrs A.
Edge, G.	Madden, M.	Thomas, R.
English, M.	Maynard, Miss J.	Thorne, S.
Evans, J.	Mikardo, I.	Wise, Mrs A.

Conservatives to vote against the clause:

| Bell, R. | Lawrence, I. | Stanbrook, I. |
| Fookes, Miss J.| Rees-Davies, W. | |

HC Deb. 893, 1465–8
1974–5, No. 239.

SEX DISCRIMINATION BILL   [78]

Report: 18 June 1975

Clause 11 (Partnerships)

R. Bell (C., Beaconsfield) moved an amendment to leave out the clause.

Mr Bell contended that it was quite unreasonable that so personal relationship as a partnership should be governed by the Bill. 'One could understand the clause better in relation to large limited companies, but when it is dealing with small partnerships and saying that people cannot decide that they are a men's club, or a women's club for that matter, this again shows the doctrinaire extremism of the Bill.'

The Under-Secretary of State at the Home Office, Dr S. Summerskill, replied that it was because of close personal relationships that existed in small partnerships that the latter had been excluded from the Bill. 'Leaving small partnerships aside, I see no reason why the larger partnerships should lawfully be able to turn away a prospective woman partner simply because she is a woman, or should lawfully be able to treat an existing woman partner less favourably than her male partners, again simply because she is a woman. The converse would apply.' She asked the House to reject the amendment.

The amendment was negatived by 142 votes to 8, with the Opposition abstaining from voting. The 10 Members (including tellers) to support the amendment comprised 6 Conservative and 4 UUUC. 1 Conservative entered the Government lobby to vote against the amendment.

Conservatives to vote for the amendment:

Bell, R.   Fry, P.   Grist, I.
Biggs-Davison, J.*   Gray, H.   Stanbrook, I.*

Conservative to vote against the amendment:

Fookes, Miss J.

HC Deb. 893, 1509–10
1974–5, No. 240.

SEX DISCRIMINATION BILL   [79]

Report: 18 June 1975

Clause 12 (Trade Unions etc.)

The Under-Secretary of State for Education and Science, Miss J. Lestor, moved an amendment to delete the provision exempting from the provisions of the clause trade unions which already existed on a single-sex basis and were the counterpart of a similar body limited to members of the other sex. [The provision had been inserted in committee against the wishes of the Government.]

Miss Lester explained that the exemption covered six bodies, all of them in the field of education. The clause laid down that it was unlawful for trade unions, employers' organizations and similar bodies to discriminate on grounds of sex in admission to membership or in their treatment of members, and the Government could not accept that there was a case for treating the six bodies differently from every other trade union and professional association in the country. The clause gave exemption to those who were least in need of it; women teachers were in a majority and were an exceptionally intelligent and articulate group of women.

For the Opposition, I. Gilmour rose to oppose the amendment. Voting in committee had been nine votes to one against the Government, and it was, he said, quite wrong for the Government, without any new arguments, to seek to undo what was done in committee.

The amendment was carried by 129 votes to 112, on a whipped party vote. The 131 Members (including tellers) in the Government lobby comprised 130 Labour and 1 SDLP. The 114 Members (including tellers) in the Opposition lobby comprised 90 Conservative, 8 Liberal, 7 Scottish National, 5 UUUC, 3 Labour and 1 Plaid Cymru.

Labour Members to vote against the amendment:

Colquhoun, Mrs M.   Richardson, Miss J.   Stewart, M.

HC Deb. 893, 1527–30
1974–5, No. 241.

SEX DISCRIMINATION BILL   [80]

Report: 18 June 1975

Clause 20 (Midwives)

The Minister of State for Health and Social Security, Dr D. Owen, moved an amendment designed to remove the statutory barriers to men becoming midwives. [The provision had been contained in the original Bill, but had been deleted, against the wishes of the Government, in committee.]

Dr Owen said that the Government saw the matter as being one of principle. It was the purpose of the Bill to uphold the right of women and, equally, of men to have access to the work of their choice, unimpeded by the fact of their sex. The Government did not wish to see the Bill weakened in its effect by enlarging the area of exceptions. As to practical objections that had been raised, he explained that the Government proposed to limit the training and the employment of men as midwives to a few selected centres where it would be possible to ensure that there could be choice by the patient. He commended the amendment to the House.

For the Opposition, I. Gilmour rose to oppose the amendment. There was no public demand for male midwives, and very few people wanted to become male midwives. All the medical bodies in the country were against the Minister on this issue. He hoped the House would reject the amendment.

Mrs A. Wise (Lab., Coventry, South-West) also rose to oppose the amendment. She did not believe that the mother would have a choice. In their search for abstract equality, they would greatly offend the susceptibilities of many women by the clause. 'I strongly urge the House to reject the amendment, not in a spirit of prudery but because

I believe that after childbirth women are entitled to—and want—the services of their own sex.'

The amendment was carried by 104 votes to 96, on a whipped party vote. The 106 Members (including tellers) in the Government lobby comprised 102 Labour, 3 Conservative and 1 SDLP. The 98 Members (including tellers) in the Opposition lobby comprised 65 Conservative, 14 Labour, 7 Scottish National, 6 Liberal, 5 UUUC and 1 Plaid Cymru.

Conservatives to vote for the amendment:

Brotherton, M.   Mudd, D.   Young, Sir G.

Labour Members to vote against the amendment:

Ashton, J.	Lamborn, H.	Rodgers, G.
Bray, J.	McElhone, F.	Small, W.
Campbell, I.	Madden, M.	Thomas, R.
Cant, R.	Mitchell, R.	Wise, Mrs A.
Craigen, J.	Noble, M.	

HC Deb. 893, 1551–4
1974–5, No. 242.

INDUSTRY BILL   **[81]**

Report: 1 July 1975

Clause 2 (General Purposes and Functions)

Dr J. Bray (Lab., Motherwell and Wishaw) moved formally an amendment to require the National Enterprise Board to consult the employees of each enterprise it owned as to the form of management they wanted, and, if the employees so chose, to permit the enterprise to be run by the workers as a workers' co-operative.

The amendment had been discussed in conjunction with other amendments, and had been resisted by the Government.[1]

The amendment was negatived by 336 votes to 72, the Opposition voting with the Government. The 338 Members (including tellers) to oppose the amendment comprised 178 Conservative, 159 Labour and 1 UUUC. The 74 Members (including tellers) to support the amendment comprised 63 Labour, 10 Liberal and 1 Plaid Cymru. At least a further 3 Labour Members abstained from voting.[2]

Labour Members to vote for the amendment:

Allaun, F.	Hart, Mrs J.	Prescott, J.
Ashton, J.	Hatton, F.	Richardson, Miss J.
Atkinson, N.	Heffer, E.	Roberts, G.
Bean, R.	Hoyle, D.	Roderick, C.
Bennett, A.	Hughes, R. J.	Rodgers, G.
Bray, J.*	Kerr, R.	Sandelson, N.
Buchan, N.	Kilroy-Silk, R.	Sedgemore, B.
Campbell, I.	Kinnock, N.	Selby, H.
Canavan, D.	Lambie, D.	Shaw, A.
Cook, R.	Leadbitter, T.	Short, Mrs R.
Corbett, R.	Lee, J.	Sillars, J.
Cryer, R.	Litterick, T.	Silverman, J.
Davies, B.	Loyden, E.	Skinner, D.
Edge, G.	Madden, M.	Spearing, N.
English, M.	Marshall, J.	Stallard, A.
Evans, J.	Maynard, Miss J.	Taylor, Mrs A.
Fernyhough, E.	Mikardo, I.	Thomas, R.*
Flannery, M.	Miller, M.	Thorne, S.
Fletcher, T.	Newens, S.	Torney, T.
Garrett, J.	Noble, M.	Wilson, A.
Hamilton, W.	Ovenden, J.	Wise, Mrs A.

HC Deb. 894, 1319–24
1974–5, No. 254

[1] The Under-Secretary of State for Industry, G. Kaufman, had said that the Government were actively considering the proposal to establish a co-operative development agency. They wanted co-operatives to have every chance of success. There was a considerable prospect that if the amendment was carried, they would go forward more sporadically than would be helpful to the situation. He did not think the Bill was an appropriate vehicle to carry out as an offshoot experiments on workers' co-operatives. If the Board's undertakings were turned into co-operatives the Board would lack the base from which to carry out its employment promoting functions.

[2] The three were: I. Evans, H. Gourlay and J. Watkinson. All three participated in a preceding and a subsequent division.

INDUSTRY BILL   [82]

New Clause 2 (The Board and the Media)

A guillotine motion was operating for the Bill, and at 9.30 p.m. the Deputy Speaker proceeded to put forthwith amendments moved by the Government which had to be completed at that time.

The new clause provided that neither the Board nor any of its subsidiaries should commence a business of publishing newspapers or other periodicals or enter into any contract with the Independent Broadcasting Authority for the provision of programmes, or acquire share capital in a body corporate if that body was substantially engaged in newspaper or periodical publication or acting as a programme contractor. The clause was moved formally by the Industry Secretary, E. Varley.

The clause was approved by 332 votes to 66, the Opposition voting with the Government. The 334 Members (including tellers) to vote in the Government lobby comprised 166 Conservative, 150 Labour, 10 Liberal, 6 Scottish National, 1 UUUC and 1 Plaid Cymru. The 68 Members (including tellers) to oppose the clause were all Labour Members.

Labour Members to vote against the clause:

Allaun, F.	Hart, Mrs J.	Prescott, J.
Ashton, J.	Hatton, F.	Price, C.
Atkins, R.	Heffer, E.	Richardson, Miss J.
Atkinson, N.	Hoyle, D.	Roberts, G.
Barnett, G.	Hughes, R. J.	Roderick, C.
Bennett, A.	Kerr, R.*	Rodgers, G.
Bray, J.	Kilroy-Silk, R.	Sedgemore, B.
Buchan, N.	Kinnock, N.	Selby, H.
Callaghan, J.	Lambie, D.	Short, Mrs R.
Canavan, D.	Lamond, J.	Sillars, J.
Cook, R.	Lee, J.	Skinner, D.
Corbett, R.	Litterick, T.	Spriggs, L.
Cryer, R.	Loyden, E.*	Stallard, A.
Davies, B.	McCartney, H.	Taylor, Mrs A.
Edge, G.	Madden, M.	Thomas, R.
Evans, I.	Marshall, J.	Thorne, S.
Evans, J.	Maynard, Miss J.	Torney, T.
Fernyhough, E.	Mikardo, I.	Watkinson, J.
Flannery, M.	Miller, M.	Wilson, A.
Fletcher, T.	Molloy, W.	Wise, Mrs A.
Garrett, J.	Newens, S.	Woof, R.
Garrett, W.	Noble, M.	Young, D.
Hamilton, W.	Ovenden, J.	

HC Deb. 894, 1327-30
1974-5, No. 255.

BUSINESS OF THE HOUSE [83]

1 July 1975

At 10.00 p.m., a Government whip moved the business motion to allow the Motion relating to the European Parliament (Membership) to be proceeded with, though opposed, at that sitting until any hour.

The Liberals divided the House on the motion, which was carried by 220 votes to 17, the Opposition abstaining from voting. The Government lobby comprised solely Labour Members. The 19 Members (including tellers) to oppose the motion comprised 13 Liberal, 4 Conservative, 1 UUUC and 1 Plaid Cymru.

Conservatives to vote against the motion:

Brotherton, M.   Meyer, Sir A.   Winterton, N.
Farr, J.

HC Deb. 894, 1333-6
1974-5, No. 256.

See subsequent divisions, nos. 262 & 263 (below) [88].

INDUSTRY BILL [84]

Report: 1 July 1975

Clause 10 (Power to make orders)

The Industry Secretary, E. Varley, moved an amendment to provide that where 30 per cent or more of the share capital of a body corporate was vested under a vesting order in the Secretary of State or National Enterprise Board, the remaining shareholders would be informed and given the right to require the Secretary of State or the Board to acquire the share capital held by them.

Mr Varley said the provision would give the shareholders a free and fair choice, and ensured that their interests were protected.

The Liberals divided against the amendment, which was carried by 222 votes to 13, the Opposition abstaining from voting. The 224 Members (including tellers) in the Government lobby comprised 213 Labour, 10 Scottish National, and, according to the division list (apparently a mistake) 1 Conservative.[1] The 15 Members (including tellers) to vote against the amendment comprised 13 Liberal, 1 Conservative and 1 UUUC.

Conservative to vote against the amendment:

Winterton, N.

HC Deb. 894, 1361–4
1974–5, No. 258.

¹ The division list records M. C. Hutchison (C., Edinburgh, South) as voting in the Government lobby, but apparently he did not so vote. M. C. Hutchison to author.

INDUSTRY BILL [85]

Report: 1 July 1975

Clause 11 (Contents of vesting orders)

At 11.00 p.m. the Speaker proceeded to put forthwith amendments moved by the Government which had to be dealt with by that time under the guillotine motion operating for the Bill.

The Industry Secretary, E. Varley, moved formally an amendment to amend the provisions concerning the setting aside of a transfer of capital or assets by a vesting order.

The Liberals divided against the amendment, which was carried by 222 votes to 15, the Opposition abstaining from voting. The 17 Members (including tellers) to vote against the amendment comprised 13 Liberal, 3 Conservative and 1 UUUC.

Conservatives to vote against the amendment:

Brotherton, M.   Lester, J.   Winterton, N.

HC Deb. 894, 1365–8
1974–5, No. 259.

INDUSTRY BILL [86]

Report: 1 July 1975

Clause 16 (Increase in limit on credits)

The Under-Secretary for Industry, G. Kaufman, moved formally an amendment to delete two lines of the clause. A guillotine motion was in operation, and the amendment was put forthwith.

The amendment was carried by 199 votes to 14, the Opposition abstaining from voting. The 16 Members (including tellers) to oppose the amendment comprised 12 Liberal, 3 Conservative and 1 UUUC.

Conservatives to vote against the amendment:

Brotherton, M.   Gower, Sir R.   Winterton, N.

HC Deb. 894, 1371–4
1974–5, No. 260.

INDUSTRY BILL [87]

Report: 1 July 1975

Clause 17 (Renewal of guarantees)

The Under-Secretary for Industry, G. Kaufman, moved formally an amendment to delete three words ('of that section') from one line of the clause. A guillotine motion was in operation, and the amendment was put forthwith.

The amendment was carried by 208 votes to 13, the Opposition abstaining from voting. The 15 Members (including tellers) to vote against the amendment comprised 12 Liberal and 3 Conservative.

Conservatives to vote against the amendment:

Brotherton, M.   Gower, Sir R.   Winterton, N.

HC Deb. 894, 1371–4
1974–5, No. 261.

EUROPEAN PARLIAMENT (MEMBERSHIP) [88]

1 July 1975

The Government Chief Whip, R. Mellish, moved 'That Mr Guy Barnett, Miss Betty Boothroyd, Mr Tam Dalyell, Sir Geoffrey de Freitas, Mrs Gwyneth Dunwoody, Mr Tom Ellis, Mr John Evans, Mr William Hamilton, Mr Mark Hughes, Mr R. C. Mitchell, Mr John Prescott and Mr Michael Stewart be designated members of the

European Parliament: That this Order be a Standing Order of the House.'

J. Thorpe (Lib., Devon, North) rose to oppose the motion. He said the House was being asked to approve a third of the British delegation, without any indication as to the remaining two-thirds. There had been no indication as to what the Government had in mind in relation to Liberal representation, though the 'suggestion' being put forward was that it should be reduced from two members to one. The Liberals had not been consulted, and he thought the matter had been handled appallingly. With 13 MPs and 5⅓ million votes behind them, he felt it would be manifestly unfair for the Liberal representation to be cut.

The Government Chief Whip, replying to the debate, said that they had employed the principle used to arrive at the delegation for the Council of Europe. The Government had decided to take 18 seats, and had offered 16 seats to the Conservatives. Had it decided upon the Committee of Selection formula, the Government could have had 19 seats. He had some sympathy for Mr Thorpe's feeling on the matter, but did not know of any immediate solution. There was nothing malicious in the arrangement, and he was still prepared to discuss with the Liberal and Scottish National parties how the difficulty could be overcome.

(1) At 2.45 a.m., after more than two-and-a-half hours of debate, the Government Deputy Chief Whip moved the closure, which was carried by 119 votes to 11, the Opposition abstaining from voting. The 121 Members (including tellers) in the Government lobby comprised 112 Labour, 8 Scottish National and 1 Conservative. The 13 Members (including tellers) to oppose closure comprised 12 Liberal and 1 Conservative.

Conservative to vote for closure:

Winterton, N.

Conservative to vote against closure:

Brotherton, M.

(2) The motion was then put and carried by 119 votes to 11. The 121 Members (including tellers) in the Government lobby comprised 110 Labour, 9 Scottish National and 2 Conservative. The 13 Members (including tellers) to vote against the motion comprised 12 Liberal and 1 Labour.

Conservatives to vote for the motion:

Brotherton, M.   Winterton, N.

Labour Member to vote against the motion:

Skinner, D.

HC Deb. 894, 1425-30
1974-5, Nos. 262 & 263.

The debate took place following a late-night sitting on report stage of the Industry Bill (see preceding divisions).

INDUSTRY BILL   [89]

Report: 2 July 1975

Clause 20 (Persons to whom duty to disclose information applies)

Shortly before the guillotine was to fall on remaining amendments to be concluded that evening, the Government Deputy Chief Whip moved formally an amendment to delete subsection (4) of the clause. [The subsection provided that, before companies gave information about their forward intentions, the Government would provide them with detailed forecast information about the economic parameters.]

The amendment was *negatived* by 220 votes to 149, *a majority against the Government of 71.* The 222 Members (including tellers) in the Opposition lobby comprised 157 Conservative, 41 Labour, 11 Scottish National, 10 Liberal and 3 Plaid Cymru. The 151 Members (including tellers) in the Government lobby comprised 150 Labour and 1 UUUC.

Labour Members to vote against the amendment:

Allaun, F.	Heffer, E.	Radice, G.*
Ashton, J.	Hoyle, D.	Richardson, Miss J.
Atkinson, N.	Hughes, R. J.	Rooker, J.
Bennett, A.	Kelley, R.	Rose, P.
Bidwell, S.	Kerr, R.	Sandelson, N.
Bray, J.	Kilroy-Silk, R.	Sedgemore, B.
Callaghan, J.	Litterick, T.	Selby, H.
Campbell, I.	Loyden, E.	Skinner, D.
Canavan, D.	Madden, M.	Snape, P.
Davies, B.	Maynard, Miss J.	Spearing, N.

Edge, G.	Mikardo, I.*	Thomas, R.
Garrett, J.	Miller, M.	Thorne, S.
Gould, B.	Noble, M.	Wise, Mrs A.
Hamilton, W.	Prescott, J.	

HC Deb. 894, 1623-8
1974-5, No. 267.

INDUSTRY BILL [90]

Report: 2 July 1975

Clause 22 (Information for trade unions)

The Industry Secretary, E. Varley, moved formally an amendment to the clause to provide that the Minister 'may serve' notice upon companies to provisionally require them to disclose information under section 21 of the clause to a representative of each relevant trade union within 28 days.

The amendment had been discussed earlier in conjunction with others, and had been objected to by a number of Labour Members because of its discretionary element; they contended that disclosure should be mandatory.[1]

The amendment was negatived by 164 votes to 58, the Opposition abstaining from voting. The 166 Members (including tellers) in the Government lobby comprised 145 Labour, 11 Scottish National and 10 Liberal. The 60 Members (including tellers) to oppose the amendment comprised 57 Labour and 3 Plaid Cymru.

Labour Members to vote against the amendment:

Allaun, F.	Grocott, B.	Richardson, Miss J.
Ashton, J.	Hatton, F.	Roderick, C.
Atkins, R.	Heffer, E.	Rodgers, G.
Atkinson, N.	Hoyle, D.	Rooker, J.
Bennett, A.	Hughes, R. J.	Rose, P.
Bidwell, S.	Jeger, Mrs L.	Sedgemore, B.
Bray, J.	Kerr, R.*	Selby, H.
Buchan, N.	Kilroy-Silk, R.	Sillars, J.
Callaghan, J.	Lamond, J.	Silverman, J.
Campbell, I.	Litterick, T.	Skinner, D.
Canavan, D.	Loyden, E.	Snape, P.
Cook, R.	Madden, M.	Swain, T.

Corbett, R.	Marshall, J.	Thomas, R.
Cryer, R.	Maynard, Miss J.	Thorne, S.
Davies, B.	Mikardo, I.	Tierney, T.
Fernyhough, E.	Molloy, W.	Walker, T.
Flannery, M.*	Noble, M.	Watkins, D.
Garrett, J.	Parry, R.	Wise, Mrs A.
George, B.	Prescott, J.	Young, D.

HC Deb. 894, 1629–32
1974–5, No. 268.

[1] See the speeches of I. Mikardo (Lab., Bethnal Green and Bow), E. Heffer (Lab., Liverpool, Walton), Mrs A. Wise (Lab., Coventry, South-West), D. Hoyle (Lab., Nelson and Colne), *HC Deb.* 894, c. 1563–70, 1573–7, 1585–9, 1592–6. The Industry Secretary had contended that the powers, from the beginning, had been regarded as reserve powers, and he argued that voluntary agreements were preferable to mandatory and compulsory arrangements. *HC Deb.* 894, c. 1599–1605.

INDUSTRY BILL [91]

Report: 2 July 1975

Schedule 3 (Disclosure of information by Government)

At 11.00 p.m., the guillotine fell and the Speaker proceeded to put forthwith remaining Government amendments which had to be dealt with by that time.

The Industry Secretary, E. Varley, moved formally an amendment to delete the schedule, which made planning agreements conditional upon the Government disclosing certain information.

The amendment was *negatived* by 230 votes to 147, *a majority against the Government of 83.* The 232 Members (including tellers) to oppose the amendment comprised 160 Conservative, 50 Labour, 11 Scottish National, 8 Liberal and 3 Plaid Cymru. The 149 Members (including tellers) in the Government lobby comprised 147 Labour and 2 UUUC.

Labour Members to vote against the amendment:

Allaun, F.	Heffer, E.	Radice, G.*
Ashton, J.	Hoyle, D.	Richardson, Miss J.
Atkins, R.	Hughes, R. J.	Rooker, J.
Atkinson, N.	Jeger, Mrs L.	Rose, P.
Bennett, A.	Kelley, R.	Sandelson, N.
Bidwell, S.	Kerr, R.*	Sedgemore, B.
Bray, J.	Kilroy-Silk, R.	Selby, H.

Callaghan, J.	Litterick, T.	Skinner, D.
Campbell, I.	Loyden, E.	Snape, P.
Canavan, D.	Madden, M.	Spearing, N.
Cook, R.	Marquand, D.	Swain, T.
Cryer, R.	Maynard, Miss J.	Thomas, R.
Davies, B.	Mikardo, I.	Thorne, S.
Edge, G.	Miller, M.	Tinn, J.
Evans, I.	Noble, M.	Wainwright, E.
Garrett, J.	Parry, R.	Wise, Mrs A.
Gould, B.	Prescott, J.	

HC Deb. 894, 1631–6
1974–5, No. 269.

BUSINESS OF THE HOUSE [92]

4 July 1975

At the commencement of public business, a Government whip formally moved 'That at this day's Sitting, proceedings on or relating to the proposed Motion (Aids to Shipbuilding), if not previously concluded, shall lapse one and a half hours after they have been entered upon, and may be proceeded with after Four o'clock, though opposed'. [The motion was being moved on a Friday.]

The motion was carried by 35 votes to 14, Conservative Members voting with the Government. The 37 Members (including tellers) in the Government lobby comprised 25 Labour, 9 Conservative and 3 Scottish National. The 16 Members (including tellers) to oppose the motion comprised 8 Labour, 5 Liberal, 2 Conservative and 1 UUUC.

Labour Members to vote against the motion:

Atkinson, N.	Jay, D.	Skinner, D.
Buchan, N.	Lee, J.	Spearing, N.
Flannery, M.	Richardson, Miss J.	

Conservatives to vote against the motion:

| Brotherton, M. | Winterton, N. |

HC Deb. 894, 1857–8
1974–5, No. 274.

The motion covered by this business resolution was a 'take note' motion of an EEC Commission Document concerning the EEC Directive on Aids to Shipbuilding. (The motion was, in the event, to be 'talked out' by the Minister concerned; *HC Deb.* 894, c. 1969.) The Labour Members to oppose the business resolution were known opponents of Britain's membership of the EEC.

COAL INDUSTRY BILL [93]

Lords Amendment: 15 July 1975

Clause 2 (New Right of Board to withdraw support to enable coal to be worked)

The House of Lords had amended the clause to provide that the National Coal Board was required to pay compensation or make good the damage where damage was incurred on land in consequence of the exercise of the right to withdraw support conferred by the clause.

The Under-Secretary of State for Energy, A. Eadie, moved for the House to disagree with the Lords amendment.

Mr Eadie said the Government had never envisaged the Bill as the right vehicle for making fundamental changes in the compensation provisions for subsistence damage. In response to the argument that the Board should have to pay increased compensation as a balance to the new powers given it by the clause, he contended that the powers were simply a clarification of existing rights. To pass the amendment would upset existing procedures, which provided a stable basis for operations.

Opposition Members rose to support the Lords amendment, as did some Labour backbenchers. M. Edelman (Lab., Coventry, North-West) spoke of the concern of manufacturers in Coventry that they may be disadvantaged because of undermining. The Lords, he said, had produced a sensible recommendation which should have the non-partisan support of the House. W. Wilson (Lab., Coventry, South-East) echoed Mr Edelman's support for the Lords amendment. He could see no reason why the common law in respect of support and of damages should be broken, even by the National Coal Board. G. Park (Lab., Coventry, North-East) declared that if the Minister could not reconsider the situation, he would have no option but to vote against the Government's motion.

The Government motion to disagree with the Lords amendment was carried by 159 votes to 129. The 161 Members (including tellers) in the Government lobby were all Labour Members. The 131 Members (including tellers) in the Opposition lobby comprised 122 Conservative, 6 Liberal and 3 Labour.

Labour Members to vote against the motion:

Edelman, M.   Park, G.   Wilson, W.

HC Deb. 895, 1441–6
1974–5, No. 284.

FINANCE (No. 2) BILL [94]

Report: 17 July 1975

Schedule 7 (VAT: higher rate)

J. MacGregor (C., Norfolk, South) moved an amendment to exclude television sets supplied under a contract of hire (entered into prior to 16th April 1975) from the 25 per cent rate of value added tax.

Mr MacGregor explained that the higher rate of VAT on the televisions covered affected especially the poorer sections of the community; the extra burden on the television rental was serious. The imposition of the higher rate was discriminatory and retrospective, and was also affecting the manufacture of television sets.

R. Kilroy-Silk (Lab., Ormskirk) rose to support a Liberal amendment being discussed at the same time to exclude all television sets obtained on hire from the higher rate. The tax on rentals would hit hardest those on the lowest incomes. Many pensioners and housebound people relied upon their televisions for companionship. 'To enact, as is proposed, a much higher, punitive rate of tax on their single and only pleasure seems to be unnecessary and regrettable.' He also drew attention to the consequences for employment prospects. S. Tierney (Lab., Birmingham, Yardley) said his main objection to the clause was the inequality of treatment it provided as between purchasers and renters. 'I received from a constituent a letter that was reprinted in the local paper under the heading: "We have been fiddled". I agree with her.' M. Noble (Lab., Rossendale) said he wished that the Government had not put forward these proposals and that they recognized that ordinary people, especially the old and deprived, regarded television as essential. He supported the Liberal amendment.

The Financial Secretary to the Treasury, R. Sheldon, replied that the Chancellor had decided that he needed that revenue at that time and had fixed the rate accordingly. The amendment would cost £90 million in the first full year, and would create problems because two rates would then be in force; also, he argued, it would not help the problems of the radio industry. In the existing economic situation, he said, he had to ask his hon. Friends to oppose the amendment.

The amendment was *carried*, on a whipped party vote, by 108 votes to 106, *a majority against the Government of 2*. The 110 Members (including tellers) in the Opposition lobby comprised 96 Conservative, 7 Scottish National, 6 Liberal and 1 Labour. The 108 Members (including tellers) in the Government lobby comprised 108 Labour and 2 UUUC. Between five and ten Labour Members also appear to have abstained from voting.[1]

Labour Member to vote for the amendment:

Campbell, I.

HC Deb. 895, 1821–4
1974–5, No. 287.

The Liberal amendment to which Mr Kilroy-Silk and Mr Noble had spoken had not been chosen for a division by the Speaker.

[1] The abstainers included: R. Kilroy-Silk, M. Madden, M. Noble, N. Spearing and S. Tierney.

POLICYHOLDERS PROTECTION BILL [95]

Second Reading: 18 July 1975

The Secretary of State for Trade and President of the Board of Trade, P. Shore, moved the Second Reading of the Bill.

Mr Shore explained that the main purpose of the Bill was to ensure that policy holders did not suffer major loss and hardship when an insurance company failed. Clause 1 established the Policyholders Protection Board, which had the duty to protect policy holders of a company in liquidation. After outlining other provisions, he said he had had useful discussions about all aspects of the Bill with the trade unions concerned, the companies and the insurance industry. He did not think it would have an adverse effect, other than a slight one, upon workers in the industry; the scheme would be a source of strength to the industry and thus of benefit to its employees. He asked the House to give the Bill a Second Reading. 'It will, at a very small cost indeed, give necessary and extra security to millions of insurance policy holders.'

For the Opposition, T. Higgins said there were a number of matters they would press in Committee, but the Opposition would not oppose Second Reading.

From the Labour backbenches, W. Williams (Lab., Warrington) moved a reasoned amendment for rejection: 'That this House declines to give a Second Reading to a Bill which discriminates against the policyholders of reputable life assurance companies and societies and consequently against small savers, does not deal with a major source of distress in an insurance company failure, namely the cumbersome and costly liquidation processes, takes no action to recover any of the large payments made to the proprietors of failed insurance companies shortly before their failure, does nothing to prevent the reckless practices by speculative insurance companies, and, in consequence, signally neglects to give genuine protection to policy holders.'[1]

Mr Williams spoke to his amendment, and was supported from the Labour benches by J. Roper (Lab., Farnworth) and S. Tierney (Lab., Birmingham, Yardley). E. Perry (Lab., Battersea, South) also rose to argue that the Bill did not touch the real problem, which was the spurious selling of insurance policies which had little prospect of ever paying off.

From the Conservative benches, R. Taylor (C., Croydon, North-West) rose to add his support for the amendment. He opposed the Bill, he said, because it made no contribution to the efficiency of the industry and failed to tackle its problems. He was joined in opposition to the measure by R. Moate (C., Faversham), who objected to it because it would effectively tax policy-holders of reputable companies, would encourage irresponsible underwriting, and would get the worst of all worlds. The Bill, he said, offended almost everyone.

The reasoned amendment for rejection was negatived by 55 votes to 19, the Opposition abstaining from voting. The 57 Members (including tellers) in the Government lobby comprised 56 Labour and 1 Conservative. The 21 Members (including tellers) to support the amendment comprised 19 Labour and 2 Conservative.

Conservative to vote against the amendment:

Tugendhat, C.

Conservatives to vote for the amendment:

Moate, R.   Taylor, R.

Labour Members to vote for the amendment:

Atkinson, N.   Evans, I.   Palmer, A.
Boardman, H.   Graham, T.*   Richardson, Miss J.
Brown, R.   Irving, S.   Roper, J.
Butler, Mrs J.   Mikardo, I.   Skinner, D.
Cartwright, J.   Newens, S.   Tierney, S.*
Clemitson, I.   Ovenden, J.   Williams, W.
Edwards, R.

HC Deb. 895, 2019–20
1974–5, No. 289.

The Bill was then given a Second Reading without a division. The debate took place on a Friday, hence the low turnout.

[1] The Minister had attempted to respond to the points contained in the amendment in advance. See *HC Deb.* 895, c. 1949–56.

ATTACK ON INFLATION   [96]

21–2 July 1975

The Chancellor of the Exchequer, D. Healey, moved 'That this House approves the White Paper on The Attack on Inflation (Command Paper No. 6151)'.

   Mr Healey reminded the House that he had reached agreement with the General Council of the TUC on new guidance to negotiators—£6 a week limit with an upper cut-off point—which was within the Government's 10 per cent target. The £6, he said, would be progressive throughout the income scale— with the cut-off point being salaries of £8,500 a year—and would be an upper limit for wage increases, not an automatic entitlement. The Government proposed to employ a battery of weapons to ensure that the limit was observed in the public and the private sector. If the pay limit was endangered due to breaches of it by a selfish minority, the Government would introduce legislation which had already been prepared. Existing price controls already ensured that the reduction in wage costs produced by the new guidelines would be passed on to the consumer in lower prices. The groundswell of support among the British people for the policy he had put forward was, he declared, approaching the dimensions of a tidal wave. He asked all Members to join the battle against inflation.

Opposition Members rose to support an amendment moved by the Leader of the Opposition, while a number of Labour backbenchers rose to oppose the motion. E. Heffer (Lab., Liverpool, Walton) said that the Labour manifesto at the previous election had opposed the policy that the Government had now introduced. Inflation was not primarily wage-led, and the Government were adopting a policy with no real future. 'Let us back away now. There is still time. We need an alternative economic strategy.' Mrs J. Hart (Lab., Lanark) argued that the Government's policy was based on a wrong analysis, and the next few months would show that those who opposed the policy were right. N. Atkinson (Lab., Tottenham) contended that the wage limit would result in wage deflation and a cut in living standards by an enormous amount. Statutory wage control was not the answer to the problems being faced. D. Hoyle (Lab., Nelson and Colne) said the proposal before them 'is the same well-worn book that, so often in the past, has been taken down from the library shelf, read, put into practice, and has failed'. I. Mikardo (Lab., Bethnal Green and Bow) said he would vote against the motion because of the unpublished Bill mentioned in the White Paper and in the debate; if there was not a division, the Chancellor would be in a position to query, later on when the Bill was introduced, why opponents had not used the opportunity to divide on the issue.

An Opposition amendment to the motion was negatived, on a straight party vote, by 327 votes to 269.

The motion was then put, and carried by 262 votes to 54 with the Opposition abstaining from voting. The 264 Members (including tellers) in the Government lobby comprised 248 Labour, 12 Liberal, 2 Conservative (1 apparently listed by mistake, hence excluded below[1]), 1 UUUC and 1 Irish Independent. The 56 Members (including tellers) to oppose the motion comprised 36 Labour, 9 Scottish National, 6 UUUC, 3 Conservative and 2 Plaid Cymru. A further 20 Labour Members abstained from voting.[2]

Conservative to vote for the motion:

Dodsworth, G.

Conservatives to vote against the motion:

Brotherton, M.   Fell, A.   Skeet, T.

Labour Members to vote against the motion:

Allaun, F.	Hoyle, D.	Miller, Mrs M.
Atkins, R.	Hughes, R.	Newens, S.
Atkinson, N.	Hughes, R. J.	Parry, R.
Bennett, A.	Kerr, R.*	Richardson, Miss J.
Bidwell, S.	Lambie, D.	Rodgers, G.
Buchan, N.	Lee, J.	Sedgemore, B.
Callaghan, J.	Lewis, A.	Selby, H.
Canavan, D.	Litterick, T.	Skinner, D.
Cryer, R.	Loyden, E.	Swain, T.
Flannery, M.	Madden, M.	Thomas, R.
Hart, Mrs J.	Maynard, Miss J.	Thorne, S.
Heffer, E.	Mikardo, I.*	Wise, Mrs. A.

HC Deb. 896, 435–40
1974–5, No. 292.

[1] R. Mawby (C., Totnes). Although *The Times* reported Mr Mawby as voting in the Government lobby on the basis of the division lists, Mr Mawby has confirmed to the author that the inclusion of his name must have been a mistake. Ray Mawby MP to author. The inclusion of Mr Dodsworth's name in the Government lobby is correct. Geoffrey Dodsworth MP to author.

[2] The twenty, having voted in the division on the Opposition amendment, were: J. Ashton, G. Barnett, A. Bottomley, R. Cook, G. Edge, F. Evans, T. Fletcher, J. Garrett, R. Kelley, N. Kinnock, J. Lamond, J. Marshall, M. Miller, J. Prescott, J. Robertson, C. Roderick, Mrs R. Short, J. Sillars, P. Snape and T. Torney. Some *Tribune* Members put the number of abstentions at more than thirty. *The Times*, 23 July 1975.

REMUNERATION, CHARGES AND GRANTS BILL [97]

Second Reading: 23 July 1975

The Chancellor of the Exchequer, D. Healey, moved the Second Reading of the Bill. He said it was designed to support the voluntary policy for incomes which the House had approved, and removed the legal obstacles to the effective operation of the policy. Clause 1 relieved employers of contractual obligations to give remuneration in excess of the pay limit, while clause 3 looked to an amendment of the Price Code which would ensure that applications for price increases were supported by the relevant information on pay settlements and would provide for the sanction through the Code whereby the whole amount of any pay settlement which broke the pay limit could be disallowed for price increases. After further detailing the provisions of the Bill, he responded to the amendment tabled by the Opposition, and argued that there was no practical alternative to the policy the Government had put forward.

For the Opposition, Sir G. Howe moved a reasoned amendment for rejection: 'That this House declines to give a Second Reading to a Bill which provides for existing contractual rights to be over-ridden by a White Paper which is not open to Parliamentary amendment; for the legal obligations imposed by the White Paper to be interpreted by a member of the Cabinet instead of by the Courts; which leaves to a further unpublished Bill the specification of additional sanctions referred to in the White Paper; and provides for an undefined increase in indiscriminate housing subsidies'.

During the debate, S. Thorne (Lab., Preston, South) declared that he would have to withhold his support for what he considered to be 'a piece of anti-working class legislation'. J. Sillars (Lab., South Ayrshire) said that when he went electioneering in South Ayrshire he said he would never vote for a statutory incomes policy, and he would not vote for one that evening.

(1) The Opposition amendment was negatived, on a straight party vote, by 320 votes to 260. 1 Conservative cross-voted to oppose the amendment.

Conservative to vote against the amendment:

Mudd, D.

(2) The motion was then put, and carried by 294 votes to 16, the Opposition abstaining from voting. The 296 Members (including tellers) in the Government lobby comprised 281 Labour, 12 Liberal, 1 Conservative, 1 SDLP, and 1 UUUC. The 18 Members (including tellers) to oppose Second Reading comprised 8 Scottish National, 7 UUUC, 2 Plaid Cymru and 1 Labour. A further 22 Labour Members abstained from voting.[1]

Conservative to vote for Second Reading:

Mudd, D.

Labour Member to vote against Second Reading:

Lambie, D.

HC Deb. 896, 693–700
1974–5, Nos. 296 & 297.

[1] The 22, having voted on the Opposition amendment, were: F. Allaun, R. Atkins, A. Bottomley, J. Callaghan, D. Canavan, I. Davies, R. Edwards, F. Evans, M. Flannery,

E. Loyden, M. Madden, Miss J. Maynard, S. Newens, J. Robertson, H. Selby, J. Sillars, D. Skinner, W. Small, P. Snape, S. Thorne, F. Tomney and Mrs A. Wise. (All bar Davies, Edwards and Small had failed to support the Government in the previous evening's division on its White Paper *The Attack on Inflation*; 13 had voted against, 5 were known abstainers, and Tomney had been absent from the evening's voting. See above, division no. 292.) A large number of the abstainers 'ostentatiously remained in the Chamber' during the division. *The Times*, 24 July 1975.

REMUNERATION, CHARGES AND GRANTS BILL   [98]

Committee: 24 July 1975

Clause 2 (Duration of section 1 and of certain provisions of Counter-Inflation Act 1973)

E. Heffer (Lab., Liverpool, Walton) moved an amendment for the duration of the provisions of clause 1 to be reduced from one year to six months.

Mr Heffer said his amendment constituted a compromise. In six months, he suggested they would have a pretty clear indication whether or not the Government was right about its policy. 'We do not like this policy, but we recognize that it will be put into effect because it is clear that the Front Benches on both sides of the Committee are basically in favour of it. Therefore, we suggest that this compromise could be accepted by the Government.'

R. Thomas (Lab., Bristol, North-West) supported the amendment and related amendments. 'I do so because they will inject flexibility into the legislation so that at the end of six months we may seriously reconsider it.' I. Mikardo (Lab., Bethnal Green and Bow) said that to argue that a year was needed before they could fully know or do anything was giving a shade too much hostage to fortune. It would be in the Government's own interest to look at the thing a bit earlier. A. Fell (C., Yarmouth) also rose to support the amendment. 'I support it because I am pretty frightened of this move by the present Government. I am pretty frightened it will not work.'

The Paymaster-General, E. Dell, said they had to think in the context of a whole wage round at least, and it would appear to make nonsense of the policy if it ceased to be effective halfway through the wage round. People who settled claims early would settle under uncertainty. The amendment would also have the effect of removing the option of continuing the policy for a further year by order, subject to approval by the House, if the Government so wished. If they were to enter into a policy for reducing inflation it seemed sensible that they should have the option of proceeding without further main legislation.

The amendment was negatived by 229 votes to 33, with the Opposition abstaining from voting. The 231 Members (including tellers) in the Government lobby comprised 226 Labour, 4 Liberal and 1 Conservative (who voted in both lobbies, in the Government lobby apparently by error). The 35 Members (including tellers) to support the amendment comprised 26 Labour, 8 Conservative and 1 UUUC.

Labour Members to vote for the amendment:

Allaun, F.	Heffer, E.	Newens, S.
Atkins, R.	Hoyle, D.	Richardson, Miss J.
Bennett, A.	Hughes, R.	Sedgemore, B.
Bidwell, S.*	Lambie, D.	Selby, H.
Buchan, N.	Lee, J.	Skinner, D.
Callaghan, J.	Litterick, T.	Thomas, R.*
Canavan, D.	Loyden, E.	Thorne, S.
Cryer, R.	Madden, M.	Wise, Mrs A.
Flannery, M.	Mikardo, I.	

Conservatives to vote for the amendment:

Budgen, N.	Fell, A.	Rees-Davies, W.[1]
Clark, W.	Morgan, G.	Ridley, N.
Emery, P.	Osborn, J.	

HC Deb. 896, 1079–84
1974–5, No. 302.

[1] Voted in both lobbies, apparently by mistake in the Government lobby.

PETROLEUM AND SUBMARINE PIPE-LINES BILL [99]

Report: 28 July 1975

Clause 1 (Constitution of the Corporation)

G. Wilson (SNP, Dundee, East) moved an amendment to divide the British National Oil Corporation into four divisions (Scottish, English, Welsh and Northern Irish).

Mr Wilson explained that the amendment sought to create a devolved structure for the BNOC, and if the Government did not accept it they would be back-tracking on some of their manifesto proposals for devolution in Scotland.

The Under-Secretary of State for Energy, J. Smith, said the Government's view was that they should approach the development of energy resources on a United Kingdom basis for the benefit of the whole of the United Kingdom. To the extent that the amendment opposed that principle, he hoped that the House would vote against it.

The amendment was negatived by 287 votes to 16, the Opposition abstaining from voting. The 18 Members (including tellers) to support the amendment comprised 10 Liberal, 7 Scottish National and 1 Plaid Cymru. The 289 Members (including tellers) in the Government lobby comprised 283 Labour and 6 Conservative.

Conservatives to vote against the amendment:

Fairgrieve, R.	Kimball, M.	Rifkind, M.
Fletcher, A.	Monro, H.	Sproat, I.

HC Deb. 896, 1469–72
1974–5, No. 306.

EMPLOYMENT PROTECTION BILL [100]

Report: 30 July 1975

New Clause 7 (Peaceful Picketing)

J. Rooker (Lab., Birmingham, Perry Barr) moved the new clause, designed to permit persons to peacefully picket on a highway or other public place 'without this constituting any offence or involving any civil liability'.

Mr Rooker reminded the House that the issue had been debated in Committee. He argued that where persons involved in an industrial dispute were picketing lawfully it was wholly unnecessary that they should be caught on technical breaches of the highway. He explained the drafting of the clause, and declared that if it came to a vote 'I shall consider it to be a vote of no confidence in those who run the Home Office whose responsibility it was to fulfil the promise made in the October manifesto by the Labour Party that something meaningful would be put into the Bill to advance the rights of those taking part in a dispute.'

The Employment Secretary, M. Foot, replied that there were difficulties with the clause as drafted. The legal position on the immunities intended would be uncertain and could lead to some difficult judgments.

The Government was seeking for a solution, and was committed to doing so. The fact they had not yet secured a solution demonstrated the difficulties involved. The Government could not accept the clause in its existing form.

P. Rose (Lab., Manchester, Blackley) said there could be nothing worse than the existing imprecision of the law, and contended that supporters of the clause had drafted a framework within which it could be possible for pickets to go about their peaceful business. T. Urwin (Lab., Houghton-le-Spring) said it was not fair to tell Labour Members that it was not the time to include the provisions being suggested. The Minister had to be more forthcoming or face the prospect of a substantial number of Labour Members voting against the Government. J. Evans (Lab., Newton) said the Minister's speech was the worst he had ever heard him make. His brief could only be described 'as a nit-picking one drawn up by the Home Office and not by his Department'. He hoped the Minister would retract and accept the clause.

The clause was negatived by 335 votes to 91, the Opposition voting with the Government. The 337 Members (including tellers) in the Government lobby comprised 172 Conservative, 161 Labour, 3 Liberal and 1 UUUC. The 93 Members (including tellers) to support the clause comprised 85 Labour,[1] 6 Liberal, 1 Plaid Cymru and 1 SDLP. A further ten to fifteen Labour Members appear to have abstained from voting.[2]

Labour Members to vote for the clause:

Allaun, F.	Hatton, F.	Price, C.
Ashton, J.	Heffer, E.	Richardson, Miss J.
Atkins, R.	Hooley, F.	Roberts, A.
Atkinson, N.	Hoyle, D.	Roberts, G.
Bean, R.	Hughes, R.	Robertson, J.
Bennett, A.	Hughes, R. J.	Rodgers, G.
Bidwell, S.	Kilroy-Silk, R.	Rooker, J.
Buchan, N.	Kinnock, N.	Rose, P.
Callaghan, J.	Lambie, D.	Ryman, J.
Canavan, D.	Latham, A.	Sedgemore, B.
Cartwright, J.	Leadbitter, T.	Selby, H.
Clemitson, I.	Lee, J.*	Sillars, J.
Cook, R.	Lewis, A.	Silverman, J.
Corbett, R.	Litterick, T.	Skinner, D.
Cryer, R.	Loyden, E.	Snape, P.
Davies, B.	McMillan, T.	Spriggs, L.
Dean, J.	McNamara, K.	Swain, T.

Edge, G.	Madden, M.	Thomas, R.
Edwards, R.	Maynard, Miss J.	Thorne, S.
Evans, F.	Mendelson, J.	Tierney, S.
Evans, J.	Mikardo, I.*	Torney, T.
Fernyhough, E.	Miller, M.	Watkins, D.
Flannery, M.	Newens, S.	Watkinson, J.
Fletcher, T.	Noble, M.	White, F.
Garrett, J.	Ovenden, J.	Wilson, A.
George, B.	Parker, J.	Wilson, W.
Grocott, B.	Parry, R.	Wise, Mrs A.
Hart, Mrs J.	Prescott, J.	Young, D.

HC Deb. 896, 1990–2
1974–5, No. 313.

¹ The 85 included a Government whip, J. Hamilton, who voted in both lobbies, in the dissenting lobby by mistake; his name is therefore excluded from the dissenters listed.

² On the basis of voting in preceding and succeeding divisions, the abstainers would appear to have included: B. Douglas-Mann, R. Kerr, R. Mitchell, W. Molloy, W. Padley, A. Stallard, T. Urwin, J. Wellbeloved and F. Willey.

HOUSING FINANCE (SPECIAL PROVISIONS) BILL   [101]

Lords Amendment: 4 August 1975

New Clause A (Repayment and Disqualification)

The new clause had been inserted by the Lords (see succeeding division).

I. Percival (C., Southport) moved an amendment to the new clause to provide that any person who was surcharged in respect of an item of account or loss attributable to a council's failure to implement the 1972 Housing Finance Act could make an application to the court in respect of the surcharge, the application to be treated as if it were made in respect of a certificate under the section.

Mr Percival said they had to uphold the rule of law, to temper justice with mercy, to treat all those who offended in precisely the same way, and to take the whole matter out of party politics. 'We can achieve all four by passing the amendment and agreeing with the other place in the first amendment [the clause itself] which we shall then go on to consider.'

R. Crawshaw (Lab., Liverpool, Toxteth) rose to support the amendment. He said he had always believed they should mitigate the punishment against the Clay Cross councillors, 'provided that this can be done through a court of law and not by an arbitrary decision taken by the Government Front Bench'. That was the element to which he had always objected in the Bill. He would vote for the amendment.

The Under-Secretary of State for the Environment, E. Armstrong, said the amendment was blatantly retrospective; it provided for the reopening of a case which had already gone through the courts. It would be unwise to put the whole matter through the courts again, and he invited the House to reject the amendment.

The amendment was negatived by 271 votes to 257. 1 Labour Member cross-voted to support the amendment.

Labour Member to vote for the amendment:

Crawshaw, R.

HC Deb. 897, 187–92
1974–5, No. 319.

The new clause itself was then discussed and divided upon; see below.

HOUSING FINANCE (SPECIAL PROVISIONS) BILL   [102]

Lords Amendment: 4 August 1975

New Clause A (Repayment and Disqualification)

The new clause had been inserted by the Lords, providing that where a district auditor decided to issue a rent loss certificate he should also issue a further certificate stating the sum and the people who would have been surcharged under the 1933 Local Government Act, this certificate to be sent to the courts for them to consider whether the councillors responsible for any surchargeable loss should be required to make good any part of such loss up to £1,000 each.

The Under-Secretary of State for the Environment, E. Armstrong, moved for the House to disagree with the Lords in the amendment.

Mr Armstrong said the effect of the clause would be to draw out the sorry affair. Month after month, year after year, local government would receive the verdicts on events which were already in most cases more than three years old. The clause would probably impose extra legal costs to be borne by the authorities, and would increase bitterness and cynicism about local government; it would bring benefit to no-body, and he asked the House to reject it.

R. Crawshaw (Lab., Liverpool, Toxteth) rose to support the Lords amendment. If a person said he would not obey the law, he should stand by what he had done and take the punishment accordingly. He was amazed to hear Ministers say that the House should decide guilt or otherwise. 'The new clause is essential because it restores to the courts the job which is theirs to do—to decide whether a person should be surcharged or disqualified.'

The motion to disagree with the Lords amendment was carried by 271 votes to 261. 1 Labour Member cross-voted to oppose the motion.

Labour Member to vote against the motion:

Crawshaw, R.

HC Deb. 897, 191–6
1974–5, No. 320.

HOUSING FINANCE (SPECIAL PROVISIONS) BILL   [103]

Lords Amendment: 4 August 1975

Clause 4 (Termination of disqualification for failure to implement Housing Finance Act 1972)

The House of Lords had passed an amendment to delete the clause. The Secretary of State for the Environment, A. Crosland, moved a motion for the House to disagree with the Lords amendment.

Mr Crosland explained that the clause removed the disqualification from the only councillors who had actually been disqualified for their failure to implement the 1972 Act, namely, those at Clay Cross. On grounds of consistency, he said, it seemed right to lift the disqualifica-tion, in the same way as the Bill removed the threat to it elsewhere. Since the matter was debated on report, the situation had changed, and the Clay Cross councillors had been disqualified on other matters unconnected with the Housing Finance Act. The clause would thus have no effect, but it was decided to try to restore it for the sake of internal consistency and in order to make it explicit that the councillors were not disqualified for what took place under the 1972 Act. He therefore asked the House to reject the Lords amendment.

For the Opposition, T. Raison said the issue had become one purely of principle. It was a wrong thing that the Commons was being asked to do, and it was essential for the rule of law that the House should reject the Government's proposal and uphold the Lords amendment.

G. Strauss (Lab., Vauxhall) said he could not accept the view that it did not matter whether the clause was retained or not. The Clay Cross councillors had ignored the law; they had said they did not recognize the law of Parliament. The removal of the disqualification would be a gesture of support to their point of view, and they should not do it. 'Everyone here who believes in the supremacy of Parliament and carrying out the laws which Parliament passes—that is the most important purpose we should have in mind—and everyone who believes in democracy should say that we must accept the Lords amendment.'

The motion to disagree with the Lords amendment was put, and *negatived* by 268 votes to 261, *a majority against the Government of 7.* The 270 Members (including tellers) in the Opposition lobby comprised 252 Conservative, 10 Liberal, 6 UUUC and 2 Labour. The 263 Members (including tellers) in the Government lobby were all Labour Members. A minimum of five to ten Labour Members would also appear to have abstained from voting.[1]

Labour Members to vote against the motion:

Crawshaw, R.
Strauss, G.

HC Deb. 897, 199–204
1974–5, No. 322.

[1] The following nine backbenchers were absent from the division, having participated in an earlier one: A. Faulds, D. Jay, M. Lipton, E. Luard, E. Lyons, R. MacFarquhar, B. Magee, D. Marquand and B. Walden. Some Labour Members also accused the Minister for Overseas Development, R. Prentice, of having abstained; Labour whips claimed that he was paired for the division, but Conservative whips denied this. *The Daily Telegraph,* 6 August 1975.

EMPLOYMENT PROTECTION BILL [104]

Report: 5 August 1975

Clause 36 (Rights of employee in connection with pregnancies and confinement)

Miss J. Richardson (Lab., Barking) moved an amendment to reduce from two years to one year the period for which a woman had to have continuous service with an employer to qualify for maternity pay.

Miss Richardson said the original consultative document had proposed a one-year qualifying period, and she wanted to know what was behind the increase to two years. She pointed out that the turnover in

manual and clerical jobs was quite high; it was quite unrealistic to
have a two-year qualifying period.

The Under-Secretary of State for Employment, H. Walker, replied
that the only way it had been possible to increase the four-weeks'
maternity pay to six weeks was by extending the qualifying period to
two years. To reduce the period to one year while maintaining the six
weeks' pay provision would boost the cost to approximately £17½
million. It was a straightforward issue of costs, and he hoped Miss
Richardson would withdraw her amendment.

Mrs H. Hayman (Lab., Welwyn and Hatfield) said the women who
would not qualify under the Bill were the most vulnerable; she could not
accept the assurances that had been given. Mrs A. Wise (Lab., Coventry,
South-West) said employers should be faced squarely with the fact that
maternity was a responsibility of society. The Government should accept
the amendment.

The amendment was negatived by 181 votes to 56, the Opposition
abstaining from voting. The 183 Members (including tellers) in the
Government lobby comprised 171 Labour and 12 Liberal. The 58
Members (including tellers) to support the amendment comprised 52
Labour and 6 Scottish National.

Labour Members to vote for the amendment:

Allaun, F.	Hughes, R.	Rodgers, G.
Ashton, J.	Hughes, R. J.	Rooker, J.
Atkinson, N.	Janner, G.	Shaw, A.
Bennett, A.	Kilroy-Silk, R.	Skinner, D.
Bidwell, S.	Lamond, J.	Snape, P.
Cook, R.	Litterick, T.	Taylor, Mrs A.
Davies, B.	Loyden, E.	Thomas, R.
Dean, J.	Madden, M.	Torney, T.
Edge, G.	Maynard, Miss J.	Walden, B.
Evans, J.	Mendelson, J.	Walker, T.
Faulds, A.	Mikardo, I.	Watkinson, J.
Flannery, M.	Miller, M.	White, F.
Fletcher, T.	Miller, Mrs M.	Whitehead, P.
Grocott, B.	Newens, S.	Wilson, A.
Hatton, F.	Noble, M.	Wilson, W.
Hayman, Mrs H.*	Parry, R.	Wise, Mrs A.
Heffer, E.	Richardson, Miss J.*	
Hoyle, D.	Roberts, G.	

HC Deb. 897, 283–6
1974–5, No. 324.

TRADE UNION AND LABOUR RELATIONS (AMENDMENT) BILL   [105]

Lords Amendment: 15 October 1975

Clause 2 (Amendments of the principal Act)

The Lords had inserted an amendment to the clause to provide that it was unfair to dismiss an employee who was not a union member in a closed shop if the employee objected to joining a union on 'reasonable grounds of conscience'.

The Minister of State for Employment, A. Booth, moved a motion for the House to disagree with the Lords in the said amendment.

The motion was carried by 292 votes to 254. 1 Labour Member cross-voted to oppose the motion.

Labour Member to vote against the motion:

Stonehouse, J.

HC Deb. 897, 1409–14
1974–5, No. 337.

TRADE UNION AND LABOUR RELATIONS (AMENDMENT) BILL   [106]

Lords Amendment: 15 October 1975

New Clause B (Freedom of the press)

The clause provided for a press charter on matters relating to freedom of the press.

The Government moved an amendment to the clause to provide that matters relating to the freedom of the press included 'such matters as the avoidance of improper pressure to distort or suppress news, comment, or criticism, the application of union membership agreements to journalists (and in particular the position of editors) and the question of access for contributors.'

G. Wilson (SNP, Dundee, East) moved formally an amendment to the Government amendment to delete all words after 'in particular', and insert instead 'right of editors to discharge their duties free from any obligation to join a trade union) and the right of editors to commission and publish any article'. The amendment had been discussed in conjunction with a preceding one, and had been opposed by the Government.[1]

The amendment to the Government amendment was negatived by 275 votes to 31, with the Opposition abstaining from voting. The 277 Members (including tellers) in the Government lobby comprised 275 Labour, 1 SDLP and 1 Irish Independent. The 33 Members (including tellers) to support the amendment comprised 13 Liberal, 9 Scottish National, 4 UUUC, 3 Labour, 2 Conservative and 2 Plaid Cymru.

Labour Members to vote for the amendment:

Crawshaw, R.   Mackintosh, J.   Magee, B.

Conservatives to vote for the amendment:

Aitken, J.   Lester, J.

HC Deb. 897, 1545–8
1974–5, No. 339.

[1] The Employment Secretary, M. Foot, had opposed the amendment on the grounds that it went too wide and did not strengthen the position of contributors; rather, it weakened it. (Instead, he later advised the House to support a separate amendment on the same subject.) The amendment originally stood in the name of J. Horam (Lab., Gateshead, West), who subsequently voted against it.

SCOTTISH DEVELOPMENT AGENCY (No. 2) BILL   [107]

Report: 21 October 1975

New Clause 1 (The Agency and the media)

The Minister of State at the Scottish Office, B. Millan, moved the new clause, which extended the provisions of section 9 of the 1975 Industry Act to the Scottish Development Agency as well as the National Enterprise Board.[1]

Mr Millan said the issue had implications for freedom of the press. The Government had made it clear, when the matter was discussed in the Lords, that employment grounds were the only justification for the Agency being involved in the news media, and that a clause would be inserted making that clear. He pointed out that even after the clause was passed there would still be provision for the Government to help a newspaper business in Scotland by loans or grants through the Agency or by selective assistance under the Industry Act.

For the Opposition, M. Rifkind said they generally welcomed the new clause as being an improvement on the Bill.

D. Canavan (Lab., West Stirlingshire) rose to oppose the clause. 'I hope that the Minister will take it back and try to reword it so as to guarantee editorial freedom without precluding the possibility of an investment by the Scottish Development Agency in any part of the media.' By opposing it, they would help to ensure the right to work among Scottish newspaper workers and at the same time would be fighting for freedom of expression in the Scottish press. J. Sillars (Lab., South Ayrshire) said he believed it would be a good thing for the media if the Agency assisted in the promotion of industrial democracy in the Scottish press as part of its operation.

The new clause was carried by 291 votes to 30, the Opposition voting with the Government. The 293 Members (including tellers) to support the clause comprised 208 Labour, 67 Conservative, 8 Scottish National, 7 Liberal and 3 Plaid Cymru. The 32 Members (including tellers) to oppose the clause comprised 31 Labour and, according to the division lists, 1 Conservative Front Bencher apparently voting in the 'No' lobby by mistake.[2]

Labour Members to vote against the clause:

Abse, L.	Lambie, D.	Rose, P.
Allaun, F.	Latham, A.	Sedgemore, B.
Atkinson, N.	Lee, J.	Sillars, J.*
Bennett, A.	Litterick, T.	Skinner, D.
Canavan, D.*	Loyden, E.	Swain, T.
Cryer, R.	Luard, E.	Thomas, R.
Flannery, M.	Madden, M.	Thorne, S.
Heffer, E.	Mikardo, I.	Wise, Mrs A.
Hughes, R.	Newens, S.	Woof, R.
Hughes, R. J.	Richardson, Miss J.	
Kinnock, N.	Rodgers, G.	

HC Deb. 898, 279–82
1974–5, No. 344.

[1] The clause in the Industry Bill had prohibited the National Enterprise Board from commencing a business of publishing newspapers or other periodicals or entering into any

contract with the Independent Broadcasting Authority for the provision of programmes, or acquiring share capital in a body corporate if that body was substantially engaged in the publication of newspapers or periodicals or was acting as a programme contractor. It, too, had attracted dissent from a number of Labour Members when introduced; see above, division no. 255, 1 July 1975.
  [2] N. St. John-Stevas, a member of the Shadow Cabinet, is listed as voting against the clause.

SCOTTISH DEVELOPMENT AGENCY   [108]
(No. 2) BILL

Report: 21 October 1975

New Clause 6 (Decentralization of Scottish Development Agency activities)

D. Crawford (SNP, Perth and East Perthshire) moved the new clause, which laid down that the Scottish Development Agency should, as soon as practicable, examine the means whereby the activities of the Agency would be decentralized to local offices in the major centres of Scotland and to arrange the provision of a fixed annual level of spending autonomy to the local offices.

  The Minister of State at the Scottish Office, B. Millan, opposed the clause. They were not willing to write such an organizational matter into the Bill, he said. It was an area in which the Agency must decide for itself.

  The clause was negatived by 229 votes to 13, with the Opposition abstaining from voting. The 15 Members (including tellers) to support the clause comprised 9 Scottish National, 3 Liberal and 3 Plaid Cymru. 1 Conservative entered the Government lobby to vote against the clause.

Conservative to vote against the clause:

Sproat, I.

HC Deb. 898, 339–42
1974–5, No. 347.

SCOTTISH DEVELOPMENT AGENCY   [109]
(No. 2) BILL

Report: 21 October 1975

Clause 1 (The Scottish Development Agency)

D. Crawford (SNP, Perth and East Perthshire) moved an amendment to insert 'democratic' before a reference to 'the development of the

Scotland's economy' in subsection (1) of the clause. The amendment was discussed in conjunction with one designed to make the Agency 'answerable to the Scottish Assembly, immediately upon establishment of that Assembly'.

Having rejected a similar amendment in committee, Mr Crawford said the amendment gave the Government and the Conservatives a second chance to make the Agency answerable to the Assembly.

The Scottish Secretary, W. Ross, said the amendments did not make very much sense. He queried what the insertion of 'democratic' actually meant. The insertion of the word 'answerable' did not mean anything legally, and there was at that time no Scottish Assembly.

The amendment was negatived by 228 votes to 12. The Opposition abstained from voting. The 14 Members (including tellers) to support the amendment comprised 9 Scottish National, 3 Plaid Cymru, 1 Liberal and 1 UUUC. 1 Conservative entered the Government lobby to vote against the amendment.

Conservative to vote against the amendment:

Sproat, I.

HC Deb. 898, 375–8
1974–5, No. 348.

CHILDRENS BILL [110]

Report: 28 October 1975

Clause 53 (Restriction on removal of child from care)

The Minister of State for Health and Social Security, Dr D. Owen, moved an amendment to require that a parent intending removing a child from the care of a local authority or voluntary organization should give not less than 28 days' notice. [This was to replace an amendment passed in committee, against Government advice, providing for variable periods of notice.]

Dr Owen explained that the different organizations involved had different views on the subject, and the amendment was designed to go some way to meeting the differing views expressed. The amendment would enable the Minister, by order subject to parliamentary approval, to vary the period should it prove not to be the most suitable. He urged the House to accept the compromise.

A. Stallard (Lab., St. Pancras, North) thought that 28 days' notice after six months was too long. The scale ought to be graded down, even going right to the bottom. He hoped the House would accept the clause as it stood. J. Robertson (Lab., Paisley) also supported the clause as it stood. He felt the period laid down in the Bill was better than the Minister's proposal.

The amendment was carried by 94 votes to 24, with the Opposition abstaining from voting. The 96 Members (including tellers) in the Government lobby comprised 94 Labour and 2 Liberal. The 26 Members (including tellers) to oppose the amendment comprised 13 Labour, 7 Conservative, 5 Scottish National and 1 Liberal.

Labour Members to vote against the amendment:

Cryer, R.	Robertson, J.	Thomas, R.
Hughes, R.	Sillars, J.	White, F.
Loyden, E.	Skinner, D.	Whitehead, P.*
Mitchell, R.*	Stallard, A.	Woof, R.
Newens, S.		

Conservatives to vote against the amendment:

Bowden, A.	Montgomery, F.	Winterton, N.
Douglas-Hamilton, Lord J.	Sims, R.	
Knight, Mrs J.	Steen, A.	

HC Deb. 898, 1501–4
1974–5, No. 371.

POLICYHOLDERS PROTECTION BILL   [111]

Report: 30 October 1975

Clause 5 (Application of sections 6 to 11)

R. Taylor (C., Croydon, North-West) moved an amendment to provide for the provisions of the measure to have effect from 1st June 1974 instead of 29th October 1974.

Mr Taylor declared that the purpose of the amendment (and related amendments) was to include the unfortunate policyholders of Nation Life within the Bill's provisions. He conceded that this would make the Bill retrospective, but pointed out that it was already, to a certain extent, retrospective. He pointed out that very quickly after the collapse of the Nation Life company the Government announced its intention to help companies in suψɔ periods of difficulty. There had to be a period of uncertainty between a Government announcing its intentions and producing detailed legislation. There were grounds for believing some of the Nation Life policyholders would have found support from the insurance industry but for the fact of the Government announcement. He believed it was the sense of the House that the amendment should be passed.

For the Opposition, T. Higgins said the crucial point was one of retrospection. Retrospective action was proposed which would impose a levy on other policyholders in other companies, many of whom may have taken out policies on less favourable terms than those by which they would be compensated under the amendment. 'On balance, while recognizing the very human problems involved here, I think it would be wrong to support my hon. Friend's amendment.'

The Under-Secretary of State for Trade, C. Davies, agreed with Mr Higgins. He did not believe the policy suggested by Mr Taylor would be in the interest of policyholders, and he asked the House to reject it.

The amendment was negatived by 117 votes to 48, with the Opposition abstaining from voting. The 119 Members (including tellers) in the Government lobby comprised 117 Labour, 1 Conservative, and 1 Liberal. The 50 Members (including tellers) to support the amendment comprised 40 Conservative, 5 Liberal, 4 Scottish National and 1 UUUC

Conservative to vote against the amendment:

Tebbit, N.

Conservatives to vote for the amendment:

Aitken, J.	Hordern, P.	Meyer, Sir A.
Arnold, T.	Hurd, D.	Miller, H.
Banks, R.	Hutchison, M. C.	Morgan, G.
Bell, R.	James, D.	Mudd, D.
Bottomley, P.	Jessel, T.	Newton, T.
Braine, Sir B.	Knight, Mrs J.	Page, R. G.
Douglas-Hamilton, Lord J.	Knox, D.	Rifkind, M.
Dykes, H.	Lane, D.	Shepherd, C.
Fookes, Miss J.	McAdden, Sir S.	Spicer, J.
Gardner, E.	Macfarlane, N.	Taylor, R.*
Glyn, A.*	McNair-Wilson, M.	Warren, K.
Grist, I.	Mather, C.	Young, Sir G.
Hannam, J.	Maxwell-Hyslop, R.	
Hawkins, P.	Mayhew, P.	

HC Deb. 898, 1863–6
1974–5, No. 379.

RHODESIA

Prayer: 31 October 1975

The Foreign and Commonwealth Secretary, L. J. Callaghan, moved 'That the Southern Rhodesia Act 1965 (Continuation) Order 1975, a draft of which was laid before this House on 13th October, be approved'.

The order renewed section 2 of the 1965 Act, empowering Her Majesty in Council to take measures to deal with the situation created by Rhodesia's unilateral declaration of independence; the measures taken, and to be maintained, included the application of sanctions. Mr Callaghan said that the renewal of sanctions was a reaffirmation 'of our commitment—a commitment accepted by successive administrations—to settle a debt of honour to the people of Rhodesia as a whole and in particular to the African majority whose legitimate aspirations remain thwarted'.

For the Opposition, R. Maudling said that, although economic sanctions had had precious little effect, it would be wrong to oppose the continuation of the order.

From the Conservative backbenches, a number of opponents of sanctions rose to oppose the order. P. Wall (C., Haltemprice) said sanctions would not help a settlement, and hurt Africans most. He suggested they remain aloof from the situation until the Rhodesians had themselves reached agreement. J. Biggs-Davison (C., Epping Forest) described the order as a 'pitiful irrelevancy'. R. Bell (C., Beaconsfield) said he would show, in the lobby, 'my disapproval of ten years of idiocy'; he would vote happily against the order. N. Winterton (C., Macclesfield) said he was convinced the best service they could do the people of Rhodesia was to accept that sanctions were simply encouraging terrorism, benefitting Britain's trade rivals, and not helping the very people in the country that the House wanted to help. M. Brotherton (C., Louth) thought the time had come to tell the United Nations that after ten years sanctions had been a complete failure.

The order was approved by 83 votes to 13, the Opposition abstaining officially from voting. The 85 Members (including tellers) in the Government lobby comprised 83 Labour, 1 Conservative and 1 Liberal. The 15 Members (including tellers) to oppose the order were all Conservatives.

Conservative to vote for the order:

Knox, D.

Conservatives to vote against the order:

Bell, R.	Lloyd, I.	Skeet, T.
Biggs-Davison, J.	Morgan-Giles, M.	Stokes, J.
Brotherton, M.	Rees-Davies, W.	Taylor, R.
Gardiner, G.	Rodgers, Sir J.	Wall, P.
Hastings, S.*	Rost, P.	Winterton, N.*

HC Deb. 898, 2037–40
1974–5, No. 380.

The division took place on a Friday, hence encouraging the low turnout.

STANDING ORDER No. 73A (STANDING COMMITTEE ON STATUTORY INSTRUMENTS) [113]

3 November 1975

The Lord President and Leader of the House, E. Short, moved a number of amendments to Standing Order No. 73A designed to bring European Commission Documents within its scope.

N. Spearing (Lab., Newham, South) moved an amendment to the Minister's proposals to provide that the Standing Committee on Statutory Instruments would consider Commission Documents upon a motion made by a Minister to which amendments could be made.

The amendment had been discussed along with others in a 'take note' debate on the First Report from the Select Committee on Procedure, Session 1974–5, on European Secondary Legislation.[1]

The amendment was negatived, with the Government whips on against it, by 152 votes to 64, with the Opposition abstaining from voting.[2] The 153 Members (including tellers) in the Government lobby comprised 148 Labour, 4 Liberal and 1 Conservative. The 66 Members (including tellers) to support the amendment comprised 55 Labour, 7 Conservative, 2 UUUC and 2 Plaid Cymru.

Conservative to vote against the amendment:

Renton, Sir D.

Labour Members to vote for the amendment:

Allaun, F.	Latham, A.	Roper, J.
Barnett, G.	Lee, J.	Sedgemore, B.
Bennett, A.	Litterick, T.	Skinner, D.
Bidwell, S.	Loyden, E.	Spearing, N.
Canavan, D.	Lyons, E.	Spriggs, L.
Clemitson, I.	Mackintosh, J.	Stewart, M.
Cunningham, G.	Madden, M.	Stott, R.
Dunwoody, Mrs G.	Maynard, Miss J.	Taylor, Mrs A.
Fletcher, T.	Mikardo, I.	Thomas, R.
George, B.	Molloy, W.	Thorne, S.
Gould, B.*	Newens, S.	Tomlinson, J.
Heffer, E.	Noble, M.	Torney, T.
Hooley, F.*	Prescott, J.	Tuck, R.
Hoyle, D.	Radice, G.	Ward, M.
Jay, D.	Richardson, Miss J.	Watkins, D.
Jeger, Mrs L.	Roberts, G.	Whitehead, P.
Kerr, R.	Rodgers, G.	Wilson, A.
Kilroy-Silk, R.	Rooker, J.	Wise, Mrs A.
Kinnock, N.		

Conservatives to vote for the amendment:

Biffen, J.	Mayhew, P.	Page, R. G.
Finsberg, G.	Moate, R.	Wells, J.
Maxwell-Hyslop, R.		

HC Deb. 899, 109–12
1974–5, No. 381.

In view of the result of the division, Mr Spearing did not move a second amendment designed to permit discussion on Commission Documents in the Committee to exceed one-and-a-half hours.

[1] The Minister had said that the Government's view on considering Documents in the Committee was that they should be on formal motions ('That the Committee has considered the document'). It was the House alone to which the Government was responsible for the conduct of affairs. 'It would be quite inappropriate, and contrary to the precedents to which the House has adhered in establishing other Standing Committees, to delegate the authority which belongs to the whole House to a small and inevitably less than representative number of hon. Members in Committee.' Mr Spearing had argued that the Committee would wish to come to an opinion on each Document or groups of Documents referred to it. The Committee might say that certain Documents should have further consideration or be debated in the House. Under the Lord President's proposals, that would not be admissable. 'The Lord President is denying the Committee the tools for the job in that it can only discuss the

legislation. A specific vote cannot be taken, specific amendments cannot be moved and a specific resolution cannot be reached.'

² Although strictly a House of Commons matter, the Lord President had presented the proposals as Government proposals, and the whips were on for the division. The tone of the debate itself also suggests that Labour backbenchers viewed themselves as dissenting from the wishes of the Treasury Bench.

TRADE UNION AND LABOUR RELATIONS [114] (AMENDMENT) BILL

Lords Amendment: 6 November 1975

New Clause B (Freedom of the press)

The clause provided for a press charter on matters relating to the freedom of the press. In the Commons, the clause had been amended to provide a different stipulation to the original Lords' one as to what was to be included as constituting 'matters relating to the freedom of the press' for the purposes of the clause.¹ The Lords had disagreed with the amendment, and proposed another one which included details of what was to be included in the application of union membership agreements to journalists.

The Employment Secretary, M. Foot, moved a motion for the House to disagree with the Lords in the amendment. (The amendment was discussed in conjunction with several others.)

Mr Foot said that the Lords amendment spelled out specific rights of editors and others which had to be included in the charter without negotiation. The Government could not accept that, and wanted to insist upon the original amendment which spelled out the matters to be covered in the charter while leaving the parties concerned to decide how they should be covered. The major Government proposal to the House, he said, was that they should send the Bill back to the Lords in the form in which it left the Commons previously. 'We take that view because we deliberately reached our conclusions then and we do not see any reasons for varying them.'

For the Opposition, J. Prior said it was an issue involving press freedom, and contended that the Lords had been conciliatory in their approach. He argued the case for amendments being discussed at the same time for compensation for those who suffered loss as a result of a breach of the charter.

At the end of the debate, J. Stonehouse (Lab., Walsall, North) rose to declare: 'On other occasions I have attacked the excesses of the Press, but I believe that the freedom of the Press is a most precious quality that we must fight to protect. I believe that on this occasion their Lordships have spoken for the public good. The House should support the Lords Amendment.'

The motion to disagree with the Lords amendment was carried by 290 votes to 241. 1 Labour Member cross-voted to oppose the motion.

Labour Member to vote against the motion:

Stonehouse, J.

HC Deb. 899, 689–94
1974–5, No. 388.

The House then approved a motion for the House to insist on its amendment to the Lords amendment to which the Lords had disagreed; the motion was agreed without a division.

¹ For text of amendment, see above, division no. 339, 15 October 1975.

TRADE UNION AND LABOUR RELATIONS [115]
(AMENDMENT) BILL

Lords Amendment: 6 November 1975

New Clause B (Freedom of the press)

The Lords had inserted an amendment to provide that the supervisory body set up to oversee the workings of the charter made possible under the clause had to award compensation to anyone who suffered material loss as a result of a breach of the charter.

The Employment Secretary, M. Foot, moved an amendment to delete the insertion made in the Lords.

The amendment had been discussed in conjunction with other amendments (see above, division no. 388, 6 November 1975).

The amendment was carried by 290 votes to 243. 1 Labour Member cross-voted to oppose the Government's amendment.

Labour Member to vote against the amendment:

Stonehouse, J.

HC Deb. 899, 695–700
1974–5, No. 389.

TRADE UNION AND LABOUR RELATIONS (AMENDMENT) BILL [116]

Lords Amendment: 6 November 1975

New Clause B (Freedom of the press)

The Lords had inserted an amendment to provide that any rule, agreement, act or conduct which was contrary to the press charter 'shall be deemed to be contrary to public policy'.

The Employment Secretary, M. Foot, moved that the House disagree with the Lords in the amendment.

The amendment had been discussed in conjunction with others (see above, division no. 388, 6 November 1975).

The motion was carried by 281 votes to 250. 1 Labour Member cross-voted to oppose the Government's motion.

Labour Member to vote against the motion:

Stonehouse, J.

HC Deb. 899, 699–704
1974–5, No. 390.

COMMUNITY LAND BILL [117]

Lords Amendment: 11 November 1975

Schedule 4 (Acquisition and appropriation of land)

The Lords had inserted an amendment to provide that a certificate provided with a compulsory purchase order under paragraph 1(2) of the schedule 'shall not be questioned in any legal proceedings whatsoever'.

The Minister for Planning and Local Government, J. Silkin moved formally for the House to agree with the Lords amendment.

The amendment had been discussed in conjunction with earlier amendments.[1]

The motion to agree with the amendment was carried by 273 votes to 30, with the Opposition abstaining from voting. The 275 Members (including tellers) in the Government lobby comprised 274 Labour and

1 SDLP. The 32 Members (including tellers) to vote against the motion comprised 11 Conservative, 9 Liberal, 9 Scottish National and 3 Plaid Cymru.

Conservatives to vote against the motion:

Bulmer, E.	Fairgrieve, R.	Latham, M.
Costain, A.	Fletcher, A.	Rawlinson, Sir P.
Drayson, B.	Gray, H.	Stainton, K.
Durant, T.	Griffiths, E.	

HC Deb. 899, 1247–50
1974–5, No. 394.

¹ The Minister had contended that the amendment was helpful in that it helped make the position clearer. For the Opposition, R. G. Page said he was highly suspicious of the amendment. He did not think it was better than what was already in the Bill. (Despite Mr Page's comments, the Opposition did not vote against the motion, preferring instead to abstain.)

COMMUNITY LAND BILL   [118]

Lords Amendment: 11 November 1975

Clause 16 (Land acquisition and management schemes)

The Lords had passed a number of amendments designed to create a separate land acquisition and management scheme (LAMS) for the Peak District National Park.

The Minister for Planning and Local Government, J. Silkin, moved for the House to disagree with the Lords in the amendments.

Mr Silkin said the question involved was a difficult and finely balanced one, but he had come to the conclusion that he should advise the House to disagree with the amendments. The proposal for a separate board could be administratively difficult, and given the compromise solution which had been produced by the constituent authorities, the Government did not feel there was any real need for any amendment.

P. Whitehead (Lab., Derby, North) rose to oppose the motion. He said the elected members who served on the Peak District National Park Council were unanimous in believing that they should have the powers proposed by the Lords amendments. He invited other Labour Members to join him in the lobby against the motion in order to protect a precious amenity. A. Bennett (Lab., Stockport, North) said the whole idea behind the Bill was positive planning, making the purchase of land go hand in hand with the planning authority. If they rejected the amendments, they would separate the two functions. He asked the Minister to reconsider. N. Winterton (C., Macclesfield) said he was undecided how to vote. He thought the task of the Peak Park Planning Board would be made much more difficult by the Minister's decision.

For the Opposition, R. G. Page said he was in the same difficulty as the Minister in deciding between two evenly balanced arguments. If co-ordinated planning in the Peak Park area could be achieved, he thought the Minister was probably right in saying that they should not accept the amendment, and instead go for another arrangement.

The motion to disagree with the Lords amendments was carried by 281 votes to 80, the Opposition voting with the Government. The 283 Members (including tellers) in the Government lobby comprised 217 Labour, 62 Conservative and 2 UUUC. The 82 Members (including tellers) to vote against the motion comprised 44 Labour, 27 Conservative, 10 Liberal and 1 SDLP.

Labour Members to vote against the motion:

Allaun, F.	Lambie, D.	Rose, P.
Ashton, J.	Latham, A.	Sandelson, N.
Bennett, A.	Lee, J.	Sedgemore, B.
Canavan, D.	Madden, M.	Short, Mrs R.
Cryer, R.	Marquand, D.	Silverman, J.
Edge, G.	Maynard, Miss J.	Spearing, N.
Flannery, M.	Mikardo, I.	Taylor, Mrs A.
Hatton, F.	Moonman, E.	Thomas, R.
Hayman, Mrs H.	Newens, S.	Thorne, S.
Hooley, F.	Price, C.	Walden, B.
Horam, J.	Radice, G.	Ward, M.
Hoyle, D.	Richardson, Miss J.	Whitehead, P.*
Kelley, R.	Rodgers, G.	Wise, Mrs A.
Kerr, R.	Rooker, J.	Young, D.
Kinnock, N.	Roper, J.	

Conservatives to vote against the motion:

Bennett, Sir F.	du Cann, E.	Rees, P.
Body, R.	Gardiner, G.	Ridsdale, J.
Boscawen, R.	Gow, I.	Royle, Sir A.
Bottomley, P.	Grylls, M.	Shaw, G.
Brittan, L.	Irving, C.	Stainton, K.
Brown, Sir E.	Langford-Holt, Sir J.	Taylor, E.
Budgen, N.	Macmillan, M.	Wells, J.
Clarke, K.	Mitchell, D.	Winterton, N.*
Crouch, D.	Mudd, D.	
Drayson, B.		

HC Deb. 899, 1339-44
1974-5, No. 399.

The Session of 1975-6

PREVENTION OF TERRORISM   [119]
(TEMPORARY PROVISIONS) BILL

Second Reading: 26 November 1975

A Bill designed to replace, with minor modifications, the 1974 Act of
the same name. It was supported both by the Government and the
Opposition.

The Bill was given a Second Reading by 183 votes to 14, with the
Opposition supporting the Government. The 185 Members (including
tellers) in the Government lobby comprised 138 Labour, 34 Conservative, 7 UUUC and 6 Liberal. The 16 Members (including tellers) to
oppose Second Reading were all Labour Members.

Labour Members to vote against Second Reading:

Bennett, A.	Latham, A.	Richardson, Miss J.
Bidwell, S.	Litterick, T.	Rose, P.
Canavan, D.	Loyden, E.	Selby, H.
Colquhoun, Mrs M.	Maynard, Miss J.	Thomas, R.
Corbett, R.*	Mikardo, I.	Thorne, S.*
Flannery, M.		

HC Deb. 901, 1001–4
1975–6, No. 5.

CIVIL LIST BILL   [120]

Second Reading: 4 December 1975

A short Bill, the main purpose of which was to provide that future
increases in provision for the Civil List should be subject to the usual
House of Commons' Supply procedure.

In moving Second Reading, the Prime Minister explained that the
Government believed that that was the best way to make provision for

the Civil List in view of the wide range of official duties of the Queen and the Royal Household and because of the effect of inflation. W. Hamilton (Lab., Fife, Central) opposed the Bill. He wanted the tax position of members of the Royal Family to be looked at. Paul Dean (C., Somerset, North), who had tabled a motion to reject the Bill, objected to the annual involvement of Parliament. It opened up the possibility of an annual wrangle over the Queen's expenses; he saw it, he said, as the thin end of a dangerous wedge. Objection on similar grounds was also expressed by E. Powell (UUUC, Down, South) and J. Stokes (C., Halesowen and Stourbridge).

Supported by both the Government and Opposition, the Bill was given a Second Reading by 247 votes to 16. The 249 Members (including tellers) to support Second Reading comprised 159 Conservative, 85 Labour, 4 SNP and 1 Liberal. The 18 Members (including tellers) to vote against comprised 17 Labour and 1 UUUC (E. Powell). A number of Members on both sides of the House, including Dean and Stokes on the Conservative side, abstained from voting.

Labour Members to vote against Second Reading:

Canavan, D.*	Latham, A.	Rodgers, G.
Cryer, R.	Madden, M.	Skinner, D.
Dunwoody, Mrs G.	Mikardo, I.	Taylor, Mrs A.
Edge, G.	Newens, S.	Thomas, R.
Hamilton, W.*	Noble, M.	Wise, Mrs A.
Hoyle, D.	Richardson, Miss J.	

HC Deb. 901, 2015–18
1975–6, No. 9.

MONEYLENDERS (CROWN AGENTS) BILL [121]

Committee: 10 December 1975

Clause 1 (Moneylenders Acts not to apply to Crown Agents, Etc.)

The Clause, the central one in the two-clause Bill, provided that the Moneylender Acts would not apply and would be deemed never to have applied to loans made by the Crown Agents either directly or through their wholly owned companies.

On the motion 'That the clause stand part of the Bill', Eldon Griffiths, from the Opposition Front Bench, announced that the Opposition agreed, without enthusiasm, 'that the clause should stand part of a disagreeable Bill'.[1] A number of Members on the opposition benches, however, forced the motion to a division.

The 'stand part' motion was carried by 73 votes to 9, with the Opposition abstaining from voting. The 11 Members (including tellers) to vote against comprised 6 Liberal, 3 Conservative and 2 UUUC.

Conservatives to vote against the Clause:

Boscawen, R.*   Wiggin, J.*   Winterton, N.

HC Deb. 902, 609–10
1975–6, No. 14.

The Bill was then reported, without amendment, and given an unopposed Third Reading.

---

[1] The main debate on the issue involved had taken place on Second Reading on 27 November. Conservative disquiet was aroused by the measure being taken in advance of the Government's promised White Paper on the Crown Agents, by the retrospective element of the Bill, and the amount of money involved. Second Reading debate, *HC Deb.* 901, 1139–77.

CIVIL ESTIMATES, 1976–77 (VOTE ON ACCOUNT)   [122]

Supply: 16 December 1975

Motion to grant a sum, not exceeding £11,704,621,000, out of the Consolidated Fund, on account, for or towards defraying the charges for Civil Services for the year ending on 31st March 1977.

For the Liberals, J. Pardoe (Lib., Cornwall, North) objected to the House not having had the opportunity for detailed debate, and protested 'at the failure of the House to do its job in controlling the spending powers of the Executive'.

The Liberals divided the House on the motion. Although the Opposition abstained from voting, they were joined by several Conservative backbenchers. The motion was carried by 234 votes to 59. The Government lobby comprised Labour Members. The 61 Members (including tellers) to vote against comprised 42 Conservative, 10 Liberal, 6 SNP, 2 Plaid Cymru and 1 UUUC.

Conservatives to vote against the motion:

Biffen, J.
Body, R.
Bottomley, P.
Boyson, R.
Braine, Sir B.
Brotherton, M.
Clark, A.
Cormack, P.
Critchley, J.
Eden, Sir J.
Fletcher, A.
Gow, I.
Grylls, M.
Hastings, S.

Hawkins, P.
Hicks, R.
Jessel, T.
Jones, A.
Kershaw, A.
Knight, Mrs J.
Langford-Holt, Sir J.
Latham, M.
Lawrence, I.
Lawson, N.
Macfarlane, N.
MacGregor, J.
Maxwell-Hyslop, R.
Mayhew, P.

Meyer, Sir A.
Miller, H.
Miscampbell, N.
Mitchell, D.
Mudd, D.
Price, D.
Ridley, N.
Rost, P.
Smithy, D.
Spence, J.
Tebbit, N.
Warren, K.
Winterton, N.
Young, Sir G.

HC Deb. 902, 1181–4
1975–6, No. 16.

HILL LIVESTOCK (COMPENSATORY ALLOWANCES) [123]

Prayer: 17 December 1975

For the Government, the Minister of State for Agriculture, Fisheries and Food, E. Bishop, moved: 'That the Hill Livestock (Compensatory Allowances) Regulations 1975, a draft of which was laid before this House on 27th November, be approved.'

For the Opposition, R. Hicks announced that his party accepted the need to approve the regulations, and would not divide the House. However, opposition to the regulations was expressed from the Liberal and Scottish National benches on the grounds that they excluded farms of less than three hectares, while R. Body (C., Holland-with Boston) objected to the provision of compensatory allowances. He argued that the effect of them would be to induce marginal producers to produce more than they would otherwise produce. 'That will have the effect of weakening the market and making it more difficult for the efficient producers to operate. At the same time, it will have the effect of forcing up the price of meat to the public.'

Liberal and Nationalist Members took the motion to a division, in which the Opposition abstained from voting. The motion was carried by 66 votes to 19. The 68 Members (including tellers) in the Government lobby comprised 60 Labour, 4 Conservative and 4 UUUC. The 21 Members (including tellers) to vote against comprised 9 Liberal, 8 SNP, 2 Plaid Cymru and 2 Conservative.

Conservatives to vote for the motion:

Gray, H.   Rippon, G.   Winterton, N.
Monro, H.

Conservatives to vote against the motion:

Body, R.   Temple-Morris, P.

HC Deb. 902, 1593–6
1975–6, No. 21.

The division took place at 1.30 a.m.

DEVOLUTION (SCOTLAND AND WALES) [124]

19 January 1976

The House had a four-day debate on devolution. On the fourth day, the Paymaster-General, E. Dell, moved 'That this House takes note of the White Paper on Our Changing Democracy, Devolution to Scotland and Wales (Command Paper No. 6348).'

For the Opposition, Sir D. Renton moved to add at the end of the motion: 'affirms the need for an Assembly in Scotland, but rejects the Government's particular proposals for Scotland and Wales which will lead to confusion and conflict, and which will threaten the unity of the United Kingdom'.

The Opposition addendum was defeated by 315 votes in 244 on a straight party vote. The 317 Members (including tellers) in the Government lobby comprised 291 Labour, 11 Liberal, 11 Scottish National, 3 Plaid Cymru and 1 UUUC Member. The 246 Members (including tellers) in the Opposition lobby comprised 238 Conservative and 8 UUUC.

(1) For the Scottish National Party, D. Stewart (SNP Western Isles) moved to add at the end of the motion: 'but regrets that the

Scottish and Welsh Assemblies are given no meaningful control over their respective economies'.

The addendum was negatived by 304 votes to 27, with the Opposition abstaining from voting. The 306 Members (including tellers) in the Government lobby comprised 286 Labour, 13 Conservative and 7 UUUC. The 29 Members (including tellers) in the Nationalist lobby comprised 11 Liberal, 11 Scottish National, 3 Plaid Cymru, 3 Labour and 1 UUUC.

Conservatives to vote against the amendment:

Bowden, A.	Gow, I.	Marten, N.
Brotherton, M.	Hutchison, M. C.	Ridley, N.
Clark, A.	Irving, C.	Tebbit, N.
Cormack, P.	Kershaw, A.	Winterton, N.
Fell, A.		

Labour Members to vote for the amendment:

Lambie, D.	Robertson, J.[1]	Sillars, J.[1]

(2) The main Question (moved by the Paymaster-General) was then put and carried by 295 votes to 37, with the Opposition abstaining from voting. The 297 Members (including tellers) in the Government lobby comprised 271 Labour, 11 Liberal, 11 Scottish National, 3 Plaid Cymru and 1 UUUC. The 39 Members (including tellers) to oppose the motion comprised 29 Conservative, 7 UUUC and 3 Labour. 16 Members abstained from voting.[2]

Conservatives to vote against the motion:

Banks, R.	Hicks, R.	Shepherd, C.
Brotherton, M.	Hutchison, M. C.	Sproat, I.*
Churchill, W.	Jones, A.	Stanbrook, I.
Clark, A.	Kershaw, A.	Stokes, J.
Durant, T.	Marten, N.	Tapsell, P.
Eden, Sir J.	Meyer, Sir A.*	Taylor, R.
Emery, P.	Miller, H.	Tebbit, N.
Galbraith, T.	Moate, R.	Wiggin, J.
Gow, I.	Morrison, P.	Winterton, N.
Hannam, J.	Rees, P.	

Labour Members to vote against the motion:

Lamond, J.   Leadbitter, T.   Stonehouse, J.

HC Deb. 903, 1069–70
1975–6, nos. 23 and 24

¹ In September 1975, Mr Sillars formed a breakaway Scottish Labour Party, joined in January 1976 by Mr Robertson, though both still remaining for the time being in receipt of the Labour whip.
² The abstainers were: L. Abse, D. Anderson, G. Cunningham, T. Dalyell, J. Dean, B. Ford, J. Lee, A. Lewis, E. Lyons, J. Mendelson, W. Molloy, A. Palmer, C. Phipps, N. Sandelson, T. Swain and F. Tomney.

IMPORT DUTIES   [125]

Prayer: 19 January 1976

From the Labour backbenches, N. Spearing (Lab., Newham, South) moved: 'That an humble address be presented to Her Majesty, praying that the Import Duties (General) (No. 5) Order 1975 (S.I., 1975, No. 1744), dated 27th October 1975, a copy of which was laid before the House on 12th November 1975, in the last Session of Parliament, be annulled.'

The Prayer was opposed by both the Government and the Opposition but supported by anti-EEC backbenchers on both sides of the House on the grounds that the duties involved would constitute a tax on food and would have the effect of putting up food prices.

With the Government whips put on against it, the Prayer was negatived by 107 votes to 64. The Opposition abstained from voting. The 109 Members (including tellers) in the Government lobby comprised 107 Labour and 2 Liberal. The 66 Members (including tellers) to vote for the Prayer comprised 49 Labour, 6 UUUC, 5 Conservative, 3 SNP and 3 Plaid Cymru.

Labour Members to vote for the motion:

Allaun, F.	Heffer, E.	Ovenden, J.
Ashton, J.	Hooley, F.*	Parry, R.
Atkinson, N.	Hoyle, D.	Richardson, Miss J.
Barnett, G.	Hughes, R. J.	Roderick, C.
Bean, R.	Kerr, R.	Rodgers, G.
Buchan, N.	Kinnock, N.	Rooker, J.

Callaghan, J.	Lambie, D.	Sedgemore, B.
Canavan, D.	Lamond, J.	Skinner, D.
Cook, R.	Latham, A.	Spearing, N.
Cryer, R.*	Litterick, T.	Stallard, A.
Dunwoody, Mrs G.	Loyden, E.	Taylor, Mrs A.
Evans, J.	Madden, M.	Thomas, R.
Fernyhough, E.	Maynard, Miss J.	Thorne, S.
Flannery, M.	Mikardo, I.	Wise, Mrs A.
Fletcher, T.	Miller, Mrs M.	Woof, R.
George, B.	Newens, S.	
Hart, Mrs J.	Noble, M.	

Conservatives to vote for the motion:

Bell, R.	Hutchison, M. C.	Moate, R.
Body, R.	Marten, N.	

HC Deb. 903, 1095–6
1975–6, No. 25.

TRADE UNION AND LABOUR RELATIONS   [126] (AMENDMENT) BILL

Suggested Amendments: 21 January 1976

Following Report and before Third Reading of the Bill—reintroduced under the provisions of the Parliament Act—the House debated amendments to be suggested to the House of Lords.

The Opposition moved an amendment to a Government amendment to provide that the proposed Charter on Freedom of the Press should contain provision for journalists to belong to the union of their choice and for editors to be free from any obligation to join a union.

The amendment was opposed by the Government, and negatived by 299 votes to 240. 1 Labour Member cross-voted to support it.

Labour Member to vote for the amendment:

Stonehouse, J.

HC Deb. 903, 1417–22
1975–6, No. 30.

TRADE UNION AND LABOUR RELATIONS   [127]
(AMENDMENT) BILL

Suggested Amendments: 21 January 1976

Following Report and before Third Reading of the Bill, the House debated amendments to be suggested to the House of Lords.

For the Liberals, J. Thorpe (Lib., Devon, North) moved an amendment to a Government amendment to provide that the decisions of the body set up to hear complaints under the proposed Press Charter should be binding.

The amendment was opposed by the Government, and supported by the Opposition. It was negatived by 294 votes to 253. 1 Labour Member cross-voted to support it.

Labour Member to vote for the amendment:

Stonehouse, J.

HC Deb. 903, 1437–42
1975–6, No. 31.

PREVENTION OF TERRORISM (TEMPORARY   [128]
PROVISIONS) BILL

Report: 28 January 1976

New Clause 3 (Information about acts of terrorism)

The Clause provided that it would be an offence for anyone who knew or believed that they had information which could be of assistance in preventing acts of terrorism or apprehending those involved in acts of terrorism to fail to disclose that information as soon as reasonably practicable to the authorities. The Clause was introduced by the Government, and supported by the Opposition.

A number of Labour backbenchers opposed the Clause, and took it it to a division. The Clause was given a Second Reading by 196 votes to 25,[1] the Opposition voting with the Government. The 27 Members (including tellers) to vote against comprised 24 Labour, 2 Plaid Cymru and 1 SDLP.

Labour Members to vote against the Clause:

Bennett, A. Fletcher, T. Newens, S.
Bidwell, S. Heffer, E. Noble, M.
Callaghan, J. Lamond, J. Parry, R.
Canavan, D. Latham, A. Rodgers, G.
Colquhoun, Mrs M. Lee, J. Skinner, D.
Corbett, R. Litterick, T.* Thomas, R.
Cryer, R. Marshall, E. Thorne, S.
Flannery, M. Mikardo, I.* Wise, Mrs A.

HC Deb. 904, 493–6
1975–6, No. 42.

¹ *Hansard* gives the number as 24, but lists 25 names.

PREVENTION OF TERRORISM (TEMPORARY PROVISIONS) BILL [129]

Report: 28 January 1976

Clause 3 (Exclusion Orders: General)

From the Labour backbenches, A. Bennett (Lab., Stockport, North) moved an amendment to delete the provision for exclusion orders.

The amendment was opposed by both the Government and the Opposition, and negatived by 140 votes to 21, the Opposition voting with the Government. The 28 Members (including tellers) to support the amendment comprised 21 Labour and 2 Plaid Cymru.

Labour Members to vote for the amendment:

Bennett, A.* Flannery, M. Parry, R.
Bidwell, S. Fletcher, T. Rodgers, G.
Canavan, D. Lamond, J. Short, Mrs R.
Colquhoun, Mrs M. Latham, A. Skinner, D.
Cook, R. Litterick, T. Thomas, R.*
Corbett, R. Mikardo, I. Thorne, S.
Cryer, R. Noble, M. Wise, Mrs A.

HC Deb. 904, 517–20
1975–6, No. 43.

PREVENTION OF TERRORISM (TEMPORARY   [130] PROVISIONS) BILL

Report: 28 January 1976

Clause 5 (Right to make representations etc. to Secretary of State)

A. Beith (Lib., Berwick-upon-Tweed) moved an amendment to provide that an exclusion order should be accompanied by the 'general reasons' for its issuance.

Mr Beith argued that it was fundamental to British justice that people should know what they were supposed to have done. The Home Secretary, R. Jenkins, responded that, under the Bill, he could only issue exclusion orders on those he was satisfied had been concerned in, or intended to be concerned in, terrorist acts, and hence the general reasons were already known; if one was more specific there was the difficulty of safeguarding information.

With the Government whips on against it, the amendment was negatived by 116 votes to 35, the Opposition voting with the Government. The 118 Members (including tellers) in the Government lobby comprised 84 Labour, 22 Conservative, 7 UUUC and 5 Scottish National. The 37 Members (including tellers) to support the amendment comprised 23 Labour, 12 Liberal and 2 Plaid Cymru.

Labour Members to vote for the amendment:

Bennett, A.	Hooley, F.	Parry, R.
Bidwell, S.	Lamond, J.	Rodgers, G.
Canavan, D.	Latham, A.	Rooker, J.
Colquhoun, Mrs M.	Litterick, T.	Skinner, D.
Cook, R.	Madden, M.	Thomas, R.
Corbett, R.	Mikardo, I.	Thorne, S.
Cryer, R.	Newens, S.	Wise, Mrs A.
Flannery, M.	Noble, M.	

HC Deb. 904, 535–8.
1975–6, No. 44.

PREVENTION OF TERRORISM (TEMPORARY   [131] PROVISIONS) BILL

Report: 28 January 1976

Clause 9 (Power of arrest and detention)

A. Bennett (Lab., Stockport, North) moved an amendment to provide that any person arrested under that section of the Bill should be entitled to inform a relative of their detention, and, where the Home Secretary extended the period of detention, to consult in private a solicitor.

The Home Secretary, R. Jenkins, opposed the amendment. He pointed out that the provisions of the Judges' Rules applied to those detained under the prevention of terrorism legislation, and he did not think it right to put them in statutory form in respect of terrorists but not of other criminals.

The amendment was negatived by 109 votes to 35, with the Opposition supporting the Government. The 111 Members (including tellers) in the Government lobby comprised 75 Labour, 21 Conservative, 7 UUUC, 7 SNP and 1 Plaid Cymru. The 37 Members (including tellers) to support the amendment comprised 23 Labour, 12 Liberal, 1 Plaid Cymru and 1 SDLP.

Labour Members to vote for the amendment:

Bennett, A.	Hughes, R.	Parry, R.
Bidwell, S.	Lamond, J.	Rodgers, G.
Canavan, D.	Latham, A.	Rooker, J.
Cook, R.	Litterick, T.	Skinner, D.
Corbett, R.	Madden, M.	Thomas, R.*
Cryer, R.	Mikardo, I.	Thorne, S.*
Cunningham, G.	Newens, S.	Wise, Mrs A.
Flannery, M.	Noble, M.	

HC Deb. 904, 557–60
1975–6, No. 45.

PREVENTION OF TERRORISM (TEMPORARY PROVISIONS) BILL [132]

Report: 28 January 1976

Clause 14 (Duration, expiry and revival of Act)

I. Mikardo (Lab., Bethnal Green and Bow) moved an amendment to provide that the Act would expire six months after the date of its coming into force unless continued for a further period of not more than six months by an Order under that section of the measure.

Mr Mikardo contended that the Bill should be as temporary as reasonably possible. For the Government, the Under-Secretary of State at the Home Office, Mrs S. Summerskill, declared that twelve months was considered appropriate as a renewal period.

The amendment was negatived by 105 votes to 31, the Opposition voting with the Government. The 107 Members (including tellers) in the Government lobby comprised 75 Labour, 19 Conservative, 7 SNP and 6 UUUC. The 33 Members (including tellers) to support the amendment comprised 22 Labour, 7 Liberal, 2 Plaid Cymru, 1 SDLP and 1 UUUC (J. Kilfedder).

Labour Members to vote for the amendment:

Bennett, A.	Lamond, J.	Noble, M.
Bidwell, S.	Latham, A.	Parry, R.
Canavan, D.	Litterick, T.	Rooker, J.
Cook, R.	McGuire, M.	Skinner, D.
Corbett, R.*	Madden, M.	Thomas, R.
Cryer, R.	Mikardo, I.*	Thorne, S.
Flannery, M.	Newens, S.	Wise, Mrs A.
Fletcher, T.		

HC Deb. 904, 583-6
1975-6, No. 46.

PREVENTION OF TERRORISM (TEMPORARY PROVISIONS) BILL   [133]

Third Reading: 28 January 1976

After completing the report stage of the Bill, the House gave the Bill a Third Reading by 118 votes to 11, the Opposition voting with the Government. The 120 Members (including tellers) to support Third Reading comprised 84 Labour, 15 Conservative, 7 Liberal, 7 UUUC and 7 SNP. The 13 Members (including tellers) to oppose the Bill comprised 11 Labour and 2 Plaid Cymru.

Labour Members to vote against Third Reading:

Bennett, A.	Latham, A.	Skinner, D.
Bidwell, S.	Litterick, T.	Thomas, R.*
Canavan, D.	Mikardo, I.	Thorne, S.*
Flannery, M.	Parry, R.	

HC Deb. 904, 591-4
1975-6, No. 47.

The division took place at 11.53 p.m.

WALES (ECONOMIC INFRASTRUCTURE)   [134]

Supply: 5 February 1976

The House debated a Plaid Cymru motion: 'That this House deplores the failure of successive Governments in not creating an industrial infrastructure for Wales which includes a road, rail and air communications system and which would make possible the development of a balanced Welsh economy'.

The motion was defeated by 242 votes to 19, with the Opposition abstaining from voting. 1 Conservative took part in the division, and voted in *both* lobbies.

Conservative to vote in both lobbies:

Farr, J.

HC Deb. 904, 1489–92
1975–6, No. 54.

Mr Farr did not speak during the debate. His voting in both lobbies was intentional.[1]

[1] 'I recall the occasion quite clearly and I voted in both lobbies, and intended so to do.' John Farr MP to author.

DOCK WORK REGULATION BILL   [135]

Second Reading: 10 February 1976

The House debated the Second Reading of the Dock Work Regulation Bill. At 10.00 p.m. the Government Deputy Chief Whip moved the closure motion, 'That the Question be now put'.

The closure motion was carried by 312 votes to 305. 1 Labour Member cross-voted to oppose the motion.

Labour Member to vote against closure:

Stonehouse, J.

*HC Deb.*905, 365–70
1975–6, No- 57.

The Bill was then given a Second Reading by 312 votes to 304, with no cross-voting. Mr Stonehouse, who had not taken part in the debate (other than to ask a question of the Employment Secretary, in which he indicated concern for the effect the Bill might have on consumers), abstained from voting. He abstained also in the succeeding division on the motion to commit the Bill to a Committee of the Whole House, negatived by 312 votes to 303. *HC Deb.* 905, c. 371–82.

FAIR EMPLOYMENT (NORTHERN IRELAND) BILL [136]

Second Reading: 16 February 1976

The Bill was designed to establish a Fair Employment Agency for Northern Ireland to promote equality of opportunity in employment, and to make it unlawful for an employer to discriminate on the grounds of religious belief and political opinion in the recruitment of new, and treatment of existing, employees.

UUUC Members opposed the Bill on the grounds that it would probably do more harm than good, and would intensify the problem.

The Bill was given a Second Reading by 156 votes to 8, the Opposition voting with the Government. The 158 Members (including tellers) in the Government lobby comprised 132 Labour, 21 Conservative, 3 Liberal and 2 Scottish National. The 10 Members (including tellers) to oppose the Bill comprised 9 UUUC and 1 Conservative.

Conservative to vote against Second Reading:

Winterton, N.

HC Deb. 905, 1067–70
1975–6, No. 64.

CIVIL AVIATION POLICY [137]

26 February 1976

The House debated both a Government and an Opposition motion on the Government's Civil Aviation Authority. The Government motion, to approve the Statement on Civil Aviation Policy Guidance given by the Secretary of State to the Civil Aviation Authority in pursuance of section 3(2) of the Civil Aviation Act 1971 with respect to the performance of its functions, was approved without a division.

The Opposition motion, 'That this House rejects the Secretary of State for Trade's decision to cancel Laker Airways Skytrain designation and to require the Civil Aviation Authority to revoke the Skytrain licence contrary to the Authority's considered view that it should be allowed to stand', was divided upon, and negatived by 262 votes to 232. 1 Labour Member cross-voted to support the motion.

Labour Member to vote for the motion:

Stonehouse, J.

HC Deb. 906, 695–700
1975–6, No. 71.

During the debate, Mr Stonehouse had argued that nothing the Secretary of State had said justified the decision to overrule the decision taken by the CAA only the previous year. 'It is deplorable for the Secretary of State to overturn a verdict of the CAA, which went into this matter very much more closely than he could have done.' In the absence of an explanation from the Under-Secretary for 'this extraordinary decision', he indicated he would vote with the Opposition. (Mr Stonehouse had briefly been Minister of Aviation in 1967.)

This was the last dissenting vote Mr Stonehouse cast as a Labour Member. On 7 April 1976, he resigned the Labour whip. He was subsequently to introduce a Private Member's motion calling for 'inspired leadership' and an early general election (9 April),[1] and to vote against the Budget (12 April).[2] He continued to sit in the House, as an English National Party member, until he was convicted and gaoled for seven years on theft and false pretenses charges on 6 August 1976, resigning his seat on 27 August. *The Times*, 28 August 1976.

---

[1] The motion was defeated by 40 votes to 0, with the Government whips on against it. *HC Deb.* 909, c. 807–8. In moving the motion, Mr Stonehouse spoke for over an hour, delivering part of his speech from the Treasury bench until instructed to return to his seat by Mr Speaker. *HC Deb.* 909, c. 792.

[2] *HC Deb.* 909, c. 1105–10.

STATUTORY INSTRUMENTS ETC. [138]

2 March 1976

A Government whip moved formally: 'That the Glanford and Scunthorpe (Areas) Order 1976 (S.I., 1976, No. 188) be referred to a Standing Committee on Statutory Instruments, Etc.'

A number of Labour Members objected to the motion and divided the House. The motion was carried, with the Government whips on, by 138 votes to 12, the Opposition abstaining from voting. The 14 Members (including tellers) to oppose the motion were all Labour Members.

Labour Members to vote against the motion:

Canavan, D.	Lambie, D.	Skinner, D.
Colquhoun, Mrs M.	Lipton, M.	Thomas, R.
Cryer, R.*	Maynard, Miss J.	Thorne, S.
Cunningham, G.*	Phipps, C.	Wise, Mrs A.
Kerr, R.	Sedgemore, B.	

HC Deb. 906, 1105–8
1975–6, No. 74.

FISHWATER AND SALMON FISHERIES (SCOTLAND) BILL   [139]

Report: 2 March 1976

New Clause 1 (Area Boards)

D. Steel (Lib., Roxburgh, Selkirk and Peebles) moved the new clause, which provided that 'The Secretary of State for Scotland shall within the next two years introduce a measure to set up Area Boards based on the recommendations of Command Paper No. 2691 of August 1965'.

The Under-Secretary of State for Scotland, H. Brown, indicated sympathy for the idea of introducing area boards in the long term; he felt there was little dividing the Government and supporters of the clause, and hoped that the clause would be withdrawn.

The Liberals pressed the clause to a division, in which it was negatived by 135 votes to 18 with the Government whips on against it. The Opposition abstained from voting. The 20 Members (including tellers) to support the clause comprised 11 Scottish National, 5 Liberal, 3 Labour and 1 Plaid Cymru.

Labour Members to vote for the clause:

Lambie, D.   Robertson, J.[1]   Sillars, J.[1]

HC Deb. 906, 1185–8
1975–6, No. 76.

[1] In September 1975, Mr Sillars had formed the Scottish Labour Party, joined in January 1976 by Mr Robertson, but both Members were still in receipt of the Labour whip.

FRESHWATER AND SALMON FISHERIES (SCOTLAND) BILL   [140]

Report: 2 March 1976

New Clause 5 (Register relating to Freshwater Fishing)

D. Steel (Lib., Roxburgh, Selkirk and Peebles) moved the new clause, which required the Secretary of State to make up a register of all persons who occupied the right to fish within a protection area, and to define the terms and conditions under which fishing within the areas in which the owners had not co-operated would be made open to the public.

From the Labour backbenches, both N. Buchan (Lab., Renfrewshire, West) and D. Canavan (Lab., West Stirlingshire) expressed the hope that the Minister would accept the principle behind the clause. For the Government, the Under-Secretary of State for Scotland, H. Brown, opposed the clause. The Bill was based on the voluntary principle, and the Government had gone as far as it could, bearing in mind the limitations of a voluntary system. The issue had been discussed at length in committee, and nothing new had been said.

The motion to read the clause a Second time was approved without a division, but the motion to add the clause to the Bill was negatived by 118 votes to 20, with the Government whips on against it. The Opposition abstained from voting. The 22 Members (including tellers) to support the clause comprised 11 Scottish National, 7 Labour and 4 Liberal.

Labour Members to vote for the clause:

Buchan, N.   Hunter, A.   Skinner, D.
Canavan, D.   Lambie, D.   Wise, Mrs A.
Cryer, R.

HC Deb. 906, 1201–2
1975–6, No. 77.

FRESHWATER AND SALMON FISHERIES   [141]
(SCOTLAND) BILL

Third Reading: 2 March 1976

On the motion for Third Reading, two Labour Members rose to speak against the Bill. Both D. Lambie (Lab., Central Ayrshire) and D. Canavan (Lab., West Stirlingshire) argued that it was not an improvement upon existing legislation, and both felt it should be opposed. 'Will it help make things better for the ordinary working-class angler?', asked Mr Canavan. 'Will it give him more access? Is it an improvement on the present situation? I do not think that it is, and I am sure that the majority of Scottish anglers would agree with me.'

The Under-Secretary of State for Scotland, H. Brown, replied that the Government was trying to create better opportunities for more anglers in Scotland. 'We are the first Government since publication of the Hunter Report to make a start in doing something positive about brown trout fishing in Scotland. I am sure that the Bill will command support from anglers when they understand better what we are after. I hope that it will command support from the House.'

The Bill was given a Third Reading by 99 votes to 16, the Opposition abstaining from voting. The Liberals voted with the Government. The 18 Members (including tellers) to vote against Third Reading comprised 11 Scottish National and 7 Labour.

Labour Members to vote against Third Reading:

Canavan, D.*	Sillars, J.[1]	Thorne, S.
Lambie, D.*	Thomas, R.	Wise, Mrs A.
Robertson, J.[1]		

HC Deb. 906, 1241–4
1975–6, No. 78.

[1] Members of the Scottish Labour Party, but still in receipt of the Labour whip.

RATING (CARAVAN SITES) BILL   [142]

Second Reading: 3 March 1976

The Under-Secretary of State for the Environment, G. Oakes, moved the Second Reading of the Bill, which was designed to amend the law concerning the valuation and rating of leisure caravans and caravan sites, providing that sites and individual caravans with their pitches could in future be valued and rated as one unit. For the Opposition, M. Morris indicated that, although critical of certain aspects of the measure, his side of the House would not resist it at that stage.

From the Conservative benches, a number of Members rose to oppose the Bill. M. Latham (C., Melton) thought the measure would create an extra burden for caravan owners, many of whom were elderly and of modest means. D. Mudd (C., Falmouth and Camborne) argued that it was premature and deficient. R. Moate (C., Faversham) felt that it would make the existing situation worse rather than better. 'It will certainly not improve the situation for site operators, and it may not ease the burdens of district valuers and local authorities generally. It will perpetuate burdens of caravan owners at a time when they face rapidly rising costs. This is a bad measure, and I regret that the Minister has chosen to go about the situation in this way.'

The Bill was given a Second Reading by 210 votes to 19, the Opposition abstaining from voting. The 21 Members (including tellers) to vote against comprised 11 Scottish National, 8 Conservative and 2 UUUC. Three Conservatives entered the Government lobby to vote for the Bill.

Conservatives to vote against Second Reading:

Brotherton, M.	Latham, M.	Mudd, D.
Clark, A.	Mills, P.	Taylor, R.
Fell, A.	Moate, R.	

Conservatives to vote for Second Reading:

Goodhart, P.	Gow, I.	Spence, J.

HC Deb. 906, 1383–6
1975–6, No. 79.

RACE RELATIONS BILL [143]

Second Reading: 4 March 1976

The Home Secretary, R. Jenkins, moved the Second Reading of the Bill. The Bill made several changes in the definition of 'discrimination', made discrimination unlawful in the fields of employment, training

and related matters, and, among other provisions, established a Race
Relations Commission. For the Opposition, W. Whitelaw announced
that, although they would seek to amend certain parts of the Bill in
committee, the Opposition would not divide the House on Second
Reading.

During the debate, R. Bell (C., Beaconsfield) rose to oppose the Bill.
He did not believe legislation should be used to outlaw discrimination,
and in particular opposed clause 69 of the Bill. It would, he said, make
it an offence to publish in a public place matter that was threatening,
abusive or insulting; the Bill proposed to eliminate the need for intent.
The clause 'will be the greatest infringement of freedom of speech or
writing since the days of religious persecution'. N. Budgen (C., Wolverhampton, South-West) and J. Stokes (C., Halesowen and Stourbridge)
also rose to speak against Second Reading.

The Bill was given a Second Reading by 132 votes to 8, with the
Opposition abstaining from voting. The 10 Members (including tellers)
to vote against Second Reading comprised 6 Conservative, 3 UUUC
and 1 Labour Member who appears to have voted in both lobbies by
mistake.

Conservatives to vote against Second Reading:

Bell, R.*	Ridley, N.	Stokes, J.
Budgen, N.	Stanbrook, I.*	Winterton, N.

HC Deb. 906, 1667–70
1975–6, No. 81.

PETROL (LEAD CONTENT)   [144]

4 March 1976

The Minister of State for the Environment, D. Howell, moved a motion
to take note of the proposals for EEC Directives for limiting the lead
content of petrol and for biological and air quality standards for lead
as contained in documents R/3113/73 and R/1150/75, and the outcome
of the Government review of lead in petrol.

Mrs J. Butler (Lab., Wood Green) moved an amendment to add at
the end of the motion: 'accepts the principle of reducing the maximum
lead content of petrol to 0.40 grams per litre as proposed by the EEC;
and, whilst recognizing that this will have an adverse effect on the United
Kingdom balance of payments, nevertheless calls on Her Majesty's

Government to take appropriate steps to achieve this aim by staged reductions'.

In moving the motion, the Minister indicated his support for the amendment, and advised the House to accept it. From the backbenches, A. Bates (Lab., Bebington and Ellesmere Port) argued that there was no serious evidence that they ought to go ahead with the proposed level (0.4 grams per litre), and indicated his intention to divide the House.

The amendment was taken to a division, in which voting was 20 votes for to 6 against, with the Government whips on in support of it. The Opposition abstained from voting. The 8 Members (including tellers) to oppose the amendment comprised 5 Conservative and 3 Labour.

Conservatives to vote against the amendment:

Cockcroft, J.   Goodlad, A.*   Winterton, N.
Davies, J.   Skeet, T.

Labour Members to vote against the amendment:

Bates, A.*   Dunwoody, Mrs G.   Taylor, Mrs A.

HC Deb. 906, 1699–700
1975–6, No. 82.

40 Members not having taken part in the division, the Question was not decided, and the business under consideration stood over until the next sitting.

The motion and the amendment were subsequently approved without a division on 5 April 1976. *HC Deb.* 909, c. 165–93.

PUBLIC EXPENDITURE   [145]

Supply: 9/10 March 1976

The Chancellor of the Exchequer, D. Healey, moved: 'That this House, in rejecting the demand for massive and immediate cuts in public expenditure which would increase both unemployment and the cost of living, recognizes the need to ensure that manufacturing industry can take full advantage of the upturn in world trade by levelling off total public expenditure from April 1977 while keeping under continuous review the priority between programmes.'

The two-day debate provided the opportunity to debate the Government's Expenditure White Paper, containing the Government's proposed spending limits, and during the debate a number of Labour backbenchers rose to oppose the Government's proposals. B. Sedgemore (Lab., Luton, West) declared that what was needed was to introduce planned reflation behind wide-ranging but selective import controls. Miss J. Lestor (Lab., Eton & Slough) argued that the Government had failed to make its policies live up to the commitments on education in the party's manifesto. J. Garrett (Lab., Norwich, South) declared that the Government had got its priorities all wrong. 'I trust that Labour Members and the Labour movement in the country will fight to see that the cuts in education expenditure are restored.' E. Heffer (Lab., Liverpool, Walton) claimed that the Government approach to the country's economic problems was 'the traditional Treasury and Tory answer to the problem'; he thought it might not be a bad thing if the Government lost the White Paper, because it would then have to come back with other projects. D. Hoyle (Lab., Nelson and Colne) thought the White Paper would mean a real cut in the standard of living for many who supported the Government; he thought the Government was setting out on the wrong road. S. Thorne (Lab., Preston, South) argued that the Government was pursuing 'Tory policies', and it was because of that that his constituency party rejected them, 'as I shall reject them in the vote tonight'.

An Opposition amendment to the Government motion was negatived by 304 votes to 274, with no cross-votes.

The Government motion was then put, and *negatived* by 284 votes to to 256, *a majority against the Government of 28*. Two Labour Members cross-voted to oppose the motion, and a further 37 abstained from voting.[1]

Labour Members to vote against the motion:

Robertson, J.   Sillars, J.

HC Deb. 907, 561–6
1975–6, No. 84.

Both Members were Scottish Labour Party Members (the breakaway party formed by Mr Sillars) but were still in receipt of the Labour whip.

The following evening, in consequence of the defeat, the Government sought and obtained a vote of confidence (on an adjournment motion) by 297 votes to 280. *HC Deb.* 907, c. 751–8. See also Philip Norton, 'The Government Defeat: 10 March 1976', *The Parliamentarian*, LVII (3), pp. 174–5.

¹ The 37 abstainers were: F. Allaun, J. Ashton, R. Atkins, N. Atkinson, A. Bennett, S. Bidwell, J. Callaghan, D. Canavan, Mrs M. Colquhoun, R. Cook, R. Cryer, G. Edge, M. Flannery, T. Fletcher, E. Heffer, D. Hoyle, R. Kerr, N. Kinnock, D. Lambie, A. Latham, J. Lee, Miss J. Lestor, T. Litterick, E. Loyden, Miss J. Maynard, I. Mikardo, M. Miller, S. Newens, Miss J. Richardson, G. Rodgers, B. Sedgemore, H. Selby, Mrs R. Short, D. Skinner, R. Thomas, S. Thorne and Mrs A. Wise.

LOCAL LOANS (INCREASE OF LIMIT) [146]

Prayer: 15 March 1976

For the Government, the Minister of State at the Treasury, D. Davies, moved: 'That the Local Loans (Increase of Limit) Order 1976, a draft which was laid before the House on 18th February, be approved.'

The order increased by £2,000 million the amount available to the Public Works Loan Commissioners for lending to local authorities and other eligible authorities.

The prayer was carried by 111 votes to 7, with the Opposition abstaining apparently from voting.¹ The 9 Members (including tellers) to vote against comprised 8 Conservative and 1 UUUC.

Conservatives to vote against the prayer:

Clark, A.	Gow, I.*	Rees, P.
Cooke, R.	Lawson, N.*	Tebbit, N.
Dodsworth, G.	Morrison, P.	

HC Deb. 907, 1091–2
1975–6, No. 87.

¹ The Opposition Front Bench spokesman to take part in the debate, J. Nott, did not participate in the division, having made an interogatory speech without saying whether the Opposition would support or oppose the order.

CIVIL AND DEFENCE ESTIMATES, [147]
SUPPLEMENTARY ESTIMATES, 1975–76

Supply: 17 March 1976

Civil and Defence Estimates, Supplementary Estimates, 1975–76

The Financial Secretary to the Treasury, R. Sheldon, moved formally: 'That a further Supplementary sum not exceeding

£951,518,000 be granted to Her Majesty out of the Consolidated Fund, to defray the charge which will come in course of payment during the year ending on 31st March 1976, for expenditure on Civil and Defence Services, as set out in House of Commons Papers Nos. 173, 174, 238 and 239.'

The Liberals divided the House on the motion. It was carried by 188 votes to 19[1] with the Opposition abstaining from voting. The 21 Members (including tellers) to oppose the supplementary estimate comprised 11 Liberal, 8 Scottish National, 1 Plaid Cymru and 1 UUUC. 6 Conservatives entered the Government lobby to vote for the estimates.

Conservatives to vote for the supplementary estimate:

Glyn, A.	Loveridge, J.	Page, R. G.
Gow, I.	Mills, P.	Winterton, N.

HC Deb. 907, 1341–4
1975–6, No. 90.

[1] *Hansard* records the number as 20 but lists only 19 names.

RATING (CARAVAN SITES) BILL [148]

Report: 29 March 1976

New Clause 1 (Information for caravanners about rating of caravan sites mentioned in section 1)

Conservative new clause to provide that if a valuation officer altered the valuation list under section 1(1) of the Bill so as to include an area of a caravan site as a single hereditament, he would send information relevant to this (name of site, number of pitches, rateable value, etc.) to each occupier of a pitch for a leisure caravan within the area so included.

The new clause was opposed by the Government and carried to a division. Voting on the clause was 32 votes against to 2 for, with the Opposition abstaining. The Government lobby comprised solely Labour Members. The 4 Members (including tellers) to support the clause comprised 3 Conservative and 1 Labour.

Conservatives to vote for the clause:

Clark, K.*	Latham, M.*	Mudd, D.

Labour Member to vote for the clause:

Whitehead, P.

HC Deb. 908, 1065–6
1975–6, No. 100.

Forty Members not having taken part in the division the Question was not decided, and the business stood over until the next sitting.

RATING (CARAVAN SITES) BILL [149]

Third Reading: 31 March 1976

A number of Opposition Members divided the House on the Third Reading of the Bill, though the Opposition abstained from voting.
The Bill was given a Third Reading by 100 votes to 10. The 12 Members (including tellers) to vote against comprised 8 Conservative, 3 Liberal and 1 Scottish National. 1 Conservative entered the Government lobby to vote for Third Reading.

Conservative Members to vote against Third Reading:

Bottomley, P.   Lawson, N.   Ridley, N.
Fairgrieve, R.   Moate, R.*   Shaw, G.
Latham, M.   Mudd, D.*

Conservative to vote for Third Reading:

Madel, D.

HC Deb. 908, 1509–12
1975–6, No. 103.

BUDGET RESOLUTIONS AND ECONOMIC [150]
SITUATION

Ways and Means: 12 April 1976

Following the Chancellor of the Exchequer's Budget speech, the Ways and Means resolutions on which the Finance Bill would be brought in were put.

On the resolution (*Spirits*), to increase the rates of duty specified in section 9 of the 1975 Finance (No. 2) Act from £22.0900 to £22.1650 per proof gallon to £24.6300 and £24.7050 per gallon respectively, the Scottish National Members divided the House.

The resolution was approved by 295 votes to 19, with the Opposition abstaining from voting. The 21 Members (including tellers) to vote against the resolution comprised 11 Scottish National, 6 Conservative, 1 Labour, 1 English National Party Member,[1] 1 UUUC and 1 Liberal.

Conservatives to vote against the resolution:

Brotherton, M.	Gray, H.	Maxwell-Hyslop, R.
Gilmour, Sir J.	Hutchison, M. C.	Mudd, D.

Labour Member to vote against the resolution:

Sillars, J.[2]

HC Deb. 909, 1109–12
1975–6, No. 109.

[1] J. Stonehouse. See above: 26 February 1976.
[2] Mr Sillars was the founder member of the breakaway Scottish Labour Party, but was still in receipt of the Labour whip. He subsequently resigned the whip (along with J. Robertson, the other SLP Member) in July 1976.

BUDGET RESOLUTIONS AND ECONOMIC   **[151]**
SITUATION

Ways and Means: 12 April 1976

Following the Chancellor of the Exchequer's Budget speech, the Ways and Means resolutions on which the Finance Bill would be brought in were put.

On the resolution (*Hydrocarbon Oil Etc.*) that as from 6.00 p.m. on 9 April 1976 the rate of duty specified in section 11 of the 1975 Finance (No. 2) Act would be increased from £0.2250 a gallon to £0.3000, the Scottish National Members divided the House.

The resolution was carried by 284 votes to 22 with the Opposition abstaining from voting. The 24 Members (including tellers) to oppose the resolution comprised 11 Scottish National, 7 Liberal, 3 Plaid Cymru, 2 Conservative and 1 UUUC.

Conservatives to vote against the resolution:

Hicks, R.   Mudd, D.

HC Deb. 909, 1111-16
1975-6, No. 110.

AGRICULTURE (MISCELLANEOUS PROVISIONS) BILL [152]

Report: 10 May 1976

Clause 17 (Application of following sections of Part II)

Dr C. Phipps (Lab., Dudley, West) moved an amendment to provide that a family tenancy of a tenant farm should last for thirty years since the first occasion when there died a tenant.

The amendment was opposed by both Government and Opposition, and negatived by 226 votes to 56, the Opposition voting with the Government. The 228 Members (including tellers) in the Government lobby comprised 119 Conservative, 108 Labour and 1 Liberal. The 58 Members (including tellers) to support the amendment comprised 42 Labour, 5 Liberal, 3 Plaid Cymru, 1 Conservative, and 7 Conservatives who voted in both lobbies, entering this lobby in error.[1]

Labour Members to vote for the amendment:

Bennett, A.	Heffer, E.	Roderick, C.
Buchan, N.	Hughes, R.	Rodgers, G.
Callaghan, J.	Hughes, R. J.	Rooker, J.
Clemitson, I.	Kilroy-Silk, R.	Selby, H.
Colquhoun, Mrs M.	Lambie, D.	Skinner, D.
Cryer, R.*	Lipton, M.	Spriggs, L.
Davies, B.	Litterick, T.	Taylor, Mrs A.
Edge, G.	Lyon, A.	Thomas, R.
Edwards, R.	Madden, N.	Thorne, S.
Evans, F.	Maynard, Miss J.	Watkinson, J.
Fernyhough, E.	Noble, M.	Wilson, W.
Forrester, J.	Ovenden, J.	Wise, Mrs A.
George, B.	Phipps, C.*	Woof, R.
Hart, Mrs J.	Richardson, Miss J.	Young, D.

Conservative to vote for the amendment:

Gow, I.[2]

HC Deb. 911, 171–6
1975–6, No. 127.

[1] Confirmed to the author by one of those involved.
[2] The division list appears to be correct in recording Mr Gow's vote, but he himself does not recollect the event: he suspects his vote was cast in error rather than by design. I. Gow MP to author.

NATIONAL FREIGHT CORPORATION   [153]

12 May 1976

In order to force a debate on the subject, the Opposition tabled a motion, 'That this House takes note of the National Freight Corporation (Commencing Capital Debt) Order 1976 (S.I., 1976, No. 329).'

At the end of the debate, the Government whips were put on in support of the motion, while the Opposition abstained from voting. The motion was carried by 88 votes to 15. The Government lobby comprised solely Labour Members. The 17 Members (including tellers) to oppose the motion comprised 9 Conservative, 6 Scottish National and 2 Liberal.

Conservatives to vote against the motion:

Douglas-Hamilton, Lord J.   Moate, R.   Rost, P.
Gow, I.*   Rathbone, T.   Wall, P.
Marten, N.   Ridley, N.*   Winterton, N.

HC Deb. 911, 611–12
1975–6, No. 132.

EUROPEAN ASSEMBLY (DIRECT ELECTIONS)   [154]

12 May 1976

After the House had approved a motion to establish a Select Committee to consider proposals for Direct Elections to the European Assembly, and one to appoint six named Members to it, D. Jay (Lab., Battersea, North) moved an amendment to add the name of E. Heffer (Lab., Liverpool, Walton) to the committee's membership. The amendment was discussed briefly in conjunction with another tabled by Mr Jay to add also the name of N. Marten (C., Banbury) to the committee's membership.

For the Government, the Minister of State for Foreign and Commonwealth Affairs opposed the amendments. He argued that it was not possible to appoint to the committee all those who were qualified to serve on it. The committee had to be of such a size which would enable it to work speedily.

(1) The amendment to appoint Mr Heffer to the committee was negatived by 76 votes to 25, with the Government whips on against it. The Opposition was not whipped, although the Opposition Front Bench spokesman had indicated his opposition to the amendment. The 78 Members (including tellers) in the Government lobby comprised 65 Labour, 10 Conservative and 3 Liberal. The 27 Members (including tellers) to support the amendment comprised 17 Labour, 5 Scottish National, 3 Conservative[1] and 2 UUUC.

Labour Members to vote for the amendment:

Buchan, N.	Hooley, F.*	Noble, M.
Cook, R.	Jay, D.	Robinson, G.
Cryer, R.	Lamond, J.	Rodgers, G.
English, M.	Loyden, E.	Spearing, N.
George, B.	Mackintosh, J.	Taylor, Mrs A.
Heffer, E.	Madden, M.*	

(2) The amendment to appoint Mr Marten to the committee was negatived by 67 votes to 27. The Government whips were on against it. The Government lobby comprised solely Labour Members. The 29 Members (including tellers) to support the amendment comprised 16 Labour, 5 Scottish National, 3 Conservative,[2] 3 Liberal and 2 UUUC.

Labour Members to vote for the amendment:

Buchan, N.	Hooley, F.*	Noble, M.
Cook, R.	Jay, D.	Robinson, G.
Cryer, R.	Lamond, J.	Rodgers, G.
English, M.	Loyden, E.	Spearing, N.
George, B.	Madden, M.*	Taylor, Mrs A.
Heffer, E.		

HC Deb. 911, 631–4
1975–6, Nos. 133 and 134.

[1] The three Conservatives to vote for the amendment were: N. Marten, R. Moate and N. Winterton.
[2] The three Conservatives were again N. Marten, R. Moate and N. Winterton.

FINANCE BILL [155]

Committee: 13 May 1976

Clause 26 (Alteration of Personal Reliefs)

G. Dodsworth (C., Hertfordshire, South-West) moved an amendment to increase the figure for child allowances contained in the clause.

The amendment was opposed by the Government and taken to a division. The Opposition abstained from voting. The Government lobby comprised solely Labour Members. The 24 Members (including tellers) to support the amendment comprised 9 Scottish National, 9 Liberal, 3 Conservative, 1 Plaid Cymru, 1 UUUC and 1 English National Party Member (J. Stonehouse).

Conservatives to vote for the amendment:

Dodsworth, G.   Fell, A.   Fookes, Miss J.

HC Deb. 911, 719–20
1975–6, No. 136.

POLICE BILL [156]

Report: 20 May 1976

New Clause 1 (Disciplinary charges in criminal cases)

After the clause had been read a second time, a Conservative amendment was moved to provide that a disciplinary charge would not be preferred against a member of the police force (or, if already preferred, would be withdrawn) if the charge was in substance the same as a possible criminal charge on which the Director of Public Prosecutions had decided, on evidential grounds, not to prosecute.

The Government opposed the amendment, and it was negatived on a party vote by 140 votes to 102. 1 Labour Member cross-voted to support the amendment.

Labour Member to support the amendment:

Cunningham, G.

HC Deb. 911, 1763–6
1975–6, No. 149.

POLICE BILL [157]

Report: 20 May 1976

New Clause 3 (Complaints against the police of a person accused or convicted of a criminal offence)

P. Whitehead (Lab., Derby, North) moved the new clause, which laid down the procedure to be followed by the Police Complaints Board in the event of a complaint made by or on behalf of an accused or convicted person about the conduct of a police officer in relation to the former's arrest, charge or prosecution.

For the Government, the Parliamentary Secretary to the Law Officers' Department, A. Davidson, opposed the clause. He contended that there were serious practical difficulties involved in the provisions contained in the clause. He felt it provided a wrong role for the Board, and that it was inappropriate that, except in certain cases, complaints of the nature involved should precede the trial of a related criminal charge.

The clause was negatived by 68 votes to 28, with the Opposition abstaining from voting. The 70 Members (including tellers) in the Government lobby comprised 67 Labour and 3 Liberal. The 30 Members (including tellers) to support the clause were all Labour Members.

Labour Members to vote for the clause:

Bennett, A.*	Jenkins, H.	Richardson, Miss J.
Cook, R.	Kilroy-Silk, R.	Roberts, G.
Corbett, R.	Lamond, J.	Rooker, J.
Cryer, R.	Latham, A.	Sedgemore, B.
Davies, B.	Lestor, Miss J.	Silverman, J.
Douglas-Mann, B.	Madden, M.	Skinner, D.
Evans, J.	Mikardo, I.	Taylor, Mrs A.
Garrett, J.	Noble, M.	Thomas, R.
Hayman, Mrs H.	Parry, R.	Whitehead, P.
Hooley, F.*	Price, C.	Wise, Mrs A.

HC Deb. 911, 1817–18
1975–6, No. 150.

BUSINESS OF THE HOUSE [158]

26 May 1976

At 10.00 p.m., during the Second Reading debate of the Public Lending Right Bill, the Government moved the procedural exemption motion to allow Government business, though opposed, to be proceeded with until any hour.

A number of Conservative backbenchers divided the House. The motion was carried by 115 votes to 12, with the Opposition abstaining from voting. The 14 Members (including tellers) to oppose the motion were all Conservatives.

Conservatives to vote against the motion:

Bottomley, P.	Moate, R.*	Taylor, E.
Clark, A.	Monro, H.	Tebbit, N.
Clarke, K.	Mudd, D.	Walder, D.
Durant, T.	Rippon, G.	Winterton, N.
Lawrence, I.	Sproat, I.*	

HC Deb. 912, 567–70
1975–6, No. 155.

EDUCATION [159]

10 June 1976

During a late-night sitting, the Secretary of State for Education and Science, F. Mulley, moved a motion to note with approval the Resolution of the Council and of the Ministers of Education within the Council comprising an action programme in the field of education (Commission Document R/263/76) and the draft directive on the education of the children of migrant workers (Commission Document No. R/2085/75), and also to urge the Government to ensure that any instrument adopted by the Council on that subject did not impose unacceptable obligations on those responsible for the provision of education in this country.

An amendment to the motion to make it clear that it took note only of the second document, and not with approval, was accepted; the Minister explained that such words had been left out due to an error.

From the Labour backbenches, N. Spearing (Lab., Newham, South) voiced his objections to both documents under discussion, and to the short amount of time allowed to debate them. D. Jay (Lab., Battersea, North) thought that the proposals involved were *ultra vires* of the Treaty of Rome. He did not approve of either the Resolution or the directive.

At 1.40 a.m. the motion was put and taken to a division, with the Government whips on and the Opposition abstaining from voting. Voting was 6 votes for to 1 against. The 8 Members (including tellers) to support the motion were all Labour Members, including 4 whips and 3 Ministers. The 3 Members (including tellers) to oppose the motion comprised 2 Labour and 1 UUUC.

Labour Members to oppose the motion:

Jay, D.*   Spearing, N.*

HC Deb. 912, 1879–80
1975–6, No. 174.

40 Members not having taken part in the division, the Question was not decided, and the business stood over until the next sitting of the House.

FAIR EMPLOYMENT (NORTHERN IRELAND) BILL   [160]

Report: 11 June 1976

Clause 4 (The Fair Employment Appeals Board)

H. McCusker (UUUC, Armagh) moved an amendment to delete clause 4, and related amendments, designed to do away with the proposed Appeals Board.

The Government opposed the amendment, and it was negatived by 84 votes to 6, with the Opposition abstaining from voting. The 8 Members (including tellers) to support the amendment were all UUUC Members. 1 Conservative Member entered the Government lobby to oppose the amendment.

Conservative to vote against the amendment:

Van Straubenzee, W.

HC Deb. 912, 1919–22
1975–6, No. 175.

FAIR EMPLOYMENT (NORTHERN IRELAND) BILL   [161]

Report: 11 June 1976

Schedule 4 (Conduct of investigations by the Agency)

H. McCusker (UUUC, Armagh) moved an amendment to provide that no person could be compelled to disclose to the Agency the religious beliefs of other persons.

The Minister of State for Northern Ireland, R. Moyle, opposed the amendment. It would, he argued, unduly restrict the ability of the Fair Employment Agency to conduct its functions.

The amendment was negatived by 41 votes to 7, with the Opposition abstaining from voting. The 9 Members (including tellers) to support the amendment comprised 6 UUUC, 2 Conservative and 1 English National Party Member. 1 Conservative entered the Government lobby to oppose the amendment.

Conservatives to vote for the amendment:

Stanbrook, I.   Steen, A.

Conservative to vote against the amendment:

Van Straubenzee, W.

HC Deb. 912, 2001–2
1975–6, No. 176.

ARMED FORCES (RE-COMMITTED) BILL   [162]

Committee: 16 June 1976

Clause 5 (Increased powers of summary punishment)

On the motion 'That the clause stand part of the Bill', a number of Labour Members rose to oppose it. R. Thomas (Lab., Bristol, North-West) objected to the fact that, under the clause, a commanding officer could unilaterally put someone in detention for 60 days without the latter having being involved in the procedure and having no right of appeal or representation. G. Roberts (Lab., Cannock) complained that the clause dealt 'with a closed procedure in which justice is dispensed arbitrarily by a god-like figure'. J. Ashton (Lab., Bassetlaw) felt that members of the armed forces should have a right of appeal to an outside body.

For the Government, the Under-Secretary of State for Defence for the Royal Air Force, J. Wellbeloved, contended that a majority of men in the armed services would welcome the proposals which provided that, for swifter justice, summary procedures were to be used in a number of cases where courts-martial were then the rule, and where the relatively slower and cumbersome procedure of the latter was seen to be unnecessarily long drawn out and heavy handed from the point of view of the serviceman. 'The Government would not have put forward these proposals for increased powers to be given to commanding officers if they had not been satisfied about the protection that will be given to the accused Service man.'

After further Labour Members had indicated dissatisfaction with the clause, the 'stand part' motion was divided upon and carried by 197 votes to 54, the Opposition voting with the Government. The 199 Members (including tellers) in the Government lobby comprised 145 Labour, 46 Conservative, 8 Liberal and 1 UUUC. The 56 Members (including tellers) to oppose the clause comprised 55 Labour and 1 Plaid Cymru.

Labour Members to vote against the clause:

Allaun, F.	Hart, Mrs J.	Ovenden, J.
Ashton, J.	Heffer, E.	Parry, R.
Atkinson, N.	Hooley, F.	Pavitt, L.
Bennett, A.	Hoyle, D.	Prescott, J.
Bidwell, S.	Hughes, R.	Richardson, Miss J.*
Buchan, N.	Kinnock, N.	Roberts, G.
Canavan, D.	Lamond, J.	Roderick, C.
Clemitson, I.	Latham, A.	Rodgers, G.
Cook, R.	Lestor, Miss J.	Rooker, J.
Corbett, R.	Litterick, T.	Sedgemore, B.
Cryer, R.	Loyden, E.	Skinner, D.
Davies, B.	McNamara, K.	Thomas, R.
Evans, I.	Madden, M.	Thorne, S.*
Evans, J.	Maynard, Miss J.	Ward, M.
Fernyhough, E.	Mendelson, J.	Watkins, D.
Flannery, M.	Mikardo, I.	Whitehead, P.
Garrett, J.	Newens, S.	Wise, Mrs A.
George, B.	Noble, M.	Young, D.
Grocott, B.		

HC Deb. 913, 689–92
1975–6, No. 186.

WEIGHTS AND MEASURES (SALE OF WINE)   [163]

Prayer: 21 June 1976

The Minister of State, Department of Prices and Consumer Protection, J. Fraser, moved: 'That the Weights and Measures (Sale of Wine) Order 1976, a draft of which was laid before this House on 8th June, be approved.'

The order, which prescribed a range of quantities for wine that was sold in carafes and for the information to be displayed, was criticized from both the Opposition Front and Back benches, and at 1.26 a.m. was taken to a division by Conservative Members.

The order was carried by 174 votes to 32, with the Government whips on. The Opposition lobby was apparently unwhipped; 30 Conservatives voted against[1] and 1 voted for.[2] 1 Labour Member entered the Conservative lobby to oppose the order.

Labour Member to vote against the order:

Skinner, D.

HC Deb. 913, 1307–10
1975–6, No. 189.

[1] The 30 were: R. Adley*, R. Banks, P. Bottomley, A. Bowden, L. Brittan, M. Brotherton, R. Cooke, T. Durant, A. Glyn, V. Goodhew, Sir R. Gower, H. Gray, M. Grylls, K. Hampson, J. Hannam, P. Hawkins, R. Hicks*, I. Lawrence, N. Marten, D. Mitchell, R. Moate, T. Rathbone, Sir B. Rhys Williams, M. Roberts, G. Shaw, T. Skeet, A. Steen, E. Taylor, J. Wiggin, and N. Winterton.
[2] J. Ridsdale.

BUSINESS OF THE HOUSE   [164]

5 July 1976

At 10.00 p.m. a Government whip moved the procedural exemption motion to allow the Public Lending Rights Bill [Lords] to be proceeded with, though opposed, until any hour at that day's sitting.

The motion was divided upon and carried by 68 votes to 18, with the whips applied on the Government side of the House. The 70 Members (including tellers) in the Government lobby comprised 65 Labour, 4 Liberal and, according to the division lists, 1 Conservative (R. Mawby). The 20 Members (including tellers) to oppose the motion comprised 19 Conservatives and 1 Labour Member.

Labour Member to oppose the motion:

English, M.*

HC Deb. 914, 1093–4
1975–6, No. 218.

PUBLIC LENDING RIGHTS BILL [165]

Second Reading: 5 July 1976

At 11.55 p.m., after nearly two hours' debate on the Second Reading of the Bill (resumed from debate adjourned on 26 May), the Government moved that the debate be adjourned.

The Opposition opposed the motion. The motion was carried by 30 votes to 20, with the whips applied on both sides of the House. The 32 Members (including tellers) in the Government lobby comprised 27 Labour and 5 Liberal. The 22 Members (including tellers) in the Opposition lobby comprised 18 Conservative and 4 Labour.

Labour Members to vote against adjournment:

Faulds, A.   Jeger, Mrs L.   Whitehead, P.
Hughes, R.

HC Deb. 914, 1127–30
975–6, No. 219.

PAY AND PRICES POLICY [166]

6/7 July 1976

The Chancellor of the Exchequer, D. Healey, moved 'That this House takes note of the White Paper entitled "The Attack on Inflation, The Second Year" (Command Paper No. 6507) and "Modifications to the Prices Code" (Command Paper No. 6540).'

After a two-day debate, an Opposition amendment to the motion was negatived by 286 votes to 251 with no dissenting votes by Members of either main party.

The Government motion was then carried by 279 votes to 13, the Opposition abstaining from voting. The 15 Members (including tellers) to oppose the motion comprised 8 Scottish National, 3 Plaid Cymru, 2 Labour, 1 Conservative and 1 UUUC.

Labour Members to vote against the motion:

Robertson, J.   Sillars, J.

Conservative to vote against the motion:

Stanbrook, I.

HC Deb. 914, 1509–12
1975–6, No. 221.

Mr Robertson and Mr Sillars were the two Members of the break-away Scottish Labour Party, but still in receipt of the Labour whip. They both resigned the Labour whip on 26 July 1976. *The Times*, 27 July 1978.

BUSINESS OF THE HOUSE   [167]

8 July 1976

At 10.00 p.m. a Government whip moved the procedural exemption motion to allow the Race Relations Bill, though opposed, to be proceeded with at that day's sitting until any hour.

A number of Conservative backbenchers forced the motion to a division, in which the Opposition Front Bench abstained from voting. The motion was carried by 90 votes to 41. The 43 Members (including tellers) to oppose the motion comprised 40 Conservative, 2 UUUC and 1 Liberal.

Conservatives to vote against the motion:

Bell, R.	Gow, I.	Neubert, M.
Bennett, Sir F.	Hannam, J.	Page, J.
Biggs-Davison, J.	Hawkins, P.	Page, R. G.
Boscawen, R.	Hayhoe, B.	Sainsbury, T.
Bowden, A.	Holland, P.	Sims, R.
Brotherton, M.*	Knight, Mrs J.	Spicer, M.
Budgen, N.*	Langford-Holt, Sir J.	Stanbrook, I.
Bulmer, E.	Lawrence, I.	Stokes, J.
Burden, F.	Lawson, N.	Taylor, R.
Cope, J.	Lloyd, I.	Tebbit, N.

Dean, P.
Fletcher-Cooke, C.
Fraser, H.
Goodhew, V.

Maxwell-Hyslop, R.
Moate, R.
Morrison, C.

Viggers, P.
Wall, P.
Winterton, N.

HC Deb. 914, 1733–4
1975–6, No. 224.

RACE RELATIONS BILL [168]

Report: 8 July 1976

Clause 12 (Qualifying bodies)

R. Bell (C., Beaconsfield) moved an amendment to restrict the qualifying bodies under the clause to those that could confer authorization or qualifications needed for engagement in a particular profession and not to encompass (as the clause provided for) those that provided qualifications which merely facilitated engagement in a particular profession or trade. (Under the clause, discrimination by such bodies was declared unlawful.)

The Government opposed the amendment, and it was negatived by 84 votes to 23. The Opposition Front Bench spokesmen abstained from voting. The 25 Members (including tellers) to support the amendment comprised 23 Conservative and 2 UUUC.

Conservatives to vote for the amendment:

Bell, R.
Bennett, Sir F.
Boscawen, R.
Brotherton, M.
Budgen, N.
Bulmer, E.
Cope, J.
Fraser, H.

Goodhew, V.
Gow, I.
Hannam, J.
Lawrence, I.
Lawson, N.
Moate, R.
Morrison, C.
Neubert, M.

Page, J.
Stanbrook, I.*
Stokes, J.*
Tebbit, N.
Viggers, P.
Wall, P.
Winterton, N.

HC Deb. 914, 1759–60
1975–6, No. 225.

The division took place at 11.57 p.m.

RACE RELATIONS BILL [169]

Report: 8 July 1976

At 3.45 a.m., during an all-night sitting on the Bill, R. Bell (C., Beaconsfield) moved that further consideration of the Bill be adjourned.

The Home Secretary, R. Jenkins, opposed the motion, and for the Opposition W. Whitelaw announced that if the Government wished to go on with the Bill 'we are ready to do so'.

Conservative backbenchers divided the House on the motion, which was negatived by 78 votes to 13. The Opposition Front Bench abstained from voting. The 15 Members (including tellers) to vote for adjournment comprised 13 Conservative, 1 UUUC and 1 Liberal.

Conservatives to vote for adjournment:

Bell, R.	Gow, I.	Stanbrook, I.
Bennett, Sir F.	Hall-Davis, A.	Stokes, J.
Boscawen, R.	Lane, D.	Tebbit, N.
Budgen, N.*	Lawrence, I.	Winterton, N.
Fraser, H.		

HC Deb. 914, 1831–4
1975–6, No. 227.

RACE RELATIONS BILL [170]

Report: 8 July 1976

Clause 20 (Discrimination in provision of goods, facilities or services)

The clause provided that it was unlawful for anyone concerned with the provision (for payment or not) of goods, facilities and services to the public to discriminate against a person who sought to obtain or use those goods, facilities or services.

R. Bell (C., Beaconsfield) moved an amendment to delete 'or not' after 'payment', to restrict the clause to those goods, facilities and services provided to the public for payment.

The amendment was opposed by the Government and negatived by 77 votes to 10.[1] The Opposition Front Bench abstained from voting. The 12 Members (including tellers) to support the amendment comprised 11 Conservative and 1 UUUC.

Conservatives to vote for the amendment:

Bell, R.   Budgen, N.   Stokes, J.
Bennett, Sir F.   Fraser, H.   Tebbit, N.
Biffen, J.   Page, J.*   Winterton, N.
Boscawen, R.   Stanbrook, I.*

HC Deb. 914, 1855–6
1975–6, No. 228.

¹ *Hansard* records the number as 9 voting for, but lists 10 names.

RACE RELATIONS BILL   [171]

Report: 8 July 1976

Clause 43 (Establishment and duties of Commission [S.53])

For the Opposition, M. Alison moved an amendment to delete the name of the Commission for Racial Equality and replace it with the name of the Equal Rights Commission.

During discussion on the amendment, E. Lyons (Lab., Bradford, West) indicated his dislike with the name of the Commission for Racial Equality. He felt the reference to 'racial' should be left out of the title. He felt his proposal of 'Equal Status Commission' or the title proposed by the Opposition would have advantages over that proposed by the Government.

For the Government, the Under-Secretary of State for Employment, J. Grant, argued that the Government's proposed name was better than those suggested by others. He hoped the House would reject the amendment.

The amendment was negatived on a whipped party vote by 71 votes to 28. 2 Labour Members cross-voted to support the amendment.

Labour Members to vote for the amendment:

Lyons, E.   Short, Mrs R.

HC Deb. 914, 1935–6
1975–6, No. 230.

The division took place at 11.05 a.m. following an all-night sitting.

RACE RELATIONS BILL [172]

Third Reading: 8 July 1976

The Home Secretary, R. Jenkins, moved the Third Reading of the Bill. For the Opposition, W. Whitelaw announced that his side of the House would not vote against it.

From the Conservative backbenches, R. Bell (C., Beaconsfield) rose to oppose Third Reading, and indicated his intention to divide the House. J. Stokes (C., Halesowen and Stourbridge) attacked the Bill as striking at the freedom of the individual and argued that it would diminish respect for the rule of law. P. Wall (C., Haltemprice) expressed the view that the Bill was bad and would not help race relations.

The Bill was given a Third Reading by 82 votes to 3, with the Opposition abstaining from voting. The 84 Members (including tellers) in the Government lobby comprised 81 Labour, 2 Liberal and 1 SNP. The 5 Members (including tellers) to oppose Third Reading comprised 4 Conservative and 1 UUUC.

Conservatives to vote against Third Reading:

Bell, R.*   Page, J.*   Stokes, J.
Brotherton, M.

HC Deb. 914, 1967–8
1975–6, No. 232.

The division took place at 1.00 p.m. after an all-night sitting, Report Stage having commenced at 4.17 p.m. the previous afternoon.

EUROPEAN PARLIAMENT (DIRECT ELECTIONS) [173]

12 July 1976

On a motion for adjournment, the House debated the Report of the Select Committee on Direct Elections to the European Parliament.

During the debate, a number of backbenchers on both sides of the House rose to object to the Report being discussed on an adjournment motion and to oppose the Committee's Report. N. Spearing (Lab., Newham, South) argued that there should be a full debate on a substantive motion with the opportunity for amendments. Until then, it should be made clear that the House had not reached a decision on the issue of direct elections. D. Jay (Lab., Battersea, North) claimed that the Select Committee failed to weigh the arguments for and against direct elections. There was no legal obligation under the Rome Treaty to introduce direct elections, and another directly-elected Parliament would blur the responsibility of Ministers. Mrs G. Dunwoody (Lab., Crewe) declared that she believed strongly that they should not accept either the principle of direct elections or the machinery that was being thrust upon them. 'I only wish that there were a motion that we could vote against so that we could make it plain how strongly we believe that the sovereignty of this Parliament should not be challenged. It has survived 900 years because it is a democratic system, and it must be protected at all costs.' N. Marten (C., Banbury) expressed his disagreement with the Committee's Report. 'The Committee acted irresponsibly and was the lackey of the Government. It bent to the Government's will which a Select Committee should never do.'

Just before 10.00 o'clock, when the motion for adjournment would lapse, Mr Jay moved that the Question be put.

The closure was opposed by the Government and, with the whips on, was negatived by 196 votes to 109. The Opposition abstained from voting. The 198 Members (including tellers) in the Government lobby comprised 189 Labour, 6 Liberal and 3 Conservative. The 111 Members (including tellers) to support closure comprised 80 Labour, 22 Conservative, 6 Scottish National, 2 Plaid Cymru, and 1 UUUC.

Conservatives to vote against closure:

Drayson, B.	Grant, A.	Macfarlane, N.

Labour Members to vote for closure:

Ashton, J.	Hooley, F.	Newens, S.
Atkins, R.	Hoyle, D.	Noble, M.
Atkinson, N.	Hughes, R. J.	Orbach, M.
Bennett, A.	Jay, D.	Ovenden, J.
Buchan, N.	Jeger, Mrs L.	Parry, R.
Callaghan, J.	Kelley, R.	Pavitt, L.
Canavan, D.	Kerr, R.	Price, C.
Carmichael, N.	Kilroy-Silk, R.	Richardson, Miss J.
Castle, Mrs B.	Kinnock, N.	Roberts, G.
Colquhoun, Mrs M.	Lambie, D.	Rodgers, G.
Cook, R.	Lamond, J.	Rooker, J.
Corbett, R.	Latham, A.	Sedgemore, B.
Crowther, S.	Leadbitter, T.	Selby, H.

Cryer, R.
Cunningham, G.
Dean, J.
Dunwoody, Mrs G.
Evans, I.
Evans, J.
Flannery, M.
Fletcher, T.
Forrester, J.
George, B.
Gould, B.
Hart, Mrs J.
Hatton, F.
Heffer, E.

Lee, J.
Lewis, A.*
Lewis, R.
Lipton, M.
Litterick, T.
McNamara, K.
Madden, M.
Marshall, J.
Maynard, Miss J.
Mendelson, J.
Mikardo, I.
Miller, M.
Miller, Mrs M.
Molloy, W.

Short, Mrs R.
Sillars, J.[1]
Silverman, J.
Skinner, D.
Swain, T.
Thomas, R.*
Thorne, S.
Tuck, R.
Urwin, T.
Wilson, W.
Wise, Mrs A.
Woof, R.
Young, D.

Conservatives to vote for closure:

Bell, R.
Body, R.
Boyson, R.
Brotherton, M.
Clark, A.
Cormack, P.
Douglas-Hamilton, Lord J.
Durant, T.

Fell, A.
Gow, I.
Gray, H.
Hutchison, M. C.
Irving, C.
Lewis, K.
McNair-Wilson, M.

Marten, N.
Moate, R.
More, J.
Smith, D.
Taylor, E.
Taylor, R.
Winterton, N.

HC Deb. 915, 175–8
1975–6, No. 233.

It being after 10.00 p.m., and the closure not having been carried, the motion for adjournment lapsed without Question put.

[1] Mr Sillars, founder member of the Scottish Labour Party, resigned the Labour whip on 26 July 1976.

BUSINESS OF THE HOUSE [174]

12 July 1976

At 10.13 p.m., a Government whip moved the procedural exemption motion to allow Government business to be proceeded with at that day's sitting, though opposed, until any hour. (The main business involved was the Development Land Tax Bill and the Iron and Steel (Amendment) Bill.)

Conservative backbenchers forced the motion to a division, in which the Opposition Front Bench abstained from voting. The motion was carried by 280 votes to 70. The 72 members (including tellers) to oppose the motion comprised 64 Conservative, 6 SNP and 2 Plaid Cymru.

Conservatives to vote against the motion:

Bell, R.	Gower, Sir R.	More, J.
Body, R.	Griffiths, E.	Morrison, C.
Bottomley, P.	Hall, Sir J.	Newton, T.
Bowden, A.	Hannam, J.	Nott, J.
Brotherton, M.	Harvie Anderson, Miss B.	Osborn, J.
Budgen, N.	Hawkins, P.	Page, J.
Burden, F.	Hutchison, M. C.	Rathbone, T.
Clarke, K.	Irving, C.	Renton, T.
Clegg, W.	Kaberry, Sir D.	Shaw, G.
Cope, J.	Kellett-Bowman, Mrs E.	Shepherd, C.
Cordle, J.	Kershaw, A.	Sims, R.
Cormack, P.*	Knight, Mrs J.	Skeet, T.
Critchley, J.	Lane, D.	Smith, D.
Dodsworth, G.	Latham, M.	Spence, J.
Drayson, B.	Lawrence, I.	Sproat, I.
Durant, T.	Lloyd, I.	Stanbrook, I.
Fell, A.	McNair-Wilson, M.	Taylor, R.
Fletcher, A.*	Marshall, M.	Wakeham, J.
Fletcher-Cooke, C.	Maxwell-Hyslop, R.	Wall, P.
Gilmour, Sir J.	Mayhew, P.	Winterton, N.
Glyn, A.	Moate, R.	Young, Sir G.
Gow, I.		

HC Deb. 915, 179–82
1975–6, No. 234.

FINANCE BILL [175]

Report: 13 July 1976

New Clause 13 (War widows' pensions: 50 per cent exemption)

R. Kilroy-Silk (Lab., Ormskirk) moved the new clause, which provided that for the purposes of calculating taxable income the first 50 per cent of war widows' pensions would be exempt.

Mr Kilroy-Silk argued that the clause would constitute a small, moderate and very justifiable concession, particularly in view of the fact that that year for the first time the war widows in receipt of only a war widow's pension had come into the tax bracket. It affected only a relatively small group of elderly women. 'They are the forgotten women. The cost would be minimal.'

Various Members rose to support the clause (though a number rose to oppose it). Dr C. Phipps (Lab., Dudley, West) asked the House to consider war widows as a special case. Mrs A. Wise (Lab., Coventry, South-West) suggested it was quite reasonable and logical for the House to say that, since society had inflicted premature widowhood on the women involved, they should remit 50 per cent of the income tax on their pensions. That was little enough, and if there were amendments to help those widowed through industrial accidents she would have voted for those as well.

The Financial Secretary to the Treasury, R. Sheldon, opposed the clause. War widows' pensions had been increased, and he contended that the best way to assist those who had the least was through benefits and pensions rather than through tax allowances. 'The advantage of these tax allowances would have little or no effect on the number of people involved.'

The clause was negatived by 170 votes to 119, the Government lobby being whipped in opposition to it. The Opposition lobby was not whipped, but all voting Conservatives, with one exception,[1] entered the lobby to support it, as did 17 Labour Members.

Labour Members to vote for the clause:

Bidwell, S.	Lambie, D.	Phipps, C.*
Craigen, J.	Leadbitter, T.	Richardson, Miss J.
Edwards, R.	Marshall, J.	Rooker, J.*
Hooley, F.	Maynard, Miss J.	Sandelson, N.
Jackson, C.	Molloy, W.	Wise, Mrs A.
Kilroy-Silk, R.	Parry, R.	

HC Deb. 915, 619–22
1975–6, No. 243.

[1] The division list records H. Fraser (C., Stafford and Stone) as voting against.

FINANCE BILL [176]

Report: 14 July 1976

Clause 24 (Charge of Income Tax for 1976–7)

The Financial Secretary to the Treasury, R. Sheldon, moved an amendment to increase from £4,500 to £6,000 the level at which the higher rate of income tax would be applied.

R. Thomas (Lab., Bristol, North-West) argued that the Government should leave the position unchanged. He intended to vote against the amendment. He was supported in this view by Mrs A. Wise (Lab., Coventry, South-West), T. Litterick (Birmingham, Selly Oak) and J. Rooker (Lab., Birmingham, Perry Barr). 'We are being asked by the Government to give tax relief—extra money—to the better-off in our society', declared Mr Rooker. He was not prepared to accept the Government amendment.

The amendment was carried by 255 votes to 47, with the Opposition officially voting with the Government. The 257 Members (including tellers) in the Government lobby comprised 147 Labour, 91 Conservative, 9 Liberal, 9 SNP and 1 UUUC. The 49 Members (including tellers) to oppose the amendment comprised 46 Labour and 3 Plaid Cymru.

Labour Members to vote against the amendment:

Allaun, F.	Flannery, M.	Maynard, Miss J.
Ashton, J.	Garrett, J.	Molloy, W.
Atkins, R.	Grocott, B.	Ovenden, J.
Bennett, A.	Heffer, E.	Parry, R.
Bidwell, S.	Hoyle, D.	Prescott, J.
Boardman, H.	Hughes, R.	Richardson, Miss J.
Buchan, N.	Jeger, Mrs L.	Rodgers, G.
Canavan, D.	Kelley, R.	Rooker, J.
Carmichael, N.	Kilroy-Silk, R.	Rose, P.
Clemitson, I.	Lambie, D.	Selby, H.
Cook, R.	Lamond, J.	Short, Mrs R.
Corbett, R.	Latham, A.	Skinner, D.
Cryer, R.	Lee, J.	Thomas, R.*
Dean, J.	Litterick, T.*	Wise, Mrs A.
Douglas-Mann, B.	Loyden, E.	Young, D.
Fernyhough, E.		

HC Deb. 915, 747–50
1975–6, No. 246.

FINANCE BILL [177]

Report: 14 July 1976

Clause 29 (Alteration of personal reliefs)

D. Wigley (Plaid Cymru, Caernarvon) moved a manuscript amendment to increase the personal relief for married persons from the proposed £1,085 to £1,275.

The amendment was opposed by the Government and negatived by 191 votes to 24, the Opposition abstaining officially from voting. The 26 Members (including tellers) to support the amendment comprised 9 Scottish National, 8 Liberal, 3 Ulster Unionist, 3 Plaid Cymru and 2 Conservative.[1]

Conservatives to vote for the amendment:

Brotherton, M.   Winterton, N.

HC Deb. 915, 795-8
1975-6, No. 249.

[1] The *Hansard* division lists record one Conservative, P. Goodhart (C., Beckenham) as voting in the Government lobby, but his name appears to have been added to the list in error. The correct list appears in *Votes and Proceedings*.

KEARNEY AND TRECKER MARWIN LIMITED   [178]
(FINANCIAL ASSISTANCE)

19 July 1976

The Minister of State for Industry, A. Williams, moved 'That this House authorizes the Secretary of State to pay, or undertake to pay, sums not exceeding £1,900,000 by way of financial assistance, as to £1 million in respect of a loan to Kearney & Trecker Marwin Limited and as to £900,000 in respect of the acquisition of share capital in that Company, under section 8 of the Industry Act 1972, as amended by section 22 of, and Part I of Schedule 4 to, the Industry Act 1975.'

Although the Opposition was to abstain on the motion, one Conservative rose to support the motion. A. Bowden (C., Brighton, Kemptown) said he believed it was both in the national and local interest that the motion should be supported. R. Taylor (C., Croydon, North-West) expressed opposition to the motion. He did not regard the proposals as a fair deal for the taxpayer.

The motion was carried by 41 votes to 4, with the Opposition abstaining from voting. The 43 Members (including tellers) in the Government lobby comprised 41 Labour, 1 Conservative and 1 Scottish National. The 6 Members (including tellers) to oppose the motion comprised 3 Conservative, 2 Liberal and 1 Labour.

Conservative to vote for the motion:

Bowden, A.

Conservatives to vote against the motion:

Gow, I.*   Taylor, R.*   Winterton, N.

Labour Member to vote against the motion:

Skinner, D.

HC Deb. 915, 1463–4
1975–6, No. 258[1].

The division took place at 12.15 a.m.

[1] *Hansard* incorrectly lists it as division number 257.

RENT (AGRICULTURE) BILL   [179]

Report: 22 July 1976

Clause 6 (No statutory tenancy where landlord's interest belongs to Crown or to local authority, etc.)

Miss J. Maynard (Lab., Sheffield, Brightside) moved an amendment to provide that the provisions of the Bill would apply to the Crown, the Government and the City of London.

Miss Maynard argued that it was wrong that farm workers who worked for the Crown, the Government or the City of London should be excluded from the full provisions of the Bill. Apart from possible legal reasons, she could see no argument against the amendment. She was supported by W. Hamilton (Lab., Fife, Central), R. Cryer (Lab., Keighley) and B. Douglas-Mann (Lab., Merton, Mitcham and Mordern).

For the Government, the Under-Secretary of State for the Environment, E. Armstrong, opposed the amendment. He explained that the bodies in question were exempt from the Bill because they had, as far as possible, followed the precedents in the Rent Acts, from which the bodies were exempt. He assured the House, though, that there was no question of the bodies mentioned being given special status under the Bill. It was intended that agricultural workers housed and employed by those bodies should in practice enjoy the same benefits and protection of those who were covered by the Bill.

The amendment was negatived by 432 votes to 121, with the Opposition voting with the Government. The 434 Members (including tellers) in the Government lobby comprised 261 Conservative, 168 Labour and 5 UUUC. The 123 Members (including tellers) to support the amendment comprised 110 Labour, 12 Liberal and 1 Plaid Cymru.

Labour Members to vote for the amendment:

Abse, L.
Allaun, F.
Ashton, J.
Atkins, R.
Atkinson, N.
Bean, R.
Bennett, A.
Bidwell, S.
Blenkinsop, A.
Bradley, T.
Bray, J.
Brown, R.
Buchan, N.
Callaghan, J.
Canavan, D.
Carmichael, N.
Cartwright, J.
Castle, Mrs B.
Clemitson, I.
Colquhoun, Mrs M.
Cook, R.
Corbett, R.
Crawshaw, R.
Cryer, R.*
Davies, B.
Dean, J.
Douglas-Mann, B.
Dunwoody, Mrs G.
Edge, G.
Edwards, R.
Evans, I.
Evans, J.
Fernyhough, E.

Grocott, B.
Hamilton, W.*
Hart, Mrs J.
Hatton, F.
Heffer, E.
Hooley, F.
Hoyle, D.
Hughes, R.
Hughes, R. J.
Hunter, A.
Jeger, Mrs L.
Kelley, R.
Kerr, R.
Kilroy-Silk, R.
Kinnock, N.
Lambie, D.
Lamond, J.
Latham, A.
Lee, J.
Lestor, Miss J.
Lewis, A.
Lipton, M.
Litterick, T.
Loyden, E.
Lyons, E.
McDonald, O.
McGuire, M.
Madden, M.
Marshall, J.
Maynard, Miss J.
Mendelson, J.
Mikardo, I.
Miller, M.

Orbach, M.
Ovenden, J.
Parry, R.
Pavitt, L.
Prescott, J.
Price, C.
Richardson, Miss J.
Roberts, G.
Roderick, C.
Rodgers, G.
Rooker, J.
Roper, J.
Rose, P.
Sedgemore, B.
Selby, H.
Shaw, A.
Short, Mrs R.
Silverman, J.
Skinner, D.
Spearing, N.
Swain, T.
Taylor, Mrs A.
Thomas, R.
Thorne, S.
Tierney, S.
Tuck, R.
Wainwright, E.
Watkins, D.
Watkinson, J.
Weetch, K.
Whitehead, P.
Wilson, W.
Wise, Mrs A.

Flannery, M.	Miller, Mrs M.	Woodall, A.
Fletcher, T.	Mitchell, R.	Woof, R.
Garrett, J.	Newens, S.	Young, D.
Garrett, W.	Noble, M.	

HC Deb. 915, 2173–8
1975–6, No. 271.

MEMBERS' REMUNERATION AND ALLOWANCES   [180]

23 July 1976

The Lord President of the Council and Leader of the House of Commons, M. Foot, moved a motion to increase the salary of Members of £5,750 a year by £312 from 13 June 1976, to reduce the pension contribution supplement introduced in 1975, and to increase the secretarial allowance rate.

N. Lawson (C., Blaby) moved an amendment to delete the provision for the £312 increase from 13th June and to replace it with one for a £208 increase from 1 October 1976. The aim of the amendment was to go straight to stage 2 of the Government's income policy and avoid stage 1, in so doing avoiding different rates of pay for Members as the £8,500 limit on pay increases would not then apply.

After three-and-a-half hours' discussion, the Government moved the closure which was carried on a party vote by 115 votes to 31.

(1) The amendment was then put and negatived by 110 votes to 35. The Government whips were on against the amendment, while Opposition Front Bench advice was to support it. The 112 Members (including tellers) in the Government lobby comprised 109 Labour, 1 Conservative, 1 UUUC and 1 SDLP. The 37 Members (including tellers) to support the amendment comprised 34 Conservative, 2 Labour and 1 UUUC.

Conservative to vote against the amendment:

Rodgers, Sir J.

Labour Members to vote for the amendment:

Lee, J.*   Skinner, D.

(2) The motion was then put and carried by 111 votes to 17. The Government whips were on in support of the motion, while the Opposition Front Bench abstained from voting. The 113 Members (including

tellers) in the Government lobby comprised 110 Labour, 1 Conservative, 1 UUUC and 1 SDLP. The 19 Members (including tellers) to oppose the motion comprised 11 Conservative, 5 UUUC and 3 Labour.

Conservative Member to vote for the motion:

Sims, R.

Conservatives to vote against the motion:

Biggs-Davison, J.	Grylls, M.	Morrison, P.
Boscawen, R.	Luce, R.	Ridley, N.
Cormack, P.	Mitchell, D.	Stanbrook, I.
Dykes, H.	Moate, R.	

Labour Members to vote against the motion:

Cryer, R.*   Madden, M.*   Skinner, D.

HC Deb. 915, 2315–20
1975–6, Nos. 274 and 275.

The division took place on a Friday, hence the low vote.

PARLIAMENTARY AND OTHER PENSIONS AND SALARIES BILL [181]

Report: 23 July 1976

Clause 1 (Member's Pensionable Salary)

R. Cryer (Lab., Keighley) moved an amendment to leave out the date on which the measure would have effect. It was discussed in conjunction with a related amendment, tabled by Mr Cryer, that it would only have effect when the state pension for a single person was one-half of average male earnings and for a married couple two-thirds that of average male earnings.

The Minister of State, Civil Service Department, C. Morris, questioned whether the amendment was the most effective way of achieving the object sought by Mr Cryer. He hoped the amendment would be withdrawn or rejected.

The amendment was negatived by 65 votes to 3, with the Government whips on. The Opposition did not participate in the division. The 67 Members (including tellers) in the Government lobby comprised 65 Labour, 1 UUUC and 1 SDLP. The 5 Members (including tellers) to support the amendment comprised 4 Labour and 1 UUUC.

Labour Members to vote for the amendment:

Cryer, R.*   Madden, M.*   Skinner, D.
Latham, A.

HC Deb. 915, 2349–52
1975–6, No. 277.

AIRCRAFT AND SHIPBUILDING INDUSTRIES BILL   [182]

Report: 28 July 1976

Clause 2 (General duties of the Corporations)

The Secretary of State for Industry, E. Varley, moved an amendment to provide that 'it shall be the duty of each Corporation to promote industrial democracy in a strong and organic form'.

G. Wilson (SNP, Dundee, East) moved an amendment to the proposed amendment to add after 'democracy': 'in which adequate powers of decision-making are shared by the Corporation and their subsidiaries with members of the relevant workforces'.

The amendment to the proposed amendment was opposed by the Government, and negatived by 302 votes to 26, with the Opposition abstaining from voting. The 28 Members (including tellers) to support the amendment comprised 12 Liberal, 9 SNP, 3 Conservative, 3 Plaid Cymru and 1 UUUC.

Conservatives to vote for the amendment:

Hawkins, P.   Mawby, R.   Mudd, D.

HC Deb. 916, 785–90
1975–6, No. 295.

AIRCRAFT AND SHIPBUILDING INDUSTRIES BILL [183]

Report: 29 July 1976

Clause 19 (Vesting in British aerospace or British shipbuilders of securities of scheduled companies)

K. McNamara (Lab., Hull, Central) moved an amendment to provide that where a company named in schedule 2 of the Bill of whose property a receiver had been appointed, 'the Corporation shall purchase from the receiver its existing assets at a value to be determined by agreement between the Corporation and the receiver as on the date of the coming into operation of this Act.'

The amendment, which was designed to deal particularly with the position of the Drypool Group, was opposed by the Government. The Minister of State, Department of Industry, G. Kaufman, argued that the amendment (along with others tabled by Mr McNamara) was not only unacceptable but positively damaging. The financial effect of the amendment moved would be disastrous.

The amendment was negatived by 248 votes to 42, with the Opposition abstaining from voting. The 250 Members (including tellers) in the Government lobby comprised 236 Labour, 11 Liberal, 1 SDLP, 1 Scottish Labour (J. Robertson) and 1 Irish Independent. The 44 Members (including tellers) to support the amendment comprised 43 Labour and 1 Scottish Labour (J. Sillars).

Labour Members to vote for the amendment:

Ashton, J.
Bennett, A.
Bidwell, S.
Canavan, D.
Clemitson, I.
Colquhoun, Mrs M.
Dunwoody, Mrs G.
Edge, G.
Evans, J.
Flannery, M.
Garrett, W.
Grocott, B.
Heffer, E.
Hoyle, D.
Johnson, J.*

Kerr, R.
Kilroy-Silk, R.
Kinnock, N.
Lambie, D.
Latham, A.
Lee, J.
Lewis, A.
Litterick, T.
Loyden, E.
McDonald, O.
McNamara, K.
Madden, M.
Mikardo, I.
Noble, M.

Ovenden, J.
Parry, R.
Prescott, J.*
Richardson, Miss J.
Roberts, G.
Roderick, C.
Rodgers, G.
Rooker, J.
Skinner, D.
Swain, T.
Taylor, Mrs A.
Thomas, R.
Thorne, S.
Wise, Mrs A.

HC Deb. 916, 915–8
1975–6, No. 297.

BAIL BILL **[184]**

Report: 3 August 1976

Schedule 1 (Persons entitled to bail: supplementary provisions)

R. Kilroy-Silk (Lab., Ormskirk) moved an amendment to delete paragraph 7 of Part I of the schedule (which permitted a court to refuse bail if it had formed the intention of passing a custodial sentence, subject to reports), discussed in conjunction with another amendment he had tabled to delete paragraph 8 (which permitted a court to refuse bail if it appeared that it would be impracticable to complete inquiries or obtain a report without keeping the defendant in custody). Mr Kilroy-Silk urged the Government to genuinely consider both amendments, 'and to strengthen the Bill accordingly, not only to make sure that the principle of presumption of bail is applied—and applied particularly to those who are least able to defend themselves and are most in need of this kind of protection—but so that we shall not feel it necessary to rewrite the Bill in the next Session.'

The Under-Secretary of State for the Home Department, Dr S. Summerskill, announced that having listened carefully to what Members had said—'the majority apparently wishing to see paragraph 7 deleted'—she was prepared to accept the amendment to delete paragraph 7 in deference to the views of the House. However, she argued against the second amendment under discussion, contending that there were circumstances in which it would be impracticable to obtain a report except by remanding the defendant in custody. The Government agreed with the objective of the amendment (that before remanding in custody for inquiries or report the court should seek all available information on whether there was any practicable alternative to a custodial remand), and would emphasize this in a circular if the amendment was withdrawn. The amendment would introduce too much inflexibility.

The amendment to delete paragraph 7 was agreed to without a division. Mr Kilroy-Silk then moved formally the second amendment (to delete paragraph 8) and forced it to a division. The amendment was negatived by 102 votes to 53, the Opposition voting with the Government. The 104 Members (including tellers) in the Government lobby comprised 85 Labour, 18 Conservative and 1 Liberal. The 55 Members (including tellers) to support the amendment comprised 49 Labour, 5 Liberal and, according to the division list, 1 Conservative.

Labour Members to vote for the amendment:

Allaun, F.	Heffer, E.	Pavitt, L.
Atkinson, N.	Jenkins, H.	Perry, E.
Bennett, A.*	Kerr, R.	Price, C.
Bidwell, S.	Kilroy-Silk, R.	Richardson, Miss J.*
Brown, R.	Kinnock, N.	Rodgers, G.
Buchan, N.	Litterick, T.	Rooker, J.
Callaghan, J.	Loyden, E.	Roper, J.
Carmichael, N.	Lyons, E.	Shaw, A.
Colquhoun, Mrs M.	McDonald, O.	Skinner, D.
Cook, R.	Madden, M.	Spearing, N.
Corbett, R.	Maynard, Miss J.	Taylor, Mrs A.
Cryer, R.	Mikardo, I.	Thomas, R.
Dunwoody, Mrs G.	Miller, M.	Thorne, S.
Edge, G.	Miller, Mrs M.	Whitehead, P.
Edwards, R.	Newens, S.	Wilson, W.
Flannery, M.	Parry, R.	Wise, Mrs A.
Hart, Mrs J.		

Conservative to vote for the amendment:

Fox, M.

HC Deb. 916, 1515–18
1975–6, No. 310.

HEALTH SERVICES BILL [185]

Report: 12 October 1976

New Clause 2 (Complete withdrawal of N.H.S. beds from resident private patients and transfer of Board's functions to Secretary of State)

L. Pavitt (Lab., Brent, South) moved the new clause which provided that, if the Board under the provisions of the measure had not submitted to the Secretary of State by 1 January 1980 proposals for the complete withdrawal of N.H.S. facilities from private patients, then, notwithstanding the provisions of the Bill for securing the progressive withdrawal of accommodation and services at N.H.S. hospitals from use in connection with treatment of private patients, the Secretary of State would not later than 1 January 1980 reduce to nil the number of beds authorized under section 1(1) of the 1968 Act to be made available to resident private patients.

Although a number of Labour backbenchers rose to speak in support of the new clause, the Secretary of State for Social Services, D. Ennals, asked Members not to vote for it. He argued that it would be a mistake to tie the Board's hand by imposing a particular date. Members of the Board would be under an obligation to ensure the carrying through of the purposes of the Bill, which was to phase pay beds out of the National Health Service.

The new clause was negatived by 144 votes to 50, with the Government whips on. The Opposition abstained from voting. The 146 Members (including tellers) in the Government lobby comprised 126 Labour, 7 Liberal, 7 Scottish National and 6 Conservative. The 52 Members (including tellers) to support the new clause comprised 48 Labour, 3 Plaid Cymru and 1 Scottish Labour.

Conservatives to vote against the clause:

Chalker, Mrs. L.	Gray, H.	Stewart, I.
Douglas-Hamilton, Lord J.	Hutchison, M. C.	Young, Sir G.

Labour Members to vote for the clause:

Allaun, F.	Hatton, F.	Noble, M.
Anderson, D.	Heffer, E.	Pavitt, L.*
Buchan, N.	Hoyle, D.	Richardson, Miss J.*
Callaghan, J.	Hughes, R.	Roberts, G.
Carmichael, N.	Hughes, R. J.	Roderick, C.
Clemitson, I.	Kilroy-Silk, R.	Rooker, J.
Colquhoun, Mrs M.	Lambie, D.	Rose, P.
Cook, R.	Lestor, Miss J.	Short, Mrs R.
Corbett, R.	Litterick, T.	Silverman, J.
Davies, B.	Lomas, K.	Skinner, D.
Edge, G.	Loyden, E.	Spearing, N.
Evans, I.	McDonald, O.	Taylor, Mrs A.
Fernyhough, E.	McMillan, T.	Thomas, R.
Flannery, M.	Madden, M.	Thorne, S.
George, B.	Maynard, Miss J.	Wise, Mrs A.
Grocott, B.	Mendelson, J.	Woof, R.

HC Deb. 917, 359–60
1975–6, No. 313.

MAPLIN DEVELOPMENT AUTHORITY (DISSOLUTION) BILL [186]

Third Reading: 14 October 1976

The Under-Secretary of State for the Environment, G. Barnett, moved the Third Reading of the Bill.

A number of Conservative backbenchers rose to speak for and against the Bill. T. Jessel (C., Twickenham) said the Bill meant there would be no Maplin Airport in the foreseeable future, which would be a disaster for many people living around the existing airports of Heathrow, Gatwick and Luton. Dr A. Glyn (C., Windsor and Maidenhead) thought Maplin was an imaginative project which should have been carried out. R. Moate (C., Faversham) thought the Bill was one of the most excellent Bills he had ever seen presented in the House.

For the Opposition, N. Tebbit announced that his side did not intend to vote against the Bill.

The Bill was given a Third Reading by 115 votes to 4, with the Government whips on. The 117 Members (including tellers) to support Third Reading comprised 109 Labour, 5 Conservative and 3 Liberal. The 6 Members (including tellers) to oppose Third Reading were all Conservatives.

Conservatives to vote for Third Reading:

Body, R.	Gow, I.	Winterton, N.
Clark, A.	Moate, R.	

Conservatives to vote against Third Reading:

Bell, R.*	Fry, P.	Jessel, T.
Fookes, Miss J.	Glyn, A.*	Montgomery, F.

HC Deb. 917, 739–40
1975–6, No. 321.

BUSINESS OF THE HOUSE   **[187]**

14 October 1976

At 10.00 p.m., during discussion on the Second Reading of the Public Lending Right Bill, a Government whip moved the procedural exemption motion to allow Government business to be proceeded with at that sitting, though opposed, until any hour.

A number of Conservative opponents of the Public Lending Right Bill—the Opposition itself being committed to the principle of the Bill —divided the House.

The motion was carried by 123 votes to 13, the Opposition voting with the Government. The 125 Members (including tellers) in the

Government lobby comprised 105 Labour, 11 Conservative, 5 SNP, 3 Liberal and 1 UUUC. The 15 Members (including tellers) to vote against were all Conservative.

Conservatives to vote against the motion:

Bell, R.*	Fookes, Miss J.	Lawrence, I.
Body, R.*	Fry, P.	Montgomery, F.
Clark, A.	Glyn, A.	Renton, Sir D.
Eyre, R.	Gow, I.	Shersby, M.
Fell, A.	Hall, Sir J.	Winterton, N.

HC Deb. 917, 759–62
1975–6, No. 322.

PUBLIC LENDING RIGHT BILL   [188]

Second Reading: 14 October 1976

The Second Reading debate on the Bill was resumed after having been adjourned on previous occasions.

   Although the Opposition was committed to the principle of the Bill, a number of Conservative backbenchers opposed it. R. Body (C., Holland-with-Boston) questioned the administration of the scheme and the timing of the measure. I. Sproat (C., Aberdeen, South) felt the Bill embodied a bad principle and had been produced at a bad time. R. Bell (C., Beaconsfield) noted that the Bill was designed to approve a principle, but contended that the principle had not been proved.

   At 10.00 p.m. Conservative opponents of the measure divided the House on the procedural exemption motion (see above).

   (1) At 11.18 p.m. the Government Chief Whip moved the closure. With the Government whips on, voting was 99 to 7 in favour, the Opposition abstaining from voting. The 101 Members (including tellers) in the Government lobby comprised 88 Labour, 4 Conservative, 4 Liberal, 4 Scottish National and 1 SDLP. The 9 Members (including tellers) to vote against were all Conservative.

Conservatives to vote for closure:

Jessel, T.	Wiggin, J.	Young, Sir G.
Stainton, K.		

Conservatives to vote against closure:

Bell, R.*   Fry, P.   Montgomery, F.
Body, R.   Hannam, J.   Sproat, I.
Fell, A.   Moate, R.*   Winterton, N.

100 Members not having voted for closure, the Question was not decided in the affirmative, and the debate continued.

(2) At 1.17 a.m. the House divided finally on Second Reading. The Bill was given a Second Reading by 99 votes to 0, the Opposition voting with the Government. The 101 Members (including tellers) in the Government lobby comprised 61 Labour, 35 Conservative, 3 Liberal, 1 UUUC and 1 Scottish National. The 2 Members to act as tellers against were both Conservatives.

Conservatives to act as tellers against Second Reading:

Moate, R.*   Sproat, I.*

HC Deb. 917, 781–4 and 817–20
1975–6, Nos. 323 and 324.

WEIGHTS AND MEASURES ETC. (No. 2) BILL   [189]

Second Reading: 18 October 1976

The Minister of State, Department of Prices and Consumer Protection, J. Fraser, moved the Second Reading of the Bill. He explained that the main purpose of the measure was to repeal the provision of the 1963 Weights and Measures Act which effectively obliged the Government to maintain the use of imperial units, and also to provide the Government with more flexible powers to bring forward proposals to remove or restrict weights and measures for the purposes of trade, necessary in order to make a sector-by-sector approach to metrication possible.

For the Opposition, Mrs S. Oppenheim moved a reasoned amendment for rejection. The amendment was negatived on a whipped party vote by 194 votes to 171, with no cross-voting taking place.

The Bill was then given a Second Reading by 181 votes to 21, with the Opposition abstaining officially from voting. The 183 Members (including tellers) in the Government lobby comprised 175 Labour, 6 Liberal and 2 Conservative. The 23 Members (including tellers) to oppose Second Reading comprised 10 Conservative, 9 Labour, 2 Liberal and 2 UUUC.

Conservatives to vote for Second Reading:

Sainsbury, T.	Scott, N.

Conservatives to vote against Second Reading:

Brotherton, M.	McAdden, Sir S.	Morgan, G.
Fell, A.	Marten, N.	Taylor, R.
Hutchison, M. C.	Moate, R.	Winterton, N.
Lawson, N.		

Labour Members to vote against Second Reading:

Heffer, E.	Maynard, Miss J.	Skinner, D.*
Lamond, J.	Rodgers, G.	Torney, T.
Madden, M.*	Rooker, J.	Wise, Mrs A.

HC Deb. 917, 1023–6
1975–6, No. 326.

COMPANIES (No. 2) BILL [190]

Report: 19 October 1976

New Clause 1 (Appointment and removal of auditors)

The Under-Secretary of State for Trade, C. Davis, moved the new clause which was designed to reshape the provisions dealing with the appointment and resignation of auditors.

The new clause was approved by 120 votes to 14, with the Opposition Front Bench abstaining from voting. The 16 Members (including tellers) to oppose the clause comprised 9 Conservative, 6 Liberal and 1 Plaid Cymru.

Conservatives to vote against the clause:

Farr, J.	Luce, R.	Rhys-Williams, Sir B
Knight, Mrs J.	Mitchell, D.	Shaw, G.
Loveridge, J.	Morrison, P.	Winterton, N.

HC Deb. 917, 1413–16
1975–6, No. 335.

SOUTHERN RHODESIA   [191]

Prayer: 20 October 1976

The Secretary of State for Foreign and Commonwealth Affairs, A. Crosland, moved 'That the Southern Rhodesia Act 1965 (Continuation) Order 1976, a draft of which was laid before this House on 14th October, be approved.'

The order, as with orders in preceding years, extended section 2 of the Southern Rhodesia Act 1965 for a further year, and, as in previous years, it was opposed by Conservative backbench opponents of sanctions.

The order was approved by 191 votes to 21,[1] the Opposition abstaining officially from voting. The 23 Members (including tellers) to vote against comprised 19 Conservative and 4 UUUC. 1 Conservative entered the Government lobby to vote for the order.

Conservatives to vote against the order:

Amery, J.	Fletcher, A.	Page, J.
Boyson, R.	Hastings, S.*	Rees, P.
Brotherton, M.	Lloyd, I.	Skeet, T.
Churchill, W.	Meyer, Sir A.	Taylor, R.
Clark, A.	Morgan-Giles, M.*	Wakeham, J.
Dodsworth, G.	Normanton, T.	Winterton, N.
Fell, A.		

Conservative to vote for the order:

Temple-Morris, P.

HC Deb. 917, 1617–20
1975–6, No. 337.

[1] *Hansard* records the number as 20, but 21 names are listed.

BUSINESS OF THE HOUSE [192]

25 October 1976

A Government whip moved 'That, at this day's Sitting, proceedings on any Bill set down for consideration at Seven o'clock by direction of the Chairman of Ways and Means shall, instead of being considered at that hour, be considered as soon as a member of the Government shall have signified his intention to move, That this House do now adjourn, for the purpose of bringing the sitting to a conclusion.'

The Opposition did not officially oppose the motion, but a number of backbenchers rose to query the motion and express objections to it. N. Ridley (C., Cirencester and Tewkesbury) thought the procedure proposed was 'utterly unacceptable'. He thought it was necessary to have an orderly procedure, and asked the House to throw out the motion. J. Rooker (Lab., Birmingham, Perry Bar) said that he treated the motion with suspicion, and he did not think it was a satisfactory procedure.

The motion was carried by 149 votes to 34, with the Opposition abstaining from voting. The 36 Members (including tellers) to oppose the motion comprised 27 Conservative, 6 Liberal, 1 Labour and 2 UUUC. 1 Conservative entered the Government lobby to support the motion. 1 Labour Member abstained from voting.[1]

Conservatives to vote against the motion:

Alison, M.	Fookes, Miss J.	Moate, R.
Arnold, T.	Gow, I.	Morrison, P.
Bennett, R.	Hampson, K.	Nelson, A.
Bottomley, P.	Hutchison, M. C.	Neubert, M.
Boyson, R.	Jopling, M.	Ridley, N.*
Buck, A.	Knight, Mrs J.	Rost, P.
Cormack, P.	Latham, M.	Sims, R.
Dodsworth, G.	Macfarlane, N.	Skeet, T.
Eyre, R.	Maxwell-Hyslop, R.	Winterton, N.

Labour Member to vote against the motion:

Skinner, D.

Conservative to vote for the motion:

Gray, H.

HC Deb. 918, 49–50
1975–6, No. 340.

¹ T. Dalyell. J. Rooker voted in the Government lobby. According to the *Hansard* division lists R. Mitchell (Lab., Southampton, Itchin) voted against the motion, but his name has been added by mistake. The correct list appears in the *Votes and Proceedings*.

STRANGERS [193]

28 October 1976

During Prime Minister's Question Time, Opposition Members voiced objections to the Prime Minister's decision to meet Mr Ponomaryov, a member of a Soviet Union delegation invited to Britain by the National Executive of the Labour Party.

During the exchanges, Mr Ponomaryov entered the Stranger's Gallery, and N. Ridley (C., Cirencester and Tewkesbury) rose on a point of order to declare 'In view of the presence in the Chamber of a man who holds this free Parliament in contempt, I beg to move, That Strangers do withdraw.'

Pursuant to Standing Order No. 115, Mr Speaker immediately put the Question, 'That Strangers do withdraw'. The motion was negatived by 192 votes to 80, with the Government whips on against it and the Opposition Front Bench abstaining from voting. The 82 Members (including tellers) to support the motion comprised 77 Conservative, 3 Liberal and 2 UUUC.

Conservatives to support the motion:

Adley, R.	Finsberg, G.	Moate, R.
Alison, M.	Fookes, Miss J.	Morgan, G.
Baker, K.	Fry, P.	Morgan-Giles, M.
Banks, R.	Goodhart, P.	Mudd, D.
Bell, R.	Griffiths, E.	Onslow, C.
Bennett, Sir F.	Grist, I.	Page, J.
Benyon, W.	Grylls, M.	Page, R. G.
Biggs-Davison, J.	Hall, Sir J.	Rathbone, T.
Boscawen, R.	Hamilton, M.	Rees-Davies, W.
Bottomley, P.	Hannam, J.	Ridley, N.*
Brotherton, M.	Hastings, S.	Roberts, M.
Brown, Sir E.	Hayhoe, B.	Rost, P.
Churchill, W.	Hicks, R.	Shepherd, C.
Clark, A.	Holland, P.	Spence, J.

Clegg, W.
Cope, J.
Critchley, J.
Dodsworth, G.
du Cann, E.
Dykes, H.
Eden, Sir J.
Elliott, Sir W.
Eyre, R.
Fairgrieve, R.
Farr, J.
Fell, A.

Jessel, T.
Kershaw, A.
King, T.
Knight, Mrs J.
Lamont, N.
Latham, M.*
Lloyd, I.
McAdden, Sir S.
McCrindle, R.
Madel, D.
Mawby, R.
Maxwell-Hyslop, R.

Spicer, M.
Steen, A.
Stewart, I.
Taylor, E.
Tebbit, N.
Townsend, C.
Wall, P.
Walters, D.
Wells, J.
Wiggin, J.
Young, Sir G.

HC Deb. 918, 699–704
1975–6, No. 351.

During the division, Mr Ponomaryov left the Gallery.

CONDUCT OF MEMBERS [194]

1 November 1976

The Prime Minister, L. J. Callaghan, moved a motion to establish a Select Committee to inquire into the conduct and activities of Members in connection with the affairs of Mr John Poulson.

Mr Speaker put each paragraph of the motion separately.

(1) The paragraph, 'That a Select Committee be appointed to inquire into the conduct and activities of Members of this House in connection with the affairs of Mr J. G. L. Poulson; to consider whether any such conduct or activities amounted to a contempt of the House or was inconsistent with the standards which the House is entitled to expect from its Members; and to report', was put. It was carried by 274 votes to 21. The Government whips were on in support of it, with the Opposition also officially supporting it. The 276 Members (including tellers) to support the motion comprised 133 Labour, 123 Conservative, 10 Liberal, 5 Scottish National, 3 Plaid Cymru and 2 UUUC. The 23 Members (including tellers) to oppose the motion comprised 22 Labour and 1 Conservative.

Conservative to vote against the motion:

Clark, A.

Labour Members to vote against the motion:

Bean, R.	Lee, J.*	Richardson, Miss J.
Bidwell, S.	Lewis, A.	Roberts, G.
Evans, F.	Litterick, T.	Rooker, J.*
Evans, J.	McDonald, O.	Sedgemore, B.
Fletcher, R.	Maynard, Miss J.	Skinner, D.
Garrett, W.	Parry, R.	Wise, Mrs A.
Kerr, R.	Price, C.	Woof, R.
Lamond, J.		

The paragraphs approving the membership, quorum, powers of the Select Committee and attendance of the Attorney-General were approved without a division.

(2) On the paragraph that the Select Committee should meet in private, D. Skinner (Lab., Bolsover) moved an amendment to provide that it should meet in public. The amendment was negatived by 256 votes to 35, with the Government and Opposition voting against it. The 37 Members (including tellers) to support the amendment comprised 31 Labour, 3 Plaid Cymru, 2 Scottish National and 1 Liberal.

Labour Members to vote for the amendment:

Canavan, D.	Latham, A.	Price, C.
Clemitson, I.	Lee, J.*	Richardson, Miss J.
Evans, F.	Lestor, Miss J.	Roberts, G.
Evans, J.	Lewis, A.	Rooker, J.*
Garrett, W.	Litterick, T.	Sedgemore, B.
Hatton, F.	McDonald, O.	Skinner, D.
Heffer, E.	Maynard, Miss J.	Thomas, R.
Hooley, F.	Mikardo, I.	Tierney, S.
Hughes, R. J.	Ogden, E.	Wise, Mrs A.
Kerr, R.	Parry, R.	Woof, R.
Lamond, J.		

(3) R. Maxwell-Hyslop (C., Tiverton) moved to insert an additional paragraph, 'That no witness summoned to appear before the Committee shall claim Crown Privilege as a justification for refusing to answer questions asked by the Committee.' The paragraph was negatived by 143 votes to 45, with the Government whips on against it and the Opposition abstaining from voting. The 47 Members (including tellers) to support the motion comprised 28 Labour, 8 Conservative, 4 Scottish National, 3 Plaid Cymru, 3 Liberal and 1 UUUC. 11 Conservatives entered the Government lobby to vote against it.

Labour Members to vote for the motion:

Allaun, F.	Hughes, R. J.	Richardson, Miss J.
Atkins, R.	Kerr, R.	Roberts, G.
Callaghan, J.	Lamond, J.	Rooker, J.
Canavan, D.	Latham, A.	Sedgemore, B.
Clemitson, I.	Lee, J.	Skinner, D.
Evans, F.	Lewis, A.*	Thomas, R.
Evans, J.	Litterick, T.	Tierney, S.
Garrett, W.	McDonald, O.	Wise, Mrs A.
Hatton, F.	Maynard, Miss J.	Woof, R.
Heffer, E.		

Conservatives to vote for the motion:

Clark, A.	Kellett-Bowman, Mrs E.	Meyer, Sir A.
Drayson, B.	Lawrence, I.	Miller, H.
Jessel, T.	Maxwell-Hyslop, R.*	

Conservatives to vote against the motion:

Carlisle, M.	James, D.	Miscampbell, N.
Gow, I.	Lester, J.	Morgan, G.
Gray, H.	Lewis, K.	Stewart, I.
Hutchison, M. C.	Mawby, R.	

(4) D. Steel (Lib., Roxburgh, Selkirk and Peebles) moved to insert an additional paragraph, 'That the Committee shall at their discretion sit in public if they consider that at any stage of the inquiry the requirements of justice or of the public interest requires them to do so notwithstanding any of the foregoing.' The motion to add the paragraph was negatived by 219 votes to 63, with the Opposition supporting the Government. The 65 Members (including tellers) to support the motion comprised 46 Labour, 8 Liberal, 5 Scottish National, 3 Plaid Cymru, 2 Conservative and 1 UUUC.

Labour Members to vote for the motion:

Abse, L.	Heffer, E.	Pavitt, L.
Allaun, F.	Hooley, F.	Richardson, Miss J.
Atkins, R.	Hughes, R. J.	Roberts, G.
Bean, R.	Kerr, R.	Robinson, G.
Bidwell, S.	Lamond, J.	Rooker, J.

Callaghan, J.	Latham, A.	Sedgemore, B.
Canavan, D.	Lee, J.	Shaw, A.
Clemitson, I.	Lewis, A.	Skinner, D.
Corbett, R.	Litterick, T.	Spearing, N.
Cunningham, G.	McDonald, O.	Thomas, R.
English, M.	Mallalieu, J.	Tierney, S.
Evans, F.	Maynard, Miss J.	Whitlock, W.
Evans, I.	Mikardo, I.	Willey, F.
Evans, J.	Ogden, E.	Wise, Mrs A.
Garrett, W.	Parry, R.	Woof, R.
Hatton, F.		

Conservatives to vote for the motion:

Hunt, J.   McNair-Wilson, M.

HC Deb. 918, 1095–8, 1099–1102, 1103–8
1975–6, Nos. 356, 357, 358 and 359.

WEIGHTS AND MEASURES ETC. (No. 2) BILL   [195]

Third Reading: 2 November 1976

The Minister of State, Department of Prices and Consumer Protection, J. Fraser, moved the Third Reading of the Bill.

The Bill was given a Third Reading by 159 votes to 35, with the Opposition abstaining from voting. The 37 Members (including tellers) to vote against comprised 13 Labour, 7 Conservative, 6 UUUC, 4 Liberal, 4 Scottish National, 2 Plaid Cymru and 1 Scottish Labour. 3 Conservatives entered the Government lobby to support Third Reading.

Labour Members to vote against Third Reading:

Atkins, R.	Lamond, J.	Rooker, J.
Colquhoun, Mrs M.	Lewis, A.	Skinner, D.*
Fletcher, T.	Madden, M.	Thomas, R.
Heffer, E.	Newens, S.*	Wise, Mrs A.
Kerr, R.		

Conservatives to vote against Third Reading:

Body, R.   Hutchison, M. C.   Marten, N.
Budgen, N.   Lawson, N.   Moate, R.
Gow, I.

Conservatives to vote for Third Reading:

Drayson, B.   Miscampbell, N.   Morgan, G.

HC Deb. 918, 1283–6
1975–6, No. 364.

POULTRY MEAT HYGIENE   [196]

Prayer: 2 November 1976

For the Opposition, M. Jopling moved 'That an humble Address be
presented to Her Majesty, praying that the Poultry Meat (Hygiene)
Regulations 1976 (S.I., 1976, No. 1209), dated 29th July 1976, a copy
of which was laid before this House on 4th August, be annulled'.

The Opposition had tabled the prayer in order that there could be a
discussion of the regulations. When the prayer was divided upon,
though, the Opposition abstained from voting. A number of backbenchers on both sides of the House entered the lobby to support it.

The prayer was negatived by 115 votes to 108, with the Government
whips on against it. The 110 Members (including tellers) to support
the prayer comprised 51 Labour, 35 Conservative, 10 Liberal, 6 UUUC,
6 Scottish National and 2 Plaid Cymru. 14 Conservatives entered the
Government lobby to oppose the prayer; had they not done so, the
Government would have been defeated in the division.

Labour Members to vote for the prayer:

Bean, R.   Irving, S.   Richardson, Miss J.
Blenkinsop, A.   Jay, D.   Roberts, A.
Brown, R.   Kelley, R.   Robinson, G.
Canavan, D.   Kilroy-Silk, R.   Sedgemore, B.
Cant, R.   Lamborn, H.   Selby, H.
Carter-Jones, L.   Lamond, J.   Shaw, A.
Castle, Mrs B.   Lewis, R.   Silverman, J.
Craigen, J.   Lyon, A.   Skinner, D.

Crowther, S.	McDonald, O.	Spearing, N.
Cunningham, G.	McNamara, K.	Spriggs, L.
Dempsey, J.	Madden, M.	Thomas, R.
Evans, J.	Newens, S.	Torney, T.
Fletcher, T.	Orbach, M.	Watkinson, J.
Forrester, J.	Ovenden, J.	Whitehead, P.
Fowler, G.	Pavitt, L.	Wise, Mrs A.
Hatton, F.	Prescott, J.	Woodall, A.
Hughes, R. J.	Price, C.	Young, D.

Conservatives to vote for the prayer:

Body, R.*	Gower, Sir R.	Nelson, A.
Bowden, A.	Grist, I.	Neubert, M.
Braine, Sir B.	Hampson, K.	Newton, T.
Brotherton, M.	Hannam, J.	Nott, J.
Budgen, N.	Hutchison, M. C.	Onslow, C.
Clark, A.	Lawrence, I.	Pattie, G.
Douglas-Hamilton, Lord J.	Lawson, N.	Ridley, N.
Drayson, B.	Marten, N.	Shaw, G.
Durant, T.	Mitchell, D.	Walder, D.
Farr, J.	Moate, R.	Walker-Smith, Sir D.
Glyn, A.	Morgan, G.	Wall, P.
Gow, I.	Morris, M.	

Conservatives to vote against the prayer:

Costain, A.	Kimball, M.	Mills, P.
Emery, P.	Latham, M.	Page, J.
Hawkins, P.	Lester, J.	Rippon, G.
Hurd, D.	Mawby, R.	Spicer, J.
Johnson Smith, G.	Maxwell-Hyslop, R.	

HC Deb. 918, 1365–8
1975–6, No. 366.

FIREARMS (VARIATION OF FEES) [197]

Prayer: 2 November 1976

M. Kimball (C., Gainsborough) moved 'That an humble Address be presented to Her Majesty praying that the Firearms (Variation of Fees)

Order 1976 (S.I., 1976, No. 1400), dated 26th August 1976, a copy of which was laid before this House on 7th September, be annulled.'

The prayer was negatived on a party vote by 144 votes to 130. The division lists record 2 Labour Members as cross-voting to support the prayer, and 1 Conservative entering the Government lobby to oppose it.

Labour Members to vote for the prayer:

Brown, R.   Craigen, J.

Conservative to vote against the prayer:

Benyon, W.

HC Deb. 918, 1367–70
1975–6, No. 367.

FIREARMS (VARIATION OF FEES) (SCOTLAND)   [198]

Prayer: 2 November 1976

Sir J. Gilmour (C., Fife, East) moved 'That an humble Address be presented to Her Majesty praying that the Firearms (Variation of Fees) (Scotland) Order 1976 (S.I., 1976, No. 1446), dated 2nd September 1976, a copy of which was laid before this House on 10th September, be annulled.'

The prayer was negatived on a party vote by 137 votes to 90. 1 Labour Member cross-voted to support the prayer.

Labour Member to vote for the prayer:

Craigen, J.

HC Deb. 918, 1369–72
1975–6, No. 368.

SEXUAL OFFENCES (SCOTLAND) BILL   [199]

Committee: 3 November 1976

Clause 7 (Gross indecency between males)

On the motion 'That the Clause stand part of the Bill', M. Rifkind (C., Edinburgh, Pentlands) rose to oppose it. He argued that it was 'totally wrong as a matter of basic constitutional principle that Parliament should be asked to approve in a consolidation measure of an activity's continuing to be a criminal offence while at the same time the Lord Advocate informs the House that the Crown has not the slightest intention of treating such activity as a criminal offence despite Parliament so deciding.'

The Lord Advocate, R. King Murray, asked the House to support the clause. He argued that to leave it out would go completely against the spirit of consolidation; he pointed out also that all of what was struck at by the clause would remain unlawful until a substantive change in the law was made, and that could not be done by consolidation.

From the Opposition Front Bench, E. Taylor supported the Lord Advocate. If people wanted to change the law on homosexuality, he said they should present a Private Member's or a Government Bill.

The 'stand part' motion was carried by 37 votes to 27, with the Government whips on. The 39 Members (including tellers) in the Government lobby comprised 30 Labour, 7 Conservative and 2 Scottish National. The 29 Members (including tellers) to oppose the motion comprised 18 Labour, 5 Conservative, 4 Liberals and 2 Scottish National.

Labour Members to vote against the clause:

Bidwell, S.	Evans, J.	Marshall, J.
Buchan, N.	Forrester, J.	Ogden, E.
Canavan, D.	Fowler, G.	Prescott, J.
Carmichael, N.	Lambie, D.	Skinner, D.
Cook, R.	Lamond, J.	Taylor, Mrs A.
English, M.	McNamara, K.	Wise, Mrs A.

Conservatives to vote against the clause:

Hicks, R.	Lester, J.	Rifkind, M.
Knox, D.	Morrison, C.	

HC Deb. 918, 1583–4
1975–6, No. 373.

PUBLIC LENDING RIGHT BILL [200]

Report: 16 November 1976

Clause 1 (Establishment of public lending right)

The Under-Secretary of State for Education and Science, Miss M.

Jackson, moved an amendment to replace the word 'works' in the Bill with 'books'. She explained that the amendment was designed to restrict the scope of the Bill; if they were to retain any hope of early implementation of the Bill it was essential to keep to proposals which they knew to be practicable, at reasonable cost.

During debate on the amendment, N. St. John-Stevas, from the Opposition Front Bench, explained that, although Conservative backbenchers were allowed free votes on the measure—'I have long ago given up attempting to impose a party line upon voting on the Bill'—it was nevertheless the decision of the Shadow Cabinet 'that the Bill be given every support'.

The amendment was carried by 154 votes to 23, with the Opposition Front Bench abstaining from voting. The 25 Members (including tellers) to oppose the amendment (opponents of the Bill who believed that to defeat it would lead to the Government abandoning the Bill) comprised 14 Conservative, 7 Scottish National, 3 Labour and 1 UUUC. 8 Conservatives entered the Government lobby to support the amendment.

Conservatives to vote against the amendment:

Benyon, W.	Lawson, N.	Ridley, N.*
Body, R.	Moate, R.	Sproat, I.*
Brotherton, M.	Morrison, P.	Stewart, I.
Gow, I.	Nott, J.	Taylor, E.
Hannam, J.	Parkinson, C.	

Labour Members to vote against the amendment:

Anderson, D.	English, M.	Kinnock, N.

Conservatives to vote for the amendment:

Bennett, R.	Fisher, Sir N.	James, D.
Biggs-Davison, J.	Fookes, Miss J.	Walder, D.
Dean, P.	Gray, H.	

HC Deb. 919, 1193–6
1975–6, No. 407.

PUBLIC LENDING RIGHT BILL [201]

Report: 16 November 1976

Clause 1 (Establishment of public lending right)

From the Opposition Front Bench, N. St. John-Stevas moved an amendment to provide that the proposed scheme could cover books held in public libraries for consultation on library premises.

No Minister replied to the debate on the amendment, but the Government whips were put on to oppose it when divided upon.

The amendment was negatived on a party vote by 125 votes to 33. 3 Labour Members cross-voted to support the amendment.

Labour Members to vote for the amendment:

Cook, R.   English, M.   Faulds, A.

HC Deb. 919, 1229–32
1975–6, No. 408.

BUSINESS OF THE HOUSE [202]

16 November 1976

At 10.00 p.m. during Report stage of the Public Lending Right Bill, a Government whip moved the procedural exemption motion to provide that the Bill could be proceeded with, though opposed, until any hour.

Conservative backbench opponents of the measure divided the House. The motion was carried by 140 votes to 9, with Conservative supporters of the Bill voting with the Government.[1] The 11 Members (including tellers) to oppose the motion comprised 10 Conservative and 1 Labour.

Conservatives to vote against the motion:

Benyon, W.	Gow, I.	More, J.
Biggs-Davison, J.	Jones, A.	Sproat, I.
Body, R.*	Moate, R.	Taylor, E.
Brotherton, M.		

Labour Member to vote against the motion:

English, M.*

HC Deb. 919, 1235–8
1975–6, No. 409.

[1] In a thinly attended House, 14 Conservatives, including members of the Front Bench, voted in the Government lobby.

QUESTION OF PRIVILEGE (MOTION)   [203]

17 November 1976

On 16 November, A. Latham (Lab., Paddington) raised as a question of privilege a public speech by I. Sproat (C., Aberdeen, South) in which he had claimed that there were at least 30 Labour Members who he believed had views which were the same as those of Communists and similar bodies.

After giving the matter the traditional 24-hours' consideration, Mr Speaker announced that he was prepared to give a motion concerning the complaint precedence over the Orders of the Day. The Lord President of the Council and Leader of the House, M. Foot, thereupon moved 'That the matter of the complaint be referred to the Committee of Privileges'.

Mr Foot asked the House to pass the motion, as did J. Peyton for the Opposition. 'We accept the motion and we shall support it', declared Mr Peyton.

The motion was carried by 370 votes to 110. The Government whips were on, and the Opposition supported the Government. The 112 Members (including tellers) to oppose the motion comprised 96 Conservative, 10 Liberal, 5 UUUC and 1 Labour.

Conservatives to vote against the motion:

Adley, R.	Hampson, K.	Morrison, P.
Aitken, J.	Hannam, J.	Mudd, D.
Awdry, D.	Hastings, S.	Nelson, A.
Bell, R.*	Hawkins, P.	Oppenheim, Mrs S.[1]
Bennett, Sir F.	Hodgson, R.	Page, R.
Body, R.	Holland, P.	Page, R. G.
Boyson, R.	Hunt, D.	Price, D.
Brittan, L.	Hurd, D.	Ridley, N.
Brocklebank-Fowler, C.	Irving, C.	Rifkind, M.
Brotherton, M.	Jessel, T.	Rodgers, Sir J.
Budgen, N.	Kaberry, Sir D.	Scott, N.
Carlisle, M.	Kimball, M.	Shaw, G.
Channon, P.	King, E.	Shepherd, C.
Churchill, W.	Kitson, Sir T.	Shersby, M.
Clark, A.	Latham, M.	Sims, R.
Clegg, W.	Lawrence, I.	Sinclair, Sir G.
Cockroft, J.	Lewis, K.	Smith, D.
Cormack, P.	Lloyd, I.	Spence, J.
Dean, P.	McAdden, Sir S.	Spicer, M.
Drayson, B.	Macfarlane, N.	Stokes, J.

Eden, Sir J.	MacGregor, J.	Tapsell, P.
Fairbairn, N.	Madel, D.	Taylor, E.
Fairgrieve, R.	Mates, M.	Tebbit, N.
Fell, A.	Mayhew, P.	Temple-Morris, P.
Fookes, Miss J.	Meyer, Sir A.	Vaughan, G.
Fry, P.	Miscampbell, N.	Wakeham, J.
Gilmour, Sir J.	Moate, R.	Walder, D.
Glyn, A.	Monro, H.	Walker, P.
Goodlad, A.	Montgomery, F.	Warren, K.
Gorst, J.	More, J.	Winterton, N.
Gow, I.	Morgan, G.	Young, Sir G.
Gower, Sir R.	Morrison, C.	Younger, G.

Labour Member to vote against the motion:

Cunningham, G.

HC Deb. 919, 1381–4 and 1467–8
1975–6, No. 411.

On 17 November, a related question of privilege was raised. The following day, Mr Speaker again allowed a motion on the subject to take precedence over the Orders of the Day, and the Lord President moved an identical motion. A closure motion was carried on a free vote (Cabinet Members voting in different lobbies) by 243 votes to 230, and the motion approved without a division. *HC Deb.* 919, c. 1587–92.

[1] A member of the Shadow Cabinet.

The Session of 1976-7

VALUE ADDED TAX [204]

29 November 1976

The Financial Secretary to the Treasury, R. Sheldon, moved 'That this House takes note of Commission Documents Nos. R/1746/73 and R/2268/74 on Value Added Tax'.

The documents related to proposals by the European Commission for a common system of assessment and administration of value added tax in the member states.

A number of Members queried the decisions they were being asked to comment upon, since further discussions were still to be held by the European Fiscal Council, and whether or not Britain would have power to zero-rate items for value added tax that were not previously zero-rated.

The motion was approved by 86 votes to 37, with the Government whips on and the Opposition abstaining. The 88 Members (including tellers) in the Government lobby comprised 86 Labour and 2 Liberal. The 39 Members (including tellers) to oppose the motion comprised 27 Labour, 5 Scottish National, 3 Conservative, 2 UUUC and the 2 Scottish Labour Members.

Labour Members to vote against the motion:

Callaghan, J.	Jay, D.	Parry, R.
Canavan, D.	Kerr, R.	Richardson, Miss J.
Cook, R.	Kinnock, N.	Roderick, C.
Crowther, S.	Loyden, E.	Rodgers, G.
Dunwoody, Mrs G.	McCartney, H.	Skinner, D.
Evans, J.	McDonald, O.	Spearing, N.
Fernyhough, E.	Madden, M.*	Spriggs, L.*
Flannery, M.	Mikardo, I.	Thomas, R.
Hoyle, D.	Noble, M.	Thorne, S.

Conservatives to vote against the motion:

Clark, A.	Marten, N.	Moate, R.

HC Deb. 921, 649–52
1976–7, No. 2.

SOCIAL SECURITY (MISCELLANEOUS PROVISIONS) BILL [205]

Second Reading: 2 December 1976

The Bill was a wide-ranging one, and proposed changes in the earnings rule, the provisions for student support, occupational pensioners' unemployment benefit, mobility allowances and the child benefit scheme.

A number of Members on both sides of the House expressed opposition to certain provisions, and in particular to clause 4 which placed restrictions on the unemployment benefit of occupational pensioners.

(1) A Liberal reasoned amendment for rejection—'That this House declines to give a Second Reading to a Bill that proposes to make small savings in public expenditure at the expense of increased hardship for an already disadvantaged section of society'—was negatived by 172 votes to 26. The 174 Members (including tellers) in the Government lobby comprised solely Labour Members, the Opposition abstaining officially from voting. The 28 Members (including tellers) to vote for the amendment comprised 9 Liberal, 9 Conservative, 8 Scottish National, 1 Labour and 1 UUUC.

Conservatives to vote for the amendment:

Benyon, W.	Budgen, N.	Page, R. G.
Bottomley, P.	Gow, I.	Steen, A.
Brotherton, M.	Page, R.	Winterton, N.

Labour Member to vote for the amendment:

Skinner, D.

(2) The Bill was then given a Second Reading by 158 votes to 43, the Opposition abstaining from voting. The 160 Members (including tellers) in the Government lobby comprised solely Labour Members. The 46 Members (including tellers) to vote against Second Reading comprised 30 Labour, 9 Liberal, 5 Conservative and 1 UUUC.

Conservatives to vote against Second Reading:

Bottomley, P.	Clark, A.	Winterton, N.
Budgen, N.	Steen, A.	

Labour Members to vote against Second Reading:

Callaghan, J.	Hooley, F.	Ovenden, J.
Canavan, D.	Kilroy-Silk, R.	Price, C.
Corbett, R.	Kinnock, N.	Richardson, Miss J.
Edge, G.	Latham, A.	Roberts, G.
Flannery, M.	Litterick, T.*	Rooker, J.
Fletcher, R.	McDonald, O.	Skinner, D.
Fletcher, T.	Madden, M.	Thomas, R.
Fowler, G.	Marshall, J.	Ward, M.
Garrett, J.	Maynard, Miss J.	Wilson, W.
Hatton, F.	Mikardo, I.*	Wise, Mrs A.

HC Deb. 921, 1297–1300
1976–7, Nos. 9 & 10.

NATIONAL INSURANCE SURCHARGE BILL [206]

Second Reading: 6 December 1976

The Bill imposed a surcharge of two percentage points on employers' national insurance contributions.

A number of Labour Members rose to voice doubts about the measure and S. Thorne (Lab., Preston, South) argued that its effect would be to increase unemployment.

The Bill was given a Second Reading by 280 votes to 278, a Government majority of 2. For the division, the Government had issued at three-line whip. 1 Labour Member (joined by SLP Member J. Sillars) entered the Opposition lobby to vote against the Bill.

Labour Member to vote against Second Reading:

Thorne, S.

HC Deb. 922, 155–62
1976–7, No. 11.

Other Labour Members to voice criticisms of the measure in debate entered the Government lobby.

Mr Thorne abstained in the subsequent division on the Money resolution for the Bill.

DEFENCE SUPPLEMENTARY ESTIMATES, 1976–77 [207]

Supply: 14 December 1976

The Financial Secretary to the Treasury, R. Sheldon, formally moved 'That a further Supplementary sum, not exceeding £517,309,000, be granted to Her Majesty out of the Consolidated Fund to defray the charges which will come in course of payment during the year ending on 31st March 1977 for expenditure on Defence Services, as set out in House of Commons Paper No. 9'.

From the Government backbenches, R. Thomas (Lab. Bristol, North-West) moved an amendment 'That the sum be reduced by £272,859,000 in respect of Votes 5, 7, 8, 9, 10, 11 and 12'.

Mr Thomas argued that with cuts in education, health, social services and housing, 'it is unacceptable for the Government to come and ask for over another £300 million-plus for defence'.

The amendment was negatived by 299 votes to 51, with the Opposition voting with the Government. The 301 Members (including tellers) in the Government lobby comprised 144 Labour, 142 Conservative, 9 Liberal, 4 UUUC and 2 Scottish National. The 53 Members (including tellers) to support the amendment comprised 47 Labour, 3 Scottish National, 2 Scottish Labour and 1 Plaid Cymru.

Labour Members to vote for the amendment:

Allaun, F.*	Hart, Mrs J.	Ovenden, J.
Atkinson, N.	Hatton, F.	Parry, R.
Bennett, A.	Heffer, E.	Pavitt, L.
Bidwell, S.*	Hooley, F.	Richardson, Miss J.
Buchan, N.	Hoyle, D.	Roberts, G.
Canavan, D.	Hughes, R.	Rodgers, G.
Carmichael, N.	Jenkins, H.	Rooker, J.
Colquhoun, Mrs M.	Kerr, R.	Rose, P.
Corbett, R.	Lamond, J.	Selby, H.
Craigen, J.	Latham, A.	Short, Mrs R.
Ellis, J.	Lee, J.	Silverman, J.
Evans, I.	Loyden, E.	Skinner, D.
Flannery, M.	Lyon, A.	Thomas, R.
Fletcher, T.	Madden, M.	Torney, T.
Garrett, J.	Mikardo, I.	Wise, Mrs A.
Grocott, B.	Newens, S.	

HC Deb. 922, 1243–8
1976–7, No. 20.

The motion was then agreed to without a division.

ROAD TRAFFIC (SPEED LIMITS) [208]

Prayer: 15 December 1976

From the Opposition Front Bench, N. Fowler moved 'That an humble Address be presented to Her Majesty praying that the 60 miles per hour and 50 miles per hour (Temporary Speed Limit) Order 1976 (S.I., 1976, No. 1872), dated 9th November 1976, a copy of which was laid before this House on 10th November 1976 in the last session of Parliament, be annulled'.

The order continued the existing 50 and 60 miles per hour temporary speed limits on roads for a period of six months, while the Government entered into consultations as to future policy. The Opposition tabled the prayer in order that the issue could be debated.

The prayer was negatived by 65 votes to 51, with the Government whips on. The Government lobby comprised solely Labour Members. The 53 Members (including tellers) to vote for the prayer comprised 42 Conservative, 6 Liberal and 5 Labour.

Labour Members to vote for the prayer:

Canavan, D.   Lambie, D.   Ovenden, J.
Gourlay, H.   McCartney, H.

HC Deb. 922, 1691–4
1976–7, No. 21.

The division took place at 11.30 p.m.

SCOTLAND AND WALES BILL [209]

Second Reading: 13–16 December 1976

The House had a four-day debate on the Bill—designed to establish Assemblies with devolved powers in Scotland and Wales—with the Opposition and a number of Labour Members opposing the measure as unworkable and likely to have an adverse effect upon the unity of the United Kingdom. A number of Conservative Members supported the Government on the grounds that the measure would strengthen the unity of the United Kingdom; failure to devolve powers, it was believed, could lead to pressure for the break-up of the UK.

The Bill was given a Second Reading by 292 votes to 247 on a whipped party vote. The 294 Members (including tellers) to vote for Second Reading comprised 257 Labour, 13 Liberal, 11 Scottish National, 5 Conservative, 3 Plaid Cymru, 2 UUUC, 2 Scottish Labour and 1 SDLP. The 249 Members (including tellers) to vote against the Bill comprised 231 Conservative, 10 Labour and 8 UUUC. 31 Labour Members (including a member of the Cabinet)[1] and 29 Conservative Members[2] also abstained from voting.

Labour Members to vote against Second Reading:

Cowans, H.	Lamond, J.	Moonman, E.
Cunningham, G.	Leadbitter, T.	Phipps, C.
Dalyell, T.	Mendelson, J.	Urwin, T.
Garrett, W.		

Conservatives to vote for Second Reading:

Buchanan-Smith, A.[3]	Knox, D.	Rifkind, M.[3]
Gray, H.	Mudd, D.	

HC Deb. 922, 1871–6
1976–7, No. 22.

[1] The Labour abstainers were: L. Abse, D. Anderson, A. Bottomley, Mrs M. Colquhoun, S. Crowther, I. Davies, J. Dean, B. Douglas-Mann, F. Evans, I. Evans, R. Fletcher, E. Heffer, D. Hoyle, N. Kinnock, A. Lewis, R. Lewis, K. Lomas, A. Lyon, Mrs M. Miller, E. Ogden, J. Ovenden, A. Palmer, J. Parker, R. Prentice, J. Prescott, G. Roberts, H. Selby, Mrs R. Short, D. Skinner, T. Torney, and W. Whitlock. Mr Prentice was a Cabinet Minister. No action was taken against him, but he resigned from the Cabinet of his own volition on 21 December. *The Times,* 17 and 22 December 1976.

[2] The Conservative abstainers were: R. Adley, P. Blaker, N. Brocklebank-Fowler, J. Corrie, D. Crouch, P. Dean, Lord J. Douglas-Hamilton, R. Fairgrieve, A. Fletcher. N. Forman, P. Fry, Sir J. Gilmour, E. Heath, R. Hicks, D. James, R. Hodgson, K. Lewis, R. Luce, D. Madel, R. McCrindle, H. Monro, T. Sainsbury, N. Scott, J. Spence, P. Temple-Morris, C. Townsend, P. Walker, K. Warren and G. Younger. *The Times,* 17 December 1976.

[3] Mr Buchanan-Smith had resigned as Shadow Scottish Secretary on 8 December in order to support the Bill; he was joined in resignation by his deputy, Mr Rifkind. John Corrie, Hector Monro, and George Younger also offered their resignations as Opposition spokesmen, but these were refused; Mr Corrie, though, did insist on resignation prior to Second Reading.

ECONOMIC SITUATION   [210]

21 December 1976

On 15 December, the Chancellor of the Exchequer, D. Healey, announced Government measures designed to reduce public expenditure and to obtain approval for a standby loan by the International Monetary Fund. *HC Deb.* 922, c. 1525–37.

On 21 December, on a motion for adjournment, the House debated the Government's measures, and a number of Labour Members rose to oppose them, arguing that what was required was, in the words of R. Thomas (Lab., Bristol, North-West) 'a fundamentally different economic strategy'.

At 11.02 p.m., Labour backbench opponents of the Government measures divided the House. The adjournment motion was negatived by 219 votes to 51, with the Opposition abstaining from voting. The Government lobby comprised solely Labour Members. The 53 Members (including tellers) to enter the lobby for adjournment comprised 28 Labour, 11 Scottish National, 10 Liberal, 2 Plaid Cymru, 1 Scottish Labour and 1 UUUC.

Labour Members to vote for adjournment:

Allaun, F.	Lambie, D.	Newens, S.
Atkins, R.	Latham, A.	Parry, R.
Bennett, A.	Lee, J.	Richardson, Miss J.
Canavan, D.	Litterick, T.	Rodgers, G.
Colquhoun, Mrs M.	Loyden, E.	Selby, H.
Cook, R.	Lyon, A.*	Skinner, D.
Edge, G.	McDonald, O.	Thomas, R.
Flannery, M.	Maynard, Miss J.	Thorne, S.
Hoyle, D.	Mikardo, I.*	Wise, Mrs A.
Kerr, R.		

HC Deb. 923, 627–30
1976–7, No. 23.

CUSTOMS AND EXCISE [211]

Prayer: 21 December 1976

The Financial Secretary to the Treasury, R. Sheldon, formally moved 'That the Surcharge on Revenue Duties Order 1976 (S.I. 1976, No. 2133), a copy of which was laid before this House on 15th December, be approved'.

Scottish and Welsh National Members divided the House on the prayer, which was carried by 265 votes to 16 with the Opposition abstaining from voting. The 18 Members (including tellers) to oppose the prayer comprised 11 Scottish National, 2 Plaid Cymru, 2 Liberal,[1] 1 Conservative, 1 UUUC and 1 Scottish Labour.

Conservative to vote against the prayer:
Brotherton, M.

HC Deb. 923, 629–32
1976–7, No. 24.

[1] 8 Liberals voted for the prayer.

RATE SUPPORT GRANT [212]

Prayer: 22 December 1976

The Secretary of State for the Environment, P. Shore, moved 'That the Rate Support Grant Order 1976, a copy of which was laid before this House on 6th December, be approved'.

Although critical of the order, the Opposition did not divide the House. A number of backbenchers, however, did force a division.

The order was carried by 90 votes to 15, the Opposition abstaining from voting. The Government lobby comprised solely Labour Members. The 17 Members (including tellers) to oppose the order comprised 12 Conservative, 4 Liberal and 1 Plaid Cymru.

Conservatives to vote against the order:

Brotherton, M.	Raison, T.	Shepherd, C.*
Hannam, J.	Rees, P.	Smith, D.*
Jopling, M.	Rhodes James, R.	Sproat, I.
Newton, T.	Rippon, G.	Winterton, N.

HC Deb. 923, 847–50
1976–7, No. 25.

RATE SUPPORT GRANT (SCOTLAND) [213]

Prayer: 22 December 1976

The Secretary of State for Scotland, B. Millan, moved 'That the Rate Support Grant (Scotland) Order 1976, a copy of which was laid before this House on 6th December, be approved'.

Although critical of the order, the Opposition did not divide against it. However, a number of Government backbenchers representing Scottish seats did force a division.

The order was approved by 66 votes to 19, the Opposition abstaining from voting. The Government lobby comprised solely Labour Members. The 21 Members (including tellers) to oppose the order comprised 9 Labour, 8 Scottish National, 3 Liberal and 1 Plaid Cymru.

Labour Members to vote against the order:

Buchan, N.
Canavan, D.*
Carmichael, N.

Cook, R.
Craigen, J.
Hughes, R.*

Lambie, D.
McMillan, T.
Selby, H.

HC Deb. 923, 879–82
1976–7, No. 26.

COVENT GARDEN MARKET (FINANCIAL PROVISIONS) BILL   [214]

Money Resolution: 11 January 1977

A Government whip formally moved the Money Resolution for the Covent Garden (Financial Provisions) Bill.

A number of Members divided the House on the Resolution, which was carried by 150 votes to 23, the Opposition abstaining from voting. The 152 Members (including tellers) in the Government lobby comprised 146 Labour and 6 Liberal. The 25 Members (including tellers) to oppose the Resolution comprised 17 Labour and 8 Conservative.

Labour Members to vote against the Resolution:

Bennett, A.
Carmichael, N.
Cook, R.
Craigen, J.
English, M.
Hatton, F.

Lambie, D.
Litterick, T.*
Loyden, E.
McDonald, Dr O.
Maynard, Miss J.
Mikardo, I.

Rooker, J.
Silverman, J.
Skinner, D.
Thorne, S.
Wise, Mrs A.

Conservatives to vote against the Resolution:

Body, R.
Budgen, N.
Gow, I.

Gower, Sir R.
Meyer, Sir A.
Miller, H.

Morris, M.
Silvester, F.

HC Deb. 923, 1343–4
1976–7, No. 27.

DEFENCE   [215]

Supply: 12 January 1977

For the Opposition, I. Gilmour moved 'That the salary of the Secretary of State for Defence should be reduced by half'.

From the Labour backbenches, F. Allaun (Lab., Salford, East) moved an amendment designed to make the motion read 'That this House believes that arms expenditure should be reduced, not increased; notes that, far from the illusion that arms spending has been seriously reduced, there has been a real increase since 1974; welcomes the proposed cuts of 1½ per cent next year, and 3 per cent the following year, but considers these inadequate; asks the Government instead to carry out its election commitment to reduce the proportion of Great Britain's resources devoted to arms to that of the major European NATO powers; urges that the savings be devoted to housing, health, education, social services, overseas aid and the re-equipment of British industry; and further calls upon the Government to draw up immediate plans for the redeployment of workers and resources from arms production to socially useful purposes, along the lines of the suggestions made by the Lucas Aerospace Shop Stewards' Combine Committee and the Vickers Shop Stewards' Combine Committee'.

The amendment was opposed by the Government, and negatived by 214 votes to 77, the Opposition abstaining from voting. The 216 Members (including tellers) to oppose the amendment comprised 203 Labour, 11 Liberal, 1 Conservative and 1 Scottish Labour (who voted in both lobbies, in the Government lobby apparently by mistake). The 79 Members (including tellers) to support the amendment comprised 76 Labour, 2 Plaid Cymru and 1 Scottish Labour.

Conservative to vote against the amendment:

Bowden, A.

Labour Members to vote for the amendment:

Allaun, F.	Hatton, F.	Maynard, Miss J.
Atkins, R.	Hayman, Mrs H.	Mikardo, I.
Atkinson, N.	Heffer, E.	Miller, Mrs M.
Bennett, A.	Hooley, F.	Newens, S.
Bidwell, S.	Hoyle, D.	Ovenden, J.
Buchan, N.	Hughes, R.	Parry, R.
Butler, Mrs J.	Hughes, R. J.	Pavitt, L.
Callaghan, J.	Jeger, Mrs L.	Price, C.

Canavan, D.	Jenkins, H.	Richardson, Miss J.*
Carmichael, N.	Kelley, R.	Roberts, G.
Carter-Jones, L.	Kerr, R.	Rodgers, G.
Clemitson, I.	Kilroy-Silk, R.	Rooker, J.
Colquhoun, Mrs M.	Kinnock, N.	Ryman, J.
Cook, R.	Lambie, D.	Sedgemore, B.
Corbett, R.	Lamond, J.	Selby, H.
Crowther, S.	Latham, A.	Silverman, J.
Edge, G.	Lee, J.	Skinner, D.
Edwards, R.	Lestor, Miss J.	Small, W.
Ellis, J.	Litterick, T.	Swain, T.
Evans, I.	Loyden, E.	Thomas, R.
Fernyhough, E.	Lyon, A.	Thorne, S.
Flannery, M.	McDonald, O.*	Tierney, S.
Fletcher, T.	McMillan, T.	Torney, T.
Garrett, J.	Madden, M.	Wilson, W.
Grocott, B.	Marshall, J.	Wise, Mrs A.
Hart, Mrs J.		

HC Deb. 923, 1563–6
1976–7, No. 29.

The motion was then negatived, on a whipped party vote, by 288 votes to 265. There were no apparent abstentions, all the above Labour Members voting in the Government lobby. *HC Deb.* 923, c. 1565–72.

Seven of the Members to vote for the amendment—B. Grocott, J. Lamond, Mrs M. Miller, G. Roberts, S. Tierney, J. Rooker, and I. Clemitson—were Parliamentary Private Secretaries to various Ministers, and were subsequently rebuked for their actions. *The Times*, 18 January 1977. The matter had been discussed in Cabinet. *See The Daily Mail*, 18 January 1977.

SCOTLAND AND WALES BILL   [216]

Committee: 13 January 1977

Clause 1 (Effect of Act)

From the Conservative backbenches, I. Sproat (C., Aberdeen, South) moved an amendment to exclude Scotland from the effects of the Bill.

The amendment was opposed by the Government, and the Opposition decided to abstain officially from voting. However, a number of the Bill's opponents forced it to a division.

The amendment was negatived by 162 votes to 30. The 164 Members (including tellers) in the Government lobby comprised 139 Labour, 12 Liberal, 7 Scottish National, 2 Plaid Cymru, 2 UUUC and 2 Scottish Labour. The 32 Members (including tellers) to support the amendment comprised 30 Conservative and 2 Labour.

Labour Members to vote for the amendment:

Dalyell, T.   Garrett, W.

Conservatives to vote for the amendment:

Aitken, J.	Gardiner, G.*	Montgomery, F.
Boscawen, R.	Goodhew, V.	Morrison, C.
Brotherton, M.	Gow, I.	Page, J.
Crowder, F. P.	Harvie Anderson, Miss B.	Page, R. G.
Dodsworth, G.	Hutchison, M. C.	Raison, T.
Eyre, R.	Jones, A.	Rees, P.
Fisher, Sir N.	Macmillan, M.	Sproat, I.*
Fox, M.	Marshall, M.	Stanbrook, I.
Fraser, H.	Marten, N.	Tebbit, N.
Galbraith, T.	Maxwell-Hyslop, R.	Wiggin, J.

HC Deb. 923, 1795–8
1976–7, No. 31.

SCOTLAND AND WALES BILL   [217]

Committee: 18 January 1977

Clause 1 (Effect of Act)

N. Edwards (C., Pembroke) moved an amendment to exclude Wales from the provisions of the Bill.

(1) After nearly seven hours' debate on the amendment, the Government moved the closure. The Opposition did not divide the House, but a number of backbenchers did. Closure was carried by 277 votes to 25, with the Opposition abstaining from voting. The 27 Members (including tellers) to oppose closure comprised 13 Conservative, 12 Labour and 2 UUUC. According to the division lists,[1] 1 Conservative (a known opponent of devolution) entered the Government lobby to support closure.

Conservative to vote for closure:

Brotherton, M.

Conservatives to vote against closure:

Budgen, N.	Grist, I.	Morgan, G.
Cormack, P.	Hutchison, M. C.	Renton, T.
Crowder, F. P.	Knight, Mrs J.	Tebbit, N.
Gardiner, G.	Langford-Holt, Sir J.	Winterton, N.
Gow, I.		

Labour Members to vote against closure:

Abse, L.	Garrett, W.	Moonman, E.
Anderson, D.	Heffer, E.	Ovenden, J.
Dalyell, T.	Kinnock, N.*	Phipps, C.
Evans, I.	Mendelson, J.	Skinner, D.

(2) The amendment was then negatived, on a whipped party vote, by 287 votes to 263. 4 Labour Members cross-voted to support the amendment.

Labour Members to vote for the amendment:

Cunningham, G.	Moonman, E.	Phipps, C.
Dalyell, T.		

HC Deb. 924, 235–44
1976–7, Nos. 33 & 34.

¹ Also according to the division lists, 26 Members had voted against closure, but only 25 names are listed.

SCOTLAND AND WALES BILL [218]

Committee: 19 January 1977

Clause 1 (Effect of Act)

Miss B. Harvie Anderson (C., Renfrewshire, East) moved an amendment to provide that the government of the Shetland and Orkney islands would not be altered by the measure and that the proposed Scottish Assembly would have no jurisdiction over them.

The amendment was negatived, on a whipped party vote, by 189 votes to 170. 16 Labour Members entered the Opposition lobby to support the amendment.

Labour Members to vote for the amendment:

Colquhoun, Mrs M.   Heffer, E.   Ovenden, J.
Cunningham, G.   Kilroy-Silk, R.   Palmer, J.
Dalyell, T.   Kinnock, N.   Parker, J.
Dean, J.   Latham, A.   Rooker, J.
Ellis, J.   Lestor, Miss J.   Skinner, D.
Evans, I.

HC Deb. 924, 411–14
1976–7, No. 38.

SCOTLAND AND WALES BILL   [219]

Committee: 19 January 1977

Clause 1 (Effect of Act)

From the Opposition Front Bench, L. Brittan moved an amendment to amend the declaration in the clause that the provisions of the Bill 'do not affect the unity of the United Kingdom' to read that 'Nothing in these provisions shall be construed as impairing or in any way affecting the unity of the United Kingdom', and related amendments.

The Opposition argued that the amendment would help provide some guidance to the courts in the case of any ambiguities in provisions that appeared to affect the unity of the United Kingdom.

The amendment was negatived, on a whipped party vote, by 151 votes to 128. 5 Labour Members entered the Opposition lobby to support the amendment.

Labour Members to vote for the amendment:

Dalyell, T.   Kinnock, N.   Urwin, T.
Hughes, R.   Mendelson, J.

HC Deb. 924, 577–80
1976–7, No. 39.

SCOTLAND AND WALES BILL [220]

Committee: 19 January 1977

Clause 1 (Effect of Act)

G. Wilson (SNP, Dundee, East) moved an amendment to provide that devolved powers would not be subject to interference or erosion by the Government or Parliament of the United Kingdom, save with the consent of the Assemblies.

The amendment was opposed by the Government and negatived by 146 votes to 14, with the Opposition abstaining from voting. The 16 Members (including tellers) to support the amendment comprised 11 Scottish National, 2 Plaid Cymru, 1 Scottish Labour, 1 Liberal and 1 UUUC. 7 Conservatives entered the Government lobby to oppose the amendment.

Conservatives to vote against the amendment:

Budgen, N.	Kershaw, A.	Renton, T.
Channon, P.	Page, R. G.	Sproat, I.
Emery, P.		

HC Deb. 924, 579–82
1976–7, No. 40.

SCOTLAND AND WALES BILL [221]

Committee: 19 January 1977

Clause 1 (Effect of Act)

On the motion 'That the Clause stand part of the Bill', a number of the Bill's opponents divided the House.

The 'stand part' motion was carried by 132 votes to 5, with the Opposition abstaining from voting. The 134 Members (including tellers) in the Government lobby comprised 132 Labour, 1 Liberal and 1 Scottish Labour. The 7 Members (including tellers) to oppose the motion comprised 6 Conservative and 1 Labour.

Conservatives to vote against the motion:

Emery, P.	Fraser, H.	Newton, T.
Fairbairn, N.	Hutchison, M. C.*	Winterton, N.*

Labour Member to vote against the motion:

Dalyell, T.

HC Deb. 924, 595–6
1976–7, No. 41.

The division took place at 5.45 a.m.

WATER CHARGES EQUALIZATION BILL   [222]

Second Reading: 24 January 1977

In moving Second Reading, the Minister of State at the Department of the Environment, D. Howell, explained that the Bill was based upon the need for more equitable charges. 'As a result of the Bill no household in the country will be asked to pay more than 2½p a week, and in most cases where people have to pay, they will have to pay about 1p a week.'

A number of Members on both sides of the House opposed the Bill on a number of grounds. It was contended that it would upset the good management techniques of the regional authorities, that the equalization proposed was not a true equalization, and, in various cases, that it would harm Members' constituencies, a view expressed by some Labour Members representing London seats. Some Members on both sides of the House rose to indicate their support for the measure.

The Bill was given a Second Reading by 228 votes to 133, with the Government whips on in support of Second Reading and the Opposition side not being whipped.[1] The 230 Members (including tellers) in the Government lobby comprised 204 Labour, 19 Conservative,[2] 4 Liberal and 3 Plaid Cymru. The 135 Members (including tellers) to vote against Second Reading comprised 115 Conservative, 17 Labour and 3 Liberal.

Labour Members to vote against Second Reading:

Atkinson, N.	Latham, A.	Pavitt, L.
Bidwell, S.	Lestor, Miss J.	Perry, E.*
Brown, R.	Mellish, R.	Richardson, Miss J.
Butler, Mrs J.	Mikardo, I.	Shaw, A.*
English, M.	Mitchell, R.	Stewart, M.
Jeger, Mrs L.	Ovenden, J.	

HC Deb. 924, 1099–102
1976–7, No. 43.

1 *See The Times*, 22 January 1977.
2 R. Body, Miss J. Fookes, Sir R. Gower, I. Grist, J. Hannam, R. Hicks, J. MacGregor, R. Maxwell-Hyslop, Sir A. Meyer, P. Mills, M. Morris, T. Newton, J. Ridsdale, M. Roberts, W. Roberts, C. Shepherd, T. Skeet, K. Stainton and J. Stradling Thomas.

SCOTLAND AND WALES BILL [223]

Committee: 25 January 1977

During an all-night sitting on the Scotland and Wales Bill, A. Beith (Lib., Berwick-upon-Tweed) moved at 1.50 a.m., 'That the Chairman do report Progress and ask leave to sit again'.

The motion was negatived, with the Government whips on against it and Opposition Members supporting it, by 240 votes to 79. 1 Conservative is recorded as having cross-voted to oppose the motion (and another as having voted in both lobbies[1]).

Conservative to vote against the motion:

Fry, P.

HC Deb. 924, 1399–404
1976–7, No. 45.

1 J. Lester. Mr Fry has confirmed to the author the accuracy of the division list in recording his vote.

SCOTLAND AND WALES BILL [224]

Committee: 25 January 1977

Clause 2 (The Assemblies)

J. Mackintosh (Lab., Berwick and East Lothian) moved an amendment to provide that members of the proposed Assemblies should be elected by a system of 'proportional voting' and to increase the number of members.

(1) G. Evans (Plaid Cymru, Carmarthen) moved an amendment to increase the number of additional members of the Welsh Assembly proposed by Mackintosh's amendment from 14 to 24.

The amendment to the amendment was negatived by 221 votes to 25, with the Government opposing it and the Opposition abstaining from voting. The 27 Members (including tellers) to support the amendment comprised 12 Liberal, 10 Scottish National, 3 Plaid Cymru, 1 Scottish Labour and 1 Conservative. 1 Conservative entered the Government lobby to vote against the amendment.

Conservative to vote for the amendment:

Rees-Davies, W.

Conservative to vote against the amendment:

Budgen, N.

(2) Mr Mackintosh's amendment was then divided upon, and negatived by 244 votes to 62. The Government side was whipped against it, while the Opposition allowed a free vote. The 246 Members (including tellers) in the Government lobby comprised 221 Labour, 17 Conservative[1] and 8 UUUC. The 64 Members (including tellers) to support the amendment comprised 35 Conservative,[2] 12 Liberal, 10 Scottish National, 3 Plaid Cymru, 3 Labour and 1 Scottish Labour. The majority of Conservative Members absented themselves from the division.

Labour Members to vote for the amendment:

Ellis, T.   Mackintosh, J.*   Thorne, S.

HC Deb. 924, 1445–50
1976–7, Nos. 46 and 47.

The divisions took place at 4.11 a.m. and 4.23 a.m. respectively.

[1] R. Banks, M. Brotherton, N. Budgen, P. Emery, A. Fell, P. Fry, T. Galbraith, G. Gardiner, Sir J. Gilmour, A. Glyn, I. Grist, Miss B. Harvie Anderson, M. Macmillan, R. Maxwell-Hyslop, R. G. Page, I. Sproat and I. Stanbrook.
[2] K. Baker, W. Benyon, P. Bottomley, C. Brocklebank-Fowler, A. Buchanan-Smith, Lord J. Douglas-Hamilton, R. Fairgrieve, Sir N. Fisher, A. Fletcher, Sir R. Gower, A. Hall-Davis, B. Hayhoe, D. Hurd, D. James, A. Kershaw*, Sir P. Kirk, D. Knox, M. Latham, P. Mayhew, Sir A. Meyer, H. Monro, C. Morrison, D. Mudd, T. Newton, T. Rathbone, P. Rees, W. Rees-Davies, Sir D. Renton, Sir B. Rhys-Williams, M. Rifkind, G. Shaw, Sir G. Sinclair, I. Stewart, R. Wood and G. Younger.

SCOTLAND AND WALES BILL   [225]

Committee: 26 January 1977

Clause 2 (The Assemblies)

D. Steel (Lib., Roxburgh, Selkirk and Peebles) moved an amendment to provide for the proposed Assemblies to be re-named Parliaments.

(1) After three hours of debate on the amendment, the Government moved the closure which was carried by 155 votes to 63, the Opposition voting against. 6 Labour Members entered the Opposition lobby to oppose closure.

Labour Members to vote against closure:

Dalyell, T.	Hamilton, W.	Leadbitter, T.
Evans, I.	Kinnock, N.	Skinner, D.

(2) The amendment was then negatived by 156 votes to 24, with the Opposition abstaining from voting. The 26 Members (including tellers) to support the amendment comprised 12 Liberal, 11 Scottish National and 3 Plaid Cymru. 17 Conservatives entered the Government lobby to vote against it.

Conservatives to vote against the amendment:

Brotherton, M.	Gow, I.	Page, R. G.
Clark, A.	Gower, Sir R.	Raison, T.
Drayson, B.	Grist, I.	Sproat, I.
Emery, P.	Holland, P.	Tebbit, N.
Gardiner, G.	Jones, A.	Winterton, N.
Goodhew, V.	Macfarlane, N.	

HC Deb. 924, 1593–8
1976–7, Nos. 49 and 50.

SCOTLAND AND WALES BILL [226]

Committee: 1 February 1977

Clause 3 (Time of election and term of office of members of Assembly)

Miss B. Harvie Anderson (C., Renfrewshire, East) moved an amendment to provide that the first ordinary election of Members to the Scottish or Welsh Assemblies should not be held until after the next general election.

The amendment was opposed by the Government and negatived by 264 votes to 123. The Opposition was apparently unwhipped, but all voting Conservative Members supported the amendment; they were joined by 6 Labour Members.

Labour Members to vote for the amendment:

Dalyell, T.   Leadbitter, T.   Phipps, C.
Heffer, E.   Mendelson, J.   Spearing, N.

HC Deb. 925, 321–14
1976–7, No. 52.

SCOTLAND AND WALES BILL   [227]

Committee: 1 February 1977

Clause 3 (Time of election and term of office of members of Assembly)

J. Mackintosh (Lab., Berwick and East Lothian) moved an amendment
to provide that the Secretary of State should not perform certain
functions, the functions to be carried out instead by a Commissioner
appointed by the Queen in Council.

The Government opposed the amendment and it was negatived by
293 votes to 26, the Opposition abstaining from voting. The 28 Members (including tellers) to support the amendment comprised 11
Liberal, 11 Scottish National, 2 Scottish Labour, 2 Plaid Cymru, 1
Labour and 1 UUUC. 16 Conservatives entered the Government lobby
to oppose the amendment.

Labour Member to vote for the amendment:

Mackintosh, J.

Conservatives to vote against the amendment:

Bell, R.   Grist, I.   Morgan, G.
Brotherton, M.   Kaberry, Sir D.   Rees, P.
Budgen, N.   Mawby, R.   Rees-Davies, W.
Fletcher-Cooke, C.   Meyer, Sir A.   Spence, J.
Gow, I.   Miscampbell, N.   Stanbrook, I.
Gower, Sir R.

HC Deb. 925, 369–74
1976–7, No. 53.

IMPORT DUTIES [228]

Prayer: 1 February 1977

D. Jay (Lab., Battersea, North) moved formally (under S.O. 73A), 'That an humble Address be presented to Her Majesty, praying that the Import Duties (General) (No. 10) Order 1976 (S.I., 1976, No. 2077), dated 2nd December 1976, a copy of which was laid before this House on 7th December, be annulled.'

The prayer was negatived by 175 votes to 92, with the Government whips on against it and the Opposition abstaining from voting. The 177 Members (including tellers) in the Government lobby comprised 164 Labour, 6 Liberal, 3 Scottish National, 3 Plaid Cymru and 1 Conservative. The 94 Members (including tellers) to support the prayer comprised 71 Labour, 9 UUUC, 7 Scottish National, 5 Conservative and 2 Scottish Labour. Approximately 20 Labour Members appear to have abstained from voting.[1]

Conservative to vote against the prayer:

Emery, P.

Labour Members to vote for the prayer:

Allaun, F.	Flannery, M.	Mendelson, J.
Bagier, G.	Fletcher, T.	Mikardo, I.
Bean, R.	Forrester, J.	Miller, M.
Bennett, A.	Gould, B.	Molloy, W.
Bidwell, S.	Hart, Mrs J.	Newens, S.
Buchan, N.	Heffer, E.	Ovenden, J.
Callaghan, J.	Hooley, F.	Parry, R.
Canavan, D.	Hoyle, D.	Pavitt, L.*
Carmichael, N.	Hughes, R.	Price, C.
Carter-Jones, L.	Hunter, A.	Richardson, Miss J.
Castle, Mrs B.	Jay, D.	Robinson, G.
Colquhoun, Mrs M.	Jenkins, H.	Rodgers, G.
Cook, R.	Kerr, R.	Silverman, J.
Corbett, R.	Kinnock, N.	Skinner, D.
Craigen, J.	Lambie, D.	Spearing, N.
Crowther, S.	Latham, A.	Swain, T.
Davies, B.	Leadbitter, T.	Thomas, R.
Dempsey, J.	Lestor, Miss J.	Thorne, S.
Dunwoody, Mrs G.	Lewis, A.	Torney, T.

Edge, G.	Litterick, T.	Whitlock, W.
Ellis, J.*	Loyden, E.	Wilson, W.
Evans, F.	McNamara, K.	Wise, Mrs A.
Evans, I.	Madden, M.	Woof, R.
Fernyhough, E.	Maynard, Miss J.	

Conservatives to vote for the prayer:

Fell, A.	Marten, N.	Winterton, N.
Hutchison, M. C.	Moate, R.	

HC Deb. 925, 511–4
1976–7, No. 55.

Three of the Members to vote for the prayer—B. Gould, B. Davies, and R. Bean—were Parliamentary Private Secretaries, and in consequence of their votes were dismissed on the instructions of the Prime Minister. *The Times*, 5 February 1977.

[1] Among Labour Members absent from the division after having participated in an immediately preceding one were: R. Atkins, N. Atkinson, R. Brown, I. Clemitson, B. Conlan, I. Davies, B. Ford, D. Ginsburg, E. Ogden, G. Roberts, C. Roderick, B. Sedgemore, A. Shaw, S. Tierney, D. Watkins, J. Watkinson, K. Weetch and F. Willey.

NUCLEAR INDUSTRY (FINANCE) BILL   [229]

Second Reading: 8 February 1977

The Secretary of State for Energy, A. Benn, moved the Second Reading of the Bill. The measure sought to raise the financial limits laid down in the 1971 Act, to permit Government loan guarantees necessary for the raising of money by British Nuclear Fuels Limited, to provide some Government guarantee for British Nuclear Fuels in the event of it being necessary to refund any advance payments, and to authorize the Government itself to acquire shares in the National Nuclear Corporation.

The debate was used also for a wider discussion of nuclear policy, and a number of Members rose to express the fear that the Bill might constitute part of a progression to dependence on nuclear power, with other options for energy sources being foreclosed.

The Bill was given a Second Reading by 196 votes to 22, with the Government whips on in support and the Opposition abstaining officially from voting. The Government lobby comprised solely Labour

Members. The 24 Members (including tellers) to oppose the Bill comprised 12 Liberal, 4 Scottish National, 3 Conservative, 2 Labour, 2 Plaid Cymru and 1 Scottish Labour. A number of Labour Members (including R. Cook and F. Willey) abstained from voting.

Conservatives to vote against the Bill:

Lawrence, I.   Maxwell-Hyslop, R.   Stainton, K.

Labour Members to vote against the Bill:

Skinner, D.   Thorne, S.

HC Deb. 925, 1357–60
1976–7, No. 59.

LOTTERIES [230]

Prayer: 8 February 1977

The Under-Secretary of State at the Home Office, Dr S. Summerskill, moved 'That the Lotteries Regulations 1977, a draft of which was laid before this House on 18th January, be approved.'

The regulations introduced requirements as to provisions which had to be included in a scheme for a promotion of a lottery and introduced restrictions on the sale of tickets in a lottery, as well as limiting the amount of proceeds that could be appropriated on account of expenses. The regulations were necessary also to bring into force outstanding provisions of the 1975 Lotteries Act.

A number of Members objected to the delay in bringing in the regulations and in their implementation, and argued also that they were still too restrictive. There was some confusion as to whether 'instant lotteries' would be banned or not.

The prayer was carried by 151 votes to 26, with the Government lobby whipped in support and the Opposition voting against. The 153 Members (including tellers) in the Government lobby comprised 152 Labour and 1 Conservative. The 28 Members (including tellers) to vote against comprised 16 Conservative,[1] 7 Labour and 5 Liberal.

Conservative to vote for the prayer:

Rees-Davies, W.

Labour Members to vote against the prayer:

Canavan, D.　　　　　Lamond, J.　　　　　McCartney, H.
Gourlay, H.　　　　　Lipton, M.　　　　　Wilson, A.
Lambie, D.

HC Deb. 925, 1391–4
1976–7, No. 60.

¹ The division took place at 11.41 p.m., and there were apparently few Conservatives present.

LOTTERIES (SCOTLAND) [231]

Prayer: 8 February 1977

Following debate on the Lotteries Regulations 1977 (see preceding division), the Under-Secretary of State for Scotland, H. Ewing, moved formally 'That the Lotteries (Scotland) Regulations 1977, a draft of which was laid before this House on 18th January, be approved.'

The prayer was carried by 149 votes to 28, with the Government whips on and the Opposition voting against. The Government lobby comprised solely Labour Members. The 30 Members (including tellers) to oppose the regulations comprised 17 Conservative,¹ 5 Labour, 5 Liberal and 3 Scottish National.

Labour Members to vote against the prayer:

Canavan, D.*　　　　Lambie, D.　　　　　McCartney, H.
Gourlay, H.　　　　　Lamond, J.

HC Deb. 925, 1393–6
1976–7, No. 61.

¹ The division took place at 11.52 p.m. and apparently there were few Conservative Members present.

RENT (AGRICULTURE) (AMENDMENT) BILL [232]

Second Reading: 9 February 1977

The Bill sought to amend the 1976 Rent (Agriculture) Act in order to rectify a minor clerical error which had taken place in the House of

Lords' Public Bill Office which resulted in three lines of text being deleted which should not have been.

The Opposition did not divide against the Bill, but two Conservative backbenchers forced it to a division. It was given a Second Reading by 50 votes to o. The 2 Members to act as tellers against the Bill were both Conservatives.

Conservatives to act as tellers against Second Reading:

Glyn, A.*   Ridley, N.*

HC Deb. 925, 1621–2
1976–7, No. 64.

SCOTLAND AND WALES BILL   [233]

Committee: 10 February 1977

Prior to discussion on a motion tabled by the Leader of the House, M. Foot, to bring forward a proposed new schedule to provide for referendums in Scotland and Wales for debate prior to clause 4, M. Macmillan (C., Farnham) rose on a point of order to contend that, on the basis of precedent, it was out of order to propose amendments to provide for mandatory (as opposed to advisory) referendums. The Chairman, O. Murton, ruled that it would be in order; in his view, the 1975 Referendum Act had largely destroyed the basis upon which previous rulings had been given.

After an hour had been taken up with points of order on this matter, F. Pym, from the Opposition Front Bench, said that many Members would wish to consider in greater depth the Chair's ruling, and moved 'That the Chairman do report Progress and ask leave to sit again'.

The motion was negatived on a whipped party vote by 248 votes to 197. 11 Labour Members cross-voted to support the motion. On the Conservative benches, at least one Member, E. Heath (C., Sidcup), abstained from voting.

Labour Members to vote for the motion:

Abse, L.	Hamilton, W.	Mendelson, J.
Brown, R.	Lamond, J.	Prentice, R.
Cunningham, G.	MacFarquhar, R.	Rooker, J.
Dalyell, T.	Mackintosh, J.	

HC Deb. 925, 1693–8
1976–7, No. 65.

The motion tabled by the Leader of the House was subsequently debated and divided upon: see below.

SCOTLAND AND WALES BILL   [234]

Committee: 10 February 1977

The Leader of the House, M. Foot, moved 'That the Order of the Committee (13th January) be amended and that the new Clause (Referendums in Scotland and Wales) in the name of Mr Michael Foot and the new Schedule (Referendums in Scotland and Wales) in the name of Mr Michael Foot be considered before Clause 4.'

(1) After nearly four hours of debate, the Government moved the closure. Although the Opposition did not officially divide the House, a number of Conservative backbenchers did. The closure was carried by 253 votes to 51. The 53 Members (including tellers) to oppose closure were all Conservatives.

Conservatives to vote against closure:

Amery, J.	Goodhew, V.	Rathbone, T.
Banks, R.	Gow, I.	Rawlinson, Sir P.
Brocklebank-Fowler, C.	Grist, I.	Rees, P.
Budgen, N.*	Harvie Anderson, Miss B.	Renton, T.
Chalker, Mrs L.	Higgins, T.	Rhodes James, R.
Clarke, K.	Hutchison, M. C.	Roberts, W.
Cope, J.	Lawrence, I.	Shaw, G.
Crouch, D.	Macfarlane, N.	Shersby, M.
Dean, P.	MacGregor, J.	Sproat, I.
Drayson, B.	Macmillan, M.	Stainton, K.
du Cann, E.	Miller, H.	Stanbrook, I.
Emery, P.*	Mills, P.	Steen, A.
Farr, J.	Monro, H.	Tebbit, N.
Fisher, Sir N.	Morgan-Giles, M.	Wakeham, J.
Fookes, Miss J.	Onslow, C.	Wall, P.
Fraser, H.	Page, J.	Wiggin, J.
Gardiner, G.	Page, R. G.	Winterton, N.
Glyn, A.	Raison, T.	

(2) The motion moved by Mr Foot was then carried by 269 votes to 64. Although the Opposition did not divide against it—the Front Bench spokesman, F. Pym, indicating that he did not intend to press

the matter, and that the issues raised previously on points of order (see preceding division) could not be dealt with by voting on the motion—a number of Conservative backbenchers did divide the House. The 66 Members (including tellers) to oppose the motion comprised 53 Conservative, 9 Liberal and 4 Labour.

Conservatives to vote against the motion:

Amery, J.
Banks, R.
Brocklebank-Fowler, C.
Budgen, N.*
Clarke, K.
Cope, J.
Crouch, D.
Drayson, B.
du Cann, E.
Emery, P.
Farr, J.
Fisher, Sir N.
Fletcher-Cooke, C.
Fookes, Miss J.
Fraser, H.
Gardiner, G.
Glyn, A.
Goodhew, V.

Gow, I.
Grist, I.
Harvie Anderson, Miss B.
Higgins, T.
Hutchison, M. C.
Lawrence, I.
Macfarlane, N.
MacGregor, J.
Macmillan, M.
Miller, H.
Mills, P.
Monro, H.
Morgan-Giles, M.
Morrison, C.
Onslow, C.
Page, J.
Page, R. G.
Raison, T.

Rathbone, T.
Rawlinson, Sir P.
Rees, P.
Renton, T.
Rhodes James, R.
Roberts, W.
Shaw, G.
Shersby, M.
Sproat, I.
Stainton, K.
Stanbrook, I.
Steen, A.
Tebbit, N.
Wakeham, J.
Wall, P.
Wiggin, J.
Winterton, N.*

Labour Members to vote against the motion:

Brown, R.
Cunningham, G.

Lamond, J.

Leadbitter, T.

HC Deb. 925, 1781–8
1976–7, Nos. 66 and 67.

SOCIAL SECURITY (MISCELLANEOUS PROVISIONS) BILL [235]

Report: 14 February 1977

Clause 4 (Alteration of earnings rule)

C. Smith (Lib., Rochdale) moved formally an amendment to alter the time period involved in the clause.

The amendment was negatived by 161 votes to 21, with the Opposition abstaining from voting. The Government lobby comprised solely Labour Members. The 23 Members (including tellers) to support the amendment comprised 9 Scottish National, 8 Liberal and 6 Conservative.

Conservatives to vote for the amendment:

Bell, R.	Glyn, A.	Page, R. G.
Bottomley, P.	Newton, T.	Winterton, N.

HC Deb. 926, 149–52
1976–7, No. 68.

SOCIAL SECURITY (MISCELLANEOUS PROVISIONS) [236] BILL

Report: 14 February 1977

Clause 12 (Amendments of Supplementary Benefits Act)

The Minister for Social Security, S. Orme, moved an amendment to provide that the parental contribution be taken into account in assessing the resources of a full-time student seeking supplementary benefits. The Minister explained that the amendment was to provide legislative authority for what was already done in practice.

The amendment was carried by 116 votes to 23. The Opposition abstained from voting. The Government lobby comprised solely Labour Members. The 25 Members (including tellers) to oppose the amendment comprised 9 Liberal, 9 Scottish National and 7 Labour.

Labour Members to vote against the amendment:

Canavan, D.	Mikardo, I.	Richardson, Miss J.
Latham, A.	Ovenden, J.	Skinner, D.
Maynard, Miss J.		

HC Deb. 926, 197–200
1976–7, No. 69.

The division took place at 11.40 p.m.

SOCIAL SECURITY (MISCELLANEOUS PROVISIONS) BILL

[237]

Report: 14 February 1977

Clause 18 (Other miscellaneous amendments)

From the Opposition Front Bench, Mrs L. Chalker moved an amendment to provide that the Occupational Pensions Board should be responsible for the alternative solvency test rather than the Secretary of State.

The amendment was opposed by the Government. The Opposition did not officially divide the House on the amendment, but a number of backbenchers did.

The amendment was negatived by 105 votes to 14, with the Opposition abstaining from voting. The Government lobby comprised solely Labour Members. The 16 Members (including tellers) to support the amendment comprised 7 Liberal, 6 Conservative and 3 Scottish National.

Conservatives to support the amendment:

Boscawen, R.	Glyn, A.	Monro, H.
Bottomley, P.*	Gray, H.	Newton, T.*

HC Deb. 926, 211–4
1976–7, No. 70.

The division took place at 12.26 a.m.

SCOTLAND AND WALES BILL

[238]

Committee: 15 February 1977

New Clause 40 (Referendums in Scotland and Wales)

Debate on the new clause was resumed, after having been adjourned on 10 February. Upon resuming the debate, several Members rose on various points of order. The Lord President of the Council and Leader of the House, M. Foot, then rose to announce that it was the Government's intention that the referendums should now be consultative and not mandatory, and that the necessary amendments would be moved at Report stage.

A number of Members rose on points of order, contending that Mr Foot's statement had put the House in a difficult situation if the relevant amendments were not to be moved until Report stage.

After nearly an hour's discussion, E. Heffer (Lab., Liverpool, Walton) rose to suggest that the Government should withdraw the clause and return with a new one, and in order to facilitate that he moved 'That the Chairman do report progress and ask leave to sit again'.

Mr Heffer's motion to report progress was opposed by the Government, and negatived by 231 votes to 202. The Opposition supported the motion, and were joined in the 'Aye' lobby by 15 Labour Members.

Labour Members to vote for the motion:

Cunningham, G.	Hayman, Mrs H.	Mendelson, J.
Dalyell, T.	Heffer, E.	Moonman, E.*
Evans, F.	Lamond, J.	Palmer, A.
Garrett, W.	Lestor, Miss J.	Phipps, C.
Hamilton, W.	Litterick, T.	Spearing, N.

HC Deb. 926, 301–4
1976–7, No. 71.

Debate on the new clause then resumed: see below.

SCOTLAND AND WALES BILL [239]

Committee: 15 February 1977

New Clause 40 (Referendums in Scotland and Wales)

The new clause provided for referendums to be held in Scotland and Wales on the question of whether or not effect was to be given to the provisions of the Bill.

Debate on the new clause commenced on 10 February, and was then adjourned to the 15th. After the Leader of the House, M. Foot, announced that the Government had decided that the referendums should be consultative and not mandatory (the clause provided that the Act should not take effect if the decisions in the referendums were negative ones), and several Members rose on points of order followed by an attempt to adjourn the debate: see preceding division.

After a further seven-and-a-half hours of discussion on the clause, the Chair accepted a closure motion by the Government.

(1) The closure was carried by 230 votes to 32, with the Opposition abstaining from voting. The 34 Members (including tellers) to oppose closure comprised 29 Conservative, 3 Labour, 1 Liberal and 1 UUUC.

Conservatives to vote against closure:

Boscawen, R.	Goodhew, V.	Mayhew, P.
Budgen, N.*	Griffiths, E.	Meyer, Sir A.
Channon, P.	Grist, I.	Morrison, C.
Cooke, R.	Harvie Anderson, Miss B.	Newton, T.
Crouch, D.	Higgins, T.*	Rathbone, T.
Emery, P.	Hutchison, M. C.	Rees, P.
Fairgrieve, R.	Latham, M.	Sproat, I.
Fisher, Sir N.	MacGregor, J.	Wiggin, J.
Gardiner, G.	Macmillan, M.	Winterton, N.
Glyn, A.	Maxwell-Hyslop, R.	

Labour Members to vote against closure:

Cunningham, G.	Dalyell, T.	Lamond, J.

(2) The new clause was then put, and carried by 231 votes to 24, with the Opposition abstaining from voting. The 26 Members (including tellers) to oppose the clause comprised 24 Conservative, 1 Labour and 1 Scottish Labour. 1 Conservative entered the Government lobby to support the clause.

Conservatives to vote against the clause:

Boscawen, R.	Glyn, A.	Macmillan, M.
Budgen, N.*	Goodhew, V.	Maxwell-Hyslop, R.
Channon, P.	Griffiths, E.	Mayhew, P.
Cooke, R.	Harvie Anderson, Miss B.	Newton, T.
Crouch, D.	Higgins, T.*	Rathbone, T.
Emery, P.	Hutchison, M. C.	Sproat, I.
Fairgrieve, R.	Latham, M.	Wiggin, J.
Gardiner, G.	MacGregor, J.	Winterton, N.

Labour Member to vote against the clause:

Lamond, J.

Conservative to vote for the clause:

Meyer, Sir A.

HC Deb. 926, 451–6
1976–7, Nos. 72 and 73.

SCOTLAND AND WALES BILL [240]

Committee: 16 February 1977

New Clause 40 (Referendums in Scotland and Wales)

G. Gardiner (C., Reigate) moved an amendment to provide for a referendum to be held in the whole of the United Kingdom (and not just in Scotland and Wales) on the question of whether or not effect should be given to the provisions of the Bill.

The amendment was opposed by the Government, and for the Opposition, L. Brittan announced that, while he was impressed by the logic of the amendment, 'I fear that the disease with which we have been presented by the Government is incapable of being cured by this means'.

The amendment was negatived by 249 votes to 69, with the Opposition abstaining from voting. The 71 Members (including tellers) to support the amendment comprised 57 Conservative, 9 Liberal, 4 UUUC and 1 Labour.

Conservatives to vote for the amendment:

Benyon, W.*	Harvie Anderson, Miss B.	Page, J.
Braine, Sir B.	Howell, D.	Page, R. G.
Brotherton, M.	Hunt, J.	Price, D.
Carlisle, M.	Hutchison, M. C.	Raison, T.
Channon, P.	Jones, A.	Rathbone, T.
Cooke, R.	Jopling, M.	Rees, P.
Cope, J.	Knight, Mrs J.	Renton, T.*
Cormack, P.	Lawrence, I.	Ridley, N.
Dodsworth, G.	Macmillan, M.	Rippon, G.
Emery, P.	Marten, N.	Sainsbury, T.

Eyre, P.	Meyer, Sir A.	Shepherd, C.
Fletcher-Cooke, C.	Mitchell, D.	Sims, R.
Fox, M.	Montgomery, F.	Skeet, T.
Gardiner, G.	More, J.	Smith, D.
Glyn, A.	Morgan-Giles, M.	Stanbrook, I.
Goodhew, V.	Morris, M.	Tebbit, N.
Gow, I.	Mudd, D.	van Straubenzee, W.
Griffiths, E.	Nelson, A.	Walder, D.
Grylls, M.	Normanton, T.	Winterton, N.

Labour Member to vote for the amendment:

Dalyell, T.
HC Deb. 926, 637–42
1976–7, No. 74.

SCOTLAND AND WALES BILL [241]

Committee: 22 February 1977

The Lord President of the Council and Leader of the House of Commons, M. Foot, moved an allocation of time (guillotine) motion for the remaining stages of the Scotland and Wales Bill.

Opposition Members rose to oppose the motion, as did K. Lomas (Lab., Huddersfield, West), E. Moonman (Lab., Basildon), L. Abse (Lab., Pontypool), F. Evans (Lab., Caerphilly), Dr C. Phipps (Lab., Dudley, West) and J. Mendelson (Lab., Penistone). Mr Lomas declared that he was not going to vote for the Government. His loyalty, he declared, was to the United Kingdom. Mr Mendelson announced that he was opposed to the motion on constitutional and political grounds. He would vote against it. E. Heffer (Lab., Liverpool, Walton) said he was in a dilemma as to how to vote. He would not vote for it, and would either abstain or vote against.

The motion was *defeated*, on a whipped party vote, by 312 votes to 283, *a majority against the Government of 29*. The 285 Members (including tellers) in the Government lobby comprised 264 Labour, 11 Scottish National, 3 Plaid Cymru, 2 Liberal, 2 UUUC, 2 Scottish Labour and 1 SDLP. The 314 Members (including tellers) in the Opposition lobby comprised 274 Conservative, 22 Labour, 11 Liberal and 7 UUUC. 21 Labour Members abstained from voting.[1]

Labour Members to vote against the motion:

Abse, L.	Evans, F.	Mendelson, J.
Brown, R.	Garrett, W.	Moonman, E.
Cowans, H.	Hamilton, W.	Ovenden, J.
Cunningham, G.	Lamond, J.	Parker, J.
Dalyell, T.	Leadbitter, T.	Phipps, C.
Dean, J.	Lewis, A.	Prentice, R.
Douglas-Mann, B.	Lomas, K.	Urwin, T.
Dunwoody, Mrs G.		

HC Deb. 926, 1361–6
1976–7, No. 79.

[1] The 21 abstainers were: D. Anderson, G. Bagier, A. Bottomley, R. Buchanan, B. Conlan, R. Crawshaw, I. Evans, J. Evans, F. Hatton, E. Heffer, R. Hughes, N. Kinnock, J. Lee, R. Mitchell, W. Molloy, G. Roberts, J. Rooker, J. Ryman, N. Spearing, D. Watkins and W. Whitlock. *The Times* 23 February 1977. (*The Guardian* 23 February 1977 lists 20 abstainers —the foregoing less F. Hatton—but other sources support the figure of 21. *The Economist* 19 November 1977, *Politics Today*, 14 March 1977, no. 4, p. 72.)

As a consequence of losing the guillotine motion, the Government decided not to proceed with the Bill as it stood, and subsequently introduced two separate Bills, one to provide for devolution to Scotland and the other to provide for a more limited form of devolution to Wales. (See divisions on the Scotland Bill and the Wales Bill below.)

WALES   [242]

Supply: 28 February 1977

The Opposition used one of its Supply Days to debate Wales on an adjournment motion.

At the end of the debate, the Liberals forced the adjournment motion to a division. It was negatived by 100 votes to 13, the Opposition abstaining from voting. The Government lobby comprised solely Labour Members. The 15 Members (including tellers) to vote for adjournment comprised 9 Liberals, 4 Conservatives and 2 Plaid Cymru.

Conservatives to vote for adjournment:

Marten, N.	Rodgers, Sir J.	Stanbrook, I.
Rees-Davies, W.		

HC Deb. 927, 105–6.
1976–7, No. 83.

PREVENTION OF TERRORISM **[243]**

Prayer: 9 March 1977

The Home Secretary, M. Rees, moved 'That the Prevention of Terrorism (Temporary Provisions) Act 1976 (Continuance) Order 1977, a draft of which was laid before this House on 24th February, be approved.'

The Order extended for a further twelve months the 1976 Prevention of Terrorism (Temporary Provisions) Act. The Home Secretary argued that it was necessary in view of the continuing threat of Provisional IRA activities in Britain.

A number of Labour backbenchers rose to criticize and oppose the Order, arguing that, on grounds of civil liberties, it was undesirable, and pressing for an inquiry into its operation.

The motion was approved by 140 votes to 15, the Opposition voting with the Government. The 142 Members (including tellers) in the Government lobby comprised 103 Labour, 25 Conservative, 8 UUUC and 6 Liberal. The 17 Members (including tellers) oppose the motion comprised 16 Labour and 1 SDLP.

Labour Members to vote against the motion:

Bennett, A.	Latham, A.	Parry, R.
Bidwell, S.	Litterick, T.	Richardson, Miss J.
Canavan, D.	Loyden, E.	Skinner, D.
Flannery, M.	Maynard, Miss J.	Thomas, R.
Fletcher, T.	Mikardo, I.*	Thorne, S.
Lamond, J.		

HC Deb. 926, 1567–70
1976–7, No. 86.

The division took place at 11.29 p.m.

NUCLEAR INDUSTRY (FINANCE) BILL **[244]**

Report: 21 March 1977

Clause 1 (Government guarantee of companies' borrowing, etc.)

D. Penhaligon (Lib., Truro) moved an amendment to delete subsection (2) of the clause which provided for a guarantee of up to £500m. to cover repayments to those who had invested in a reprocessing plant should British Nuclear Fuels Limited be unable to repay in certain circumstances.

The Government opposed the amendment, and from the Opposition Front Bench, H. Gray announced that it was not the intention of the official Opposition to vote on it.

The amendment was negatived by 171 votes to 28, with the Opposition abstaining from voting. The Government lobby comprised solely Labour Members. The 30 Members (including tellers) to support the amendment comprised 22 Conservative, 6 Liberal and 2 Scottish National. At least 2 Labour Members (R. Cook and F. Hooley) abstained from voting.

Conservatives to vote for the amendment:

Bottomley, P.
Clark, A.
Cooke, R.
Fisher, Sir N.
Fookes, Miss J.
Glyn, A.
Gow, I.
Grylls, M.

Hodgson, R.
Knight, Mrs J.
Lawrence, I.
Marshall, M.
Mates, M.
Miscampbell, N.
Nelson, A.

Onslow, C.
Rathbone, T.
Rees-Davies, W.
Stainton, K.
Stanbrook, I.
Trotter, N.
Wakeham, J.

HC Deb. 928, 977–80
1976–7, No. 90.

NUCLEAR INDUSTRY (FINANCE) BILL [245]

Report: 21 March 1977

Clause 1 (Government guarantees of companies' borrowing, etc.)

G. Dodsworth (C., Hertfordshire, South-West) moved an amendment to provide that before any guarantee was given under the clause an order made by statutory instrument showing the extent, character and amount of the guarantee should be laid before and approved by the Commons.

The Government opposed the amendment on the grounds that they were following precedent, and that it would complicate unnecessarily the giving of guarantees and might prejudice British Nuclear Fuel Limited's commercial interest.

The amendment was negatived by 145 votes to 40, the Opposition abstaining apparently from voting. The Government lobby comprised solely Labour Members. The 42 Members (including tellers) to support the amendment comprised 31 Conservative, 9 Liberal and 2 Scottish National. At least one Labour Member (F. Hooley) abstained from voting.

Conservatives to vote for the amendment:

Boscawen, R.
Bottomley, P.
Buck, A.
Budgen, N.
Clarke, K.
Cockcroft, J.
Dodsworth, G.*
Fairgrieve, R.
Fisher, Sir N.
Fookes, Miss J.
Fox, M.

Gardner, E.
Glyn, A.*
Hampson, K.
Hicks, R.
Hodgson, R.
Knight, Mrs J.
Lawrence, I.
Macfarlane, N.
Morris, M.
Nelson, A.

Newton, T.
Nott, J.
Page, R. G.
Rathbone, T.
Sainsbury, T.
Shersby, M.
Skeet, T.
Stanbrook, I.
Trotter, N.
Viggers, P.

HC Deb. 928, 991–4
1976–7, No. 91.

NUCLEAR INDUSTRY (FINANCE) BILL [246]

Third Reading: 21 March 1977

The Under-Secretary of State for Energy, A. Eadie, moved the Third Reading of the Bill. The Bill, he explained, provided the basis for financing British Nuclear Fuel Ltd's large investment programme.

For the Opposition. H. Gray welcomed the Bill, and indicated they would be happy to give it a Third Reading.

The Bill was given a Third Reading by 140 votes to 11, the Liberals having divided the House against it. Despite H. Gray's comments in debate, the Opposition abstained from voting. The 13 Members (including tellers) to oppose Third Reading comprised 10 Liberal and 3 SNP. 3 Conservatives entered the Govt lobby to vote for Third Reading. At least one Labour Member (F. Hooley) abstained from voting.

Conservatives to vote for Third Reading:

Hodgson, R.   Langford-Holt, Sir J.   Stanbrook, I.

HC Deb. 928, 1003–6
1976–7, No. 92.

SOCIAL SECURITY (MISCELLANEOUS PROVISIONS) BILL   [247]

Lords Amendment: 24 March 1977

New Clause A (Amendment of regulations for crediting contributions)

The Minister for Social Security, S. Orme, moved the new clause, which was designed to extend the existing power to make regulations on credits in order that the Government could restrict the use of credits given for 1975–6 and 1976–7 in establishing future benefit rights. The Minister explained that the purpose was to avoid the unintended and expensive effect of changes to the national insurance scheme since 1975 which would have enabled people to acquire contributory benefit rights although they had not paid contributions or received contributory benefit for many years.

From the Opposition Front Bench, P. Jenkin, although expressing unhappiness with the way the matter had been dealt with, stated that the Opposition did not intend to oppose the Government in trying to put matters right.

The clause was approved by 229 votes to 47, with the Opposition abstaining from voting. The 49 Members (including tellers) to oppose the clause were all Conservatives.

Conservatives to vote against the clause:

Arnold, T.	Harvie Anderson, Miss B.	Newton, T.
Bennett, Sir F.	Hordern, P.	Onslow, C.
Bennett, R.	Hutchison, M. C.	Osborn, J.
Body, R.	James, D.	Page, R. G.
Bottomley, P.*	Jessel, T.	Rees, P.
Brittan, L.	Jones, A.	Rees-Davies, W.
Buck, A.	Lawrence, I.	Rodgers, Sir J.
Clarke, K.	McNair-Wilson, M.	Scott-Hopkins, J.
Cooke, R.	Marshall, M.	Sinclair, Sir G.
Cormack, P.	Mates, M.	Smith, D.
Durant, T.	Maxwell-Hyslop, R.	Steen, A.*

Eden, Sir J.
Eyre, R.
Fairbairn, N.
Farr, J.
Fookes, Miss J.
Fry, P.

Mayhew, P.
Miller, H.
Mills, P.
Montgomery, F.
Morris, M.

Tebbit, N.
Viggers, P.
Walker, P.
Warren, K.
Winterton, N.

HC Deb. 928, 1497–1500
1976–7, No. 95.

EUROPEAN COMMUNITIES ACT 1972 [248]

Private Member's Motion: 1 April 1977

J. Lee (Lab., Birmingham, Handsworth) moved a motion calling upon the Government to institute a review of the 1972 European Communities Act, and to amend the provisions of Standing Order 73(A) dealing with the scrutiny of EEC Commission documents. Under his proposed amendments, the EEC Scrutiny Committee would be given power to decide on the merits of Commission documents, either approving, disapproving or taking note of them.

Although a Private Member's motion, it was opposed by the Government, and the Parliamentary Secretary to the Privy Council Office, W. Price, moved an amendment to amend the provisions in the motion. The amendment was designed in particular to remove the power to decide on the merits of documents and to prevent the Scrutiny Committee becoming master of its own time.

At 3.18 p.m. (the motion being taken on a Friday), the amendment was put, and Government whips acted as tellers in support of it. Voting on the amendment was 28 against to 0 for. The 30 Members (including tellers) to vote against the amendment comprised 16 Labour, 13 Conservative and 1 Scottish National. Opposition Members were not whipped, Opposition whips being among those voting against.

Labour Members to vote against the amendment:

Atkinson, N.
Bidwell, S.*
Callaghan, J.
English, M.
Jay, D.
Kelley, R.

Kerr, R.
Lee, J.*
McCartney, H.
Mendelson, J.
Price, C.

Rooker, J.
Silverman, J.
Spearing, N.
Tuck, R.
Wise, Mrs A.

HC Deb. 929, 815–16
1976–7, No. 99.

Forty Members not appearing present on the report of the division, the Question was not decided and the business stood over to the next sitting. This would appear to have been the result sought by the Government in forcing the division, and not having its supporters vote.

BUDGET RESOLUTIONS AND ECONOMIC SITUATION [249]

Ways and Means: 4 April 1977

Following the Chancellor of the Exchequer's Budget speech, the Ways and Means motions on which the Finance Bill would be brought in were put.

After the Opposition had divided the House on motion no. 11 (*Hydrocarbon oil, etc.*), increasing the excise duty on hydrocarbon oil, a number of backbenchers divided the House on motion no. 15 (*Vehicles Excise Duty*) which amended the definition of a goods vehicle and increased rates of vehicle excise duty.

The motion was approved by 290 votes to 61, with the Opposition abstaining from voting. The 292 Members (including tellers) in the Government lobby comprised 291 Labour and 1 SDLP. The 63 Members (including tellers) to oppose the motion comprised 49 Conservative, 10 Scottish National, 2 Plaid Cymru, 1 Scottish Labour and 1 Ulster Unionist.

Conservatives to vote against the motion:

Adley, R.	Kitson, Sir T.	Morrison, C.
Brocklebank-Fowler, C.	Knox, D.	Mudd, D.
Brotherton, M.	Langford-Holt, Sir J.	Nelson, A.
Burden, F.	Madel, D.	Normanton, T.
Clegg, W.	Marten, N.	Page, J.
Emery, P.	Mates, M.	Price, D.
Eyre, R.	Mawby, R.	Rees, P.
Fairbairn, N.	Maxwell-Hyslop, R.	Shaw, G.
Fairgrieve, R.	Meyer, Sir A.	Shepherd, C.
Fry, P.	Miller, H.	Shersby, M.
Glyn, A.	Miscampbell, N.	Smith, D.
Goodhew, V.	Moate, R.	Spicer, J.
Gower, Sir R.	Monro, H.	Stanbrook, I.

Grieve, P.
Hannam, J.
Hicks, R.
Kershaw, A.

Montgomery, F.
Morgan, G.
Morris, M.

Steen, A.
Stewart, I.
Wiggin, J.

HC Deb. 929, 1023-6
1976-7, No. 101.

BUDGET RESOLUTIONS AND ECONOMIC SITUATION [250]

Ways and Means: 4 April 1977

Following the Chancellor of the Exchequer's Budget speech, the Ways and Means motions on which the Finance Bill would be brought in were put.

A number of Labour Members divided the House on motion no. 16, *Income Tax* (charge and rates for 1977-78), which provided that the basic rate of income tax would be 35 per cent and with the higher rates applying on incomes in excess of £6,000.

The motion was approved by 369 votes to 54, with the Opposition supporting the Government. The 371 Members (including tellers) in the Government lobby comprised 224 Labour, 137 Conservative, 7 Liberal, 2 Ulster Unionist and 1 Scottish National. The 56 Members (including tellers) to vote against the motion comprised 55 Labour backbenchers and one Minister voting in error in the wrong lobby.[1] Ten or more Labour Members appear to have abstained from voting.

Labour Members to vote against the motion:

Allaun, F.
Atkinson, N.
Bennett, A.
Bidwell, S.*
Callaghan, J.
Canavan, D.
Carter-Jones, L.
Colquhoun, Mrs M.
Cook, R.
Craigen, J.
Edge, G.
Ellis, J.

Hughes, R. J.
Jeger, Mrs L.
Jenkins, H.
Kelley, R.
Kerr, R.
Kilroy-Silk, R.
Kinnock, N.
Lambie, D.
Lamond, J.
Latham, A.
Lee, J.
Loyden, E.

Newens, S.
Ovenden, J.
Parry, R.
Prescott, J.
Price, C.
Richardson, Miss J.
Roberts, G.
Rodgers, G.
Rooker, J.
Rose, P.
Selby, H.
Skinner, D.

Evans, F.	Lyon, A.	Swain, T.
Evans, J.	McDonald, O.	Thomas, R.
Fernyhough, E.	Madden, M.	Thorne, S.
Flannery, M.	Marshall, J.	Torney, T.
Fletcher, T.	Maynard, Miss J.	Wise, Mrs A.
Heffer, E.	Mikardo, I.*	Woof, R.
Hoyle, D.		

HC Deb. 929, 1027–32
1976–7, No. 102.

¹ The division lists record the Minister of State at the Privy Council Office, J. Smith, as voting in the 'No' lobby.

DENTISTS (RIGHTS OF ESTABLISHMENT) [251]

22 April 1977

A Government whip moved formally 'That this House takes note of Commission Document No. R/2196/76 on Rights of Establishment of Dentists'.

In order to object apparently to the Government bringing forward such matters on a Friday, and also in order to draw attention to the closure of a ward in a hospital in the constituency of Islington, South and Finsbury,¹ two Labour Members divided the House on the motion.

The voting was 14 to 0 in favour of the motion. The 16 Members (including tellers) in the Government lobby comprised 9 Labour, 6 Conservative and 1 Scottish National. The 2 Members to act as tellers against the motion were Labour Members.

Labour Members to act as tellers against the motion:

Cunningham, G.*   Lewis, A.*

HC Deb. 930, 675–8
1976–7, No. 106.

¹ See the preceding debate on the Money Resolution for the Rentcharges Bill. *HC Deb.* 930, c. 659–76.

Forty Members not being present, the Question was not decided in the affirmative and was held over until the next sitting. The division took place at 4.52 p.m. on a Friday.

DENTISTS AND PUBLIC HEALTH OFFICIALS   [252]
(ADVISORY COMMITTEES)

22 April 1977

A Government whip moved formally 'That this House takes note of Commission Document No. R/103/77 on Advisory Committees on Dentists and Senior Public Health Officials.'

After having divided the House on an immediately preceding 'takes note' motion (see above), two Labour Members again divided the House.

The voting was 18 votes to 0 in support of the motion. The 20 Members (including tellers) in the Government lobby comprised 12 Labour, 7 Conservative and 1 Scottish National. The two Members to act as tellers against the motion were Labour Members.

Labour Members to act as tellers against the motion:

Cunningham, G.*   Lewis, A.*

HC Deb. 930, 677–8
1976–7, No. 107.

Forty Members not being present, the Question was not decided in the affirmative and was held over until the next sitting. The division took place at 5.02 p.m. on a Friday.

DATA PROCESSING   [253]

22 April 1977

A Government whip moved formally 'That this House takes note of Commission Document No. R/2697/76 on Data Processing.'

After having divided the House on two preceding 'take note' motions (see above), two Labour Members again divided the House.

The voting was 13 votes to 0 in support of the motion. The 15 Members (including tellers) in the Government lobby comprised 9 Labour, 5 Conservative and 1 Scottish National. The two Members to act as tellers against the motion were Labour Members.

Labour Members to act as tellers against the motion:

Cunningham, G.*   Lewis, A.*

HC Deb. 930, 677-8
1976-7, No. 108.

Forty Members not being present, the Question was not decided in the affirmative and was held over until the next sitting. The division took place at 5.12 p.m. on a Friday.

EUROPEAN COMMUNITIES (TREATIES)   [254]

Prayer: 25 April 1977

The Under-Secretary of State for Foreign and Commonwealth Affairs, J. Tomlinson, moved 'That the European Communities (Definition of Treaties) Order 1977, a draft of which was laid before this House on 3rd March, be approved.'

The order sought approval for five treaties, and with it was discussed a prayer to approve the European Communities (Definition of Treaties) (No. 2) Order 1977.

A number of Members rose to criticize the prayer, objecting to the lack of information on the documents concerned, the lumping together of several treaties in the order, and questioning what effects they would have.

With Opposition support, the prayer was carried by 71 votes to 21. The 73 Members (including tellers) to support it comprised 60 Labour, 9 Conservative and 3 Liberal. The 23 Members (including tellers) to vote against it comprised 21 Labour, 1 UUUC and 1 Scottish National.

Labour Members to vote against the order:

Allaun, F.	Garrett, W.	Madden, M.
Bennett, A.	Hooley, F.*	Mikardo, I.
Callaghan, J.	Jay, D.	Richardson, Miss J.
Canavan, D.	Kerr, R.	Rooker, J.
English, M.	Lambie, D.	Skinner, D.
Evans, J.	Leadbitter, T.*	Spearing, N.
Flannery, M.	Loyden, E.	Wise, Mrs A.

HC Deb. 930, 991-2
1976-7, No. 109.

The division took place at 11.30 p.m. The European Communities (Definition of Treaties) (No. 2) Order 1977 was then approved without a division.

SOUTHERN RHODESIA [255]

Prayer: 28 April 1977

The Minister of State for Foreign and Commonwealth Affairs, E. Rowlands, moved 'That the Southern Rhodesia (United Nations Sanctions) Order 1977 (S.I., 1977, No. 591), a copy of which was laid before this House on 5th April, be approved.'

The Order enabled the Government to enforce paragraph 2 of Security Council Resolution No. 388, and to close loopholes in sanctions enforcement concerning trade marks and registered designs.

A number of Conservative opponents of sanctions opposed the Order, and carried their opposition to a division. The motion was carried by 46 votes to 6, with the Opposition abstaining from voting. The Government lobby comprised solely Labour Members. The 8 Members (including tellers) to vote against the motion comprised 7 Conservative and 1 UUUC (E. Powell).

Conservatives to vote against the Order:

Amery, J.	Fell, A.	Goodhew, V.
Bell, R.	Glyn, A.*	Hastings, S.
Brotherton, M.*		

HC Deb. 930, 1687–90
1976–7, No. 114.

The division took place at 1.12 a.m.

CRIMINAL LAW BILL [256]

Second Reading: 3 May 1977

The Home Secretary, M. Rees, moved the Second Reading of the Bill. The Bill contained 50 clauses and 11 schedules. Part I of the Bill dealt with the law of conspiracy, and arose from the recommendations of the Law Commission in its report on the subject; Part II modernized and amended the criminal law on entering and remaining on property; Part III gave effect to the main recommendations contained in the James Committee's report on the Distribution of Criminal Business between the Crown Court and Magistrates' Courts.

During the course of the debate, a number of Labour backbenchers rose to criticize certain provisions of the Bill, and one, S. Crowther (Lab., Rotherham), indicated that he would be unable to vote for the measure. 'What I simply cannot support', he said, 'is the reduction of the right of people to be tried by jury.' Some Members also expressed reservations about the provisions relating to forcible entry.

The Bill was given a Second Reading by 188 votes to 15, the Opposition voting with the Government. The 190 Members (including tellers) in the Government lobby comprised 152 Labour, 31 Conservative, 6 Liberal and 1 Scottish Labour. The 17 Members (including tellers) to oppose the Bill were all Labour Members.

Labour Members to vote against Second Reading:

Ellis, J.	Loyden, E.	Selby, H.
Hoyle, D.	Marshall, J.*	Skinner, D.
Kerr, R.	Maynard, Miss J.	Thomas, S.*
Lamond, J.	Parry, R.	Thorne, S.*
Latham, A.	Richardson, Miss J.	Wise, Mrs A.
Lee, J.	Rodgers, G.	

HC Deb. 931, 363–6
1976–7, No. 119.

MR AGEE AND MR HOSENBALL [257]

3 May 1977

On an adjournment motion, the House debated the decision of the Home Secretary to deport from Britain two American citizens, Mr Agee and Mr Hosenball.

In opening the debate, the Home Secretary, M. Rees, emphasized that the decision had been his and his alone, and that it was taken solely in the interests of this country.

The Opposition supported the Home Secretary's decision, but a number of Labour Members rose to oppose it. S. Newens (Lab., Harlow) considered that unless the Home Secretary produced some evidence, his decision would be regarded as unjust. A. Lyon (Lab.,

York) argued that the Home Secretary did not know whether the two men were guilty or not because he had not heard their answers to the charges made. P. Rose (Lab., Manchester, Blackley) hoped that the Minister would admit that he was wrong. He contended that the procedure against which the two men had to struggle was a farce. One Conservative, J. Aitken (C., Thanet, East) also argued that the Minister's case remained 'non-proven'.

At the conclusion of the debate, a number of Labour backbench opponents of the Home Secretary's decision forced a division. The motion to adjourn was negatived by 138 votes to 34, with the Opposition supporting the Government. The 140 Members (including tellers) in the Government lobby comprised 111 Labour, 24 Conservative and 5 Liberal. The 36 Members (including tellers) to vote for adjournment were all Labour Members. At least 1 Conservative Member (J. Aitken) abstained from voting.

Labour Members to vote for adjournment:

Allaun, F.	Heffer, E.	Maynard, Miss J.
Atkinson, N.	Hooley, F.	Mendelson, J.
Bennett, A.	Hoyle, D.	Mikardo, I.
Bidwell, S.	Kerr, R.	Newens, S.*
Carter-Jones L.	Lamond, J.	Price, C.
Cook, R.	Latham, A.	Richardson, Miss J.*
Corbett, R.	Lestor, Miss J.	Rose, P.
Crowther, S.	Loyden, E.	Skinner, D.
Ellis, J.	Lyon, A.	Thomas, R.
Fletcher, T.	Lyons, E.	Thorne, S.
Fowler, G.	McDonald, O.	Whitehead, P.
Garrett, J.	Madden, M.	Wise, Mrs A.

HC Deb. 931, 409–12
1976–7, No. 120.

The division took place at 12.10 a.m.

FINANCE BILL [258]

Committee: 10 May 1977

Clause 15 (Charge for income tax for 1977–78)

Dr O. McDonald (Lab., Thurrock) moved an amendment to provide that the rates of income tax for these people in the higher income brackets should remain the same in 1977–78 as in 1976–77.

The Government opposed the amendment, and the Minister of State at the Treasury, D. Davies, asked the Committee to reject it. The amount that would be saved by it, he said, would be so small that it would not make much contribution to solving the problem.

The amendment was negatived by 205 votes to 53, with the Opposition abstaining from voting. The 207 Members (including tellers) in the Government lobby comprised 187 Labour, 10 Liberal, 9 Scottish National and 1 Plaid Cymru.[1] The 55 Members (including tellers) to support the amendment were all Labour Members.

Labour Members to vote for the amendment:

Allaun, F.	Heffer, E.	Maynard, Miss J.
Atkins, R.	Hoyle, D.	Mikardo, I.
Atkinson, N.	Hughes, R.	Miller, M.
Bennett, A.	Hughes, R. J.	Miller, Mrs M.
Bidwell, S.	Jeger, Mrs L.	Newens, S.
Buchan, N.	Jenkins, H.	Ovenden, J.
Canavan, D.	Kelley, R.	Richardson, Miss J.
Carmichael, N.	Kerr, R.*	Roberts, G.
Cohen, S.	Kilroy-Silk, R.	Rooker, J.
Colquhoun, Mrs M.	Kinnock, N.	Rose, P.
Cook, R.	Lamond, J.	Selby, H.
Cowans, H.	Latham, A.	Silverman, J.
Edge, G.	Lee, J.	Skinner, D.
Flannery, M.*	Loyden, E.	Spearing, N.
Fletcher, T.	Lyon, A.	Thomas, R.
Fowler, G.	McDonald, O.	Thorne, S.
Garrett, J.	Madden, M.	Wilson, W.
Gould, B.	Marshall, J.	Wise, Mrs A.
Hayman, Mrs H.		

HC Deb. 931, 1147–50
1976–7, No. 128.

[1] The *Hansard* division lists record one Conservative, P. Dean (C., Somerset, North), as voting in the Government lobby. This is a mistake, the name appearing in error for J. Dean (Lab., Leeds, West).

FINANCE BILL [259]

Committee: 10 May 1977

Clause 15 (Charge for income tax for 1977–78)

J. Pardoe (Lib., Cornwall, North) moved formally an amendment to provide that the tax payable by an individual in respect of his earned income would not exceed one half of such income.

The amendment was negatived by 199 votes to 16, with the Opposition abstaining from voting. The Government lobby comprised solely Labour Members. The 18 Members (including tellers) to support the amendment comprised 8 Liberal, 7 Conservative and 3 Plaid Cymru.

Conservatives to vote for the amendment:

Carlisle, M.	Hunt, D.	Newton, T.
Cope, J.	MacGregor, J.	Sinclair, Sir G.
Durant, T.		

HC Deb. 931, 1247–50
1976–7, No. 131.

FINANCE BILL [260]

Committee: 10 May 1977

Clause 15 (Charge for income tax for 1977–78)

Mrs A. Wise (Lab., Coventry, South-West) moved an amendment designed to exclude from the reckoning of taxable income the taxable dependency allowance for dependent children of widows and others.

The Government opposed the amendment, the Financial Secretary to the Treasury, R. Sheldon, arguing that if Members felt that the child benefits were inadequate, they should press for increased benefits.

The amendment was negatived by 129 votes to 41, with the Opposition abstaining from voting. The Government lobby comprised solely Labour Members. The 43 Members (including tellers) to support the amendment comprised 34 Labour, 5 Liberal, 3 Scottish National and 1 Plaid Cymru.

Labour Members to vote for the amendment:

Allaun, F.	Kinnock, N.	Ovenden, J.*
Atkinson, N.	Lambie, D.	Richardson, Miss J.
Bennett, A.	Latham, A.	Rodgers, G.
Bidwell, S.	Lestor, Miss J.	Rooker, J.
Canavan, D.	Loyden, E.	Selby, H.
Cook, R.	McDonald, O.*	Skinner, D.
Evans, I.	Madden, M.	Spearing, N.

Flannery, M.
Hooley, F.
Hoyle, D.
Kerr, R.
Kilroy-Silk, R.

Maynard, Miss J.
Mendelson, J.
Miller, M.
Newens, S.

Thomas, R.
Thorne, S.
Watkins, D.
Wise, Mrs A.

HC Deb. 931, 1265–8
1976–7, No. 132.

The division took place at 11.35 p.m.

FINANCE BILL [261]

Committee: 12 May 1977

New Clause 4 (Taxation of Directors and others in respect of cars)

Sir J. Hall (C., Wycombe) moved formally the new clause, which provided that to qualify for the 50 per cent reduction in the flat-rate cash equivalent for business travel the distance of 12,500 miles had to be travelled, instead of 25,000 miles.

The clause was opposed by the Government, and negatived by 156 votes to 116. The division lists record 1 Labour Member as cross-voting to support the amendment.

Labour Member to vote for the clause:

Lambie, D.

HC Deb. 931, 1683–8
1976–7, No. 136.

STATUTORY INSTRUMENTS, ETC. [262]

17 May 1977

A Government whip formally moved 'That the draft Pool Competitions Act 1971 (Continuance) Order 1977 be referred to a Standing Committee on Statutory Instruments, Etc.'

The motion was approved by 130 votes to 1. The 132 Members (including tellers) in the 'Aye' lobby comprised 112 Labour, 7 Conservative, 6 Liberal, 6 SNP and 1 SLP Member. The 3 Members (including tellers) to oppose the motion were Labour Members.

Labour Members to oppose the motion:

Cunningham, G.*   Skinner, D.*   Thorne, S.

Conservatives to vote for the motion:

Finsberg, G.   Morgan, G.   Page, R.
Glyn, A.   Mudd, D.   Warren, K.
Lewis, K.

HC Deb. 932, 237–40
1976–7, No. 140.

IMMIGRATION RULES   [263]

24 May 1977

The Under-Secretary of State at the Home Office, Dr S. Summerskill, moved 'That this House takes note of the Statement of Changes in Immigration Rules for Control on Entry of Commonwealth Citizens, the Statement of Changes in Immigration Rules for Control after Entry of Commonwealth Citizens, the Statement of Changes in Immigration Rules for Control on Entry of EEC and other non-Commonwealth Nationals and the Statement of Changes in Immigration Rules for Control after Entry of EEC and other non-Commonwealth Nationals.'

From the Labour backbenches, A. Lyon (Lab., York) moved a manuscript amendment to leave out 'takes note' and to insert 'disapproves'.

Mr Lyon argued that under the proposed rules, designed to deal with the problem of 'marriages of convenience', a non-indigenous person who entered the country for a genuine marriage, but whose marriage broke down within 12 months ending in separation or divorce, would be deported. 'There is no provision in the rules which allows the exercise of discretion, as a normal form, in respect of that power.' He argued also that there was no abuse on the scale that would justify the rules being introduced.

Dr Summerskill argued that the rules were necessary and that they were aimed at 'marriages of convenience'. She commended the rules to the House.

The amendment was negatived by 140 votes to 65, Conservative Members supporting the Government. The 142 Members (including tellers) in the Government lobby comprised 122 Labour, 15 Conservative, 4 Liberal and 1 Ulster Unionist. The 67 Members (including tellers) to support the amendment comprised 66 Labour backbenchers and, according to the division list, one Minister who voted in both lobbies by mistake.

Labour Members to vote for the amendment:

Allaun, F.
Atkinson, N.
Bean, R.
Bennett, A.
Bidwell, S.
Bray, J.
Brown, R.
Buchan, N.
Callaghan, J.
Canavan, D.
Carmichael, N.
Carter-Jones, L.
Clemitson, I.
Colquhoun, Mrs M.
Cronin, J.
Crowther, S.
Davies, B.
Douglas-Mann, B.
Ellis, J.
English, M.
Faulds, A.
Fernyhough, E.

Flannery, M.
Fletcher, T.
George, B.
Gould, B.
Hatton, F.
Hayman, Mrs H.
Hooley, F.
Hoyle, D.
Hughes, R.
Jeger, Mrs L.
Kerr, R.
Kinnock, N.
Lamond, J.
Latham, A.
Lestor, Miss J.
Loyden, E.
Lyon, A.
McDonald, O.
McNamara, K.
Madden, M.
Magee, B.
Marshall, J.

Maynard, Miss J.
Mendelson, J.
Mikardo, I.*
Miller, M.
Mitchell, A.
Newens, S.
Ovenden, J.
Parry, R.
Pavitt, L.
Richardson, Miss J.
Rodgers, G.
Rooker, J.
Sandelson, N.
Selby, H.
Skinner, D.
Spearing, N.
Thomas, R.
Thorne, S.*
Torney, T.
Whitehead, P.
Wilson, W.
Wise, Mrs. A.

HC Deb. 932, 1357–62
1976–7, No. 146.

The division took place at 11.30 p.m.

EUROPEAN COMMUNITY (DENTISTS) [264]

24 May 1977

A Government whip moved formally 'That this House takes note of Commission Document R/2196/76 on Rights of Establishment of Dentists.'

A number of Labour backbenchers divided the House on the motion.

The motion was approved by 128 votes to 49, with the Opposition abstaining from voting. The 130 Members (including tellers) in the

Government lobby comprised 127 Labour and 3 Liberal. The 51 Members (including tellers) to oppose the motion comprised 49 Labour, 1 Conservative and 1 Ulster Unionist.

Labour Members to vote against the motion:

Allaun, F.

Atkinson, N.

Bennett, A.

Bidwell, S.

Buchan, N.

Callaghan, J.

Canavan, D.

Carmichael, N.

Carter-Jones, L.

Crowther, S.

Ellis, J.*

Evans, J.

Fernyhough, E.

Flannery, M.

Fletcher, T.

Forrester, J.

Gould, B.

Hatton, F.

Hooley, F.

Hoyle, D.

Jeger, Mrs L.

Kerr, R.

Kinnock, N.

Lamond, J.

Latham, A.

Lestor, Miss J.

Loyden, E.

McDonald, O.

McMillan, T.

Madden, M.

Marshall, J.

Maynard, Miss J.

Mikardo, I.

Mitchell, A.

Newens, S.

Ovenden, J.

Parry, R.

Pavitt, L.*

Price, C.

Richardson, Miss J.

Rodgers, G.

Rooker, J.

Skinner, D.

Spearing, N.

Thomas, R.

Thorne, S.

Torney, T.

Wilson, W.

Wise, Mrs A.

Conservative to vote against the motion:

Moate, R.

HC Deb. 932, 1359–62
1976–7, No. 147.

The division took place at 11.41 p.m.

QUESTION OF PRIVILEGE [265]

25 May 1977

On 24 May, R. Adley (C., Christchurch and Lymington) raised as a possible breach of privilege a motion passed at the annual conference of the National Union of Public Employees that unless the six NUPE-sponsored Members of Parliament opposed Government cuts in public expenditure the union's executive was to withdraw their sponsorship.

The following day, Mr Speaker announced that he considered it a proper case for him to allow a motion relating to it to have precedence over the Orders of the Day, and the Lord President of the Council and Leader of the House, M. Foot, then moved 'That the matter of the complaint made by the hon. Member for Christchurch and Lymington be referred to the Committee of Privileges'.

D. Skinner (Lab., Bolsover) rose to oppose the motion. He contended that there were many Members who got involved in sponsorships, consultancies, directorships and the like. While a trade union might take a decision which was democratic and open for all to see, there could be instances where firms might decide secretly to stop sponsorships; in such circumstances the matter could not be raised. It was time that those with sponsorships and the like were treated in the same manner. R. Prentice (Lab., Newham, North-East) rose to support the motion. The situation was more unique and serious than might be assumed from Mr Skinner's remarks, he said. 'The resolution passed at the NUPE conference yesterday if allowed to prevail and become a precedent, would be a dangerous intervention in the normal democratic traditions of this country.'

The motion was carried by 203 votes to 45, with the Government whips on and with both Government and Opposition Front Bench advice being to support the motion. The 205 Members (including tellers) in the Government lobby comprised 117 Conservative, 77 Labour, 10 Liberal and 1 Plaid Cymru. The 47 Members (including tellers) to oppose the motion were all Labour Members.

Labour Members to vote against the motion:

Allaun, F.	Grocott, B.	Miller, M.
Atkinson, N.	Hatton, F.	Ovenden, J.
Bidwell, S.	Hughes, R.	Prescott, J.
Buchan, N.	Hughes, R. J.	Richardson, Miss J.
Callaghan, J.	Kelley, R.	Roberts, G.
Carter-Jones, L.	Kerr, R.*	Rodgers, G.
Castle, Mrs B.	Lamond, J.	Rooker, J.
Clemitson, I.	Latham, A.	Rose, P.
Dean, J.	Lee, J.	Sedgemore, B.
Edge, G.	Lipton, M.	Short, Mrs R.
Edwards, R.	Loyden, E.	Skinner, D.*
Ellis, J.	Lyon, A.	Spriggs, L.
Evans, F.	McDonald, O.	Thomas, R.
Flannery, M.	Madden, M.	Wilson, W.
Fletcher, T.	Marshall, J.	Wise, Mrs A.
Garrett, J.	Maynard, Miss J.	

HC Deb. 932, 1423–6
1976–7, No. 148.

EUROPEAN SOCIAL FUND [266]

13 June 1977

The Under-Secretary of State for Employment, J. Grant, moved 'That this House takes note of Commission Document No. R/752/77 on the European Social Fund.'

From the Labour backbenches, N. Spearing (Lab., Newham, South) moved an amendment to leave out all from 'House' to the end of the motion and to insert instead 'declines to take note of Commission Document No. R/752/77 concerning the EEC Social Fund as it believes that assistance to persons or areas with particular needs should be the responsibility of national Parliaments and national Governments.'

The amendment was negatived by 59 votes to 23, with the Government and Opposition opposing it. The 61 Members (including tellers) to oppose the amendment comprised 56 Labour and 5 Conservative. The 25 Members (including tellers) to support the amendment comprised 23 Labour and 2 Ulster Unionist.

Labour Members to vote for the amendment:

Allaun, F.	Kerr, R.	Mikardo, I.
Bidwell, S.	Lambie, D.	Skinner, D.
Canavan, D.	Lamond, J.	Spearing, N.
Carter-Jones, L.	Leadbitter, T.	Spriggs, L.
Crowther, S.	Lestor, Miss J.	Thorne, S.
Fernyhough, E.	Loyden, E.	Wise, Mrs A.
Flannery, M.*	Madden, M.*	Woof, R.
Hooley, F.	Maynard, Miss J.	

HC Deb. 933, 189–90
1976–7, No. 150.

The motion was then put and carried without a division. The division took place at 11.14 p.m.

PRICE COMMISSION BILL [267]

Report: 21 June 1977

Shortly after 3.30 a.m., during a late-night sitting, Mrs S. Oppenheim, from the Opposition Front Bench, moved 'That further consideration of the Bill, as amended, be adjourned.'

After an hour's debate, a Scottish National Member moved the closure, which was carried on a party vote by 251 votes to 219. 1 Labour Member cross-voted to oppose closure.

Labour Member to vote against closure:

Leadbitter, T.

HC Deb. 933, 1615–20
1976–7, No. 163.

The motion was then negatived by 249 votes to 221, with no cross-votes. Mr Leadbitter did not take part in the division.[1]

[1] Mr Leadbitter's absence from the division might be taken to suggest the possibility of a mistake in the names in the Opposition lobby on the closure motion, but the Member has confirmed to the author the accuracy of *Hansard* on this occasion.

PRICE COMMISSION BILL [268]

Report: 21 June 1977

Clause 2 (Commission's duty to have regard to specified matters)

Mrs M. Bain (SNP, Dumbartonshire, East) moved an amendment to provide that the Price Commission should have 'the function of carrying out, and of preparing a report in consequence of an investigation into the wholesale and retail trades of the reasons for the imbalance of pricing in the various parts of the United Kingdom and in pursuance of such a report of issuing guidelines and recommendations for the eradication of such an imbalance.'
The Government opposed the amendment, and it was negatived by 238 votes to 14, with the Opposition abstaining from voting. The 16 Members (including tellers) to support the amendment comprised 9 Conservative and 7 Scottish National. 1 Conservative entered the Government lobby to vote against the amendment.

Conservatives to vote for the amendment:

Fraser, H.	Lawrence, I.	Sinclair, Sir G.
Hamilton, M.	Mates, M.	Stanbrook, I.
Johnson Smith, G.	Mudd, D.	Townsend, C.

Conservative to vote against the amendment:

Sainsbury, T.

HC Deb. 933, 1631–4
1976–7, No. 167.

The division took place at 8.00 a.m. during an all-night sitting.

EUROPEAN ASSEMBLY ELECTIONS BILL [269]

Second Reading: 6 July 1977

The Home Secretary, M. Rees, moved the Second Reading of the Bill, designed to provide for direct election of British representatives to the European Assembly. Mr Rees explained that the Bill contained provision for the regional list system to be employed as the method of election, but Members would have the opportunity to decide between that and the simple majority system when the relevant clause was debated.

After a two-day debate, the Bill was given a Second Reading by 394 votes to 147. Members were permitted a free vote, but the advice of both the Government and Opposition was to support the Bill (the principle of collective responsibility being suspended, though, in order that Ministers may vote as they wished). The 396 Members (including tellers) to support the Bill comprised 241 Conservative, 132 Labour, 12 Liberal, 9 Scottish National, 1 SDLP, and 1 Ulster Unionist. The 149 Members (including tellers) to oppose Second Reading comprised 126 Labour (including six members of the Cabinet), 15 Conservative, 6 Ulster Unionist, 1 Scottish Labour, and 1 Plaid Cymru.

Labour Members to vote against Second Reading:

Allaun, F.
Ashton, J.[2]
Atkins, R.
Atkinson, N.
Barnett, G.[2]
Benn, A.[1]
Bennett, A.
Bidwell, S.
Booth, A.[1]

Freeson, R.[2]
Garrett, J.
Garrett, W.
Gilbert, J.[2]
Gould, B.*
Grocott, B.
Hamilton, J.[2]
Harrison, W.[2]
Hatton, F.

Mitchell, A.
Molloy, W.
Morris, A.[2]
Newens, S.
Noble, M.
O'Halloran, M.
Orbach, M.
Orme, S.[1]
Ovenden, J.

Buchan, N.
Butler, Mrs J.
Callaghan, J.
Canavan, D.
Carmichael, N.
Carter-Jones, L.
Castle, Mrs B.
Clemitson, I.
Colquhoun, Mrs M.
Cook, R.
Cowans, H.
Cox, T.[2]
Craigen, J.
Crowther, S.
Cryer, R.[2]
Cunningham, G.
Davidson, A.[2]
Davies, B.
Davis, C.[2]
Deakins, E.[2]
Dean, J.
Dormand, J.[2]
Eadie, A.[2]
Edge, G.
Ellis, J.
Evans, F.
Evans, I.
Ewing, H.[2]
Flannery, M.
Fletcher, T.
Foot, M.[1]
Forrester, J.
Fraser, J.[2]

Heffer, E.
Hooley, F.
Hoyle, D.
Huckfield, L.[2]
Hughes, R.
Hughes, R. J.
Jackson, Miss M.[2]
Jeger, Mrs L.
Jenkins, H.
Kelley, R.
Kilroy-Silk, R.
Kinnock, N.
Lambie, D.
Lamond, J.
Latham, A.
Leadbitter, T.
Lee, J.
Lestor, Miss J.
Litterick, T.
Loyden, E.
McCartney, H.
McDonald, O.
McElhone, F.[2]
McMillan, T.
McNamara, K.
Madden, M.*
Marshall, J.
Maynard, Miss J.
Meacher, M.[2]
Mendelson, J.
Mikardo, I.
Miller, M.
Miller, Mrs M.

Park, G.
Pavitt, L.
Pendry, T.
Prescott, J.
Richardson, Miss J.
Roberts, G.
Robinson, G.
Roderick, C.
Rodgers, G.
Rooker, J.
Ross, W.
Sedgemore, B.
Shaw, A.
Shore, P.[1]
Short, Mrs R.
Silkin, J.[1]
Silverman, J.
Skinner, D.
Snape, P.[2]
Spearing, N.
Spriggs, L.
Stallard, A.[2]
Stoddart, D.[2]
Taylor, Mrs A.[2]
Thomas, R.
Thorne, S.
Torney, T.
Walker, H.[2]
Watkinson, J.
Wellbeloved, J.[2]
Wilson, W.
Wise, Mrs A.
Young, D.

Conservatives to vote against Second Reading:

Bell, R.
Biffen, J.
Body, R.
Budgen, N.
Clark, A.

Fraser, H.
Fry, P.
Hutchison, M. C.
Marten, N.
Maxwell-Hyslop, R.

Moate, R.
More, J.
Stokes, J.
Taylor, R.
Winterton, N.

HC Deb. 934, 1563–70
1976–7, No. 189.

The Bill made no further progress during the session, and was re-introduced in the following session (see below: 24 November 1977).

¹ Cabinet Minister.
² Member of the Government.

CRIMINAL LAW BILL [270]

Report: 13 July 1977

New Clause 5: 'Where any person has been arrested, other than under the Prevention of Terrorism Act 1976, and is being held in custody in a police station or other premises, he shall be entitled to have intimation of his arrest and of the place where he is being held sent to a person of his choosing.'

The new clause was moved by G. Cunningham (Lab., Islington, South and Finsbury). He said he drew the line at not being prepared to see a person who was taken to a police station told that he could not communicate with anyone outside. The right involved was a fundamental one.

C. Price (Lab., Lewisham, West) hoped all parties would join together in supporting the clause as a matter of sheer common sense. F. Hooley (Lab., Sheffield, Heeley) said it was right that there should be immediate, quick communication with somebody else by the person who had been arrested. He was prepared to vote for the clause. R. G. Page (C., Crosby) said the clause was narrow, but worthy of support.

The Home Secretary, M. Rees, said the clause sought to embody part of the Judges' Rules in legislation. A Royal Commission had been set up to look at the prosecuting process. It was important that they should not make changes piecemeal. He had no reason to believe that there was an overwhelming number of cases in which people were held in communicado. As it stood, it was not clear what would happen if the provisions were not observed. To proceed by means of the clause would be wrong.

The clause was *carried* by 89 votes to 86, *a majority against the Government of 3*. The Opposition abstained officially from voting. The 88 Members (including tellers) in the Government lobby comprised 85 Labour and 3 Conservative. The 91 Members (including tellers) to support the clause comprised 68 Labour, 11 Conservative and 12 Liberal.

Conservatives to vote against the clause:

Mawby, R.	Mudd, D.	Stanbrook, I.

Labour Members to vote for the clause:

Atkins, R.
Atkinson, N.
Bennett, A.*
Bidwell, S.
Brown, R.
Callaghan, J.
Carmichael, N.
Carter-Jones, L.
Clemitson, I.
Cook, R.
Corbett, R.
Crawshaw, R.
Cunningham, G.
Davies, B.
Dean, J.
Dempsey, J.
Douglas-Mann, B.
Dunwoody, Mrs G.
Ellis, J.
Evans, I.
Evans, J.
Flannery, M.
Fletcher, T.

Gould, B.
Hooley, F.*
Hoyle, D.
Hughes, R.
Hughes, R. J.
Janner, G.
Jeger, Mrs L.
Jenkins, H.
Kerr, R.
Kilroy-Silk, R.
Kinnock, N.
Lamond, J.
Lee, J.
Lestor, Miss J.
Lewis, R.
Loyden, E.
Lyon, A.
McCartney, H.
McDonald, O.
McGuire, M.
Madden, M.
Marshall, J.
Maynard, Miss J.

Mendelson, J.
Mikardo, I.
Miller, Mrs. M.
Mitchell, A.
Ovenden, J.
Parry, R.
Pavitt, L.
Phipps, C.
Price, C.
Richardson, Miss J.
Robinson, G.
Rodgers, G.
Rooker, J.
Rose, P.
Selby, H.
Silverman, J.
Skinner, D.
Thomas, R.
Thorne, S.
Whitehead, P.
Willey, F.
Wise, Mrs A.

Conservatives to vote for the clause:

Bowden, A.
Crowder, F. P.
Fairbairn, N.
Fookes, Miss J.

Irving, C.
Kellett-Bowman, Mrs E.
Meyer, Sir A.
Moate, R.

Page, R. G.
Rees-Davies, W.
Rhys-Williams, Sir B.

HC Deb. 935, 531–4
1976–7, No. 192.

The issue was to be raised again on a Lords Amendment: see below,
27 July 1977.

CRIMINAL LAW BILL　　　　　　　　　　　　　　　　　　[271]

Report: 13 July 1977

Schedule 12 (Repeals)

R. Kilroy-Silk (Lab., Ormskirk) moved an amendment to remove the legal powers that enabled the Government, local authorities and the courts to remand school children to prisons and Prison Department establishments.

Mr Kilroy-Silk said that they all agreed that sending schoolchildren to prison (on remand) was intolerable and wrong. If one route was closed, he thought an alternative would be found to deal with the problem.

The Minister of State at the Home Office, B. John, said he could not accept the amendment because it did not constitute the right approach to the subject to summarily close off all the options without the necessary accommodation being available.

The amendment was negatived by 83 votes to 15, the Conservatives voting with the Government. The 85 Members (including tellers) in the Government lobby comprised 75 Labour, 9 Conservative and 1 Liberal. The 17 Members (including tellers) to support the amendment were all Labour Members.

Labour Members to vote for the amendment:

Bennett, A.*	Kerr, R.	Richardson, Miss J.
Callaghan, J.	Kilroy-Silk, R.	Robinson, G.
Corbett, R.	Maynard, Miss J.	Skinner, D.
Davies, B.	Mikardo, I.*	Ward, M.
Evans, J.	Ovenden, J.	Wise, Mrs A.
Flannery, M.	Parry, R.	

HC Deb. 935, 741–2
1976–7, No. 194.

The division took place at 7.10 a.m.

FINANCE BILL [272]

Report: 25 July 1977

Clause 22 (Alteration of personal reliefs)

J. Pardoe (Lib., Cornwall, North) moved an amendment to delete the power to vary the effect of the clause by Treasury order.

Mr Pardoe argued that there had been no need for the power to have been included (it had been inserted in Committee). He said it would be sensible for Parliament to stick to its guns and remove the power.

The Minister of State at the Treasury, D. Davies, asked the House to reject the amendment. It was open to the objection that it was clearly in favour of the kind of indexation that the Liberal Party wanted, a system which related not only to personal allowances but to the rest of the tax system.

The amendment was negatived by 268 votes to 24, the Opposition abstaining from voting. The Government lobby comprised solely Labour Members. The 26 Members (including tellers) to support the amendment comprised 11 Liberal, 10 Scottish National, 3 Plaid Cymru and 2 Labour.

Labour Members to vote for the amendment:

Loyden, E.   Thorne, S.

HC Deb. 936, 147-50
1976-7, No. 209.

CRIMINAL LAW BILL [273]

Lords Amendment: 27 July 1977

New Clause (Right to have someone informed when arrested)

The Home Secretary, M. Rees, moved to agree with the Lords in an amendment to provide that where any person had been arrested and was being held in custody that person should be entitled to have intimation of his arrest and place of detention to 'one person reasonably named by him, without delay or, where some delay is necessary in the interest of the investigation or prevention of crime or the apprehension of offenders, with no more delay than is necessary'. (The amendment sought to amend the clause carried against the Government on Report stage: see above, 13 July.)

Mr Rees explained that the reference to 'one person reasonably named' was to avoid the police having to inform someone outside the categories one would expect. The categories would be provided in a circular. The provision for the possibility of some delay in sending the intimation was that an unqualified right would impose a serious handicap on the police in dealing with crime. He would make arrangements for monitoring the new provision.

C. Price (Lab., Lewisham, West) objected to the new wording since it put them back to square one regarding the behaviour of the police. The wording gave a 'carte blanche to the police that they already possess in the Judges' Rules to decide on the spot to deny the right of information to a relative.'

Mr Price moved an amendment to delete all words after the first 'delay'.

The amendment was opposed by the Government and the Opposition and negatived by 242 votes to 68. The 246 Members (including tellers) in the Government lobby comprised 160 Labour, 79 Conservative and 7 Liberal. The 70 Members (including tellers) to support the amendment comprised 67 Labour and 3 Conservative.

Labour Members to support the amendment:

Allaun, F.	Hayman, Mrs H.	Molloy, W.
Bennett, A.	Heffer, E.	Newens, S.
Buchan, N.	Hoyle, D.	Orbach, M.
Callaghan, J.	Hughes, R.	Parry, R.
Canavan, D.	Janner, G.	Pendry, T.
Carmichael, N.	Jeger, Mrs L.	Phipps, C.
Carter-Jones, L.	Jenkins, H.	Prescott, J.
Castle, Mrs B.	Kilroy-Silk, R.	Price, C.
Clemitson, I.	Lamond, J.	Richardson, Miss J.
Cook, R.	Latham, A.	Roberts, G.
Corbett, R.	Lestor, Miss J.	Robinson, G.
Crawshaw, R.	Lewis, A.	Rodgers, G.
Davies, B.	Litterick, T.	Rooker, J.
Douglas-Mann, B.*	Lyon, A.	Rose, P.
Edge, G.	McDonald, O.	Shaw, A.
Ellis, J.	McGuire, M.	Skinner, D.
English, M.	McNamara, K.	Spriggs, L.
Evans, J.	Madden, M.	Thomas, R.
Flannery, M.	Mendelson, J.	Thorne, S.
Fletcher, T.	Mikardo, I.*	Torney, T.
Forrester, J.	Miller, M.	Weitzman, D.
Fowler, G.	Mitchell, A.	Wise, Mrs. A.
Garrett, J.		

Conservatives to vote for the amendment:

Fry, P.	Moate, R.	Steen, A.

HC Deb. 936, 739–42
1976–7, No. 226.

The motion moved by the Home Secretary was then agreed to without a division.

CONTROL OF OFFICE DEVELOPMENT BILL   [274]

Lords Amendment: 27 July 1977

Clause 1 (Continuance in force of provisions relating to control of office development)

The Government moved an amendment to restore to five years the period for which office control powers would be extended (under the Lords amendment, the period was reduced to three years).

The amendment was carried on a straight party vote by 235 votes 179. 1 Conservative cross-voted to support the amendment.

Conservative to vote for the amendment:

Meyer, Sir A.

HC Deb. 936, 749–52
1976–7, No. 227.

The dissenting vote had been cast for constituency reasons.[1]

---

[1] 'I wanted the Government to retain control over office building since this would increase the chances of getting badly needed Government clerical jobs in North Wales.' Sir A. Meyer to author.

REMUNERATION   [275]

Prayer: 27 July 1977

The Secretary of State for Employment, A. Booth, moved formally 'That the draft Limits of Remuneration Order 1977, which was laid before this House on 22nd July, be approved.' The order was designed to continue the provisions in relation to employers in the Remuneration, Charges and Grants Act 1975 to the extent needed to enforce and support the T.U.C. guidance for the 12-month rule. The order was framed on the same basis as the order approved by the House in 1976, and dealt with the pay limits as set out in the White Paper 'The Attack on Inflation after 31st July 1977'.

The order was discussed in conjunction with two preceding orders (debate concentrating on the Counter-Inflation (Continuation of

Enactments) Order). During the debate, R. Thomas (Lab., Bristol, North-West) had said that he was not happy with the 12-month rule, and J. Rooker (Lab., Birmingham, Perry Bar) had commented that in some ways the order was 'a fradulent document'. He wanted on record the fact that it applied only to a highly selected group of people.

The order was approved by 172 votes to 1, with the Opposition abstaining from voting. The 174 Members (including tellers) in the Government lobby comprised 168 Labour and 6 Liberal. The 3 Members (including tellers) to oppose the order were Labour Members. In addition, 25 to 30 Labour Members appear to have abstained from voting.[1]

Labour Members to vote against the order:

Canavan, D.*	Leadbitter, T.[2]	Skinner, D.*

HC Deb. 936, 815–18
1976–7, No. 229.

[1] The following Labour Members were absent from the division having voted in an immediately preceding one: F. Allaun, R. Atkins, A. Bennett, R. Brown, Mrs. B. Castle, F. Evans, A. Faulds, M. Flannery, B. Grocott, D. Hoyle, H. Jenkins, R. Kerr, A. Latham, A. Lewis, J. Mendelson, I. Mikardo, W. Molloy, S. Newens, C. Price, Miss J. Richardson, G. Roberts, G. Rodgers, J. Ryman, T. Torney, J. Watkinson, F. Willey and Mrs A. Wise.

[2] According to the division lists, Mr Leadbitter voted in both lobbies, in the Government lobby apparently by mistake.

CONSOLIDATED FUND (APPROPRIATION) BILL [276]

Second Reading: 28 July 1977

The Second Reading debate was taken up, as usual, by topics raised by Private Members.

After eleven and a half hours of debate (at 8.25 a.m.) the Government moved the closure, but failed due to not having 100 Members present to vote for it. *HC Deb.* 936, c. 1275–6.

Two hours later, the Government again moved the closure, which was carried on a straight party vote by 106 votes to 32.

The Bill was then given a Second Reading by 103 votes to 21, the Opposition Front Bench abstaining from voting. The 104 Members (including tellers) in the Government lobby comprised 100 Labour, 3 Liberal and 1 Scottish National. The 23 Members (including tellers) to oppose Second Reading were all Conservatives.

Conservatives to vote against Second Reading:

Adley, R.	Hamilton, M.	Rees-Davies, W.
Bottomley, P.	Hunt, D.	Rhodes James, R.
Braine, Sir B.	MacGregor, J.	Ridley, N.
Clark, A.	Mates, M.	Shaw, M.
Durant, T.	Moate, R.	Sims, R.
Eyre, R.	Morgan-Giles, M.	Tebbit, N.*
Fairbairn, N.	Osborn, J.	Townsend, C.
Gow, I.*	Rees, P.	

HC Deb. 936, 1315–18
1976–7, No. 233.

REDUNDANCY PAYMENTS [277]

Prayer: 28 July 1977

A Government whip moved formally: 'That the draft Redundancy Payments (Variation of Rebates) Order 1977, which was laid before this House on 25th July, be approved.'

(Debate on the prayer had been adjourned on 27 July because of the unavailability of copies of the Act under which the order was made.)

D. Mitchell (C., Basingstoke) questioned the timing of the order. He argued that it would take money from the part of the private sector which could least sustain it.

The Employment Secretary, A. Booth, contended that it was one of the measures designed to reduce the public sector borrowing requirement. From the Opposition Front Bench, J. Prior said that the Opposition saw no urgency for the provisions.

The order was approved by 102 votes to 6, with the Opposition abstaining from voting. The 108 Members (including tellers) in the Government lobby comprised 107 Labour and 1 Liberal. The 8 Members (including tellers) to oppose the order were all Conservatives.

Conservatives to vote against the order:

Biggs-Davison, J. Finsberg, G.* Tebbit, N.
Butler, A. Mitchell, D.* Temple-Morris, P.
Durant, T. Neubert, M.

HC Deb. 936, 1393–6
1976–7, No. 234.

The Session of 1977-8

SOUTHERN RHODESIA [278]

Prayer: 11 November 1977

The Secretary of State for Foreign and Commonwealth Affairs, Dr D. Owen, moved 'That the draft Southern Rhodesia Act 1965 (Continuation) Order 1977, which was laid before this House on 3rd November, be approved.'

As in previous years, a number of Conservative backbenchers rose to express opposition to the continuation of Rhodesian sanctions. M. Mates (C., Petersfield) said that the effect of sanctions had been to damage the blacks, and the whites had taken a much harder attitude than they otherwise would have done. J. Amery (C., Brighton, Pavilion) contended that sanctions made it more difficult for the Rhodesians to defend the civilian population against guerrillas. H. Fraser (C., Stafford and Stone) believed they should vote against the order 'for the simple reason that those who are suffering are those inside Rhodesia of all races.'

Although critical of the Foreign Secretary's policy, the Shadow Foreign Secretary, J. Davies, asked his supporters not to oppose the order. He argued that it would not be desirable to encourage those who wished to delay affairs at that juncture.

The order was approved by 77 votes to 26, with the Opposition abstaining from voting. The 79 Members (including tellers) in the Government lobby comprised 78 Labour Members and 1 Liberal. The 28 Members (including tellers) to vote against comprised 27 Conservatives and 1 Ulster Unionist.

Conservatives to vote against the order:

Amery, J.	Goodhew, V.*	Pink, R. B.
Bell, R.	Gow, I.	Shelton, W.
Boscawen, R.	Hastings, S.	Skeet, T.
Brotherton, M.	Jessel, T.	Spicer, J.
Clark, A.	Mates, M.	Stainton, K.
Dodsworth, G.	Meyer, Sir A.	Taylor, R.
Fell, A.	Moate, R.	Wall, P.
Gardiner, G.	Morgan-Giles, M.	Wiggin, J.*
Glyn, A.	Page, J.	Winterton, N.

HC Deb. 938, 1139–40
1977–8, No. 3.

SCOTLAND BILL   [279]

Second Reading: 14 November 1977

The Secretary of State for Scotland, B. Millan, moved the Second Reading of the Bill. The Bill provided for the creation of a directly-elected Scottish Assembly with powers to make primary and sub-ordinate legislation. Mr Millan argued that within the continuing unity of the United Kingdom there was room for diversity and for giving greater scope for the expression of Scottish identity. 'We propose, within the continuing union, to give the people of Scotland much improved democratic participation in making their own choice on matters which primarily are of concern to themselves.'

For the Opposition, F. Pym moved a reasoned amendment for rejection, calling for a Constitutional Conference to consider defects in the process of governing Scotland. Mr Pym contended that no measure of general agreement had been reached on the subject and that it was wrong to approach a major constitutional reform in a party political way. He criticized the Bill, and argued that it would not bring government closer to the people.

During the debate, T. Dalyell (Lab., West Lothian) rose to oppose the Bill. It did not provide the remotest chance of a lasting settlement between Scotland and England, and if it was passed they would be on 'a motorway without exit roads to a separate Scottish state.' He was joined in his opposition by J. Mendelson (Lab., Penistone) and T. Leadbitter (Lab., Hartlepool). Mr Mendelson argued that the Government's proposals had been put together, in the main, for immediate political purposes; they were not worthy of the occasion. E. Heffer

(Lab., Liverpool, Walton) and B. Douglas-Mann (Lab., Mitcham and Morden) expressed strong reservations about the measure. Mr Heffer expressed the hope that the Bill might be stopped in a democratic manner. From the Conservative benches, A. Buchanan-Smith (C., North Angus and Mearns) argued that there was a basic dissatisfaction with the machinery of government of our unitary state, and what they needed more than anything else was the dispersal of power. 'I support the Second Reading of the Bill. I welcome the fact that the Government are at least attempting to meet the very big challenge which faces the country at present.'

(1) At 11.00 p.m., the Government moved the closure, which was carried by 313 votes to 274. One Labour Member cross-voted to oppose closure. At least three Labour Members (L. Abse, G. Cunningham and T. Leadbitter) abstained from voting.

Labour Member to vote against closure:

Garrett, W.

The Opposition reasoned amendment was then put and negatived by 313 votes to 265, with no cross-voting. At least five Labour Members (L. Abse, F. Evans, W. Garrett, T. Leadbitter and J. Ovenden) and three Conservatives (A. Buchanan-Smith, D. Knox and D. Mudd) abstained from voting.

(2) The Second Reading of the Bill was carried by 307 votes to 263. The 309 Members (including tellers) in the Government lobby comprised 278 Labour, 11 Scottish National, 10 Liberal, 4 Conservative, 3 Plaid Cymru, 2 Scottish Labour, and 1 Ulster Unionist (W. Craig). The 265 Members (including tellers) in the Opposition lobby comprised 249 Conservative, 11 Labour, 3 Ulster Unionist, 1 Liberal and 1 Democratic Unionist. At least 15 Conservative and 4 Labour Members abstained from voting.[1]

Conservatives to vote for Second Reading:

Buchanan-Smith, A.	Knox, D.	Mudd, D.
Gray, H.		

Labour Members to vote against Second Reading:

Abse, L.	Evans, F.	Mendelson, J.
Brown, R.	Garrett, W.	Ovenden, J.
Cunningham, G.	Lamond, J.	Phipps, C.
Dalyell, T.	Leadbitter, T.	

HC Deb. 939, 197–204, 207–14
1977–8, Nos. 4 & 6.

¹ The known Conservative abstainers were: R. Adley, P. Blaker, C. Brocklebank-Fowler, H. Dykes, R. Fairgrieve, Sir J. Gilmour, R. Hodgson, D. Hunt, K. Lewis, R. McCrindle, H. Miller, M. Rifkind, N. Scott, J. Spence, C. Townsend and P. Walker. The Labour abstainers were: A. Bottomley, R. Edwards, I. Evans and E. Heffer.

FIRE SERVICE (DISPUTE)   [280]

15 November 1977

On 14 November, J. Sillars (SLP, South Ayrshire) had been granted leave under Standing Order 9 to discuss 'The grave threat to public safety and the future of the Fire Service now that the firemen are on strike.'

In moving the adjournment motion, Mr Sillars argued that the firemen were a special case because of the nature of their job. The fault for the strike, he said, lay firmly with the Government. He asked the Government to call in the local authorities and the Fire Brigades Union and tell them they were free to negotiate. 'There is room for negotiation.'

The Home Secretary, M. Rees, outlined what had been offered by the employers' side in negotiations, and pointed out that they were dealing with a claim for an immediate 31 per cent rise. He noted that others could make a claim to be special cases, and said it was important for the Government to stay within the pay guidelines which they controlled or on which they had influence. The firemen could not be considered in isolation.

E. Heffer (Lab., Liverpool, Walton) expressed disappointment with the Minister's speech, and asked him to be flexible and not make hard and fast statements. N. Kinnock (Lab., Bedwellty) argued that the National Joint Council should be given freedom to negotiate realistically. D. Skinner (Lab., Bolsover) wanted the 10 per cent pay rule disposed of. 'Let us see the strike called off, and to hell with the 10 per cent rule and any form of incomes policy in future.' Mrs A. Wise (Lab., Coventry, South-West) stressed the importance of the Labour Party not being seen as at war with the firemen. The issue had to be solved. J. Page (C., Harrow, West) expressed agreement with Mr Sillar's speech. The demands of the firemen were not inflexible. M. Morris (C., Northampton, South) expressed his fears at the degree of inflexibility over the guidelines. He wanted the Minister to get some positive suggestions into the negotiations.

At the end of the debate, Mr Sillars forced the adjournment motion to a division, in which it was negatived by 211 votes to 58 with the Opposition abstaining from voting. The 213 Members (including tellers) in the Government lobby comprised 205 Labour and 8 Liberal. The 60 Members (including tellers) to vote for adjournment comprised 38 Labour, 8 Scottish National, 7 Conservative, 3 Plaid Cymru, 2 Scottish Labour, 1 Ulster Unionist and 1 Democratic Unionist. At least one Labour Member (N. Kinnock) abstained from voting.

Labour Members to vote for adjournment:

Allaun, F.
Atkins, R.
Atkinson, N.
Bennett, A.
Bidwell, S.
Buchan, N.
Canavan, D.
Craigen, J.
Edwards, R.
Flannery, M.
Fletcher, T.
Hamilton, W.
Hatton, F.

Heffer, E.
Hoyle, D.
Hughes, R. J.
Kerr, R.
Lambie, D.
Latham, A.
Leadbitter, T.
Loyden, E.
Madden, M.
Maynard, Miss J.
Mikardo, I.
Moonman, E.
Newens, S.

O'Halloran, M.
Parry, R.
Richardson, Miss J.
Rodgers, G.
Rooker, J.
Selby, H.
Skinner, D.
Spriggs, L.
Swain, T.
Thomas, R.
Thorne, S.
Wise, Mrs A.

Conservatives to vote for adjournment:

Costain, A.
Durant, T.
Fell, A.

Griffiths, E.
Morris, M.

Page, J.
Winterton, N.

HC Deb. 939, 353–4
1977–8, No. 7.

WALES BILL [281]

Second Reading: 15 November 1977

The Secretary of State for Wales, J. Morris, moved the Second Reading of the Bill. The Bill provided for the creation of a directly-elected Welsh Assembly, with certain decision-making powers (primarily concerning environmental and social issues) devolved to it. Mr Morris explained that it was designed to increase democracy and account-ability, 'to give people a bigger say in decision-making.' Devolution was an essential reform, and he believed that the Government's proposals were needed in Wales.

Conservative Members rose to oppose the Bill, as did a number of Labour Members. L. Abse (Lab., Pontypool) said that they knew the Bill was 'conceived out of opportunism and reared in expediency.' He saw it as a capitulation to the nationalists. I. Evans (Lab., Aberdare) subjected the Bill to various criticisms, and expressed the opinion that the measure, if passed, would undermine the political and economic unity of the United Kingdom. N. Kinnock (Lab., Bedwellty) said his feelings on devolution were summed up in the words of Bevin: 'If you open that Pandora's Box, you will find it full of Trojan horses.'

The Bill was given a Second Reading by 295 votes to 264. The 297 Members (including tellers) in the Government lobby comprised 269 Labour, 11 Liberal, 9 Scottish National, 3 Plaid Cymru, 2 Scottish Labour, 1 SDLP, 1 Conservative, 1 Ulster Unionist. The 266 Members (including tellers) in the Opposition lobby comprised 253 Conservative, 6 Labour, 6 Ulster Unionist and 1 Democratic Unionist. At least two Labour Members (I. Evans and N. Kinnock) abstained from voting.

Conservative to vote for Second Reading:

Mudd, D.

Labour Members to vote against Second Reading:

Abse, L.	Dalyell, T.	Lamond, J.
Cunningham, G.	Evans, F.	Phipps, C.

HC Deb. 939, 507–12
1977–8, No. 8.

The division took place at 2.00 a.m.

SCOTLAND BILL (ALLOCATION OF TIME) [282]

16 November 1977

The Lord President of the Council and Leader of the House, M. Foot, moved a timetable (guillotine) motion for the Scotland Bill. The detailed motion provided for the remaining stages of the Bill (Committee, Report and Third Reading) to be completed in seventeen allotted days.

The motion was opposed by the Opposition, and by a number of Labour backbench opponents of devolution. G. Cunningham (Lab., Islington, South and Finsbury) appealed to Members to defeat the motion as a means of stopping the Bill. 'Members who could be counted on just two hands could kill this thing tonight.' E. Moonman (Lab., Basildon) argued that the case for the guillotine had not been made out. 'It is very important to remember the English connection when we allocate time for the debate. It should not have the limits that a guillotine motion imposes.'

The timetable motion was approved by 313 votes to 287, a Government majority of 26. The 315 Members (including tellers) in the Government lobby comprised 285 Labour, 12 Liberal, 11 Scottish National, 3 Plaid Cymru, 2 Scottish Labour, 1 SDLP and 1 Irish Independent. The 289 Members (including tellers) in the Opposition lobby comprised 270 Conservative, 9 Labour, 8 Ulster Unionist, 1 Democratic Unionist and 1 Liberal.[1]

Labour Members to vote against the motion:

Abse, L.	Evans, F.	Mendelson, J.
Cunningham, G.	Garrett, W.	Moonman, E.
Dalyell, T.	Leadbitter, T.	Phipps, C.

HC Deb. 939, 647–54
1977–8, No. 9.

[1] With the exceptions of A. Buchanan-Smith and D. Knox on the Conservative side, and R. Brown on the Labour side, the division list suggests few abstentions.

WALES BILL (ALLOCATION OF TIME) [283]

16 November 1977

The Minister of State at the Privy Council Office, J. Smith, moved a timetable (guillotine) motion for the Wales Bill. The motion provided for the remaining stages of the Bill (Committee, Report and Third Reading) to be completed in eleven allotted days.

The motion was opposed by the Opposition and by a number of Labour opponents of devolution. Dr C. Phipps (Lab., Dudley, West) contended that it was legitimate to try to defeat the Bill through voting against the guillotine motion. He realized the vote would be a victory for the Government, but declared that the fight was not over. L. Abse (Lab., Pontypool) said it was a sad occasion for him. 'We shall continue to fight and, in the end, Wales will make up its mind and repudiate the Bill—or the Act, if it is passed.'

The motion was approved by 314 votes to 287. The 316 Members (including tellers) in the Government lobby comprised 286 Labour, 12 Liberal, 11 Scottish National, 3 Plaid Cymru, 2 Scottish Labour, 1 SDLP and 1 Irish Independent. The 289 Members (including tellers) in the Opposition lobby comprised 275 Conservative, 7 Ulster Unionist, 6 Labour and 1 Democratic Unionist. There were no apparent Conservative abstentions; at least three Labour Members (W. Garrett, J. Mendelson and E. Moonman) abstained from voting.

Labour Members to vote against the motion:

Abse, L.	Dalyell, T.	Leadbitter, T.
Cunningham, G.	Evans, F.	Phipps, C.

HC Deb. 939, 721–6
1977–8, No. 10.

PENSIONERS PAYMENT BILL   [284]

Committee: 17 November 1977

Clause 2 (Interpretation)

R. Kilroy-Silk (Lab., Ormskirk) moved an amendment to provide that the Christmas bonus for pensioners was paid annually and not just in 1977 as provided for in the clause.

Mr Kilroy-Silk argued that such a bonus was a very effective means of giving aid directly to the people who needed it most. It was morally indefensible for the Government to hold out the hope of a similar bonus in future years and then decide in later years not to pay it. He asked the Government to ensure that it was paid every year. He was supported by a number of Members on both sides of the House. J. Rooker (Lab., Birmingham, Perry Barr) wanted the amendment written in to the Bill so that all knew where they stood. The commitment was not great. T. Newton (C., Braintree) argued that it was better to make a lump sum payment rather than smaller payments during the year. He would vote for the amendment.

The Minister for Social Security, S. Orme, said that the Bill was designed to give money to pensioners immediately. The argument put forward for the amendment would have to be considered by the

Government; the Cabinet would take the decision. He asked Mr Kilroy-Silk not to press his amendment.

The amendment was negatived by 46 votes to 21, with the Opposition abstaining from voting. The 48 Members (including tellers) in the Government lobby comprised 47 Labour and 1 Conservative.[1] The 23 Members (including tellers) to vote for the amendment comprised 13 Labour, 9 Conservative, and 1 Liberal.

Labour Members to vote for the amendment:

Hamilton, W.*	Newens, S.	Skinner, D.
Kilroy-Silk, R.	Prescott, J.	Spriggs, L.*
Lamond, J.	Richardson, Miss J.	Thomas, R.
Madden, M.	Rooker, J.	Wise, Mrs A.
Maynard, Miss J.		

Conservative Members to vote for the amendment:

Brooke, P.	Hodgson, R.	Sainsbury, T.
Cope, J.	Mills, P.	Shersby, M.
Drayson, B.	Newton, T.	Stanbrook, I.

HC Deb. 939, 935–6
1977–8, No. 11.

[1] M. Kimball (C., Gainsborough). Apparently it was discovered that one of the Conservative Members who voted for the amendment (and who had left after voting) had been paired for the evening by the whips, so 'to balance the books' Mr Kimball voted in the Government lobby. 'There was no political significance whatsoever in my vote.' Marcus Kimball MP to author.

SCOTLAND BILL [285]

Committee: 22 November 1977

Clause 1 (Effect of Act)

The clause provided that the provisions of the Bill 'do not affect the unity of the United Kingdom'. For the Opposition, F. Pym moved an amendment to provide that it should read: 'Nothing in these provisions shall be construed as impairing or in any way affecting the unity of the United Kingdom'.

Mr Pym contended that the sentence as it stood was a bland assertion, which sought to give reassurance where none was possible. The unity of the United Kingdom would be affected, and the Opposition would prefer to have the sentence removed altogether. They put forward the amendment in a constructive way as a guide to the courts in the future.

From the Labour benches, E. Ogden (Lab., Liverpool, West Derby) indicated a preference for some of the other amendments being discussed at the same time, but, failing those, the amendment proposed by Mr Pym would be preferable to the clause as it stood.

The Minister of State at the Privy Council Office, J. Smith, said the clause was a declaratory one, which could not be used as a rule of construction. It was not without precedent. He felt the amendment might have the effect of politicising the courts if it made it a rule of construction.

The amendment was negatived by 206 votes to 178. The 208 Members (including tellers) in the Government lobby comprised 184 Labour, 11 Scottish National, 8 Liberal, 3 Plaid Cymru, 1 Scottish Labour and 1 Ulster Unionist. The 180 Members (including tellers) in the Opposition lobby comprised 174 Conservative, 5 Ulster Unionist and 1 Labour.

Labour Member to vote for the amendment:

Ogden, E.

HC Deb. 939, 1397–402.
1977–8, No. 13.

SCOTLAND BILL [286]

Committee: 22 November 1977

Clause 1 (Effect of Act)

The clause provided that the provisions of the Bill 'do not affect the unity of the United Kingdom'.

The motion 'That the clause stand part of the Bill' was put without debate, the guillotine having fallen for the remaining proceedings on the clause.

The 'stand part' motion was put and *negatived* by 199 votes to 184, *a majority against the Government of 15*. The 186 Members (including tellers) in the Government lobby comprised 184 Labour, 1 Scottish Labour and 1 Ulster Unionist. The 201 Members (including tellers) in the Opposition lobby comprised 175 Conservative, 11 Scottish National,

6 Liberal, 5 Ulster Unionist, 3 Plaid Cymru and 1 Labour.[1] Two Labour Members (G. Cunningham and E. Ogden) appear to have abstained from voting.

Labour Member to vote against the clause:

Dalyell, T.

HC Deb. 939, 1401–4
1977–8, No. 14.

The Government accepted the decision of the House, and made no subsequent attempt to restore the clause. See *HC Deb.* 944, c. 1445–6.

[1] According to the division lists, two Labour Members voted in both lobbies, but their names appear to have been recorded in error for Conservative Members in the 'No' lobby.

SCOTLAND BILL [287]

Committee: 23 November 1977

Clause 2 (The Scottish Assembly)

The clause dealt with the size, composition and method of election for the Scottish Assembly.

At 7.00 p.m., during debate on a proposed amendment, the guillotine fell for the remaining stages of the clause.

The motion 'That the clause stand part of the Bill' was put, and carried by 208 votes to 180. The 210 Members (including tellers) in the Government lobby comprised 182 Labour, 12 Liberal, 11 Scottish National, 3 Plaid Cymru, 1 Scottish Labour and 1 Ulster Unionist. The 182 Members (including tellers) in the Opposition lobby comprised 162 Conservative, 7 Ulster Unionist, 1 Liberal and 4 Labour, plus a further 8 Labour Members recorded by *Hansard* as having voted in both lobbies.[1]

Labour Members to vote against the clause:

Abse, L.   Dalyell, T.   Ovenden, J.
Cunningham, G.

HC Deb. 939, 1603–6
1977–8, No. 16.

[1] The eight were: M. Flannery, T. Litterick, E. Loyden, Miss J. Maynard, I. Mikardo, R. Thomas, S. Thorne, and Mrs A. Wise. (The Weekly *Hansard* also records A. Latham as voting in both lobbies, but this is presumed to be in error for M. Latham in the 'No' lobby.)

EUROPEAN ASSEMBLY ELECTIONS BILL   **[288]**

Second Reading: 24 November 1977

The Bill, except for a few textual and minor amendments, was in the
same form as the Bill given a Second Reading by the House in July
1977. The Bill provided for the election of members to the European
Assembly.

Members on both sides of the House were permitted a free vote on
the Second Reading,[1] but the view of both the Government and the
Opposition was that the Bill should be supported.

The Bill was given a Second Reading by 381 votes to 98, Government
whips acting as tellers for the 'Aye' lobby. The 383 Members (including
tellers) in the 'Aye' lobby comprised 227 Conservative, 134 Labour, 11
Liberal, 9 Scottish National, 1 Ulster Unionist and 1 SDLP Member.
The 100 Members (including tellers) to oppose Second Reading
comprised 74 Labour, 16 Conservative, 7 Ulster Unionist and 3 Plaid
Cymru. More than 90 Labour Members, and over 30 Conservatives,
were absent from the division.

Labour Members to vote against Second Reading:

Allaun, F.	Gould, B.	Mendelson, J.
Ashton, J.	Heffer, E.	Mikardo, I.
Atkins, R.	Hooley, F.	Mitchell, A.
Atkinson, N.	Hoyle, D.	Newens, S.
Bean, R.	Hughes, R. J.	Ovenden, J.
Bennett, A.	Hunter, A.	Pavitt, L.
Bidwell, S.	Jay, D.	Price, C.
Canavan, D.	Jeger, Mrs L.	Richardson, Miss J.
Carmichael, N.	Jenkins, H.	Roberts, G.
Carter-Jones, L.	Kelley, R.	Robinson, G.
Castle, Mrs B.	Kerr, R.	Rodgers, G.
Colquhoun, Mrs M.	Kilroy-Silk, R.	Rooker, J.
Cook, R.	Kinnock, N.	Shaw, A.
Crowther, S.	Lambie, D.	Silverman, J.
Cunningham, G.	Latham, A.	Skinner, D.
Davies, B.	Leadbitter, T.	Spearing, N.
Dean, J.	Lee, J.	Stoddart, D.
Dunwoody, Mrs G.	Lestor, Miss J.	Thomas, R.
Ellis, J.*	Lewis, A.	Thorne, S.
Evans, I.	Litterick, T.	Torney, T.
Fernyhough, E.	Loyden, E.	Urwin, T.

Flannery, M.	McCartney, H.	Wilson, W.
Fletcher, T.	McMillan, T.	Wise, Mrs A. ·
Forrester, J.	Madden, M.*	Woof, R.
Garrett, W.	Maynard, Miss J.	

Conservatives to vote against Second Reading:

Aitken, J.	Cormack, P.	Marten, N.
Bell, R.	Fraser, H.	Maxwell-Hyslop, R.
Biffen, J.	Fry, P.	Moate, R.
Body, R.	Gow, I.	Stokes, J.
Budgen, N.	Hutchison, M. C.	Winterton, N.
Clark, A.		

HC Deb. 939, 1887–92
1977–8, No. 20.

[1] See *HC Deb.* 939, c. 1782. However, according to one source, the Government had issued a two-line whip, and the Prime Minister had made it clear that Ministers were expected to support the measure. *Daily Telegraph* 23 November 1977. In the division on the original Bill, Ministers had been permitted a free vote (see above: 6 July 1977).

EUROPEAN ASSEMBLY ELECTIONS (MONEY)   [289]

Money Resolution: 24 November 1977

The Minister of State at the Home Office, B. John, moved the Money Resolution for the European Assembly Elections Bill.

A number of backbenchers on both sides of the House rose to express doubts about the resolution, the general complaint being that the House was being asked to provide a blank cheque. Mrs G. Dunwoody (Lab., Crewe) said it was clear from the resolution that there was little control over the sums of money to be expended in relation to the European elections. R. Moate (C., Faversham) urged the Government to come clean on the public expenditure effects of the measure. 'I urge the Government to cut this item of public expenditure.' N. Kinnock (Lab., Bedwellty) felt that not as much as a halfpenny should be spent on an obligation imposed solely by membership of the EEC.

Mr John replied that it was not possible to predict with certainty the exact costs involved in the conduct of the election, and maximum sums would be prescribed by statutory instruments to be brought into force nearer the time.

The resolution was approved by 156 votes to 64, the Opposition Front Bench supporting the Government. The 158 Members (including tellers) in the Government lobby comprised 82 Labour, 66 Conservative, 5 Liberal, 3 Scottish National, 1 Ulster Unionist and 1 SDLP. The 66 Members (including tellers) to oppose the resolution comprised 47 Labour, 11 Conservative, 7 Ulster Unionist and 1 Plaid Cymru Member.

Labour Members to vote against the resolution:

Allaun, F.	Forrester, J.	Newens, S.
Ashton, J.	Gould, B.	Ovenden, J.
Atkinson, N.	Hoyle, D.	Pavitt, L.
Bean, R.	Hughes, R. J.	Richardson, Miss J.
Bennett, A.	Jay, D.	Robinson, G.
Bidwell, S.	Jeger, Mrs L.	Rodgers, G.
Castle, Mrs B.	Kerr, R.	Rooker, J.*
Colquhoun, Mrs M.	Kilroy-Silk, R.	Skinner, D.
Cook, R.	Kinnock, N.	Spearing, N.
Crowther, S.	Latham, A.	Stoddart, D.
Cunningham, G.	Lee, J.	Thomas, R.
Dean, J.	Litterick, T.	Torney, T.
Dunwoody, Mrs G.	Loyden, E.	Urwin, T.
Evans, I.	Madden, M.*	Wise, Mrs A.
Fernyhough, E.	Maynard, Miss J.	Woof, R.
Flannery, M.	Mikardo, I.	

Conservatives to vote against the resolution:

Bell, R.	Clark, A.	Marten, N.
Biffen, J.	Fraser, H.	Moate, R.
Body, R.	Gow, I.	Winterton, N.
Budgen, N.	Marshall, M.	

HC Deb. 939, 1911–14
1977–8, No. 21.

SCOTLAND BILL [290]

Committee: 29 November 1977

Clause 18 (Scottish Assembly Acts)

Under the clause, the Scottish Assembly was given power to pass Acts which could amend or repeal a provision made by or under an Act of Parliament.

E. Griffiths (C., Bury St. Edmunds) moved an amendment to provide that such amendment or repeal could only have effect after a draft had been laid and approved by affirmative resolution of each House of Parliament.

The amendment was moved formally, having been discussed in conjunction with another amendment moved by Mr Griffiths. During the debate on Mr Griffiths' amendments, the junior Opposition spokesman on devolution, L. Brittan, rose briefly to declare 'that in our view the amendments raise profound matters at the absolute centre of the Government's scheme for devolution, but matters that can be dealt with most effectively by Amendment No. 247.'[1]

The amendment was negatived by 189 votes to 69, the Opposition abstaining from voting. The 191 Members (including tellers) in the Government lobby comprised 169 Labour, 10 Liberal, 10 Scottish National, 1 Plaid Cymru and 1 Scottish Labour. The 71 Members (including tellers) to support the amendment comprised 66 Conservative and 5 Ulster Unionist.

Conservatives to vote for the amendment:

Benyon, W.*
Biffen, J.
Biggs-Davison, J.
Boscawen, R.
Bottomley, P.
Braine, Sir B.
Buck, A.
Carlisle, M.
Cooke, R.
Drayson, B.
Dykes, H.
Eden, Sir J.
Fell, A.
Fisher, Sir N.
Fookes, Miss J.
Fox, M.
Gardiner, G.
Glyn, A.
Goodhew, V.
Gow, I.

Grist, I.
Hall, Sir J.
Hamilton, M.
Holland, P.
Howell, R.
James, D.
Kaberry, Sir D.
King, E.
Lawrence, I.
Lloyd, I.
McCrindle, R.
Macfarlane, N.
Marten, N.
Maxwell-Hyslop, R.
Miller, H.
Moate, R.
Montgomery, F.
Moore, J.
More, J.
Morgan, G.

Neubert, M.
Page, R. G.
Price, D.
Rathbone, T.
Rees, P.
Rhys Williams, Sir B.
Rost, P.
Shaw, G.
Shelton, W.
Shepherd, C.
Skeet, T.
Sproat, I.*
Stainton, K.
Stanbrook, I.
Steen, A.
Stokes, J.
Tebbit, N.
Temple-Morris, P.
Wall, P.
Wells, J.

Gower, Sir R.   Mudd, D.   Wiggin, J.
Griffiths, E.   Nelson, A.   Winterton, N.

HC Deb. 940, 311–14
1977–8, No. 22.

¹ Amendment no. 247 was an Opposition amendment which was discussed following the division on the Griffiths' amendment. The amendment provided that any future Act of Parliament which expressly stated that it extended to Scotland would result in any Scottish Assembly Act provision which was repugnant to the Act being void. The amendment was negatived on a party vote by 169 votes to 131. *HC Deb.* 940, c. 355–8.

SCOTLAND BILL   [291]

Committee: 30 November 1977

Clause 21 (The Scottish Executive)

I. Sproat (C., Aberdeen, South) moved an amendment to remove from the Assembly the power to create Assistant Secretaries of State.

The amendment was negatived by 276 votes to 246. 1 Labour Member cross-voted to support the amendment, and at least one other (G. Cunningham) abstained from voting.

Labour Member to vote for the amendment:

Ogden, E.

HC Deb. 940, 639–44
1977–8, No. 30.

EUROPEAN ASSEMBLY ELECTIONS BILL   [292]

Committee: 1 December 1977

Clause 1 (Election of representatives to the European Assembly)

D. Jay (Lab., Battersea, North) moved an amendment to provide that the terms of the measure would cease to have effect when there was any alteration in the powers of the European Assembly.

Mr Jay contended that his amendment sought to give effect to what Ministers had said. He hoped they could reach agreement in the Committee that there must not be increases in the powers of the Assembly without full legislation and discussion in the House. 'That is the only safeguard that matters.' He was supported by E. Powell (UU, Down, South) and J. Ellis (Lab., Brigg and Scunthorpe). Mr Ellis said they should put in all the checks and balances they thought appropriate. N. Budgen (C., Wolverhampton, South-West) rose to add his support, expressing the view that the amendment was a necessary beginning.

The Secretary of State for Foreign and Commonwealth Affairs, Dr D. Owen, contended that the amendment was defective in a number of respects. The Government accepted that it should be made clear that no extension of the Assembly's powers which would encroach on the legislative powers of the House could be agreed by the Government without an authorizing Act of Parliament, and a new clause would be introduced later to that effect.

The amendment was carried to a division and negatived by 122 votes to 49, Opposition Members voting with the Government. The 124 Members (including tellers) in the Government lobby comprised 81 Labour, 34 Conservative, 5 Liberal and 4 Scottish National. The 51 Members (including tellers) to support the amendment comprised 40 Labour, 6 Ulster Unionist, 4 Conservative and 1 Scottish Labour.

Labour Members to support the amendment:

Atkins, R.	Heffer, E.	Madden, M.
Atkinson, N.	Hooley, F.	Maynard, Miss J.
Bidwell, S.	Hoyle, D.	Mendelson, J.
Buchan, N.	Jay, D.	Mikardo, I.
Castle, Mrs B.	Jeger, Mrs L.	Miller, M.
Cook, R.	Jenkins, H.	Richardson, Miss J.
Corbett, R.	Kerr, R.	Robinson, G.
Cunningham, G.	Lamond, J.	Short, Mrs R.
Ellis, J.*	Latham, A.	Skinner, D.
Fernyhough, E.	Lee, J.	Spearing, N.
Flannery, M.	Lewis, R.	Stoddart, D.*
Fowler, G.	Litterick, T.	Thomas, R.
George, B.	McMillan, T.	Wise, Mrs A.
Gould, B.		

Conservatives to vote for the amendment:

Body, R.	Marten, N.	Moate, R.
Budgen, N.		

HC Deb. 940, 825–6
1977–8, No. 32.

BUSINESS OF THE HOUSE [293]

1 December 1977

At 10.00 p.m., during discussion on the European Assembly Elections Bill, a Government whip moved the procedural exemption motion to allow the Bill to be proceeded with at that sitting, though opposed, until any hour.

Opponents of the European Assembly Elections Bill divided the House, and the motion was carried by 116 votes to 44,[1] Opposition Members voting with the Government. The 118 Members (including tellers) in the Government lobby comprised 79 Labour, 33 Conservative, 5 Liberal and 1 Ulster Unionist. The 46 Members (including tellers) to oppose the motion comprised 28 Labour, 6 Ulster Unionist, 5 Scottish National, 4 Conservative, 2 Plaid Cymru and 1 Scottish Labour.

Labour Members to vote against the motion:

Atkins, R.	Jenkins, H.	Richardson, Miss J.
Atkinson, N.	Lamond, J.	Robinson, G.
Bidwell, S.	Latham, A.	Rooker, J.
Cook, R.	Lee, J.*	Skinner, D.
Ellis, J.	Lewis, R.	Spearing, N.
Fernyhough, E.	Litterick, T.	Stoddart, D.
Flannery, M.	McMillan, T.	Thomas, R.
Gould, B.*	Madden, M.	Mrs A. Wise
Hoyle, D.	Maynard, Miss J.	
Jay, D.	Mikardo, I.	

Conservatives to vote against the motion:

Body, R.	Marten, N.	Moate, R.
Budgen, N.		

HC Deb. 940, 847–50
1977–8, No. 33.

[1] *Hansard* records the figures as 116 votes to 45, but only 44 names are listed in the 'No' lobby.

CROWN AGENTS [294]

5 December 1977

On 1 December, J. Mendelson (Lab., Penistone) was given leave under Standing Order 9 to discuss 'The loss of more than £200 million through the operations of the Crown Agents'.

In moving the motion for adjournment, Mr Mendelson said his purpose was to establish the response of the House to the facts so far revealed, and to allow the House to express its judgment as to the type of inquiry that should take place. On the latter point, he said he did not think that the Government's proposal was adequate: a committee sitting in private was not adequate, and the nature of the committee proposed was inadequate. He argued for an inquiry under the procedure of the 1921 Tribunal of Inquiry (Evidence) Act. He felt it was justified by the nature of the case and the purposes of the inquiry. If the Government did not accept his proposal, he would divide the House.

The Minister of State for Overseas Development, Mrs J. Hart, gave the House further information concerning the loss of £200 million by the Crown Agents, and explained why the Government preferred not to use the procedure of the 1921 Act. It would not be justified to go over matters already comprehensively investigated by the Fay Committee. The Government had decided to appoint the Aarvold inquiry, which was in line with the precedents of Crichel Down and the Bossard case. It would operate with much greater speed, and witnesses would know what they said was in private.

Support for a public inquiry came from both sides of the House. R. Wood (C., Bridlington), the Minister for Overseas Development 1970–4, urged the Minister to reconsider. There were dangers in a secret trial which it was in the Minister's power to avoid. D. Skinner (Lab., Bolsover) said the people who had returned Members to Westminster would not be treated to a private inquiry if they were involved in pilfering from Woolworths. It had been a sordid matter, and he wanted a public inquiry. During the debate, Sir H. Wilson (Lab., Huyton) also expressed the view 'that there is a strong case—to put it no higher than that—for an open inquiry'.

At the end of the debate, the Minister said she would be prepared to consider the matter further, but Mr Mendelson said that if she could not give a commitment to appoint a tribunal under the 1921 Act he would divide the House.

Mr Mendelson divided the House on his motion to adjourn, and it was *carried* by 158 votes to 126, *a majority against the Government of 32.* The Opposition Front Bench abstained from voting. The 128 Members (including tellers) in the Government lobby comprised solely Labour Members. The 160 Members (including tellers) to support the motion comprised 79 Labour, 65 Conservative,[1] 9 Liberal, 6 Scottish National and 1 Plaid Cymru. Over 90 Labour Members were absent from the division; among those abstaining was Sir H. Wilson.

Labour Members to vote for adjournment:

Abse, L.
Allaun, F.
Atkins, R.
Atkinson, N.
Bean, R.
Bidwell, S.
Bray, J.
Brown, R.
Buchan, N.
Canavan, D.
Carmichael, N.
Castle, Mrs B.
Clemitson, I.
Cohen, S.
Colquhoun, Mrs M.
Cook, R.
Craigen, J.
Crawshaw, R.
Davies, B.*
Dean, J.
Doig, P.
Edge, G.
Ellis, J.
English, M.
Evans, I.
Evans, J.
Flannery, M.

Fletcher, T.
Fowler, G.
Garrett, J.
Grant, G.
Hamilton, W.
Heffer, E.
Hooley, F.
Hughes, M.
Hughes, R.
Hughes, R. J.
Hunter, A.
Jeger, Mrs L.
Jenkins, H.
Johnson, J.
Kerr, R.
Kinnock, N.
Lamond, J.
Latham, A.
Leadbitter, T.
Lee, J.
Lestor, Miss J.
Lewis, R.
Litterick, T.
Lyon, A.
MacFarquhar, R.
McNamara, K.*

Madden, M.
Maynard, Miss J.
Mendelson, J.
Mikardo, I.
Miller, M.
Molloy, W.
O'Halloran, M.
Pendry, T.
Richardson, Miss J.
Roberts, G.
Rooker, J.
Roper, J.
Skinner, D.
Small, W.
Spearing, N.
Spriggs, L.
Stoddart, D.
Thomas, R.
Thorne, S.
Torney, T.
Ward, M.
Watkinson, J.
Whitehead, P.
Wilson, A.
Wise, Mrs A.
Wrigglesworth, I.

Conservatives to vote for adjournment:

Adley, R.
Aitken, J.
Baker, K.
Benyon, W.
Biffen, J.
Blaker, P.
Bowden, A.
Braine, Sir B.
Brocklebank-Fowler, C.
Brooke, P.
Channon, P.
Clark, W.

Gow, I.
Grylls, M.
Haselhurst, A.
Hodgson, R.
Holland, P.
Hordern, P.
Howell, R.
Hutchison, M. C.
Jessel, T.
Kellett-Bowman, Mrs E.
Knight, Mrs J.
Lawrence, I.

Onslow, C.
Raison, T.
Rathbone, T.
Rees, P.
Rees-Davies, W.
Rhodes James, R.
Rifkind, M.
Rodgers, Sir J.
Rost, P.
Royle, Sir A.
Shaw, G.
Sims, R.

Cope, J.	Loveridge, J.	Smith, D.
Costain, A.	Macfarlane, N.	Spence, J.
Crouch, D.	MacKay, A.	Stanbrook, I.
Dodsworth, G.	Marshall, M.	Taylor, R.
Durant, T.	Marten, N.	Temple-Morris, P.
Dykes, H.	Mayhew, P.	Townsend, C.
Gardiner, G.	Miller, H.	Viggers, P.
Gardner, E.	Moate, R.	Walder, D.
Glyn, A.	Montgomery, F.	Wood, R.
Goodhew, V.	Nelson, A.	

HC Deb. 940, 1093–6.
1977–8, No. 34.

The motion having been carried, the House was adjourned. Subsequently, the Government accepted the decision of the House and announced that the inquiry into the Crown Agents' affair would be held, in public, under the provisions of the 1921 Act. See *HC Deb.* 945, c. 253–73.

1 Although no official Front Bench advice was offered to Conservative Members, the Opposition Front Bench abstained from voting (as did Opposition whips, an indication of a non-free vote), and the vote was notably one of backbenchers asserting their wishes against the Government and acquiesence of the Opposition Front Bench. For that reason, the names of Conservative Members voting for the motion are recorded.

SHERIFF PETER THOMSON [295]

Prayer: 6 December 1977

D. Canavan (Lab., West Stirlingshire) moved 'That an humble Address be presented to Her Majesty, praying that the Sheriff (Removal from Office) Order 1077, dated 22nd July 1977, a copy of which was laid before this House on 27th July in the last Session of Parliament, be annulled'.

The order removed Sheriff Peter Thomson from his office of sheriff. Mr Canavan contended that Sheriff Thomson had been removed on the basis of a pamphlet he had written, which was of a non-party nature. If he was not allowed to state his case before the House[1] the case for dismissal must at best be doubtful. 'That reason alone, to my mind, is enough to justify voting tonight for the annulment of the dismissal order.'

The Secretary of State for Scotland, B. Millan, said that he had decided to make the order after Sheriff Thomson had been found guilty of misbehaviour on two occasions by a judges' inquiry and declared unfit for office. The sheriff had not put arguments in support of his conduct before the inquiry. He had been involved in campaigning for a Scottish plebiscite for some time, and had previously been warned about his activities. Mr Millan asked the House to accept his decision and to reject the prayer.

The prayer was negatived by 170 votes to 52, with Opposition Members being allowed a free vote. The 172 Members (including tellers) in the Government lobby comprised 158 Labour, 13 Conservative and 1 Liberal. The 55 Members (including tellers) to support the prayer comprised 36 Conservative, 10 Scottish National, 3 Labour, 2 Ulster Unionist, 2 Liberal and 1 Scottish Labour.

Labour Members to vote for the prayer:

Canavan, D.*	English, M.	Mackintosh, J.

HC Deb. 940, 1329–32
1977–8, No. 37.

---

[1] An unsuccessful attempt had been made to allow Sheriff Thomson to state his case at the Bar of the House.

SCOTLAND BILL [296]

Committee: 7 December 1977

Clause 39 (Industrial and Economic Guidelines)

The clause made provision for the Secretary of State to issue guidelines to the Scottish Secretary in respect of certain stipulated matters, including the Scottish Development Agency.

At 11.00 p.m., during debate on an amendment to the clause, the guillotine fell for the remaining stages of the clause, and the motion 'That the clause stand part of the Bill' was put without debate.

The 'stand part' motion was carried by 168 votes to 163, a Government majority of 5. The 170 Members (including tellers) in the Government lobby comprised 161 Labour and 9 Liberal. The 165 Members (including tellers) in the Opposition lobby comprised 146 Conservative, 10 Scottish National, 3 Ulster Unionist, 3 Plaid Cymru, 2 Labour and 1 Scottish Labour.

Labour Members to vote against the clause:

Canavan, D.   Mackintosh, J.

HC Deb. 940, 1553–8
1977–8, No. 43.

SCOTLAND BILL [297]

Committee: 7 December 1977

Clause 40 (National Pay Policy)

The clause provided that the Scottish Secretary should have regard to national pay policy.

At 11.00 p.m., the guillotine fell, and the 'stand part' motion for the clause was put without debate.

The motion for the clause to stand part of the Bill was *negatived* by 161 votes to 160, *a majority against the Government of 1*. The 162 Members (including tellers) in the Government lobby comprised 154 Labour and 8 Liberal. The 163 Members (including tellers) in the Opposition lobby comprised 144 Conservative, 10 Scottish National, 3 Ulster Unionist, 3 Plaid Cymru, 2 Labour and 1 Liberal. Seven Labour Members appear also to have abstained from voting.[1]

Labour Members to vote against the clause:

Canavan, D.   Mackintosh, J.

HC Deb. 940, 1557–60
1977–8, No. 44.

The Government accepted the decision of the House, and made no subsequent attempt to restore the clause to the Bill. See *HC Deb.* 944, c. 1445–6.

---

[1] The seven abstainers were: F. Allaun, N. Atkinson, D. Hoyle, A. Latham, Miss J. Richardson, D. Skinner and R. Thomas. Two Conservative Members (C. Brocklebank-Fowler and D. Mudd) who participated in an immediately preceding division were also absent from the division.

SCOTLAND BILL   [298]

Committee: 7 December 1977

Clause 41 (Minister's consent to terms and conditions of service of certain persons)

At 11.00 p.m. the guillotine fell, and the 'stand part' motion for clause 41 was put without debate.

The motion for the clause to stand part of the Bill was carried by 162 votes to 16, with the Opposition abstaining from voting. The 164 Members (including tellers) in the Government lobby comprised 156 Labour and 8 Liberal. The 18 Members (including tellers) to oppose the clause comprised 10 Scottish National, 3 Ulster Unionist, 3 Plaid Cymru, 1 Labour and 1 Conservative.

Labour Member to vote against the clause:

Canavan, D.

Conservative to vote against the clause:

Stanbrook, I.

HC Deb. 940, 1559–62
1977–8, No. 45.

BUSINESS OF THE HOUSE (SUPPLY)   [299]

12 December 1977

A Government whip moved formally 'That, at this day's sitting, Mr Speaker shall put forthwith any questions necessary to dispose of the proceedings on the Motions in the name of Mr Robert Sheldon relating to Civil and Defence Estimates as soon as the House has entered upon the business of Supply'.

A number of backbenchers on both sides of the House rose to oppose the motion. F. Allaun (Lab., Salford, East) said he wished to oppose passing on the nod, without debate, the spending of an additional £427 million on defence. They were entitled to an explanation of the items covered in the Estimates. I. Gow (C., Eastbourne) declared that the control of public expenditure was a matter of key importance for backbenchers. 'If we allow this motion to go through without debate,

I believe that we shall betray the trust of those who are opposed to it.'
Miss J. Richardson (Lab., Barking) said the situation struck her as
being ridiculous. The House expected to be able to question and ask
for clarification of many of the items in the Supplementary Estimates.

No Minister or Opposition Front Bencher spoke. The motion was
put and carried by 243 votes to 82, the Opposition supporting the
Government.[1] The 245 Members (including tellers) in the Government
lobby comprised 139 Labour, 100 Conservative and 6 Liberal. The 84
Members (including tellers) to oppose the motion comprised 53
Labour, 19 Conservative, 8 Scottish National, 3 Ulster Unionist and 1
Scottish Labour.

Labour Members to vote against the motion:

Allaun, F.*	Flannery, M.	Madden, M.
Ashton, J.	Fletcher, T.	Maynard, Miss J.
Atkinson, N.	Garrett, J.	Mikardo, I.
Bidwell, S.	Gould, B.	Miller, M.
Butler, Mrs J.	Hayman, Mrs H.	Newens, S.
Canavan, D.	Heffer, E.	Pavitt, L.
Carmichael, N.	Hooley, F.	Richardson, Miss J.
Castle, Mrs B.	Hoyle, D.	Robinson, G.
Clemitson, I.	Hughes, R.	Rodgers, G.
Colquhoun, Mrs M.	Hughes, R. J.	Rooker, J.
Cook, R.	Kelley, R.	Selby, H.
Corbett, R.	Kerr, R.*	Short, Mrs R.
Davies, B.	Lambie, D.	Silverman, J.
Edge, G.	Lamond, J.	Spriggs, L.
Ellis, J.	Latham, A.	Thomas, R.
English, M.	Litterick, T.	Wise, Mrs A.
Evans, F.	McMillan, T.	Woof, R.
Evans, I.	McNamara, K.	

Conservatives to vote against the motion:

Bell, R.	Hordern, P.	Moate, R.
Burden, F.	Jessel, T.	Rost, P.
Clark, A.	Johnson Smith, G.	Shelton, W.
Costain, A.	Lloyd, I.	Sims, R.
Dodsworth, G.	McCrindle, R.	Skeet, T.
Drayson, B.	Mayhew, P.	Townsend, C.
Gow, I.		

HC Deb. 941, 47–50
1977–8, No. 46.

EUROPEAN ASSEMBLY ELECTIONS BILL [300]

Committee: 12 December 1977

Clause 1 (Election of representatives to the European Assembly)

On the motion for clause 1 to stand part of the Bill, a number of backbenchers on both sides of the House rose to oppose it. A. Clark (C., Plymouth, Sutton) said that they had no idea what members of the European Assembly would do when they got there. He felt it would be better if they were to take another look at the whole question. B. Gould (Lab., Southampton, Test) expressed the fear that direct elections could lead to a transfer of powers to the European Assembly. 'If political expediency can produce this Bill, what guarantee do we have that in the end political expediency will not also produce the extension of powers implicit in the whole concept of direct elections?' N. Spearing (Lab., Newham, South) argued that if the clause was agreed to it would put an effective weapon in the hands of the elected Assembly members to change EC budgets and project them into an arena in which the emergence of a European party was already happening. R. Moate (C., Faversham) contended that the existing system was better than the proposal for direct elections; he felt MPs would more truly represent the people of this country than directly-elected members.

The Minister of State at the Foreign and Commonwealth Office, F. Judd, said points made by Members would be borne in mind by the Government in formulating the new clause promised by the Foreign Secretary,[1] and hoped Members would be patient for a little longer.

The 'stand part' motion was carried by 219 votes to 79, the Opposition voting with the Government. The 221 Members (including tellers) in the Government lobby comprised 122 Labour, 84 Conservative, 9 Liberal, 4 Scottish National, 1 Ulster Unionist and 1 SDLP. The 81 Members (including tellers) to oppose the motion comprised 69 Labour, 6 Ulster Unionist, 5 Conservative and 1 Plaid Cymru.

Labour Members to vote against the clause:

Allaun, F.
Ashton, J.
Atkins, R.
Atkinson, N.
Bean, R.
Bennett, A.
Bidwell, S.
Buchan, N.
Canavan, D.
Cant, R.
Carmichael, N.
Carter-Jones, L.
Castle, Mrs B.
Clemitson, I.
Cook, R.
Crowther, S.
Cunningham, G.
Davies, B.
Ellis, J.*
Evans, I.
Fernyhough, E.
Flannery, M.
Fletcher, T.

Forrester, J.
Garrett, W.
Gould, B.
Heffer, E.
Hooley, F.
Hoyle, D.
Hughes, R.
Hughes, R. J.
Jay, D.
Jenkins, H.
Kerr, R.
Kilroy-Silk, R.
Kinnock, N.
Lambie, D.
Lamond, J.
Latham, A.
Leadbitter, T.
Lee, J.
Lewis, R.
Loyden, E.
McCartney, H.
McNamara, K.
Madden, M.*

Maynard, Miss J.
Mendelson, J.
Mikardo, I.
Miller, M.
Ovenden, J.
Parry, R.
Pavitt, L.
Pendry, T.
Richardson, Miss J.
Roberts, G.
Robinson, G.
Rodgers, G.
Rooker, J.
Short, Mrs R.
Silverman, J.
Skinner, D.
Spearing, N.
Spriggs, L.
Stoddart, D.
Thomas, R.
Thorne, S.
Wise, Mrs A.
Woof, R.

Conservatives to vote against the clause:

Budgen, N.
Clark, A.

Marten, N.
Moate, R.

Winterton, N.

HC Deb. 941, 179–82
1977–8, No. 48.

¹ In debate on an amendment to the clause on 1 December (see above) the Foreign Secretary had agreed to introduce a new clause to make clear that no extension of the European Assembly's powers which would encroach on the legislative powers of the House could be agreed by the Government without an authorizing Act of Parliament. Opponents of the clause made it clear they would have preferred to have seen the new clause before the 'stand part' motion was taken.

EUROPEAN ASSEMBLY ELECTIONS BILL [301]

Committee: 12 December 1977

The Home Secretary, M. Rees, moved 'That Clause 3 be considered before Clause 2'.

Mr Rees explained that the motion was put forward in order to allow the House to consider and vote upon the electoral system to be employed for the Assembly elections before rising for the Christmas recess, and to allow for practical arrangements to start being made by those with responsibility for organizing the elections.

A number of Members expressed doubts about the motion. D. Jay (Lab., Battersea, North) said the Minister gave no sufficient reason for such a drastic change in procedure. I. Mikardo (Lab., Bethnal Green and Bow) wondered what the relevance was of a decision being reached before Christmas. 'Is it any more than a bit of flapdoodle verbiage, and is it not a fact that the so-called reasons given by the Home Secretary are devoid of any serious political substance?' D. Skinner (Lab., Bolsover) argued that the motion had nothing to do with Christmas and was an attempt to placate the Liberal Party, so that the Liberals could claim that sooner rather than later they had been able to achieve something through the Lib–Lab pact. E. Heffer (Lab., Liverpool, Walton) said he did not understand the idea behind the motion. He wanted clause 2 taken in the normal way.

The motion was carried by 180 votes to 56, the Opposition supporting the Government. The 182 Members (including tellers) in the Government lobby comprised 112 Labour, 62 Conservative, 7 Liberal and 1 SDLP. The 58 Members (including tellers) to oppose the motion comprised 46 Labour, 7 Ulster Unionist, 3 Scottish National, 1 Conservative and 1 Plaid Cymru.

Labour Members to vote against the motion:

Allaun, F.	Forrester, J.	Madden, M.*
Ashton, J.	Gould, B.	Maynard, Miss J.
Atkins, R.	Heffer, E.	Mendelson, J.
Atkinson, N.	Hooley, F.	Mikardo, I.
Bennett, A.	Hoyle, D.	Richardson, Miss J.
Bidwell, S.	Hughes, R.	Robinson, G.
Buchan, N.	Jay, D.	Rodgers, G.
Canavan, D.	Kerr, R.	Rooker, J.
Carmichael, N.	Kilroy-Silk, R.	Skinner, D.
Castle, Mrs B.	Kinnock, N.	Spearing, N.
Clemitson, I.	Lamond, J.	Spriggs, L.
Ellis, J.	Latham, A.	Stoddart, D.*
Evans, I.	Leadbitter, T.	Thomas, R.
Fernyhough, E.	Loyden, E.	Thorne, S.
Flannery, M.	McNamara, K.	Wise, Mrs A.
Fletcher, T.		

Conservative to vote against the motion:

Moate, R.

HC Deb. 941, 201–4
1977–8, No. 49.

SCOTLAND BILL   [302]

Committee: 10 January 1978

Clause 42 (Scottish Consolidated Fund and Loans Fund)

J. Mackintosh (Lab., Berwick and East Lothian) moved an amendment to provide that the Scottish Consolidated Fund should have three sources of revenue, including a personal income tax levied upon Scottish residents with the Scottish Assembly having power to reduce the rate at which the tax was levied.

Mr Mackintosh argued that if the Bill was to be made to work, if Members wanted devolution, the Scottish Assembly had to be given its own source of revenue together with the right to alter, to some extent, the rate of taxation. 'An Assembly with these powers would be responsible to its electorate. Without these powers, the plan is half-baked.'

The amendment received some support (and opposition) from both sides of the House. A. Buchanan-Smith (C., Angus, North and Mearns) said that for his part he would like to see a larger element of discretion and responsibility in relation to revenue sharing within the budget of a Scottish Assembly. R. Cook (Lab., Edinburgh, Central) argued by declining to give the Assembly a revenue-raising power they were making it more likely that the Assembly would demand more money. If they were to have an Assembly it was important that it should have a revenue-raising power. N. Buchan (Lab., Renfrewshire, West) believed that without such an amendment they would be creating an enormous danger for the future.

The Minister of State, Privy Council Office, J. Smith, pointed out that no one had come forward with a system of revenue raising which was economical and practical. It would be very difficult to have national or regional variations in tax collection without very high cost. The Government believed the best way to deal with the question was on the basis of the block grant.

The amendment was negatived by 306 votes to 61, the Opposition allowing apparently a free vote.[1] The 308 Members (including tellers) in the Government lobby comprised 203 Labour and 105 Conservative. The 63 Members (including tellers) to vote for the amendment comprised 19 Labour, 19 Conservative, 11 Liberal, 10 Scottish National, 3 Plaid Cymru and 1 Ulster Unionist.

Labour Members to vote for the amendment:

Bray, J.	Ellis, T.	Mackintosh, J.*
Buchan, N.	Hughes, R.	Miller, M.
Canavan, D.	Hughes, R. J.	Thorne, S.
Carmichael, N.	Kerr, R.	Whitehead, P.
Cook, R.	Lambie, D.	Wise, Mrs A.
Craigen, J.	Lamond, J.	
Douglas-Mann, J.	MacFarquhar, R.	

HC Deb. 941, 1607–10
1977–8, No. 52.

¹ Various members of the Shadow Cabinet voted with the Government, while others were among the more than 70 Conservative Members who took no part in the division (while voting in an immediately succeeding division). The 19 Conservatives to vote for the amendment were: R. Adley, M. Brotherton, A. Buchanan-Smith, A. Buck, P. Cormack, D. Crouch, R. Fairgrieve, H. Gray, R. Hicks, D. Knox, K. Lewis, M. Marshall, C. Morrison, D. Mudd, N. Scott, T. Smith, I. Stewart, D. Walder and J. Wells.

SCOTLAND BILL [303]

Committee: 10 January 1978

Clause 42 (Scottish Consolidated Fund and Loans Fund)

At 11.00 p.m., during discussion of an amendment to the clause (see preceding division), the guillotine fell for the remaining stages of the clause, and the motion 'That the clause stand part of the Bill' was put without debate.

The 'stand part' motion was carried by 229 votes to 210. The 231 Members (including tellers) in the Government lobby comprised 206 Labour, 11 Liberal, 10 Scottish National, 3 Plaid Cymru and 1 Ulster Unionist. The 212 Members (including tellers) in the Opposition lobby comprised 196 Conservative, 11 Labour and 5 Ulster Unionist.

Labour Members to vote against the clause:

Abse, L.	Evans, I.	Moonman, E.
Atkins, R.	Garrett, W.	Parker, J.
Cunningham, G.	Kinnock, N.	Phipps, C.
Dalyell, T.	Lamond, J.	

HC Deb. 941, 1609–14
1977–8, No. 53.

SCOTLAND BILL [304]

Committee: 10 January 1978

Clause 46 (Payments into Scottish Consolidated Fund out of moneys provided by Parliament)

Following the falling of the guillotine at 11.00 p.m. the motions necessary for the conclusion of certain clauses were put forthwith.

The 'stand part' motion for clause 46 was carried by 236 votes to 201. Three Labour Members cross-voted to oppose the clause, and at least a further three (L. Abse, G. Cunningham and N. Kinnock) abstained from voting.

Labour Members to vote against the clause:

Garrett, W.	Johnson, J	Phipps, C.

HC Deb. 941, 1613–18
1977–8, No. 54.

SCOTLAND BILL [305]

Committee: 11 January 1978

Clause 61 (Devolved Matters)

J. Mackintosh (Lab., Berwick and East Lothian) moved an amendment to provide for the devolution of the statutory duties, functions and obligations of the Secretary of State for Scotland and the Scottish Office.

Mr Mackintosh contended that the Bill should follow the 1920 Government of Ireland Act and retain certain functions for Westminster, with it being clear that all other functions were transferred to the devolved Parliament. He felt the Government had created a subdivision within the Secretary of State's responsibilities for political reasons. He was of the opinion that it would be much more satisfactory to have a Scottish Office with all the powers of the Secretary of State devolved to the Assembly.

The Minister of State at the Privy Council Office, J. Smith, argued that certain matters should not be devolved, including some that would be if the amendment was passed. The Government considered that it would be better to concentrate on the positive and focus on what was to be devolved: that method permitted greater accuracy. The Assembly and Executive would be clear about what they could or could not do.

The amendment was negatived by 133 votes to 35, with the Opposition abstaining from voting. The 135 Members (including tellers) in the Government lobby comprised 133 Labour and 2 Conservative. The 37 Members (including tellers) to support the amendment comprised 10 Conservative, 10 Scottish National, 12 Liberal, 2 Labour, 2 Plaid Cymru and 1 Ulster Unionist.

Conservatives to vote for the amendment:

Buchanan-Smith, A.*	Jessel, T.	Onslow, C.
Fairgrieve, R.	Knox, D.	Renton, T.
Gilmour, Sir J.	Macfarlane, N.	Rifkind, M.
Glyn, A.		

Labour Members to vote for the amendment:

McCartney, H.   Mackintosh, J.*

Conservatives to vote against the amendment:

Fookes, Miss J.   Irving, C.

HC Deb. 941, 1763-4
1977-8, No. 59.

EUROPEAN ASSEMBLY ELECTIONS BILL [306]

Committee: 12 January 1978

Clause 3 (Method of voting)

G. Reid (SNP, Clackmannan and East Stirlingshire) moved an amendment to provide for voting in the European Assembly elections to be by the 'alternative vote' method of election.[1]

The advice of both Government and Opposition Front Benchers was to oppose the amendment, and during the debate no Conservative or Labour Members rose to support it.

The amendment was negatived by 226 votes to 22, the Opposition voting with the Government. The 228 Members (including tellers) in the Government lobby comprised 176 Labour, 43 Conservative, 7 Ulster Unionist, 1 Irish Independent and 1 Democratic Unionist. The 24 Members (including tellers) to support the amendment comprised 10 Scottish National, 8 Liberal, 3 Plaid Cymru, 1 Ulster Unionist, 1 Labour and 1 Conservative.

Labour Member to vote for the amendment:
Jenkins, H.

Conservative to vote for the amendment:

Biffen, J.

HC Deb. 941, 1961–4
1977–8, No. 60.

---

[1] Under the alternative vote method an elector can indicate his preference by listing candidates in order of preference by writing 1, 2, 3 etc. up to the total number of candidates. If no candidate receives an overall majority on first preferences, the candidate at the bottom of the poll is eliminated and his votes redistributed according to second preferences, the process being repeated until a candidate receives an overall majority. On 13 December 1977, the House had rejected also the regional list system as the method of election: voting was 319–222 on a free vote. *HC Deb.* 941, c. 417–22.

SCOTLAND BILL   [307]

Committee: 17 January 1978

Schedule 10 (Matters within legislative competence of Assembly, and within powers of Scottish Executive)

Lord J. Douglas-Hamilton (C., Edinburgh, West) moved an amendment to exclude family planning and abortion from the list of matters within the legislative competence of the Scottish Assembly and powers of the Executive.

The amendment was moved formally, having been discussed in conjunction with a previous amendment. In the preceding discussion, Lord Douglas-Hamilton had explained that the British Medical Association felt that the matter was one that should be dealt with on a uniform basis throughout the whole of the United Kingdom. The objection to devolving the issue was on grounds of practicalities and not morals. Members on both sides of the House, in discussing the amendment, were divided on the matter. For the Government, the Under-Secretary of State for Scotland, H. Ewing, said it would be both strange and dangerous to devolve all other child-bearing functions (maternity and the like) and hold on to abortion. He felt there were no dangers involved in devolving abortion. If Lord Douglas-Hamilton's amendment was taken to a division, he asked the House to reject it.

The amendment was negatived by 179 votes to 162, with the Opposition allowing a free vote. The 181 Members (including tellers) in the Government lobby comprised 154 Labour, 10 Scottish National, 10 Liberal, 3 Conservative,[1] 2 Plaid Cymru, 1 Ulster Unionist and 1 Scottish Labour. The 164 Members (including tellers) to support the amendment comprised 99 Conservative, 63 Labour and 2 Ulster Unionist.

Labour Members to vote for the amendment:

Abse, L.	Fowler, G.	Newens, S.
Allaun, F.	Garrett, J.	Ogden, E.
Atkins, R.	Garrett, W.	Orbach, M.
Bennett, A.	Heffer, E.	Ovenden, J.
Buchan, N.	Hughes, R.	Palmer, A.
Carmichael, N.	Hughes, R. J.	Parker, J.
Castle, Mrs B.	Jeger, Mrs. L.	Pavitt, L.
Clemitson, I.	Kerr, R.	Richardson, Miss J.
Cook, R.	Kilroy-Silk, R.	Robinson, G.
Corbett, R.	Kinnock, N.	Roderick, C.
Cowans, H.	Lamond, J.	Rodgers, G.
Crawshaw, R.	Latham, A.	Ryman, J.
Dalyell, T.	Lee, J.	Sedgemore, B.
Dean, J.	Litterick, T.	Shaw, A.
Douglas-Mann, B.	Loyden, E.	Short, Mrs R.
Edge, G.	Madden, M.	Skinner, D.
Ellis, J.	Maynard, Miss J.	Spearing, N.
Evans, I.	Mendelson, J.	Spriggs, L.
Flannery, M.	Mikardo, I.	Thomas, R.
Fletcher, T.	Molloy, W.	Thorne, S.
Ford, B.	Moonman, E.	Wise, Mrs A.

HC Deb. 942, 289–92
1977–8, No. 61.

[1] The three Conservatives to vote against the amendment were: A. Fell, R. Mawby and H. Monro.

SCOTLAND BILL [308]

Committee: 17 January 1978

Schedule 10 (Matters within legislative competence of Assembly, and within powers of Scottish Executive)

D. Henderson (SNP, Aberdeenshire, East) moved an amendment to include industrial promotion, regulation and monitoring of investment grants, aids and incentives, and other topics, in the list of matters within the competence of the Assembly and Executive.

During the debate, J. Mackintosh (Lab., Berwick and East Lothian) indicated his support for the amendment. He explained that the changes it involved were limited, but would be of benefit: they could be wielded more quickly if they were in the hands of a Scottish administration. A. Buchanan-Smith (C., Angus, North and Mearns) and D. Canavan (Lab., West Stirlingshire) both rose to say that they had sympathy with the amendment.

The Under-Secretary of State for Scotland, H. Ewing, asked the Committee to reject the amendment because of the dangers it posed to the economic unity of the United Kingdom. Other parts of the UK would suffer if the Assembly had competence to legislate on matters such as the regulation of investment grants.

The amendment was rejected by 202 votes to 23, the Opposition voting with the Government. The 204 Members (including tellers) in the Government lobby comprised 173 Labour, 28 Conservative and 3 Ulster Unionist. The 25 Members (including tellers) to support the amendment comprised 10 Scottish National, 9 Liberal, 2 Labour, 2 Plaid Cymru and 2 Scottish Labour. Among those absent from the division was A. Buchanan-Smith.

Labour Members to vote for the amendment:

Canavan, D.   Mackintosh, J.

HC Deb. 942, 409–12
1977–8, No. 63.

SCOTLAND BILL [309]

Committee: 18 January 1978

Schedule 10 (Matters within legislative competence of Assembly, and within powers of Scottish Executive)

G. Wilson (SNP, Dundee, East) moved an amendment to include

electricity coal, gas, oil exploration, and other items, in the list of matters within the competence of the Assembly and Executive.

The amendment was opposed by both Government and Opposition. The Minister of State at the Privy Council Office, J. Smith, described it as a 'separatist amendment'.

The amendment was negatived by 289 votes to 14, the Opposition voting with the Government. The 291 Members (including tellers) in the Government lobby comprised 167 Labour, 109 Conservative, 10 Liberal and 5 Ulster Unionist. The 16 Members (including tellers) to support the amendment comprised 10 Scottish National, 3 Plaid Cymru, 2 Scottish Labour and 1 Conservative.

Conservative to vote for the amendment:

Prentice, R.[1]

HC Deb. 942, 537–40
1977–8, No. 65.

Although Mr Prentice cast his vote, hence a dissenting vote, for the amendment, he did so unaware that the Opposition was not supporting it.[2]

[1] Mr Prentice was Labour Member for Newham, North-East until October 1977 when he crossed the Floor of the House to join the Conservatives.

[2] He had been engaged in discussions with a constituent and had hurried to take part in the division, arriving just before the doors closed, and had entered the lobby for the amendment unaware that the Opposition was not supporting it. Reg Prentice MP to author.

SCOTLAND BILL [310]

Committee: 18 January 1978

Schedule 10 (Matters within legislative competence of Assembly, and within powers of Scottish Executive)

At 9.00 p.m., the guillotine fell for the remaining stages of the schedule, and the motion 'That this Schedule, as amended, be the Tenth Schedule to the Bill' was put without debate. The schedule dealt with the matters that were to be within the competence of the Assembly and Executive (see e.g., preceding divisions).

The motion was carried on a whipped party vote by 186 votes to 164. 1 Labour Member cross-voted to oppose the motion, and at least one other (G. Cunningham) abstained from voting.

Labour member to vote against the schedule:

Dalyell, T.

HC Deb. 942, 563-8
1977-8, No. 66.

SCOTLAND BILL [311]

Committee: 24 January 1978

Clause 65 (Rate Support Grants)

On the motion 'That the clause stand part of the Bill', T. Dalyell (Lab., West Lothian) rose to express doubts about the clause. Under the proposed new system, the Scottish Executive would negotiate with the Secretary of State and central government to establish what element in the rate support grant would be relevant to the reserved functions. Under section (2) of the clause the Scottish Secretary would have to 'have regard to such considerations affecting reserved functions as the Secretary of State may bring to his notice after consulting with such associations of local authorities as appear to him to be concerned'. Mr Dalyell wanted to know what was meant by 'shall have regard to'. It was a grey area, he said. The wording was very loose. It was a recipe for conflict.

The Secretary of State for Scotland, B. Millan, replied that there had to be a form of words which gave the Secretary of State a statutory locus on the issue. 'The form of words we have seems to be as good as any other.'

The 'stand part' motion was carried by 161 votes to 147. 1 Labour Member cross-voted to oppose the clause.

Labour Member to oppose the clause:

Dalyell, T.

HC Deb. 942, 1317-20
1977-8, No. 74.

SCOTLAND BILL [312]

Committee: 25 January 1978

Clause 82 (Referendum)

W. Hamilton (Lab., Fife, Central) moved an amendment to provide that the referendum on devolution should be a United Kingdom, and not solely a Scottish, one.

Mr Hamilton contended that the case for having a UK referendum was overwhelming. It was a facetious argument to suggest that the issue did not affect the United Kingdom as a whole. There was a great deal of concern about the matter in England, and he asked the Committee to support the amendment.

The Minister of State at the Privy Council Office, J. Smith, said the proposals in the Bill would affect more directly the people living in Scotland. 'As it is they who will be most directly affected, we thought it wise to consult them before the Bill, which Parliament has to pass on behalf of the whole United Kingdom, is put into effect.' For practical reasons, there was little merit in the amendment.

The amendment was negatived by 184 votes to 122, with the Opposition allowing a free vote. The 186 Members (including tellers) in the Government lobby comprised 152 Labour, 10 Conservative,[1] 10 Scottish National, 9 Liberal, 3 Plaid Cymru, 1 Ulster Unionist and 1 Scottish Labour. The 124 Members (including tellers) to support the amendment comprised 114 Conservative, 7 Labour, 2 Ulster Unionist and 1 Liberal.

Labour Members to vote for the amendment:

Dalyell, T.	Heffer, E.	Moonman, E.
Evans, I.	Latham, A.	Torney, T.
Hamilton, W.*		

HC Deb. 942, 1457–60
1977–8, No. 77.

[1] The ten Conservatives to vote against the amendment were: A. Buchanan-Smith, D. Crouch, H. Dykes, E. Heath, R. Hicks, D. Knox, K. Lewis, C. Morrison, J. Spence and P. Walker.

SCOTLAND BILL　　　　　　　　　　　　　　　　　[313]

Committee: 25 January 1978

Clause 82 (Referendum)

B. Douglas-Mann (Lab., Mitcham and Mordern) moved an amendment to provide that if 'it appears to the Secretary of State that less than one-third of the persons entitled to vote on the referendum has voted "Yes" in reply to the question posed in the Appendix to Schedule 17 to this Act he shall lay before Parliament the draft of an Order in Council for the repeal of this Act'.

G. Cunningham (Lab., Islington, South and Finsbury) moved an amendment to the amendment, to delete 'one-third' and insert '40 per cent'.

Mr Cunningham said there was nothing magical about the figures involved. He was suggesting the modest figure of 40 per cent. If the Government and the SNP were right in saying that the people of Scotland overwhelmingly wanted devolution there was no problem. 'If they overwhelmingly want devolution, far more than 40 per cent will presumably vote for it.' If only 37 per cent voted 'Yes' it did not mean that devolution necessarily stopped. All it meant was that the Minister would have to lay the order, and it would be up to the House whether to pass it. He suggested the test was a reasonable one for such a fundamental and irrevocable change as that being proposed.

R. Hughes (Lab., Aberdeen, North) said it was essential to have a threshold. They had to ask people to show positively that they wanted devolution, and they had to be prepared to take the trouble to go out and vote for it. I. Evans (Lab., Aberdare) said he supported the amendments, but felt the figure of 40 per cent was too low. He felt they could go to a figure of 50 per cent. T. Dalyell (Lab., West Lothian) said Mr Cunningham's amendment was a modest one compared to some of the majorities required in other countries for constitutional amendments. It deserved to be supported.

The Minister of State at the Privy Council Office, J. Smith, said the supporters of the amendments wanted to get the abstainers on their side. There had not been any such percentage requirement imposed in the EEC referendum. He did not think the supporters of the amendment had put forward a convincing explanation. 'First, what is involved in the amendment is that we would be changing the rules. Secondly, no convincing reason has been given for such a change in the rules. In those circumstances, it would be unwise if the Committee were to accept the amendment.'

(1) Mr Cunningham's amendment to the amendment was put, and *carried* by 166 votes to 151, *a majority against the Government of 15.* The Opposition allowed a free vote. The 153 Members (including tellers) in the Government lobby comprised 124 Labour, 11 Liberal, 10 Scottish National, 4 Conservative,[1] 3 Plaid Cymru and 1 Scottish Labour. The 168 Members (including tellers) to support the amendment comprised 127 Conservative, 35 Labour, 5 Ulster Unionist and 1 Liberal.

Labour Members to vote for the amendment:

Abse, L.	Fletcher, T.	Ogden, E.
Bidwell, S.	Garrett, W.	Palmer, A.
Boothroyd, Miss B.	Hamilton, W.*	Parker, J.
Carter-Jones, L.	Hayman, Mrs H.	Richardson, Miss J.
Colquhoun, Mrs M.	Heffer, E.	Robinson, G.
Cunningham, G.	Hughes, R.	Rodgers, G.
Dalyell, T.	Hunter, A.	Short, Mrs R.
Dean, J.	Lyon, A.	Skinner, D.
Doig, P.	Maynard, Miss J.	Spriggs, L.
Douglas-Mann, B.	Mendelson, J.	Thomas, R.
Evans, I.	Moonman, E.	Wise, Mrs A.
Flannery, M.	Newens, S.	

(2) The main amendment, as amended, was then put, and *carried* by 168 votes to 142, *a majority against the government of 26*. The Opposition allowed a free vote. The 144 Members (including tellers) in the Government lobby comprised 117 Labour, 10 Liberal, 8 Scottish National, 5 Conservative,[2] 3 Plaid Cymru and 1 Scottish Labour. The 170 Members (including tellers) to support the amended amendment comprised 127 Conservative, 37 Labour, 4 Ulster Unionist and 1 Liberal.

Labour Members to vote for the amended amendment:

Abse, L.	Garrett, W.	Orbach, M.
Bidwell, S.	Hamilton,, W.*	Palmer, A.
Boothroyd, Miss B.	Hayman, Mrs H.	Parker, J.
Colquhoun, Mrs M.	Heffer, E.	Richardson, Miss J.
Cook, R.	Hughes, R.	Robinson, G.
Cunningham, G.	Jay, D.	Rodgers, G.
Dalyell, T.	Lyon, A.	Short, Mrs R.
Dean, J.	Maynard, Miss J.	Skinner, D.
Doig, P.	Mendelson, J.	Spriggs, L.
Douglas-Mann, B.	Moonman, E.	Thomas, R.
Evans, I.	Newens, S.	Torney, T.
Flannery, M.	Ogden, E.	Wise, Mrs A.
Fletcher, T.		

HC Deb. 942, 1541–4, 1545–8
1977–8, Nos. 78 and 79.

[1] The four Conservatives to vote against the amendment to the amendment were: A. Buchanan-Smith, D. Crouch, E. Heath and D. Knox.
[2] The five Conservatives to vote against the amended amendment were: A. Buchanan-Smith, D. Crouch, E. Heath, D. Knox, and J. Spence.

SCOTLAND BILL [314]

Committee: 25 January 1978

Clause 82 (Referendum)

J. Grimond (Lib., Orkney and Shetland) moved formally an amendment to provide that if a majority of voters in the Orkney Islands area or in the Shetland Islands area voted 'No' in the referendum the Secretary of State would lay an order providing that in the area or areas concerned the Act would not apply, and providing also for the establishment of a commission to recommend such changes in the government of that area or areas as might be desirable.

The House divided on the amendment, with the Government lobby being whipped in opposition to it. The amendment was *carried* by 204 votes to 118, *a majority against the Government of 86.* The 120 Members (including tellers) in the Government lobby comprised 107 Labour, 9 Scottish National, 3 Plaid Cymru and 1 Conservative. The 206 Members (including tellers) to support the amendment comprised 140 Conservative, 50 Labour, 11 Liberal and 5 Ulster Unionist.

Conservative to vote against the amendment:

Spence, J.

Labour Members to vote for the amendment:

Abse, L.	Flannery, M.	Ogden, E.
Atkins, R.	Fletcher, T.	Orbach, M.
Blenkinsop, A.	Ford, B.	Palmer, A.
Boothroyd, Miss B.	Fowler, G.	Parker, J.
Buchan, N.	Garrett, W.	Richardson, Miss J.
Butler, Mrs. J.	Hamilton, W.	Roberts, A.
Canavan, D.	Hayman, Mrs H.	Robinson, G.
Carmichael, N.	Heffer, E.	Rodgers, G.
Carter-Jones, L.	Hughes, R.	Rooker, J.
Colquhoun, Mrs M.	Jay, D.	Rose, P.
Cook, R.	Kerr, R.	Short, Mrs R.
Cunningham, G.	Lewis, R.	Skinner, D.
Dalyell, T.	Lyon, A.	Spriggs, L.
Dean, J.	Maynard, Miss J.	Thomas, R.
Douglas-Mann, B.	Mendelson, J.	Watkins, D.
English, M.	Moonman, E.	Wise, Mrs A.
Evans, I.	Newens, S.	

HC Deb. 942, 1547–52
1977–8, No. 80.

SCOTLAND BILL [315]

Committee: 25 January 1978

Clause 82 (Referendum)

At 11.00 p.m. the guillotine fell for the remaining stages of clause 82, and the motion 'That the clause, as amended, stand part of the Bill' was put without debate.

The 'stand part' motion was carried by 242 votes to 18, with the Opposition allowing apparently a free vote. The 244 Members (including tellers) in the Government lobby comprised 152 Labour, 82 Conservative and 10 Liberal. The 20 Members (including tellers) to oppose the motion comprised 10 Scottish National, 3 Plaid Cymru, 3 Conservative,[1] 2 Labour and 2 Liberal.

Labour Members to vote against the clause:

Lambie, D.   Rose, P.

HC Deb. 942, 1551-4
1977-8, No. 81.

---

[1] The three Conservatives to vote against were: N. Budgen, T. Higgins and J. Spence.

EUROPEAN ASSEMBLY ELECTIONS BILL (ALLOCATION OF TIME) [316]

26 January 1978

The Home Secretary, M. Rees, moved a timetable (guillotine) motion for the European Assembly Elections Bill. The detailed motion provided that the remaining stages in Committee should be completed in two allotted days and Report and Third Reading in one allotted day.

The Home Secretary contended that it was important that the Bill be passed in that session and that the Government had to protect the rest of its legislative timetable; he argued that the remaining parts of the Bill to be discussed covered largely topics which had been discussed in the House over the years.

D. Stoddart (Lab., Swindon) felt that the Government was trying to get the Bill through 'with indecent haste'. He could not understand why there was such haste; there was no precedent for it. E. Heffer (Lab.,

Liverpool, Walton) said that in introducing the Bill the Government had ignored the views of the Labour Party, and introducing a guillotine 'adds insult to injury'. W. Molloy (Lab., Ealing, North) declared that the guillotine 'contains all the dangers of a tyrannical majority rule, with an added threat of being progressively used to curtail the rights of Private Members'. J. Rooker (Lab., Birmingham, Perry Bar) said that it was a black day for parliamentary democracy and the powers of the House. He would vote against the motion.

The timetable motion was approved by 314 votes to 137, with the Opposition allowing a free vote for its Members. The 316 Members (including tellers) in the Government lobby comprised 155 Conservative, 151 Labour, 9 Liberal and 1 Ulster Unionist. The 139 Members (including tellers) to vote against comprised 63 Labour, 61 Conservative, 7 Ulster Unionist, 6 Scottish National, 1 Democratic Unionist and 1 SDLP. More than 80 Labour Members (and 60 Conservatives) were absent from the division.

Labour Members to vote against the motion:

Allaun, F.	Heffer, E.	Molloy, W.
Ashton, J.	Hooley, F.	Newens, S.
Atkinson, N.	Hoyle, D.	Orbach, M.
Bidwell, S.	Hughes, R.	Ovenden, J.
Buchan, N.	Hughes, R. J.	Pendry, T.
Callaghan, J.	Jay, D.	Richardson, Miss J.
Canavan, D.	Jeger, Mrs L.	Roberts, G.
Carmichael, N.	Jenkins, H.	Robinson, G.
Carter-Jones, L.	Kelley, R.	Rodgers, G.
Castle, Mrs B.	Kerr, R.	Rooker, J.*
Cook, R.	Kilroy-Silk, R.	Ryman, J.
Cunningham, G.	Kinnock, N.	Short, Mrs R.
Davies, B.	Latham, A.	Skinner, D.
Dean, J.	Lee, J.	Spearing, N.
Ellis, J.	Litterick, T.	Spriggs, L.*
Evans, I.	Loyden, E.	Stoddart, D.
Fernyhough, E.	Madden, M.	Thomas, R.
Flannery, M.	Maynard, Miss J.	Thorne, S.
Fletcher, T.	Mendelson, J.	Torney, T.
Garrett, W.	Mikardo, I.	Wise, Mrs A.
Gould, B.	Miller, M.	Woof, R.

HC Deb. 942, 1689–94
1977–8, No. 82.

EUROPEAN COMMUNITY (EXCISE DUTY HARMONIZATION) [317]

30 January 1978

The Financial Secretary to the Treasury moved: 'That this House takes note of Commission Documents Nos. COM (72) 225, R/2113/73 and R/1966/77 on Excise Duty Harmonization.'

Mr Sheldon explained that the proposals involved were designed as a means to achieve some harmonization in the structure of excise duties, and were not proposals for harmonizing the rates of duty.

During the debate, a number of Labour backbenchers rose to criticize the proposals. D. Jay (Lab., Battersea, North) asked a number of questions, including the question of what was the purpose of the exercise anyway. 'Is there any reason why we should not set aside all the suggestions in these papers before us tonight?' Mrs G. Dunwoody (Lab., Crewe) expressed the fear that the directive would lead inevitably to measures which were not examined in depth in the House before they were accepted. F. Hooley (Lab., Sheffield, Heeley) said that he approached the proposals 'with considerable scepticism'; they impinged on the tax-raising powers of the House. Mrs A. Wise (Lab., Coventry, South-West) felt they were opening the door to something that would gravely distort social policies 'as well as our ability to control taxation'.

The motion was carried by 74 votes to 25, Conservative Members supporting the Government. The 76 Members (including tellers) in the Government lobby comprised 60 Labour, 14 Conservative and 2 Liberal. The 27 Members (including tellers) to oppose the motion comprised 25 Labour, 1 Conservative and 1 Ulster Unionist.

Labour Members to vote against the motion:

Ashton, J.	Flannery, M.	Madden, M.
Atkins, R.	Forrester, J.	Mikardo, I.
Canavan, D.	Hooley, F.*	Parry, R.
Cook, R.	Hoyle, D.	Richardson, Miss J.
Craigen, J.	Jay, D.	Skinner, D.
Dunwoody, Mrs G.	Kerr, R.	Spearing, N.*
Evans, I.	Lambie, D.	Thomas, R.
Evans, J.	Loyden, E.	Wise, Mrs A.
Fernyhough, E.		

Conservative to vote against the motion:

Marten, N.

HC Deb. 943, 205–6
1977–8, No. 88.

SCOTLAND BILL [318]

Committee: 1 February 1978

New Clause 4 (Bill of Rights for Scotland)

From the Opposition Front Bench, L. Brittan moved the New Clause which (in conjunction with other amendments being discussed at the same time) sought to incorporate the rights and freedoms set out in the European Convention of Human Rights as a Bill of Rights for Scotland.

During the debate, one Conservative backbencher rose to declare his opposition to the clause. F. Silvester (C., Manchester, Withington) said that the trouble with a Bill of Rights was that it was too vague and general. The items included would have to be interpreted, and it would result in political matters being decided by the courts.

The Government opposed the clause, and it was negatived on a whipped party vote by 251 votes to 227. 2 Conservative Members cross-voted to oppose the clause.[1] 1 Labour Member (T. Dalyell) abstained from voting; given Liberal and Scottish Nationalist support for the clause, the voting figures suggest a number of Conservative abstentions as well.

Conservatives to vote against the clause:

Silvester, F.   Sproat, I.

HC Deb. 943, 579–84
1977–8, No. 90.

[1] According to the division lists, 1 Conservative also voted in both lobbies.

EUROPEAN ASSEMBLY ELECTIONS BILL [319]

Committee: 2 February 1978

Clause 3 (Method of election)

E. Powell (UU, Down, South) moved an amendment to provide that the elections for the European Assembly should be by the same method throughout the United Kingdom. (The clause, as amended, provided for elections in Northern Ireland to be by proportional representation, and by the simple majority, first-past-the-post system in the rest of the United Kingdom.)

The amendment was supported on behalf of the Opposition by D. Hurd from the Opposition Front Bench, and opposed by the Home Secretary, M. Rees. Mr Hurd argued that the Government's proposals touched the raw nerve of the relationship between Northern Ireland and the remainder of the United Kingdom and could cause pain and harm. The Home Secretary opposed the amendment on the grounds that only on the basis of proportional representation could the minority community in Northern Ireland have any chance of direct representation in the European Assembly.

During the debate, a Labour backbencher, J. Lamond (Lab., Oldham, East), rose to query why Northern Ireland should be treated differently. The non-representation of people from certain areas was not unique to the province. 'Since I object to PR as a whole, I do not want to see it in any form.' He indicated his intention to support the amendment.[1]

The amendment was negatived by 241 votes to 150. The 243 Members (including tellers) in the Government lobby comprised 215 Labour, 14 Conservative, 9 Liberal, 2 Plaid Cymru, 1 Scottish National, 1 SDLP, and 1 Irish Independent. The 152 Members (including tellers) to support the amendment comprised 140 Conservative,[2] 4 Labour, 7 Ulster Unionist and 1 Democratic Unionist.

Conservatives to vote against the amendment:

Bottomley, P.	Hunt, J.	Smith, T.
Chalker, Mrs L.	Meyer, Sir A.	Temple-Morris, P
Dykes, H.	Morrison, C.	Townsend, C.
Fairgrieve, R.	Renton, T.	Wood, R.
Fisher, Sir N.	Sainsbury, T.	

Labour Members to vote for the amendment:

Gould, B.	Skinner, D.	Spearing, N.
Lamond, J.		

HC Deb. 943, 749–54
1977–8, No. 92.

[1] Mr Lamond was speaking on 12 January, when the amendment was first moved. See *HC Deb.* 941, c. 1983–7.
[2] The figures would appear to suggest several Conservative abstentions, but a subsequent division suggests a low Conservative attendance.

EUROPEAN ASSEMBLY ELECTIONS BILL [320]

Committee: 2 February 1978

Clause 3 (Method of election)

At 6.00 p.m. the guillotine fell for the remaining stages of clause 3, and the motion 'That the clause, as amended, stand part of the Bill' was put without debate. The clause stipulated the method by which elections to the European Assembly were to take place (see preceding division and that of 12 January, above).

The motion was carried by 170 votes to 59, Conservative Members voting with the Government. The 172 Members (including tellers) in the Government lobby comprised 144 Labour, 17 Conservative,[1] 8 Liberal, 2 Plaid Cymru and 1 Irish Independent. The 61 Members (including tellers) to oppose the motion comprised 43 Labour, 11 Conservative, 6 UU, and 1 Democratic Unionist.

Labour Members to vote against the clause:

Ashton, J.	Jenkins, H.	Newens, S.
Bean, R.	Kerr, R.	Ovenden, J.
Butler, Mrs J.	Kilroy-Silk, R.	Richardson, Miss J.
Carmichael, N.	Kinnock, N.	Robinson, G.
Castle, Mrs B.	Lamond, J.	Rodgers, G.
Ellis, J.*	Latham, A.	Rooker, J.
Evans, F.	Lestor, Miss J.	Ryman, J.
Evans, I.	Litterick, T.	Short, Mrs R.
Evans, J.	Loyden, E.	Skinner, D.
Flannery, M.	Madden, M.	Spearing, N.
Fletcher, T.	Maynard, Miss J.	Stoddart, D.
Gould, B.	Mendelson, J.	Thomas, R.
Heffer, E.	Mikardo, I	Thorne, S.
Hoyle, D.	Molloy, W.	Wise, Mrs A.
Jay, D.		

Conservatives to vote against the clause:

Bell, R.	McNair-Wilson, M.	Renton, Sir D
Biffen, J.	Marten, N.	Scott, N.
Fraser, H.	Moate, R.*	Winterton, N.
Gow, I.	Rathbone, T.	

HC Deb. 943, 753–6
1977–8, No. 93.

[1] There appears to have been a low attendance by Conservative Members for the debate

EUROPEAN ASSEMBLY ELECTIONS BILL [321]

Committee: 2 February 1978

Clause 2 (Number of representatives)

G. Reid (SNP, Clackmannan and East Stirlingshire) moved an amendment, discussed in conjunction with a number of related amendments, to increase the number of representatives to the Assembly from Scotland to sixteen.

The amendment was opposed from the Opposition Front Bench by D. Hurd, and opposed for the Government by the Minister of State at the Privy Council Office, J. Smith. Mr Smith contended that although Wales and Scotland were nations, they were not nation states. He thought the clause as drafted was the best that could be achieved.

The amendment was negatived by 132 votes to 47, the Opposition voting with the Government. The 134 Members (including tellers) in the Government lobby comprised 91 Labour, 38 Conservative and 5 Liberal. The 49 Members (including tellers) to support the amendment comprised 30 Labour, 7 Conservative, 6 Ulster Unionist, 4 Scottish National, 1 Dem. U. and 1 PC.

Labour Members to vote for the amendment:

Atkinson, N.	Fletcher, T.	Molloy, W.
Bidwell, S.	Heffer, E.	Ovenden, J.
Castle, Mrs B.	Jay, D.	Richardson, Miss J.
Colquhoun, Mrs M.	Jenkins, H.	Short, Mrs R.
Crowther, S.	Kerr, R.	Skinner, D.
Ellis, J.	Latham, A.	Spearing, N.
Evans, F.	Lee, J.	Stoddart, D.
Evans, I.	Madden, M.	Thomas, R.
Evans, J.	Maynard, Miss J.	Torney, T.
Flannery, M.	Mikardo, I.	Wise, Mrs A.

Conservatives to vote for the amendment:

Bell, R.	Fraser, H.	Moate, R.
Body, R.	Marten, N.	Winterton, N.
Budgen, N.		

HC Deb. 943, 789–92
1977–8, No. 94.

EUROPEAN ASSEMBLY ELECTIONS BILL [322]

Committee: 2 February 1978

Clause 2 (Number of representatives)

At 8.00 p.m. the guillotine fell for the remaining stages of clause 2, and the motion 'That the clause stand part of the Bill' was put without debate. The clause provided for the number of representatives to the European Assembly and their distribution in the United Kingdom.

The 'stand part' motion was carried by 122 votes to 47, the Opposition voting with the Government. The 124 Members (including tellers) in the Government lobby comprised 85 Labour, 34 Conservative and 5 Liberal. The 49 Members (including tellers) to oppose the clause comprised 30 Labour, 7 Ulster Unionist, 6 Conservative, 5 Scottish National and 1 Plaid Cymru.

Labour Members to vote against the clause:

Atkinson, N.	Heffer, E.	Ovenden, J.
Buchan, N.	Jay, D.	Richardson, Miss J.
Castle, Mrs B.	Jenkins, H.	Short, Mrs R.
Colquhoun, Mrs M.	Kerr, R.	Skinner, D.
Ellis, J.*	Kinnock, N.	Spearing, N.
Evans, F.	Latham, A.	Stoddart, D.
Evans, I.	Lee, J	Thomas, R.
Evans, J.	Madden, M.	Torney, T.
Flannery, M.	Maynard, Miss J.	Wise, Mrs A.
Fletcher, T.	Mikardo, I.	Woof, R.

Conservatives to vote against the clause:

Bell, R.	Budgen, N.	Moate, R.*
Body, R.	Marten, N.	Winterton, N.

HC Deb. 943, 791–2
1977-78, No. 95.

EUROPEAN ASSEMBLY ELECTIONS BILL [323]

Committee: 8 February 1978

Schedule 1 (Simple majority system (for Great Britain) with S.T.V. (for Northern Ireland))

For the Opposition, D. Hurd moved an amendment designed to enfranchise for European Assembly elections only British nationals and their wives or husbands who were living or working in the European Community.

Mr Hurd said that the people concerned felt strongly that they should not be excluded from the franchise. Their lives and prospects would probably be more deeply affected than those of most people by the decisions of the Community which the Assembly, once directly elected, would influence more strongly than was then the case.

Dr C. Phipps (Lab., Dudley, West) supported the amendment, and said he was basically in favour of allowing UK citizens who were non-resident to have a vote in elections in this country and in the EEC. M. Stewart (Lab., Fulham) felt that until the EEC agreed on a uniform method for election throughout the Community the amendment offered the nearest approach to justice and common sense. R. MacFarquhar (Lab., Belper) said that it seemed only right and proper that all people who were residents and citizens within the European Community on election day should have the right to vote. R. Moate (C., Faversham) opposed the amendment, arguing that its supporters were advancing a limited case on the basis of special pleading and not on the basis of principle. N. Budgen (C., Wolverhampton, South-West) opposed it because he considered it defective in detail and because he viewed it as a step along the road to a federal Europe.

The Minister of State, Privy Council Office, J. Smith, said that the amendment would involve a significant extension of the franchise and would have some potential repercussions for the internal franchise; he suggested that they should first have recourse to a Speaker's Conference. He argued also that voters should have a connection with their constituencies. He could not advise the House to accept the amendment.

The amendment was negatived on a whipped party vote by 160 votes to 149. The 162 Members (including tellers) in the Government lobby comprised 142 Labour, 7 Conservative, 7 Ulster Unionist, 4 Scottish National, 1 Democratic Unionist and 1 Plaid Cymru. The 151 Members (including tellers) in the Opposition lobby comprised 136 Conservative, 9 Liberal, 5 Labour and 1 Ulster Unionist.

Conservatives to vote against the amendment:

Biffen, J.	Hutchison, M. C.	Moate, R.
Budgen, N.	Marten, N.	Winterton, N.
Gow, I.		

Labour Members to vote for the amendment:

Crawshaw, R.	Stewart, M.	Williams, A. L.
MacFarquhar, R.	Ward, M.	

HC Deb. 943, 1523–6
1977–8, No. 103.

EUROPEAN ASSEMBLY ELECTIONS BILL [324]

Committee: 8 February 1978

Schedule 1 (Simple majority system (for Great Britain) with S.T.V. (for Northern Ireland))

At midnight, the guillotine fell for the remaining stages of the committee stage, and the motion 'That this schedule be the First Schedule to the Bill' was put without debate.

The motion was carried by 86 votes to 38, Conservative Members supporting the Government. The 88 Members (including tellers) in the Government lobby comprised 71 Labour, 16 Conservative and 1 Liberal. The 40 Members (including tellers) to oppose the schedule comprised 24 Labour, 7 Ulster Unionist, 4 Conservative, 2 Scottish National, 2 Plaid Cymru and 1 Democratic Unionist.

Labour Members to vote against the Schedule:

Callaghan, J.	Lamond, J.	Robinson, G.
Cook, R.	Latham, A.	Rodgers, G.
Dean, J.	Lee, J.	Skinner, D.
Ellis, J.*	Loyden, E.	Spearing, N.
Fernyhough, E.	Madden, M.	Stoddart, D.
Flannery, M.	Mendelson, J.	Thomas, R.
Gould, B.	Pendry, T.	Wilson, A.
Jay, D.	Richardson, Miss J.	Wise, Mrs A.

Conservatives to vote against the schedule:

Biffen, J.	Marten, N.	Moate, R.*
Budgen, N.		

HC Deb. 943, 1627–30
1977–8, No. 104.

EUROPEAN ASSEMBLY ELECTIONS BILL [325]

Committee: 8 February 1978

Clause 14 (Expenses)

At midnight, the guillotine fell for the remaining committee stage. The 'stand part' motion for clause 14, covering expenses, was put without debate.

The motion was carried by 83 votes to 38, Conservative Members supporting the Government. The 85 Members (including tellers) to support the clause comprised 67 Labour, 17 Conservative and 1 Liberal. The 40 Members (including tellers) to oppose the clause comprised 24 Labour, 7 Ulster Unionist, 4 Conservative, 2 Scottish National and 2 Plaid Cymru.

Labour Members to vote against the clause:

Cook, R.	Latham, A.	Rodgers, G.
Dean, J.	Lee, J.	Skinner, D.
Ellis, J.*	Loyden, E.	Spearing, N.
Fernyhough, E.	Madden, M.	Stoddart, D.
Flannery, M.	Mendelson, J.	Thomas, R.
Gould, B.	Pendry, T.	Wilson, A.
Jay, D.	Richardson, Miss J.	Wise, Mrs A.
Lamond, J.	Robinson, G.	Woof, R.

Conservatives to vote against the clause:

Biffen, J.	Marten, N.	Moate, R.*
Budgen, N.		

HC Deb. 943, 1629–30
1977–8, No. 105.

OPPOSITION PARTIES (FINANCIAL ASSISTANCE) [326]

13 February 1978

The Parliamentary Secretary to the Privy Council Office, W. Price, moved a motion to increase the rates on which the annual grant paid to opposition parties was based. [The rates were £1 for every 200 votes cast for the party at the preceding general election plus £500 for each seat won, up to a maximum entitlement of £150,000 per annum. Under the motion the rates were increased to £1.10 per every 200 voters and £550 for each seat won, with a maximum entitlement of £165,000, with effect from 1 January 1978.]

Mr Price explained that the motion proposed a ten per cent rise in the level of financial aid provided to opposition parties to assist them in carrying out their parliamentary duties at Westminster. Given that costs had risen more than ten per cent in the three years since the scheme was introduced he thought the increase was justified and, indeed, overdue.

A. Lewis (Lab., Newham, North-West) opposed the motion. 'I am strongly against my already hard-pressed taxpayers having to pay their hard-earned taxed money to political parties which they violently oppose.' M. Madden (Lab., Sowerby) said that the money involved was not insignificant, and he felt there was a need for proper accounting. D. Canavan (Lab., West Stirlingshire) said that no one could argue that the opposition parties were essential 'because the only constructive opposition in this place is the Tribune Group, which receives nothing from public funds'. The opposition parties did not perform a social service, and he was opposed to the motion.

J. Rooker (Lab., Birmingham, Perry Barr) moved an amendment for the increase to take effect from 1 January 1979 instead of 1 January 1978. He argued that no case had been made for a change in the amounts paid between general elections. When the next election came, the matter would be put to the public. He said the money should be spent on the Library.

(1) The amendment moved by Mr Rooker was put and negatived by 124 votes to 15. The Government whips were on, and the Opposition supported the Government. The 126 Members (including tellers) in the Government lobby comprised 94 Labour, 15 Conservative, 9 Liberal, 6 Scottish National and 2 Ulster Unionist. The 17 Members (including tellers) to support the amendment comprised 16 Labour and 1 Ulster Unionist (E. Powell).

Labour Members to vote for the amendment:

Canavan, D.*	Lewis, A.	Rooker, J.
Flannery, M.	Madden, M.*	Skinner, D.
Hoyle, D.	Mikardo, I.	Spearing, N.
Kerr, R.	Parry, R.	Thomas, R.
Lamond, J.	Richardson, Miss J.	Wise, Mrs A.
Latham, A.		

(2) The motion was then put and carried by 118 votes to 15, the Opposition again supporting the Government. The 120 Members (including tellers) in the Government lobby comprised 92 Labour, 12 Conservative, 9 Liberal, 6 Scottish National and 1 Ulster Unionist. The 17 Members (including tellers) to oppose the motion comprised 15 Labour, 1 Conservative and 1 Ulster Unionist (E. Powell).

Labour Members to vote against the motion:

Canavan, D.*	Lewis, A.	Rooker, J.*
Flannery, M.	Madden, M.	Skinner, D.
Kerr, R.	Mikardo, I.	Spearing, N.
Lamond, J.	Parry, R.	Thomas, R.
Latham, A.	Richardson, Miss J.	Wise, Mrs A.

Conservative to vote against the motion:

Moate, R.

HC Deb. 944, 201–4
1977–8, Nos. 107 and 108.

SCOTLAND BILL [327]

Report: 14 February 1978

New Clause 1 (Period between General Election and Referendum)

T. Dalyell (Lab., West Lothian) moved the new clause, which provided that if Parliament was dissolved before a referendum, 'that referendum shall not be held until a period of three months has elapsed after the polling day of the ensuing general election'.

Mr Dalyell argued that it would be wrong for a general election to be intertwined with the referendum: one could be reversed four or five years later, while the decision on a subordinate Parliament would be irrevocable during the lifetime of Members. 'This is a solemn decision which should be taken in a referendum which is separate in time from a General Election.' He argued also that holding the two at the same time could set a precedent: it would be a step towards a plebiscatory democracy.

The Minister of State at the Privy Council Office, J. Smith, said it was not the Government's intention for the dates of the general election and the referendum to coincide. However, he saw difficulties with the clause. He did not see the need for it to be three months. In any event, the date of the referendum was subject to an affirmative resolution of both Houses. The clause introduced an element of rigidity, and he felt the House should not tie itself down to a period of three months.

The clause was *carried* by 242 votes to 223, with the Government whips on against it, *a majority against the Government of 19.* The 225 Members (including tellers) in the Government lobby comprised 207

Labour, 10 Scottish National, 6 Liberal and 2 Plaid Cymru. The 244 Members (including tellers) to support the clause comprised 210 Conservative, 25 Labour, 5 Ulster Unionist and 4 Liberal.

Labour Members to vote for the clause:

Boothroyd, Miss B.
Cunningham, G.
Dalyell, T.
Dean, J.
Douglas-Mann, B.
Ellis, J.
Evans, I.*
Flannery, M.
Garrett, W.

Hoyle, D.
Hughes, R.
Jeger, Mrs L.
Lamond, J.*
Latham, A.
Leadbitter, T.
Lewis, A.
Ovenden, J.

Parker, J.
Richardson, Miss J.
Rooker, J.
Sandelson, N.
Spearing, N.
Stoddart, D.
Urwin, T.
Wise, Mrs A.

HC Deb. 944, 297–302.
1977–8, No. 110.

SCOTLAND BILL [328]

Report: 15 February 1978

Clause 80 (Referendum)

D. Canavan (Lab., West Stirlingshire) moved an amendment to delete the 40 per cent requirement inserted in committee, and to return the clause to its original state. [See above, 25 January 1978]
Mr Canavan contended that the Bill as it stood was unworkable; the clause talked about 40 per cent of an unknown quantity. He also drew attention to the outburst that would be caused in Scotland if 66 per cent voted yes in a 60 per cent turnout, producing a yes vote by 39.6 per cent of the electorate. It was wrong to build in an arithmetical hurdle, particularly an ill-defined one, in advance of the referendum.

The Lord President of the Council and Leader of the House, M. Foot, supported the amendment. If they retained the 40 per cent provision they would to some extent impair the consultative nature of the referendum. He pointed out that the provision could mean that there might be a substantial voting majority for devolution but one which failed to satisfy the 40 per cent rule. If that happened, they would be inviting a very serious constitutional crisis.

G. Cunningham (Lab., Islington, South and Finsbury) opposed the amendment. He argued that all the demerits of devolution had been countered with the argument that devolution was an irresistible Scottish demand. In the circumstances, the 40 per cent test was a reasonable one to be imposed. 'More than that, we are not only entitled to have this kind of evidence of irresistible demand, but we are failing in our duty to Britain, Scotland and the areas we represent in England if we do not require that test.'

The amendment was *negatived* by 298 votes to 243, *a majority against the Government of 55*; the Opposition lobby was not whipped.[1] The 245 Members (including tellers) in the lobby to support the amendment comprised 214 Labour, 10 Scottish National, 9 Liberal, 7 Conservative,[2] 3 Plaid Cymru, 1 Ulster Unionist and 1 Scottish Labour. The 300 Members (including tellers) to oppose the amendment comprised 238 Conservative, 51 Labour, 8 Ulster Unionist, 2 Liberal and 1 Democratic Unionist. According to one report, approximately 20 Labour Members abstained from voting.[3]

Labour Members to vote against the amendment:

Abse, L.	Fletcher, T.	Newens, S.
Bennett, A.	Forrester, J.	Ogden, E.
Boothroyd, Miss B.	Garrett, W.	Ovenden, J.
Bottomley, A.	Hamilton, W.	Palmer, A.
Buchanan, R.	Hayman, Mrs H.	Parker, J.
Cohen, S.	Heffer, E.	Phipps, C.
Cowans, H.	Hughes, R.	Richardson, Miss J.
Crowther, S.	Kilroy-Silk, R.	Roberts, G.
Cunningham, G.	Kinnock, N.	Robinson, G.
Dalyell, T.	Lamond, J.	Rooker, J.
Davies, I.	Latham, A.	Short, Mrs R.
Dean, J.	Leadbitter, T.	Skinner, D.
Doig, P.	Lewis, A.	Spearing, N.
Douglas-Mann, B.	Lyon, A.	Spriggs, L.*
Evans, F.	Mendelson, J.	Stoddart, D.
Evans, I.	Molloy, W.	Thomas, R.
Flannery, M.	Moonman, E.	Wise, Mrs A.

HC Deb. 944, 597–602
1977–8, No. 115.

[1] Strictly speaking, neither lobby was whipped: the amendment was moved by a Labour backbencher, and Labour backbenchers acted as tellers for it. However, the Leader of the House made it clear beyond doubt that the Government supported the amendment. On the Opposition side, F. Pym said that he thought it was essentially a 'House of Commons matter', and made no specific recommendation.

[2] The seven Conservatives to vote for the amendment were: R. Adley, A. Buchanan-Smith, H. Dykes, E. Heath, R. Hicks, D. Knox and P. Walker.

[3] *The Times*, 17 February 1978.

SCOTLAND BILL   **[329]**

Réport: 15 February 1978

Clause 80 (Referendum)

Following an unsuccessful attempt to delete the provision of the clause requiring the laying of a repeal order if 40 per cent of eligible voters failed to vote 'yes' in the referendum (see preceding division), the Minister of State at the Privy Council Office, J. Smith, moved formally an amendment to delete '40 per cent' and insert 'one in three'.

The amendment was *negatived* by 285 votes to 240, *a majority against the Government of 45*; the Opposition lobby was unwhipped.[1] The 242 Members (including tellers) in the Government lobby comprised 225 Labour, 9 Liberal, 5 Conservative[2] and 3 Plaid Cymru. The 287 Members (including tellers) to oppose the amendment comprised 239 Conservative, 38 Labour, 8 Ulster Unionist, 1 Liberal and 1 Democratic Unionist. Scottish National Members abstained from voting.

Labour Members to vote against the amendment:

Abse, L.	Hamilton, W.	Moonman, E.
Bennett, A.	Hayman, Mrs H.	Newens, S.
Boothroyd, Miss B.	Heffer, E.	Ogden, E.
Cohen, S.	Kilroy-Silk, R.	Ovenden, J.
Cowans, H.	Kinnock, N.	Palmer, A.
Cunningham, G.	Lamond, J.	Phipps, C.
Dalyell, T.	Latham, A.	Robinson, G.
Dean, J.	Leadbitter, T.	Rooker, J.
Doig, P.	Lestor, Miss J.	Short, Mrs R.
Douglas-Mann, B.	Lewis, A.	Spearing, N.
Evans, F.	Lyon, A.	Spriggs, L.*
Evans, I.	Mendelson, J.	Stoddart, D.
Garrett, W.	Molloy, W.	

HC Deb. 944, 601–6
1977–8, No. 116.

[1] As in the preceding division, neither lobby strictly speaking was whipped, with Labour backbenchers acting as tellers for the amendment. However, the Government made clear its support for the amendment which was moved by a Government Minister. The Opposition spokesman on devolution, F. Pym, had said that he thought it was a 'House of Commons matter' and offered no specific advice.

[2] The five Conservatives to vote for the amendment were: A. Buchanan-Smith, E. Heath, R. Hicks, D. Knox and P. Walker.

EUROPEAN ASSEMBLY ELECTIONS BILL [330]

Report: 16 February 1978

New Clause 2 (Approval of Salaries, Etc.)

M. Madden (Lab., Sowerby) moved the new clause, which provided that: 'This Act shall not come into force until the House of Commons has considered and approved the salaries and expenses to be paid to Members of the European Assembly.'

Mr Madden said little information was available on salaries and expenses. The allowances of existing Assembly members and newspaper reports indicated that the views on the matter of those who controlled the Assembly was far from niggardly. It was essential that the House had clear information on the matter. The position as it stood was unsatisfactory.

A number of Members on both sides of the House rose to support the clause. W. Hamilton (Lab., Fife, Central) said the clause underlined the fact that the House wanted some control, and he was wholly in sympathy with the principle underlying it. J. Farr (C., Harborough) thought there was a great deal to be said for having such a clause in the Bill; he felt the Fees Office should have a say in the remuneration of European Members. He thought it was nonsense that European Members should be paid more than their Westminster counterparts.

From the Opposition Front Bench, D. Howell said he did not favour the new clause. It linked the fortunes of the Bill to a decision about salaries, and the decision itself was one for the Council of Ministers: '. . . our view clearly is that it is a decision for the Council of Ministers, and that is why I would not recommend support for the new clause'.

The Minister of State for Foreign and Commonwealth Affairs, F. Judd, replied that the Council of Ministers acting unanimously would have the final say on the level of salaries. The Government would not agree to a salary scale that would be inflationary by Westminster standards. 'The clause seeks to assume an authority which is neither present nor necessary. It is far better that we should seek a satisfactory agreement in the Council of Ministers to pay a reasonable rate for the job which representatives to the Assembly will be required to undertake.' He asked the House to reject the clause.

The new clause was negatived by 166 votes to 58, Opposition Members supporting the Government. The 168 Members (including tellers) in the Government lobby comprised 107 Labour, 52 Conservative, 6 Liberal and 3 Scottish National. The 60 Members (including tellers) to support the clause comprised 42 Labour, 8 Conservative, 7 Ulster

Unionist, 1 Scottish National, 1 Plaid Cymru and 1 Democratic Unionist.

Labour Members to vote for the clause:

Buchan, N.	Garrett, W.	Newens, S.
Callaghan, J.	Gould, B.	Richardson, Miss J.
Canavan, D.	Heffer, E.	Roberts, G.
Castle, Mrs B.	Hoyle, D.	Rodgers, G.
Clemitson, I.	Hughes, R.	Rooker, J.
Cowans, H.	Jay, D.	Short, Mrs R.
Crowther, S.	Lamond, J.	Skinner, D.
Davies, B.	Leadbitter, T.	Spearing, N.
Ellis, J.*	Lee, J.	Spriggs, L.
Evans, F.	Litterick, T.	Stoddart, D.
Evans, I.	Madden, M.	Thomas, R.
Fernyhough, E.	Maynard, Miss J.	Whitlock, W.
Flannery, M.	Mendelson, J.	Wilson, A.
Fletcher, T.	Mikardo, I.	Wise, Mrs A.

Conservatives to vote for the clause:

Bell, R.	Farr, J.	Moate, R.*
Biffen, J.	Fraser, H.	Winterton, N.
Budgen, N.	Marten, N.	

HC Deb. 944, 759–62
1977–8, No. 117.

EUROPEAN ASSEMBLY ELECTIONS BILL   [331]

Third Reading: 16 February 1978

The Home Secretary, M. Rees, moved the Third Reading of the Bill. He mentioned the changes made to the Bill in Committee, including the decision in favour of a system of election by simple majority. He said it was important that the Bill reached the statute book in good time, so that they could be prepared to hold elections on the date that was to be agreed with other partners in the Community. The Bill enabled them to meet international obligations without calling into question unnecessarily the framework of elections to Westminster. 'The Government have taken very much in mind what the House has said in recent months, and I trust that the Bill will be given a Third Reading.'

For the Opposition, D. Howell said that the Bill was a much improved one. 'I welcome the amended Bill and believe, with my right hon. and hon. Friends, that it should be read the Third time.'

During the debate, a number of backbenchers rose to oppose Third Reading. N. Spearing (Lab., Newham, South) said that the EEC wished to create a super-State and to derive its powers from the powers of the House. He contended that whether the Assembly was active or not, the result would be a loss of influence in the House which would otherwise be retained. D. Jay (Lab., Battersea, North) contended that no case had been made out for the Bill. N. Marten (C., Banbury) said that if the powers of the Assembly were to be increased, it would try to gain legislative powers; if there was not to be any increase in powers, he could not see the need for the Bill. J. Ellis (Lab., Brigg and Scunthorpe) declared that in many respects the Bill was lacking. 'We are setting up a procedure for sending men to the European Parliament. We should consider what they are to do and their purpose in being there. Surely we should find in the Bill a contract of employment or a job specification.' He felt it was a bad Bill that should not be given a Third Reading.

The Bill was given a Third Reading by 159 votes to 45, Opposition Members voting with the Government. The 161 Members (including tellers) in the Government lobby comprised 101 Labour, 54 Conservative and 6 Liberal. The 47 Members (including tellers) to oppose Third Reading comprised 29 Labour, 9 Conservative, 7 Ulster Unionist, 1 Plaid Cymru and 1 Democratic Unionist.

Labour Members to vote against Third Reading:

Buchan, N.	Heffer, E.	Richardson, Miss J.
Canavan, D.	Jay, D.	Roberts, G.
Castle, Mrs B.	Lamond, J.	Rodgers, G.*
Crowther, S.	Latham, A.	Skinner, D.
Dean, J.	Lee, J.	Spearing, N.
Ellis, J.	Litterick, T.	Spriggs, L.
Fernyhough, E.	Madden, M.	Stoddart, D.
Flannery, M.	Maynard, Miss J.	Thomas, R.
Fletcher, T.	Mendelson, J.	Wise, Mrs A.
Gould, B.	Mikardo, I.	

Conservatives to vote against Third Reading:

Aitken, J.	Farr, J.	Marten, N.
Biffen, J.	Fraser, H.	Moate, R.*
Budgen, N.	Gow, I.	Winterton, N.

HC Deb. 944, 845–8
1977–8, No. 118.

SCOTLAND BILL [332]

Third Reading: 22 February 1978

The Secretary of State for Scotland, B. Millan, moved the Third Reading of the Bill. He argued that there was overwhelming evidence that the Scots wanted change and that what they wanted was devolution within the United Kingdom.

For the Opposition, F. Pym argued that the Bill could not in the event satisfy the people of Scotland. The Bill was riddled with inconsistencies. When the laws in the Bill were discovered in Scotland there would be a bitter sense of disappointment. He asked the House to reject the Bill.

J. Mendelson (Lab., Penistone) contended that the Bill was being promoted by people who were not convinced of its merits. It had been created in response to an immediate political need and not as part of a grand design to reform the constitution of the United Kingdom. A. Buchanan-Smith (C., Angus, North and Mearns) said that on balance he thought the Bill was workable, and gave the opportunity to work towards a more stable type of constitutional structure for the United Kingdom. E. Ogden (Lab., Liverpool, West Derby) said his conclusion was 'that the Bill was born of reaction, not anticipation; of expediency and despair, not hope; and of panic, in an attempt to halt the nationalist tide.' T. Dalyell (Lab., West Lothian) said that if one believed, as he did, that the creation of an Assembly in Edinburgh would lead inevitably to a separate Scottish state, he had a duty to vote against the Bill.

The Bill was given a Third Reading, on a three-line whip, by 297 votes to 257, a Government majority of 40. The 299 Members (including tellers) in the Government lobby comprised 269 Labour, 11 Scottish National, 11 Liberal, 3 Plaid Cymru, 2 Conservative, 2 Scottish Labour and 1 Ulster Unionist. The 259 Members (including tellers) to vote against the Bill comprised 241 Conservative, 9 Ulster Unionist, 7 Labour, 1 Liberal and 1 Democratic Unionist. The voting figures suggest several abstentions (possibly twenty or more) on both sides of the House.[1]

Conservatives to vote for Third Reading:

Buchanan-Smith, A.   Knox, D.

Labour Members to vote against the Third Reading:

Cunningham, G.	Leadbitter, T.	Ogden, E.
Dalyell, T.	Mendelson, J.	Phipps, C.
Garrett, W.		

HC Deb. 944, 1599–1606
1977–8, No. 124.

¹ The Conservative abstainers would appear to have included: R. Adley, C. Brocklebank-Fowler, H. Dykes, E. Heath, K. Lewis, R. McCrindle, M. Rifkind, N. Scott, J. Spence and P. Walker. Labour abstainers would appear to have included L. Abse, R. Brown, R. Edwards, F. Evans, E. Heffer and J. Ovenden.

HOUSING (SCOTLAND) BILL   [333]

Report: 28 February 1978

Clause 15 (Reserve power to limit rents)

D. Lambie (Lab., Ayrshire, Central) moved an amendment to delete the clause.

Mr Lambie said he wished to reinstate section 2 of the 1975 Housing (Rents and Subsidies) (Scotland) Act which gave the Secretary of State reserve powers to limit rent increases to £39 a year or 75p a week as a maximum. [Under clause 15, there was no fixed limit, the Secretary of State being given the power to determine annually the maximum level of rents.] He contended that the clause had been introduced without consultation, and objected to the power that it would place in the hands of any future Conservative Secretary of State.

The Under-Secretary of State for Scotland, H. Brown, replied that under the clause they were not abandoning the power to limit rent increases, but he contended that if precise limits were decided they would be seen as an instruction to local authorities to increase rents up to those limits. They had had that situation before. 'The sooner we get shot of any fixed limit the better.'

The amendment was negatived by 128 votes to 11, with the Opposition abstaining from voting. The 130 Members (including tellers) in the Government lobby comprised 119 Labour, 10 Liberal and 1 Conservative. The 13 Members (including tellers) to support the amendment comprised 12 Labour and 1 Plaid Cymru.

Conservative to vote against the amendment:

Jessel, T.

Labour Members to vote for the amendment:

Bennett, A.	Lamond, J.	Newens, S.
Canavan, D.*	Litterick, T.	Skinner, D.
Flannery, M.	McMillan, T.	Thomas, R.
Lambie, D.*	Maynard, Miss J.	Wise, Mrs A.

HC Deb. 945, 363–6
1977–8, No. 129.

HOUSING (SCOTLAND) BILL   [334]

Report: 28 February 1978

Clause 15 (Reserve power to limit rents)

R. Cook (Lab., Edinburgh, Central) moved formally an amendment to provide that under the clause a local authority could not increase rents by more than an average of £39 for the houses concerned in any one year.

The amendment had been discussed in conjunction with another (see preceding division), and opposed by the Government. [Mr Cook's amendment sought to limit the rise to an average increase of £39, whereas the Lambie amendment was designed to limit it to £39 per house. The comments of the Under-Secretary of State for Scotland, H. Brown, in reply to the Lambie amendment covered also Mr Cook's amendment: see above.]

The amendment was negatived by 119 votes to 25, with the Opposition abstaining from voting. The 121 Members (including tellers) in the Government lobby comprised 107 Labour, 10 Liberal, 2 Conservative and 2 Ulster Unionist. The 27 Members (including tellers) to support the amendment comprised 21 Labour, 5 Scottish National and 1 Plaid Cymru.

Conservatives to vote against the amendment:

Bottomley, P.   Jessel, T.

Labour Members to vote for the amendment:

Bennett, A.	Flannery, M.	Madden, M.
Buchan, N.	Gourlay, H.	Maynard, Miss J.
Buchanan, R.	Hughes, R.	Newens, S.
Canavan, D.*	Lambie, D.*	Rooker, J.
Cook, R.	Litterick, T.	Skinner, D.
Dempsey, J.	Loyden, E.	Thomas, R.
Ellis, J.	McMillan, T.	Wise, Mrs A.

HC Deb. 945, 365–8
1977–8, No. 130.

CIVIL AVIATION BILL [335]

Third Reading: 28 February 1978

On the motion for the Third Reading of the Bill, H. Jenkins (Lab., Putney) rose to say that he would be unable to support the Bill's Third Reading. The Under-Secretary of State, he said, had refused consistently every attempt in Committee to strengthen the clauses which would have given greater protection against aircraft noise. He would divide the House.

A number of Conservative backbenchers rose also to oppose the Bill. Sir G. Sinclair (C., Dorking) felt that the Bill failed to protect those who were suffering from aircraft noise. Sir A. Royle (C., Richmond, Surrey) and T. Jessel (C., Twickenham) rose to voice a similar complaint.

The Under-Secretary of State for Trade, C. Davis, said that he had sought to achieve a balance, and pointed out the cost of some of the proposals that had been put forward. He believed the Government was dealing with the matter sensibly and rationally.

The Bill was given a Third Reading by 73 votes to 6, with the Opposition lobby not being whipped.[1] The 75 Members (including tellers) in the Government lobby comprised 74 Labour and 1 Liberal. The 8 Members (including tellers) to oppose Third Reading comprised 7 Conservative and 1 Labour.

Labour Member to vote against Third Reading:

Jenkins, H.

HC Deb. 945, 421–2
1977–8, No. 131.

The division took place at 12.16 a.m.

[1] Given the lateness of the division, few Conservative Members appear to have been present. Of the 7 Conservatives to vote against Third Reading, one was an Opposition whip.

WALES BILL **[336]**

Committee: 7 March 1978

Clause 13 (Review of Local Government structure)

At 7.00 p.m. the guillotine fell for discussion on a number of clauses to the Bill, and the 'stand part' motion for clause 13 was put without debate.[1]

The clause was carried on a whipped party vote by 213 votes to 206. The 215 Members (including tellers) in the Government lobby comprised 189 Labour, 10 Liberal, 10 Scottish National, 3 Ulster Unionist and 3 Plaid Cymru. The 208 Members (including tellers) to oppose the clause comprised 190 Conservative, 16 Labour and 2 Ulster Unionist.

Labour Members to vote against the clause:

Abse, L.	Davies, I.	Lee, J.
Anderson, D.	Dean, J.	Molloy, W.
Atkins, R.	Evans, F.	Parker, J.
Cowans, H.	Evans, I.	Phipps, C.
Cunningham, G.	Garrett, W.	Robinson, G.
Dalyell, T.		

HC Deb. 945, 1309–14
1977–8, No. 137.

[1] The clause read: 'The Assembly shall review the structure of local government in Wales and shall report its conclusions to the Secretary of State.'

WALES BILL **[337]**

Committee: 8 March 1978

Clause 25 (Staff)

At 7.00 p.m. the guillotine fell for the remaining stages of the clause, and the motion 'That the clause stand part of the Bill' was put without debate.[1]

The 'stand part' motion was carried on a whipped party vote by 196 votes to 169. The 198 Members (including tellers) in the Government lobby comprised 169 Labour, 12 Liberal, 11 Scottish National, 3 Ulster Unionist and 3 Plaid Cymru. The 171 Members (including tellers) in the Opposition lobby comprised 163 Conservative, 4 Labour and 4 Ulster Unionist.

Labour Members to vote against the clause:

Abse, L.	Evans, F.
Atkins, R.	Kinnock, N.

HC Deb. 945, 1489–92
1977–8, No. 140.

¹ The clause read: 'The Assembly may appoint such officers and servants as it considers appropriate.'

PREVENTION OF TERRORISM   [338]

Prayer: 15 March 1978

The Home Secretary, M. Rees, moved 'That the draft Prevention of Terrorism (Temporary Provisions) Act 1976 (Continuance) Order 1978, which was laid before this House on 23rd February, be approved.'

Mr Rees outlined the extent to which the Act had been used in the past year. The past year had been free of terrorist attacks, but while to the public at large the situation was normal and peaceful under the surface the IRA might be planning its next campaign. He had set up an inquiry under Lord Shackleton to assess the effectiveness of the legislation and its effect on the liberties of the subject; the report of the inquiry would be debated by the House. He believed that the Act continued to have an important role to play, and recent events in Northern Ireland had reminded them of the continuing danger. 'We must maintain our vigilance.'

A number of Labour Members rose to oppose the order. A. Bennett (Lab., Stockport, North) voiced a number of objections to it, and said the real practice of the legislation tended to be used to harry the Irish community. R. Parry (Lab., Liverpool, Scotland Exchange) said he had never supported renewal of the provisions, and that there was still a lot of concern in Merseyside about them. M. Flannery (Lab., Sheffield, Hillsborough) spoke of the injustice of exclusion orders. 'They are really deportation orders.' He believed the legislation was born in panic, that it was unnecessary for it to be continued, and if it was it should be for a period of only three months. R. Thomas (Lab., Bristol, North-West) said he thought the police had enough powers before the legislation was brought in.

The order was approved by 118 votes to 21, the Opposition supporting the Government. The 120 Members (including tellers) in the Government lobby comprised 92 Labour, 20 Conservative, 5 Liberal and 3 Ulster Unionist. The 23 Members (including tellers) to oppose the order were all Labour Members.

Labour Members to vote against the order:

Bennett, A.*	Lamond, J.	Parry, R.
Canavan, D.	Latham, A.	Price, C.
Clemitson, I.	Litterick, T.	Richardson, Miss J.*
Cook, R.	Loyden, E.	Rodgers, G.
Corbett, R.	McGuire, M.	Skinner, D.
Ellis, J.	Maynard, Miss J.	Thomas, R.
Flannery, M.	Mikardo, I.	Thorne, S.
Kerr, R.	Ovenden, J.	

HC Deb. 946, 595–8
1977––, No. 150.

WINDSCALE INQUIRY REPORT [339]

22 March 1978

On an adjournment motion, the Government initiated a debate on the report of the Windscale inquiry under Mr Justice Parker.

The debate was opened by the Secretary of State for the Environment, P. Shore, who outlined the background to the inquiry and the considerations that he had to take into account in considering it. In summing up his points, he said that 'the Government believe that Mr Justice Parker's Report, based upon all the mass of evidence submitted, and assisted, as he was, by the great expertise of the most distinguished radiological and chemical engineering assessors we could find, has shown that this reprocessing can be carried out without any significant increase in radiological risk; that environmentally it offers a better option than the alternative of storing our spent fuel for disposal in a form which includes the plutonium and unused uranium; that the security risks can be contained in ways compatible with our democratic way of life; and that the reprocessing of foreign fuel does not run counter to our policy to prevent the proliferation of nuclear weapons. For all these reasons I commend the report to the House.'

The Government was supported by the Opposition, but a number of Members rose to express opposition to the report. L. Abse (Lab.,

Pontypool) felt they were being rushed into a decision. He contended that the reason was an economic one, and argued that once plutonium had been exported they no longer had any control over it. Justice Parker, he said, 'reacts to the hazards of the twenty-first century, if we ever reach it, with all of the dated chauvinism of the nineteenth century.' R. Cook (Lab., Edinburgh, Central) expressed his concern about environmental pollution, civil liberties, and, in particular, the dangers of proliferation. He felt it might be valuable to have a division on the matter. F. Hooley (Lab., Sheffield, Heeley) felt that the report failed to heed the warning not to ignore other options. Ms M. Colquhoun (Lab., Northampton, North) felt the inquiry was like other inquiries, and was meaningless nonsense to people outside.

Opponents of the report forced the adjournment motion to a division, in which it was negatived by 186 votes to 56, the Opposition supporting the Government. The 188 Members (including tellers) in the Government lobby comprised 123 Labour, 64 Conservative and 1 Ulster Unionist. The 58 Members (including tellers) to support the motion comprised 35 Labour, 9 Liberal, 6 Conservative, 4 Scottish National, 3 Plaid Cymru and 1 Scottish Labour.

Labour Members to vote for adjournment:

Abse, L.	Gould, B.	Molloy, W.
Bidwell, S.	Hooley, F.*	Ovenden, J.
Blenkinsop, A.	Jeger, Mrs L.	Price, C.
Butler, Mrs J.	Jenkins, H.	Richardson, Miss J.
Canavan, D.	Kinnock, N.	Ryman, J.
Colquhoun, Ms M.	Latham, A.	Skinner, D.
Cook, R.	Lee, J.	Spearing, N.
Corbett, R.	Lewis, A.	Thomas, R.
Crowther, S.	Loyden, E.	Whitehead, P.
Davies, B.	Madden, M.	Whitlock, W.
Flannery, M.	Mendelson, J.	Wise, Mrs A.
Fletcher, T.	Mikardo, I.	

Conservatives to vote for adjournment:

Braine, Sir B.	Gow, I.	Stainton, K.
Brown, Sir E.	Grist, I.	Stanbrook, I.

HC Deb. 946, 1673–6
1977–8, No. 153.

WALES BILL   **[340]**

Committee: 4 April 1978

Clause 42 (Welsh Consolidated Fund and Loans Fund)

At 7.45 p.m., the 'stand part' motion for clause 42 of the Bill was proposed.[1]

At 11.00 p.m., after more than three hours of discussion, the Government Deputy Chief Whip moved the closure.

The closure motion was carried on a whipped party vote by 142 votes to 125. 4 Labour Members cross-voted to oppose closure.

Labour Members to vote against closure:

Anderson, D.   Evans, I.   Kinnock, N.
Dalyell, T.

HC Deb. 947, 395–8
1977–8, No. 157.

The 'stand part' motion was then carried by 142 votes to 121, with no cross-voting. Mr Anderson and Mr Evans voted for the motion, and Mr Dalyell and Mr Kinnock abstained from voting.

[1] The clause provided that there would be a Welsh Consolidated Fund and a Welsh Loans Fund, and that the Executive Committee of the Assembly could from time to time cause sums to be transferred from one to the other of those Funds.

WALES BILL   **[341]**

Committee: 5 April 1978

Clause 60 (Rate Support and Other Grants)

On the motion 'That the clause, as amended, stand part of the Bill', N. Edwards, from the Opposition Front Bench, rose to oppose it. He said if the clause was allowed to stand, local authorities would be removed from the negotiation of the rate support grant; he contended that the arrangements set out in the clause were complex and obscure.

I. Evans (Lab., Aberdare) said one of the fundamental weaknesses of the Bill was that district authorities and county councils were in danger of suffering from the centralization of local government power within

Wales. T. Dalyell (Lab., West Lothian) rose to question aspects of the clause, and to ask who wanted the Bill. N. Kinnock (Lab., Bedwellty) said his most profound reason for disagreeing with the Bill, coming from a constituency with a significant dependence upon the rate support grant, was that it would be of immense material disadvantage to the people he represented.

The Under-Secretary of State at the Welsh Office, A. Jones, replied that in negotiating the block fund the Assembly would take into account representations from local authorities. The Assembly would negotiate a separate rate support grant settlement with the authorities. Welsh local authorities would be able to play a much more influential role than they could at that time.

The 'stand part' motion was carried on a whipped party vote by 128 votes to 112. 2 Labour Members cross-voted to oppose the clause, and a third (T. Dalyell) abstained from voting.

Labour Members to vote against the clause:

Evans, I.   Kinnock, N.

HC Deb. 947, 583–6
1977–8, No. 163.

WALES BILL   [342]

Committee: 18 April 1978

Clause 61 (Power to make new provision as to certain bodies)

For the Opposition, L. Brittan moved an amendment to exclude the British Waterways Board, the Forestry Commissioners, the Housing Corporation and other bodies, from the provisions of the clause.

During the debate on the amendment, T. Dalyell (Lab., West Lothian) rose to express doubts about the contents of the clause, and drew attention to the view of the British Waterways Board that the inland waterways should continue to be dealt with primarily on a Great Britain basis. J. Parker (Lab., Dagenham) rose also to suggest that all those who were interested in the waterways in Wales wanted them not to be devolved but to remain under the control of the United Kingdom.

The Minister of State at the Privy Council Office, J. Smith, announced a number of concessions on the points raised in debate, but resisted the amendment as such.

The amendment was negatived on a whipped party vote by 165 votes to 146. 1 Labour Member cross-voted to support the amendment, and at least 1 other (T. Dalyell) abstained from voting.

Labour Member to vote for the amendment:

Parker, J.

HC Deb. 948, 325–8
1977–8, No. 172.

WALES BILL [343]

Committee: 19 April 1978

Clause 75 (Orders)

At 5.00 p.m., the guillotine fell for discussion on a number of clauses, and the motion 'That the clause stand part of the Bill' was moved formally.[1]

The 'stand part' motion for clause 75 was carried by 236 votes to 16, with the Opposition abstaining from voting. The 238 Members (including tellers) in the Government lobby comprised 227 Labour, 10 Liberal and 1 Conservative. The 18 Members(including tellers) to oppose the motion comprised 11 Scottish National, 3 Plaid Cymru, 2 Conservative and 2 Ulster Unionist.

Conservative to vote for the motion:

Glyn, A.

Conservatives to vote against the motion:

Gow, I.   Mitchell, D.

HC Deb. 948, 487–90
1977–8, No. 178.

[1] The Clause provided that any power to make orders under the Act conferred on a Minister could be exercised by statutory instrument.

WALES BILL [344]

Committee: 19 April 1978

Clause 81 (Interpretation)

At 5.00 p.m., the guillotine fell for discussion on a number of clauses, and the Minister of State at the Privy Council Office, J. Smith, moved formally an amendment to the clause to insert a reference to 'a Scottish Act'.

The amendment was carried by 235 votes to 15, with the Opposition abstaining from voting. The 17 Members (including tellers) to oppose the amendment comprised 11 Scottish National, 3 Plaid Cymru and 1 Ulster Unionist. 1 Conservative entered the Government lobby to support the amendment.

Conservative to vote for the amendment:

Glyn, A.

HC Deb. 948, 489-92
1977-8, No. 179. ·

WALES BILL   [345]

Committee: 19 April 1978

Clause 82 (Commencement)

G. Howells (Lib., Cardigan) moved an amendment to delete subsection (4) of the clause, which provided that orders made under the clause should be subject to the affirmative resolution procedure.

The amendment was opposed by the Government, and was negatived by 220 votes to 18, with the Opposition abstaining from voting. The 20 Members (including tellers) to support the amendment comprised 11 Scottish National, 6 Liberal and 3 Plaid Cymru. 1 Conservative entered the Government lobby to oppose the amendment.

Conservative to vote against the amendment:

Morgan, G.

HC Deb. 948, 577-80
1977-8, No. 182.

WALES BILL   [346]

Committee: 19 April 1978

Clause 82 (Commencement)

D. Wigley (Plaid Cymru, Caernarvon) moved formally an amendment to provide that the first order made under the clause should be made within 120 days of the measure receiving the Royal Assent.

The amendment was opposed by the Government, and negatived by 222 votes to 18. The Opposition abstained from voting. The 20 Members (including tellers) to support the amendment comprised 10 Scottish National, 7 Liberal and 3 Plaid Cymru. 1 Conservative entered the Government lobby to oppose the amendment.

Conservative to vote against the amendment:

Morgan, G.

HC Deb. 948, 579–82
1977–8, No. 183.

WALES BILL [347]

Committee: 19 April 1978

Clause 83 (Referendum)

The Minister of State at the Privy Council Office, J. Smith, moved formally an amendment to provide that 'If it appears to the Secretary of State that less than 40 per cent of the persons entitled to vote in the referendum have voted 'Yes' in reply to the question posed in the Appendix of Schedule 12 of this Act or that a majority of the answers given in the referendum have been 'No' he shall lay before Parliament the draft of an Order in Council for the repeal of this Act.'

Mr Smith had explained earlier in the day that if it was not possible to debate and divide upon the amendment, as many Members wanted, because of the operation of the guillotine motion, he would move formally the amendment when the guillotine fell in order to allow a division upon it. Hosever, he made clear that the Government were opposed to it, and would advise the Committee not to accept it.

The amendment was *carried* against the Government by 280 votes to 208, *a majority against the Government of 72.* The 210 Members (including tellers) in the Government lobby comprised 182 Labour, 11 Liberal, 10 Scottish National, 4 Conservative and 3 Plaid Cymru. The 282 Members (including tellers) to support the amendment comprised 225 Conservative, 51 Labour and 6 Ulster Unionist.

Conservatives to vote against the amendment:[1]

Adley, R.	Knox, D.	Walker, P.
Buchanan-Smith, A.		

Labour Members to vote for the amendment:

Abse, L.	Ford, B.	Newens, S.
Atkins, R.	Garrett, W.	Ogden, E.
Bean, R.	Hamilton, W.	Palmer, A.
Bennett, A.	Heffer, E.	Price, C.
Bidwell, S.	Irving, S.	Richardson, Miss J.
Boothroyd, Miss B.	Jeger, Mrs L.	Robinson, G.
Cohen, S.	Jones, D.	Rooker, J.
Colquhoun, Ms M.	Kilroy-Silk, R.	Short, Mrs R.
Cowans, H.	Kinnock, N.	Skinner, D.
Crawshaw, R.	Litterick, T.	Spearing, N.
Dean, J.	Lyon, A.	Spriggs, L.
Doig, P.	Madden, M.	Stoddart, D.
Douglas-Mann, B.*	Maynard, Miss J.	Thomas, R.
Evans, F.	Mendelson, J.	Torney, T.
Evans, I.	Mikardo, I.	Willey, F.
Evans, J.	Molloy, W.	Wise, Mrs A.
Fletcher, T.	Moonman, E.	Woodall, A.

HC Deb. 948, 619–24
1977–8, No. 185.

[1] Technically, the Opposition lobby was not whipped, apparently as a means of encouraging as many Labour Members to dissent as possible. The Conservative Members to vote for the Government nevertheless were dissenting clearly from the wishes of their Front Bench and backbench colleagues.

WALES BILL [348]

Committee: 19 April 1978

Clause 83 (Referendum)

At 11.00 p.m., the guillotine fell for remaining discussion on the clause, and, following a division on the 40 per cent requirement in the Welsh referendum (see preceding division), the motion 'That the clause, as amended, stand part of the Bill' was moved formally.

The 'stand part' motion was carried by 269 votes to 30, the Opposition allowing apparently an unwhipped vote.[1] The 271 Members (including tellers) in the Government lobby comprised 220 Labour, 49 Conservative and 2 Liberal. The 32 Members (including tellers) to

oppose the motion comprised 10 Scottish National, 10 Liberal, 7 Conservative,² 3 Plaid Cymru and 2 Labour. At least 10 Labour Members
appear to have abstained from voting.

Labour Members to vote against the clause:

Canavan, D.   Fowler, G.

HC Deb. 948, 623–8
1977–8, No. 186.

---

¹ Most Conservatives absented themselves from the division (over 170 who had voted in
the immediately preceding division failed to enter a lobby), but among those voting for the
clause were a member of the Shadow Cabinet and two Opposition whips.
² R. Adley, A. Buchanan-Smith, N. Budgen, T. Higgins, D. Knox, M. Marshall, and
T. Rathbone.

WALES BILL [349]

Report: 3 May 1978

New Clause No. 1 (Commencement)

The Minister of State at the Privy Council Office, J. Smith, moved the
Second Reading of the clause, which allowed provisions of the measure
to come into force on days appointed by the Secretary of State by order.
(Introduced to replace the old clause 82, defeated in Committee, which
brought the provisions into force upon the measure receiving the Royal
Assent.)

Although F. Pym rose to welcome the new clause for the Opposition,
the Opposition nevertheless abstained from voting in the division upon
it.

The new clause was approved by 235 votes to 17. The 19 Members
(including tellers) to oppose the clause comprised 8 Scottish National,
8 Liberal and 3 Plaid Cymru. Two Conservatives entered the Government lobby to support the clause. At least 1 Labour Member (T.
Dalyell) abstaining from voting.

Conservatives to vote for the clause:

Gower, Sir R.   Grieve, P.

HC Deb. 949, 277–80
1977–8, No. 195.

FINANCE BILL [350]

Committee: 10 May 1978

Clause 11 (Charge of Income Tax for 1978-79)

J. Pardoe (Lib., Cornwall, North) moved an amendment to provide that the investment income surcharge would not apply below the figure of £2,500 for single-parent families. Mr Pardoe explained that single-parent families suffered various disadvantages, and the amendment brought them into line with those of retirement age.

The Financial Secretary to the Treasury, R. Sheldon, replied that the Government had implemented the Finer Report which produced the proper way of handling these problems. That meant giving the additional personal allowance. Accepting the amendment, he said, would help a minority with investment income.

The amendment was negatived by 277 votes to 101, with Opposition Members (apparently on a free vote) supporting the Liberals. The 279 Members (including tellers) in the Government lobby comprised 277 Labour, 1 SDLP and 1 Scottish Labour. The 103 Members (including tellers) in the Liberal lobby comprised 76 Conservative, 12 Liberal, 10 Scottish National, 3 Plaid Cymru, 1 Ulster Unionist and 1 Labour.

Labour Member to vote for the amendment:

Canavan, D.

HC Deb. 949, 1341-6
1977-8, No. 204.

WINDSCALE (SPECIAL DEVELOPMENT ORDER) [351]

Prayer: 15 May 1978

D. Steel (Lib., Roxburgh, Selkirk and Peebles) moved 'That the Town and Country Planning (Windscale and Calder Works) Special Development Order 1978 (S.I., 1978, No. 523), dated 3rd April 1978, a copy of which was laid before this House on 3rd April, be withdrawn.'

Mr Steel said he opposed the order because, once they passed that stage, future Parliaments or Governments could not easily review it and draw back, and because of public concern about safeguards. Further investigation into the safety and security of nuclear materials on site and in transit and of waste storage was needed. If they went ahead, he felt they would be giving an international lead in the wrong direction.

The Secretary of State for the Environment, P. Shore, replied to the various objections that had been raised to the proposed Windscale development, and pointed out that no country in the world had had a more searching inquiry into major nuclear issues than they had had during the Parker inquiry. The recommendations calling for an independent check on security precautions at Windscale were to be accepted. He asked the House to reject the motion.

R. Cook (Lab., Edinburgh, Central) supported the motion, contending that the development would encourage proliferation. A. Blenkinsop (Lab., South Shields) said he did not think they could afford the kind of commitment involved if they wished to preserve the opportunity for commitments in other fields. L. Abse (Lab., Pontypool) declared that 'Windscale is a staging point on the road to Armageddon'.

For the Opposition, T. King said that in all the circumstances they supported the conclusions drawn from the Parker Report, and given certain conditions would support the Government.

The motion was negatived by 224 votes to 80, with the Opposition supporting the Government. The 226 Members (including tellers) in the Government lobby comprised 143 Labour, 82 Conservative and 1 Ulster Unionist. The 82 Members (including tellers) to support the motion comprised 46 Labour, 18 Conservative, 11 Liberal, 3 Scottish National, 3 Plaid Cymru and 1 Scottish Labour.

Labour Members to vote for the motion:

Abse, L.	Garrett, J.	Pavitt, L.
Bidwell, S.	Gould, B.	Price, C.
Blenkinsop, A.	Grocott, B.	Richardson, Miss J.
Buchan, N.	Hayman, Mrs H.	Rodgers, G.
Butler, Mrs J.	Jenkins, H.	Shaw, A.
Canavan, D.	Kilroy-Silk, R.	Skinner, D.
Castle, Mrs B.	Latham, A.	Spearing, N.
Clemitson, I.	Lee, J.	Thomas, R.
Colquhoun, Ms M.	Litterick, T.	Thorne, S.
Cook, R.	Madden, M.	Tilley, J.
Corbett, R.	Maynard, Miss J.	Torney, T.
Dean, J.	Mendelson, J.	Whitehead, P.
Edge, G.	Mikardo, I.	Whitlock, W.
Ellis, J.	Moonman, E.	Willey, F.
Flannery, M.	Parry, R.	Wise, Mrs A.
Fletcher, T.		

Conservatives to vote for the motion:

Biffen, J.
Body, R.
Bowden, A.
Fookes, Miss J.
Forman, N.
Gow, I.

Grist, I.
Hicks, R.
Hunt, D.
Irving, C.
Langford-Holt, Sir J.
Mills, P.

Morris, M.
Mudd, D.
Newton, T.
Rhodes James, R.
Smith, D.
Stanbrook, I.

HC Deb. 950, 179–82
1977–8, No. 208.

TRANSPORT BILL [352]

Report: 17 May 1978

Clause 1 (Passenger transport policies in county areas)

I. Gow (C., Eastbourne) moved an amendment to reduce from six months to three months the period which district councils would have to wait for reimbursement of expenditure incurred in accordance with county council instructions, and on which there was a dispute as to the amount involved.

Mr Gow said he did not see why the Government had chosen a period of six months. 'Why should a district council be out of pocket, getting no interest on the money it has laid out, for a period of six months before it even goes to arbitration?' He considered it a modest amendment.

The Secretary of State for Transport, W. Rodgers, replied that the provision came from the 1972 Local Government Act. If anything, the Association of District Councils would have preferred a longer period. He hoped the amendment would not be pressed.

The amendment was negatived by 103 votes to 6, with the Opposition abstaining apparently from voting. The 105 Members (including tellers) in the Government lobby comprised 100 Labour and 5 Liberal. The 8 Members (including tellers) to support the amendment were all Conservatives. Two Labour Members (E. Loyden and R. Thomas) appear to have abstained from voting.

Conservatives to vote for the amendment:

Adley, R.
Brooke, P.
Fry, P.

Gow, I.*
Hicks, R.
Knox, D.

Moate, R.*
Montgomery, F.

HC Deb. 950, 691
1977–8, No. 217.

EUROPEAN COMMUNITIES (TREATIES) [353]

23 May 1978

During debate on a prayer to approve the draft European Communities (Definition of Treaties) (No. 4) Order 1978, D. Jay (Lab., Battersea, North) moved that the debate be adjourned.

A number of Members had objected to the fact that Command Paper No. 6623 (comprising a text of the European Assembly Elections Act and Decision of the Council of the European Communities of 20 September 1976) was not readily available. It was argued that, as it was central to the debate, it should be available, and Mr Jay moved that the debate be adjourned until such time as the relevant documents were available.

The Minister of State for Foreign and Commonwealth Affairs, F. Judd, opposed the motion. He said the relevant documents had been available, and he understood that many Members who had raised the issue had managed to obtain copies.

The motion to adjourn was negatived by 119 votes to 61, with Opposition Members supporting the Government. The 121 Members (including tellers) in the Government lobby comprised 71 Labour, 46 Conservative and 4 Liberal. The 63 Members (including tellers) to vote for adjournment comprised 45 Labour, 10 Conservative, 4 Ulster Unionist, 3 Scottish National and 1 Plaid Cymru.

Labour Members to vote for adjournment:

Atkinson, N.	Forrester, J.	Noble, M.
Bean, R.	Fowler, G.	Price, C.
Bennett, A.	Grocott, B.	Richardson, Miss J.
Bidwell, S.	Hoyle, D.	Robinson, G.
Buchan, N.	Jay, D.	Rodgers, G.
Callaghan, J.	Lamond, J.	Rooker, J.
Canavan, D.	Leadbitter, T.	Skinner, D.
Clemitson, I.	Lestor, Miss J.	Spearing, N.
Cook, R.	Loyden, E.	Spriggs, L.
Craigen, J.	McDonald, O.	Stoddart, D.
Ellis, J.	Madden, M.	Thomas, R.
Evans, J.	Maynard, Miss J.	Tilley, J.
Fernyhough, E.	Mikardo, I.	Torney, T.
Flannery, M.	Mitchell, A.	Wise, Mrs A.
Fletcher, T.	Newens, S.	Woof, R.

Conservatives to vote for adjournment:

Aitken, J.	Budgen, N.	Marten, N.
Bell, R.	Gow, I.	Maxwell-Hyslop, R.
Biffen, J.	Latham, M.	Moate, R.
Body, R.		

HC Deb. 950, 1463–6
1977–8, No. 224.

The prayer was subsequently divided upon: see below.

EUROPEAN COMMUNITIES (TREATIES) [354]

Prayer: 23 May 1978

The Minister of State at the Foreign and Commonwealth Office, F. Judd, moved 'That the draft European Communities (Definition of Treaties) (No. 4) Order 1978, which was laid before this House on 11th May, be approved.'

The order effectively ratified the provisions of the European Assembly Elections Act and the Decision of the Council of the European Communities of 20 September 1976 (published together in Cmnd. Paper 6623). A number of Members rose to complain that the relevant documents, such as copies of the Command Paper, were not available (see preceding division), and also to oppose it on the grounds that it was one of the moves necessary to ensure direct elections to the European Assembly. N. Marten (C., Banbury) thought the Assembly would be toothless; he also opposed it as he thought it was a large step towards a federal Europe. D. Jay (Lab., Battersea, North) thought it was unsatisfactory to approve the order without knowing the salaries or expenses that Assembly Members would receive. J. Biffen (C., Oswestry) argued that it would not be in the long-term interests of those who wanted to promote a working Community partnership to proceed with a directly-elected Assembly. An elected Assembly would likely wish to reinforce its spending power and enter into some form of partnership with the Commission.

The order was approved by 111 votes to 52, the Opposition supporting the Government. The 113 Members (including tellers) in the Government lobby comprised 73 Labour, 35 Conservative and 5 Liberal. The 54 Members (including tellers) to oppose the order comprised 40 Labour, 9 Conservative and 5 Ulster Unionist.

Labour Members to vote against the order:

Atkinson, N.	Grocott, B.	Richardson, Miss J.
Bennett, A.*	Hoyle, D.	Robinson, G.
Bidwell, S.	Jay, D.	Rodgers, G.
Buchan, N.	Kerr, R.	Rooker, J.
Callaghan, J.	Lamond, J.	Skinner, D.
Canavan, D.	Leadbitter, T.	Spearing, N.*
Cook, R.	Loyden, E.	Spriggs, L.
Cowans, H.	Madden, M.	Stoddart, D.
Ellis, J.	Maynard, Miss J.	Thomas, R.
Evans, J.	Mikardo, I.	Tilley, J.
Fernyhough, E.	Mitchell, A.	Urwin, T.
Flannery, M.	Newens, S.	Wise, Mrs A.
Fletcher, T.	Price, C.	Woof, R.
Forrester, J.		

Conservatives to vote against the order:

Bell, R.	Brotherton, M.	Gow, I.
Biffen, J.	Budgen, N.	Marten, N.
Body, R.	Clark, A.	Moate, R.

HC Deb. 950, 1503–4
1977–8, No. 225.

EMPLOYMENT (CONTINENTAL SHELF) BILL [355]

Second Reading: 6 June 1978

The Under-Secretary of State for Employment, J. Grant, moved the Second Reading of the Bill. He explained that the Bill provided the power to extend certain enactments concerned with employment law to the oil and gas fields that straddled the median line drawn in the North Sea between the United Kingdom sector of the Continental Shelf and the sectors of other countries. It would permit the Government to plug a small gap in the existing coverage of employment law.

For the Opposition, B. Hayhoe said that they were not opposed to the provisions of the Bill, and felt it reasonable that such action should be taken.

R. Bell (C., Beaconsfield) opposed the measure. 'All that we are doing in the Bill is extending three of the most controversial and foolish pieces of modern legislation [Sex Discrimination Act, Race Relations Act and

Employment Protection Act] to those on the storm-tossed and remote sections of the North Sea. We are fouling what would otherwise be a nice clean landscape.' He thought the Bill was totally unnecessary. N. Fairbairn (C., Kinross and West Perthshire) described it as a stupid Bill. "It is a Bill designed purely to get the influence of ACAS on to the rigs."

The Bill was given a Second Reading by 107 votes to 13, with the Opposition abstaining from voting. The 109 Members (including tellers) in the Government lobby comprised 100 Labour, 5 Scottish National and 4 Liberal. The 15 Members (including tellers) to oppose the Bill comprised 12 Conservative and 3 Ulster Unionist.

Conservatives to vote against Second Reading:

Bell, R.*	Macfarlane, N.	Ridley, N.
Fairbairn, N.*	Moate, R.	Tebbit, N.
Gow, I.	Page, R. G.	Walder, D.
Holland, P.	Renton, T.	Winterton, N.

HC Deb. 951, 125–6
1977–8, No. 228.

NORTHERN IRELAND (PAYMENTS FOR DEBT) [356]

Prayer: 20 June 1978

The Minister of State for Northern Ireland, J. Concannon, moved 'That the draft Payments for Debt (Amendment) (Northern Ireland) Order 1978, which was laid before this House on 11th May, be approved.'

The Minister explained that the non-payment of gas and electricity bills was a serious problem, especially in comparison to the rest of the United Kingdom. The objectives were being pursued of encouraging people not to fall into debt and to catch up with arrears, but they still had to deal with consumers who would not respond to that sympathetic approach. For those who were not in employment, and who failed to pay rent and rate debts, certain deductions could be made from their social security benefits—the benefit allocation procedure—and the Government had decided that the gas and electricity undertakings should be allowed to explore this route when all others had failed.

Miss J. Maynard (Lab., Sheffield, Brightside) opposed the order. She said the people in debt in Northern Ireland were in debt because of their poverty. Instead, the Government should do something about unemployment. R. Thomas (Lab., Britsol, North-West) felt that the order discriminated against Northern Ireland and against the under-privileged. T. Litterick (Lab., Birmingham, Selly Oak) considered enough had been said to indicate that there was no rational basis for the original Act, let alone the order made under it. Ministers knew that it violated the basic principles of the welfare system.

The order was approved by 166 votes to 23, with the Opposition supporting the Government. the 168 Members (including tellers) in the Government lobby comprised 128 Labour, 22 Conservative, 9 Ulster Unionist, 8 Liberal and 1 Democratic Unionist. The 25 Members (including tellers) to oppose the order comprised 24 Labour and 1 SDLP Member.

Labour Members to vote against the order:

Atkinson, N.	Lamond, J.	Noble, M.
Bennett, A.	Lestor, Miss J.	Parry, R.
Callaghan, J.	Litterick, T.*	Richardson, Miss J.
Canavan, D.	Loyden, E.	Rodgers, G.
Flannery, M.	Madden, M.	Skinner, D.
Fletcher, T.	Maynard, Miss J.	Thomas, R.*
Gould, B.	Mitchell, A.	Thorne, S.
Hoyle, D.	Newens, S.	Wise, Mrs A.

HC Deb. 952, 309–12
1977–8, No. 233.

NORTHERN IRELAND (MATRIMONIAL CAUSES) [357]

Prayer: 20 June 1978

The Under-Secretary of State for Northern Ireland, J. Dunn, moved 'That the draft Matrimonial Causes (Northern Ireland) Order, which was laid before this House on 8th June, be approved.'

In a detailed speech, Mr Dunn explained that the order sought to reform the law of Northern Ireland relating to divorce, annulment of marriage, judicial separation and other matters connected with marriage, and to bring it into line broadly with the law of England and Wales.

From the Opposition Front Bench, I. Gow expressed support for the order, and said he would vote for it.

The only backbenchers to participate in the debate were Northern Ireland Members, who were divided on the order.

The order was approved by 110 votes to 16, with the Opposition supporting the Government. The 112 Members (including tellers) in the Government lobby comprised 98 Labour, 6 Conservative, 4 Ulster Unionist and 4 Liberal. The 18 Members (including tellers) to oppose the order comprised 9 Conservative, 5 Ulster Unionist, 3 Labour and 1 Democratic Unionist.

Conservatives to vote against the order:

Alison, M.	Hamilton, M.	More, J.
Body, R.*	Marten, N.	Page, R. G.
Biggs-Davison, J.	Mawby, R.	Roberts, M.

Labour Members to vote against the order:

Buchanan, R.	Dempsey, J.	Woof, R.

HC Deb. 952, 365–6
1977–8, No. 234.

The division took place at 11.08 p.m.

EUROPEAN COMMUNITY (FOUNDATION AND CULTURAL SECTOR) [358]

23 June 1978

The Under-Secretary of State at the Foreign and Commonwealth Office, J. Tomlinson, moved 'That this House takes note of EEC Documents Nos. COM(77) 600, R/325/78, R/734/78, R/774/78 and R/2982/77 on the European Foundation and Cultural Sector.'

Mr Tomlinson explained that the documents dealt with a European Foundation and Community action in the cultural sector. The Government, he explained, was committed only to the principle of establishing a European Foundation, and that it should be in Paris. They were committed to no more than that. As to action in the cultural sector, the Community enjoyed no automatic competence in that sector, and the Government had put forward its scepticism about the need to extend Community competence.

H. Jenkins (Lab., Putney) objected to the two subjects being taken together, and said that he regarded the Foundation as 'a sinister body for the purpose of promoting a federal Europe.' N. Spearing (Lab., Newham, South) also argued that it was clearly designed to promote

European union, and 'in a very clever and effective manner' through
its grant-giving power. R. Moate (C., Faversham) felt that once the
Foundation was established, it would be beyond the Government's
control. It seemed to him that they were setting up a propaganda
machine for the Common Market. D. Jay (Lab., Battersea, North) said
if the Foundation intended to finance political propaganda for a federal
EEC with public money it was a vicious proposal. If it did not, it was
unnecessary. Other bodies already provided for cultural exchanges and
the like.

The motion was approved by 28 votes to 10. The 30 Members (including tellers) in the Government lobby comprised 23 Labour and
7 Conservative. The 12 Members (including tellers) to oppose the
motion comprised 10 Labour and 2 Conservative.

Labour Members to vote against the motion:

Atkinson, N.	Jenkins, H.	Pavitt, L.
Crowther, S.	Lee, J.	Spearing, N.*
Cunningham, G.	Litterick, T.	Wise, Mrs A.
Jay, D.		

Conservatives to vote against the motion:

Bell, R.	Moate, R.*

HC Deb. 952, 999–1000
1977–8, No. 238.

SCOTLAND BILL [359]

4 July 1978

The Minister of State at the Privy Council Office, J. Smith, moved a
detailed allocation of time (guillotine) motion to provide that consideration of Lords amendments to the Scotland Bill be completed in three
allotted days.

The motion was carried on a whipped party vote by 292 votes to 274.
The 294 Members (including tellers) in the Government lobby comprised 268 Labour, 11 Scottish National, 9 Liberal, 2 Plaid Cymru,
2 Scottish Labour, 1 SDLP and 1 Ulster Unionist. The 276 Members
(including tellers) in the Opposition lobby comprised 260 Conservative,
8 Ulster Unionist, 7 Labour and 1 Democratic Unionist.

Labour Members to vote against the motion:

Abse, L.   Evans, F.   Lee, J.
Cunningham, G.   Garrett, W.   Phipps, C.
Dalyell, T.

HC Deb. 953, 405–12
1977–8, No. 244.

SCOTLAND BILL   [360]

Lords Amendments: 6 July 1978

Clause 1 (The Scottish Assembly)

The Lords had inserted an amendment that members of the Scottish Assembly should be elected by a system of proportional representation. On a free vote, the House rejected the amendment by 363 votes to 155.[1] *HC Deb.* 953, c. 733–8.

The Lords had inserted also an amendment to provide that, notwithstanding any provisions of the Bill, 'the Assembly may at any time after the first ordinary election of members of the Assembly review the system of voting prescribed by this Act and may by Bill amend that system'.

The Minister of State at the Privy Council Office, J. Smith, moved formally (the guillotine having fallen), 'That this House doth disagree with the Lords in the said amendment'.

The motion to disagree with the Lords amendment was carried by 467 votes to 39, with the Opposition supporting the Government. The 469 Members (including tellers) in the Government lobby comprised 245 Labour, 218 Conservative, 5 Ulster Unionist and 1 Democratic Unionist. The 41 Members (including tellers) to oppose the motion comprised 12 Conservative, 11 Scottish National, 9 Liberal, 3 Labour, 3 Plaid Cymru, 2 Ulster Unionist, and 1 Scottish Labour.

Conservatives to vote against the motion:

Blaker, P.   Fisher, Sir N.   Meyer, Sir A.
Brocklebank-Fowler, C.   Hunt, D.   Morrison, C.
Buchanan-Smith, A.   Knox, D.   Rathbone, T.
Fell, A.   Lewis, K.   Rifkind, M.

Labour Members to vote against the motion:

Canavan, D.   Lambie, D.   Thorne, S.

HC Deb. 953, 743–8
1977–8, No. 248.

¹ The 365 Members (including tellers) to vote against the amendment comprised 204 Labour, 153 Conservative, 7 Ulster Unionist and 1 Democratic Unionist. The 157 Members (including tellers) to support the motion comprised 86 Conservative, 44 Labour, 11 Scottish National, 11 Liberal, 3 Plaid Cymru and 1 Scottish Labour and 1 Ulster Unionist.

SCOTLAND BILL   [361]

Lords Amendments: 6 July 1978

Clause 20 (The Scottish Assembly)

The Lords had deleted subsection (3) of the clause, which made provision for the devolving of executive powers.

The Minister of State at the Privy Council Office, J. Smith, moved an amendment to re-insert subsection (3) in the clause.

The amendment was carried on a whipped party vote by 272 votes to 258. 1 Labour Member cross-voted to oppose the amendment.

Labour Member to vote against the amendment:

Dalyell, T.

HC Deb. 953, 805–10
1977—8, No. 215.

SCOTLAND BILL   [362]

Lords Amendments: 6 July 1978

Clause 26 (Committees)

The Lords had amended the clause to provide that the Assembly could not appoint a Committee with functions not relating to devolved matters.

The Secretary of State for Scotland, B. Millan, moved formally 'That this House doth disagree with the Lords in the said amendment'.

Earlier, the Minister had argued that it would be difficult to prevent the Assembly or its Committees from discussing non-devolved matters if they wished to.

The motion to disagree with the Lords amendment was carried by 248 votes to 229. 2 Labour Members cross-voted to oppose the motion.

Labour Members to vote against the Motion:

Dalyell, T.　　　　　　　Ogden, E.

HC Deb. 953, 837–42
1977–8, No. 253.

FINANCE BILL　　　　　　　　　　　　　　　　　　　　[363]

Report: 13 July 1978

Clause 63 (Disclosures of information to tax authorities in other member States)

D. Stoddart (Lab., Swindon) moved an amendment to delete the clause. He said that the clause sought to legislate on the basis of an EEC directive, one which was very wide. The tax, and therefore the personal affairs, of every individual and enterprise in the land could be made available to eight alien States. 'That is an unprecedented intrusion into the lives of British people by foreign Governments.' He went on to contend that the clause represented only the thin end of the wedge, and he hoped the House would realize the serious implications of it.

The Financial Secretary to the Treasury, R. Sheldon, replied that the worries of Mr Stoddart as to what might follow on from the clause were problems that would not have to be faced for many years. A Government amendment would make it clear that the Inland Revenue was not authorised to disclose information unless satisfied that the tax authorities of the other member States were bound by rules of confidentiality not less strict than those applying in the United Kingdom. The exchange of information would help stop tax evasion. He believed that the House should accept the clause.

The amendment was negatived by 209 votes to 81, with the Opposition abstaining from voting. The 211 Members (including tellers) in the Government lobby comprised 186 Labour, 17 Conservative and 8 Liberal. The 83 Members (including tellers) to support the amendment comprised 58 Labour, 15 Conservative, 5 Ulster Unionist, 4 Scottish National and 1 Plaid Cymru.

Conservatives to vote against the amendment:

Banks, R.
Bottomley, P.
Brooke, P.
Churchill, W.
Clarke, K.
Costain, A.

Dykes, H.
Godber, J.
Knox, D.
Meyer, Sir A.
Mills, P.
Miscampbell, N.

Newton, T.
Renton, Sir D.
Rifkind, M.
Scott, N.
Wood, R.

Labour Members to vote for the amendment:

Atkins, R.
Atkinson, N.
Bean, R.
Bidwell, S.
Buchan, N.
Callaghan, J.
Canavan, D.
Castle, Mrs B.
Corbett, R.
Dunwoody, Mrs G.
Ellis, J.
Evans, F.
Evans, J.
Fernyhough, E.
Flannery, M.
Fletcher, T.
Fowler, G.
Garrett, W.
Gould, B.
Heffer, E.

Hooley, F.
Hughes, R. J.
Jay, D.
Jeger, Mrs L.
Kerr, R.
Kinnock, N.
Lambie, D.
Lamond, J.
Latham, A.
Leadbitter, T.
Lee, J.
Lestor, Miss J.
Litterick, T.
McNamara, K.
Madden, M.*
Maynard, Miss J.
Mikardo, I.
Miller, M.
Mitchell, A.

Molloy, W.
Parry, R.
Pavitt, L.
Price, C.
Richardson, Miss J.
Roberts, G.
Robinson, G.
Rodgers, G.
Short, Mrs R.
Skinner, D.
Spearing, N.
Spriggs, L.
Stoddart, D.*
Thomas, R.
Thorne, S.
Tilley, J.
Torney, T.
Watkins, D.
Wise, Mrs A.

Conservative Members to vote for the amendment:

Aitken, J.
Bell, R.
Biffen, J.
Body, R.
Budgen, N.

Farr, J.
Fell, A.
Gow, I.
Jessel, T.
King, E.

Marten, N.
Maxwell-Hyslop, R.
Moate, R.
Morgan, G.
Winterton, N.

HC Deb. 954, 1885–8
1977–8, No. 269.

SCOTLAND BILL [364]

Lords Amendments: 17 July 1978

Clause 48 (Limitation of capital expenditure financed by borrowing)

The Lords had deleted reference in the clause to the British Waterways Board. The Secretary of State for Scotland, B. Millan, moved formally (the guillotine having fallen), 'That this House doth disagree with the Lords in the said amendment'.

The motion was carried by 295 votes to 267. 1 Labour Member crossvoted to oppose the motion.

Labour Member to vote against the motion:

Dalyell, T.

HC Deb. 954, 105–12
1977–8, No. 273.

SCOTLAND BILL [365]

Lords Amendments: 17 July 1978

New Clause 'E' (Proposals for powers to raise moneys)

The Lords had inserted the new clause which read: 'If the Assembly decides that it wishes to make proposals that power should be conferred on the Assembly to raise by taxation moneys to be paid into the Scottish Consolidated Fund, it may communicate such proposals to the Secretary of State who shall lay such proposals before both Houses of Parliament.'

The Minister of State at the Privy Council Office, J. Smith, moved 'That this House doth disagree with the Lords in the said amendment.' He explained that it was a declaratory clause, and contended that it was misleading and was likely to cause misunderstanding. It assumed a formalistic relationship between the devolved administration and the Government, and he did not know what purpose it would serve.

R. Cook (Lab., Edinburgh, Central) and T. Renton (C., Mid-Sussex) both spoke in support of the new clause. Both wanted tax-raising powers included; without them, they would be putting a false prospectus before the electorate in the referendum. 'We are telling the electorate that we will give them better public services through an Assembly but that it will not cost them a penny. That is', said Mr Cook, 'irresponsibility in every sense of the word, and it will not solve the problem in any way.'

The motion to disagree with the Lords amendment was carried by 266 votes to 35, with the Opposition abstaining officially from voting. The 268 Members (including tellers) in the Government lobby comprised 258 Labour, 6 Conservative, 3 Ulster Unionist and 1 Plaid Cymru Member who voted in both lobbies (in this lobby apparently in error). The 37 Members (including tellers) to oppose the motion comprised 11 Scottish National, 10 Liberal, 9 Labour, 3 Plaid Cymru, 2 Scottish Labour, 1 Conservative and 1 Ulster Unionist.

Conservatives to vote for the motion:

Budgen, N.	Drayson, B.	Morgan, G.
Crowder, F. P.	Fookes, Miss J.	Stanbrook, I.

Labour Members to vote against the motion:

Canavan, D.	Craigen, J.	Lambie, D.
Carmichael, N.	Dalyell, T.	Rose, P.
Cook, R.*	Hughes, R.	Thorne, S.

Conservative to vote against the motion:

Renton, T.

HC Deb. 954, 153-6
1977-8, No. 274.

SCOTLAND BILL [366]

Lords Amendments: 17 July 1978

New Clause 'F' (Voting of Scottish Members of Parliament)

The Lords had inserted the new clause, which provided that if the Commons passed a Bill for which there would not have been a majority if Members representing Scottish seats had been excluded from the voting on Third Reading, then the Bill would not be deemed to have been read a Third time unless the House confirmed its decision after the next fourteen days (to apply to Bills which did not concern Scotland).

From the Opposition Front Bench, F. Pym moved an amendment to delete the reference to 'Third Reading' and to insert 'Second Reading'.

Mr Pym contended that the delay for second thoughts provided by the clause was a good idea, but he and his colleagues felt it would be best if the process occurred on Second Reading before all the work had been done on a Bill. The Minister of State at the Privy Council Office, J. Smith, opposed the amendment. He said the Government were opposed to the proposal for a delay on the grounds of both principle and practice.

The amendment was negatived by 288 votes to 282, a Government majority of six. The 290 Members (including tellers) in the Government lobby comprised 279 Labour and 11 Liberal. The 284 Members (including tellers) in the Opposition lobby comprised 264 Conservative, 11 Scottish National, 5 Ulster Unionist, 2 Labour, 1 Scottish Labour and 1 Liberal.

Labour Members to vote for the amendment:

Cunningham, G.   Dalyell, T.

HC Deb. 954, 197–202
9177–8, No. 275.

See also the succeeding division (below), and division [378].

SCOTLAND BILL [367]

Lords Amendments: 17 July 1978

New Clause 'F' (Voting of Scottish Members of Parliament)

The Lords had amended the Bill to include new clause 'F' [for details, see preceding division].

The Minister of State at the Privy Council Office, J. Smith, moved formally 'That this House doth disagree with the Lords in the said amendment'.

The motion was voted upon, with the Opposition voting against. The voting was 286 votes for to 286 votes against. The 288 Members (including tellers) in the Government lobby comprised 278 Labour and 10 Liberal. The 288 Members (including tellers) in the Opposition lobby comprised 264 Conservative, 11 Scottish National, 5 Ulster Unionist, 3 Labour, 3 Plaid Cymru and 2 Liberal.

Labour Members to vote against the motion:

Cunningham, G.   Dalyell, T.   Garrett, W.

HC Deb. 954, 201–6
1977–8, No. 276.

In line with precedent (to vote to support the Bill in the form in which it left the House), the Deputy Speaker gave his casting vote in favour of the motion.

SCOTLAND BILL · [368]

Lords Amendments: 17 July 1978

Clause 67 (Transfer of property)

The Lords had deleted subsection (4) of the clause which devolved the subject of forestry to the Scottish Assembly.

The Secretary of State for Scotland, B. Millan, moved 'That this House doth disagree with the Lords in the said amendment'.

Mr Millan said the subject had been debated at some length at Committee stage. Forestry was a subject of proportionately more interest in Scotland than in England, and was a subject which, with certain reservations, was suitable for devolution.

For the Opposition, G. Younger opposed the motion. The forestry industry, he argued, was one with great potential which operated in one market and which ought to operate under one system of support.

The motion was carried by 285 votes to 279. The 287 Members (including tellers) in the Government lobby comprised 262 Labour, 11 Liberal, 8 Scottish National, 1 Conservative, 2 Plaid Cymru, 2 Scottish Labour and 1 Ulster Unionist.[1] The 281 Members (including tellers) in the Opposition lobby comprised 266 Conservative, 10 Labour, 4 Ulster Unionist and 1 Liberal.

Conservative to vote for the motion:

Buchanan-Smith, A.

Labour Members to vote against the motion:

Buchanan, R.   Hughes, R.   Parker, J.
Dalyell, T.   Lewis, R.   Sandelson, N.
Evans, I.   Molloy, W.   Wilson, W.
Garrett, W.

HC Deb. 954, 215–20
1977–8, No. 277.

[1] The Weekly edition of *Hansard* lists D. Atkinson (C., Bournemouth, East) as voting in the Government lobby. This is a printing error.

SCOTLAND BILL   [369]

Lords Amendments: 18 July 1978

Schedule 10 (Matters within legislative competence of Assembly, and within powers of Scottish Executive)

The Lords had deleted aerodromes from the list of subjects devolved to the Scottish Assembly.

The Under-Secretary of State for Scotland, H. Ewing, moved 'That this House doth disagree with the Lords in the said amendment'.

Mr Ewing said the Government believed it was right that the Assembly should have responsibility for aerodromes in Scotland as part of its wide-ranging responsibilities for communications, transport and physical infrastructure.

T. Dalyell (Lab., West Lothian) considered that the reason the Government sought to restore aerodromes to the list of devolved subjects was in order to give the Scottish Assembly something to do. Up to then, they had a perfectly good system under the British Airports Authority.

The motion was carried by 292 votes to 259. The 294 Members (including tellers) in the Government lobby comprised 268 Labour, 11 Scottish National, 9 Liberal, 3 Plaid Cymru, 2 Scottish Labour and 1 Ulster Unionist. The 261 Members (including tellers) to oppose the motion comprised 254 Conservative, 4 Ulster Unionist and 3 Labour.

Labour Members to vote against the motion:

Dalyell, T.   Kerr, R.   Urwin, T.

HC Deb. 954, 473–80
1977–8, No. 281.

SCOTLAND BILL [370]

Lords Amendments: 18 July 1978

Schedule 10 (Matters within legislative competence of Assembly, and within powers of Scottish Executive)

The Lords had passed an amendment designed to reserve to the Government responsibility 'for special purchase grants in respect of Scottish libraries.

The Under-Secretary of State for Scotland, H. Ewing, moved 'That this House doth disagree with the Lords in the said amendment'. He explained that special purchase grants were ad hoc and without prejudice. To say that they were matters which could be decided only by the Government and to exclude the devolved Administration would be contrary to the basic principles of devolution.

R. Cook (Lab., Edinburgh, Central) opposed the motion. He said the argument for retaining the functions of the annual and special grants at United Kingdom level was that that was the area where the financial arrangements made sense.

The motion to disagree with the Lords amendment was carried by 293 votes to 262. 3 Labour Members cross-voted to oppose the motion.

Labour Members to vote against the motion:

Cook, R.   Dalyell, T.   Kinnock, N.

HC Deb. 954, 479–84
1977–8, No. 282.

WALES BILL [371]

18 July 1978

The Minister of State at the Privy Council Office, J. Smith, moved a detailed allocation of time (guillotine) motion to provide for consideration of Lords amendments to the Wales Bill to be completed in two allotted days.

The motion was carried by 291 votes to 260, a Government majority of 31. The 293 Members (including tellers) in the Government lobby comprised 266 Labour, 11 Liberal, 10 Scottish National, 3 Plaid Cymru, 2 Scottish Labour and 1 SDLP. The 262 Members (including tellers) in the Opposition lobby comprised 255 Conservative, 5 Ulster Unionist and 2 Labour. A small number of Labour Members (including I. Evans and N. Kinnock) abstained from voting.

Labour Members to vote against the motion:

Abse, L.   Dalyell, T.

HC Deb. 954, 501–6
1977–8, No. 287.

The division took place at 1.30 a.m.

WALES BILL [372]

Lords Amendments: 19 July 1978

Clause 5 (Disqualification for membership)

The Lords had inserted a provision that Members of Parliament were disqualified from being elected to the Welsh Assembly.

The Minister of State at the Privy Council Office, J. Smith, moved formally (the guillotine having fallen), 'That this House doth disagree with the Lords in the said amendment'.

The motion to disagree with the Lords amendment was *negatived* by 293 votes to 260, *a majority against the Government of 33*. The 262 Members (including tellers) in the Government lobby comprised 248 Labour, 10 Liberal, 2 Conservative, 1 Democratic Unionist, and 1 Conservative who voted in both lobbies (in this lobby apparently in error). The 295 Members (including tellers) in the Opposition lobby comprised 263 Conservative, 20 Labour, 9 Ulster Unionist and 3 Plaid Cymru.

Conservative Members to vote for the motion:

Mitchell, D.   Morgan, G.

Labour Members to vote against the motion:

Abse, L.	Kinnock, N.	Molloy, W.
Cowans, H.	Lee, J.	Parry, R.
Evans, F.	Lestor, Miss J.	Richardson, Miss J.
Evans, I.	Loyden, E.	Short, Mrs R.
Evans, J.	McGuire, M.	Tomney, F.
Fernyhough, E.	Maynard, Miss J.	Wise, Mrs A.
Kilroy-Silk, R.	Mitchell, R.	

HC Deb. 954, 727–32
1977–8, No. 289.

WALES BILL [373]

Lords Amendments: 19 July 1978

Clause 12 (Review of Local Government Structure)

The clause conferred upon the Welsh Assembly the power to review the structure of local government in Wales and to report its conclusions to the Secretary of State. The Lords passed an amendment to delete the clause from the Bill.

The Secretary of State for Wales, J. Morris, moved 'That this House doth disagree with the Lords in the said amendment'. He contended that the clause should be restored. The Assembly was a suitable body to carry out such a review, he said, and allowing it to do so was a democratic solution to the problem of which body should undertake such a review.

I. Evans (Lab., Aberdare) felt it was dangerous to give such a task to the Assembly. The Secretary of State, he said, should set up a commission instead to review local government in Wales. D. Anderson (Lab., Swansea, East) said the clause was unnecessary. If the Assembly wanted to make local government proposals, it could do so anyway. He felt the clause was being supported as a sweetening process for the referendum campaign. N. Kinnock (Lab., Bedwellty) said that what was proposed was the most superficial and misleading way in which to conduct the whole exercise of local government reorganization. If the Assembly made representations, the whole process would have to be gone through in the Commons in order to change local government.

The motion to disagree with the Lords amendment was carried by 278 votes to 277, a Government majority of 1. The 280 Members (including tellers) in the Government lobby comprised 248 Labour, 11 Liberal, 8 Scottish National, 8 Ulster Unionist, 3 Plaid Cymru and 2 Scottish Labour. The 279 Members (including tellers) to oppose the motion comprised 263 Conservative, 15 Labour and 1 Democratic Unionist.

Labour Members to vote against the motion:

Abse, L.	Evans, F.	Mitchell, R.
Anderson, D.	Evans, I.	Molloy, W.
Atkins, R.	Evans, J.	Parker, J.
Dalyell, T.	Hughes, R.	Richardson, Miss J.
Davies, I.	Kinnock, N.	Urwin, T.

HC Deb. 954, 731–6
1977–8, No. 290.

WALES BILL   [374]

Lords Amendments: 19 July 1978

Clause 37 (Industrial and economic guidelines)

The Lords had passed an amendment deleting reference to the Welsh Development Agency, the Development Board for Rural Wales and the Land Authority for Wales from the list of bodies to be devolved to the Welsh Assembly.

The Secretary of State for Wales, J. Morris, moved 'That this House doth disagree with the Lords in the said amendment'. He said that all three bodies dealt with matters which had major planning and social content, and were of major concern to people living in Wales. He believed that the Government's original proposals in the Bill provided a realistic and coherent devolution of powers to the Assembly without prejudicing the Government's responsibility for economic and other matters with wider United Kingdom implications.

N. Kinnock (Lab., Bedwellty) felt that allocating the powers of the Welsh Development Agency to the Assembly would significantly jeopardise the possibilities of obtaining the kind of money needed by the agency. I. Evans (Lab., Aberdare) felt the three bodies had done a tremendous job, and hoped the Government would reconsider the matter.

The motion to disagree with the Lords amendment was carried by 285 votes to 280, a Government majority of 5. The 287 Members (including tellers) in the Government lobby comprised 268 Labour, 8 Liberal, 8 Scottish National and 3 Plaid Cymru. The 282 Members (including tellers) to oppose the motion comprised 269 Conservative, 8 Ulster Unionist, 4 Labour and 1 Democratic Unionist. A small number of Labour Members (including D. Anderson and F. Evans) apparently abstained from voting.

Labour Members to vote against the motion:

Dalyell, T.	Evans, I.	Kinnock, N.
Davies, I.		

HC Deb. 954, 749–56
1977–8, No. 294.

WALES BILL [375]

Lords Amendments: 20 July 1978

Clause 60 (Power of Assembly to assume functions of certain bodies)

The Lords had passed an amendment to delete clause 60.

The Secretary of State for Wales, J. Morris, moved 'That this House doth disagree with the Lords in the said amendment.' He said the Government believed bodies operating solely within Wales covered by the clause should be dissolved and appointed by the Assembly and not by a Minister. The aim was to replace the indirect control of nominated bodies with the control and scrutiny of the Assembly. He asked the House to reject the Lords amendment.

T. Dallyell (Lab., West Lothian) opposed the motion. He queried the possibility of the Assembly selecting some of its own members to serve on the bodies concerned. He contended that what was proposed was a recipe for confusion. I. Evans (Lab., Aberdare) felt it better that the Welsh Development Agency should be answerable to the House. The people appointed by the Minister to the bodies in question were doing a first-class job for Wales.

The motion to disagree with the Lords amendment was carried by 261 votes to 233. 2 Labour Members cross-voted to oppose the motion.

Labour Members to vote against the motion:

Dalyell, T.   Evans, I.

HC Deb. 954, 839–44
1977–8, No. 296.

WALES BILL [376]

Lords Amendments: 20 July 1978

Clause 70 (Determination of issues as to Assembly's powers)

The House of Lords had inserted a provision in the clause to provide that the Attorney-General or any other person could institute proceedings seeking a determination of any question whether the Assembly was in default in the fulfilment of any duty placed upon it by the Act, and seek an order requiring the fulfilment of that duty, provided that the person (other than the Attorney-General) would be aggrieved by such default or had an interest in the fulfilment of the duty.

The Attorney-General, S. Silkin, moved 'That this House doth disagree with the Lords in the said amendment'.

Mr Silkin said that the power given to the individual was unnecessary, as the power would be provided in due course by the Crown Proceedings Act, and he objected to the coercive part of the amendment.

The motion was carried on a whipped party vote by 286 votes to 272. The 288 Members (including tellers) in the Government lobby comprised 279 Labour, 10 Liberal, 5 Scottish National, 3 Plaid Cymru and 1 Ulster Unionist. The 274 Members (including tellers) to oppose the motion comprised 264 Conservative, 6 Ulster Unionist, 3 Labour and 1 Democratic Unionist.

Labour Members to vote against the motion:

Abse, L.   Dalyell, T.   Evans, F.

HC Deb. 954, 867–74
1977–8, No. 298.

WALES BILL [377]

Lords Amendments: 20 July 1978

Schedule 2 (Legislative competence of Assembly)

The Lords had deleted Part X of the schedule, which transferred forestry to the legislative competence of the Welsh Assembly.

The Under-Secretary of State for Wales, A. Jones, moved 'That this House doth disagree with the Lords in the said amendment'.

Mr Jones said the Government felt it would be undesirable if forestry was not transferred while the subjects of planning, land use, the countryside and tourism were. Forestry was of considerable importance to Wales, and the Government's view was that the Assembly should have the power under the 1967 Forestry Act to determine the extent and form of afforestation to be undertaken.

For the Opposition, N. Edwards said that forestry should be dealt with on a United Kingdom basis, and those involved in the industry were agreed on that point. J. Parker (Lab., Dagenham) and I. Evans (Lab., Aberdare) rose also to argue that it should be dealt with on a United Kingdom basis. Dividing the island into three parcels, as the devolution Bills proposed, would be gravely detrimental, said Mr Evans. 'Every forestry expert and the Forestry Commission itself know that this is crazy.' T. Dalyell (Lab., West Lothian) briefly rose to say that it would be a sad day for the unions if the Lords amendment was rejected, as they too did not want forestry devolved.

The motion was *negatived* by 280 votes to 247, *a majority against the Government of 33.* The 249 Members (including tellers) in the Government lobby comprised 236 Labour, 6 Liberal, 3 Scottish National, 3 Plaid Cymru and 1 Ulster Unionist. The 282 Members (including tellers) in the Opposition lobby comprised 252 Conservative, 22 Labour, 6 Ulster Unionist, 1 Liberal and 1 Democratic Unionist.

Labour Members to vote against the motion:

Anderson, D.
Buchanan, R.
Carter-Jones, L.
Dalyell, T.
Douglas-Mann, B.
Dunwoody, Mrs G.
Evans, F.
Evans, I.

Heffer, E.
Hughes, R.
Kinnock, N.
Latham, A.
Molloy, W.
Newens, S.
Ovenden, J.

Parker, J.
Sandelson, N.
Short, Mrs R.
Spearing, N.
Torney, T.
Williams, A. L.
Woodall, A.

HC Deb. 954, 919–24
1977–8, No. 301.

SCOTLAND BILL [378]

Lords Amendments: 26 July 1978

New Clause A (Voting of Scottish Members of Parliament)

The Lords had inserted the new clause, which provided that (once the Scottish Assembly had met) if a Bill was given a Second Reading due to the voting behaviour of Members from Scottish constituencies (i.e. if without them, there would not be a majority for Second Reading) the Bill would be deemed not to have been read a Second time unless after the next fourteen days there was a second division which confirmed the decision that the Bill be read a Second time.

The Minister of State at the Privy Council Office, J. Smith, moved 'That this House doth disagree with the Lords in the said amendment'.

Mr Smith said the Government's view was that they opposed the proposition in principle, and suggested it was unrealistic as a practical proposition. He argued that the proposal was not sensible and should not be included in the Bill. 'I think the propoosal is a bit of a gimmick.'

For the Opposition, F. Pym supported the new clause. He thought it would help reduce slightly the divisiveness inherent in the Bill. It would allow a pause for second thoughts.

T. Dalyell (Lab., West Lothian) asked his colleagues to support the clause. He said that it did at least do something in the direction of pinning a constitutional price tag on the neck of the Assembly, and would act as a warning signal to the electors of Scotland during the referendum campaign.

The motion to disagree with the Lords amendment was *negatived* by 276 votes to 275, *a majority against the Government of 1*. The 277 Members (including tellers) in the Government lobby comprised 268 Labour and 9 Liberal. The 278 Members (including tellers) in the Opposition lobby comprised 255 Conservative, 9 Scottish National, 5 Labour, 4 Ulster Unionist, 3 Plaid Cymru and 2 Liberal. A small number of Conservative Members abstained from voting.[1]

Labour Members to vote against the motion:

Cunningham, G.	Evans, F.	Phipps, C.
Dalyell, T.	Garrett, W.	

HC Deb. 954, 1659–66
1977–8, No. 313.

[1] The Conservative abstainers included: C. Brocklebank-Fowler, A. Buchanan-Smith, M. Rifkind, J. Spence and P. Walker.

SCOTLAND BILL [379]

Lords Amendments: 26 July 1978

Clause 67 (Transfer of property)

The Lords had inserted an amendment to the clause, to provide that the provisions of the clause would not apply to land acquired by the Secretary of State as land suitable or for purposes connected with forestry or as land necessarily acquired with such land. (Under the original wording of the clause, the provisions would 'with the necessary modifications' apply.)

The Under-Secretary of State for Scotland, H. Ewing, moved formally 'That this House doth disagree with the Lords in the said amendment'.

The motion to disagree with the Lords amendment was *negatived* by 286 votes to 266, *a majority against the Government of 20*. The 268 Members (including tellers) in the Government lobby comprised 243 Labour,

11 Liberal, 10 Scottish National, 3 Plaid Cymru and 1 Conservative. The 288 Members (including tellers) in the Opposition lobby comprised 265 Conservative, 18 Labour and 5 Ulster Unionist.

Conservative to vote for the motion:

Buchanan-Smith, A.

Labour Members to vote against the motion:

Buchanan, R.	Evans, I.	Maynard, Miss J.
Cant, R.	Forrester, J.	Parker, J.
Dalyell, T.	Garrett, W.	Roberts, G.
Douglas-Mann, B.	Kelley, R.	Rodgers, G.
Dunwoody, Mrs G.	Kinnock, N.	Skinner, D.
Evans, F.	Lewis, R.	Wilson, W.

HC Deb. 954, 1665–70
1977–8, No. 314.

WALES BILL [380]

Lords Amendments: 26 July 1978

Clause 12 (Review of Local Government structure)

The House of Lords had suggested amendments in lieu of certain amendments to which the Commons had disagreed. On clause 12, the Lords proposed an amendment to provide that the Assembly would not (unless authorized by the Secretary of State) review the structure of local government in Wales (the authorization of the Secretary of State to be by order subject to the approval of each House).

The Under-Secretary of State for Wales, A. Jones, moved 'That this House doth disagree with the Lords in the said amendment'.

The Under-Secretary contended that the amendment was totally inappropriate given the substantial functions which the Bill conferred on the Assembly in relation to local government and to important services provided by local authorities.

I. Davies (Lab., Gower) said he could see nothing offensive in the amendment, and he thought it was a reasonable one in so far as it sought to re-establish the authority of the Secretary of State as to the timing of the review. I. Evans (Lab., Aberdare) put forward several reasons why he felt the Assembly should not have the power to carry out such a review. Having gone through a reorganization of local government not so long ago, he felt the counties and districts should be left alone.

The motion to disagree with the Lords amendment was carried by 292 votes to 271. The 294 Members (including tellers) in the Government lobby comprised 263 Labour, 11 Liberal, 9 Scottish National, 6 Ulster Unionist, 3 Plaid Cymru, 1 SDLP and 1 Irish Independent. The 273 Members (including tellers) in the Opposition lobby comprised 266 Conservative and 7 Labour.

Labour Members to vote against the motion:

Abse, L.	Evans, F.	Evans, J.
Dalyell, T.	Evans, I.	Kinnock, N.
Davies, I.		

HC Deb. 954, 1729–36
1977–8, No. 315.

WALES BILL [381]

Lords Amendments: 26 July 1978

Clause 37 (Industrial and economic guidelines)

The Lords deleted two sub-sections of the clause which required the Secretary of State, with Treasury approval, to prepare guidelines as to the exercise by the Assembly of its powers with respect to functions of the Welsh Development Agency relating to the promotion, financing, establishment, carrying on, growth, reorganization, modernization or development of industrial or commercial activities or undertakings, and any other functions of the Development Board for Rural Wales relating to economic development.

The Minister of State at the Privy Council Office, J. Smith, moved formally 'That this House doth disagree with the Lords in the said amendment.'

The motion was carried by 293 votes to 273. 3 Labour Members cross-voted to oppose the motion.

Labour Members to vote against the motion:

Abse, L.	Davies, I.	Evans, I.

HC Deb. 954, 1735–40
1977–78, No. 316.

CONSOLIDATED FUND (APPROPRIATION) BILL [382]

Second Reading: 1 August 1978

As usual, the Second Reading debate was given over to topics raised by Private Members.

After three-and-a-half hours' debate, the Government moved the closure. The closure was carried by 139 votes to 5, Opposition Members (including member of the Shadow Cabinet) supporting the Government. The 141 Members (including tellers) in the Government lobby comprised 127 Labour, 7 Conservative,[1] 5 Liberal, 1 Scottish National and 1 SDLP. The 7 Members (including tellers) to oppose the closure comprised 4 Conservative and 3 Ulster Unionist.

Conservatives to vote against closure:

Bottomley, P.*   Lawrence, I.   Neubert, M.
Hodgson, R.*

HC Deb. 955, 711–2
1977–8, No. 322.

The Division took place at 12.14 p.m. Second Reading was then agreed without a division.

[1] M. Carlisle, N. Edwards, P. Fry, Mrs J. Knight, T. Newton, M. Rifkind and Sir G. Sinclair.

The Session of 1978-9

SOUTHERN RHODESIA [383]

Prayer: 8 November 1978

The Secretary of State for Foreign and Commonwealth Affairs, Dr D. Owen, moved 'That the draft Southern Rhodesia Act 1965 (Continuation) Order 1978, which was laid before this House on 24th October 1978, in the last Session of parliament, be approved.'

As in previous years, a number of Conservative backbench opponents of Rhodesian sanctions rose to oppose the order.

The debate followed a two-day debate on Rhodesia, during which a senior Conservative Member, R. Maudling (C., Chipping Barnet), had announced his intention to vote against the continuation of sanctions. 'I have not done so before. I shall do so tonight for the first time, for two reasons. My first reason is that the situation has completely changed since the March settlement. My second reason is that the Government have totally failed to seize the opportunity presented by the March settlement.'

In the debate on the order, F. Pym for the Opposition said that they felt, notwithstanding their criticisms of the Government, that for the moment things were best left as they were.

The order was approved by 320 votes to 121, with the Opposition abstaining officially from voting. The 322 Members (including tellers) in the Government lobby comprised 304 Labour, 9 Liberal, 5 Scottish National, 2 Plaid Cymru, 1 SDLP and 1 Scottish Labour. The 123 Members (including tellers) to vote against the order comprised 116 Conservative, 6 Ulster Unionist and 1 Democratic Unionist.

Conservatives to vote against the order:

Aitken, J.
Amery, J.
Atkinson, D.
Bell, R.*
Bendall, V.
Bennett, Sir F.
Benyon, W.
Biggs-Davison, J.
Boscawen, R.
Braine, Sir B.
Brotherton, M.
Brown, Sir E.
Budgen, N.*
Burden, F.
Channon, P.
Churchill, W.
Clark, A.
Clark, W.
Dodsworth, G.
Drayson, B.
Durant, T.
Eden, Sir J.
Fairbairn, N.

Harvie Anderson, Miss B.
Hastings, S.
Hawkins, P.
Holland, P.
Hordern, P.
Howell, R.
Hutchison, M. C.
Irving, C.
James, D.
Jessel, T.
Jones, A.
Kaberry, Sir D.
Kellett-Bowman, Mrs E.
Kershaw, A.
Kimball, M.
King, E.
Knight, Mrs J.
Langford-Holt, Sir J.
Latham, M.
Lawrence, I.
Lewis, K.
Lloyd, I.
Loveridge, J.

Nelson, A.
Newton, T.
Normanton, T.
Osborn, J.
Page, J.
Pattie, G.
Pink, R. B.
Price, D.
Rees-Davies, W.
Rhys Williams, Sir B.
Ridley, N.
Ridsdale, J.
Rodgers, Sir J.
Rost, P.
Scott-Hopkins, J.
Shaw, G.
Shelton, W.
Shepherd, C.
Shersby, M.
Sims, R.
Skeet, T.
Smith, D.
Spence, J.

Farr, J.	McAdden, Sir S.	Spicer, M.
Fell, A.	Macfarlane, N.	Sproat, I.
Fookes, Miss J.	MacKay, A.	Stainton, K.
Fraser, H.	Macmillan, M.	Stokes, J.
Fry, P.	Mates, M.	Taylor, R.
Galbraith, T.	Maudling, R.	Tebbit, N.
Gardiner, G.	Mawby, R.	Wakeham, J.
Gilmour, Sir J.	Mayhew, P.	Walker-Smith, Sir D.
Glyn, A.	Meyer, Sir A.	Wall, P.
Goodhart, P.	Mitchell, D.	Warren, K.
Goodhew, V.	Moate, R.	Wells, J.
Gorst, J.	Montgomery, F.	Whitney, R.
Gow, I.	Morgan, G.	Wiggin, J.
Griffiths, E.	Morgan-Giles, M.	Winterton, N.
Hamilton, A.	Morris, M.	Wood, R.
Hannam, J.	Mudd, D.	

HC Deb. 957, 1141–6
1978–9, No. 2.

The Conservative dissenting lobby represented the largest dissenting lobby in Conservative post-war history, the first occasion on which more than 100 Conservatives dissented in a whipped division.[1] Of the dissenters, J. Biggs-Davison and W. Churchill were junior Opposition spokesmen. After the division, Mr Biggs-Davison resigned his Front Bench post, and Mr Churchill was dismissd from his.

[1] Over 100 Conservatives had dissented from Front Bench advice in the 1966 Parliament and voted, on two occasions, against proposals for reform of the House of Lords, but on neither occasion was the whip applied. See Philip Norton, *Dissension in the House of Commons 1945–74* (1975), pp. 304–5 and 313–14. The two most sizable dissenting Conservative lobbies after the above were those on the American loan in 1945 and on Rhodesian oil sanctions in 1965. See Norton, *op. cit.*, pp. 3–4 and 256.

HOUSE OF COMMONS (REDISTRIBUTION OF SEATS) BILL [384]

Second Reading: 28 November 1978

The Secretary of State for Northern Ireland, R. Mason, moved the Second Reading of the Bill. The Bill was to give effect to the recommendation of a Speaker's Conference on electoral law, and provided that the number of parliamentary seats for Northern Ireland should be 'not greater than 18 or less than 16', giving the Boundary Commissioners a target figure of 17 at which to aim. The background of the Bill, Mr Mason explained, was that the province's parliamentary representation was set at 12 at a time when it had a devolved Parliament; given the decisions now taken centrally, and the responsibilities of central government, there was a need for a broadly similar standard of representation at Westminster for every part of the United Kingdom. He contended that Northern Ireland's representation should be increased on grounds of equity, and to allow electors the same access to their Members as elsewhere; he also contended that it would reduce the burden on the Members themselves.

During the debate, a number of Labour backbenchers rose to oppose the Bill. R. Mellish (Lab., Bermondsey) declared that he would vote against the Bill. 'My principles and loyalties, not only to the Labour Party but to the people who are associated with me, will not allow me to support and perpetuate a system that was started in 1920, with the representation of the Ulster Unionists. I never wanted them, I do not want them now, and I live for the day when they are out of this House for ever.' K. McNamara (Lab., Hull, Central) claimed the Government had reversed its policy on representation, and had been influenced by the powerful position in the House of the Ulster Unionists. P. Rose (Lab., Manchester, Blackley) felt the Bill would exacerbate hostility, provoke antagonism and cause a greater distrust of the Government.

(1) A Liberal reasoned amendment for rejection, on the grounds that the Bill failed to provide an opportunity for the House to determine whether or not the Members from Northern Ireland should be elected by a system of proportional representation, was negatived by 355 votes to 27, the Opposition supporting the Government. The 357 Members (including tellers) in the Government lobby comprised 195 Labour, 151 Conservative, 8 Ulster Unionist, 1 Democratic Unionist, 1 SDLP and 1 Irish Independent. The 29 Members (including tellers) to support the amendment comprised 12 Conservative, 11 Liberal, 3 Scottish National, 2 Labour and 1 Scottish Labour. Over thirty Conservative Members would appear also to have abstained from voting.[1]

Conservatives to vote for the amendment:

Buchanan-Smith, A.	Knox, D.	Rathbone, T.
Dean, P.	Meyer, Sir A.	Sinclair, Sir G.
Fisher, Sir N.	Morris, M.	Walker, P.
Kershaw, A.	Morrison, C.	Young, Sir G.[2]

Labour Members to vote for the amendment:

Colquhoun, Ms M.	Home Robertson, J.

(2) The Bill was then given a Second Reading by 350 votes to 48,[3] the Opposition supporting the Government. The 352 Members (including tellers) in the Government lobby comprised 153 Labour, 186 Conservative, 8 Ulster Unionist, 2 Scottish National, 1 Liberal, 1 Democratic Unionist and 1 Scottish Labour. The 50 Members (including tellers) to oppose the Bill comprised 38 Labour, 9 Liberal, 1 Scottish National, 1 SDLP and 1 Irish Independent. A Government whip abstained from voting.[4]

Labour Members to vote against Second Reading:

Atkinson, N.	Kerr, R.	Ovenden, J.
Buchan, N.	Latham, A.	Price, C.
Canavan, D.	Lee, J.	Richardson, Miss J.
Carmichael, N.	Litterick, T.*	Rodgers, G.
Carter-Jones, L.	Loyden, E.	Rose, P.
Clemitson, I.[5]	Lyon, A.	Sandelson, N.
Colquhoun, Ms M.	McGuire, M.	Short, Mrs R.
Corbett, R.	McNamara, K.	Skinner, D.
Ellis, J.*	Maynard, Miss J.	Spriggs, L.
Flannery, M.	Mellish, R.	Thomas, R.
Fletcher, T.	Mikardo, I.	Thorne, S.
Grocott, B.[5]	Newens, S.	Woodall, A.
Home Robertson, J.	Orbach, M.	

HC Deb. 959, 353–62
1978–9, Nos. 4 and 5.

[1] For the Opposition, A. Neave had made it clear that 'Our view is that the effect of introducing a proportional representation system for parliamentary elections would be completely against the view that we have always adopted, that there should be one uniform system for all parts of the United Kingdom.' The Liberal amendment, he said, 'must be resisted'. Among the Conservatives apparently abstaining (absent from the division but voting in the subsequent one) were two members of the Shadow Cabinet, Sir I. Gilmour and F. Pym. Among those voting for the amendment was an Opposition whip.

[2] An Opposition whip.

[3] According to *Hansard*, 49 Members voted against, but only 48 names are listed.

[4] A. Stallard, an assistant whip. He was subsequently seen by the Government Chief Whip 'and was let off with a reprimand'. *The Times*, 30 November 1978.

[5] Mr Grocott was Parliamentary Private Secretary to the Minister of Agriculture, and Mr Clemitson P.P.S. to the Secretary of State for Employment. The day following the division they resigned their respective positions. *The Times*, 30 November 1978.

EUROPEAN ASSEMBLY CONSTITUENCIES (ENGLAND) [385]

Prayer: 4 December 1978

The Minister of State at the Home Office, B. John, moved 'That the draft European Assembly Constituencies (England) Order 1978, which was laid before this House on 23rd November, be approved.'

Mr John explained that the Government had accepted the final proposals of the Boundary Commissions (for England, Scotland and Wales) and had laid them before the House without modification.

R. Cryer (Lab., Keighley) said that 'I object to this sort of order, which is a stage further towards a federal State of Europe in which the power will shift away from the United Kingdom Parliament'. The order was against Labour Party Policy; it represented the end of a miserable road of abrogation of Labour Party policies. D. Skinner (Lab., Bolsover) contended that members of the European Assembly would cease to be accountable once they got to the Assembly, and said that the House was faced now with the appalling proposition that the taxpayers would be asked to finance the elections in some form of state aid. 'What a carry on!'

The order was approved by 112 votes to 23, the Opposition supporting the Government. The 114 Members (including tellers) in the Government lobby comprised 99 Labour and 15 Conservative. The 25 Members (including tellers) to oppose the order comprised 16 Labour, 6 Liberal, 2 Plaid Cymru and 1 Ulster Unionist.

Labour Members to vote against the order:

Allaun, F.	Lee, J.	Short, Mrs R.
Bidwell, S.	Loyden, E.*	Skinner, D.
Cryer, R.*	Madden, M.	Spriggs, L.
Ellis, J.	Maynard, Miss J.	Tilley, J.
Hoyle, D.	Rodgers, G.	Wise, A.
Kerr, R.		

HC Deb. 959, 1177–80
1978–9, No. 7.

EUROPEAN ASSEMBLY CONSTITUENCIES (SCOTLAND)
[386]

Prayer: 4 December 1978

A Government whip moved formally 'That the draft European Assembly Constituencies (Scotland) Order 1978, which was laid before this House on 23rd November, be approved.'

The order had been discussed in conjunction with the order for England (see preceding division). The order embodied the recommendations of the Boundary Commissioners for the constituencies in Scotland for the elections to the European Assembly.

The order was approved by 113 votes to 22, with the Opposition supporting the Government. The 115 Members (including tellers) in the Government lobby comprised 101 Labour and 14 Conservative. The 24 Members (including tellers) to oppose the order comprised 15 Labour, 6 Liberal, 2 Plaid Cymru and 1 Scottish National.

Labour Members to vote against the order:

Allaun, F.	Kerr, R.	Rodgers, G.
Bidwell, S.	Lee, J.*	Short, Mrs R.
Cryer, R.	Loyden, E.	Skinner, D.
Ellis, J.	Madden, M.*	Spriggs, L.
Hoyle, D.	Maynard, Miss J.	Wise, Mrs A.

HC Deb. 959, 1181–2
1978–9, No. 8.

EUROPEAN ASSEMBLY CONSTITUENCIES (WALES) [387]

Prayer: 4 December 1978

A Government whip moved formally 'That the draft European Assembly Constituencies (Wales) Order 1978, which was laid before this House on 23rd November, be approved.'

The order had been discussed in conjunction with the order for England (see above). The order embodied the recommendations of the Boundary Commissioners for the Welsh constituencies for the election of members to the European Assembly.

The order was approved by 113 votes to 26, with the Opposition supporting the Government. The 115 Members (including tellers) in the Government lobby comprised 102 Labour and 13 Conservative. The 28 Members (including tellers) to oppose the order comprised 16 Labour, 8 Liberal, 2 Plaid Cymru, 1 Conservative and 1 Scottish National.

Labour Members to vote against the order:

Allaun, F.	Lee, J.	Short, Mrs R.
Bidwell, S.	Loyden, E.	Skinner, D.
Cryer, R.	Madden, M.	Spriggs, L.
Ellis, J.	Maynard, Miss J.	Torney, T.
Hoyle, D.*	Rodgers, G.*	Wise, Mrs A.
Kerr, R.		

Conservative to vote against the order:

Moate, R.

HC Deb. 959, 1183–4
1978–9, No. 9.

NORTHERN IRELAND (EMERGENCY PROVISIONS)   [388]

Prayer: 6 December 1978

The Secretary of State for Northern Ireland, R. Mason, moved 'That the draft Northern Ireland (Emergency Provisions) Act 1978 (Continuance) (No. 2) Order 1978, which was laid before this House on 21st November, be approved.'

Mr Mason explained that the purpose of the order was to extend for a further six months the availability of the powers provided by the Emergency Provisions Act. He did not lightly ask for their renewal. There had been prolonged lulls in terrorist activity since June but the Provisional IRA continued to indulge in violence for the sake of violence. He hoped the time would not be too far off when the Government would be able to recommend that one or more of the Act's provisions be allowed to lapse.

S. Thorne (Lab., Preston, South) felt that by ending emergency powers there might be a response towards bringing an end to the reign of violence in Northern Ireland. T. Litterick (Lab., Birmingham, Selly Oak) objected to the kind of power that the Act was giving an executive arm of the State. The Act was about relying on a military power to get political solutions, and virtually guaranteed that there would be no political solution while it was on the statute book. M. Flannery (Lab., Sheffield, Hillsborough) felt that the emergency provisions 'have not a snowball in hell's chance of contributing to or solving the problems in Northern Ireland'. He would vote against them.

The order was approved by 113 votes to 10, with the Opposition supporting the Government. The 115 Members (including tellers) in the Government lobby comprised 94 Labour, 9 Conservative, 8 Ulster Unionist and 4 Liberal. The 12 Members (including tellers) to oppose the order comprised 11 Labour and 1 SDLP.

Labour Members to vote against the order:

Flannery, M.	Madden, M.	Skinner, D.
Lamond, J.	Mikardo, I.	Thomas, R.
Litterick, T.*	Richardson, Miss J.	Thorne, S.*
Loyden, E.	Selby, H.	

HC Deb. 959, 1583–6
1978–9, No. 11.

BUSINESS OF THE HOUSE (SUPPLY) [389]

7 December 1978

A Government whip moved formally 'That at this day's sitting, Mr Speaker shall put forthwith any Questions necessary to dispose of the proceedings on the Motions in the name of Mr Robert Sheldon relating to Civil and Defence Estimates as soon as the House has entered upon the business of Supply.'

R. Thomas (Lab., Bristol, North-West) rose to oppose the motion. He said that many Labour Members felt it was indefensible that they should be expected, on the nod, to vote for or against the substantial sums of money involved.

The Lord President of the Council and Leader of the House, M. Foot, pointed out that there would be a minimum of three days of debate on the individual services, two days on the Defence White Paper in the Spring, and a debate on discipline in July. All the Votes before the House would come up again, and any one of them could be the subject of the remaining 26 Supply Days. He hoped his hon. Friends would take this matter into account.

F. Allaun (Lab., Salford, East) rose to say that he repudiated what the Lord President had said. If the motion was carried, they would pass a large sum of money without debate. M. English (Lab., Nottingham, West) said that it could not be right that the whole of public expenditure was ignored because it could not be discussed anywhere once it had been decided to discuss another subject on a Supply Day. That day was a good example. S. Newens (Lab., Newens) argued that the Supplementary Estimates should be debated, as they would affect the attitude of Members to the public expenditure package they were being asked to approve, and needed to consider their effects upon the global sum of public expenditure and upon inflation.

After further discussion, the Opposition Chief Whip moved 'That the Question be now put'. [Discussion on the motion was eating into the time of the Opposition's Supply Day Debate.] The closure motion was carried by 266 votes to 106, with the Opposition side being whipped in support and the Government allowing apparently an unwhipped vote (Ministers present in both lobbies and some whips abstaining). The 268 Members (including tellers) to support closure comprised 159 Conservative, 99 Labour, 7 Liberal and 3 Ulster Unionist. The 108 Members (including tellers) to oppose closure comprised 96 Labour, 7 Scottish National, 2 Plaid Cymru, 1 SDLP, 1 Ulster Unionist and 1 Liberal.

Closure having been carried, the motion was then put, and the Government whips put on in support of the motion. The motion was carried by 338 votes to 92, with both the Government and Opposition supporting it. The 340 Members (including tellers) in the Government lobby comprised 170 Conservative, 167 Labour and 3 Ulster Unionist. The 94 Members (including tellers) to oppose the motion comprised 75 Labour, 9 Liberal, 7 Scottish National, 2 Plaid Cymru and 1 Ulster Unionist.

Labour Members to vote against the motion:

Allaun, F.	Grocott, B.	Pavitt, L.
Ashton, J.	Hayman, Mrs H.	Price, C.
Atkins, R.	Heffer, E.	Richardson, Miss J.
Bennett, A.	Hoyle, D.	Roberts, G.
Bidwell, S.	Hughes, R.	Robertson, G.
Boothroyd, Miss B.	Hughes, R. J.	Robinson, G.
Bray, J.	Jeger, Mrs L.	Rodgers, G.
Buchan, N.	Jenkins, H.	Rooker, J.
Butler, Mrs J.	Jones, D.	Ryman, J.
Carmichael, N.	Kelley, R.	Sedgemore, B.
Carter-Jones, L.	Kilroy-Silk, R.	Selby, H.
Castle, Mrs B.	Kinnock, N.	Short, Mrs R.
Cook, R.	Lamond, J	Silverman, J
Corbett, R.	Lee, J.*	Skinner, D.
Cryer, R.	Lestor, Miss J.	Spearing, N.
Dewar, D.	Litterick, T.	Spriggs, L.
Edge, G.	Loyden, E.	Stoddart, D.
Ellis, J.	Madden, M.	Thomas, R.
English, M.	Maynard, Miss J.	Thorne, S.*
Evans, F.	Mikardo, I.	Torney, T.
Evans, I.	Mitchell, A.	Tuck, R.
Fernyhough, E.	Morton, G.	Watkinson, J.
Flannery, M.	Newens, S.	White, F.
Fowler, G.	Orbach, M.	Wilson, W.
George, B.	Parry, R.	Wise, Mrs A.

HC Deb. 959, 1663–8
1978–9, No. 13.

The Estimates were then put (see below).

CIVIL ESTIMATES, 1979–80 (VOTE ON ACCOUNT) [390]

Supply: 7 December 1978

The Financial Secretary to the Treasury, R. Sheldon, moved 'That a sum, not exceeding £17,470,584,900, be granted to Her Majesty out of the Consolidated Fund, on account, for or towards defraying the charges for Civil Services for the year ending on 31st March 1980, as set out in House of Commons Paper No. 55.'

The motion was moved formally, and the Question put forthwith (see preceding division).

The motion was carried by 190 votes to 52, with the Opposition abstaining from voting. The 192 Members (including tellers) in the Government lobby comprised 189 Labour and 3 Conservative. The 54 Members (including tellers) to oppose the motion comprised 43 Labour, 9 Liberal, 1 Ulster Unionist and 1 SDLP.

Conservatives to vote for the motion:

Braine, Sir B.	Mitchell, D.	Morgan, G.

Labour Members to vote against the motion:

Atkins, R.	Fowler, G.	Roberts, G.
Atkinson, N.	George, B.	Rodgers, G.
Bennett, A.	Grocott, B.	Rooker, J.
Bidwell, S.	Hughes, R. J.	Ryman, J.
Boothroyd, Miss B.	Jeger, Mrs L.	Selby, H.
Buchan, N.	Kelley, R.	Short, Mrs R.
Butler, Mrs J.	Kilroy-Silk, R.	Skinner, D.
Carmichael, N.	Kinnock, N.	Spriggs, L.
Cook, R.	Lamond, J.	Thomas, R.*
Corbett, R.	Lee, J.*	Thorne, S.
Edge, G.	Loyden, E.	Tomney, F.
Ellis, J.	Maynard, Miss J.	Tuck, R.
English, M.	Parry, R.	Wilson, W.
Evans, F.	Richardson, Miss J.	Wise, Mrs A.
Flannery, M.		

HC Deb. 959, 1669–72
1978–9, No. 14.

CIVIL ESTIMATES (CLASS XIII A), 1979-80
(VOTE ON ACCOUNT)   [391]

Supply: 7 December 1978

The Financial Secretary to the Treasury, R. Sheldon, moved 'That a sum, not exceeding £2,726,000 be granted to Her Majesty out of the Consolidated Fund, on account, for or towards defraying the charges for House of Commons: Administration for the year ending on 31st March 1980, as set out in House of Commons Paper No. 59.'

The motion was moved formally, and the Question put forthwith (see above).

The motion was carried by 192 votes to 57, with the Opposition abstaining from voting. The 194 Members (including tellers) in the Government lobby comprised 193 Labour and 1 Conservative. The 59 Members (including tellers) to oppose the motion comprised 44 Labour, 9 Liberal, 3 Scottish National, 2 Plaid Cymru and 1 Ulster Unionist.

Conservative to vote for the motion:

Morgan, G.

Labour Members to vote against the motion:

Atkins, R.	Fowler, G.	Roberts, G.
Atkinson, N.	George, B.	Robertson, G.
Bennett, A.	Hughes, R. J.	Rodgers, G.
Bidwell, S.	Jeger, Mrs L.	Rooker, J.
Butler, Mrs J.	Kerr, R.	Ryman, J.
Carter-Jones, L.	Kilroy-Silk, R.	Short, Mrs R.
Castle, Mrs B.	Kinnock, N.	Skinner, D.
Cook, R.	Lamond, J.	Spriggs, L.
Corbett, R.	Lee, J.*	Thomas, R.*
Cryer, R.	Litterick, T.	Thorne, S.
Edge, G.	Loyden, E.	Tuck, R.
Ellis, J.	Maynard, Miss J.	White, F.
English, M.	Newens, S.	Wilson, W.
Evans, F.	Parry, R.	Wise, Mrs A.
Flannery, M.	Richardson, Miss J.	

HC Deb. 959, 1671-4
1978-9, No. 15.

CIVIL SUPPLEMENTARY ESTIMATES, 1978–79 [392]

Supply: 7 December 1978

The Financial Secretary to the Treasury, R. Sheldon, moved 'That a further Supplementary sum, not exceeding £1,860,115,000 be granted to Her Majesty out of the Consolidated Fund to defray the charges which will come in course of payment during the year ending on 31st March 1979 for expenditure on Civil Services, as set out in House of Commons Paper No. 53.'

The motion was moved formally, and the Question put forthwith (see above).

The motion was carried by 201 votes to 46, with the Opposition abstaining from voting. The 203 Members (including tellers) to support the motion comprised 200 Labour and 3 Conservative. The 48 Members (including tellers) to oppose the motion comprised 36 Labour, 9 Liberal, 2 Plaid Cymru and 1 Ulster Unionist.

Conservatives to vote for the motion:

Forman, N.   Maxwell-Hyslop, R.   Morgan, G.

Labour Members to vote against the motion:

Atkins, R.	George, B.	Rooker, J.
Bennett, A.	Jones, D.	Ryman, J.
Bidwell, S.	Kelley, R.	Selby, H.
Carter-Jones, L.	Kilroy-Silk, R.	Short, Mrs R.
Castle, Mrs B.	Kinnock, N.	Spriggs, L.
Cook, R.	Lamond, J.	Thomas, R.*
Corbett, R.	Lee, J.*	Thorne, S.
Edge, G.	Maynard, Miss J.	Torney, T.
English, M.	Newens, S.	Tuck, R.
Evans, F.	Parry, R.	White, F.
Flannery, M.	Richardson, Miss J.	Wilson, W.
Fowler, G.	Roberts, G.	Wise, Mrs A.

HC Deb. 959, 1673–6
1978–9, No. 16.

DEFENCE ESTIMATES, 1979–80 (VOTE ON ACCOUNT) [393]

Supply: 7 December 1978

The Financial Secretary to the Treasury, R. Sheldon, moved 'That a sum, not exceeding £3,155,066,000, be granted to Her Majesty out of the Consolidated Fund, on account, for or towards defraying the charges for Defence Services for the year ending on 31st March 1980, as set out in House of Commons Paper No. 54.'

The motion was moved formally, and the Question put forthwith (see above).

The motion was carried by 342 votes to 68, the Opposition supporting the Government. The 344 Members (including tellers) in the Government lobby comprised 183 Labour, 156 Conservative and 5 Ulster Unionist. The 70 Members (including tellers) to oppose the motion comprised 58 Labour, 10 Liberal and 2 Plaid Cymru.

Labour Members to vote against the motion:

Allaun, F.*	Garrett, J.	Parry, R.
Ashton, J.	Grocott, B.	Pavitt, L.
Atkins, R.	Hayman, Mrs H.	Price, C.
Atkinson, N.	Hoyle, D.	Richardson, Miss J.
Bennett, A.	Hughes, R.	Roberts, G.
Bidwell, S.	Jeger, Mrs L.	Rodgers, G.
Buchan, N.	Jenkins, H.	Rooker, J.
Butler, Mrs J.	Kelley, R.	Ryman, J.
Carmichael, N.	Kilroy-Silk, R.	Sedgemore, B.
Cook, R.	Kinnock, N.	Selby, H.
Corbett, R.	Lamond, J.	Short, Mrs R.
Cryer, R.	Lee, J.	Silverman, J.
Edge, G.	Litterick, T.	Skinner, D.
Ellis, J.	Madden, M.	Thomas, R.
English, M.	Maynard, Miss J.	Thorne, S.*
Evans, F.	Mikardo, I.	Torney, T.
Evans, I.	Moonman, E.	Tuck, R.
Fernyhough, E.	Morton, G.	Wilson, W.
Flannery, M.	Newens, S.	Wise, Mrs A.
Fowler, G.		

HC Deb. 959, 1677–80
1978–9, No. 17.

DEFENCE SUPPLEMENTARY ESTIMATES, 1978–79   [394]

Supply: 7 December 1978

The Financial Secretary to the Treasury, R. Sheldon, moved 'That a further Supplementary sum, not exceeding £248,547,000, be granted to Her Majesty out of the Consolidated Fund to defray the charges which will come in course of payment during the year ending on 31st March 1979 for expenditure on Defence Services, as set out in House of Commons Paper No. 52.'

The motion was moved formally, and the Question put forthwith (see above).

The motion was carried by 335 votes to 69, the Opposition voting with the Government. The 337 Members (including tellers) in the Government lobby comprised 179 Labour, 152 Conservative and 6 Ulster Unionist. The 71 Members (including tellers) to oppose the motion comprised 59 Labour, 10 Liberal and 2 Plaid Cymru.

Labour Members to vote against the motion:

Allaun, F.	Flannery, M.	Newens, S.
Ashton, J.	Fowler, G.	Parry, R.
Atkins, R.	Garrett, J.	Pavitt, L.
Atkinson, N.	Grocott, B.	Price, C.
Bennett, A.	Hayman, Mrs H.	Richardson, Miss J.
Bidwell, S.	Hoyle, D.	Roberts, G.
Buchan, N.	Hughes, R.	Rodgers, G.
Butler, Mrs J.	Hughes, R. J.	Rooker, J.
Carmichael, N.	Jeger, Mrs L.	Ryman, J.
Carter-Jones, L.	Jenkins, H.	Sedgemore, B.
Castle, Mrs B.	Kelley, R.	Selby, H.
Cook, R.	Kilroy-Silk, R.	Short, Mrs R.
Corbett, R.	Kinnock, N.	Skinner, D.
Cryer, R.	Lamond, J.	Thomas, R.*
Edge, G.	Lee, J.	Thorne, S.*
Ellis, J.	Litterick, T.	Torney, T.
English, M.	Loyden, E.	Tuck, R.
Evans, F.	Maynard, Miss J.	Wilson, W.
Evans, I.	Mikardo, I.	Wise, Mrs A.
Fernyhough, E.	Morton, G.	

HC Deb. 959, 1681–4
1978–9, No. 18.

DEFENCE ESTIMATES [395]

7 December 1978

Following the putting of a series of Estimates votes formally, pursuant to a motion agreed by the House preceding the votes (see preceding divisions), a number of Labour Members rose on various points of order—requesting a Government reply to the debate on the motion that resulted in the Estimates being taken without debate, regretting that a longer debate on the motion had not been allowed, and related points—as a means apparently of demonstrating opposition to the Estimates having been required to be taken formally, without debate.

After points of order had been raised for over twenty minutes, Mr Speaker declared that he thought the time had come to stop points of order 'because, clearly, there have been frivolous points of order'. J. Lee (Lab., Birmingham, Handsworth) then rose, and moved 'That Strangers do withdraw'.

Notice having been taken of the presence of Strangers, Mr Speaker put the Question forthwith, as required under S.O. 115.

The motion was negatived by 223 votes to 2, the Opposition voting with the Government. The 225 Members (including tellers) in the Government lobby comprised 108 Labour, 100 Conservative, 9 Liberal, 5 Ulster Unionist, 2 Scottish National and 1 Plaid Cymru. The 4 Members (including tellers) to support the motion were Labour Members.

Labour Members to vote for the motion:

Lamond, J.   Selby, H.   Thomas, R.*
Lee, J.*

HC Deb. 959, 1689–92
1978–9, No. 19.

As a result of the amount of time taken up on the motion for the Estimates to be taken without debate, on the divisions on the Estimates themselves (see above), and on the points of order and division on Mr Lee's motion, there was insufficient time for debate on the Opposition Supply Day subject of Government economic sanctions, and, after discussions during a brief suspension of the sitting, the debate was re-arranged. See *HC Deb.* 959, c. 1693–99.

ADJOURNMENT (CHRISTMAS AND WINTER) [396]

12 December 1978

On the Christmas and Winter adjournment motion (for the House to adjourn from 15 December to 15 January 1979 and from 23 February to 5 March), a number of backbenchers rose to pose various questions, recommending that the adjournment should be shortened in order to allow for debates to take place on them. D. Crouch (C., Canterbury) wanted a debate on parliamentary reform. G. Younger (C., Ayr) raised the question of the rate support grant for Scotland, contending that the time allocated for its debate was insufficient. J. Stokes (C., Halesowen and Stourbridge) did not want the House to adjourn until it had debated the state of the nation.

At the end of the debate, the motion was approved by 143 votes to 23, with the Opposition abstaining from voting. The 145 Members (including tellers) in the Government lobby comprised 136 Labour, 5 Liberal, 3 Scottish National and 1 Plaid Cymru. The 25 Members (including tellers) to oppose the motion comprised 23 Conservative and 2 Ulster Unionist.

Conservatives to vote against the motion:

Adley, R.*	Glyn, A.	Rhodes James, R.
Atkinson, D.	Hamilton, A.	Smith, D.
Baker, K.	Hodgson, R.	Smith, T.
Buchanan-Smith, A.*	Marten, N.	Sproat, I.
Clarke, K.	Maxwell-Hyslop, R.	Vaughan, G.
Costain, A.	Montgomery, F.	Winterton, N.
Crouch, D.	Page, J.	Younger, G.
Eyre, R.	Page, R. G.	

HC Deb. 960, 337–40
1978–9, No. 21.

CONSOLIDATED FUND BILL [397]

Second Reading: 12 December 1978

Following discussion on various Private Members' topics under the auspices of the Second Reading debate of the Consolidated Fund Bill, during an all-night sitting, the Government moved the closure at 10.20 a.m.

The closure was carried by 152 votes to 43. 1 Labour Member cross-voted to oppose closure.[1]

Labour Member to vote against closure:

Ogden, E.

HC Deb. 960, 617–8
1978–9, No. 22.

The Bill was then given a Second Reading without a division.

Mr Ogden voted against closure as a protest, as he had planned to take part in debate on one of the later items down for debate (on outer-city policy).[2]

---

[1] According to the division lists, N. Fairbairn (C., Kinross and West Perthshire) entered the Government lobby to support closure, but the inclusion of his name is a mistake. N. Fairbairn QC, MP to author. According to the division lists, the Solicitor-General, P. Archer, voted in both lobbies.

[2] E. Ogden MP to author.

BUSINESS OF THE HOUSE [398]

14 December 1978

A Government whip moved a motion to allow various Rate Support Grant motions to be proceeded with, though opposed, after ten o'clock, though limiting debate on them to a total of four hours.

P. Emery (C., Honiton) moved an amendment designed to ensure separate debates on the orders covering England and Scotland.

The amendment was negatived on a party vote by 217 votes to 177. 1 Labour Member cross-voted to support the amendment.

Labour Member to vote for the amendment:

Hooley, F.

HC Deb. 960, 915–8
1978–9, No. 27.

Mr Hooley voted for the amendment as he wanted adequate time to be devoted to debating the order for England.[1]

---

[1] 'This matter caused acute controversy in Sheffield in 1978 and I felt that adequate time should be given to debating the whole matter—especially as about £7.5 billion of public money was involved.' Frank Hooley MP to author.

BUSINESS OF THE HOUSE [399]

17 January 1979

At 10.00 p.m., during Committee stage of the House of Commons (Redistribution of Seats) Bill, a Government whip moved the procedural exemption motion to allow the Bill to be proceeded with at that sitting, though opposed, until any hour.

The motion was carried by 162 votes to 32, with the Opposition supporting the Government. The 164 Members (including tellers) in the Government lobby comprised 131 Labour, 23 Conservative, 9 Ulster Unionist and 1 Democratic Unionist. The 34 Members (including tellers) to oppose the motion comprised 27 Labour, 5 Liberal, 1 SDLP, and (according to the division lists) one Conservative who voted in both lobbies, in this lobby in error.

Labour Members to vote against the motion:

Canavan, D.	Loyden, E.	Richardson, Miss J.
Corbett, R.	McNamara, K.*	Rodgers, G.
Cryer, R.	Madden, M.	Skinner, D.
Ellis, J.	Mahon, S.	Stallard, A.
Flannery, M.	Maynard, Miss J.	Thomas, R.*
Fletcher, T.	Mikardo, I.	Thorne, S.
Home Robertson, J.	O'Halloran, M.	White, F.
Latham, A.	Ovenden, J.	Wise, Mrs A.
Litterick, T.	Parry, R.	Woodall, A.

HC Deb. 960, 1835–8
1978–9, No. 34.

HOUSE OF COMMONS (REDISTRIBUTION OF SEATS) BILL [400]

Committee: 17 January 1979

Clause 1 (Increase of number of constituencies in Northern Ireland)

I. Paisley (Dem. U., Antrim, North) moved an amendment to provide that the number of parliamentary constituencies in Northern Ireland should be not more than 24 or less than 21. [Under the clause, the number of Northern Ireland constituencies was raised from 12 to not more than 18 or less than 16.]

After more than five hours of debate on the amendment, the Government moved the closure. A number of Labour backbenchers who wished to speak on the amendment and related amendments but had not been called[1] opposed the motion.

The closure was carried by 150 votes to 27, with the Opposition supporting the Government. The 152 Members (including tellers) in the Government lobby comprised 126 Labour, 15 Conservative, 8 Ulster Unionist and 3 Liberal. The 29 Members (including tellers) to oppose the motion comprised 23 Labour, 3 Liberal, 1 SDLP, 1 Ulster Unionist and 1 Democratic Unionist.

Labour Members to vote against closure:

Canavan, D.	McNamara, K.*	Skinner, D.
Corbett, R.	Madden, M.	Stallard, A.
Cryer, R.	Mahon, S.	Thomas, R.
Ellis, J.	Mikardo, I.	Thorne, S.*
Flannery, M.	O'Halloran, M.	White, F.
Home Robertson, J.	Parry, R.	Wise, Mrs A.
Litterick, T.	Richardson, Miss J.	Woodall, A.
Loyden, E.	Rodgers, G.	

HC Deb. 960, 1847–50
1978–9, No. 35.

The amendment was then negatived by 179 votes to 0, the Opposition voting with the Government. The two tellers to act for the amendment comprised 1 Ulster Unionist and 1 Democratic Unionist. Of the 23 Labour Members to vote against closure, all bar one (R. Corbett) entered the Government lobby.

¹ See the comments of K. McNamara (Lab., Hull, Central), *HC Deb.* 960, c. 1841–2.

HOUSE OF COMMONS (REDISTRIBUTION OF SEATS) BILL [401]

Committee: 17 January 1979

Clause 1 (Increase of number of constituencies in Northern Ireland)

K. McNamara (Lab., Hull, Central) moved an amendment to provide that the number of constituencies for Northern Ireland should be not more than 16 or less than 14, instead of not more than 18 or less than stipulated in the clause.

The amendment was moved formally, having been discussed in conjunction with another amendment (see above). In the preceding discussion, Mr McNamara said that if they granted Northern Ireland more seats, it should be the minimum number. He thought the Government's proposal was a shabby compromise produced in shabby circumstances. The Minister of State at the Northern Ireland Office, J. Concannon, resisted the amendment. He said the Government's proposal would put

Northern Ireland on a par with the rest of the country. A Speaker's Conference was the traditional way of deciding such matters, and the Government accepted the recommendations of the Conference.

The amendment was negatived by 151 votes to 17, the Opposition supporting the Government. The 153 Members (including tellers) in the Government lobby comprised 124 Labour, 19 Conservative 9 Ulster Unionist and 1 Democratic Unionist. The 19 Members (including tellers) to support the amendment comprised 13 Labour and 6 Liberal.

Labour Members to vote for the amendment:

Canavan, D.	Mikardo, I.	Stallard, A.
Ellis J.	O'Halloran, M.	Thorne, S.
Home Robertson, J.	Ovenden, J.	Wise, Mrs A.
Loyden, E.*	Skinner, D.	Woodall, A.
McNamara, K.*		

HC Deb. 960, 1851–2
1978–9, No. 37.

HOUSE OF COMMONS (REDISTRIBUTION OF SEATS) BILL [402]

Committee: 17 January 1979

Clause 1 (Increase of number of constituencies in Northern Ireland)

K. McNamara (Lab., Hull, Central) moved an amendment to delete subsection (3) of the clause (discussed in conjunction with an amendment to delete subsection (4), also tabled by Mr McNamara). [Under the subsections, the Boundary Commissioners were to arrive at the electoral quota by dividing the aggregate electorate by 17, the electorate to be the number of electors on the electoral register in force at the passing of the Act.]

Mr McNamara said his amendment was designed to test the intentions of the Secretary of State, who he thought had indicated that the boundaries would be drawn in such a way as to determine the results of the election.

The Minister of State at the Northern Ireland Office, J. Concannon, resisted the amendment. The subsections in question were in the Bill so that the Commissioners could determine the electoral quota by dividing the electorate by 17, which was the proposed number of seats; otherwise, they would have to divide by 12. The provisions also ensured that the electoral register used would be an up-to-date one; otherwise, the Commissioners would have to use the one in force in February 1976. The amendments tabled by McNamara would complicate life for the Commissioners, and he urged the House to reject them.

Mr McNamara rose to say that he had received no reply to the question he raised.

The amendment was negatived by 113 votes to 19, the Opposition supporting the Government. The 115 Members (including tellers) in the Government lobby comprised 94 Labour, 9 Conservative, 9 Ulster Unionist, 2 Liberal and 1 Democratic Unionist. The 21 Members (including tellers) to support the amendment comprised 19 Labour, 1 SDLP and 1 Liberal.

Labour Members to support the amendment:

Canavan, D.	McNamara, K.	Rodgers, G.*
Cryer, R.	Mahon, S.	Skinner, D.
Ellis, J.*	Mikardo, I.	Stallard, A.
Flannery, M.	O'Halloran, M.	Thomas, R.
Home Robertson, J.	Parry, R.	Thorne, S.
Litterick, T.	Richardson, Miss J.	Woodall, A.
Loyden, E.		

HC Deb. 960, 1877–8
1978–9, No. 38.

The Division took place at 12.49 a.m.

HOUSE OF COMMONS (REDISTRIBUTION OF SEATS) BILL   [403]

Committee: 17 January 1979

Clause 1 (Increase of number of constituencies in Northern Ireland)

Following discussion on a number of amendments to the clause (see preceding divisions), the Chairman decided that the principle of the clause had been adequately discussed, and therefore put formally the Question 'That the Clause stand part of the Bill'.

The 'stand part' motion was carried by 114 votes to 18, the Opposition supporting the Government. The 116 Members (including tellers) in the Government lobby comprised 96 Labour, 9 Ulster Unionist, 8 Conservative, 2 Liberal and 1 Democratic Unionist. The 20 Members (including tellers) to oppose the clause comprised 19 Labour and 1 SDLP.

Labour Members to oppose the clause:

Canavan, D.	McNamara, K.*	Rodgers, G.
Cryer, R.	Mahon, S.	Skinner, D.
Ellis, J.	Mikardo, I.	Stallard, A.
Flannery, M.	O'Halloran, M.	Thomas, R.
Home Robertson, J.	Parry, R.	Thorne, S.*
Litterick, T.	Richardson, Miss J.	Woodall, A.
Loyden, E.		

HC Deb. 960, 1879–80
1978–9, No. 39.

The division took place at 1.01 a.m.

HOUSE OF COMMONS (REDISTRIBUTION OF SEATS) BILL
[404]

Committee: 17 January 1979

Clause 2 (Citation)

On the motion 'That the clause stand part of the Bill', K. McNamara (Lab. Hull, Central) rose to oppose it. He argued that the citation of the Bill should be changed to reveal the fact that they were treating Northern Ireland differently, and that it represented a change in Labour policy. 'It is not a happy day, or a happy time, and I regret that we are citing the Bill under a general heading covering membership of the whole of this House and not distinguishing between the Great Britain seats and the Northern Ireland seats. I hope that we shall vote against the clause.' R. Thomas (Lab., Bristol, North-West) also objected to the citation of the Bill; he did not think they should cite the Bill as proposed as they had not spent enough time on it. M. Flannery (Lab., Sheffield, Hillsborough) said the Bill was not a House of Commons (Redistribution of Seats) Bill. 'It has been given an aura of democracy, based upon expediency. It is an abortion.' He thought the name of the Bill should be 'More Unionist voices at Westminster'. T. Litterick

(Lab., Birmingham, Selly Oak) said the title of the Bill stuck in his throat. He thought it should be retitled the Direct Rule (Continuation) Bill.

The Minister of State at the Northern Ireland Office, J. Concannon, replied that the Bill's primary purpose was to amend rule 1 of schedule 2 of the House of Commons (Redistribution of Seats) Act 1949. It was therefore logical that the Bill should be entitled likewise.

The 'stand part' motion was carried by 113 votes to 18, the Opposition supporting the Government. The 115 Members (including tellers) in the Government lobby comprised 95 Labour, 9 Ulster Unionist, 8 Conservative, 2 Liberal and 1 Democratic Unionist. The 20 Members (including tellers) to oppose the clause comprised 19 Labour and 1 SDLP.

Labour Members to oppose the clause:

Canavan, D.	McNamara, K.	Rodgers, G.
Cryer, R.	Mahon, S.	Skinner, D.
Ellis, J.	Mikardo, I.	Stallard, A.
Flannery, M.*	O'Halloran, M.	Thomas, R.
Home Robertson, J.	Parry, R.	Thorne, S.
Litterick, T.*	Richardson, Miss J.	Woodall, A.
Loyden, E.		

HC Deb. 960, 1891–4
1978–9, No. 40.

The division took place at 1.55 a.m.

HOUSE OF COMMONS (REDISTRIBUTION OF SEATS) BILL [405]

Motion to re-commit: 17 January 1979

Following Committee stage, and the motion to report the Bill to the House, A. Stallard (Lab., Camden, St. Pancras North) moved a motion to re-commit the Bill to a Committee of the whole House.

Mr Stallard explained that he wished to re-commit the Bill due to the absence of any senior Government Minister during the debate in Committee, especially the Secretary of State for Northern Ireland, and because of the curtailment of debate by the Government on at least two occasions. 'I do not accept that the Bill has been adequately discussed by a sufficient number of hon. Members, and it has not been given the courtesy that it merited by Front Bench spokesmen from the Departments concerned.'

The Minister of State at the Northern Ireland Office, J. Concannon, objected to the motion. He said the Committee stage had been taken on the Floor of the House, and all hon. Members had had the right to be there and to put their views.

The motion was negatived by 112 votes to 18, the Opposition supporting the Government. The 114 Members (including tellers) in the Government lobby comprised 94 Labour, 9 Conservative, 9 Ulster Unionist, 1 Liberal and 1 Democratic Unionist. The 20 Members (including tellers) to support the motion comprised 19 Labour and 1 SDLP.

Labour Members to support the motion:

Canavan, D.	McNamara, K.*	Rodgers, G.
Cryer, R.	Mahon, S.	Skinner, D.
Ellis, J.	Mikardo, I.	Stallard, A.
Flannery, M.	O'Halloran, M.	Thomas, R.
Home Robertson, J.	Parry, R.	Thorne, S.
Litterick, T.	Richardson, Miss J.*	Woodall, A.
Loyden, E.		

HC Deb. 960, 1895–6
1978–9, No. 41.

The division took place at 2.11 a.m. As soon as the division had been completed K. McNamara (Lab., Hull, Central) rose to spy Strangers (see below).

HOUSE OF COMMONS (REDISTRIBUTION OF SEATS) BILL
[406]

17 January 1979

After the House had divided upon a motion to re-commit the Bill to a Committee of the whole House (negatived by 112 votes to 18: see above), K. McNamara (Lab., Hull, Central) rose to move 'That Strangers do withdraw'.

As required under S.O. 115, the Deputy Speaker put forthwith the motion. It was negatived by 112 votes to 7, the Opposition supporting the Government. The 114 Members (including tellers) in the Government lobby comprised 96 Labour, 8 Conservative, 7 Ulster Unionist,

2 Liberal and 1 Democratic Unionist. The 9 Members (including tellers) to support the motion comprised 8 Labour and 1 SDLP.

Labour Members to support the motion:

Litterick, T.*	Mahon, S.	Stallard, A.
Loyden, E.	O'Halloran, M.	Thomas, R.
McNamara, K.	Parry, R.	

HC Deb. 960, 1895–8
1978–9, No. 42.

The division took place at 2.26 a.m. The House then proceeded to the Third Reading of the Bill (see below).

HOUSE OF COMMONS (REDISTRIBUTION OF SEATS) BILL [407]

Third Reading: 17 January 1979

The Minister of State at the Northern Ireland Office, J. Concannon, moved the Third Reading of the Bill. In the debate on devolution for Scotland and Wales, the House had decided that devolved government should not be accompanied by reduced representation at Westminster. That was why the matter in relation to Northern Ireland had been referred to a Speaker's Conference. As long as Northern Ireland remained part of the United Kingdom the Government saw no justification for denying it fair representation in the UK Parliament.

K. McNamara (Lab., Hull, Central) opposed Third Reading. He thought they would regret the effects of the Bill for many days and perhaps many years. He said the Government's fine ideals had gone out of the window in a squalid desire to retain office at any price. T. Litterick (Lab., Birmingham, Selly Oak) said the Bill was welding Northern Ireland to the British body politic. It sought to make direct rule permanent. J. Ellis (Lab., Brigg and Scunthorpe) said he had heard nothing that had convinced him that the Bill would result in the years of bitterness and strife in Northern Ireland being brought to an end or the prospect improved in any way.

The Bill was given a Third Reading by 104 votes to 17, with the Opposition supporting the Government. The 106 Members (including tellers) in the Government lobby comprised 88 Labour, 9 Ulster Unionist, 8 Conservative and 1 Democratic Unionist. The 19 Members (including tellers) to oppose Third Reading comprised 18 Labour and 1 SDLP.

Labour Members to vote against Third Reading:

Canavan, D.	Loyden, E.	Richardson, Miss J.
Cryer, R.	McNamara, K.*	Rodgers, G.
Ellis, J.*	Mahon, S.	Skinner, D.
Flannery, M.	Mikardo, I.	Stallard, A.
Home Robertson, J.	O'Halloran, M.	Thomas, R.
Litterick, T.	Parry, R.	Woodall, A.

HC Deb. 960, 1915–6
1978–9, No. 43.

The division took place at 3.35 a.m.

WEIGHTS AND MEASURES BILL [408]

Second Reading: 22 January 1979

The Secretary of State for Prices and Consumer Protection, R. Hattersley, moved the Second Reading of the Bill. He explained that its main purpose was to legalize the system by which fixed weight packages were sold according to their average content rather than according to their minimum content. He pointed out that it enabled the United Kingdom to fulfil its obligations under two EEC directives, and contended that the measure would be in the interests of British industry and the consumer. It would be less wasteful for industry, and would enable producers to use the same system as applied in most of the countries to which they exported.

The Liberals opposed the Bill, and during the short debate on it one Labour backbencher, N. Spearing (Lab., Newham, South) rose to express 'grave reservations in principle' about the Bill. He thought it was an unfortunate measure which reduced protection for the consumer, increased the bureaucracy and probably increased the cost. The Bill had been forced on them because of Britain's accession to the EEC.

The Bill was given a Second Reading by 198 votes to 41, the Opposition abstaining from voting. The 200 Members (including tellers) in the Government lobby comprised 196 Labour, 2 Conservative, 1 Scottish National and 1 Plaid Cymru. The 43 Members (including tellers) to oppose the Bill comprised 23 Labour, 7 Liberal, 6 Conservative, 5

Scottish National and 2 Ulster Unionist. At least one Labour Member (N. Spearing) abstained from voting.

Conservatives to vote for Second Reading:

Morgan, G.   Shersby, M.

Labour Members to vote against Second Reading:

Bidwell, S.   Hughes, R. J.   Richardson, Miss J.
Cryer, R.   Kelley, R.   Ryman, J.
Edge, G.   Latham, A.   Skinner, D.
Flannery, M.   Litterick, T.   Spriggs, L.
Garrett, W.   Loyden, E.   Thomas, R.
Heffer, E.   Madden, M.   Thorne, S.
Hooley, F.   Maynard, Miss J.   Wise, Mrs A.
Hoyle, D.   Parry, R.

Conservatives to vote against Second Reading:

Body, R.   Grist, I   Mawby, R.
Fell, A.   Hutchison, M. C.   Winterton, N.

HC Deb. 961, 101–4
1978–9, No. 44.

PUBLIC LENDING RIGHT BILL   [409]

Report: 24 January 1979

New Clause 4 (Annual Report)

R. Moate (C., Faversham) moved the new clause, which required the Secretary of State to lay annually before Parliament a report on the workings of the public lending right scheme in addition to such other papers as may be required to be laid by the Comptroller and Auditor General under clause 2.

After two hours of debate on the clause, the Government Deputy Chief Whip moved the closure.

The closure was carried by 214 votes to 19, with Opposition Members supporting the Government [the Opposition officially being committed to the principle of the Bill]. The 216 Members (including tellers) in the Government lobby comprised 170 Labour, 33 Conservative, 9 Liberal, 3 Plaid Cymru and 1 Ulster Unionist. The 21 Members (including tellers) to oppose closure comprised 18 Conservative, 1 Labour, 1 Liberal and 1 Ulster Unionist.

Conservatives to vote against closure:

Body, R.	Holland, P.	Miller, H.
Brotherton, M.	Jessel, T.	Moate, R.*
Brown, Sir E.	King, E.	Monro, H.
Clarke, K.	Knight, Mrs J.	Ridley, N.
Goodhew, V.	Lloyd, I.	Sproat, I.*
Gow, I.	MacKay, A.	Viggers, P.

Labour Member to vote against closure:

English, M.

HC Deb. 961, 497–500
1978–9, No. 49.

The new clause was then negatived without a division.

PUBLIC LENDING RIGHT BILL [410]

Report: 24 January 1979

Clause 1 (Establishment of Public Lending Right)

I. Sproat (C., Aberdeen, South) moved an amendment to provide that benefits deriving from public lending rights were confined to live authors, and could not be passed on to their heirs. He argued that public money should not be paid out on behalf of any author after he had been dead for many years.

The Under-Secretary of State for Education and Science, Miss M. Jackson, replied that authors would have to be alive to register for public lending right and also to assign such right. The Government looked upon public lending right as a property, so authors had power to assign public lending right in their lifetime or to make bequests.

The amendment was negatived by 163 votes to 7, with Opposition Members supporting the Government. The 165 Members (including tellers) in the Government lobby 140 Labour, 14 Conservative, 5 Liberal, 3 Plaid Cymru, 2 Scottish National and 1 Ulster Unionist. The

9 Members (including tellers) to support the amendment comprised 5 Conservative, 3 Labour and 1 Ulster Unionist.

Conservatives to vote for amendment:

Kimball, M.   Moate, R.*   Viggers, P.
Knight, Mrs J.   Sproat, I.*

Labour Members to vote for amendment:

Craigen, J.   Lee, J.   Loyden, E.

HC Deb. 961, 537–40
1978–9, No. 50.

STEEL INDUSTRY [411]

25 January 1979

The Minister of State at the Foreign and Commonwealth Office, F. Judd, moved 'That this House takes note of EEC Documents Nos. R/1135/78, R/1221/78, R/1292/78 and R/3454/78 on the Steel Industry.' [The documents covered proposals for the steel industry.]

F. Hooley (Lab., Sheffield, Heeley) moved an amendment to add at the end 'but cannot accept proposals which would curtail assistance to and investment in the iron and steel industry and would damage employment in that industry.'

In the winding-up speech, the Under-Secretary for Industry, L. Huckfield, said that he accepted the spirit of the amendment, and hoped that it would be withdrawn. However, the amendment was taken to a division, in which the Government supported the amendment, with the whips on in support of it.[1]

The amendment was carried by 35 votes to 5, with the Government supporting the amendment and the Opposition abstaining apparently from voting. The 37 Members (including tellers) in the Government lobby comprised 34 Labour, 2 Conservative and 1 Scottish National. The 7 Members (including tellers) to oppose the amendment comprised 5 Conservative and 2 Liberal.

Conservatives to vote for amendment:

Marten, N.   Moate, R.

Conservatives to vote against amendment:

Fairbairn, N.	Meyer, Sir A.	Rhodes James, R.
Lester, J.[2]	Renton, T.*	

HC Deb. 961, 877–8
1978–9, No. 52.

[1] Following the division, Mr Huckfield was questioned as to the Government's action on the amendment. The Minister replied that the amendment used words which, given a choice, he would not have used. 'That is all I say. But, having said that and having voted for it, I hope that the Government's position is now clear.' *HC Deb.* 961, c. 877.

[2] A junior Opposition whip.

NURSES, MIDWIVES AND HEALTH VISITORS BILL [412]

Report: 7 February 1979

Clause 4 (The Midwifery Committee)

R. Hodgson (C., Walsall, North) moved an amendment to provide that at least two members of the general public (at least one of whom had to be a woman) should serve on the Central Midwifery Committee and also on each of the midwifery committees of the national boards being set up in consequence of the recommendations of the Briggs committee.

Mr Hodgson said women had an obvious and special interest in the operations of the midwifery committee, and the presence of a woman from outside the profession could have a balancing effect. The Bill concerned the nursing profession which sought to serve the general public, so the interest of the general public and the consumer had to be represented properly.

The Minister of State, Department of Health and Social Security, R. Moyle said there were technical defects with the amendment. He pointed out also that it was highly unlikely that the committee would be devoid of women and of women who were mothers. The question of whether babies were delivered in hospital or at home (a question raised by Mr Hodgson) was not a matter that the committee could settle.

The amendment was *carried* on a whipped party vote by 149 votes to 121, *a majority against the Government of 28*. The 123 Members (including tellers) in the Government lobby comprised 122 Labour and 1 Ulster Unionist. The 151 Members (including tellers) in the Opposition lobby comprised 119 Conservative, 13 Labour, 11 Liberal, 6 Scottish National and 2 Plaid Cymru. A number of Labour Members abstained apparently from voting.[1]

Labour Members to vote for the amendment:

Canavan, D.   Flannery, M.   Litterick, T.
Colquhoun, Ms M.   Fletcher, T.   Mitchell, A.
Cook, R.   Hayman, Mrs H.   Ovenden, J.
Corbett, R.   Latham, A.   Thomas, R.
Douglas-Mann, B.

HC Deb. 962, 463–6
1978–9, No. 73.

¹ Among those absent from the division, but voting in one half-an-hour later, were: N. Buchan, N. Carmichael, J. Ellis, D. Hoyle, R. Hughes, G. Rodgers and J. Rooker.

NURSES, MIDWIVES AND HEALTH VISITORS BILL   [413]

Report: 7 February 1979

Clause 8 (Joint Committees of Council and Boards)

D. Penhaligon (Lib., Truro) moved formally an amendment to provide that the Midwifery Committee would, on behalf of the national Boards, discharge the functions of the Boards in relation to health visitors.

The amendment was negatived by 122 votes to 12, with the Government opposing the amendment and the Opposition abstaining. The 124 Members (including tellers) in the Government lobby comprised 123 Labour and 1 Plaid Cymru. The 14 Members (including tellers) to support the amendment comprised 8 Liberal, 2 Conservative, 2 Labour, 1 Scottish National and 1 Plaid Cymru.

Conservatives to vote for the amendment:

Body, R.   Morris, M.

Labour Members to vote for the amendment:

Colquhoun, Ms M.   Mitchell, A.

HC Deb. 962, 471–2
1978–9, No. 74.

INDEPENDENT BROADCASTING AUTHORITY BILL [414]

Second Reading: 6 March 1979

The Home Secretary, M. Rees, moved the Second Reading of the Bill. He explained that the purpose of the Bill was to enable the Independent Broadcasting Authority to incur expenditure in equipping itself to transmit television broadcasts on a fourth channel. It made the necessary statutory provision for the Authority to undertake the engineering and transmitting of the fourth channel service. He made it clear that the purpose of the Bill was quite independent of the service ultimately to be transmitted by the new channel. Without the Bill, the IBA could not do the engineering necessary. 'I commend this modest Bill to the House.'

P. Whitehead (Lab., Derby, North) said that he welcomed the Bill as far as it went, but he did not think it went far enough. He said it would be a tragedy if the Parliament was to end without the introduction of the main Bill dealing with the Open Broadcasting Authority. R. Cryer (Lab., Keighley) said he could see no real reason for the introduction of the Bill at that time. He said he did not wish to assist in the process of handing over the fourth channel to the IBA. M. English (Lab., Nottingham, West) rose to argue that the IBA was an inefficient body. He hoped also that before the Bill was passed the IBA, despite its inefficiencies, would provide a separate television service to the East Midlands.

The Bill was given a Second Reading by 203 votes to 25, with the Opposition supporting the Government. The 205 Members (including tellers) to support Second Reading comprised 141 Labour, 48 Conservative, 9 Liberal, 4 Scottish National and 3 Plaid Cymru. The 27 Members (including tellers) to oppose Second Reading comprised 26 Labour, and 1 Conservative who voted in both lobbies.[1] P. Whitehead abstained from voting.

Labour Members to oppose Second Reading:

Bennett, A.	Kilroy-Silk, R.	Richardson, Miss J.
Bidwell, S.	Litterick, T.	Rooker, J.
Cook, R.	Loyden, E.	Selby, H.
Cryer, R.*	McMillan, T.	Skinner, D.
English, M.*	Madden, M.	Thomas, R.
Flannery, M.	Maynard, Miss J.	Thorne, S.
Grocott, B.	Mikardo, I.	Whitlock, W.

Hughes, R. J.   Newens, S.   Wise, Mrs A.
Jones, D.   Parry, R.

HC Deb. 963, 1165–8
1978–9, No. 84.

[1] The Deputy Leader of the Opposition, W. Whitelaw, voted by mistake against Second Reading and, realizing his mistake, then voted in the correct lobby.

BUSINESS OF THE HOUSE (SUPPLY) [415]

8 March 1979

A Government whip moved formally 'That this day, as soon as the House has entered upon the Business of Supply, Mr Speaker shall put forthwith the Questions which under the provisions of paragraph (11) of Standing Order No. 18 (Business of Supply) he is directed to put at Ten o'clock.'

A number of Labour backbenchers rose to oppose the motion. R. Thomas (Lab., Bristol, North-West) said that he and some of his colleagues found it indefensible that the motion should demand that they pass on the nod the expenditure of large sums of public money. S. Thorne (Lab., Preston, South) argued that there needed to be adequate debate on the hundreds of millions of public money involved. They were supported by other Labour backbenchers, including S. Newens (Lab., Harlow), F. Willey (Lab., Sunderland, North), Miss J. Richardson (Lab., Barking), A. Latham (Lab., Paddington) and T. Litterick (Lab., Birmingham, Selly Oak). From the Conservative benches, P. Cormack (C., Staffordshire, South-West) said he thought Mr Thomas and his colleagues had a real argument that deserved support on both sides of the House. Sir R. Gower (C., Barry) declared that they needed a new and different procedure for dealing with such matters.

No Minister rose to reply to the points made.

The motion was carried by 228 votes to 68, with the Opposition supporting the Government. The 230 Members (including tellers) in the Government lobby comprised 135 Labour, 93 Conservative and 2 Ulster Unionist. The 70 Members (including tellers) to vote against the motion comprised 57 Labour, 6 Liberal, 5 Scottish National, 1 Plaid Cymru and 1 Ulster Unionist. A number of Members (including F. Willey on the Labour benches, and P. Cormack and Sir R. Gower on the Conservative benches) abstained from voting.[1]

Labour Members to vote against the motion:

Abse, L.	Flannery, M.	McNamara, K.
Ashton, J.	Fletcher, T.	Madden, M.
Atkins, R.	Fowler, G.	Maynard, Miss J.
Atkinson, N.	Hamilton, W.	Mikardo, I.
Bennett, A.	Heffer, E.	Morton, G.
Bidwell, S.	Hooley, F.	Newens, S.
Blenkinsop, A.	Hoyle, D.	Ovenden, J.
Canavan, D.	Hughes, R. J.	Parry, R.
Carmichael, N.	Jeger, Mrs L.	Price, C.
Clemitson, I.	Jenkins, H.	Richardson, Miss J.
Cook, R.	Kelley, R.	Rodgers, G.
Corbett, R.	Kerr, R.	Rooker, J.
Cryer, R.	Kinnock, N.	Skinner, D.
Edge, G.	Lambie, D.	Spearing, N.
Ellis, J.	Lamond, J.	Stoddart, D.
English, M.	Latham, A.	Thomas, R.
Evans, F.	Lee, J.	Thorne, S.*
Evans, I.	Litterick, T.*	Tierney, S.
Fernyhough, E.	Loyden, E.	Wise, Mrs A.

HC Deb. 963, 1529–32
1978–9, No. 85.

The pertinent Estimates were then moved formally (see below).

[1] Voting figures in a succeeding division suggest that there may have been abstentions by about thirty-five Conservative Members.

DEFENCE ESTIMATES, SUPPLEMENTARY ESTIMATES, 1978-79 [416]

Supply: 8 March 1979

A number of Defence and Civil Estimates were put formally, debate being precluded by the terms of a motion agreed to by the House (see preceding division).

A number of Labour Members divided the House on the motion 'That a further Supplementary sum not exceeding £141,122,000 be granted to Her Majesty out of the Consolidated Fund, to defray the charge which will come in course of payment during the year ending on

31 March 1979 for expenditure on Defence Services, as set out in House of Commons Paper No. 198.'

The motion was carried by 276 votes to 50, the Opposition supporting the Government. The 278 Members (including tellers) in the Government lobby comprised 141 Labour, 128 Conservative, 6 Liberal and 3 Ulster Unionist. The 52 Members (including tellers) to vote against comprised 51 Labour and 1 Plaid Cymru.

Labour Members to vote against the motion:

Ashton, J.	Fowler, G.	McNamara, K.
Atkins, R.	Hamilton, W.	Madden, M.
Bennett, A.	Heffer, E.	Maynard, Miss J.
Bidwell, S.*	Hooley, F.	Mikardo, I.
Carmichael, N.	Hoyle, D.	Morton, G.
Clemitson, I.	Hughes, R. J.	Newens, S.
Colquhoun, Ms M.	Jeger, Mrs L.	Ovenden, J.
Cook, R.	Jenkins, H.	Parry, R.
Corbett, R.	Kelley, R.	Price, C.
Cryer, R.	Kerr, R.	Richardson, Miss J.
Edge, G.	Lambie, D.	Rodgers, G.
Ellis, J.	Lamond, J.	Silverman, J.
Evans, F.	Latham, A.	Skinner, D.
Evans, I.	Lee, J.	Thomas, R.
Fernyhough, E.	Lestor, Miss J.	Thorne, S.*
Flannery, M.	Litterick, T.	Tierney, S.
Fletcher, T.	Loyden, E.	Wise, Mrs A.

HC Deb. 963, 1533-6
1978-9, No. 86.

LOCAL GOVERNMENT GRANTS (ETHNIC GROUPS) BILL [417]

Second Reading: 12 March 1979

The Minister of State at the Home Office, B. John, moved the Second Reading of the Bill. The Bill sought to replace section 11 of the 1966 Local Government Act which provided for the payment by the Government of 75 per cent of local government expenditure on attempts to eliminate racial disadvantage. Mr John explained that the Bill sought to remedy a number of deficiencies in the original Act. 'We see the Bill as a significant step towards a harmonious multiracial society. This can

be achieved only by turning notional equalities and notional entitle-
ments into realities.'

Although the Opposition officially was not opposed to the Bill,[1] a
number of Conservative backbenchers rose to oppose it. A. Clark (C.,
Plymouth, Sutton) said they were being asked to approve an open-
ended commitment to provide public money to a section of the population, living side by side and in identical circumstances with the rest,
simply because they were black. 'That is reverse discrimination, and is
the most dangerous and insidious principle of all to introduce into the
distribution of public funds or public favours.' J. Stokes (C., Halesowen
and Stourbridge) said the Bill showed how out of touch both the Government and the Home Office were with ordinary people. R. Bell (C.,
Beaconsfield) described the Bill as 'the latest stage in the business of
controlling people's minds'.

The Bill was given a Second Reading by 267 votes to 7, with the
Opposition abstaining from voting. The 269 Members (including
tellers) in the Government lobby comprised 261 Labour, 4 Liberal,
2 Scottish National and 2 Plaid Cymru. The 9 Members (including
tellers) to oppose the Bill comprised 6 Conservative and 3 Ulster
Unionist.

Conservatives to vote against Second Reading:

Bell, R.	Budgen, N.*	Stokes, J.
Brotherton, M.	Clark, A.*	Winterton, N.

HC Deb. 964, 169–74
1978–9, No. 88.

---

[1] The Opposition was known to be divided on the measure, adopting abstention as a
compromise between those who supported it and those who opposed it. *See*, e.g., the *Guardian*,
7 March 1979.

EUROPEAN ASSEMBLY ELECTIONS [418]

14 March 1979

Prior to the moving of the European Assembly Elections Regulations
1979, to be discussed in conjunction with the European Assembly
Elections (Northern Ireland) Regulations 1979, a number of Members
rose on points of order to question the decision to discuss the two sets
of regulations together and the availability of relevant documents.

After points of order had been raised for almost twenty minutes, G. Fitt (SDLP, Belfast, West), who had questioned the decision to debate the two sets of regulations together, rose to move 'That Strangers do withdraw'.

As required under S.O. 115, the Deputy Speaker put the Question forthwith. It was negatived by 254 votes to 3, with the Opposition supporting the Government. The 5 Members (including tellers) to support the motion comprised 2 Labour, 1 Conservative, 1 Democratic Unionist and 1 SDLP.

Labour Members to vote for the motion:

Lee, J.*   Stoddart, D.*

Conservative to vote for the motion:

Bell, R.

HC Deb. 964, 587-92
1978-9, No. 95.

The draft regulations were then debated (see below).

EUROPEAN ASSEMBLY ELECTIONS   [419]

Prayer: 14 March 1979

The Home Secretary, M. Rees, moved 'That the draft European Assembly Elections Regulations 1979, which were laid before this House on 6 March, be approved.' (The regulations were discussed in conjunction with the regulations for Northern Ireland.)

The Home Secretary explained that the regulations provided for the detailed conduct of the first elections of United Kingdom representatives to the European Assembly. Those for Great Britain provided for election by the simple majority, first-past-the-post system, and those for Northern Ireland provided for a single transferable vote system of proportional representation. The regulations provided for the conduct of the elections to be closely related to the conduct of parliamentary elections.

For the Opposition, D. Howell said that, while not agreeing with all the details, the view of the Opposition was that the regulations should be supported.

Apart from the two Front Bench speakers, only one other Member had time to deliver a speech, G. Fitt (SDLP, Belfast, West) before the Question was put under S.O.3.

The regulations were approved by 124 votes to 73, with the Opposition supporting the Government. The 126 Members (including tellers) in the Government lobby comprised 94 Labour, 30 Conservative and 2 Scottish National. The 75 Members (including tellers) to oppose the regulations comprised 51 Labour, 8 Ulster Unionist, 7 Conservative, 6 Liberal, 1 SDLP, 1 Democratic Unionist, and 1 Member who voted in both lobbies.[1]

Labour Members to vote against the regulations:

Allaun, F.	Jenkins, H.	Ovenden, J.
Bidwell, S.	Kerr, R.	Parry, R.
Clemitson, I.	Kinnock, N.	Pavitt, L.
Cook, R.	Lambie, D.	Price, C.
Cryer, R.	Lamond, J.	Richardson, Miss J.
Ellis, J.*	Latham, A.	Roberts, G.
Evans, I.	Lee, J.	Rodgers, G.
Fernyhough, E.	Litterick, T.	Rooker, J.
Flannery, M.	McMillan, T.	Sedgemore, B.
Fletcher, T.	McNamara, K.*	Skinner, D.
Forrester, J.	Madden, M.	Spearing, N.
George, B.	Maynard, Miss J.	Spriggs, L.
Gould, B.	Mikardo, I.	Stallard, A.
Hoyle, D.	Mitchell, A.	Stoddart, D.
Hughes, R. J.	Molloy, W.	Thomas, R.
Jay, D.	Newens, S.	Wise, Mrs A.
Jeger, Mrs L.	O'Halloran, M.	Woof, R.

Conservatives to vote against the regulations:

Body, R.	Gow, I.	Moate, R.
Clark, A.	Marten, N.	Winterton, N.
Farr, J.		

HC Deb. 964, 619–22
1978–9, No. 96.

[1] The division lists record the Minister of State for Employment, H. Walker, as voting in both lobbies, clearly voting in the 'No' lobby in error.

EUROPEAN ASSEMBLY ELECTIONS   [420]

Prayer: 14 March 1979

A Government whip moved formally 'That the draft European Elections (Northern Ireland) Regulations 1979, which were laid before this House on 6th March, be approved.'

The regulations had been discussed in conjunction with the regulations for Great Britain (see above).

The regulations were approved by 108 votes to 64, with Opposition Members supporting the Government.[1] The 110 Members (including tellers) in the Government lobby comprised 87 Labour, 16 Conservative, 6 Liberal and 1 Scottish National. The 66 Members (including tellers) to oppose the regulations comprised 48 Labour, 8 Conservative, 8 Ulster Unionist, 1 SDLP and 1 Democratic Unionist.

Labour Members to vote against the regulations:

Allaun, F.	Kinnock, N.	Parry, R.
Bidwell, S.	Lambie, D.	Pavitt, L.
Clemitson, I.	Lamond, J.	Price, C.
Cook, R.	Latham, A.	Richardson, Miss J.
Cryer, R.	Lee, J.	Roberts, G.
Ellis, J.	Litterick, T.	Rodgers, G.
Evans, I.	McMillan, T.	Rooker, J.
Fernyhough, E.	McNamara, K.	Sedgemore, B.
Flannery, M.	Madden, M.*	Skinner, D.
Fletcher, T.	Maynard, Miss J.	Spearing, N.
Forrester, J.	Mikardo, I.	Spriggs, L.
Gould, B.	Mitchell, A.	Stallard, A.
Hoyle, D.	Molloy, W.	Stoddart, D.*
Jay, D.	Newens, S.	Thomas, R.
Jeger, Mrs L.	O'Halloran, M.	Wise, Mrs A.
Kerr, R.	Ovenden, J.	Woof, R.

Conservatives to vote against the regulations:

Body, R.	Gow, I.	Moate, R.
Clark, A.	McNair-Wilson, M.	Winterton, N.
Farr, J.	Marten, N.	

HC Deb. 964, 621–4
1978–9, No. 97.

[1] Several Opposition Members, including Front Benchers, appear to have absented themselves from the division. Those voting in the Government lobby included some junior Front Bench spokesmen and Opposition whips.

ADMINISTRATION OF JUSTICE (EMERGENCY PROVISIONS) (SCOTLAND) BILL [421]

Second Reading: 20 March 1979

The Secretary of State for Scotland, B. Millan, moved the Second Reading of the Bill. He explained that the need for the Bill had been brought about due to most of the executive and clerical staff in Scottish courts having withdrawn their labour. The Bill was temporary, and aimed to extend certain legal time limits, to deal with the question of the 110-day rule, to enable crimes to continue to be prosecuted, to allow the courts to extend the range of business they could undertake, and to cope with a particular problem affecting the Keeper of the Registers of Scotland. The Government had tried to keep a balance between the needs of the community in relation to law and order and the rights of the individual. He regretted the necessity to introduce the measure, but it was necessary.

The Opposition supported the measure, and it was given a Second Reading by 162 votes to 20. The 164 Members (including tellers) in the Government lobby comprised 113 Labour, 35 Conservative, 10 Scottish National, 3 Liberal and 3 Ulster Unionist. The 22 Members (including tellers) to oppose the Bill were all Labour Members.

Labour Members to vote against Second Reading:

Allaun, F.	Kerr, R.	Ovenden, J.
Atkinson, N.	Lamond, J.	Parry, R.
Bennett, A.*	Lee, J.	Richardson, Miss J.
Bidwell, S.	Litterick, T.	Rodgers, G.
Colquhoun, Ms M.	Madden, M.	Skinner, D.*
Cryer, R.	Maynard, Miss J.	Thomas, R.
Flannery, M.	Newens, S.	Wise, Mrs A.
Fletcher, T.		

HC Deb. 964, 1393–4
1978–9, No. 101.

None of the Members to vote against Second Reading had taken part in the debate.

ADMINISTRATION OF JUSTICE (EMERGENCY PROVISIONS) (SCOTLAND) BILL   [422]

Committee: 20 March 1979

Clause 5 (Arrangements for court proceedings during emergency period)

On the motion 'That the clause stand part of the Bill', R. Cook (Lab., Edinburgh, Central) said he was opposed to the principle of the clause, and would like to see it removed. The stage had not been reached where such powers were essential. The clause would raise tensions in an industrial dispute. 'We are providing specific authority and powers, either to the Secretary of State for Scotland or to the courts, to circumvent the practical effects of the dispute. I can think of nothing that is more likely to increase tensions and tempers.' His basic objection, though, was that it shifted the balance between the work force and the Government in the dispute, and created a precedent which should be avoided.

The Secretary of State for Scotland, B. Millan, said that he had certain wider responsibilities, including that of seeing that the courts continued to function, if possible, because that was in the interests of every citizen. 'That, therefore, must be my primary responsibility.' If clause 5 was eliminated from the Bill it would seriously weaken the Government's overall pursuit of their objectives. He hoped that the powers would not prove necessary.

The 'stand part' motion was carried by 116 votes to 22, with the Opposition supporting the Government. The 118 Members (including tellers) in the Government lobby comprised 97 Labour, 16 Conservative, 3 Liberal, 1 Ulster Unionist and 1 Democratic Unionist. The 24 Members (including tellers) to oppose the motion were all Labour Members.

Labour Members to vote against the clause:

Allaun, F.	Fletcher, T.	Newens, S.
Bean, R.	Hughes, R.*	Parry, R.
Bennett, A.	Kerr, R.	Richardson, Miss J.
Bidwell, S.	Lamond, J.	Rodgers, G.
Cook, R.*	Lestor, Miss J.	Skinner, D.
Cryer, R.	Litterick, T.	Thomas, R.
Ellis, J.	Loyden, E.	Torney, T.
Flannery, M.	Maynard, Miss J.	Wise, Mrs A.

HC Deb. 964, 1445–6
1978–9, No. 102.

PREVENTION OF TERRORISM [423]

Prayer: 21 March 1979

A Government whip moved formally 'That the draft Prevention of Terrorism (Temporary Provisions) Act 1976 (Continuance) Order 1979, which was laid before this House on 19 February, be approved.'

The prayer was moved formally, having been discussed in conjunction with a preceding motion to take note of the Shackleton Report on the Review of the Operation of the Prevention of Terrorism (Temporary Provisions) Acts 1974 and 1976 (Command Paper No. 7324).

As on previous occasions, a number of Labour Members expressed objection to the continuance of the Act.

The prayer was carried by 136 votes to 33, the Opposition supporting the Government. The 138 Members (including tellers) to support the prayer comprised 92 Labour, 28 Conservative, 8 Ulster Unionist, 3 Liberal, 1 Democratic Unionist and 1 Plaid Cymru. The 35 Members (including tellers) to oppose the prayer comprised 34 Labour and 1 SDLP.[1]

Labour Members to vote against the prayer:

Ashton, J.	Fowler, G.	Ovenden, J.
Atkinson, N.	Garrett, W.	Parry, R.
Bennett, A.*	Heffer, E.	Prescott, J.
Bidwell, S.	Hoyle, D.	Price, C.
Canavan, D.	Lamond, J.	Richardson, Miss J.*
Clemitson, I.	Latham, A.	Rodgers, G.
Cook, R.	Litterick, T.	Skinner, D.
Cryer, R.	Loyden, E.	Stallard, A.
Edge, G.	Madden, M.	Thomas, R.
Ellis, J.	Maynard, Miss J.	Tilley, J.
Flannery, M.	Mikardo, I.	Whitehead, P.
Fletcher, T.		

HC Deb. 964, 1623–6
1978–9, No. 103.

[1] In addition to these Members, the division lists in the *Hansard* Weekly edition include 1 Conservative and 1 Minister as voting against, apparently a printing error.

FIREARMS CERTIFICATES   [424]

Prayer: 22 March 1979

J. Farr (C., Harborough) moved 'That an humble Address be presented to Her Majesty, praying that the Firearms (Variation of Fees) Order 1979 (S.I., 1979, No. 86), dated 30 January 1979, a copy of which was laid before this House on 7 February, be annulled.'

Mr Farr said that if the order was approved, the fee for a firearm certificate, which was £3.50 in 1975, would be £18.50, and for a shotgun certificate, which was £1 in 1975, would be £8.50. He disputed the arguments used regularly to justify such increases, and said the House was totally dissatisfied with the actions of the Government.

M. Madden (Lab., Sowerby) supported the prayer. He referred to the sense of grievance and unfairness felt about the increases. 'There is a feeling that the charges are unfair and unrealistic, certainly in relation to the cost of administration by the police.'

The Under-Secretary of State at the Home Office, Dr S. Summerskill, replied that the reason for the increased fees was simple. 'The costs have risen, and someone must meet them.' In 1968, Parliament had decided that a person should be expected to pay the economic cost of issuing or renewing a licence or certificate. The amounts of the new fees had been determined solely by the need to recover higher costs, and the increases were the minimum needed to achieve that.

The prayer was *carried* by 115 votes to 26, *a majority against the Government of 89*, Opposition Members being present in force compared with the presence of Government supporters. The 28 Members (including tellers) in the Government lobby were all Labour Members. The 117 Members (including tellers) to support the prayer comprised 102 Conservative, 7 Ulster Unionist, 6 Liberal, 1 Labour and 1 Scottish National.

Labour Member to vote for the prayer:

Madden, M.

HC Deb. 964, 1857–60
1978–9, No. 105.

DEFENCE [425]

26/27 March 1979

The Secretary of State for Defence, F. Mulley, moved 'That this House endorses Her Majesty's Government's policy set out in the Statement on the Defence Estimates 1979 (Command Paper No. 7474) of basing British security on collective effort to deter aggression, while seeking every opportunity to reduce tension through international agreements on arms control and disarmament.'

From the Labour backbenches, F. Allaun (Lab., Salford, East) moved an amendment to delete all from 'House' and to insert instead 'declines to take note of the White Paper because it provides for a massive increase in military expenditure to £8,588 million in the year 1979–80, which will add to world tension, divert resources from urgent social needs and contravenes Her Majesty's Government's election pledge to give active support to policies designed to redeploy armaments industries to the manufacture of alternative socially useful products, as advocated by Lucas Aerospace and other workers; and reaffirms Labour's commitment not to proceed to a new generation of nuclear weapons.'

At the end of the two-day debate, Labour backbenchers divided the House on the amendment. It was negatived by 228 votes to 52, with the Government whips on against it and the Opposition abstaining from voting. The 230 Members (including tellers) to oppose the amendment comprised 213 Labour, 9 Liberal and 8 Ulster Unionist. The 54 Members (including tellers) to support the amendment comprised 47 Labour, 4 Scottish National and 3 Plaid Cymru.

Labour Members to vote for the amendment:

Allaun, F.	Hoyle, D.	Mitchell, A.
Atkinson, N.	Jeger, Mrs L.	Newens, S.*
Bennett, A.	Jenkins, H.	Parry, R.
Bidwell, S.	Kelley, R.	Pavitt, L.
Buchan, N.	Kerr, R.	Price, C.
Canavan, D.	Kilroy-Silk, R.	Richardson, Miss J.
Carmichael, N.	Kinnock, N.	Rodgers, G.
Clemitson, I.*	Lambie, D.	Silverman, J.
Cryer, R.	Lamond, J.	Skinner, D.
Edge, G.	Latham, A.	Thomas, R.
Ellis, J.	Lee, J.	Thorne, S.
Flannery, M.	Litterick, T.	Tilley, J.

Fletcher, T.	Loyden, E.	Torney, T.
Fowler, G.	Madden, M.	Wilson, W.
Heffer, E.	Maynard, Miss J.	Wise, Mrs A.
Hooley, F.	Mikardo, I.	

HC Deb. 964, 391–4
1978–9, No. 107.

The motion moved by Mr Mulley was then carried by 290 votes to 259, with no cross-votes.

REPRESENTATION OF THE PEOPLE BILL [426]

Second Reading: 2 April 1979

The Home Secretary, M. Rees, moved the Second Reading of the Bill. He explained that its purpose was to facilitate polling on May 3 when there was to be a general election as well as district council elections in England (excluding Greater London) and Wales.

For the Opposition, D. Howell said that, at the end of the day, they had to make the elections work, and he advised his hon. Friends not to oppose the Second Reading of the Bill, 'though I fully understand many of the worries that have been expressed by hon. Members on both sides'.

S. Ross (Lib., Isle of Wight) moved a reasoned amendment for rejection 'That this House declines to give a Second Reading to a Bill to facilitate the holding of Parliamentary elections on the date laid down for the holding of district council elections which fails to postpone the said district council elections.'

Mr Ross contended that parliamentary and district council elections should not be held on the same day, and not in such a rush as had been decided. It had not been properly thought through, and there would be a vast number of problems. He was supported from the Conservative benches by P. Cormack (C., Staffordshire, South-West). Mr Cormack drew attention to the confusion that would be caused by different ballot papers. He hoped the House would reject the Bill. R. Maxwell-Hyslop (C., Tiverton) described the Bill as 'an unprecedented mess', and one that could have been avoided. To make elections unnecessarily complicated was a service to no one. R. Moate (C., Faversham) contended that the Government should have thought more than twice before introducing a considerable constitutional innovation when it did not have the moral authority to do so at that stage in their life. The Government should have tried other options.

The Liberal amendment for rejection was negatived by 137 votes to 17, with the Opposition abstaining from voting. The 139 Members (including tellers) in the Government lobby comprised 136 Labour and 3 Ulster Unionist. The 19 Members (including tellers) to support the amendment comprised 12 Conservative, 5 Liberal and 2 Plaid Cymru.

Conservatives to vote for rejection:

Bottomley, P.*
Budgen, N.
Cormack, P.*
Durant, T.

Grist, I.
Hodgson, R.
Knox, D.
Mawby, R.

Maxwell-Hyslop, R.
Moate, R.
Shepherd, C.
Viggers, P.

HC Deb. 965, 1025-8
1978-9, No. 110.

The Bill was then given a Second Reading without a division, and completed its remaining stages in less than two hours. The division on the Liberal amendment was the last division of the Parliament.

Conclusions

With the rise of a mass electorate in the nineteenth century and the consequent advent of party government, parliamentary parties became increasingly cohesive in their voting behaviour in the House of Commons. In the post-war years from 1945 to 1970 cohesiveness of parties in the division lobbies was a well-established feature of parliamentary life, so much so that, writing in 1965, Samuel Beer was to declare that cohesion had increased 'until in recent decades it was so close to 100 per cent that there was no longer any point in measuring it',[1] adding in a variously quoted comment:

In the House of Commons were two bodies of freedom-loving Britons, chosen in more than six hundred constituencies and subject to influences that ran back to an electorate that was numbered in the millions and divided by the complex interests and aspirations of an advanced modern society. Yet day after day with a Prussian discipline they trooped into the division lobbies at the signals of their Whips and in the service of the authoritative decisions of their parliamentary parties. We are so familiar with this fact that we are in danger of losing our sense of wonder over them.[2]

There were, in Ozbudun's terminology, the 'occasional deviations' from this norm,[3] but they were occasional and rarely of a magnitude to worry unduly the party whips or the Government's business managers. Labour Members tended to dissent in greater numbers than Conservative Members,[4] but when they did so it more often than not was in divisions in which the Conservative Party either abstained from voting or else voted with the Labour Front Bench: the greater the number of Members voting against the whips, the less likelihood there was of their entering a whipped Conservative lobby. Twenty or more Labour Members voted against their own side in a total of sixty-six divisions in the years from 1945 to 1970, but in only three did the dissenters enter the official lobby of their opponent party; of these three, only one resulted in a Labour Government's majority being seriously reduced on an issue of importance.[5] Throughout the period of Conservative Government from 1951 to 1964 there was, similarly, only one occasion when Conservative backbenchers voted with the Opposition in sufficient numbers to embarrass seriously (though not remove) the Government's majority in an important division;[6] indeed, there were actually two sessions in the 1950s in which not one dissenting vote was cast by a Conservative Member. While the number of votes cast against the wishes of the whips during this period was enough to suggest that Members of Parliament were not quite as sheep-like in their behaviour as Christopher Hollis and others believed them to be[7] (and perhaps not as Prussian in their discipline as Beer believed), intra-party dissent was nevertheless far from being a common feature of parliamentary life: on those occasions when it did take place it was rarely on a serious scale and, one could argue, rarely did it have much effect.

However, the Parliament returned in June 1970 witnessed a change in parliamentary behaviour, at least on the Conservative side of the House. There was a significant increase in dissent by Government backbenchers, an increase that was significant not only in terms of its incidence (the number of divisions witnessing dissenting votes) and the size of the dissenting lobbies, but also in terms of its actual and, more important even, potential constitutional and political effects. 204 divisions in the Parliament witnessed dissenting votes by one or more Conservatives, 64 of them involving ten or more dissenters. Unusual for a party of tendencies (as opposed to factions),[8] there was almost persistent dissent by a number of Members on a range of issues: whereas in previous Parliaments the composition of a Conservative dissenting lobby was likely to change from issue to issue, in this Parliament there was a much greater likelihood of the names of the dissenters on one issue appearing in the lobby against the Government on other occasions as well.[9] In addition, Members proved willing not only to vote against the Government on more occasions than before but also to enter whipped Opposition lobbies in sufficient numbers to deprive the Government of its majority, doing so on six occasions during the life of the Parliament. Of the six defeats experienced, three were on three-line whips, the most important taking place on the immigration rules in November 1972.[10] As we have had occasion to note in the introduction, the increase in and the seriousness of this dissent by Conservative backbenchers has been attributed to one variable no longer present—the Prime Ministerial leadership of Edward Heath. The measures for which he was responsible (or with which he was closely identified), the manner in which they were introduced and pushed through the House, his failure to communicate with his own Members either at the personal level of friendship or at the intellectual level of explaining his actions, and his failure to make effective use of his powers of appointment and patronage to encourage a feeling of goodwill among his supporters, all coalesced to produce a parliamentary party that was confused and divided, and with those Members who disagreed with Government policy believing that they had no acceptable alternative but to express their opposition by voting against the Government in the division lobbies.[11] Mr Heath ceased to be Prime Minister in March 1974 (and lost the leadership of the Conservative Party in February 1975), but it has been contended, by this author, that the dissent by Conservative Members during his premiership, especially that resulting in Government defeats, was enough to provide the potential for long-term political and constitutional changes. Although much of the dissent in the Parliament had little effect in terms of achieving what the dissenters wanted (indeed, there was a rough inverse relationship between the increase in dissent and its effectiveness), the defeats imposed upon the Government did demonstrate that Government supporters could combine with Opposition Members to deny the Government a majority, and usually achieve their aims in consequence, without necessarily endangering its continuance in office. The defeat on the immigration rules was of particular importance in setting a precedent for later defeats,[12] and the number of defeats was such that one could claim a precedent had been set for future Parliaments. As one Member who opposed the Government on the immigration rules observed, once one had defeated the Government a first time, it was much easier to do it a second time.[13] Similarly, one could argue that once it had been done in one Parliament on several occasions, it would be that much less difficult to achieve in future ones.

To what extent was the change in parliamentary behaviour in the first Parliament of the 1970s continued in the two subsequent Parliaments? As the size and content of this volume demonstrate, our research has revealed that the Parliaments of 1974 and 1974–9 witnessed a high incidence of intra-party dissent in the division lobbies, especially by Labour Members in the latter Parliament, and a considerable number of Government defeats. The purpose of this chapter is to analyse that dissent, both in terms of its incidence and, in the light of the foregoing paragraph, its political and constitutional effects and implications for the future.

Incidence of intra-party dissent 1974–9

That there was a significant incidence of intra-party dissent expressed by vote in the House of Commons' division lobbies from 1974 to 1979 is demonstrated clearly by the number and the content of the pages of this work and, more succinctly, by Table 1. In the pre-1970 Parliaments, the number of divisions witnessing dissenting votes were few, as we have noted; only in the three Parliaments of 1945–50, 1959–64 and 1966–70,

TABLE 1

DIVISIONS WITNESSING DISSENTING VOTES

Parliament (Number of sessions in parenthesis)	Number of divisions witnessing dissenting votes			Number of divisions witnessing dissenting votes expressed as a percentage of all divisions
	Total:	Lab.:*	Con.:*	
1945–50 (4)	87	79	27	7
1950–1 (2)	6	5	2	2.5
1951–5 (4)	25	17	11	3
1955–9 (4)	19	10	12	2
1959–64 (5)	137	26	120	13.5
1964–6 (2)	2	1	1	0.5
1966–70 (4)	124	109	41	9.5
1970–4 (4)	221	34†	204	20
1974 (1)	·25	8	21	23
1974–9 (5)	423	309	240	28

* As one division may witness dissenting votes by Labour *and* Conservative Members, the Labour and Conservative figures do not necessarily add up to the totals on the left.

† Excluding the Labour backbench 'ginger group' votes of February–March 1971. See Philip Norton, *Dissension in the House of Commons 1945–74*, pp. 387–9.

in each of which the Government of the day had a large overall majority, did the number exceed five per cent of all divisions held. In the three Parliaments of the 1970s, the proportion has never been less than twenty per cent of all divisions. The greater willingness of Conservative Members to vote against their own side (by comparison with pre-1970 voting behaviour) appears to have been a feature of all three, though being overshadowed by the remarkable and more important incidence of dissent by Labour Members in the last Parliament. As Table 1 reveals, there were more divisions witnessing dissenting votes in the one Parliament returned in October 1974 than there were in the whole of the period, covering seven Parliaments, from 1945 to 1970. Not only were Members willing to vote against their own party in more divisions than before, they were prepared also to vote against in greater numbers. On the Labour side, this was coupled with a greater willingness to enter the Conservative lobby, a change in behaviour that was to have important political consequences: Government backbenchers were prepared to vote in the Opposition lobby, on occasion in some number, in a Parliament in which the Government had initially an overall majority of three and, from April 1976, no formal overall majority at all. The result, as we shall see, was to be several Government defeats, though on occasion the number of dissenters was such that even a sizable overall majority would have been vulnerable.

The issues which attracted intra-party dissent during the five sessions of the 1974–9 Parliament were varied, though two in particular caused serious divisions within both main parliamentary parties: British membership of the European Communities, and devolution of certain powers to elected assemblies in Scotland and Wales. The issue of Britain's accession to the European Communities (EC) had divided both parties in the Parliament of 1970–4, but the divisions continued beyond the passage of the European Communities Bill in 1972. The Conservative ranks contained a small but persistent element that remained opposed to British entry, even after entry, and the division within the Labour ranks was such that the party leadership determined upon a compromise policy of supporting a re-negotiation of the terms of membership while remaining committed (or at least not opposed) to the principle of membership. During the course of the Parliament, several measures came before the House which motivated opponents of Britain's membership to vote against their party line: the European Assembly Elections Bill, attracting the most persistent opposition from anti-EC Members, and consequent constituency orders and election regulations; the various 'take note' motions on Commission Documents; a number of prayers (to approve import duty orders for example); the Referendum Bill; and a variety of motions on substantive and procedural matters. Altogether, 56 divisions in the Parliament covering EC or EC-related matters witnessed dissenting votes by Conservative or Labour Members, Labour Members tending to dissent in more divisions than Conservatives (but only slightly so—51 divisions compared to 45)[14] and in greater numbers (notably so)[15]. The issue of devolution attracted more substantial dissent: backbenchers opposed to their Front Bench on the matter cast dissenting votes in more divisions, and—given that the two main parties were on opposite sides on this issue—the dissent by Labour Members resulted in a number of defeats for the Government. The number of divisions witnessing dissenting votes totalled ninety-one, Labour anti-devolutionists being greater in number as well as more persistent in their voting than Conservative pro-devolutionists.[16] Had a number of Labour Members not opposed the Government, the Scotland and Wales Bill would have been guillotined (and presumably passed), there would have been no referendums in Scotland and Wales with a requirement for a 'Yes' vote by forty per cent of eligible voters, and presumably there would now be Assemblies in Scotland and Wales. In effect, the Government failed to achieve the implementation of devolution, its most important constitutional proposal, because of opposition from the Conservatives and a number of its own backbenchers.

Although the issues of EC membership and devolution divided both parliamentary parties, they account for only a minority of the votes cast against their respective whips by Labour and Conservative Members in the Parliament. If one was to exclude both issues from a consideration of intra-party dissent (albeit a somewhat spurious exercise), the incidence of dissent would still be unprecedented, there would still be a marked increase in the number of large dissenting Labour lobbies, and there would still be several Government defeats wrought by Labour backbenchers voting with Opposition Members. As a browse through the pages of this volume will demonstrate, a wide range of other

TABLE 2
DIVISIONS WITNESSING DISSENTING VOTES AND THE STAGES AT WHICH THEY OCCURRED, 1974–1979[a]

Number of Divisions Witnessing Dissenting Votes:

Party:	On 2R[b]	During committee stage[c]	During report	On 3R	On Lords' Amendments	On Prayers	On motions (excluding closure)	On closure motions	Total
Lab.	22 (7%)	67 (21.5%)	50 (16%)	7 (2%)	34 (11%)	31 (10%)	86 (28%)	12 (4%)	309 (99.5)%[d]
Con.	30 (12.5%)	47 (19.5%)	39 (16%)	7 (3%)	12 (5%)	31 (13%)	64 (26.5%)	10 (4%)	240 (99.5%)[d]

Key
2R = Second Reading
3R = Third Reading
Lab. = Labour
Con. = Conservative

[a] 1974–9 Parliament only.
[b] Includes divisions held on reasoned amendments for rejection. Two divisions may thus be held on one Bill, one on the reasoned amendment and the other on the motion for Second Reading.
[c] Committee stage where taken on the Floor of the House.
[d] Less than 100 per cent due to rounding.

measures and motions encountered opposition or support from Members in defiance of the wishes of their leaders. The dissent encompassed both legislation and non-legislative motions, and took place at the various stages of the former: a few Bills attracted opposition at all stages, from Second through to Third Reading (and beyond if there were subsequent House of Lords' amendments to consider), while many more ran into trouble on specific provisions in committee or at report stage. A breakdown of the stages at which dissenting votes were cast is given in Table 2. There would appear to be no great dissimilarity between the two parties, although Conservative Members defied their party whips on Second Readings (usually to vote against when the Opposition Front Bench abstained from voting) more often than Labour Members.[17] As has been the case in previous Parliaments, fewer Bills encountered dissenting votes on Third Reading than at Second Reading;[18] this may be attributable in part to dissenters being prepared to accept the decision of the House on Second Reading; to some Second Readings encompassing two divisions (one on a reasoned amendment for rejection, the other on the motion for Second Reading); on occasion perhaps to Government concessions being made during committee or report stages; and in one or two cases to Bills not reaching Third Reading at all.[19]

The significance of the intra-party dissent in this Parliament was not confined to the fact that there was an increase in the number of divisions in which dissenting votes were cast or to the fact that they were cast at various stages; indeed, if the increase was attributable to one Member cross-voting on many occasions it would be of little importance, while votes had been cast against the whips at the various stages possible (as delineated in Table 2) in previous Parliaments. As we have touched upon already, it was significant also and more importantly because of the number of dissenters involved, their willingness to enter the lobby of their opponent party, and the consequent effect upon the Government's capacity to carry a majority for its measures in the division lobbies. Although a precedent for these changes was, in part, created by Conservative Members in the 1970–4 Parliament, the changes themselves, the important ones, took place on the Labour side of the House, and it is to a consideration of the position in each party, the Labour Party in Government and the Conservative Party in Opposition, that we now turn.

The Labour Party

During the period of this study, the Parliamentary Labour Party witnessed the most serious division lobby dissent of its post-war history, indeed of its whole history. The dissent expressed by Labour Members in the lobbies bore some similarities to that expressed in earlier Parliaments, but in other respects was markedly different.

As in previous periods of Labour Government, Labour Members proved not unwilling to vote against their own side in some number (though, as we shall see, doing so in this Parliament in greater numbers than before, on more occasions, and with more effect), and to do so on a factional basis. As in the 1966–70 Parliament, there was a strong positive association between voting against the Government on one issue and voting against it on a number of other issues.[20] The index of association between dissenting votes cast on ten separate issues in the 1974–9

Parliament is given in Table 3. The correlation was strong especially on those issues which divided the party between what are popularly described as its left and right wings, with those Members on the left voting regularly and to some extent cohesively against many of the policies pursued by a Government dominated largely by the party's right or social democratic wing.[21] Attracting regular opposition from the Members on the left were the Government's economic and defence policies, as well as a range of disparate measures introduced during the five sessions of the Parliament.

TABLE 3

YULE'S Q INDEX OF ASSOCIATION BETWEEN DISSENTING VOTES CAST BY LABOUR MEMBERS ON SELECTED ISSUES IN THE PARLIAMENT OF 1974–1979

		Issue									
		1	2	3	4	5	6	7	8	9	10
	1	////	+0.98	+0.95	+0.96	+0.99	+0.92	+0.96	+0.96	+0.93	+0.78
	2	+0.98	////	+0.95	+0.98	+0.99	+0.89	+0.94	+0.98	+0.95	+0.65
I	3	+0.95	+0.95	////	+0.99	+1.00	+0.96	+0.79	+0.99	+0.93	+0.80
s	4	+0.96	+0.98	+0.99	////	+1.00	+0.93	+0.88	+0.98	+0.92	+0.69
s	5	+0.99	+0.99	+1.00	+1.00	////	+0.98	+0.96	+0.99	+0.95	+0.92
u	6	+0.92	+0.89	+0.96	+0.93	+0.98	////	+0.84	+0.92	+0.85	+0.70
e	7	+0.96	+0.94	+0.79	+0.88	+0.96	+0.84	////	+0.86	+0.88	+0.51
	8	+0.96	+0.98	+0.99	+0.98	+0.99	+0.92	+0.87	////	+0.89	+0.71
	9	+0.93	+0.95	+0.93	+0.92	+0.95	+0.85	+0.88	+0.89	////	+0.67
	10	+0.78	+0.65	+0.80	+0.69	+0.92	+0.70	+0.51	+0.71	+0.67	////

Key:

1 Voting against the Prevention of Terrorism (Temporary Provisions) Act 1976 (Continuance) Order 1979, 21 March 1979

2 Voting against the motion to approve the White Paper 'The Attack on Inflation', 22 July 1975

3 Voting for amendment to disapprove the 1977 immigration rules, 24 May 1977

4 Voting for amendment to motion on Defence, 12 January 1977

5 Voting for adjournment following debate on deportation of Agee and Hosenball, 3 May 1977

6 Voting for new clause (on pay beds in N.H.S.) to Health Services Bill, 12 October 1976

7 Voting for prayer to annul the Civil List (Increase of Financial Provisions) Order 1975, 26 February 1975

8 Voting against motion to refer R. Adley's complaint of privilege to the Committee of Privileges, 25 May 1977

9 Voting for closure following debate on the report of the Select Committee on Direct Elections to the European Parliament, 12 July 1976

10 Voting for amended amendment stipulating 40% 'Yes' vote requirement in Scottish referendum, 25 January 1978

The test of association employed in Table 3 is that of Yule's Q,[22] and given that the value of Q can range from -1.0 to $+1.0$ the correlations are striking. In two cases, the index of association was actually $+1.0$, though in both this was produced by the process of rounding up. Ministers were included for the purpose of calculating the correlations, but even with Ministers excluded a sample calculation reveals little change in the figures, strong positive correlations remaining as such. The strength of the correlations may be illustrated also by looking at the actual voting figures upon which they were based. The following constitute some useful examples:

(1)

		Prevention of Terrorism Order 1979	
		Voting against (dissenting lobby)	Voting for (Government lobby)
Agee and Hosenball adjournment motion	Voting for (dissenting lobby)	20	1
	Voting against (Government lobby)	3	57

(2)

		Immigration rules: amendment	
		Voting for (dissenting lobby)	Voting against (Government lobby)
Motion to refer complaint of privilege 25 May 1977	Voting against (dissenting lobby)	30	0
	Voting for (Government lobby)	5	51

(3)

		Agee and Hosenball adjournment motion	
		Voting for (dissenting lobby)	Voting against (Government lobby)
Amendment to Defence motion 12 Jan. 1977	Voting for (dissenting lobby)	31	0
	Voting against (Government lobby)	4	104

(Tables confined to Members voting in both divisions)

Table 3 reveals clearly that a number of Labour Members, the same Labour Members, were voting against the whips on multiple issues, but for their dissent to be classified as factional they had to be 'self-consciously organized as a body, with a measure of discipline and cohesion thus resulting'.[23] The necessary organizational element was provided by the Tribune Group. The Group, widely accepted as representing the party's left wing, met once (and sometimes twice) a week 'to discuss—or even more frequently debate—the issues before the movement, including the current business of the House of Commons, particularly campaigns demanding attention and action, and wider questions of party policy.'[24] Although not having its own whip, and refuting allegations that it was conspiratorial, it did employ a policy of co-ordinating the action of its supporters. 'Co-ordination is a different matter: ideals must, like any other motive force, be organized if they are to be effective and the Tribune Group's most frequent and telling activity is to give an organized lead to opinion in the PLP.'[25] The cohesion resulting from this activity is revealed in the foregoing data: the cohesion was essentially that of Tribune Members. Of the ten divisions covered by Table 3, Tribune Members comprised a clear majority of the dissenters in nine of them (indeed, in some instances the dissenting lobby comprised almost exclusively Tribune Members); few Tribunites were to be found in the Government lobby and those that were were usually Ministers rather than backbenchers. In short, a majority of voting Tribune Members in each case entered the lobby against the whips, forming in so doing a majority of the dissenters. (The one exception was the division on the Scotland Bill amendment in which only forty-three per cent of Labour cross-voters were members of the Group; this helps explain the somewhat lower correlations on the issue in Table 3.) This voting behaviour by Tribune MPs was not confined to the few divisions covered by the Table. There was an element of cohesive and persistent dissent by Group Members in the short 1974 Parliament.[26] Of the sixty-nine divisions in the 1974–9 Parliament in which forty or more Labour Members voted against the whips, Tribunites constituted a clear majority of the dissenters in all by five of them.[27] The Labour Members who cast the most votes against the whips during the life of the Parliament were all members of the Group. Table 4 gives the number of dissenting votes cast by Members on both sides of the House. As it reveals, approximately one-third of Labour Members proved willing to cast twenty or more votes against their own side (as compared to one-tenth of Conservative Members), with 27 Members voting against the whips on seventy or more occasions. The more the number of dissenting votes cast, the greater the proportion of Tribune Members. Of the 86 Members who were members of the Group for all or part of the Parliament,[28] all (including Ministers, given the opportunity afforded by the votes on EC membership and the European Assembly Elections Bill) cast one or more votes against their own Government, with a majority voting against on forty or more occasions. Of the 27 Members to cast seventy

TABLE 4
NUMBER OF DISSENTING VOTES CAST
1974–1979 PARLIAMENT

Number of dissenting votes cast in the Parliament:	*Number of Members*[1]	
	Labour:	*Conservative:*
None	62 (19%)	31 (10.5%)
1 only	32 (10%)	17 (6%)
2–9	90 (27%)	144 (49%)
10–19	37 (11%)	74 (25%)
20–29	32 (10%)	11 (4%)
30–39	17 (5%)	6 (2%)
40–49	20 (6%)	4 (1.5%)
50–59	5 (1.5%)	2 (1%)
60–69	8 (2.5%)	1 (0.5%)
70–79	5 (1.5%)	1 (0.5%)
80–89	7 (2%)	0 (0%)
90–99	6 (2%)	1* (0.5%)
100 or more	9† (3%)	0 (0%)
Totals:	330 (100.5%)[2]	292 (100.5%)[2]

† D. Skinner 156; R. Thomas 137; Mrs A. Wise 136; Miss J. Richardson 132; M. Flannery 120; M. Madden 112; D. Canavan 110; I. Mikardo 108; and Miss J. Maynard 105.
* N. Winterton 92.
[1] Includes all Conservative and Labour Members, bar three, to have sat in the Parliament (including Ministers and bye-election returnees, and with R. Prentice counted twice, once as a Labour Member and subsequently as a Conservative); the three excluded are G. Thomas, O. Murton and Sir M. Galpern, each of whom held non-voting posts throughout the Parliament.
[2] Exceeds 100% due to rounding of percentages.

or more dissenting votes, all were Tribunites.[29] If one wished to identify the 'most left-wing Labour Members' in the Parliament (an exercise not without precedent),[30] then, given the number of dissenting votes cast and the issues on which they were cast, these 27 may be said to qualify for that distinction.[31]

Although the Members to vote against the whips most often and in the greatest numbers were those who were on the party's left wing, members of the Tribune Group, they were not the exclusive occupants of dissenting lobbies. They were joined usually by one or more non-Tribunites, and on occasion by a substantial number of Members drawn from various sections of the parliamentary party. On issues which could not be seen solely in left/right terms, dissenting lobbies often comprised a number of Tribune Members and several MPs drawn from the centre of the party and the right, with a number of Tribunites entering the Government lobby; examples of such would include devolution, the demand for a public inquiry into the activities of the Crown Agents, the 1975 Lotteries Bill, individual provisions of certain measures and the occasional Prayer. Although all but a handful of Tribune Members were opposed to Britain's continued membership of the EC—the Group providing the most persistent and largest contingent of opponents during the passage of the European Assembly Elections Bill—they were joined in their opposition by many non-Tribunites, so much so that Group members constituted less than half of the dissenting Labour lobby in the division on the renegotiated terms of entry in April 1975 and only a little over half of the Labour dissenters on the Second Reading of the first European Assembly Elections Bill. In addition, there were several divisions in which Tribune MPs were not among dissenting Labour voters. A number of dissenting Labour lobbies, comprising only a small number of Members and sometimes only one, were the product of Members on what is viewed as the party's right wing disagreeing with Government measures. Although the Members involved were few and were not as co-ordinated in their activities as Tribune Members,[32] their actions were potentially embarrassing for the Government given the possibility of their entering a whipped Opposition lobby. With a bare and later non-existent overall majority, the Government was vulnerable in a number of divisions to cross-votes (or abstentions) by as few as two or three of its supporters. When two Labour Members (John Mackintosh and Brian Walden) abstained in a division on a Lords amendment to the central provision of the Dock Work Regulation Bill in November 1976, their action was sufficient to deprive the Government of a majority;[33] similarly, when Richard Crawshaw and George Strauss voted against the Government on clause 4 of the Housing Finance (Special Provisions) Bill in August 1975, with another five to ten Labour Members abstaining from voting, the Government found itself in a minority by seven votes.[34] Overall, though, the most persistent, sizable and cohesive dissent in the Parliament was that expressed by Tribune Group Members, dissent that on occasion was also to produce defeats for the Government.

The factional nature of much of Labour intra-party dissent during the Parliament does not, in itself, constitute a marked change from the experience of past Parliaments. Factional disagreement has been a feature of the Labour Party's history.[35] What does constitute a significant change from the experience of previous post-war Parliaments is (a) the large number of divisions witnessing dissenting votes, (b) the size of the dissenting lobbies, as opposed to their composition, and (c) the willingness of Members to enter a whipped Opposition lobby (or vote with unwhipped Opposition backbenchers) and deprive the Government of a majority.

(*a*) The increase in the number of divisions witnessing dissenting votes by Labour Members has been identified already in Table 1. As that shows, one or more Labour Members voted against their own side in more than three-hundred divisions, almost three times as many as the number in the last Parliament of Labour Government (1966–70), and almost four times as many as the number in the first post-war Parliament of Labour Government (1945–50). The number of divisions witnessing dissenting votes represented 24 per cent of all divisions in the Parliament in which Labour Members were not permitted free votes.[36] Expressed as a proportion of non-free divisions in each session, the percentage of divisions in which Labour Members voted against the whips increased during the course of the Parliament (Table 5); although the largest number was actually in the penultimate session, the proportion was highest (45%) in the final, somewhat curtailed session.

TABLE 5

NUMBER OF DIVISIONS INVOLVING DISSENTING VOTES BY ONE OR MORE LABOUR MEMBERS EXPRESSED AS A PERCENTAGE OF ALL NON-FREE DIVISIONS IN EACH SESSION, 1974–1979:

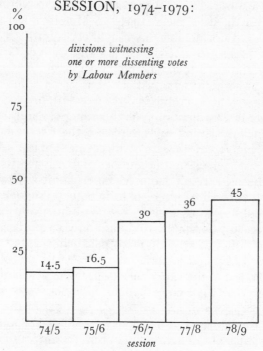

This increase cannot be attributed solely to increased activity on the part of members of the Tribune Group. Even though Tribune Members dominated most of the dissenting lobbies, we have noted already that they were rarely the exclusive occupants. On the two divisive issues to which we have earlier drawn attention—Britain's membership of the EC and devolution—opposition to the Government's measures, while drawing strength in large measure from Tribunites in the former case and to a lesser extent in the latter, was led by non-Tribunites: Douglas Jay and Nigel Spearing (among others) on EC membership, Tam Dalyell and George Cunningham (a Manifesto Group member) on devolution. The Government would have encountered opposition to both within its ranks regardless of the Tribune Group and the stance adopted by its members. Of the 309 dissenting lobbies, the number which could be described as exclusively Tribunite in composition was less than thirty.[37] Over one-third of the dissenting lobbies were manned in each case by a majority of non-Tribunites. (Of course, the converse of this latter point is that almost two-thirds of the lobbies comprised a majority who were Tribune Group Members, a fact of special relevance to the second change identified below.) Although Tribune Group MPs were clearly the most persistent and to a large extent cohesive body of Labour dissenters in the Parliament, the fact that a dissenting lobby comprised a substantial or disproportionate number of Tribune Members does not in itself mean that the Members were voting in their capacity as Group members or that the Group itself had a collective opinion on the issue in question. While the Tribune Group was opposed to the Government's economic policy, among other policies (and pursued such opposition on a factional basis), its adherents were clearly divided, for example, on the issue of devolution.

(*b*) Not only was there a remarkable increase in the number of divisions in which dissenting votes were cast, there was a notable, and more important, increase in the size of dissenting lobbies.[38] As we have noted already, if the increase in the number of divisions witnessing dissenting votes had been the result of one Member voting against his own side on multiple occasions it would be of little political significance. In fact, the dissenting lobbies were notable for the number of Members they comprised (Table 6). Of the 309 divisions, only 53 (17 per cent of the total) were the product of an individual backbencher, not always the same one of course, casting a dissenting vote.[39] Worthy of note, especially when compared to the experience of previous Parliaments, is the number of times that 20 or more Labour Members voted against their own side: 120 occasions in all, almost 39 per cent of the total. Especially striking is the figure of 44 divisions in which 50 or more Members cast dissenting votes; it is a figure without precedent, both in absolute terms

TABLE 6

SIZE OF DISSENTING LABOUR LOBBIES, 1945–1979

(Number of divisions in which Labour dissenters entered official Conservative lobby given in parenthesis)

Number of Labour dissenting voters:	Number of divisions Parliament									
	1945–50	1950–1	1951–5	1955–9	1959–64	1964–6	1966–70	1970–4	1974	1974–9 *
1 only	16 (14)	1 (0)	1 (1)	2 (0)	12 (7)	1 (1)	18 (13)	13 (7)	1 (1)	53 (32)
2 – 9	27 (15)	2 (1)	5 (0)	6 (1)	8 (0)	0 (0)	16 (4)	6 (2)	0 (0)	87 (41)
10–19	17 (4)	1 (0)	3 (0)	0 (0)	1 (0)	0 (0)	44 (1)†	5 (1)	1 (0)	49 (14)
20–29	5 (1)	0 (0)	2 (0)	0 (0)	4 (0)	0 (0)	10 (1)	1 (0)	1 (0)	31 (4)
30–39	9 (1)	1 (0)	2 (0)	1 (0)	0 (0)	0 (0)	10 (0)	3 (0)	2 (0)	20 (0)
40–49	4 (0)	0 (0)	1 (0)	0 (0)	1 (0)	0 (0)	5 (0)	3 (0)	2 (0)	25 (1)
50 or more	1 (0)	0 (0)	3 (0)	1 (0)	0 (0)	0 (0)	6 (0)	3 (1)‡	1 (0)	44 (3)
TOTAL:	79	5	17	10	26	1	109	34	8	309

* In addition, in this Parliament Labour dissenters joined with a sufficient number of unwhipped Conservative Members to impose Government defeats on six occasions.

† Labour Members voting against Government during passage of Parliament (No. 2) Bill not included as voting in official Conservative lobby (Opposition whips not being applied in the divisions).

‡ Vote on the principle of entry into the EEC when Labour dissenters entered unwhipped Conservative lobby.

and expressed as a proportion of the number of dissenting lobbies. Indeed, prior to this Parliament, the number of occasions on which 50 or more Labour Members had voted against the wishes of their Front Bench in the whole of the post-war period was only fifteen. These figures are all the more remarkable given that the votes were cast in a Parliament in which there was a Labour Government, one with a small and then non-existent overall majority. If the dissenters entered the Opposition lobby, the Government was in danger of losing its majority, sometimes badly so; in a number of divisions, albeit a minority, this is what happened.

The figures in Table 6 are significant also in that they act as a powerful demonstration of the fact that, really for the first time in recent parliamentary history, the analysis of cohesion in terms of 'party votes' as used by Lawrence Lowell at the beginning of the century may again be deemed relevant:[40] in the 1974–9 Parliament, the cohesion of the Labour Party was no longer 'so close to 100 per cent that there was no point in measuring it'.[41] Lowell defined party votes as those in which ninety per cent or more of the members of one party voting in a division entered the same lobby; a non-party vote would thus be one in which more than ten per cent of voting party members entered the lobby against the majority of their colleagues. Given that in the 1974–9 Parliament thirty or so Labour Members constituted roughly ten per cent of the Parliamentary Labour Party, the figures in the Table suggest that at least 89 divisions, approximately seven per cent of all non-free divisions, constituted non-party votes by Labour Members. Given that the Lowell definition is based on the percentage of Members actually voting, the figure is a minimum one (for example, if 200 Labour MPs vote, it takes only twenty-one of them to enter the opposite lobby to their colleagues for it to be a non-party vote), and a further analysis of the data for the 309 divisions in which Labour Members cast dissenting votes reveals the number of non-party votes to be no less than 151, 11.6 per cent of non-free Labour votes in the Parliament. In other words, the percentage of party votes on the Labour side of the House (as a percentage of all non-free Labour votes) was less than 89 per cent. The figures are even more remarkable when considered on a sessional basis. In the last session, the percentage of party votes was less than seventy per cent,[42] a figure one associates more with late nineteenth than with twentieth century Parliaments.

As to the composition of the large dissenting lobbies, we have drawn attention already to the predominance of Tribune Group MPs. Although few dissenting lobbies, and none of the large ones, comprised exclusively Tribune Members, the majority of dissenters in almost two-thirds of them were Group Members. In all but five of the sixty-nine divisions in which forty or more Members voted against their own side, Tribunites were in a majority; in thirty-three of them they constituted at least two-thirds of the occupants. Without the presence of the party's left-wing, as represented by members of the Tribune Group, there would still have been a large number of divisions witnessing dissenting votes, but the size of the dissenting lobbies would have been significantly smaller, the numbers in the highest three categories in Table 6 almost being obliterated. However, even had that been the case, it would have provided little comfort for the Government, for the activities of the Tribune Group and its supporters were responsible only in part for the third, and most important, change of the Parliament.

(*c*) Labour Members proved willing on occasion to vote with the Opposition and defeat the Government. Given its small and then, for most of the time, non-existent overall majority, and the precedent set by Conservative backbenchers during Mr Heath's premiership, the Labour Government of 1974 to 1979 was vulnerable to defeat as a result of (1) a combination of opposition parties against it when lacking an overall majority, and (2) a number of its own backbenchers cross-voting. A combination of both these factors was to result in an unprecedented number of defeats for a twentieth-century Government.

In each of the post-war Parliaments prior to 1970 the Government had an overall majority and did not experience any defeats as a result of dissent by its own Members. In the Parliament returned in June 1970, as we have recorded, the Government suffered six defeats because some of its own backbenchers voted with the Opposition. In the short 1974 Parliament, the new Labour Government—in a minority by over thirty votes—suffered a total of seventeen defeats because of opposition parties combining against it; to find a precedent for a similar number of defeats in one session one has to go back to 1868.[43] In the Parliament returned in October 1974, the Government experienced no less than 42 defeats. Of these, a minority (nineteen) were the result of opposition parties combining against a minority Government (or in one or two cases to other or related factors, as for example some mistake or confusion in the division lobbies or a miscalculation by the Government whips); a majority (twenty-three) were attributable to cross-voting by Government backbenchers. (A list of all the defeats in the two Parliaments covered by this study is provided as an appendix, with attribution as to the cause of each.) As none of those in the 1970–4 Parliament occurred before April 1972, the 65 Government defeats in the three Parliaments of the 1970s all took place in the seven-year period from April 1972 to April 1979. This compares with a total (according to our researches) of only 34 defeats in the whole of the 67-year period from July 1905 to March 1972. The figure of 65 defeats is a remarkable total by twentieth-century standards, and a noteworthy one by comparison with nineteenth-century experience. The last seven-year period to witness a similar number of defeats was that of 1863 to 1869 inclusively.[44] In short, the figure is without precedent in the history of party government since 1867.

Despite the scale and persistence of dissent by Tribune Group MPs during the life of the 1974–9 Parliament, only a small number of the twenty-three defeats inflicted upon the Government by Labour Members voting in the Opposition lobby can be attributed to cross-voting by Tribune Members. Although a large number of Group Members did vote in the Opposition lobby (or the Opposition voted at times with dissenting Labour Members, the distinction being determined by which of the two supplied the tellers), and did so for the first time in sufficient numbers to defeat the Government, the occasions were relatively few. On issues which divided the Labour left from the Government, the Opposition was likely to be closer to the Government's position, and when left-wing Labour Members divided the House tended either to vote with the Government or abstain from voting; in one or two instances, the Government was actually saved from defeat by the votes of Conservative Members.[45] Nevertheless, on those few occasions when the Labour left and the Opposition did find common ground the result usually was defeat for the Government, sometimes by substantial margins.

Given that the twenty-three defeats cannot be attributed solely to the dissent of Tribune Members on the party's left wing, to whom or what body of Members can they be attributed? An analysis of the defeats suggests that they fall into three categories. One of these, of course, is that which we have just identified: cross-voting by those on the party's left, members of the Tribune Group. Although not constituting exclusively the dissenting lobbies, the presence of Tribune Group Members in some cases was so substantial that (coupled with the issues involved) the dissent can be described as having emanated from the party's left wing. Cross-voting or abstention by a recognizable body of Tribune Members resulted in the two defeats on the Industry Bill in July 1975;[46] the defeat on the Expenditure White Paper in March 1976, the most important Government defeat to that date;[47] the loss of clause 40 of the Scotland Bill, dealing with national pay policy;[48] and, perhaps surprisingly, the defeat on an amendment to the Nurses, Midwives and Health Visitors Bill in February 1979.[49] The defeat on the amendment to the 1975 Finance Bill dealing with Value Added Tax on television sets could make a claim also to fall into this category, though the left-wing affiliations of several of the dissenters may be coincidental and not related to any great extent to their stance on the issue. Tribune Group

MPs were responsible also for a number of the many defeats suffered by the Government in standing committee, the most notable and best known of which were those on the so-called Rooker/Wise amendments to the 1977 Finance Bill, defeats which the Government accepted.[50] The Group's opposition to the Government's economic policy, as manifested in the division on the 1976 Expenditure White Paper, contributed as well to the problems encountered by the Government on its 1977 White Paper.[51]

The second category that we can identify is that of defeats which, on the basis of the composition of the dissenting lobbies and the issues involved, may be attributed to the party's right wing. There are really only two defeats on the Floor of the House which fall into this category, both involving few dissenters and to which we have drawn attention already: the loss in August 1975 of clause 4 of the Housing Finance (Special Provisions) Bill, designed to lift the disqualification from the Clay Cross councillors for failing to implement the provisions of the 1972 Housing Finance Act,[52] and the defeat on the central provision of the Dock Work Regulation Bill in November 1976. The failure of those on the party's right to dissent on a more persistent, serious or cohesive scale during the life of the Parliament as a right-wing body (there was no recognizable dissenting 'Manifesto lobby' at any time) may be attributed less to loyalty *per se* on the part of the Members concerned and more perhaps to the fact that they were in general (though not necessarily universal or unanimous) agreement[52a] with the actions and measures pursued by the Government, and were prepared to support or acquiesce in them. The assumption that they did not act out of sheer loyalty to their party would appear to be borne out to some extent by the fact that on issues which could not be seen in clear left/right terms and on which a number of right-wing Members disagreed with the line taken by the Treasury Bench, they proved willing to take their disagreement as far as the division lobbies, a point of some relevance to the third category of defeats that can be identified.

The third category is that of defeats brought about by Members from all parts of the Parliamentary Labour Party voting with the Opposition or, in some cases, unwhipped Opposition Members. Of the three categories, this is the most varied and encompasses the greatest number of defeats. With the exception of that on clause 40 of the Bill, referred to above, and one that was the result of opposition parties combining against the Government, the various defeats on the Scotland Bill fall within it, as do three of the four defeats on the Wales Bill and the loss of the guillotine motion for the original Scotland and Wales Bill. The issue of devolution was one which could not be seen in terms of left or right-wing attitudes, at least not solely so. It divided both parties, and the reasons why Members chose to support or oppose it appear to have been varied: some opponents felt it was irrelevant to the problems facing Britain, others (particularly from the North of England) were motivated to oppose it for constituency reasons, others felt it would lead to the break-up of the United Kingdom, and some may just have felt that the Bills themselves were badly-drafted pieces of legislation and not the best means of achieving an effective form of devolution; supporters believed that the peoples of Scotland and Wales deserved to have decisions taken nearer home by their own elected representatives, that it would serve to strengthen the unity of the United Kingdom and, from the point of view of the Labour Party, undermine the support for the Nationalist movement in the two countries. The result was that the various political wings and groupings within the PLP were divided; opponents of devolution included some Tribune Group Members, some Manifesto Group MPs, and Members identified with neither Group. For example, when an amendment was moved at the report stage of the Scotland Bill in February 1978 to delete the so-called 40 per cent threshold requirement for the Scottish referendum—an amendment moved by a member of the Tribune Group and supported by the Government—the 51 Labour Members to vote with the Conservatives against it included such diverse figures as George Cunningham, Tam Dalyell, Leo Abse, Stanley Cohen, Peter Doig, Eric Heffer, Neil Kinnock, Arthur Lewis, John Mendelson, Eric Ogden, Dr Colin Phipps, Denis Skinner and Mrs Audrey Wise, hardly a collection of Members that would merit description as being predominantly of one political leaning within the parliamentary party; it was one of the few large dissenting lobbies of the Parliament in which Tribunites were not in a majority. Other defeats which fall within this category include those on the inquiry into the activities of the Crown Agents in December 1977,[53] on an amendment to the Criminal Law Bill in July of the same year,[54] and on the earnings rule amendment to the Social Security Benefits Bill in January 1975.[55] In June 1976, the House debated the Government's decision to postpone introduction of its child benefits scheme, doing so on an adjournment motion. At the end of the debate, the Government failed to contest the division, and with the opposition parties entering the lobby against it went down to defeat by 259 votes to 0.[56] The Government had decided not to contest it because of the likelihood of it being defeated anyway through cross-voting or abstentions by some of its own supporters; a number of backbenchers, 'drawn from all sections of the party',[57] were opposed to the decision to delay the scheme and had threatened not to support the Government in the vote.[58] Government business managers hoped that by not contesting the division, a vote might be avoided, a hope dashed by the willingness of two Scottish National Members to act as tellers for the 'No' lobby. Although thus the result of a combination of opposition parties against it (and recorded as such in the appendix), the defeat is one that might nonetheless be considered to fall, *de facto* though not *de jure*, into this category as well.

For the Government, it was both politically and managerially a difficult Parliament. There was always the danger of a motion or legislative provision being defeated if it ran into opposition from MPs on the party's left wing, on its right wing, or from a cross-section of the parliamentary party (assuming in each case that the views of the dissenters coincided roughly with those of the Opposition or sufficient Opposition Members to mould a majority in the lobby), and, failing that, the danger of defeat at the hands of a combination of the official Opposition and the minor parties in the House. To the whips and the Government's business managers fell the task of assessing opinion within the parliamentary party on a contentious issue, finding out the positions likely to be taken by the other parties, and then trying to work out the parliamentary arithmetic, in the event not always successfully.[59] Even when the Government managed to stave off defeat after encountering opposition within the ranks of its own supporters there was still the political embarrassment of a number of its own backbenchers voting against it. An additional managerial and political problem from March 1977 through to May 1978 was that of trying to balance the demands made by the Liberal Party, as part of the limited Lib-Lab Pact agreed in 1977 as a means of avoiding defeat on a confidence vote,[60] with what it wanted to achieve and what was acceptable to its own backbenchers; even though the Pact was valuable to the Government for the purpose of maintaining itself in office, it was of a limited nature and was not sufficient to prevent various defeats during the time that it was in force.[61] The difficulties faced by the Prime Minister and his administration were to be highlighted by its final defeat. On 28 March 1979, the House debated a motion of no confidence in the Government. The motion had been tabled in the wake of the March 1st referendums in Scotland and Wales in neither of which was the forty per cent threshold requirement achieved, a requirement that existed because Labour backbenchers had voted with Opposition Members to impose it upon an unwilling Government; indeed, had it not been for the threat of dissent, there would not have been the decision to hold referendums at all. As a result of the opposition parties voting against it (and the absence of one seriously-ill Labour Member), the Government went down to defeat by 311 votes to 310.[62] It was the first time a Government had lost a confidence vote since 1924. The following day, the Prime Minister had an audience of the Queen and requested a dissolution. The forty-seventh Parliament of the United Kingdom was dissolved on 7th April 1979.

The Parliament of 1974–9 thus witnessed, on the Labour side of the House, a high incidence of intra-party dissent in the division lobbies, both in terms of the number of divisions witnessing dissenting votes and the size of the dissenting lobbies, and a willingness on the part of some Members to vote with the Opposition and defeat the Government on various (and not unimportant) occasions, something not previously experienced by post-war Labour Governments. The wider political and constitutional implications of these changes we shall consider later.

The Conservative Party

The general election of June 1970 resulted in the return of a Conservative Government under Mr Heath, and during the Government's four-year tenure of office it achieved some notable legislative enactments—British entry into the European Communities, the reorganization of the National Health Service, and reform of the structure of local government, plus some that were notable though not originally intended, as, for example, the Industry Act of 1972 and the Counter-Inflation Act of 1973. Despite, and in several cases because of, the measures it introduced and carried through, it experienced some serious problems within the ranks of its own supporters: Conservative backbenchers proved willing to vote against their own Front Bench on more occasions than before, in greater numbers and with somewhat more persistence, and to do so in the lobby of the Opposition, endangering in so doing the Government's majority.[63] The Government was defeated six times during the life of the Parliament, and was able to carry the Second Reading of its most important constitutional measure, the European Communities Bill, only on a vote of confidence and by the narrowest of margins: a majority of eight, with fifteen of its own backbenchers voting against and a further five abstaining from voting.[64] The dissent expressed by vote in the division lobbies was the most serious and public expression of a sense of dissatisfaction and unease that was felt by a number of Conservative Members; it was to find expression also in the election of critics of Government policy to the officerships of various party committees and in a lowering of morale within the parliamentary party as the Parliament progressed. As recorded already, the Prime Ministerial leadership of Mr Heath has been identified as largely responsible for the significant increase in dissent (the result of the contentious measures for which he was responsible or with which he was closely identified), its seriousness (the result of his unwillingness to listen to backbench critics, or doubters, and his insistence on pushing measures through quickly and sometimes without amendment), and the low morale in the party (a result of his failure to communicate and to use his powers of appointment and patronage as sweeteners for his supporters); so much so that in some divisions a number of Conservatives voted against their own side not only because they disagreed with the line adopted by the Front Bench but also because they wished, consciously, to 'put a shot across Mr Heath's bows'.[65] At a meeting of the 1922 Committee in October 1973, serious criticism was levelled at Mr Heath's 'presidential style of government'.[66] Of the dissent in the division lobbies, the most persistent was that by a recognizable (though not organized) body of backbenchers, whose views were articulated notably and most effectively by Enoch Powell; he provided what has been described as 'an alternative intra-party view to government policy'.[67] The picture to be painted is thus one of a Government led by a determined Prime Minister, pushing through a number of radical measures, and having to contend with a divided and, the more the Parliament progressed, uneasy parliamentary party, the line adopted by the Treasury Bench being challenged consistently by one of the House's most effective speakers. The dissent experienced by the Government, and its effects, were unprecedented.

As Tables 1 and 4 reveal, dissent by Conservative Members in the two subsequent Parliaments was to be more on a par with (in some respects, going further than) that of 1970–4 than with pre-1970 Parliaments: indeed, as some of our earlier comments and the figures in Table 1 indicate, there is really no comparison of the experience of the 1970s with that especially of the 1950s. There were more divisions witnessing dissenting votes by Conservatives in the one session of 1974/5 than there were in the whole of the post-war period up to 1959; the number for the first two sessions of the 1974–9 Parliament was greater than that for the whole of the five-session 1959–64 Parliament, a Parliament which by pre-1970 standards saw a remarkable willingness by some backbenchers to vote against their own side. As the first Table shows, there were more divisions witnessing dissenting votes by Conservatives in the 1974–9 Parliament than there were in that of 1970–4; as can be seen from Table 4, almost ninety per cent of all Conservatives to sit in the Parliament cast one or more votes against the wishes (explicit or implicit) of their Front Bench, 35 per cent of them doing so on ten or more occasions. One Member, Nicholas Winterton, cast 92 dissenting votes, a figure surpassed only in the 1970–4 Parliament by Enoch Powell.[68]

The Parliament thus saw a continuing willingness on the part of Conservative MPs to display a certain (albeit still limited) independence in their voting behaviour, a willingness that extended much beyond that experienced in pre-1970 Parliaments, especially those of the early 1950s. However, the dissent that was expressed, while significant in its incidence, was arguably not as serious in intent and effect as that which occurred in the Parliament returned in 1970. Three reasons may be advanced to explain why this might be so, all three being inter-related: firstly, the Conservative Party was no longer in Government; secondly, Mr Heath ceased to be leader of the party; and thirdly, Mr Powell changed parliamentary parties.

The first of these three factors took effect in March 1974. Although gaining more votes than the Labour Party in the February 1974 general election, the Conservatives suffered from one of those rare quirks of the electoral system and had fewer Members returned than did the Labour Party. After an unsuccessful attempt to reach an accommodation with the Parliamentary Liberal Party, Mr Heath resigned on March 4th. No longer being in office meant that the party's business managers and whips were relieved of the responsibility of ensuring the passage of legislation: if the parliamentary party was divided on the merits of a measure, the disagreement of a number of backbenchers was not by itself likely to endanger the passage of the measure. The Front Bench no longer had the responsibility of putting measures before the House which it knew might attract opposition from some of its own supporters but which it believed to be in the national interest. In Opposition, Members could be allowed somewhat greater freedom (though not too much) in their voting behaviour; dissenting votes by backbenchers could be politically embarrassing, but were unlikely to have much substantive impact. If party leaders considered a Government Bill to have some merit and were disinclined to oppose it, a decision to abstain from voting was the likely outcome. If a number of backbenchers felt strongly about the measure, they could carry their opposition (or support) to the division lobbies, although the whips would try to dissuade them from doing so. Unless it was an issue of great importance and/or the number of dissenters was substantial, their votes were not going to cause their leaders to worry unduly. A handful of Members voting with the Government against a dissenting Tribune lobby or dividing the House on the Rating (Caravan Sites) Bill were not by themselves going to attract much (if any) press attention or have an impact upon party morale—though morale could be affected if Front Bench decisions to abstain were frequent and taken in conditions in which a vote by the Opposition could affect the outcome of a division, a point of importance in the short 1974 Parliament. Overall, though, attention was focused upon, and the responsibility for legislation lay with, the Government, and it was dissent within the ranks of its supporters that could affect seriously the content and passage of measures.

When the 1970–4 Parliament came to an end so too did Mr Powell's career as a Conservative Member of Parliament. He disagreed strongly with Mr Heath's reasons for seeking a dissolution, and refused to seek re-election as a Conservative candidate in his constituency of Wolverhampton South-West. As a result, he was not a Member of the March–October Parliament of that year. He was returned to the House at the subsequent election as the Ulster Unionist Member for Down, South, and was hence a member (while it lasted) of the United Ulster Unionist Coalition in the House. Although with his return he was able once again to criticize the policies of the Conservative leadership, his impact was not as great as before. For one thing, he lacked access to the Conservative party committees, and, for another, a number of his supporters were no longer in the House.[69] Also, the Conservative Party was no longer in power (attention being focused upon Government policy), and in 1975 it chose a new leader, one generally conceded to hold views somewhat nearer to those of Mr Powell's than Mr Heath's had been. A number of Conservative neo-liberals, with views on economic policy similar to Mr Powell's, were to be promoted to the Front Bench, no longer thrown together as they had been in 1970–4 by their exclusion from office. For Mr Powell, many of the opportunities that had presented themselves when previously in the House were thus no longer present. While still a critic of Conservative policy and one of the House's most effective contributors, it was difficult to lead a body of dissenters in a parliamentary party of which he was no longer a member, and in which some of his views had been incorporated into official thinking.

Of the three factors, the last to become operative was that of Mr Heath's ceasing to be party leader. In the interval between his resignation as Prime Minister in March 1974 and his giving up the party leadership (through failing to contest the second ballot in the leadership election) in February 1975, dissent within the parliamentary party was, as before, to be influenced and encouraged by his manner of leadership. Disquiet concerning his leadership had been reinforced by the decision to go to the country in February 1974; a number of Members (about forty, according to one of their number) disagreed with his decision, and their worst fears were to be realized by the outcome of the election. A feeling that perhaps the time had come for a new leader was to gain strength also because of Mr Heath's leadership in Opposition. During the first three months of the new Parliament, the approach taken by him and the Shadow Cabinet was one of not seeking to defeat the minority Government in the division lobbies. 'Mr Heath has let his rank and file know that Opposition tactics will be to win the argument but not to win divisions and thus give Mr Wilson the excuse of saying he is prevented from governing and must fortify his mandate in another general election.'[70] Although it was an approach that initially appeared to have the support of most backbenchers, it was one that was to have some politically embarrassing manifestations—tabling an amendment to the Address on the Queen's Speech and then failing to divide upon it in March, tabling a motion on the economy and then deciding not to divide when the Government tabled an amendment to it in July—and was quickly to fall out of favour with many Members. The decision not to press the amendment to the Address was described as having 'done something to undermine the confidence of Conservative backbenchers in the tactical judgment of their leaders',[71] and a number of younger Members began to display impatience with a policy that they viewed as being too timid. 'I, along with several of my colleagues, felt it was right to oppose the measures of the Socialist Government at an early stage in the belief that an earlier election would have yielded the Conservative Party victory', wrote one. 'I am convinced that the Opposition Front Bench under Mr Heath lacked the will to fight the Labour Party.'[72] This sense of dissatisfaction among a number of Members was to find expression at meetings of the 1922 Committee: at a meeting on 9 May the strength of feeling was so strong that the chairman, Edward du Cann, agreed to convey the sentiments expressed to Mr Heath,[73] and at a meeting on 13 June the 'overwhelming feeling was that the Opposition should now do its utmost to defeat the Government in the Commons'.[74] It was a feeling that was to be reflected also in the willingness of back-bench Members to force divisions against the Government. Although opposed to the Government on the issues in question (a number of which had divided the party in the previous Parliament), some Members divided the House in order, as one of them put it, 'to instil some fighting spirit into the troops'[75] on those occasions when Front Bench advice was to abstain from voting. It was only after the passage of the opportunity for a June election that the Opposition began combining with other parties in sufficient numbers to defeat the Government, though still enjoining its supporters to abstain on a number of occasions. In the eyes of some backbenchers, the defeats came three months too late.

The loss of the October election was a further blow to Mr Heath's standing within the parliamentary party. He had led the party to defeat in two successive elections (and three altogether), and a number of Members felt that on grounds of personality and policy[76] he was no longer the right person to lead the party; 'we paid the price of Mr Heath's leadership with the loss of the October election', complained one.[77] Pressure for Mr Heath to offer himself for re-election (for which there was no provision under the existing rules) began to build up, and after initially resisting such pressure he succumbed to it. He appointed a committee under Lord Home to review the rules governing the election of the leader, and on 17 December the committee reported its recommendations: the procedure was to be based on the existing method of election (but with a requirement of 15 per cent of eligible voters on the first ballot replacing that of 15 per cent of those voting), and a leadership ballot was to be held between three and six months after a new Parliament had assembled, with annual ballots thereafter within 28 days of the start of each session.[78] The recommendations were agreed to by the 1922 Committee and by Mr Heath in January 1975, with the first ballot scheduled for 4 February. After a spirited contest, which Mr Heath expected and was expected to win, the first ballot resulted in Mrs Margaret Thatcher, the leading challenger, receiving 130 votes, as compared to 119 votes for Mr Heath and 16 votes for Hugh Fraser. Mr Heath withdrew from the contest—the first man to be elected as leader of the Conservative Party, he was the first to be voted out of the leadership—and in the second ballot in which four newcomers to the contest challenged her, Mrs Thatcher received an overall majority with seven votes to spare.[79] The Conservative Party had acquired a new leader.

Under Mrs Thatcher's leadership, Conservative Members proved willing to dissent and to carry their dissent to the lobbies, especially on those occasions when the Front Bench position was to abstain from voting. However, the disagreement that took place did so within a different environment to that which had prevailed before. When Members did dissent, their action in voting against their own side was a result of disagreement on the merits of the issues involved; it was not encouraged by a feeling of disquiet or of low morale within the parliamentary party, nor by a desire to put a shot across the bows of the party leader. Though at times criticized for having traits similar to those of Mr Heath's (as, for example, lecturing meetings of the Shadow Cabinet), Mrs Thatcher appears to have encouraged a feeling of goodwill within the parliamentary party by being prepared to promote on the basis of ability and by a capacity to communicate with her supporters through personal contact: it was, as one Member noted, 'easy to see her'.[80] Many of the dissenting votes cast in the Parliament were not on issues of great importance (several were minor), and those that were were on issues which the Opposition could not have avoided being brought on to the political agenda—devolution, the EC, and the economy, issues which, as we have seen, also divided the party in Government. Also, a case could be made for suggesting that had it not been for the line taken by the new leadership—a slightly more cautious approach to membership of the EC; an attempt, not necessarily an altogether consistent or successful one, to find some common ground between the different positions taken within the party on economic policy (an attempt finding expression in the publications *The Right Approach* and *The Right*

Approach to the Economy); and, under Mr Francis Pym's guidance, an approach to devolution which opposed the legislation before the House without jettisoning the principle, albeit aided by the fact of being in Opposition—the dissent might have been greater even than it was. Mrs Thatcher's leadership, in short, does not appear to have played the same role in relation to backbench dissent as that played by the leadership of her predecessor. When dissenting votes were cast, it would appear that they could be described as having been cast more in sorrow than in anger.

Nonetheless, the foregoing should not be taken to underestimate the importance of the votes cast against the whips and Front Bench advice by Conservative Members during the life of the Parliament. Even though the environment within the parliamentary party had changed, and many of the matters divided upon were not of great import (be it in terms of content or the number of dissenters), the incidence of dissent was significant—more Members than before were willing to vote against their own side and to do so on more occasions. As Table 4 has shown, almost ninety per cent of all Conservatives to sit in the House for the whole or part of the Parliament cast one or more dissenting votes, with a plurality of Members casting between two and nine votes against their own side. One in ten of Members proved willing to vote against the party twenty or more times. While revealing an apparent willingness on the part of backbenchers to vote against their own side on occasions when they disagreed with the line being taken, more so than in previous Parliaments, these figures are important also for demonstrating the extent to which the party remained one of tendencies rather than factions. These data, when compared with the data for the Labour Party, help reveal that, while harbouring some Members with a willingness to dissent on multiple occasions, the Conservative Party is one with many Members willing to cast dissenting votes on a few disparate occasions (as was the case, on a much smaller scale, in the 1959–64 Parliament,[81] and, despite some persistent dissent by a body of identifiable right-wing Members, that of 1970–4),[82] while the Labour Party is one with a substantial minority prepared to vote against on a consistent and fairly cohesive basis. Despite the existence within the Conservative Party of such unofficial bodies as the Monday Club, the Tory Reform Group and the Selsdon Group—none of which is confined to a parliamentary membership—there are no organized or cohesive groupings within the parliamentary party ready and able to provide a co-ordinated challenge to official policy in the same way, or on the same scale, as the Tribune Group on the other side of the House. During the Parliament, there were a few Conservatives who cast dissenting votes on particular issues on a sufficient number of occasions to be considered, for want of a better nomenclature, right-wingers (akin to those in the 1970–4 Parliament who could be subsumed under the label of 'Powellites'),[83] but there was little correlation between the composition of the dissenting lobbies, even those in which dissent might be deemed to come from the party's right; in most cases, they comprised a few consistent right-wingers joined by a much larger number of backbenchers who were not to be found in other right-wing lobbies. A scalogram was compiled listing all Members to vote against the wishes of the Front Bench on one or more of eight selected issues, the issues being chosen as ones in which the dissenting lobbies could, with one possible exception, be considered right-wing.[84] One Member headed the list as having voted against on seven of the eight occasions, followed by only thirteen others to have voted against on four or more occasions.[85] The total number of names on the scalogram was 167. 92 Members listed cast one dissenting vote only, out of the possible eight. This large number of one-only votes cannot be attributed solely to the inclusion of the division on the Rhodesian sanctions order in 1978 when 116 Members defied the whips to vote against its renewal; several Members to appear in previous right-wing lobbies failed to vote against renewal of the order. Thus, the leadership was faced with a party in which Members were entering the lobby against their advice on more occasions than before, but in which the composition of the dissenting lobbies varied from issue to issue. Also varying from issue to issue was the seriousness of the dissent.

The seriousness of dissent may be assessed in terms of the issue involved and the number of dissenters. One or two Members ignoring Front Bench advice on a minor amendment to an unimportant Bill would not fall within the category of serious dissent; a number of Members dissenting on an issue which was one of the most important and contentious issues of a Parliament would, especially so if the number of dissenters was a large one. On the Conservative side of the House, much of the dissent was, as we have noted, minor: a few dissenters on occasion entering the lobbies on matters not central to Government or Opposition policy. However, there were a few occasions of serious dissent. Two of these we have drawn attention to already: on the issues of EC membership and devolution. The issue of British membership of the EC, or Common Market, is one which has divided both parties since it came on to the political agenda. Since the decision by Harold Macmillan to apply for membership, the Conservative Party had been committed to joining, subject to suitable terms being negotiated, but with a number of Conservatives being opposed on both constitutional and economic grounds. Mr Heath's Government was to give effect to the commitment by negotiating entry and introducing the European Communities Bill in 1972, and it was on this measure that the most serious and persistent opposition was expressed by a number of Conservative backbenchers. Britain became a member of the EC on 1 January 1973, but a number of anti-Marketeers maintained their opposition, and a number of measures in the 1974–9 Parliament provided an opportunity for them to give voice and vote to this. These we have noted earlier, the most important being the European Assembly Elections Bill. However, despite the consistent opposition of a number of backbenchers, the dissent on the Conservative side was not as serious as in previous Parliaments: although the number of divisions in which anti-Marketeers dissented was 45, the size of the dissenting lobbies was not large, and on certain provisions of the Assembly Elections Bill on which more serious dissent was anticipated the party leaders allowed a free vote. Much more serious was the division within the party on the issue of devolution. The Government's devolution legislation created a rift within the party between those who supported devolution believing it to be a means of strengthening the unity of the United Kingdom and those who opposed it on the grounds that it would imperil that unity. The pro-devolutionists were in a small but important minority, and included Edward Heath and the Shadow Scottish Secretary, Alick Buchanan-Smith. The Shadow Cabinet sought to find some compromise by deciding to oppose the Second Reading of the Scotland and Wales Bill, at the same time declaring its support for the principle of Assemblies in Scotland and Wales. However, it was announced also that the whip for the Second Reading debate would be a three-line one and that the principle of collective responsibility would apply to members of the Shadow Cabinet.[86] The same evening, Mr Buchanan-Smith resigned from the Shadow Cabinet and was joined in resignation by his deputy, Malcolm Rifkind;[87] three other junior Front Bench spokesmen also offered their resignations, but had them refused.[88] In the division on the Second Reading of the Bill, five Conservatives cross-voted to support the measure and a further 29, including Mr Heath, abstained from voting. Although the number of dissenters on the Government side was greater, the standing within the party of some of the Conservative dissidents, the resignation of Mr Buchanan-Smith, and the refusal of Front Bench speakers to offer any alternatives to the Government's proposals in the debate, attracted embarrassing publicity for the party. For the dissenters, though, the Second Reading vote represented the crucial division—they were concerned to demonstrate their support for the principle of the measure, and thereafter were not vigorous in support of its specific provisions. Attention shifted to the Labour side of the House, notably so with the loss of the guillotine motion for the Bill in February 1977, and despite instances of notable disagreement in some divisions,[89] the Conservative spokesmen on devolution, Francis Pym, and his deputy Leon Brittan, managed generally to keep the party together during the passage of the Scotland and Wales Bills, with regular cross-votes or abstentions by only a very small number of pro-devolutionists and a sizable dissenting vote by anti-devolutionists in a few divisions, such disagreement being masked on occasion by the use of free votes.[90] Although Mr Pym and the party leadership were to be accused of cynically employing tactics designed solely to hold the party together (a criticism not confined to the Opposition),[91] the approach was to be successful; indeed, Mr Pym was to emerge as a leading figure within the parliamentary party and a possible future leader. With the various defeats on the Bills and the results of the subsequent referendums, attention became centred upon the Government's difficulties, and the Opposition emerged with few apparent lasting internal scars; the pro-devolutionists had at least the knowledge of the party's commitment to the principle involved—and when the party gained office in May 1979 they were to find their stand on the issue no bar to being selected for ministerial office[92]—while the anti-devolutionists were to find their opposition to the legislation largely vindicated by events. Although the division within the Conservative ranks on the issue had been serious, they did not prove as disastrous in terms of dissent in the lobbies and party morale as might initially have been expected at the time of the Second Reading of the Scotland and Wales Bill.

In addition to EC membership and devolution, an issue that was to cause a serious rift within the parliamentary party was Rhodesian sanctions. When first introduced in 1965, the party had been badly divided on the issue—dividing three ways in the division on the oil sanctions order, in the largest party split in the lobbies since the American Loan in 1945[93]—and thereafter a number of backbenchers on the party's right would normally divide the House on the annual sanctions renewal order.[94] The issue proved a sensitive one when the Conservatives returned to power in 1970. The Foreign Secretary, Sir Alec Douglas-Home, managed to negotiate an agreement for a settlement of the dispute with the Salisbury government, but this was found to be unacceptable to the population of Rhodesia by the Pearce Commission. In light of the Commission's report, the Government decided to wait upon events in Rhodesia and to maintain sanctions in the meantime. The decision not to end sanctions was opposed by those on the party's right, who continued to divide the House on the annual renewal order. After 1972, interest in the division on the order was not great, largely because the outcome was a foregone conclusion, but about twenty sanctions opponents could usually be relied upon to go into the 'No' lobby each time it came up.[95] However, opposition to sanctions began to grow during 1978 as a consequence of developments within Rhodesia and the move towards an internal settlement. By the time that sanctions came up for renewal in November the opposition to them within the parliamentary party was such as to be causing serious problems for the party leadership. Not wishing to tie the hands of a future Conservative Government, the official Opposition line was to abstain from voting, and a whip was issued enjoining abstention. It was made clear also that Opposition spokesmen would be expected to abstain in line with this decision. In the event, 116 Conservatives, constituting over forty per cent of the parliamentary party, defied the whip and entered the 'No' lobby. The dissenters included former Home Secretary Reginald Maudling, two Front Bench spokesmen, John Biggs-Davison and Winston Churchill, and Members drawn from all parts of the parliamentary party: ex-Ministers such as Richard Wood, Maurice Macmillan and Paul Channon; senior backbenchers such as Miss Betty Harvie Anderson and Sir Bernard Braine; and a number of what might be termed traditional loyalists at the heart of the party, MPs such as John Osborn, James Scott-Hopkins, Arthur Jones and Marcus Kimball. After the division, Mr Biggs-Davison resigned as a spokesman on Northern Ireland, and, after declining to resign, Mr Churchill was dismissed as a Defence spokesman. It was a serious and embarrassing rift within the party's ranks, the most sizable dissenting lobby in the party's post-war history. Although confined to one division, it had important implications for future years, serving as it did to put a shot across the bows of a future Conservative Government.

The party experienced some discord within its ranks on the issue of economic policy, with a number of Members (led by Edward Heath) being prepared to support an incomes policy and others dedicated to the pursuit of a free market economy. The tensions within the party were to find some expression in a number of divisions early in the Parliament, as on the Second Reading of the Prices Bill in 1975,[96] but mainly were to find outlets through other forums, as, for example, the annual party conference and statements by leading figures within the party. Various measures introduced in the Parliament were to be the cause of internal dissent on the Conservative side of the House, but the dissent was not to be serious, albeit occasionally causing problems for the whips and on occasion embarrassing the position taken by the Front Bench (as on the Public Lending Right Bill); the morale of the parliamentary party was not to suffer any apparent impairment as a consequence of such dissent.

The parliamentary party was thus to witness a high incidence of dissent in its period in Opposition. Much of this was to be accounted for by Members dissenting, usually not in great numbers, on fairly minor issues, though on occasion the dissent was to be serious and cause problems for the party leadership, notably on the issues of Rhodesia, devolution, and direct elections to the European Assembly, plus more generally (and away from the division lobbies) economic policy. Given Mr Heath's departure as leader and the absence from the party's ranks of Mr Powell, the dissent appears to have been confined to the merits of the issues involved, with no wider implications for the leadership and with no one to give a lead to the party's right by articulating an alternative and comprehensive intra-party view to challenge party policy.[97] When the Parliament ended, the parliamentary party—despite its recent rift on the question of Rhodesia, and some doubts as to the policies that Mrs Thatcher might decide to pursue when in office—was in apparent good spirits: the most notable dissent had tended to take place on the Government side of the House where media attention was normally focused anyway, the Government had run into trouble with its economic policy and with the result of the March referendums, and had been brought down on a vote of no confidence. On 3 May, the Conservative Party was returned to office with an overall majority of 43. However, for the new Government the experience of the last Parliament could not be forgotten: the dissent on devolution and Rhodesia (and, elsewhere, economic policy) meant that these were issues that had to be treated carefully and, in the case of Rhodesia, quickly. More generally, the dissent that occurred in the 1974–9 Parliament, on both sides of the House, was to have implications for the House of Commons that no Government could now ignore.

Parliamentary behaviour in the 1970s[98]

The Parliament returned in October 1974 witnessed a significant and unprecedented incidence of intra-party dissent in the House of Commons' division lobbies. The incidence of the dissent we have detailed above. The extent of the dissent (coupled, we would suggest, with that of the Parliament of 1970–4) has been such as to negate or undermine a number of generalizations or assumptions made about the House of Commons and parliamentary behaviour. It was assumed previously, certainly until well into the 1970s and possibly still by many, that Members of Parliament would, and did, vote loyally with their party; that they were reluctant or unwilling to engage in serious dissent because they believed that voting against one's own party, if in Government, could lead to a defeat which could bring it down: that the Government had a monopoly of or at least superior information which could not be matched by the Opposition or backbenchers; and that the whips (and constituency parties) would take disciplinary action against dissenting Members.

(1) The assumption that MPs vote loyally with their party to the extent that they comprise no more than lobby fodder would appear to have been undermined if not dispelled by the experience of the 1970s. It is the case that the cohesion of the parties in the division lobies remained and remains strong. Each Member will usually enter the lobby with his party in a whipped division, and even in the Parliaments of the 1970s the Member who voted against his party in ten per cent or more of whipped divisions was very much the exception rather than the rule. However, the cohesion has been and is largely that of those who wish to be cohesive. 'MPs', as Sir Ian Gilmour observed, 'have a predisposition to vote for their party, otherwise they would not be there.'[99] Members are returned as party Members, they are in agreement with the principles and usually the main policies of the party, and want it to do well: when they vote with like-minded colleagues in the lobbies they do so on the whole because they are in agreement with them and not because they feel forced to do so by the pressure of others. However, on those occasions, usually relatively few, when they have found themselves in disagreement with their colleagues, the assumption has been that party loyalty, and pressure from the whips and others, would carry the day and ensure that they entered the lobby with the rest of the party, and it is this assumption that the events of the 1970s have served to undermine. First in the 1970–4 Parliament and then more especially in that of 1974–9, Members proved willing to enter the lobbies against their own side on occasions when they disagreed with the line being taken by their leaders. As Table 4 has shown, a majority of Members in each parliamentary party in the latter Parliament entered the lobby against their own side on one or more occasions, over seventy per cent of them doing so more than twice. Over twenty per cent of Labour Members, finding themselves in disagreement with several policies being pursued by their Front Bench, voted against the Government thirty or more times. Where several Members disagreed with their Front Bench on a particular issue the result was often a large dissenting lobby, especially on the Government side of the House: as we have seen, the number of party votes on the Labour side was less than 90 per cent of all non-free divisions in the Parliament, and in the final session it was actually less than 70 per cent. Though pointing to the fact that cohesion remained the norm rather than the exception, these figures help reveal that reserves of party loyalty were not inexhaustible. Dissent which backbenchers had preferred previously to confine to private forums now found public expression. Though wishing to vote with their party and normally doing so, Members ceased to display the Prussian discipline in the lobbies noted by Beer, and more especially showed that they were not as sheep-like in their voting behaviour, with its attendant

implications, as Christopher Hollis and others had previously presumed them to be.

(2) Prior to the 1970s, a variable influencing Members' voting behaviour was the belief that voting against one's own party in Government could lead to its defeat and precipitate a general election. This belief, held by Members and doubtless not discouraged by the whips, resulted in a rough correlation between the size of a Government's overall majority and the extent to which backbenchers were prepared to vote against it in the lobbies. The larger the Government's majority— as in the Parliaments of 1945–50, 1959–64 and 1966–70—the less vulnerable it was to being lost as a result of cross-votes by its own supporters, and so the more willing were backbenchers to express their dissent by vote rather than confining it to other forums. The smaller the majority, as in the Parliaments of 1950–1, 1951–5 and 1964–6, the less prepared were Government backbenchers to dissent (Table 1). This rough correlation was recognized by Members and whips alike. However, it did not hold for the 1970–4 Parliament nor, more notably, for that of 1974–9. Following the precedent set by Conservative backbenchers in the former Parliament, Members came to realize that the Government could be defeated without its continuance in office necessarily being endangered. A result, as shown by the experience of the latter Parliament, was that a low or even formally non-existent overall majority ceased to be a barrier to Government backbenchers being prepared to cross-vote in sufficient numbers to jeopardize the Government's majority. As we have seen, the Government suffered twenty-three defeats as a result of some of its own backbenchers abstaining or voting with the Opposition. Of these defeats, it is pertinent to note that a number were the product of cross-voting by a substantial body of Labour Members. It was not simply a case of one or two Members making the difference between success and failure in a division in which the parties were fairly evenly balanced; as we have mentioned, the number of dissenters on occasion was such that even a sizable overall majority would have been vulnerable. For example, the Government was outvoted by 204 votes to 118 on an amendment to the Scotland Bill in January 1978 when 50 Labour Members cross-voted; it lost by 230 votes to 147 on one of the amendments to the Industry Bill in July 1975, when another 50 Labour Members had cross-voted; it went down to defeat on other occasions with majorities of 72 (on an amendment to the Wales Bill in April 1978), 71 (another amendment to the Industry Bill in July 1975) and 55 (another amendment to the Scotland Bill, in February 1978) against it. On the two most important Government defeats of the Parliament caused by Labour Members abstaining or cross-voting—the loss of the guillotine motion for the Scotland and

Wales Bill and the defeat on the 1976 Expenditure White Paper—the majorities against the Government were not insubstantial, the result of dissent by 43 and 39 Labour backbenchers respectively. In addition, the parliamentary arithmetic for the Parliament appears to have acted as no apparent discouragement to Members wishing to dissent on other occasions; indeed, as we noted earlier, the Government was saved from defeat in one or two divisions by the votes of Conservative Members, the number of Labour Members dissenting exceeding the number to be found in the Government lobby. In short, there were occasions when the Government's small and then non-existent overall majority does not appear to have acted as a constraint upon Labour Members who opposed Government policy, certainly not to the same extent as before.

The reluctance of Members previously to risk defeating the Government was given justification by the belief that a defeat had either to be reversed or else the Government must seek a vote of confidence or request a dissolution or resign, or some variant on this theme, some sources not including the discretion to reverse a defeat. In 1964, Graeme Moodie wrote that, except for free votes, 'it is now assumed as a matter of course that any defeats in the House of Commons must be reversed or else lead to the Government's resigning or dissolving Parliament'.[100] This is a point of some constitutional importance, and one which we shall consider separately. For the moment, we may note that the belief constituted something of a constitutional myth, and the defeats of the 1970s, both in number and type, and the Government's response to them—which was in line with precedent—served to help dispel it.

(3) There was a general acceptance on the part of Members that the Government had sources of information which they could not match; Government backbenchers appeared willing in consequence to acquiesce in Government policy or, if opposed, to dissent in a mood of frustrated resignation, while the Opposition, though not unwilling to enter the lobby against the Government on issues of principle that divided the parties, was conscious of the limitations of not knowing all the relevant facts and figures. Neither backbenchers nor the Opposition were privy to the consultations conducted between Departments and outside interests, and agreed Departmental measures would often go through the House with little or no opposition. 'What more effective plea can a minister make to potentially hostile MPs than that the interests which are affected by a measure have been consulted and have given their approval?'[101] The constraints imposed by not having the information and facilities that were available to the administration were recognized by Members on both sides of the House, and remain so recognized. Despite the availability of the Conservative Research

Department on the Conservative side and the recent limited provision of public funds to assist opposition parties in fulfilling their parliamentary duties, the Opposition Front Bench and backbenchers on both sides of the House cannot match the resources of the Civil Service at the disposal of the Government. These resources continue to constitute a powerful weapon in the armoury of the Government, especially useful in debate and at Question Time in the House. However, the changed parliamentary behaviour in the 1970s suggests that, while recognizing the superior resources and information enjoyed by the Government, Members (or at least some of them) were less willing to accept as a corollary of this that 'the Government knows best'. Backbenchers on both sides of the House, the Conservatives under Mr Heath and then Labour Members under Mr Wilson and Mr Callaghan, appeared more prepared than before to rely upon their own instincts and beliefs in challenging their own Front Benches. On occasion, some even challenged the assumed superiority of Government information by relying upon their own informed sources (indeed, the expert advice received by Conservative opponents of the Maplin Development Bill in 1973 was at least on a par with that available to the Government), though such examples remain exceptional.[102] There appears to have been much less willingness to accept what the Government said at face value. One may speculate that this was encouraged by the publication of Richard Crossman's *Diaries of a Cabinet Minister*, which helped reveal publicly that decision-making in Government is not necessarily a rational process based on a balanced evaluation of options and convincing objective data. As they showed, decision making may be based upon the most partisan and personal of reasons.[103] Government might possess superior sources of information, but it was clearly shown to have no monopoly of wisdom.

This increased unwillingness to accept that 'the Government knows best' was reflected in various of the defeats imposed upon the Government in the 1970s. Of special interest in this context is the defeat on the Crown Agents' affair in December 1977. For the Government, the Minister for Overseas Development, Mrs Judith Hart, argued that the inquiry into the activities of the Crown Agents should be held in private. The opposition Front Bench, the alternative Government, proved unwilling to jettison altogether the belief that on certain matters the Government of the day does know best (the two Front Benches being assumed on occasion to have more in common with one another than their own backbenchers), and in the division abstained from voting. It was left to backbenchers on both sides of the House, who wanted a public inquiry under the provisions of the 1921 Tribunal of Inquiry (Evidence) Act, to combine and impose a defeat upon the Government, doing so by 158 votes to 126. It was not the only example in the Parliament of a defeat being imposed by backbenchers on both sides of the House. This, it could be contended, constitutes a healthy development, as it could have the effect of forcing the Government to be more open, not only with its own Members but also with the House of the whole.

An increased determination by Members not to accept unquestioningly the advice of the Government could serve also to have the perhaps surprising effect of strengthening the position of Ministers in relation to their officials. Ministers are often viewed as being dominated by their own civil servants—one informed source once suggested that only about one Minister in three actually ran his Department[104]—and on occasion may not know how to overcome the views of their officials, even when they may wish to do so,[105] the result being that the advice given the House is less that of the Minister than of his permanent advisers. Backbenchers are in less close contact with civil servants than are Ministers and hence less likely to be susceptible to their influence. By being prepared to defeat the Government on a particular issue, rejecting the advice proferred from the Treasury Bench, Members can place a Minister in a position where he (or she) can inform his officials that 'the House will not accept this', and in some cases Ministers may find this to their advantage. Again, the defeat on the Crown Agents' affair serves as a useful example. Even such a strong-willed Minister as Mrs Hart appears to have been in a position of advancing the Departmental view in debate, and it took the House to defeat the Government and produce a result that she had been known to favour in pre-Ministerial days.

(4) There was a popular belief that Members who dissented would be, or ran the risk of being, disciplined by the party whips or even, in some cases, by their local parties. This belief was held and was variously expressed by a number of Members, and was perceived as being given credence by some of the events of the 1950s, some Labour Members having the whip withdrawn from them and a number of 'Suez rebels' on the Conservative side running into trouble with their constituency associations. Fear of falling foul of punishment from either source was one reason advanced for the reluctance of most Members to dissent. As late as 1968, Humphry Berkeley was to write: 'The fear of the whip is now so great in the Labour party . . . that most Labour Members fight shy of any real display of independence which would seem to disunite the party.'[106] References to 'the tyranny of the whips' were not unknown.[107] However, while both the whips and local parties did and do act as important constraints on Members' independent voting behaviour, they have not been nor are they as powerful as was popularly believed, realization of this fact being aided by the events of the 1970s.

The view of the whips as powerful disciplinarians is both misleading and, in post-war years, largely without foundation. The main functions of the whips, as they have been throughout this century and prior to it, are those of communication and management.[108] They serve as a valuable channel through which Front Benchers are kept abreast of backbench opinion, and vice versa. They serve to keep Members in-informed of business coming before the House (and other parliamentary and party activity), and to advise them of the importance attached to items of business by the party leaders. In conjunction with the Leader and Shadow Leader of the House and their officials, they play an important role in the arranging of the parliamentary timetable. 'The whips', in short, 'perform functions of value to both front and back benches and are the oil in the machine of parliamentary business.'[109] It is true that the whips serve to ensure that parliamentary parties are cohesive in their voting behaviour, but what they are doing is usually to ensure the cohesion of those who wish to be cohesive. As we have had cause to comment already, Members usually vote with their party because they want it to do well and are in agreement with it. It is only when Members indicate an unwillingness to be cohesive on a particular issue that the presumed disciplinary power of the whips is brought into play, and what this power amounts to essentially is that of persuasion. If Members express an intention to vote against their own side, the approach of the whips is to try to dissuade them from doing so by appeals to party loyalty and by putting the Front Bench case; if that fails, they often arrange for the Member or Members concerned to see the relevant Front Bencher for further discussions. On important votes, the Chief Whip and other Ministers may talk to the likely dissenters; on rare occasions, the Prime Minister (or Leader of the Opposition as appropriate) may become involved and send a note or message.[110] If these various attempts at persuasion fail to deflect dissenters from their proposed course of action then there is little in practice that the whips can do. As one senior whip succinctly expressed the position: 'we have no powers of sanction, I mean, if a Member of Parliament says he's not going to do anything, well, he jolly well doesn't do it and there's nothing I can do about it, I can't bribe him.'[111] If the number of unpersuadable Members is a large one, then far from contemplating taking action against them, the whips may advise party leaders to modify or not press ahead with the measure involved in deference to their intended dissent.

Of the various powers associated with the whips, that of withdrawing the written whip, receipt of which signifies one's membership of the parliamentary party, is generally regarded as the most important. However, on the Conservative side of the House it has fallen into desuetude: it was last employed in 1942 (the previous occasion being in

1928)[112] and apparently was last contemplated in the 1959 Parliament.[113] Even if resuscitated, it could be employed in practice only with the approval of the party leader. On the Labour side of the House, the power does not even reside with the whips: it rests with meetings of the parliamentary party, and was last employed and apparently last contemplated in the 1960s.[114] Whips on both sides of the House do enjoy the power to issue post-dissent rebukes, and on the Labour side the Chief Whip has the power to issue formal reprimands, but such rebukes, coming after the event, are of limited use and may serve only to antagonize the Members concerned. 'I missed two votes and got a letter from the Deputy Chief Whip', recalled one MP on one occasion, 'and I told him in effect to get stuffed.'[115] There are various instances of backbenchers responding in such a manner, not all confined to recent experience.[116]

Influence over promotion prospects, also associated with the whips, may have some influence (the Chief Whip being the party leader's main adviser on such matters), but a Member's voting behaviour is only one of several factors likely to be taken into account—a Member may receive promotion on the basis of ability, popularity within the parliamentary party, support from a particular section of the national party, personal ties to the party leader, or even to some limited extent because of gender (the perceived need for one or two women in Front Bench posts) or constituency representation, regardless of dissenting behaviour, while a Member with a record of voting consistently with his party may be fated to remain on the backbenches because of perceived incompetence, unpopularity within the party, personal incompatibility with the Prime Minister, or quite simply because there is no room on the Front Bench after the allocation of portfolios to the more preferred Members; and, of course, a dissenter may be promoted anyway as a means of silencing him. The extent to which independent voting behaviour is not an automatic bar to promotion is borne out by the experience of the 1970s. A number of Labour Members with records of notable dissenting behaviour, from Michael Foot downwards, were to find their way on to the Treasury Bench under the premierships of Harold Wilson and James Callaghan.[117] In May 1979, Mrs Thatcher appointed to her Cabinet John Biffen, who had been second only to Enoch Powell in the number of times he had voted against the whips in the 1970–4 Parliament and who was a not infrequent dissenter in the two subsequent ones; Angus Maude, a 'Suez rebel' who had resigned the whip in 1957 and who abstained on the Second Reading of the European Communities Bill in 1972; and George Younger, one of the Front Bench spokesmen to offer his resignation in 1976 because of his support for the Scotland and Wales Bill. Also given Ministerial posts were Neil Marten, who had dissented consistently on the issue of EC membership in preceding Parliaments, Nicholas Ridley, a leading opponent of Mr Heath's U-turn on the economy, and all bar one of those who had resigned or offered their resignations as Front Bench spokesmen in 1976 over the issue of devolution; the Member to cast the third largest number of dissenting votes in the 1974–9 Parliament became the Prime Minister's Parliamentary Private Secretary. Only John Biggs-Davison and Winston Churchill appear to have been excluded from office because of their failure to adhere to the instructions given Front Benchers for the Rhodesian sanctions division in 1978; their exclusion, though, does not invalidate our general point. If a Prime Minister was consistently to exclude dissenting backbenchers from office, as Mr Heath was accused of doing, it would fuel resentment on the backbenches and affect adversely the morale and effectiveness of the parliamentary party, as Mr Heath discovered;[118] and even Mr Heath at one point brought back into the Government a Member who had previously resigned in order to oppose the European Communities Bill.

Other powers associated with the whips, such as the distribution of honours and selection for parliamentary delegations and various committees, are useful for helping maintain an environment of goodwill within a parliamentary party and may serve to lessen a Member's willingness to dissent, especially when the case for or against dissent is fairly evenly-balanced in the Member's mind, but by themselves are hardly likely to deflect a Member determined upon dissent. As powers, they also have certain limitations: the final decisions on patronage rest with the Prime Minister, some Members may be unconcerned about committee membership, and the threat of denying a Member a knighthood or similar honour may appear both heavy-handed and, if leaked, embarrassing. Their limitations are illustrated by the case of one Conservative MP in the 1970–4 Parliament who, finding himself not selected for any parliamentary delegations abroad, proceeded to go on his own one-man delegations.[119]

The powers popularly associated with the whips are thus limited, and these limitations have been highlighted by the extent and seriousness of intra-party dissent in the Parliaments of the 1970s. There was a large and serious increase in dissent in the Conservative ranks under Mr Heath's leadership which the whips were unable to prevent and to which they could not respond with disciplinary weapons, and a significant increase in dissent by Labour Members, which the Labour whips similarly could not prevent, when Labour was in Government in the Parliaments covered by this volume. The activity of the whips was not without its effectiveness (appeals to party loyalty and the arguing of the Front Bench case can be very effective, especially when put by such skilled practitioners), and it can be and has been argued that without the whips the dissent would have been even greater than it was.[120] In this sense, whips continue to serve as constraints, important constraints, upon Members' independent voting behaviour, but if Members are determined upon dissent there is little that they can do; indeed, Members who dissented in the 1970s were more likely to end up eventually on their Front Bench than they were to be in danger of having the whip withdrawn. As one Labour Member commented in the House in 1970, 'although the Whips may be put on, not only on this side but on the other side of the House, if hon. Members want to ignore the Whips they jolly well do so. They do not appear to be afraid of the ultimate sanctions.'[121] The validity of this assertion was to be borne out by Members on both sides in the succeeding decade. It could be contended that if dissension within the parties was to reach much greater proportions than those of the 1970s then the whips might seek or be given strong disciplinary powers; for reasons given earlier, though, parties are likely to remain more cohesive than disunited; if they failed to remain so, it would be unlikely that the whips could make much difference.[122]

Much more effective as a constraint upon Members contemplating dissent is the possibility of an adverse reaction by their constituency parties. Each Member is dependent upon his local party both for his initial selection and for his consequent re-adoption as the party candidate at each election. To be denied re-adoption is tantamount usually, albeit not always, to being denied the chance of re-election. Not surprisingly, a Member will as a rule be sensitive to the likely reaction of his local party officers and activists if he is contemplating dissent on an issue, especially one central to party policy. However, the dissent of the 1970s, especially on the issue of entry into the European Communities in the 1970–4 Parliament and on the devolution legislation in the 1974–9 Parliament, suggests that local parties are not quite as ready and able to disown dissenting Members as was perhaps popularly believed. Entry into the European Communities was the central item of Government policy during Mr Heath's premiership: the European Communities Bill dominated the 1971–2 session, and the Second Reading vote was made one of confidence. Despite that, none of the Conservative Members to oppose it throughout its passage, including on Second Reading, was denied re-nomination by his local association, though most did encounter some problems, in some cases serious ones.[123] Although constituency pressure served to prevent dissent on the measure from being even greater—some Members failed to oppose, or moderated their opposition, because of the stance taken by their local parties—no local associations exacted the ultimate penalty from those who refused to comply with their wishes. On the Labour side, the issue was one which caused serious divisions also, but of the pro-Marketeers to dissent the only one effectively to be disowned by his local party was Dick Taverne at Lincoln, and even here it appears to have been an issue that tipped the balance in an internal constituency dispute rather than motivating the dispute itself. The experience of Labour Members to oppose the Government's devolution legislation is even more noteworthy. Unlike the dissenters on the EC Bill, the anti-devolutionists cross-voted in sufficient numbers to effect a defeat of their own Government on various occasions, seriously embarrassed the Government and forced it in practice to abandon its original Bill, imposed the 40 per cent require- ment for the referendums, and at the end of the day could claim to have achieved their aim. Their actions were also to set in train a series of events which were to lead to the Government's defeat in the March 1979 confidence vote. Despite this, they were to suffer no serious retribution from their local parties. Some did encounter problems (George Cun- ningham, for example, experienced some trouble, though not on any serious scale, with his local party in Islington, South and Finsbury), but none appears to have been denied re-nomination because of dissent on the issue.[124] More generally, none of the Members who dissented on multiple issues (notably, Enoch Powell in the 1970–4 Parliament, Denis Skinner and other Labour Members identified in Table 4 in the 1974–9 Parliament) appear to have encountered serious problems because of their voting behaviour.

In some cases, it is possible to contend that the attitude of local parties, far from discouraging Members from casting dissenting votes, may on occasion encourage them. This is particularly the case where constituency interests may be involved, and, on the Labour side, can result also from a left-wing orientated constituency party being opposed to measures pursued by a Labour Government. In his study of the nineteenth-century House of Commons, Hugh Berrington found that Liberal radicals who dissented stood to be applauded by their local caucuses, not disciplined:[125] the same would appear to apply to a number of Labour Members in the 1970s. Of those Labour MPs who found themselves in dispute with their local parties in the 1974–9 Parliament, none did so because of failing to support the Government in the division lobbies.

Although constituency parties can and do act as constraints, strong ones, upon Members considering entering the lobby against their own side, especially on an issue of importance, they are not quite as strong as was previously assumed. In the 1970s, Members determined upon dissent were allowed to go far further than many would previously have thought possible. Conservative opponents of EC entry who en- countered attempts to deny them re-nomination resisted such attempts (which few of the disowned Suez rebels in the 1950s did) and survived. Members who have been denied re-nomination in recent history have been few.[126] It was generally assumed that if a Member did encounter trouble with his local party, it was as likely to be because of personal problems or constituency neglect as it was for political reasons such as voting disloyalty in the division lobbies. One could contend that few MPs were refused re-adoption for political reasons because there was little serious dissent in the House. However, the Parliaments of the 1970s witnessed serious dissent within the parties, which was not accompanied by local parties responding with decisions to deny Members' re-nomination. Those Members who were not re-adopted in the 1970s fell foul instead of such things as complaints of constituency neglect or, on the Labour side, left-wing dominated local parties.

To summarize, there was a significant increase in the incidence and seriousness of intra-party dissent in the Commons' division lobbies in the Parliaments of the 1970s; Members, some more than others, showed that they could not be accused of being sheep-like in their voting behaviour, and that they were not deterred, if on the Government side of the House, from rejecting the advice of their leaders and voting with the Opposition to defeat their own side, their actions in so doing revealing that constraints presumed to operate upon such activity—the whips and local parties—were not quite as potent as was previously assumed. Though cohesion remained the norm, the outcome of divisions was not a foregone conclusion. Party loyalty was a strong but not inexhaustible commodity at the disposal of party leaders.

Government defeats
In the post-war period, and indeed for most of this century including well into the 1970s, a belief variously held by Members and others was that a Government defeat in the division lobbies had either to be reversed or else the Government must seek a vote of confidence, request a dissolution or resign, or, as we have mentioned, some variant on this theme. As early as 1905, Arthur Balfour observed that it appeared to be assumed in various parts of the House 'that the accepted constitutional principle is that, when a government suffers defeat, either in Supply or on any other subject, the proper course for His Majesty's responsible advisers is either to ask His Majesty to relieve them of their office or to ask His Majesty to dissolve Parliament'.[127] This view, or some variant of it, was to find expression throughout most of this century. In 1965, Harvey and Bather claimed that 'failure of party members to support Cabinet decisions in the division lobby will lead either to the resignation of the Government or to a dissolution',[128] and in 1971 Sir Philip de Zulueta expressed the opinion that a three-line whip was 'a formality

which warns supporters of an administration that the government will resign if the vote in question goes against them'.[129] The belief found implicit expression in the comments of some Government backbenchers in various Parliaments that they did not vote against their own party in divisions because they had no wish to put the other party in power.

The seven years from April 1972 to April 1979, as we have detailed, witnessed a total of 65 Government defeats in the division lobbies. Six of these took place during Mr Heath's premiership, all six being attributable to Conservative backbenchers cross-voting. Three took place on three-line whips. The Government sought to have only one defeat reversed in the House of Lords; it sought no votes of confidence, and no thought was given to requesting a dissolution or resigning. The minority Labour Government was defeated seventeen times in the short 1974 Parliament as a result of opposition parties combining against it; it did not respond to any of them by seeking a vote of confidence. When Mr Wilson requested a dissolution he did so because he considered it a politically opportune time to go to the country, not because he considered he was constitutionally required to do so. In the subsequent five-session Parliament, the Government suffered 42 defeats in the lobbies, most of which it accepted. Of the 42, 19 were attributable to opposition parties combining against a minority Government (or to confusion in the lobbies or miscalculations by the whips), and 23 to Labour Members combining with Opposition Members to defeat their own side. Several of the defeats took place on important items of Government legislation or policy. However, only three defeats were followed by votes of confidence (one of them tabled by the Opposition), and not until defeated on a vote of confidence did the Prime Minister request a dissolution.

The experience of these Parliaments clearly did not accord with the belief held by many as to the Government's required response in the event of a defeat in the lobbies. Either the Government was defying precedent and what some considered to be a constitutional convention, or the belief held by Members was without substance. The latter was the case. The belief held by Members, while influencing parliamentary behaviour, could be described as constituting something of a constitutional 'myth'. It had no basis in any authoritative original source, nor was it a 'convention' based on any consistent parliamentary practice. Indeed, it was belied by the experience of nineteenth and twentieth century Parliaments, including those in the period from 1945 to 1970: during that time, the Government—as we recorded in the introduction —suffered a total of ten defeats, the most important of which (on the Finance Bill in 1965) was accepted by the Government. Nevertheless, these defeats were quickly forgotten, and most Members appear to have continued in their belief.

The defeats of the 1970s helped lay this myth to rest. Following the early defeats under Mr Heath's administration, there was a much wider realization that a Government was constitutionally required to resign or request a dissolution in consequence only of losing a vote of confidence. The defeat on the immigration rules was of special importance in this context. It was reinforced by the defeats on the issues of the third London airport (the Adley amendment to the Maplin Development Bill) and the export of live animals for slaughter in 1973. These were to constitute important precedents for Labour Members in the latter half of the decade. The realization that, as Government backbenchers, they could vote with Opposition Members to defeat what they considered to be a bad measure or proposal without necessarily endangering the Government's life, was to find expression both in the speeches and votes of a number of Labour MPs. 'Some people say that if we do not vote for this motion, the Government will fall', declared George Cunningham during debate on the guillotine motion for the Scotland Bill. 'Anyone who believes that is extremely naive . . . If the motion is defeated, the Government will be able to get on with its work on more substantive issues, and people will applaud them for doing so.'[130] On various occasions, Labour Members entered the Opposition lobby in a conscious attempt to deny a majority to the motion being divided upon; the motions defeated as a result of this action included, as we have seen earlier, a number of some importance to Government policy.

The number and type of the defeats that took place and the Government response to them have served also to reinforce what has been the constitutional reality for over a century, namely that there are essentially three types of defeats in the House of Commons: those on votes of confidence (a category which may be further sub-divided),[131] in consequence of which the Government is required to resign or request a dissolution; those on issues central to Government policy, in response to which the Government may *either* seek a vote of confidence *or* request a dissolution or resign; and those on issues which are not central to Government policy (as, e.g. amendments to a measure), in response to which the Government need determine only whether to accept them or attempt their *de facto* reversal.[132] By their nature, most divisions are not matters deemed to be central to Government policy. The distinction between these types has existed really since the 1830s, and has been adhered to by succeeding Governments, those in the 1970s responding in line with precedent. None of the defeats in the 1970–4 Parliament was on a central item of Government policy, and the Government contented itself with deciding whether or not to accept them. The Labour Government survived various votes of confidence, hence surviving in office, until losing the decisive vote of 28 March 1979, as a result of which the Prime Minister requested a dissolution; it suffered a small number of defeats on issues central to Government policy—the 1976 Expenditure White Paper motion, the 1977 Expenditure White Paper in practice, and the policy of employing sanctions against firms breaking the five per cent pay limit—each of which was followed by a confidence vote (with one Cabinet Minister on one occasion raising the alternative possibility of a dissolution);[133] and the remaining defeats were on items that the Government deemed not central to its main policies, and more often than not accepted such defeats.

Realization by Members and others of what is the constitutional reality has important implications for the House of Commons. It can have the seemingly paradoxical effect of strengthening the position both of the Government and of private Members. If, with the Opposition, constituting a majority of the House, Government backbenchers know they can defeat the Government on occasion on issues which are not votes of confidence (and various constraints operate which prevent too many votes being changed into ones of confidence),[134] while the Government knows it can continue in office unless defeated on a vote of confidence: it need encounter no uncertainty as to what to do in the event of all other defeats, and if it has an overall majority it can be expected to carry confidence votes.

The result in practice, is that a majority of the House is able to force the Government to think again on certain issues, without necessarily raising any wider constitutional implications. The House may thus have its way on a particular issue; the Government remains in office. Thus, awareness of the differences between types of Government defeats in the lobbies can help ensure some element of stability in government, the Government only being required to resign if defeated on a vote of confidence, while permitting Members a degree of freedom in voting behaviour which previously many felt they did not have.[135]

This has important implications both for the future effectiveness of the House of Commons in fulfilling certain of its functions and for the movement for parliamentary reform. The return of a Government with a clear overall majority in May 1979 reduced the importance of what Anthony King has aptly termed the 'Opposition mode' of executive-legislative relations:[136] the new Government was not going to be defeated by a combination of opposition parties against it. The 'intra-party mode' of relations, however, remained and remains important. An overall majority, as we have seen, does not constitute a bar to defeats in the House of Commons.

Intra-party dissent and parliamentary reform
Various functions have been ascribed to the House of Commons, and the votes that take place in the Commons' division lobbies are important

in helping fulfil two of them, those of (a) legitimizing and (b) scrutinizing and influencing the Government and its measures. The Commons, comprising the elected representatives of the people of the United Kingdom and Northern Ireland, is responsible for maintaining the Government (between elections) and giving approval to the measures which it puts forward. The House itself no longer legislates in any significant manner; legislation is usually initiated and formulated elsewhere, and resulting measures passed through the Government's majority in the House. By passing them, by approving them, the House is nevertheless fulfilling an important function, that of legitimization. 'It represents MPs, the people's elected representatives, giving, if you like, 'the seal of approval' to measures drawn up and decided upon by the Government.'[137] Between elections, the House gives the 'seal of approval' to the Government itself. So long as the Government can maintain a majority in a vote of confidence it is free to soldier on: only if losing such a vote does it incur the obligation (by convention) to resign or request a dissolution.[138] When there is no unanimity or near-unanimity in the House, such approval is given through a majority vote in the division lobbies.

Before legitimizing the Government and its measures, a legitimation which it is free formally to deny, the House, or at least that part of it which does not form the Government, is deemed to fulfil the function of scrutinizing that part of it which does constitute the Government. Collectively and individually, Members fulfil or are supposed to fulfil this function, doing so through a variety of means, and doing so in practice in different representative capacities; concomitantly, they seek also to influence the Government to take certain action or amend proposed courses of action in order to further the interests of those that they represent.[139] The most consistent, structured and public scrutiny is provided not by House as a collective entity (Ministers excluded), but by one of its elements, the Opposition. Scrutiny by backbench Members on the Government side, though, has not been abandoned, and is performed more thoroughly in the private or semi-private confines of the parliamentary party. The Government has to withstand both the public scrutiny of the Opposition and the private scrutiny of its own supporters. If scrutiny leads to criticism and the Government fails to respond to such criticism, at least to the satisfaction of those expressing it, then at the end of the day all that Members can do is express their dissatisfaction through the division lobbies.

Members, collectively and individually, represent in practice a number of interests.[140] They seek to scrutinize and influence Government in order to protect and further the interests of constituents, local organizations and concerns, their parties locally and nationally, national organizations and interest groups with which they are associated, their political philosophies and personal values, and what they perceive to be in 'the national interest'. The means through which they can exercise scrutiny and influence are, as we have just mentioned, varied. In the twentieth century, both main parliamentary parties have developed highly organized infrastructures.[141] Through meetings of the parliamentary parties and the specialized party committees, Members can question and discuss the proposals of their leaders and legislation coming before the House; through the whips, they can make known to their Front Bench their views on pending business. If on the Government side of the House, they seek to influence directly, early and privately the actions and measures being put forward by Ministers; if on the Opposition side, they seek to influence the approach to be taken publicly by the Opposition Front Bench on such measures. Meeting privately in party forums (though details of meetings are often leaked), the factors that encourage cohesion on the floor of the House are generally absent: the result is that 'plain speaking is encouraged and differences can be aired'.[142] The importance of such forums for MPs returned under a party label should not be underestimated. In the nineteenth century, parties acted as a conduit for the transfer elsewhere of the legislative and elective functions of the Commons, the former going to the Cabinet and the latter to the electorate. '[P]ower was no longer exercised through the floor of the House but through party, and by establishing party forums within Parliament Members were, to some degree, regaining a slight measure of influence which they had lost in the nineteenth century.'[143] Party leaders generally would prefer their supporters in the House to be publicly united and not divided, for a sense of goodwill to pervade the party rather than one of bad feeling, and for their actions and measures to be acceptable rather than disliked by those interests represented by the party's MPs. For these reasons, party leaders will usually listen and often respond to criticism expressed within the confines of the parliamentary party. If they fail to do so, their backbench critics may decide to 'go public'.

The public parliamentary forums through which the Opposition and Government backbenchers may scrutinize and attempt to influence the Government include debates on the floor of the House and Question Time, and the various committees of the House: standing committees for legislation, and select committees (now restructured) for oversight of executive actions. If scrutiny leads to criticism or demands for action, the Government may respond by conceding the point at issue or offering some concession: it may do so because it recognizes the merits of the case put forward, or in order to thwart public criticism from its own supporters, or to avoid embarrassing publicity if it considers its own position to be weak, or to avoid antagonizing unduly the Opposition or some of its own supporters upon whom it relies for co-operation in the orderly despatch of parliamentary business. A prudent Government will often avoid bringing measures before the House with a closed mind. As one former Minister explained, a Government will not, as a rule, be prepared to give way on the Second Reading of a measure, but 'it will watch the Second Reading debate and consider again now at what points would it be wise to make concessions. And so on, throughout the whole process of the Bill'.[144] If the Government fails to respond to criticism or demands levelled at it, then its critics may divide the House and enter the lobby against it.

When the Opposition votes against the Government, it does so to express its disagreement with the policy or measure being pursued, part of the process of what is termed now 'adversary politics'. If Government backbenchers vote against their own side, they may do so as a form of public demonstration to be picked up by supporters outside, they may do so simply because they believe their consciences dictate such action, or they may do so as part of the continuing process of attempting to influence Government actions: party leaders often prefer to avoid if possible the embarrassment of some of its own supporters publicly voting against it, and, especially if the divisions take place on matters on which multiple divisions are possible (or which recur annually), may offer concessions to avoid further dissent. Basically, though, voting against one's own side in the division lobbies may be construed as an admission of failure: it constitutes an admission usually that attempts to influence Government (or the Opposition Front Bench as appropriate) at an earlier stage, behind closed doors, have failed. A party may be united publicly, and suffer few embarrassing dissenting votes, because of a willingness by party leaders to respond early to criticism expressed privately. 'Concord and peace', as one inside observer noted, 'may signify backbench influence, not dull obedience'.[145] A high incidence of dissent in the lobbies may thus signify a degree of voting independence on the part of Members but also a failure of backbench influence. This, it could be argued, was the case in the post-war years, and especially during the period of Conservative Government in the 1950s: the Government proved willing to make concessions and cross-voting was rare. When dissenting votes were cast, especially in some number, further (or new) concessions were sometimes forthcoming.[146] However, when they were offered, they were often of a limited nature (and, indeed, on occasion were essentially cosmetic rather than substantive), and were offered for the reasons outlined above. They do not appear to have been the product of threatened defeat in the division lobbies. The assumption was that if the Government resisted pressure from its backbench critics and pushed ahead with the measures it wished, then at the end of the day it would be able to have its way: its own supporters would give it a majority in the lobbies, fearing that failure to do so could result in a general election. Even on the Resale Prices Bill in 1964, the Government's own critics failed (apparently deliberately) to deny it a majority at report stage, even though they were sufficiently numerous to do so,[147] and contented themselves with concessions which were to be described subsequently as 'window-dressing'.[148]

The extent to which a high incidence of dissent may signify a general failure of backbench influence was to be borne out by the experience of the 1970–4 Parliament. The dissent that was expressed in the lobbies by Conservative Members was generally a response to Government unwillingness to change or abandon measures or policies following criticism expressed through meetings of the 1922 Committee, party committees, the whips and personal communications. In the 1970 Conservative manifesto, Mr Heath had declared that 'once a decision is made, once a policy is established, the Prime Minister and his colleagues should have the courage to stick to it',[149] an attitude that he was to maintain in Government. The European Communities Bill, which attracted the most persistent dissent in the Parliament from a body of Conservative backbenchers, went through the House unamended (by Government design); other measures were pushed through despite serious dissent having been expressed privately. The consequence was to be, as we have noted earlier, an inverse relationship between the increase in division lobby dissent and the effectiveness of backbenchers to influence the Government.[150] The same may be said of the 1974–9 Parliament. There was, as we have seen, a notable increase in dissenting votes on the Labour side of the House. In most cases, the dissent had little effect. In particular, one could contend that there was an inverse relationship between the incidence of dissent by Tribune Group Members and the effectiveness of that dissent.

The experience of the Parliaments of the 1970s, though, was to result in one important change. Although most dissent in the division lobbies continued to constitute an admission of earlier failure which the Government could ignore if it wished to, not all dissent continued to remain in that category. As we have seen, the assumption that if the Government persisted it could get its way in the division lobbies was to be shattered. Through pushing measures through, Mr Heath managed to achieve most of what he wanted, but it could be argued that he pushed a little too hard: a point finally came at which a number of backbenchers were prepared to enter the Opposition lobby and defeat the Government. By so doing, they were to create a precedent with important long-term implications.

... by the strongest assertion of Conservative prime ministerial dominance ... in post-war history, Mr Heath ensured that his result-orientated approach was successful in most instances, but created a situation where on occasion, through defeat on the floor of the House, it was not, and in so doing created the basis for a weakening of Government dominance in the division lobbies in future Parliaments.[151]

The Government could no longer guarantee that it could carry a division at will. Government backbenchers began to realize that, if strong enough in number, they could combine with the Opposition and deny the Government a majority without endangering its life. Once they had demonstrated a willingness to deny the Government a majority on occasion, then the threat of doing so at other times became a strong weapon in their armoury as well, one that could be used early through the private and public forums available to them. What concessions were achieved in earlier Parliaments were the product of backbench influence: the decision-making power remained with the Government. By moulding a majority against the Government in the lobbies, Members were wielding a power at their disposal: they were engaging in the decision-making process, albeit largely in the negative sense. The Government could not ignore defeats: in some instances, the defeats could be definitive, in others it could be difficult to obtain their reversal, and in all cases reversals in the same session could only be reversals *de facto* and never (without a suspension of standing orders) *de jure*. If the House were to insist upon an amendment imposed against Government wishes, then—as the Government discovered in 1978 with the 40 per cent requirement for the referendum in the Scotland Bill—there was little that could be done. '(W)hereas a government can duck any number of critical Select Committee reports', as one MP, now a Minister, wrote, 'it cannot normally duck the consequences of a defeat in the lobbies'.[152]

The defeats of 1970–4 were reinforced by those of the 1974–9 Parliament (as well as those that were the product of opposition parties combining against the Government in the 1974 Parliament), making a total of 65 in all, including a number on important issues. The Government was able to continue governing in both Parliaments—the Labour Government actually survived a full five-session Parliament despite being in a nominal minority for most of it—and could be said to have realized that element of stability to which we have referred in the preceding section; at the same time, Members were enjoying somewhat greater freedom of voting behaviour, and able to define more clearly the limits within which they were prepared (if in a majority in the House) to allow the Government to operate. It was a negative power they were employing, defeating Government proposals in the lobbies rather than one of being involved in the process of policy formulation, but it was a power nonetheless. A consequence of this has been that 'it is arguable that the period of minority Labour government after 1974 has made the Chamber more important than it had been for years'.[153] Given the factors encouraging party loyalty to which we have referred earlier, the incidence of Government defeats is not likely to increase (indeed, it will almost certainly be less given a Government returned in 1979 with an overall majority), but the precedent has been set, and on the basis of that the House has been presented with the opportunity of making itself more effective in the future. This, we would suggest, has important implications for the movement for parliamentary reform.

Calls for reform of the House of Commons are not new, and in this century have been most strident in the late 1920s and the 1930s and, more recently, from the very late 1950s (and more especially the mid 1960s) to the present day. Parliament came under close and critical scrutiny when there was a general questioning of the effectiveness of national institutions during times of economic unheaval. The House was perceived as being ineffective in fulfilling its function of scrutiny, and various reforms were advocated. The reforms suggested in the 1960s may be subsumed under the heading of internal procedural reforms, and the pressure for their implementation built up under the influential leadership of Professor Bernard Crick (especially with the publication of *The Reform of Parliament*), and was aided by the influx of a number of reform-minded Labour Members in the 1964 Parliament, encouraging the creation of the Labour Reform Group in the House. In the subsequent Parliament, Richard Crossman, as Leader of the House, introduced a package of reforms, a package designed on the one hand to facilitate Government business and on the other to introduce some new or improved methods of scrutiny. Among the reforms were the introduction of a number of specialist select committees, relaxation of the terms under which emergency debates could be sought under Standing Order No. 9, morning sittings two days a week, taking part of the Finance Bill in standing committee, and a simplifying of some of the confusing and archaic traditions in the sphere of financial procedure.[154] With the benefit of hindsight, it is possible to describe the reforms as being, in the event, either ineffective or so minor as to be irrelevant. The proposals themselves constituted something of a compromise, had neither the enthusiastic support of the Government (the reverse as far as some Ministers and officials were concerned) or of many Members, were not well thought out, and in the event achieved little. Morning sittings were a failure, and were brought to an end with few tears being shed over their demise; the Select Committee on Agriculture proved troublesome to the Foreign Office and the Department of Agriculture, and was effectively wound up; the impact of the change in S.O.9. was marginal;

and the House failed to approve a recommendation for the televising of proceedings. In terms of affecting significantly the ability of the House to scrutinize and influence the Government, they must be deemed a failure. Further internal reforms were instituted in subsequent Parliaments: the Expenditure Committee, the radio broadcasting of proceedings, the provision of limited public money to aid opposition parties in the carrying out of their parliamentary duties, and improved pay and facilities, but these too did not help affect significantly the ability of the House to influence Government; one, in fact, may have had a slightly negative rather than positive effect: the radio broadcasts of Prime Minister's Question Time were not well received, and the BBC ceased their live broadcast of them when the House rose for the summer recess in 1979.

The realization that internal procedural reforms were not having the desired effect resulted in the reform movement (in so far as it can be described as having constituted a coherent 'movement' at all) dividing roughly into two schools of thought: one which continued to press for more internal reforms, and the other to press for radical change through electoral reform. Examples of those falling in the former group would be Lisanne Radice with her pamphlet *Reforming the House of Commons*[155] and Sir Peter (now Lord) Rawlinson with his proposals as published in two articles in *The Times* in 1977.[156] The latter school of thought, which developed rapidly and gained some prominence in the latter half of the decade, was represented by such works as S. E. Finer's collection of essays, *Adversary Politics and Electoral Reform*[157] and, intellectually somewhat more weighty, various articles from the pen of S. A. Walkland.[158] The line of argument adopted, very simply, was that the procedural tinkering of the 1960s was largely irrelevant to the needs of the country and Parliament's capacity to respond to them. What was needed was electoral reform (with a system of proportional representation) which, it was thought, would put an end to the existing system of 'adversary politics'—one party coming into Government and undoing the work of its predecessor, thus encouraging uncertainty and instability in industry and economic management—and produce instead a centre-coalition government capable of making long-term decisions that would not be upset by an incoming Government of a different political persuasion; electoral reform would result also in a weakening of party ties, and so produce MPs with greater freedom of voting behaviour, responsive more to their constituencies than to the party whips.

Both schools of thought, though, suffered from a number of flaws. The internal reformers' arguments were too cautious. They adhered to the 'strong' single-party model of government, and sought in consequence to pursue two incompatible aims: 'that of strengthening the House of

Commons without detracting from the power of government'.[159] They placed too much of the onus on the Government as well for introducing the reforms. The reforms of the 1960s were the 'Crossman reforms'; when Crossman ceased to be Leader of the House, the drive for reform ended with the opposition of his successor, Fred Peart: 'He counts as much as I did'.[160] The Government was being left largely to determine what reforms it wanted introduced, reforms that were supposed to act as a means of scrutiny, of criticism, of its actions. As the Crossman *Diaries* reveal, Ministers and more especially their officials are rarely too keen on the establishment of bodies that are likely to get in their way. As S. A. Walkland observed, 'It seemed . . . inconceivable that any single-party government, secure in its voting strength on the floor of the House, would allow any significant scope to powerful investigatory agencies of the type that were being proposed.'[161] So long as it was left to the Government to determine the reforms, they were, for that very reason, likely to be ineffective.

The external reformers[162] suffered and suffer from a practical problem. Electoral reform (as Stuart Walkland has conceded)[163] is an unlikely prospect at the moment. Members would not wish to vote themselves out of their own seats, which would be the practical effect in some cases, and the Conservative and Labour Parties, the main beneficiaries of the existing system, will not embrace change. The Prime Minister, Mrs Thatcher, is a well-known opponent of PR. The extent to which it is an unlikely prospect has been demonstrated by various notes in the Commons in recent years.[164] It is not an issue whose time has come; indeed, there would appear to be less support for it now than in the 1930s. The reformers' argument is also open to criticism: policy continuity and greater freedom of voting behaviour by Members do not appear to be necessarily compatible aims. 'Even under the existing system of strong party ties, Members are capable of interrupting policy continuity . . . How much more so would it be under the system envisaged by the reformers?'[165] The 'adversary' thesis also appears to overlook the fact that policy continuity is as likely, if not more likely, to be interrupted by a Government during the life of a Parliament (note the U-turns on economic policy in the past two decades) than in consequence of a change of Government after an election. The strongest argument for proportional representation is on grounds of fairness, the traditional argument in its favour, and by adopting this new 'adversary politics' argument the reformers may even have done their cause a disservice, given that opponents of PR now have a much more vulnerable argument to respond to.

If there is to be reform of the House of Commons, giving it an effective role of scrutiny and influence, then the way lies through a majority of Members willing it and being prepared to force the issue and sustain the subsequent reforms. As Edward du Cann observed in a debate on the civil service in 1979, change generally does not come from the Government. 'What is needed is an exercise of political will on the part of the House of Commons as a whole.'[166] Members have the power to force their will upon the Government, as the experience of recent Parliaments, especially that of 1974–9, has demonstrated. The problem of parliamentary reform, as Stuart Walkland noted, 'is at bottom political—whether the Commons has the political power to make its views heeded in the decisions of government, or whether government can at all essential times control the decisions of Parliament. This was the awkward issue which the 1960s generation of reformers could only resolve by fudging.'[167] It is no longer an issue in need of fudging: the Commons has started to demonstrate that it has the power to make its views heeded.

If reforms are to be introduced and made effective as a means of scrutiny, then the developments of the 1970s have suggested that the answer lies with Members themselves. Support from Government or Opposition obviously helps, but in itself is not a sufficient condition; conversely, opposition from Front Benchers may be insufficient to prevent pressure for change. If a majority of Members wish for reforms, it is up to them to press the Government of the day to ensure their enactment and then to sustain them through their activities and, if necessary, their votes.[168]

This point was recognized and acted upon by a number of Members in the 1974–9 Parliament, most notably George Cunningham, and gained ground in the wake of the publication in August 1978 of the First Report from the Select Committee on Procedure.[169] Among its seventy-six recommendations were those for the creation of twelve new select committees, based on Departments rather than subject areas, with specialist staff and power to take evidence from interested parties. Initially, it appeared that the Report would go the way of previous Reports— ignored by the Government and consequently undebated. However, both the Opposition Front Bench and backbenchers on both sides of the House began to take an interest in its recommendations and started pressing the Government for action. As a result of this pressure, the Leader of the House, Michael Foot (known to be opposed to the proposals), agreed reluctantly to a debate, which took place in February 1979: so strongly was the view expressed by Members that they should have an opportunity to vote upon the Committee's recommendations that Mr Foot reversed his previous position and conceded the opportunity for such a vote.[170] The May general election then intervened. The Conservative manifesto contained a pledge to 'give the new House of Commons an early chance of coming to a decision' on the recommendations, and the new Government honoured that pledge on 26

June 1979. One of the Party's publications was subsequently to observe that 'by tabling a motion authorizing the establishment of twelve departmental Select Committees the Government paid prompt attention to recommendations originated by Parliament itself'.[171] By 248 votes to 12, the House approved the new committee structure. If the committees are to be effective, then it is up to backbench Members on both sides of the House to make them so. However, there is still some way to go. The power of choosing Members for the committees was put in the hands of the Committee of Selection, though the extent to which the Committee itself is free of the influence of the whips is a point of some contention.[172] The House failed to approve amendments giving the committees power to compel the attendance of Ministers, to set aside at least eight parliamentary days a session to debate their reports, and to give them power to appoint sub-committees to consider matters of detail.[173] The Leader of the House, Norman St. John-Stevas, gave a pledge that Ministers would do all in their power to co-operate with the committees (contending that he had not recommended powers to compel attendance in order to get the proposals through the House quickly);[174] however, Ministers are likely to be co-operative when they have nothing to hide, and unco-operative when they have.[175] By not giving committees power to compel attendance, the *decisions* as to attendance rest with the Ministers (or the Prime Minister): the committees can only request and influence attendance. By failing to set aside a number of days to debate committees' reports, the House is bereft largely of the necessary linkage between the committees and the floor of the House where Members' effective power, through the division lobbies, lies. They run the risk of operating, like their predecessors, 'in a sort of bi-partisan limbo, remote from the main House, unconnected with its procedures and deeply unsure of their role'.[176] The threat of action on the floor of the House in consequence of a committee's recommendations or findings is the way to ensure an effective Government response. Mr St. John-Stevas announced that he regarded the changes as a 'first instalment', but the danger inherent in this is that of the Government, through the Leader of the House, deciding what further reforms it wants introduced.[177] The pressure for further reforms to ensure an effective method of scrutinizing Government must come from Members, through 'an exercise of political will on the part of the House of Commons as a whole'.

In the 1970s—first in the 1970–4 Parliament and then, more substantially and dramatically, in that of 1974–9—Members on both sides of the House demonstrated a willingness to disagree with their parties, not out of sheer recalcitrance but out of a genuine belief that the line being taken by their leaders was wrong, and in so doing utilized the basic power available to a majority of the House: defeating the Government in the division lobbies. Basically, a negative power, but nevertheless a very important one, both in itself and as the basis on which positive changes may be achieved. The Government is the Government and governs, but Members of Parliament collectively (those not in the Government) can, *if they wish*, create an effective method of scrutiny of Government, and at the end of the day say say 'no' to its measures. The House of Commons cannot (has not and will not) govern, but it can help provide the broad parameters within which Government can govern.

[1] *Modern British Politics* (Faber, 1969 ed.), p. 350.

[2] *Ibid.*, pp. 350–1.

[3] Ergun Ozbudun, *Party Cohesion in Western Democracies: A Causal Analysis* (Sage Publications, 1970), p. 316. See the introduction to this volume.

[4] Compare Table 6 below and Table 8.7 in Philip Norton, *Conservative Dissidents* (Temple Smith, 1978), p. 212.

[5] See Philip Norton, *Dissension in the House of Commons 1945–74* (Macmillan, 1975), p. 296.

[6] On an amendment to the Resale Prices Bill in 1964. See *ibid.*, pp. 251–2.

[7] See Christopher Hollis, *Can Parliament Survive?* (Hollis & Carter, 1949), p. 64.

[8] The distinction between tendencies and factions is based on Richard Rose, 'Parties, factions and tendencies in Britain', *Political Studies*, 12, 1964, pp. 3–46.

[9] Norton, *Conservative Dissidents, op. cit.*, pp. 244–9.

[10] Philip Norton, 'Intra-Party Dissent in the House of Commons: A Case Study. The Immigration Rules 1972', *Parliamentary Affairs*, 29 (4), 1976, pp. 404–20.

[11] Norton, *Conservative Dissidents, op. cit.*, Ch. 9.

[12] Norton, 'Intra-Party Dissent in the House of Commons: A Case Study', *loc cit.*, p. 416.

[13] Conservative MP (now a Minister) to author.

[14] As the figure suggests, there was a large overlap, with Labour and Conservative anti-EC Members combining in the same lobby. The figures tend to underemphasize slightly the division within the Conservative ranks, as in a number of divisions in which Labour Members voted against the whips the Opposition allowed free votes.

[15] The Conservative dissenters usually numbered less than ten (centred on Roger Moate, Neil Marten, John Biffen and Richard Body), and the Labour dissenters more than ten, sometimes well in excess of fifty.

[16] Labour MPs cast dissenting votes in 78 divisions (on occasion the votes being cast by pro rather than anti-devolutionists) and Conservatives in 36, several of the latter involving anti-devolutionists, voting when the Opposition abstained from voting. The figures underemphasize Conservative dissent due to several free votes being allowed. The number of Conservative pro-devolutionists in a lobby (where the whips was on) never reached more than ten, while the number of Labour dissenters ranged from one to in excess of fifty.

[17] Labour MPs also cast more dissenting votes on Lords amendments, the difference here due to dissent on Lords amendments to the Scotland and Wales Bills.

[18] See Norton, *Conservative Dissidents*, Table 8.6, p. 210, for the Conservative figures in preceding Parliaments.

[19] For example, taking instances covered in this volume, the Scotland and Wales Bill and first European Assembly Elections Bill.

[20] See J. Richard Piper, 'Backbench rebellion, party government and consensus politics: the case of the Parliamentary Labour Party 1966–70', *Parliamentary Affairs*, 27, 1974, pp. 384–96.

[21] The left/right division (the terms are rarely defined but are in common usage) is sometimes distinguished in terms of Fundamentalists versus Revisionists or Socialists versus Social Democrats. See, e.g. Harry Lazer, 'Division in the Labour Party: Left and Right in

the Wilson Years', Paper presented at the American Political Science Association Conference, Chicago, 1976.

[22] For more on Yule's Q and the conventions for describing values, see Norton, *Conservative Dissidents*, *op. cit.*, p. 19, and James A. Davis, *Elementary Survey Analysis* (Prentice-Hall, 1971), pp. 33–62.

[23] Rose, *op. cit.*, p. 37.

[24] Neil Kinnock MP in *Tribune*, 29 November 1974, reprinted in Douglas Hill (ed), *Tribune 40* (Quartet, 1977), pp. 194–5. See also A. King (ed), *British Members of Parliament: A Self-Portrait* (Macmillan, 1974), p. 45, and Joe Ashton MP in *Labour Weekly*, 3 January 1975.

[25] Kinnock, *loc. cit.*, p. 195.

[26] Philip Norton, 'Intra-Party Dissent in the House of Commons: The Parliament of 1974', *The Parliamentarian*, 58 (4), 1977, pp. 243–4.

[27] In the 69 divisions, the proportion of Tribune MPs in each ranged from a low of 39 per cent to a high of 87 per cent.

[28] The figures of membership are based upon membership lists as published in *The Political Companion*, issues numbers 21 to 28.

[29] The breakdown of dissenting votes cast by Tribune MPs is as follows: No dissenting votes: 0; 1 only: 3 (constituting 9% of Labour MPs to cast 1 dissenting vote only) 2–9: 10 (11% of Labour MPs casting 2–9 dissenting votes); 10–19: 8 (21.5%); 20–29: 12 (37.5%); 30–39: 8 (47%); 40–49: 10 (50%); 50–59: 2 (40%); 60–69: 6 (75%) 70–79: 5 (100%); 80–89: 7 (100%); 90–99: 6 (100%); 100 or more: 9 (100%).

[30] S. E. Finer *et al.*, in *Backbench Opinion in the House of Commons 1955–59* (Pergamon, 1961), attempted to identify the 50 most left-wing Labour Members of that Parliament (based on Early Day Motion data)—an exercise not without its critics (and, in Hugh Berrington's later volume, its defender)—while the Conservative Research Department has displayed a not unsurprising willingness to monitor Labour Members' voting behaviour in order to identify those on the party's Left. See e.g. appendix 2 in 'The Labour Left in Marginal Seats', *Politics Today*, No. 15, 19 September 1977.

[31] In addition to the nine identified in Table 4 (Messrs Skinner, Thomas, Flannery, Madden, Canavan, Mikardo, the Misses Richardson and Maynard, and Mrs Wise), the Members, with number of dissenting votes in parenthesis, are: T. Fletcher (71), E. Heffer (71), N. Kinnock (72), D. Hoyle (76), R. Parry (79), J. Lee (80), R. Kerr (81), S. Newens (81), A. Bennett (84), R. Cook (84), A. Latham (85), J. Rooker (87), S. Bidwell (90), T. Litterick (94), E. Loyden (98), G. Rodgers (98), J. Lamond (99), and S. Thorne (99).

[32] In November 1974, the Manifesto Group had been formed and, claiming a membership of about 75 Members, it was the effective equivalent on the right to the Tribune Group on the left. However, there was no large scale or cohesive voting by Manifesto MPs during the life of the Parliament, though some of its members were prominent dissenters on occasion. (Unlike the Tribune Group, Ministers were not eligible for membership of the Manifesto Group.)

[33] *HC Deb.* 919, c. 581–92.

[34] See Division [103] in this volume.

[35] While conceding this point, R. Rose *op. cit.* suggests that in the early 1960s Harold Wilson converted the Labour Party from one of factions to one of tendencies 'temporarily, at least'. This temporary period would now appear to be at an end, though the problem of no recognized factional leader remains.

[36] Free votes as defined in this volume; all other divisions, as delineated in the introduction, are included for the purpose of this compilation and our calculations, and are referred to for convenience as 'non-free votes'.

[37] That is, where all dissenting voters were Tribune Group MPs, a total of 28 divisions; of these, 12 involved one dissenting Member only. Tribunites comprised more than 90 per cent of the dissenters in a further nine divisions.

[38] 'Dissenting lobby' is employed as a convenient term for the number of Members casting dissenting votes in one division. (The use of the word 'lobby' should not be taken to imply that the dissenters were the sole occupants of one of the division lobbies; a dissenting Labour lobby may vote with Opposition Members for example.)

[39] One Labour Member occasionally cast multiple lone dissenting votes, as e.g. John Stonehouse and (on devolution) Tam Dalyell. The numbers involved in each case are too small to be worthy of much note.

[40] A. Lawrence Lowell, *The Government of England*, Vol. II (Macmillan, 1908), pp. 74–81. It is possible now to employ more sophisticated analyses of party cohesion, but for reasons of time it has not been possible to utilize them in this study. See S. H. Beer, 'Data on party unity in British parties' (mimeo, undated), and John D. Fair, 'A Quantitative Analysis of the House of Commons Division Lists from 1886 to 1921: Method and Preliminary Results', Paper presented to British Politics Group, American Political Science Association Conference, Washington D.C., 1979.

[41] Samuel H. Beer, quoted above.

[42] The percentage of non-party votes per session was: 1974/5: 29 (almost 8 per cent of non-free Labour votes); 1975/6: 29 (again, almost 8 per cent); 1976/7: 27 (almost 14 per cent); 1977/8: 38 (14 per cent); and 1978/9: 28 (over 31 per cent). (The percentage of 11.6% overall is produced because of the large number of divisions in the first two sessions.)

[43] There were 18 defeats in the 1868 session. In the list given by Lowell for post-1847 sessions, no other session witnessed more than 15 defeats. Lowell, *op. cit.*, pp. 79–80.

[44] Based on the number of defeats per session (1847–1906) as listed by Lowell, *op. cit.*, pp. 79–80.

[45] As e.g. on the Poultry Meat Hygiene Regulations, November 1976, and, more notably, on the European Community Membership motion in April 1975; note the comments of the *Spectator*, 19 April 1975, p. 463.

[46] The sizable dissenting lobbies comprised a disproportionate number of Tribune Group MPs (about 80 per cent of the total), plus some of their like-minded sympathisers, and—despite the presence in the lobby of Manifesto MPs Giles Radice and Neville Sandelson—it was recognized as dissent by the party's left wing.

[47] Of the 37 abstainers, all bar two were members of the Tribune Group; James Sillars, one of the two Scottish Labour Members to cross-vote, was also a Group member. See also Philip Norton, 'The Government Defeat: 10 March 1976', *The Parliamentarian*, 57 (3), 1976, pp. 174–5.

[48] The seven known abstainers were all Tribune Group MPs, as was one of the two cross-voters. (The position is complicated slightly by the fact that the other cross-voter was John Mackintosh, so voting because of his stance on the issue of devolution.)

[49] Of the twenty Members to cross-vote or abstain, 14 were Tribune Group MPs, one an ex-member of the Group, and one or two others had established left-wing voting patterns, as, e.g. John Ellis.

[50] The amendments, named after Jeff Rooker and Mrs Audrey Wise, the two Tribune MPs to cross-vote to ensure that they were carried, raised the levels of income tax allowances and partially indexed them against inflation.

[51] For fear of a repetition of its 1976 defeat, the Government decided not to debate the 1977 White Paper on a substantive motion (even a 'take note' one, since that is what it had been defeated on the previous year), and tabled instead an adjournment motion in the hope that Left-wing Members might support it what was technically a procedural motion. See the comments in Alistair Michie and Simon Hoggart, *The Pact* (Quartet, 1978), p. 14. In the event, the Government seemed likely to be defeated by a combination of opposition parties against it, and decided to take the unusual course of not contesting the division, the voting being 293 votes to 0. *HC Deb.* 928, c. 763–6. As a result of this, the Leader of the Opposition tabled a motion of no confidence in the Government, and in order to avoid defeat on it the Government negotiated the Lib-Lab Pact.

[52] In addition to the cross-votes of Richard Crawshaw and Father of the House, George Strauss, the abstainers comprised Members recognized as being on the party's right wing. According to one source, Tribune Group MPs compiled a list of the abstainers for 'future reference'. *Daily Telegraph*, 6 August 1975.

[52a] On occasion, MPs on the party's right did disagree or were uneasy with some Government measures: John Mackintosh, for example, is reputed to have been saying what many others were thinking when he opposed the provisions of the Dock Work Regulation Bill (Labour MP to author). However, they would appear to have been prepared to acquiesce

in measures that were perceived as the exception to the rule; for the Tribune Group, it was more a case of opposing Government policies that were the rule rather than the exception.

[53] The Labour dissenters comprised roughly half-and-half of Tribunites and non-Tribunites; among the latter were several members of the party's right and a number normally considered party loyalists, such as James Johnson and—casting their only dissenting votes of the Parliament—George Grant and Ian Wrigglesworth.

[54] Tribune Members constituted a little over half of the dissenters, but were joined by Members from all parts of the parliamentary party, including various Manifesto Group MPs.

[55] The party's right wing was rather well represented among the dissenters, but a sufficient number of Tribunites and Members with left-wing voting patterns joined them for it to be considered a fairly diverse lobby.

[56] *HC Deb.* 914, c. 165–8.

[57] *Sunday Express*, 27 June 1976.

[58] *The Times*, 28 June 1976. It was estimated that about 30 Labour Members were prepared to abstain in the division.

[59] Some of the defeats took the whips by surprise, as e.g. that on the Dock Work Regulation Bill in 1976: John Mackintosh and Brian Walden had not told them of their intention to abstain. *Daily Express*, 12 November 1976. On occasion, though, the whips expected defeat, the decision to go ahead being taken by the Cabinet; see, e.g., Michie and Hoggart, *op. cit.*, p. 27.

[60] The Pact was one essentially in which a commitment was made by the Government to consult with the Liberals, to introduce the European Assembly Elections Bill in that session (1976/7), to make progress on legislation for devolution, to provide time for a Liberal Private Member's Bill and to limit the provisions of a Government Bill, in return for which the Liberals 'would work with the Government in pursuit of economic recovery'. The text of the agreement is reproduced in *The Political Companion*, No. 25, Winter 1976/Spring 1977, pp. 150–1. See also David Butler (ed), *Coalitions in British Politics* (Macmillan, 1978), pp. 107–9.

[61] For the background to the Pact and some of its eventual shortcomings, see Michie and Hoggart, *op. cit.*; also Butler, *op. cit.*, Ch. 5.

[62] *HC Deb.* 965, c. 583–8.

[63] Norton, *Conservative Dissidents, op. cit.*, Ch. 8.

[64] *Ibid.*, pp. 73–4, and Norton, *Dissension in the House of Commons 1945–74, op. cit.*, pp. 404–6.

[65] Norton, *Conservative Dissidents, op. cit.*, p. 83, and 'Intra-Party Dissent in the House of Commons: A Case Study', *loc cit.*, p. 414.

[66] *The Times*, 19 October 1973.

[67] Norton, *Conservative Dissidents, op. cit.*, p. 244.

[68] Mr Powell had voted against the Government in 115 divisions. However, when the number of dissenting votes is expressed as a proportion of all votes in the Parliament, Mr Winterton's percentage would rank lower than that of one or two dissenters in the 1970–4 Parliament, in addition to Mr Powell.

[69] See Philip Norton, 'Test your own Powellism', *Crossbow*, 17, February 1976, pp. 10–11.

[70] David Wood, *The Times*, 9 May 1974.

[71] *The Times*, 19 March 1974.

[72] Nicholas Winterton MP to author.

[73] *The Times*, 10 May 1974.

[74] *The Times*, 14 June 1974.

[75] Patrick Cormack MP to author. In May, Mr Cormack had written to Mr du Cann to complain of Opposition tactics in divisions, which he described as 'farces'. *The Times*, 9 May 1974.

[76] During a review of party policy undertaken at this time, a number of Members criticized Mr Heath for the extent to which they were not consulted on the deliberations and reports of the study groups undertaking the review. *Daily Telegraph*, 25 June 1974.

[77] Conservative MP to author.

[78] Sir Nigel Fisher, *The Tory Leaders* (Weidenfeld and Nicolson, 1977), appendix 2. On the first ballot, a candidate had to receive an absolute majority plus fifteen per cent of the votes of those entitled to vote to be deemed elected; failing that, a second ballot was to be held, with new nominations, but with an overall majority alone required for election; if no candidate

received an overall majority, a third ballot was to be held limited to the three candidates with the highest number of votes in the second ballot, and with the single transferable vote system of election being employed.

[79] Philip Norton, 'The Organization of Parliamentary Parties', in S. A. Walkland (ed), *The House of Commons in the Twentieth Century* (Oxford University Press, 1979), pp. 56–7.

[80] Robin Maxwell-Hyslop MP to author. Mr Maxwell-Hyslop was a noted supporter of Mrs Thatcher, but the point has been confirmed to author by less committed Members.

[81] 172 Conservatives had cast one or more dissenting votes in the 1959–64 Parliament, though none had cast more than 22 dissenting votes.

[82] Norton, *Conservative Dissidents, op. cit.*, Ch. 8 and pp. 244–54.

[83] *Ibid.*, pp. 244–54, and Norton, 'Test your own Powellism', *loc cit.*

[84] The possible exception was that on the 'take note' motion on devolution on 19 January 1976. The other seven being: British Leyland Motor Corporation Ltd. motion of 18 Dec. 1974, the Butter Prices Order of 13 Jan. 1975, the Second Reading of the Prices Bill on 30 Jan. 1975, the British Leyland (Financial Assistance) motion of 21 May 1975 (the foregoing chosen to represent occasions when the economic right, the party's neo-Liberals, would dissent); the amendment on report stage of the Race Relations Bill on 8 July 1976 (for the home affairs right); the Second Reading of the European Assembly Elections Bill on 24 Nov. 1977; and the Rhodesian sanctions order of 8 Nov. 1978 (for the foreign affairs right). The scalogram was too large to be reproduced here.

[85] If one wished to identify the 'most right-wing Conservative Members' of the Parliament, then these fourteen would probably suffice: they were Nicholas Budgen (the Member to dissent on seven of the eight occasions), Nicholas Winterton, Ivan Lawrence, Roger Moate, Michael Brotherton, Ian Gow, Norman Tebbit, John Stokes, John Biffen, Colin Shepherd, Alan Clark, John Hannam, Ivor Stanbrook and (perhaps surprisingly) Sir Anthony Meyer.

[86] *The Times*, 9 December 1976.

[87] *Ibid.*

[88] *The Times*, 10 December 1976. The three were Hector Monro, George Younger and John Corrie; the latter did resign on the eve of the Second Reading vote. Russell Fairgrieve also offered his resignation as chairman of the Scottish Conservative Party, but this too was refused.

[89] Notably on Second Reading of the Scotland Bill, with dissent from the pro-devolutionists (4 cross-voters and 15 abstainers), and on an amendment to clause 18 of the Bill on 29 November 1977, with 66 Conservative anti-devolutionists voting for it.

[90] As, e.g. on various divisions on 25 January 1975. Pro-devolutionists tended to enter the lobbies when free votes were permitted, but otherwise tended to opt for abstention.

[91] See, e.g., *The Economist*, 19 November 1977, p. 21.

[92] George Younger became Secretary of State for Scotland, and Malcolm Rifkind and Russell Fairgrieve junior Ministers in his Department; Alick Buchanan-Smith was appointed Minister of State for Agriculture, and Hector Monro Minister for Sport. (Only John Corrie was not given office.)

[93] See Norton, *Dissension in the House of Commons 1945–74, op. cit.*, pp. 255–6 (and pp. 2–4),

[94] *Ibid.*, pp. 362, 380–1, 521–2, 597–8 for pre-1974 Parliaments.

[95] See Norton, *Conservative Dissidents, op. cit.*, pp. 152–3. See this volume for dissent on the 1974, 1975, 1976 and 1977 (as well as the 1978) orders. The number of dissenters on each occasion, reinforced usually by Ulster Unionists, was 23, 15 (division on a Friday), 19 and 27 respectively.

[96] 41 Conservatives voted against Second Reading. See division [45].

[97] The MP in the best position to do so was John Biffen, but he spent part of the Parliament as a member of the Shadow Cabinet.

[98] Some of the points in this section constitute points developed from a paper, 'The Changing Face of the House of Commons in the 1970s', delivered by the author to the British Politics Group at the American Political Science Association Conference, Washington D.C., 1979.

[99] Ian Gilmour, *The Body Politic* (Hutchinson, rev. ed. 1971), p. 261.

[100] Graeme Moodie, *The Government of Great Britain* (Methuen, 1964), p. 100.

[101] Robert E. Dowse and Trevor Smith, 'Party Discipline in the House of Commons—A Comment', *Parliamentary Affairs* (16), 1962–3, p. 164.

[102] See the comments of Philip Norton, 'Government Defeats in the House of Commons: Three Restraints Overcome', *The Parliamentarian*, 59 (4), 1978, pp. 234–5.

[103] This was especially so with Volume III. Richard Crossman, *The Diaries of a Cabinet Minister*, Vol. III (Hamilton/Cape, 1977). A simple but useful example of a decision being reached for partisan and ad hoc reasons was that to lower the voting age. *Ibid.* p. 92.

[104] Gilmour, *op. cit.*, p. 201.

[105] In addition to the Crossman *Diaries*, *passim*, see also Leo Abse MP, *Private Member* (Macdonald, 1973), p. 98.

[106] Humphry Berkeley, *The Power of the Prime Minister* (Chilmark Press, 1968), p. 9 of U.S. edition.

[107] E.g. T. F. Lindsay, *Parliament from the Press Gallery* (Macmillan, 1967), p. 23; see also Max Nicholson, *The System* (McGraw-Hill, 1967), p. 155.

[108] See Norton, 'The Organisation of Parliamentary Parties', *loc cit.*, pp. 10–12.

[109] Philip Norton, 'Party Organisation in the House of Commons', *Parliamentary Affairs*, 31 (4), 1978, p. 421.

[110] Based on the author's research, cited above, and interviews and correspondence with Members of Parliament.

[111] Bernard Weatherill MP, in Radio 3 programme, 'The Parliamentary Process: Parties and Parliament', 12 February 1976.

[112] See J. A. Cross, 'Withdrawal of the Conservative Party Whip', *Parliamentary Affairs*, 21, 1967–8, pp. 166–75.

[113] R. J. Jackson, *Rebels and Whips* (Macmillan, 1968), pp. 302–3.

[114] John Lee claimed that in 1969 he was 'the last member of the Labour Party from whom it was seriously considered withdrawing the whip'. *HC Deb.* 915, c. 2289.

[115] William Hamilton MP, in A. King and A. Sloman (eds), *Westminster and Beyond* (Macmillan, 1975), p. 103. Note also his comments at p. 102.

[116] A small number of similar instances have been recounted to the author by Members of various Parliaments. In 1973, for instance, after abstaining on a three-line whip, one Conservative MP received a letter from his whip asking why he had abstained: 'I have put it in the waste paper basket and do not intend to reply.'

[117] Others so promoted included Robert Cryer, Mrs Judith Hart, Leslie Huckfield, John Ellis, Joe Ashton, Eric Heffer and James Wellbeloved, among others.

[118] Norton, *Conservative Dissidents*, *op. cit.*, Ch. 9.

[119] Former Conservative MP to author. Cited in *ibid.*, p. 173.

[120] Norton, *Conservative Dissidents*, *op. cit.*, Ch. 6.

[121] *HC Deb.* 800, c. 166.

[122] Note the comments of Norton, 'Party Organisation in the House of Commons', *loc cit.*, p. 410.

[123] Norton, *Conservative Dissidents*, *op. cit.*, Ch. 7.

[124] Reg Prentice, who was disowned by his local party in Newham North-East, was an opponent of devolution, but his stand on the issue appears totally unrelated to the dispute with his local party.

[125] 'Partisanship and Dissidence in the Nineteenth-Century House of Commons', *Parliamentary Affairs*, 21, 1967–8, p. 363.

[126] David Butler, 'The renomination of MPs: A Note', *Parliamentary Affairs*, 31 (2), 1978, pp. 210–12. For more detailed treatment of the subject see Norton, *Conservative Dissidents*, *op. cit.*, Ch. 7, and A. D. R. Dickson, 'Conflict in Constituency Parties', Unpublished PhD thesis, Council for National Academic Awards, n.d.

[127] *HC Deb.* CL, c. 49.

[128] J. Harvey and L. Bather, *The British Constitution* (Macmillan, 1965), p. 234.

[129] Letter to *The Times*, 13 July 1971.

[130] *HC Deb.* 939, c. 615.

[131] See Philip Norton, 'Government Defeats in the House of Commons: Myth and Reality', *Public Law*, Winter 1978, pp. 362–5. The three types of defeats are also drawn from this article.

[132] Should it decide upon reversal, a Government cannot table a motion identical to the one upon which the defeat took place. A motion, once defeated, cannot be reintroduced in

the same session, and so, to reverse a defeat, the language of the new motion must be materially different though, in practice, achieving the same ends as if it were the original motion. Hence, all reversals that take place are *de facto*, though never (in the same session, unless standing orders are suspended), *de jure* reversals.

[133] Philip Norton, 'The Government Defeat: March 10, 1976', *The Parliamentarian*, 57 (3), 1976, p. 175n.

[134] See Norton, 'Government Defeats in the House of Commons: Myth and Reality', *loc cit*. pp. 375–6.

[135] *Ibid.*, p. 378.

[136] Anthony King, 'Modes of Executive–Legislative Relations: Great Britain, France, and West Germany', *Legislative Studies Quarterly*, 1 (1), 1976, pp. 15–18.

[137] Philip Norton, 'The House of Commons in the 1970s: Three Views on Reform', *Hull Papers in Politics No. 3* (Hull University Politics Department, 1978), p. 4.

[138] The Government also derives a separate legitimacy as Her Majesty's Government.

[139] This is, in fact, the simplest expression of what is a complex function. See Philip Norton, *The Commons in Perspective* (Martin Robertson, forthcoming), Ch. 4.

[140] *Ibid.*, Ch. 4.

[141] See Norton, 'The Organisation of Parliamentary Parties', *loc cit.* for a detailed study of the development and structure of parliamentary parties.

[142] Sir Bernard Braine MP, book review, *The Parliamentarian*, 60 (3), 1979, p. 182.

[143] Norton, 'The Organisation of Parliamentary Parties', *loc cit.*, p. 62.

[144] Michael Stewart MP, in Radio 3 programme, 'The Parliamentary Process: Government and Opposition', 19 February 1976.

[145] Gilmour, *op. cit.*, p. 269.

[146] For some examples, see Ronald Butt, *The Power of Parliament* (Constable, 1967), Chs. 6–10.

[147] The Government had a majority of one: not only did 31 Conservatives cross-vote, but a further 20 or more abstained from voting.

[148] Butt, *op. cit.*, p. 269.

[149] Foreword to *A Better Tomorrow*, reproduced in F. W. S. Craig (ed), *British General Election Manifestos 1900–1974* (Macmillan, 1975), p. 325.

[150] See Norton, *Conservative Dissidents*, *op. cit.*, Ch. 10.

[151] *Ibid.*, p. 274.

[152] Timothy Raison MP, *Power and Parliament* (Basil Blackwell, 1979), p. 74.

[153] *Ibid.*

[154] Most of the reforms are summarised in Frank Stacey, *British Government 1966–75* (Oxford University Press, 1975), Chs. 3 and 4. See also Gavin Drewry, 'The Outsider and House of Commons Reform: Some evidence from the Crossman Diaries', *Parliamentary Affairs*, 31 (4), 1978, pp. 424–35. For reforms advocated in the pre-1960 period, see Hansard Society, *Parliamentary Reform 1933–60* (Cassell, 1967).

[155] Anthony Wigram, 1975.

[156] Fabian Pamphlet 448 (Fabian Society, 1977).

[157] *The Times*, 12 and 13 September 1977.

[158] As, e.g., 'Whither the Commons?', Ch. 12 in S. A. Walkland and M. Ryle (eds), *The Commons in the Seventies* (Fontana, 1977); 'The Politics of Parliamentary Reform', *Parliamentary Affairs*, 29 (2), 1976, pp. 190–200; 'Parliament and the economy in Britain: Some Reflections', *Parliamentary Affairs*, 32 (1), 1979, pp. 6–18.

[159] S. A. Walkland, 'The Politics of Parliamentary Reform', *loc cit.*, p. 192.

[160] Crossman, *op. cit.*, p. 355, also cited in Drewry, *loc cit.*

[161] Walkland, 'The Politics of Parliamentary Reform', *loc cit.*, pp. 192–3.

[162] The distinction between 'internal' and 'external' reformers is made in Norton, 'The House of Commons in the 1970s: Three Views on Reform', *op. cit.*

[163] Walkland, 'Whither the Commons?', *loc cit.*, pp. 255–6.

[164] In the 1974–9 Parliament, on free votes, PR for the proposed Scottish Assembly, under the Scotland Bill, was rejected by a majority of 183, and PR for the 1979 European Assembly elections by a majority of 97, despite a Government recommendation to support it.

[165] Philip Norton, 'The Influence of the Backbench Member', *The Parliamentarian*, 58 (3), 1977, p. 169.

[166] *HC Deb.* 960, c. 1342.

[167] 'Whither the Commons?' *loc cit.*, p. 244.

[168] Norton, 'The Changing Face of the House of Commons in the 1970s', *loc cit.*, p. 16.

[169] Vol. 1: Report and Minutes of Proceedings. HC 588, 1977–8.

[170] *HC Deb.* 963, c. 383–4. See also 'Parliament prepares to seize power', *The Economist*, 24 February 1979, pp. 23–4.

[171] *Politics Today*, No. 11, 16 July 1979, p. 242.

[172] The move is a step in the right direction, but close observers of the new system to whom the author has talked appear divided upon the extent to which the Committee of Selection is capable of exerting its independence.

[173] Only three of the committees (foreign; home affairs; treasury and civil service) have power to appoint sub-committees.

[174] BBC Radio 4, 'World at One', 19 June 1979, quoted in *Politics Today*, *op. cit.*, p. 243.

[175] In the wake of the debate, one Conservative Member wrote to his constituents that 'my own faith in the willingness of Ministers to co-operate is not that great'. Michael Brotherton MP, 'From the House . . .', *Louth Standard*, 6 July 1979, p. 3.

[176] Walkland, 'Whither the Commons?' *loc cit.*, p. 246.

[177] This would appear to be borne out by the content and nature of some further essentially minor reforms put before the House in October 1979. See *HC Deb.* 972, c. 1370-91. It should also be borne out by further reforms promised for summer 1980.

GOVERNMENT DEFEATS IN THE HOUSE OF COMMONS 1974-79

The Parliament of 1974

The defeats in this Parliament were the consequence of a minority Government being outvoted by opposition parties.

19 June 1974 New Clause (Trade Unions) to Finance Bill—to help restore relief to trade unions de-registered under the 1971 Industrial Relations Act—defeated 308–299.*HC Deb*. 875, c. 607–14.

20 June 1974 Government amendment to Opposition motion on Labour's plan for industry defeated 311–290. *HC Deb*. 875, c. 607–14.

27 June 1974 Government amendment to Opposition motion on Rates negatived 298–289, *and* Opposition motion then carried by the same vote. *HC Deb*. 875, c. 1865–74.

11 July 1974 Divisions on two Opposition amendments to Trade Union and Labour Relations Bill resulted in two tied votes. *HC Deb*. 876, c. 1685–92, 1715–20. In accordance with precedence, the Chair gave casting vote against each amendment. Subsequently it was disclosed that one Labour Member had been 'nodded through' on each vote without being within the precincts of the Palace of Westminster. *HC deb*. 877, c. 38–44, 248–65. House consequently declared proceedings of 11th July on the two votes null and void, and asked the Lords to return the Bill for correction. The Bill was returned, and the amendments made. *HC Deb*. 877, c. 265, 366–7.

16 July 1974 New Clause (Mitigation of Corporation Tax liability of small companies) to Finance Bill carried 292–267. *HC Deb*. 877, c. 323–30.

16 July 1974 Opposition amendment to Clause 2 (Increase of certain duties on betting) of Finance Bill carried 291–274. *HC Deb*. 877, c. 355–60.

16 July 1974 Government amendment to Clause 5 (Value Added Tax—time of supply) of Finance Bill—to remove Opposition amendment made in committee—defeated 298–280. *HC Deb*. 877, c. 385–90.

16 July 1974 Liberal amendment to Clause 7 (Charge of income tax for 1974–5) of Finance Bill carried 296–280. *HC Deb*. 977, c. 403–8.

18 July 1974 Government motion to disagree with a Lords amendment to Clause 1 of the Health and Safety at Work Etc. Bill defeated 159–153. *HC Deb*. 877, c. 823–6.

18 July 1974 Government motion to disagree with a Lords amendment to Clause 2 of Health and Safety at Work Etc. Bill defeated 147–143. *HC Deb*. 877, c. 831–4.

30 July 1974 Government motion to disagree with Lords amendment (New Clause 'A') to Trade Union and Labour Relations Bill defeated 276–270. *HC Deb*. 878, c. 513–8.

30 July 1974 Government motion to disagree with Lords amendment (New Clause 'B') to Trade Union and Labour Relations Bill defeated 280–269. *HC Deb*. c. 525–30.

30 July 1974 Government motion to disagree with a Lords amendment to Clause 5 (Lists of trade unions and employers' associations) of Trade Union and Labour Relations Bill defeated 281–271. *HC Deb*. 878, c. 529–34..

30 July 1974 Government motion to disagree with Lords amendment to Clause 10 (acts in contemplation of furtherance of trade disputes) of Trade Union and Labour Relations Bill defeated 282–272. *HC Deb*. 878, c. 543–8.

30 July 1974 Government motion to disagree with Lords amendment to Clause 26 (meaning of trade dispute) of Trade Union and Labour Relations Bill. *HC Deb*. 878, c. 551–6.

The Parliament of 1974-9

Following details of each defeat in this Parliament, an (O) indicates a defeat attributable to a combination of opposition parties against a minority Government, (D) indicates a defeat attributable to dissent (by vote and/or abstention) by Government backbenchers, and (X) indicates a defeat attributable to neither, e.g. confusion in the division lobbies.

29 Jan. 1975 Government amendment to Social Security Benefits Bill defeated 280 votes to 265. *HC Deb.* 885, c. 525–30. (D)

2 July 1975 Government amendment to clause 20 of the Industry Bill defeated by 220 votes to 149. *HC Deb.* 894, c. 1623–8. (D)

2 July 1975 Government amendment to delete schedule 3 of the Industry Bill defeated by 230 votes to 147. *HC Deb.* 894, c. 1631–6. (D)

17 July 1975 Conservative amendment to Finance Bill on VAT on television sets carried 108 votes to 106. *HC Deb.* 895, c. 1821–4. (D)

4 Aug. 1975 Government motion to disagree with Lords amendment to delete clause 4 of the Housing Finance (Special Provision) Bill defeated by 268 votes to 261. *HC Deb* 897, c. 199–204. (D)

11 Feb. 1976 Opposition motion to reduce salary of Industry Secretary carried by 214 votes to 209, following some confusion in the division lobbies. *HC Deb.* 905, c. 521–6. (X)

10 Mar. 1976 Government motion on public expenditure negatived by 284 votes to 256. *HC Deb.* 907, c. 561–6. (D)

28 Jun. 1976 Government defeat on motion for adjournment (through failing to contest it) following debate on its Child Benefits Scheme by 259 votes to 0. *HC Deb.* 914, c. 165–8. (O) [Though defeated by combination of opposition parties, Government failed to contest division for fear of defeat brought about by dissent by its own backbenchers.]

10 Nov. 1976 *Two* Lords amendments to Dock Work Regulation Bill carried against the Government by 310 votes to 308, and by 311 votes to 308, respectively, attributed to Labour abstentions. *HC Deb.* 919, c. 919, c. 581–92. (D) (O)[1]

7 Feb. 1977 Second Reading of the Reduction of Redundancy Rebates Bill negatived by 130 votes to 129. *HC Deb.* 925, c. 1183–9. (O) (X)[2]

22 Feb. 1977 Guillotine motion for the Scotland and Wales Bill defeated by 312 votes to 283. *HC Deb.* 926, 1361–6. (D)

11 Mar. 1977 Government defeated by 293 votes to 0 through failing to contest division following debate on its 1977 White Paper on Public Expenditure. *HC Deb.* 928, c. 763–6. (O)

5 Apr. 1977 Government defeated on adjournment motion by 203 votes to 185 following debate on teacher training colleges in Scotland. *HC Deb.* 929, c. 1187–90. (O) [Defeat exacerbated by some Labour abstentions.]

12 Jul. 1977 Third Reading of the Local Authority Works (Scotland) Bill negatived by 105 votes to 99. *HC Deb.* 935, c. 377–80. (O) (X)[3]

13 Jul. 1977 New clause to the Criminal Law Bill carried against the Government by 89 votes to 86. *HC Deb.* 935, c. 531–4. (D)

22 Nov. 1977 The 'stand part' motion for clause 1 of the Scotland Bill negatived by 199 votes to 184. *HC Deb.* 939, c. 1401–4. (O) [Defeat exacerbated by some Labour dissent.]

5 Dec. 1977 Government defeated on adjournment motion following emergency debate on Crown Agents' affair. *HC Deb.* 940, c. 1093–6. (D)

7 Dec. 1977 'Stand part' motion for clause 40 of the Scotland Bill negatived by 161 votes to 160. *HC Deb.* 940, c. 1557–60. (D)

23 Jan. 1978 Opposition amendment to devalue Green Pound by 7½%, instead of 5% proposed in Government motion, carried by 291 votes to 280, and amended motion then carried by 291 to 281. *HC Deb.* 942, c. 1097–1106. (O)

25 Jan. 1978 Amendment to amendment to provide 40% 'threshold' for Scottish referendum carried by 166 votes to 151, and amended amendment then carried by 168 votes to 142. *HC Deb.* 942, c. 1541–8. (D)

25 Jan. 1978 Amendment to Scotland Bill to require Secretary of State to lay order excluding Orkney and/or Shetland Islands from provisions of Act if majority of voters in relevant islands voted 'No' in referendum carried against Government by 204 votes to 118. *HC Deb.* 942, c. 1547–52. (D)

14 Feb. 1978 New clause to Scotland Bill (to provide three month gap between a general election and referendum) carried against Government by 242 votes to 223. *HC Deb.* 944, c. 297–302. (D)

15 Feb. 1978 Amendment on Report stage of Scotland Bill to delete 40% 'threshold' requirement for referendum defeated by 298 votes to 243. *HC Deb.* 944, c. 597–602. (D)

15 Feb. 1978 Government amendment to Scotland Bill to replace 40% 'threshold' requirement with one of 33⅓% of eligible voters defeated by 285 votes to 240. *HC Deb.* 944, c. 601–6. (D)

19 Apr. 1978 'Stand part' motion for clause 82 of the Wales Bill negatived by 259 votes to 232. *HC Deb*. 948, c. 615–20. (O)

19 Apr. 1978 Amendment to Wales Bill to provide a 40% 'threshold' requirement for Welsh referendum carried against the Government by 280 votes to 208. *HC Deb*. 948, c. 619–24. (D)

8 May 1978 Opposition amendment to Finance Bill to reduce basic rate of income tax from 34% to 33% carried by 312 votes to 304. *HC Deb*. 949, c. 917–22. (O)

10 May 1978 Opposition amendment to Finance Bill to raise the level at which higher rates of income tax would apply from £7,000 annual income to £8,000 carried by 288 votes to 286. *HC Deb*. 949, c. 1299–1304. (O)

10 May 1978 Government motion to report progress during consideration of Finance Bill (to allow consideration of proposed Opposition amendment to the Bill) defeated by 280 votes to 273. *HC Deb*. 949, c. 1357–62. (O)

19 July 1978 Motion to disagree with Lords amendment to Wales Bill (on qualifications for membership) negatived by 293 votes to 260. *HC Deb*. 954, c. 727–32. (D)

20 July 1978 Motion to disagree with Lords amendment to schedule 2 of the Wales Bill (removing forestry from Assembly's legislative competence) defeated by 280 votes to 247. *HC Deb*. 954, c. 919–24. (D)

24 July 1978 Prayer to approve the draft Dock Labour Scheme 1978 defeated by 301 votes to 291. *HC Deb*. 954, c. 1319–26. (O)

26 July 1978 Motion to disagree with Lords amendment to Scotland Bill (on voting of Scottish MPs in the Commons) defeated by 276 votes to 275. *HC Deb*. 954, c. 1659–66. (D)

26 July 1978 Motion to disagree with Lords amendment to clause 67 of Scotland Bill defeated by 286 votes to 266. *HC Deb*. 954, c. 1665–70. (D)

13 Dec. 1978 Opposition amendment to Government motion (opposing Government's economic policy of sanctions against firms breaking 5% pay limit) carried by 285 votes to 279, and amended motion then carried by 285 votes to 283. *HC Deb*. 960, c. 799–810. (O) [First defeat exacerbated by Labour abstentions.]

7 Feb. 1979 Amendment to clause 4 of the Nurses, Midwives and Health Visitors Bill carried against the Government by 149 votes to 121. *HC Deb*. 962, c. 463–6. (D)

22 Mar. 1979 Prayer to annul Firearms (Variation of Fees) Order 1979 carried against the Government by 115 votes to 26. *HC Deb*. 964, c. 1857–60. (O)[4]

28 Mar. 1979 Opposition motion 'That this House has no confidence in her Majesty's Government' carried by 311 votes to 310. *HC Deb*. 965, c. 583–8. (O)

---

[1] The first defeat was attributed to abstention by two Labour Members, J. Mackintosh and B. Walden. (The casting vote would have gone to the Government.)

[2] Although caused by a combination of opposition parties, there appears to have been an element of mismanagement by the Government whips. The Prime Minister was absent unpaired from the division.

[3] Although caused by a combination of opposition parties, there was an element of confusion involved, the Government believing the Opposition did not intend to contest the division.

[4] Although caused by a combination of opposition parties, there appears to have been a clear case of mismanagement by the Government whips or an effective Opposition manoeuvre.

SELECT BIBLIOGRAPHY

The following constitute a selection of the main works on, or which in important respects touch upon, intra-party dissent in the House of Commons.

Books

The main works have been touched upon in the introduction: Ronald Butt, *The Power of Parliament* (Constable, 1967), Robert J. Jackson, *Rebels and Whips* (Macmillan, 1968), Philip Norton, *Dissension in the House of Commons 1945–74* (Macmillan, 1975), and, by the same, author, *Conservative Dissidents* (Temple Smith, 1978).

Other pertinent works include Hugh Berrington, *Backbench Opinion in the House of Commons, 1945–55* (Pergamon Press, 1973) and S. E. Finer, Hugh Berrington and D. J. Bartholomew, *Backbench Opinion in the House of Commons 1955–59* (Pergamon Press, 1961). Both works analyze divisions within the parliamentary parties not through the use of division lists but through that other source of 'hard' data, Early Day Motions. See also Malcolm J. Barnett, *The Politics of Legislation: The Rent Act 1957* (Weidenfeld & Nicolson, 1969), chapter 10; Leon D. Epstein, *British Politics in the Suez Crisis* (Pall Mall Press, 1964), *passim*.; Michael Kinnear, *The Fall of Lloyd George* (Macmillan, 1973), chapter 4, which analyses the 'Die-Hards' in the 1912–22 Parliament, 'the only clear Conservative faction' of the Parliament (p. 78); Uwe Kitzinger, *Diplomacy and Persuasion* (Thames & Hudson, 1973), especially chapter 13 and Appendix 1; John D. Lees and Richard Kimber (eds), *Political Parties in Modern Britain* (Routledge & Kegan Paul, 1972), chapter 5; A. Lawrence Lowell, *The Government of England*, Vol. II (Macmillan, 1924), chapter 35 'The strength of party ties'; Gillian Peele's study of Conservative intra-party dissent on the issue of India in Gillian Peele and Chris Cook (eds), *The Politics of Reappraisal 1918–39* (Macmillan, 1975); Richard Rempel, *Unionists Divided* (David & Charles/Archon Books, 1972), *passim*; H. H. Wilson, *Pressure Group: The Campaign for Commercial Television* (Secker & Warburg, 1961), *passim*; and, of course, Samuel Beer, *Modern British Politics* (Faber, 1969 ed.,), pp. 255–66.

Monographs and articles

The following constitute a selection of useful monographs and articles, listed alphabetically by author:

Alderman, R. K., 'Parliamentary Party Discipline in Opposition: The Parliamentary Labour Party 1951–64', *Parliamentary Affairs* (21), 1967–8, pp. 124–36.

'Discipline in the Parliamentary Labour Party 1945–51', *Parliamentary Affairs* (18), 1964–5, pp. 293–305.

Aydelotte, W. O., 'Voting patterns in the British House of Commons in the 1840s', *Comparative Studies in Society and History* (V), 1962–3.

Berrington, H. B., 'The Conservative Party: Revolts and Pressures 1955–61', *Political Quarterly* (32), 1961, pp. 363–73.

'Partisanship and dissidence in the nineteenth-century House of Commons', *Parliamentary Affairs* (21), 1968, reprinted in Kimber and Lees (see above).

Christoph, J.B., 'The study of voting behavior in the British House of Commons', *Western Political Quarterly* (11), 1958, pp. 301–18.

Critchley, J., 'Strains and stresses in the Conservative Party', *Political Quarterly* (44), 1973, pp. 401–10.

Dowse, R.E. and Smith, T., 'Party Discipline in the House if Commons—A Comment', *Parliamentary Affairs* (16), 1962–3, pp. 159–64.

Epstein, L. D., 'Cohesion of British Parliamentary Parties', *American Political Science Review* (50), 1956, pp. 360–77.

'British M.P.s and their Local Parties: The Suez Cases', *American Political Science Review* (54), 1960, pp. 374–90.

'New M.P.s and the Politics of the P.L.P.', *Political Studies* (10), 1962, pp. 121–9.

Frasure, R. C., '*Backbench Opinion* revisited: The case of the Conservatives', *Political Studies* (20), 1972, pp. 325–8.

S. C. Ghosh, 'Decision-Making and Power in the British Conservative Party: A Case Study of the Indian Problem 1929–34', *Political Studies* (13), 1965, pp. 198–212.

Holt, R. T. and Turner, J. E., 'Change in British Politics: Labour in Parliament and Government', in W. G. Andrews (ed), *European Politics II: The Dynamics of Change* (Van Nostrand Reinhold, 1969), pp. 23–116.

King, A., 'The Changing Tories', *New Society*, 2 May 1968, reprinted in Kimber and Lees (see above).

Kirk, P., 'Tories in Revolt', *The Spectator*, 28 April 1961, pp. 593–4.

Lazer, H., 'British Populism: The Labour Party and the Common Market Parliamentary Debate', *Political Science Quarterly* (91), 1976, pp. 259–77.

Lynskey, J. J., 'The role of British backbenchers in the modification of Government policy', *Western Political Quarterly*, 1970, pp. 333–47.

'Backbench tactics and Parliamentary Party structure', *Parliamentary Affairs* (27), 1973, pp. 28–37.

Norton, P., 'Intra-Party Dissent in the House of Commons: A Case Study. The Immigration Rules 1972', *Parliamentary Affairs* (29), 1976, pp. 404–20.

'Dissent in Committee: Intra-Party Dissent in Commons' Standing Committees 1959–74', *The Parliamentarian* (57), 1976, pp. 15–25.

'Government Defeats in the House of Commons: Myth and Reality', *Public Law*, Winter 1978, pp. 360–77.

'Government Defeats in the House of Commons: Three Restraints Overcome', *The Parliamentarian* (59), 1978, pp. 231–8.

'The Influence of the Backbench Member', *The Parliamentarian* (58), 1977, pp. 164–71.

'Intra-Party Dissent in the House of Commons: The Parliament of 1974', *The Parliamentarian* (58), 1977, pp. 240–45.

'Test your own Powellism', *Crossbow* (17), February 1976, pp. 10–11.

'The Government Defeat: 10 March 1976', *The Parliamentarian* (57), 1976, pp. 174–5.

'The House of Commons in the 1970s: Three views on reform', *Hull Papers in Politics, No. 3* (Hull University Politics Department, 1978).

'Discipline, Dissent and the Prevalence of Unity: The Conservative Party in Opposition 1945–51', *Occasional Paper* (1975).

Ozbudun, E., *Party Cohesion in Western Democracies: A Causal Analysis* (Sage Publications, 1970).

Piper, J. R., 'Backbench rebellion, party government and consensus politics: the case of the Parliamentary Labour Party 1966–70', *Parliamentary Affairs* (27), 1974, pp. 384–96.

Rasmussen, J. S., *The Relations of the Profumo Rebels with their local parties* (University of Arizona Press, 1966).

'Government and Intra-Party Opposition: Dissent within the Conservative Parliamentary Party in the 1930s', *Political Studies* (19) 1971, pp. 172–83.

'Party Discipline in War-Time: The Downfall of the Chamberlain Government', *Journal of Politics* (32), 1970, pp. 379–406.

Rose, R., 'Parties, factions and tendencies in Britain', *Political Studies* (12), 1964, pp. 33–46.

'The Labour Party and German Rearmament: A View from Transport House', *Political Studies* (14), 1966, pp. 133–44.

Schwarz, J. E. and Lambert, G., 'The Voting Behavior of British Conservative Backbenchers', in S. C. Patterson and J. C. Wahlke (eds), *Comparative Legislative Behavior: Frontiers of Research* (Wiley, 1972), pp. 65–85. (Published originally in *Journal of Politics* (33), 1971, pp. 399–421.)

Seyd, P., 'Factionalism within the Conservative Party: The Monday Club', *Government and Opposition* (7), 1972, pp. 464–87.

Theses and unpublished material
Some useful material on intra-party dissent is to be found in unpublished, albeit variously available, sources, of which the following is a selection:

Alderman, R. K., 'Discipline in the Parliamentary Labour Party from the formation of the Labour Representation Committee in 1900 to 1964', PhD Thesis, University of London, 1971.

Beer, S. H., 'Data on Party Unity in British Politics', mimeographed research note (n.d.).

Coates, C. M., 'The course of party discipline in Parliament and the constituencies over the past thirty years, and its effect on the worth of the backbencher in British Government', MA Thesis, University of Bristol, 1959–60.

Jones, R., 'Party Voting in the English House of Commons', MA Thesis, University of Chicago, 1933.

King, A., 'Study of rebellions within the Parliamentary Labour Party 1964–70', data deposited in the SSRC Survey Archive, University of Essex (Survey number: 70002(B)).

Lazer, H., 'Division in the British Labour Party: Left and Right in the Wilson Years', Paper delivered at the American Political Science Association Conference, Chicago, 1975.

Lynskey, J. J., 'The Role of British Backbenchers in the Modification of Government policy: The issues involved, the channels utilized, and the tactics employed', PhD Thesis, University of Minnesota, 1966.

McEwen, J. M., 'Unionist and Conservative Members of Parliament 1914–1939', PhD Thesis, University of London, 1959. (Though primarily an analysis of Members' backgrounds, includes useful details of various occasions of dissenting behaviour, including an analysis of dissent on the issue of India.)

Norton, P., 'Intra-Party Dissent in the House of Commons: The Conservative Party in Government 1970–74', PhD Thesis, University of Sheffield, 1977.

'The Changing Face of the House of Commons in the 1970s', Paper delivered at British Politics Group panel, American Political Science Association Conference, Washington D.C., 1979.

Potter, A. M., 'British Party Politics: A Study of Party Discipline', PhD Thesis, Columbia University, 1955.

SUBJECT INDEX

Numbers in the index refer to division numbers—printed at the beginning of each entry—and not to page numbers.

Numbers in italics refer to page numbers in the Conclusions.

2R = Second Reading; Comm = Committee; Rep = Report; 3R = Third Reading; LA = Lords Amendments

NAME INDEX

131, 132, 157, 162, 173, 176, 179, 184, 185,
194, 205, 207, 215, 228, 257, 270, 271, 273,
292, 299, 307, 338, 339, 351, 363, 384, 389,
390, 391, 392, 393, 394, 399, 400, 412, 415,
416

Cordle, J. (Bournemouth, East), 15, 51, 174

Cormack, P. (Staffordshire, South-West), 3,
4, 11, 23, 39, 42, 43, 71, 72, 122, 124, 173,
174, 180, 192, 203, 217, 240, 247, 288,
302n, 415, 426

Corrie, J. (Ayrshire, North and Bute), 27,
40, 43, 53, 71, 74, 209n

Costain, A. (Folkestone and Hythe), 12, 43,
51, 53, 74, 117, 196, 280, 294, 299, 363, 396

Cowans, H. (Newcastle-Upon-Tyne, Central)
209, 241, 258, 269, 307, 328, 329, 330, 336,
347, 354, 372

Cox, T. (Wandsworth, Tooting), 58, 269

Craig, W. (Belfast, East), 279

Craigen, J. (Glasgow, Maryhill), 8, 52n, 80,
175, 196, 197, 198, 207, 213, 214, 228, 250,
269, 280, 294, 302, 317, 353, 365, 410

Crawford, D. (Perth and East Perthshire),
108, 109

Crawshaw, R. (Liverpool, Toxteth), 42,
44n, 101, 102, 103, 106, 179, 241n, 270,
273, 294, 307, 323, 347, *436*

Critchley, J. (Aldershot), 122, 174, 193

Cronin, J. (Loughborough), 64, 263

Crosland, A. (Grimsby), 1, 42, 103, 191

Crouch, D. (Canterbury), 3, 4, 42, 118,
209n, 234, 239, 294, 302n, 312n, 313n, 396

Crowder, F. P. (Ruislip-Northwood) 13, 39,
45, 216, 217, 270, 365

Crowther, S. (Rotherham), 173, 196, 204,
209n, 215, 228, 256, 257, 263, 264, 266,
269, 288, 289, 300, 328, 330, 331, 339, 358

Cryer, R. (Keighley), 7, 8, 12, 14, 16, 17, 22,
29, 30, 32, 36, 41, 52, 58, 63, 64, 65, 68,
77, 81, 82, 90, 91, 96, 98, 100, 107, 110,
118, 120, 125, 128, 129, 130, 131, 132, 138,
140, 145n, 152, 154, 157, 162, 173, 176,
179, 180, 181, 184, 269, 385, 386, 387, 389,
391, 393, 394, 399, 400, 402, 403, 404, 405,
407, 408, 414, 415, 416, 419, 420, 421, 422,
423, 425

Cunningham, G. (Islington, South and
Finsbury), 7, 44, 49, 58, 113, 124n, 131,
138, 156, 173, 194, 196, 203, 209, 217, 218,
233, 234, 238, 239, 241, 251, 252, 253, 262,
269, 270, 279, 281, 282, 283, 286, 287, 288,
289, 291, 292, 300, 303, 304, 310, 313, 314,
316, 327, 328, 329, 332, 336, 358, 359, 366,
367, 378, *438, 444, 467, 470, 480*

Dalyell, T. (West Lothian), 51, 88, 124n,
192n, 209, 216, 217, 218, 219, 221, 225,

226, 233, 238, 239, 240, 241, 279, 281, 282,
283, 286, 287, 303, 307, 310, 311, 312, 313,
314, 318, 327, 328, 329, 332, 336, 340, 341,
342, 349, 359, 361, 362, 364, 365, 366, 367,
368, 369, 370, 371, 373, 374, 375, 376, 377,
379, 380, *438, 444*

Davidson, A. (Accrington), 16, 157, 269

Davies, B. (Enfield, North), 7, 12, 14, 16, 29,
30, 36, 41, 49, 58, 63, 64, 65, 68, 77, 81, 82,
89, 90, 91, 100, 104, 152, 157, 162, 179,
185, 228, 263, 269, 270, 271, 273, 288, 294,
299, 300, 316, 330, 339

Davies, D. (Llanelli), 14, 58, 146, 258, 272

Davies, I. (Gower), 97n, 209n, 228n, 328,
336, 373, 374, 380, 381

Davies, J. (Knutsford), 144, 278

*d'Avigdor-Goldsmid, J. (Lichfield and
Tamworth), 6

Davis, C. (Hackney, Central), 58, 111, 190,
269, 335

Deakins, E. (Waltham Forest, Waltham-
stow), 269

Dean, J. (Leeds, West), 7, 16, 58, 100, 104,
124n, 173, 176, 179, 209n, 218, 241, 258n,
265, 269, 270, 288, 289, 294, 307, 313, 314,
316, 324, 325, 327, 328, 329, 331, 336, 347,
351

Dean, P. (Somerset, North), 71, 120, 167,
200, 203, 209n, 234, 258n, 384

De Freitas, Sir G. (Kettering), 88

Delargy, H. (Thurrock), 29, 30, 36n

Dell, E. (Birkenhead), 14, 53, 98, 124

Dempsey, J. (Coatbridge and Airdrie), 51,
58, 196, 228, 270, 334, 357

Dewar, D. (Glasgow, Garscadden), 389

Dodsworth, G. (Hertfordshire, South-West),
23, 45, 96, 146, 155, 174, 191, 192, 193,
216, 240, 245, 278, 294, 299, 383

Doig, P. (Dundee, West), 294, 313, 328, 329,
347, *444*

Dormand, J. (Easington), 269

Douglas-Hamilton, Lord J. (Edinburgh,
West), 39, 110, 111, 153, 173, 185, 196,
209n, 224n, 307

Douglas-Mann, B. (Merton, Mitcham and
Morden), 12, 44, 49, 58, 100n, 157, 176,
179, 209n, 241, 263, 270, 273, 279, 302, 307,
313, 314, 327, 328, 329, 347, 377, 379,
412

Drayson, B. (Skipton), 45, 117, 118, 173,
174, 194, 195, 196, 203, 225, 234, 284, 290,
299, 365, 383

Du Cann, E. (Taunton), 21, 58n, 118, 193,
234, *450, 480*

Duffy, P. (Sheffield, Attercliffe), 7

Dunn, J. (Liverpool, Kirkdale), 357

*Member of short 1974 Parliament only

*Member of short 1974 Parliament only

*Member of short 1974 Parliament only.

*Member of short 1974 Parliament only.

*Member of short 1974 Parliament only.

*Member of short 1974 Parliament only.

*Member of short 1974 Parliament only.